D0041122

ONE HUNDRED YEARS OF
U.S. NAVY
AIR POWER

ONE HUNDRED YEARS OF
U.S. NAVY
AIR POWER

Edited by
Douglas V. Smith

NAVAL INSTITUTE PRESS
Annapolis, Maryland

Naval Institute Press
291 Wood Road
Annapolis, MD 21402

© 2010 by Douglas V. Smith
All rights reserved. No part of this book may be reproduced or utilized in
any form or by any means, electronic or mechanical, including photocopying
and recording, or by any information storage and retrieval system, without
permission in writing from the publisher.

Library of Congress Cataloging-in-Publication Data
One hundred years of U.S. Navy air power / edited by Douglas V. Smith.
    p. cm.
  Includes bibliographical references and index.
  ISBN 978-1-59114-795-4 (hardcover : alk. paper) 1. United States. Navy—
Aviation—History. I. Smith, Douglas V. (Douglas Vaughn), 1948- II. Title:
One hundred years of United States Navy air power.
  VG93.O54 2010
  359.9'40973—dc22
                          2010034231

Printed in the United States of America on acid-free paper

14 13 12 11 10   9 8 7 6 5 4 3 2
First printing

All photographs are courtesy of the the U.S. Naval Institute Photo Archive
unless otherwise credited.

This work is dedicated to
THOSE who have worn the Wings of Gold,
Navy Wings of Silver, and THOSE who have supported them
in the air, on the ground, and in their homes;
Professor Emeritus GEORGE W. BAER, who so graciously
allowed us to use the title for his award-winning book,
One Hundred Years of Sea Power,
as an inspiration for our own;
JOYCE I. MILLER,
who has been an inspiration and
mentor to us all.

CONTENTS

List of Illustrations   ix

Foreword by George H. W. Bush   xi

Acknowledgments   xiii

Chapter 1. Introduction   1
            Douglas V. Smith

Chapter 2. The Experimental Era: U.S. Navy Aviation before 1916   5
            Stephen K. Stein

Chapter 3. Eyes of the Fleet: How Flying Boats Transformed War Plan Orange   31
            Edward S. Miller

Chapter 4. Ships in the Sky   43
            John E. Jackson

Chapter 5. Big Guns versus Wooden Decks: Naval Aviation   52
            Officer Personnel, 1911–1941
            Donald Chisholm

Chapter 6. Admiral Joseph Mason "Bull" Reeves,   79
            Father of Navy Carrier Aviation
            Douglas V. Smith

Chapter 7. Aviation in the Interwar Fleet Maneuvers, 1919–1940   94
            Albert A. Nofi

Chapter 8. The Two-Ocean Navy Act of 1940:   131
            The Impact on American Preparedness for World War II
            Timothy H. Jackson and Stanley D. M. Carpenter

Chapter 9. U.S. Aircraft Carrier Evolution, 1911–1945   153
              Norman Friedman

Chapter 10. Foundation for Victory: U.S. Navy Aircraft Development,   199
              1922–1945
              Hill Goodspeed

Chapter 11. Straight Up: Vertical Flight in the U.S. Navy   220
              Kevin J. Delamer

Chapter 12. The Transition to Swept-Wing Jets   240
              Robert C. Rubel

Chapter 13. Naval Aviation in the Korean and Vietnam Wars   269
              Gary J. Ohls

Chapter 14. By Land and Sea: Non-Carrier Naval Aviation   301
              Sterling Michael Pavelec

Chapter 15. U.S. Aircraft Carrier Evolution: 1945–2011   322
              Norman Friedman

Chapter 16. Conclusions   350
              Douglas V. Smith

Contributors   355
Index   361

ILLUSTRATIONS

F-18 Super Hornet. 1

Eugene B. Ely flies his Curtiss pusher airplane from 7
USS *Birmingham* (CV-2), 14 November 1910. The USS *Roe*,
serving as plane guard, is visible in the background.

Lieutenant John Towers was convinced of the importance of 14
an aviation program in spite of the skepticism of senior officers.

The Consolidated PBY or Catalina had a 1,000-mile range. 34
By 1941, the U.S. Navy had 330 in service.

The Honorable Frank Knox, Secretary of the Navy (right), 36
with Rear Admiral C. C. Bloch, Naval Air Station, Pearl Harbor,
Hawaii, September 1940.

The U.S. Navy's largest non-rigid airships, the ZPG-3W class, flew until 1962. 47

ZPG-2s in hangar. 49

Early naval aviators pose at the Naval Aeronautic Station, 55
Pensacola, Florida, spring 1914.

Naval Reserve Freshmen, class of 1930, University of California. 62

Admiral Joseph Mason "Bull" Reeves. 79

DT-2 taking off from USS *Langley*, circa 1925. 84

USS *Langley* in Pearl Harbor in 1928. 96

The USS *Lexington* with Martin bombers on deck. 102

Left to right: Representative Carl Vinson (D-GA); Secretary of Navy   132
Francis P. Matthews; Admiral Louis E. Denfeld, Chief of Naval Operations;
and Admiral Arthur W. Radford, Commander, Pacific Fleet, 6 October 1949.

USS *Essex* (CV-9), circa 1945.   145

The USS *Saratoga* (CV-3), recovering her aircraft, June 1935.   161

The USS *Midway* in a gale off Sicily, February 1949.   181
Photograph taken from the *Essex*-class carrier *Philippine Sea*.

The first successful torpedo plane design was Douglas Aircraft Company's DT.   202

U.S. Navy Curtiss SB2C Helldiver returns from a strike on Japanese shipping.   213

The pontoon-equipped XR-4 flights from the USS *Bunker Hill* in   221
May 1943 marked the birth of naval rotary-wing aviation.

SH-3A (HSS-2) flown publicly for first time, 24 March 1959.   231

McDonnell FH-1 Phantom.   248

A-6 Intruder on the USS *Independence*'s catapult, March 1965.   266

U.S. Navy Fighters F4U Corsairs return to carrier USS *Boxer* (CV-21)   272
after a strike over Korea, September 1951.

U.S. Navy F-4B Phantom II from the USS *Ranger*, February 1968.   285

P-3 Orion conducting ship surveillance in mid-Pacific, September 1974.   308

Consolidated B-24 Liberator designated by the U.S. Navy as the PB4Y-1.   316

Official 1948 sketch of the supercarrier *United States*, which was designed   325
to carry heavy bombers.

USS *Abraham Lincoln*, typical of modern U.S. nuclear carriers, October 1994.   336

Nimitz-class aircraft carrier USS *Ronald Reagan* (CVN 76) with   350
guided-missile cruiser USS *Chancellorsville* (CG 62).

FOREWORD

I am indeed honored to have been asked to help kick off the Centennial Year of U.S. Navy Aviation by sharing a few insights on Navy aviation's proud history. As a Navy pilot who has shared the thrills and the agonies of defending our nation in the air, I am happy to congratulate those who wear, or have worn, the Wings of Gold, and I salute the thousands of dedicated men and women in and out of uniform who keep them in the air. America's citizens owe a great debt to all who pioneered Navy aviation and brought it to such a prominent position in the nation's arsenal.

In looking back over the past century, it is incredible to see how far aviation technology has come. Within the span of one human lifetime, we have seen remarkable progress from Navy pilot Eugene Ely's first carrier landing in a fragile Curtiss pusher biplane in 1911, to Navy aviator Alan Shepard's footsteps on the moon only six decades later! I believe that America's birthrights of freedom and liberty have been in large part secured through air power. One of the first questions I always asked as Commander-in-Chief when American interests were threatened around the globe was *"Where are our aircraft carriers?"* The ability to project power from the sea—free from the restrictions of international political maneuvering—has repeatedly played a key part in crisis management and in securing vital U.S. interests.

Some of my fondest memories are of my years as a young Navy pilot, flying off USS *San Jacinto* during World War II, and of the other pilots, aircrewmen, and ship's company who shared the experience of flying aircraft in harm's way. My combat missions were marked by both triumph and tragedy, but I never felt more like a patriot than when I carried America's flag into battle in pursuit of a just cause.

You can imagine the pride I felt in January 2009 when I participated in the commissioning of the remarkable new nuclear-powered aircraft carrier that bears my name. I said at the time: *"Make no mistake, the work aboard this ship will be routinely difficult and sometimes dangerous. But the freedom we seek and the peace we desire can only be found in the countless sacrifices you will make in everyday tasks you will perform."*

It is particularly appropriate that this book, dedicated to the Navy aviator's courage, incredibly close ties to comrades in arms, sense of duty in the face of death, and loyalty to our great nation, is being published during Navy Aviation's Centennial celebration. It tells a tale rife with courage and sacrifice, dangerous experimentation and awe-inspiring innovation, tenacity, and dedication. It involves wondrous technologies that include the exhilaration of jet propulsion, the agility of rotary wings, and the iconoclastic ventures of lighter-than-air. Most of all, it is a human drama with far-reaching implications into the shaping of world events and the ultimate success of our great democratic experiment. The book is also, in a very real sense, a tribute to the military families who served quietly in their own way, through countless hours of separation and anxiety, praying for the safe return of their champions.

My life has been blessed with many wonderful experiences, but few rival my days in uniform with the United States Navy. All my best wishes as you celebrate 100 years of U.S. Navy air power!

GEORGE H. W. BUSH
Lieutenant, U.S. Navy Reserve

ACKNOWLEDGMENTS

The authors would all like to express our sincere thanks to President George Herbert Walker Bush, forty-first President of the United States, not only for providing the foreword for this book, but for his gallant service as a pilot wearing the Navy Wings of Gold in World War II in the Pacific. We thank President Bush as well for saluting all those who have worn or now wear the Wings of Gold, those who have kept and continue to keep them in the air, and those who, past and present, have kept the home fires burning while awaiting their return.

We would also like to thank Mr. Danny Pietrodangelo and his associate, Ms. Dale Harness, of Pietrodangelo Production Group in Tallahassee, Florida, for their excellent photo research and photo editing work for this project.

Dr. Al Nofi would like to add his thanks to Admiral James Hogg, USN (Ret.), and his shipmates from the CNO's Strategic Studies Group, 2001–2005; as well as the staff of the Naval War College Library and the Naval War College Archives; Editor Emeritus of the *Naval War College Review*, Frank Uhlig; and Dr. Thomas Hone, without whom his chapter and this entire book would not have been possible.

I add my thanks to all of these, but especially to Tom Hone, who helped envision this project.

Capt. John Jackson, SC USN (Ret.) would like to extend his thanks to Vice Admiral Charles E. Rosendahl, USN (Ret.), who commanded all Navy airships in World War II and was the commanding officer at Naval Air Station Lakehurst the night the German Zeppelin Hindenburg crashed. John's meeting and discussions with Vice Admiral Rosendahl provided fascinating details of the age of airships. John also thanks his loving wife, Valerie, for her untiring support and encouragement of all that he does.

Tim Jackson and Stan Carpenter thank Mr. Nathaniel Patch at the National Archives and Records Administration for his assistance in locating many essential records relating to naval legislation and appropriations bills.

Dr. Norman Friedman above all wants to thank his wife, Rhea, for her warm support throughout this project. Dr. Friedman's acquaintance with the story of U.S. carrier design dates back to a NAVSEA project sponsored by Dr. Reuven Leopold, who was then senior civilian ship designer (and who had designed the *Tarawa*-class large-deck amphibious ships and the *Spruance*-class destroyers). Dr. Leopold wanted Dr. Friedman to use the NAVSEA preliminary design files to find out why the U.S. Navy preferred large to small carriers. Through Dr. Leopold he became acquainted with the Navy's preliminary designers, including Herbert S. Meier, who led the team that produced the preliminary design for the *Nimitz*-class carriers. "I hope I have done them justice. I also want particularly to thank Dr. Evelyn Cherpak, who is responsible for the archive of the Naval War College and to thank the staff of the U.S. National Archives and Records Agency, at both the downtown Washington, D.C., and College Park locations. I would also like to thank Dr. Thomas C. Hone of the Naval War College for many valuable insights developed during our two Joint projects for the Office of Net Assessment. I am grateful to Charles Haberlein, photo curator of the Naval History and Heritage Command, for help not only with photographs but also with much wider issues of ship development and employment."

Hill Goodspeed gratefully acknowledges Captain Robert Rasmussen, USN (Ret.), and Dr. Robert R. Macon of the National Naval Aviation Museum for their longtime support of his work, and thanks those many naval aviators and aircrewmen who over the years have shared the experiences that have done so much to inspire his writing

Dr. Mike Pavelec singles out Dr. Evelyn Cherpak, Archivist of the Naval War College, for her great support of his archival research, and Hill Goodspeed, Historian of the Naval Air Museum in Pensacola, Florida, who is also a contributing author of this work, for his important help on research of all aspects of Navy aviation.

Finally, as editor of this book, I want to thank each of the authors who have shared their insights and scholarship by providing the chapters herein. Every one of them submitted their chapters on time or ahead of schedule, a rarity in the academic community. Experts all, they have made my job easy and enlightened me in the process.

My thanks go out to Dr. Evelyn Cherpak, echoing those above. She is a consummate professional and incredible resource for all scholars of U.S. Naval History. Likewise, I thank Ms. Alice Juda, Senior Reference Librarian and the strongest possible supporter of the scholarly research efforts of members of the Naval War College faculty and student body. Mr. Dennis Zambrotta, library technician at the War College, has provided an important service in locating microfilm holdings that have proven critical to this project and deserves my thanks as well. All six contributing authors of the Naval War College faculty owe a great degree of gratitude to Evelyn, Alice, and Dennis and all the staff of the War College Library.

Thanks also to Rear Admiral Jay DeLoach USN (Ret.), Director of the Navy History and Heritage Command at the Navy Yard in Washington, D.C., for his support of this project and our archival research in his fine archives; and to Captain Russ Knight, USN, Chief of Staff of the Naval War College and a senior Navy pilot, for offering us advice on aviation matters and contacts useful to this project.

I owe a special debt of gratitude to my wife, Paulette, who has assisted in proofreading this book and in so many other ways. I thank her also for keeping me flying for over twenty years.

Others who have provided help to all of the contributors but who are not named here are gratefully acknowledged.

The views expressed in this book are those of the authors alone and are not to be construed as those of the Naval War College or the Department of the Navy.

DOUGLAS V. SMITH

CHAPTER 1

Introduction

Douglas V. Smith

F-18 Super Hornet.

I f there is one aspect of the United States Navy that has defined its history, and
that stands out in its molding of American history, it is Navy Aviation. It is hard
to imagine the centrality of the U.S. Navy in America's history without the role
Navy aviation has played for almost half its existence. Thus, in 2011 when the Navy
celebrates the Centennial of Navy Aviation, it is appropriate that all Americans—
and particularly those who have worn the Wings of Gold—take time to reflect on
the monumental impact Navy aviation has had on this country and its citizens.

It is fitting that a volume be dedicated to the pilots who have proudly worn the
Wings of Gold, the Naval Flight Officers and the aircrewmen who have placed their

1

lives in their care, and to the men and women who have kept them in the air for a
century. So too is it important that the pioneers of Navy aviation be recognized, their
stories told, and that the thousands of men and women who risked everything to
make sure the airplanes in the fleet matched the skills of those who would fly them
be honored for their innovation, bravery, sacrifice, and dedication.

A poem on aviation extols the magnificence of being able to have "slipped the
surly bonds of Earth—put out my hand and touched the Face of God!"[1] Few have
ever been able to break those bonds and fly. One can only imagine how exhilarat-
ing it must have been in 1911 when some had the prospect of doing just that . . .
while serving their country and at the expense of the U.S. Navy. In one hundred
years, the prospect of the excitement of air flight has not lessened in the American
spirit. Living on the edge constantly—almost every day of one's life—creates an
exhilaration unimaginable to most young people growing up. Strapping on a flame-
throwing Mach 2+ rocket today must give a feeling not much different from nestling
into a 95-mph biplane with an engine that would not meet the requirements for a
good lawn mower a hundred years later. Landing either of these on a postage stamp
in the middle of the ocean, inhibited by forty-foot waves and a rolling deck, can
only be imagined by someone who has not experienced it. Being referred to regularly as the "best two percent of humanity"[2] for being one of the few who can do just
that has produced a confidence unmatched in any fraternity of brothers (and more
recently sisters) other than naval aviators of the United States Navy. The pages that
follow tell their story.

Today the Commander, U.S. Naval Air Forces is Vice Admiral Allen G.
Myers IV, USN. He is in the most fortunate position of leading all Navy aviators
as they reach the Centennial year of their profession. It is hoped that this volume,
which is intended to tell Navy aviation's story through its first hundred years,
might complement the commemorative activities Admiral Myers has planned for
the Centennial.

Any tribute to Navy aviation must include a consideration of the pioneers, aircraft, politics, operational concepts, and tactics that together propelled it from primitive aircraft barely capable of operations aboard ships or over vast ocean areas to the
most potent and lethal combination of aircraft represented by a modern carrier. Any
tribute to what is arguably the greatest leap in technology over a single one-hundred-
year period presents the huge problem of what to include and what not to include.
Thus the pages that follow have been organized to include as much information as
possible on topics of central importance to an understanding of the evolution of
Navy aviation as a warfighting tool in the nation's arsenal. Essential to accomplishing this is an understanding of the manner in which aircraft were embraced by the
Navy's senior leadership in their nascent state, what roles and missions were envisioned for them, and how those roles and missions evolved and expanded over time.

Additionally, with respect to the capabilities of most likely adversaries, the manner in which Navy Air was introduced into the fleet, the bureaucracy that developed to foster Navy Air capabilities and activities, and the way in which aviation was treated in American war planning—all these issues and dynamics will be addressed in the first part of this book.

The second part of the book is focused on preparations for war with Japan and the totalitarian threats in Europe. Of particular interest are aircraft carrier design and aircraft technology, capabilities and manufacturing developments. The series of twenty-one Fleet Problems and periodic Grand Joint Exercises conducted in the interwar period that enabled Navy leaders to formulate and refine aviation doctrine and tactics are examined. This book looks closely at the competing ideas on the proper mission for American carriers and their aircraft, displacement and design trade-offs, and treaty limitations affecting mission accomplishment. Also analyzed is the need to project technological advances in aircraft accurately to maximize the prospects for success in an increasingly likely war with Japan.

The third section in this volume probes developments in helicopter- and land-based Navy aviation. Most importantly, it considers the huge risk associated with the transition from straight-wing propeller-driven aircraft after World War II to high-speed swept-wing jets necessitated by the Cold War. This section puts these developments in perspective by considering the part played by Navy aviation in the Korean and Vietnam wars.

Finally, a chapter is devoted to post–World War II trade-offs in aircraft carrier design and capabilities. This chapter ties in nicely with that on the transition to swept-wing supersonic jets. The trade-off of lives lost and aircraft crashed in bringing American Navy aviation to a state of technological sophistication necessary to support their varied missions today was one realized and accepted by Navy leaders in order to make carriers effective. It is also a tribute to those who have worn the Wings of Gold and their courage and sacrifice. Through the entire hundred-year history of Navy aviation, their willingness to accept the risks of the job has been essential to preserving America's freedoms.

From the first landing and subsequent take-off from a wooden platform on the cruiser *Pennsylvania* by Eugene Burton Ely on 18 January 1911 to the first Navy pilot to set foot on the moon, Neil Alden Armstrong, on 20 July 1969, a mere fifty-eight years had passed. Never in history had such a rapid evolution in a new technology taken place. Keeping pace with this evolution was a similar one in aircraft carriers. Moreover, a blistering change from prop to jet aircraft was under way that was not complete until fleet introduction of the F-18 Hornet on 7 January 1983 and modifications to it that followed. The costs to the men who flew Navy aircraft during this period was tremendous, but progress was steady. Today, thanks to their courage, sacrifices, and tenacity, the United States Navy has carrier Air Wings capable of responding to crises anywhere around the world.

NOTES

1. John Gillespie Magee Jr. poem "High Flight."
2. This was a statement made frequently by instructor pilots while I was undergoing pilot training in Meridian, Mississippi, and Beeville, Texas. It relates to less than two percent of humans having ever landed on an aircraft carrier. At the time, few if any of us had any comprehension of or appreciation for the danger inherent in our chosen profession. Reminders such as this were, in retrospect, intended to boost our confidence psychologically beyond rational limits—an absolute necessity for all Navy pilots.

CHAPTER 2

The Experimental Era: U.S. Navy Aviation before 1916

Stephen K. Stein

INTRODUCTION

On 14 November 1910, Eugene Ely flew a fifty-horsepower Curtiss pusher biplane off an 82-foot platform hastily constructed on the cruiser *Birmingham*. The plane cleared the ship, but then dropped rapidly. Its propeller touched the water, shattering its tips, as Ely, hampered by a bulky lifejacket and blinded as water sprayed across his goggles, struggled to gain altitude. Successful, he flew his damaged plane toward the Norfolk Navy Yard. He landed his damaged aircraft at Willoughby Spit five minutes later after a two-mile flight.

The person who arranged this record-making flight, the first take-off of an airplane from a ship, was Navy Captain Washington Irving Chambers. The bureaucratic obstacles and other challenges Chambers overcame to arrange this simple demonstration exemplify the problems he and other aviation enthusiasts faced promoting aviation and building a Navy aviation program in the years before the United States entered World War I. From the first glimmerings of interest in Navy aviation in 1898 to 1916, when the United States began to prepare for major war, aviation advocates faced an uphill struggle that tested their endurance, technical skills, and their acumen for political and bureaucratic maneuvering. In this experimental era, aviation proponents had to prove aircraft both safe and of military utility before they could integrate them into existing military organizations. In the United States, they faced doubting superior officers, a skeptical and penurious Congress, rival inventors, and a slew of bureaucratic impediments and technological factors that singly and in combination hindered innovation and the dissemination of aircraft throughout the Army and Navy.

THE BEGINNINGS OF MILITARY AVIATION

Practical aviation began more than a century earlier with the balloon flights of the Montgolfier brothers who first ascended in one of their creations in 1783. A decade later, France's Revolutionary Army deployed observation balloons at several battles. Napoleon, though, found little use for them and military ballooning disappeared over the next generation. During the American Civil War, civilian aeronauts, particularly John Wise, John La Mountain, and Thaddeus S. C. Lowe, operated balloons for the Union Army. These included balloon flights off the collier *George Washington Parke Curtis* and transport *Fanny*, which marked the birth of Navy aviation. In the first of these, in August 1861, La Mountain ascended from the *George Washington Parke Curtis*, then anchored in off Sewell's Point in Hampton Roads, and sketched Confederate fortifications and artillery positions while hoping to locate the CSS *Virginia*.[1] Historian Craig Symonds jokes that this was the first American aircraft carrier.

Despite some successes, the Army abandoned balloon operations before the war's end. Yet when U.S. troops landed in Cuba in 1898, they brought an observation balloon and its crew helped direct the American advance until Spanish rifle fire brought it down. These balloon flights demonstrated the potential for aviation to transform warfare, but balloons proved too slow, vulnerable, and slow to deploy to inaugurate that transformation. Militaries needed more effective aerial units and, in the last years of the nineteenth century, funded several pioneers exploring heavier-than-air and powered flight.

Researchers around the world struggled to unravel the mysteries of flight as the nineteenth century neared its end; the more prominent included machine-gun inventor Hiram Maxim in Great Britain, Clement Ader in France, and Otto Lilienthal, the "Flying Prussian." Later revered as the father of hang gliding, Lilienthal made more than two thousand flights in a variety of gliders before dying in a crash in August 1896. Maxim lost control of his business, and with it support for aviation research, while Ader's bat-shaped *Avion III* stubbornly refused to fly in its 1898 trials. Others proved equally unsuccessful. While aeronautic research continued in Europe, attention turned to airships, which Count Ferdinand von Zeppelin in Germany and Alberto Santos-Dumont, then living in Paris, regularly demonstrated after 1900.

Beginning in 1887, Samuel Pierpont Langley, the Director of the Smithsonian Institution, built successively larger gliders and steam-powered model aircraft, one of which flew for ninety seconds on 6 May 1896, traveling three thousand feet. Langley extended this to a mile in later tests and his continued success brought him to the attention of prominent individuals including Alexander Graham Bell; Charles Walcott, the Director of the Geological Survey; and Assistant Secretary of the Navy Theodore Roosevelt who arranged a joint Army–Navy Board to examine recent

Eugene B. Ely flies his Curtiss pusher airplane from USS Birmingham *(CV-2), 14 November 1910. The USS* Roe, *serving as plane guard, is visible in the background.*

flight research on the eve of the Spanish-American War. This six-member board, chaired by Commander Charles H. Davis, the Naval Observatory's director, concluded that it would soon be possible to build a heavier-than-air craft capable of carrying a pilot and a small cargo. They recommended funding Langley's research and suggested that aircraft could soon be used for reconnaissance and spotting, carrying messages between military forces, and bombing enemy camps and fortifications. Unfortunately, the members of the Navy's Construction Board (the Chief of Naval Intelligence and the chiefs of the bureaus of Construction and Repair, Equipment, Ordnance, and Steam Engineering) declared aviation research premature and unsuited to the Navy.[2]

The Army, though, found $50,000 for Langley who over the next five years built his full-sized aircraft. Dubbed the *Aerodrome* (due to Langley's poor command of Greek), it was powered by a fifty-two-horsepower gasoline engine built by his assistants Stephen Balzer and Charles Manly who would fly the craft. Scaled up from models without sufficient redesign and testing, the fragile *Aerodrome* lacked landing gear and had only a small rudder for control. Launched by a spring catapult from a houseboat on the Potomac River on 7 October 1903, the craft plunged into the river after a strut snagged the launch mechanism. Launched again two months later on

8 December, the *Aerodrome*'s rear wings buckled after only a brief moment in the air. It crashed into the Potomac, though Manly again survived.[3]

Langley's failures confirmed the doubts of skeptics, including Rear Admiral George W. Melville, one of the most respected engineers in the Navy. Two years earlier, Melville pronounced heavier-than-air flying machines "absurd" and condemned aviation research by noting that there was "no field where so much inventive seed has been sown with so little return as in the attempts of man to fly successfully through the air."[4] Government funding for aviation met the same fate as Langley's *Aerodrome*, vanishing under a hail of criticism and condemnation. Langley, himself, died a few years later in 1906.

THE WRIGHT BROTHERS

While Langley's failures received full, and rather harsh, attention in the press, Orville and Wilbur Wright achieved the first powered, sustained, and controlled flight in relative obscurity on 17 December 1903, nine days after the second and final crash of Langley's *Aerodrome*. Through painstaking research, the Wrights corrected the errors of their predecessors and built on their successes, fusing the work of several designers. Unlike many of their predecessors, they recognized the importance of controlling flight in all three dimensions (pitch, roll, and yaw). They used glider data and wind tunnel tests to build a better airfoil and develop control mechanisms, and successfully integrated diverse technologies into a single airframe. As aviation historian Richard Hallion notes, they recognized the importance of "progressive flight research and flight testing" and followed "an incremental path from theoretical understanding through ground-based research methods" and then flight trials of a succession of models until they worked their way to piloted aircraft. After several successful flights, a wind gust smashed the *Flyer*. The Wrights returned home to Dayton, Ohio, with the wreckage and spent the next two years refining and improving their design. Their new 1905 *Flyer* seated two people and was capable of long flights, such as Wilbur's twenty-four-mile, thirty-eight-minute flight on 5 October. Finding buyers for their plane proved difficult, though, and they soon focused on the military as the only likely purchaser of significant numbers of aircraft.[5]

Despite their disappointment with Langley, several Army Signal Corps officers kept abreast of aviation developments. In 1907, Major George O. Squire toured Europe to study aviation developments.[6] That August, the Army created an Aeronautical Division within the Signal Corps. Prodded by civilian aviation enthusiasts, particularly the members of the Aero Club of America (formed in 1905 by members of the Automobile Club of America) and President Theodore Roosevelt, the division advertised the world's first specifications for a military aircraft. Of the twenty-four bidders, only the Wrights delivered a working airplane.

While Wilbur took one plane to France, where he astounded audiences, Orville flew their new *Military Flyer* for the Army in a succession of test flights at Fort Meyer, Virginia, in the summer of 1908. The several thousand witnesses included two Navy observers: Naval Constructor William McEntee and Lieutenant George W. Sweet, a radio expert who had developed an interest in aviation. Orville took several passengers aloft including Squire, but the demonstrations ended when a propeller blade shattered—its fragments sliced through bracing wires—and the plane plunged to the ground seriously injuring Orville and killing his passenger, Army Lieutenant Thomas Selfridge, the first airplane fatality. A champion of aviation who had ascended in giant kites and contributed to the work of the Aerial Experiment Association, a group led by Alexander Graham Bell, Selfridge would be missed.[7]

The crash delayed the remaining tests until the following summer when the Wrights again astounded observers with both their plane and their aeronautic acumen. Sweet, who had traded places with Selfridge the previous year, finally flew as a passenger on 9 November, becoming the first American Navy officer to fly. The Army accepted the *Military Flyer* into service that August, making it the world's first military Service with an airplane. Supported by Rear Admiral William S. Cowles, the Chief of the Bureau of Equipment, Sweet recommended that the Navy purchase airplanes. The Navy's senior leadership, though, dismissed the idea. Speaking for them, Assistant Secretary of the Navy Beekman Winthrop declared that airplanes had not "progressed sufficiently at this time for use in the Navy."[8]

France hosted the first international air show and flying competition later that summer. Twenty-five aircraft competed for prizes at the Reims Air Meet (22–29 August 1909), which showcased aeronautic progress. While American Glenn Curtiss won two trophies for speed in his *Reims Racer,* European aircraft and aviators dominated the other events. The Wrights, concerned about infringement on their patents, refused to participate, though several contestants flew Wright aircraft. The U.S. Navy's observer at the show, Commander Frederick L. Chapin, recommended deploying airplanes on battleships and building new ships with flight decks. The Navy dismissed his recommendations, as it had Sweet's, but Glenn Curtiss would prove difficult to ignore.[9]

Curtiss, who set a world speed record riding one of his motorcycles in 1907, expanded his business into aircraft engines and then airplanes over the next few years. Flying airplanes of his own design, he quickly won several prizes including the $10,000 Bennett Prize for the fastest twenty-kilometer flight and the Prix de la Vitesse for averaging 46.63 mph over thirty kilometers at Reims. The following year, the flamboyant inventor flew one of his new planes 137 miles (with two stops to refuel) down the Hudson River from Albany to New York City to win a $10,000 prize offered by the *New York World.* Afterward he told reporters that airplanes would soon take off from ships and that warships were already vulnerable to air attack. "The battles of the future," he proclaimed, would "be fought in the air." In July Curtiss flew over a battleship-sized target on Lake Keuka and dropped eight-inch lengths of lead pipe on it, striking it repeatedly. The stunt encouraged the *New York Times* to join the *World* in trumpeting the military possibilities of aviation.[10]

THE U.S. NAVY DISCOVERS AVIATION

The Wrights' 1908 demonstrations at the Reims air show and other aerial exhibitions highlighted the new possibilities of military aviation. After Reims, all of Europe's major powers increased their aviation spending and research. The U.S. Navy's leaders, though, proved slow to recognize aviation's potential and balked at funding aviation research.

A certain amount of skepticism and penny-pinching was to be expected. The U.S. Navy had just completed the greatest transformation in its history. Captivated by the writings of Alfred Thayer Mahan, Congress funded an enormous expansion of the fleet including more than two dozen new battleships, as Mahan's disciples reoriented strategy from commerce raiding and coast defense to seeking command of the sea through decisive capital ship engagements. The United States soon boasted one of the largest and most modern fleets in the world. Each new class of battleships grew in size and armament, carrying guns so large that directing accurate fire became a problem. The 12-inch guns of the new battleship *Michigan* (BB-27), for example, could fire shells out to 21,000 yards. Under the best conditions, though, the ship's spotters could only see out to 16,000 yards. The Navy experimented with sending spotters aloft in kites and kite-balloons, but as with balloons on land, these proved problematic. Practical airplanes and airships appeared as the world's navies worked to solve this problem, though most naval officers failed to see their potential.

While the fleet expanded and officers improved their technical skills, much of the Navy's administration remained rooted in the past. To simplify the Navy's convoluted administrative structure and reduce the power of its eight bureaus, which despite a generation of reform continued to operate as independent fiefdoms, Secretary of the Navy George Meyer introduced the Aide System on 1 December 1909. Four aides (operations, personnel, inspection, and material), who reported directly to the Secretary of the Navy, would oversee different bureaus and encourage their cooperation. The Aide for Material oversaw the Navy's four technical bureaus: Construction and Repair, Ordnance, Engineering, and Equipment. Congress never sanctioned this arrangement, which failed to resolve fully the centurylong problem of interbureau cooperation. Bureau chiefs maintained substantial independence, particularly over their finances, which Congress continued to allocate to individual bureaus in annual naval appropriations.[11]

Among the officers who staffed this new administrative apparatus was Captain Washington Irving Chambers. The personal choice of Rear Admiral William H. Swift, the first Aide for Material, Chambers relinquished his brief command of the battleship *Louisiana* and became Swift's assistant. An 1876 Naval Academy graduate, Chambers played a critical role in the process of reform and technological innovation that transformed the U.S. Navy into a world-class fleet. One of the Navy's leading intellectuals, Chambers taught at the Naval War College in the 1890s and later contributed to the design of torpedoes and the Navy's first all-big-gun battleships. He came to his new position with a record of technological aptitude and substantial experience in the Navy's labyrinthine administration and incessant bureaucratic squabbling.[12]

While the Navy's leaders proved slow to notice aviation developments, the growing clamor and the volume of mail promising that airplanes would revolutionize warfare overwhelmed Secretary Meyer's office. He demanded that his aides assign someone to deal with it. So, Rear Admiral Frank F. Fletcher, who had succeeded Swift as Aide for Material, added the aviation correspondence to Chambers' other duties in September 1910. A friend of Chambers since their days as Naval Academy midshipmen, Fletcher's support proved important as Chambers sought to master his new responsibilities and bring airplanes into the Navy.[13]

Curious about aviation, Chambers had discussed recent developments with Lieutenant Sweet and had observed flights of lighter-than-air craft and Wilbur Wright's flights for the 1909 Hudson-Fulton Celebration. Reading the aviation mail fired his imagination. He arranged for his friend Captain Templin Potts, the Navy's Chief Intelligence Officer, to send him copies of all reports he received on aviation, which he translated himself. The more he studied aviation, the more its potential fascinated him. Chambers became the most vocal champion of aviation within the Navy.[14]

In October 1910, Admiral George Dewey and the Navy's General Board, an advisory body of senior officers, recommended deploying airplanes on the new scout cruiser *Chester*. When this came to their attention, the Chiefs of both the Bureau of Construction and Repair and the Bureau of Engineering separately wrote Meyer requesting that he assign responsibility for aviation to his particular bureau. Chambers scrambled to maintain control of aviation and convinced Meyer's assistant, Beekman Winthrop, to intervene on his behalf. Winthrop ordered each bureau to assign an officer to coordinate with Chambers. This decision, which remained in force throughout these years, split responsibility for aviation into three parts: Chambers remained tenuously in charge of personnel, policymaking, and the general direction of the program; the Bureau of Construction took charge of the planes; while the Bureau of Engineering looked after their engines. This was a poor arrangement, made worse first, because bureau chiefs received temporary rank as rear admirals, so they outranked Chambers and routinely bypassed him to speak directly to the Secretary of the Navy; and second, because when Congress later sanctioned this arrangement, it split funding among Chambers and the two bureaus.[15]

After examining about three dozen different aircraft and discussing aviation progress with the Wrights, Curtiss, and other inventors, and with pilots at aviation meets at Belmont Park, New York, and Halethorpe, Maryland, Chambers recommended that the Navy establish a national aeronautic laboratory to research flight, assign officers to study aviation and adapt it to the fleet's needs, construct an airfield, train pilots, buy a few airplanes, and establish a distinct Naval Aeronautics Office to direct this effort. His report fell on deaf ears, so Chambers went in person, first to Rear Admiral Richard Wainwright, the Aide for Operations, and then to Secretary Meyer. Wainwright told him that "the present state of aeroplanes" did not merit funding, while Meyer dismissed airplanes as carnival toys. Glenn Curtiss received a similar response when he approached Meyer on his own.[16]

Hoping to force the issue, Chambers and Curtiss planned a demonstration for the Navy. Publisher and aviation enthusiast John Barry Ryan helped arrange a flight from a Hamburg-America passenger liner. Curtiss supplied a plane and pilot, Eugene Ely, but an accident damaged the plane, and the ship sailed before Curtiss repaired it. The liner's German registry, though, allowed Chambers to hint darkly that the Germans were pursuing naval aviation. Supported by Fletcher and civilian aviation organizations, Chambers convinced the Navy to facilitate the demonstration. So, Eugene Ely took off from an improvised flight deck paid for by Ryan and erected on the cruiser *Birmingham* on 14 November 1910. Meyer's grudging congratulatory letter arrived a few days later and spelled out further a requirement for Chambers and Curtiss to meet: "When you show me that it is feasible for an aeroplane to alight on the water alongside a battleship and be hoisted aboard without any false deck to receive it, I shall believe the airship is of practical benefit to the Navy."[17]

Essentially, Meyer asked for a seaplane, which Chambers, inspired by Henri Fabre's March 1910 seaplane flight, had already asked Curtiss to build. Fabre equipped a monoplane with three floats and completed the world's first seaplane flight, taking off from and landing on the calm waters of la Méde harbor near Marseilles. Since Curtiss' seaplane was not ready, Chambers rushed ahead with the second half of his demonstration. He arranged to land a plane on the armored cruiser *Pennsylvania* (ACR-4), then anchored in San Francisco Bay and commanded by Captain Charles Pond, another of Chambers' friends. Workers erected a 119-foot wooden platform over the ship's aft deck, attached three metal hooks to the bottom of Ely's plane, and strung twenty ropes between 50-pound sandbags along the deck for the hooks to catch. On 18 January 1911 Ely took off from shore, circled the *Pennsylvania*, and then turned to land. He cut his engine fifty feet from the ship and glided in for a landing, but a sudden gust of wind lifted the plane. Responding quickly, Ely pushed the plane's nose down and landed on the deck. The hooks caught eight of the ropes, which stopped the plane before it crashed into the canvas barrier at the end of the platform. The *Pennsylvania*'s crew refueled the plane, and Ely took off from that same short platform a few hours later after a celebratory toast with Chambers and ship's officers. Over the next few days Chambers arranged a succession of other flights and demonstrations for the officers of the Pacific Fleet, which coincided with a nearby civilian aviation meet. Captain Pond was particularly impressed and announced that he was "positively assured of the importance of the aeroplane in future naval warfare."[18] Two weeks later, John Alexander Douglas McCurdy, shadowed by a squadron of destroyers arranged by Chambers, attempted to fly from Key West to Cuba in a Curtiss biplane. While engine trouble forced him down fourteen miles from Havana, he flew an accurate course for one hundred miles, further underlining the rapid progress in aviation.[19]

THE FIRST PILOTS AND PLANES

Chambers still had no budget, but Curtiss offered to train Navy pilots for free. The Wrights made a similar offer contingent on purchasing airplanes, which Chambers promised to do. Only a handful of Navy officers had requested aviation duty—how many remains uncertain since their requests often disappeared in the Navy's bureaucracy before reaching Chambers. Nonetheless, he secured his first pilots, splitting them between Curtiss and the Wrights. Lieutenant Theodore Ellyson trained with Curtiss, and Lieutenant John Rodgers went to the Wrights.[20] Rodgers had witnessed Ely's landing while serving on *Pennsylvania* and afterward ascended in a box kite to spot and direct the ship's fire by telephone. Two more pilots arrived the following summer: Lieutenant John Towers,[21] previously the Chief Gunfire Officer on the *Michigan*, who trained with Curtiss; and Ensign Victor Herbster, who trained with the Wrights. Towers' experiences trying to direct the *Michigan*'s guns convinced him of aviation's importance despite the efforts of senior officers to discourage him from such foolishness.[22]

Chambers needed a plane better suited to the Navy's needs than either Curtiss or the Wrights manufactured, and he worked to develop good relations with both companies. Curtiss proved more responsive to his requests and, unlike the Wrights, was willing to borrow and improve upon the ideas of others. Chambers had first approached the Wrights to fly a plane off a ship, but they declined, as they had most suggestions for demonstrations and contests. Curtiss loved the idea, and his daring and outgoing nature endeared him to the Navy's pilots. Unlike the Wrights, Curtiss also brought Navy officers into his design process. Lieutenant Ellyson helped Curtiss design and build the pontoons for his first seaplane and test a number of devices and modifications to his airplanes.[23]

Stephen K. Stein

Lieutenant John Towers was convinced of the importance of an aviation program in spite of the skepticism of senior officers.

The Wrights, though, did things their own way, and frequently ignored requests and suggestions from Chambers and his pilots. Relations worsened after Wilbur died from typhoid fever on 30 May 1912. Withdrawn and taciturn, Orville lacked Wilbur's charm and had no interest in building seaplanes. He was, though, very interested in enforcing the Wrights' patents. The Wrights had filed suit against Curtiss in 1909 and they continued to sue other pilots and inventors who infringed on their pioneering work to enjoin them from building, selling, or even exhibiting aircraft. Apart from complicating the work of military and civilian aviators, the patent fight hindered aviation research and development in the United States. The federal government did not step in and settle the dispute until 1917 when preparation for war necessitated a settlement, which it arranged by cross-licensing the key patents through the newly created Manufacturers' Aircraft Association.[24]

While the Navy's aviators favored Curtiss, the Army favored the Wrights, and this may have exacerbated the tendency of Army and Navy aviation leaders to go their own way. Navy aviators, who operated from a small airfield Chambers established near the Naval Academy at Greensbury Point in the summer of 1911, occasionally socialized with Army aviators stationed at nearby College Park, Maryland, but few friendships developed between the two groups. Whatever the reasons, cooperation and resource sharing between the Services' aviation units remained slight.

The Navy's airfield was also conveniently near the Bureau of Engineering's Experiment Station. Perennially short of tools and supplies, Chambers' pilots and mechanics borrowed these in regular nighttime raids that began after the station's officers refused to support the aviation program—an all-too-common problem in these years. They also regularly wrote manufacturers, requesting samples of oil, gasoline, and other materials and equipment they needed, suggesting that lucrative contracts were in the offing. They often paid expenses out of their own pockets since the Navy proved slow to reimburse them and sometimes forgot them entirely.[25]

Seaplanes were critical both to satisfy Meyer's requirements and to prove that airplanes could operate with the fleet. While a few visionaries suggested constructing aircraft carriers, Chambers saw seaplanes as the only viable option given the state of technology, lack of funds, and scant support from Navy leadership. Early in his career, Chambers had witnessed new technologies isolated by the Navy's bureaucracy and ignored by officers, particularly torpedoes, which remained confined to the Newport Torpedo Station and its two torpedo boats before the Spanish-American War. Chambers hoped to put seaplanes on every cruiser and battleship in the Navy. This would not only spread the gospel of aviation, but also solve his financial problems by funding planes as part of a warship's regular equipment rather than through separate appropriations.

Over the winter, Chambers relocated most of the aviation unit to Curtiss' North Island base near San Diego where they could continue flying and also work with Curtiss on his new seaplane. Working with Ellyson, Curtiss developed effective pontoons and attached them to one of his planes, which they tested in several flights in late January. On 17 February 1911 Curtiss flew this new seaplane from shore and landed near the *Pennsylvania*, whose crew hoisted the plane aboard, refueled it, and lowered it back into the water. Curtiss took off without problems, satisfying Meyer's terms.

Armed with this success, Chambers convinced Meyer to support a $25,000 appropriation for naval aviation—a rather small sum when one considers that the Royal Navy had spent $175,000 on aviation the previous year. Congress passed the Navy's appropriation that March, but Chambers could not spend it until the fiscal year began in July. Meyer again refused Chambers' request to create an Office of Aeronautics with a dedicated staff, but months of additional lobbying convinced him to clarify Chambers' duties. Meyer ordered him to "keep informed" of the progress of aeronautics "with a view to advising the Department concerning the adaptability of such material for naval warfare, especially for the purpose of naval scouting." He was to guide the training of Navy aviators and consult with the bureaus involved in his work. Final authority to carry out Chambers' recommendations, though, rested "entirely with the bureaus having cognizance of the details." This arrangement actually magnified all the problems of bureau coordination that Meyer had created the aide system to resolve. It left aviation, the great marvel of the twentieth century, saddled with nineteenth-century administrative problems. Chambers continued to operate without an official title or solid place in the Navy's hierarchy, signing his correspondence with a self-made title, "Officer in Charge of Aviation."[26]

Chambers' friends continued to help him, or at least try to. On 30 March, Admiral Dewey transferred Chambers to the General Board where he would have clerical help and a voice in policymaking. Shortly afterward though, Congress assigned the $25,000 aviation appropriation to the Bureau of Navigation, which in those years oversaw personnel assignments. So Chambers had to arrange his transfer there, where no one wanted him. The Chief of the bureau, Reginald Nicholson, refused to assign him any staff and suggested that Chambers work from home, though Chambers found a corner in the dank basement of the War, State, and Navy building to set up shop. It was, he told friends, "a good place to catch a cold."[27]

Chambers' small budget proved just enough for him to order three planes, two from Curtiss and one from the Wrights, which he ordered on 8 May, generally considered the official birth of U.S. Navy Aviation. Curtiss delivered his planes in early July. One of these was a seaplane, the A-1 Triad, which had retractable wheels attached to its floats allowing it to operate from land and sea. The Wrights delivered their plane (the B-1) a few weeks later—a conventional plane rather than the requested seaplane. Naval constructors William McEntee and Holden C. Richardson, who worked closely with the aviation program, designed and built pontoons for the Wright plane. The following year, they helped Chambers' pilots and mechanics assemble another Wright plane (the B-2) from spare and scavenged parts. The Wrights, who proved increasingly difficult to deal with, would sell only two more planes to the Navy. The B-1, underpowered before the addition of floats, rarely managed to exceed thirty-five miles per hour.[28]

By the end of 1911, Chambers had acquired a small mechanical and engineering staff, and his pilots had logged about one hundred hours in each of his three airplanes, often carrying passengers to demonstrate the potential of aviation. Chambers assumed that his team would build rapidly on this foundation the following year and that new demonstrations of airplanes' growing capabilities would clear bureaucratic obstacles and yield more support and funding. Essentially he believed that all he had to do was repeat his 1911 experiences, producing new and better aviation demonstrations to overcome each new obstacle, which would open the financial floodgates and lead to the integration of aviation into the fleet. The Army's pilots did much the same, hoping to promote their own program with successful tests and demonstrations. Given the poor funding of the United States' two air Services, they could do little else.[29]

EXPANDING NAVAL AVIATION

Chambers spent the first months of 1912 lobbying Congress. He asked for $150,000, which Congress reduced to $35,000. Another round of lobbying and letters from aviation enthusiasts raised it to $65,000, split among the three bureaus ($10,000 for the Bureau of Navigation, $20,000 for the Engineering Bureau, and $35,000 for Construction and Repair). The Army did little better that year, securing only $100,000 for its larger aviation program. The European powers, of course, spent much more. Between 1908 and 1913 Germany and France both spent more than $20 million on military aviation compared to a total of $435,000 spent by the United States Army and Navy. Not only did each of the major European powers outspend the United States in these years, so did Brazil, Bulgaria, Chile, Greece, and Japan.[30]

Chambers ordered three more planes including a flying boat (C-1), a new Curtiss design with a boatlike fuselage instead of a central pontoon. Several new pilots arrived in the second half of the year: Ensign William D. Billingsley and Ensign Godfrey de Courcelles Chevalier; Lieutenant Patrick N. L. Bellinger; and Marine 1st Lieutenant Alfred A. Cunningham and Marine 1st Lieutenant Bernard L. Smith. While they were learning to fly, Chambers arranged a succession of new demonstrations. Helped by Ensign Charles H. Maddox, a radio expert, Towers and Rodgers transmitted messages to shore stations and a torpedo boat. Towers, the rising star of the aviation program, also worked with Lieutenant Chester Nimitz, then commanding the Atlantic Fleet's submarine flotilla, to demonstrate that planes could locate submarines. On 6 October 1912 Towers set an endurance record by remaining aloft for more than six hours and also bested several other American records. Commanded by Towers, the aviation unit joined the Atlantic Fleet's maneuvers off Guantanamo Bay, Cuba, in January. For the next eight weeks, the Navy's five planes spotted for gunfire, took photographs, hunted for submarines, dropped small bombs, and successfully located "enemy" ships. Encouraged by Chambers, pilots carried passengers on more than a hundred flights, among them Lieutenant Colonel John A. Lejeune and Lieutenant Ernest J. King who both received a ten-minute flight and aviation sales pitch from Towers.[31]

Chambers needed to find a way to launch aircraft from the Navy's existing warships. He studied the catapults used by Langley and the Wrights and also built on his own experience with torpedoes to design a compressed air catapult. Tested and improved over the summer of 1912, the catapult successfully launched Ellyson (in the A-3) on 12 November. Leaving the project in Richardson's capable hands, Chambers announced to reporters that a working catapult eliminated the last barrier to deploying planes to the fleet. Hoping to pressure his superiors, he predicted that each of the fleet's battleships would carry a seaplane by the end of 1913.[32]

Less than miniscule funding hindered Chambers' work. The efforts by leaders of the Bureau of Construction and Repair to gain control of aviation repeatedly obstructed Chambers and slowed the growth of Navy aviation. Toward the end of 1912, for example, Chambers discovered that the bureaus had sabotaged his lobbying efforts by telling members of Congress that they needed money for other projects and that funding aviation was premature. The same thing happened in 1913, when Congress again authorized only $65,000 for Navy aviation. So, U.S. Navy aviation grew slowly in 1912 against considerable resistance, while other navies surged ahead. Royal Navy aviators duplicated Ely's shipboard take-off, and European aviators soon matched and then surpassed other American records. The French navy moved particularly quickly, converting the destroyer *Foudre* to a seaplane tender in 1912. The Royal Navy did the same to the obsolete cruiser *Hermes* the following year.[33]

The change in administration following the 1912 election compounded Chambers' problems. New Secretary of the Navy Josephus Daniels assumed his position determined to run things strictly according to existing laws and regulation. This necessarily entailed either dismantling or making permanent Meyer's ad hoc administrative arrangements. The first indication of changes to come was Daniel's threat to retire Captain Templin Potts, the Chief of Naval Intelligence, for lack of sea duty.[34] As he had Chambers, Meyer had recalled Potts from a battleship command to assume his new post. As word spread of Potts' problems, virtually every officer on shore applied for command at sea, producing a tremendous shake-up in the Navy's administration. Hutchinson I. Cone, Chambers' strongest supporter in the bureaus, relinquished his position as Chief of the Bureau of Engineering and returned to sea as a Lieutenant Commander. Others left as well, including Ellyson, and Chambers watched most of his carefully cultivated group of supporters and contacts sail out to sea with the Atlantic Fleet. Chambers, himself short of sea duty, refused to apply for sea duty until Daniels appointed an officer to replace him in charge of aviation.[35]

Chambers also ran into problems with his new commander, Rear Admiral Bradley Fiske. A reformer appointed Aide for Operations in February 1913, Fiske desperately wanted to become the first Chief of Naval Operations, an office everyone expected Congress would soon create. In 1911, Fiske had stunned the General Board by suggesting that torpedo-armed airplanes could defend the Philippines. When he returned to Washington two years later after a tour at sea, Fiske still understood neither the complexities of aviation technology nor the intricacies of interbureau politics as they related to aviation matters. Fancying himself a master of new technology, he wrested control of the Navy's aviation program. A visionary, Fiske understood neither the "problems of builders or pilots." He routinely clashed with the pragmatic Chambers, who insisted that unless critical technical problems were solved, all of

Fiske's ideas would come to naught. Fiske quickly tired of these debates and maneuvered to replace Chambers with a more amenable officer.[36]

Internal resistance to aviation was such that Chambers spent most of 1913 working to overcome it, emphasizing struggles inside the Navy over lobbying Congress for more money or even saving his own career. In June, shortly after Chambers received a gold medal from the National Aeronautical Society for his pioneering work and aviation advocacy, the Navy announced his retirement for lack of sea service as a Captain. Chambers, in fact, had belatedly applied for sea duty, but Fiske interceded with Daniels and prevented his reassignment to a battleship command. It is also likely that Chambers' insistence that a qualified officer first relieve him in command of naval aviation had irked Daniels. While Fiske searched for an officer willing to risk his career by succeeding Chambers, Chambers launched a last desperate effort to overcome the combination of political and administrative neglect and bureaucratic competition that slowed aviation progress, focusing his efforts on improving safety, funding a national aeronautic research lab, and expanding the naval air service.

Newly appointed Assistant Secretary of the Navy Franklin D. Roosevelt—probably at Admiral Dewey's suggestion—facilitated Chambers' campaign by appointing him to chair a special aeronautics board (usually called the Chambers Board) on 7 October 1913. Chambers added Towers to the board, the Marine Corps sent Cunningham, and each of the bureaus sent a representative. Richardson represented Construction and Repair; Commander Carlo B. Brittain represented Navigation; Commander Samuel S. Robison represented Engineering; and Lieutenant Manly H. Simons represented Ordnance. The board met in mid-November for twelve days and afterward issued a unanimous report that charted the future of naval aviation. Its recommendations totaled $1,297,700 and included purchasing fifty airplanes and three dirigibles and assigning a ship to serve as a mobile aviation base, as Britain and France had. While Fiske had lobbied to create a separate aviation bureau, the existing bureaus strongly opposed this, and the Chambers Board simply recommended an Office of Naval Aeronautics, directed by a Captain and a small staff that included representatives from the Marine Corps and the four bureaus involved in aviation. Similarly, they refused to choose sides in what had become a fractious dispute and recommended funding aeronautic research at both the Navy's model basin and the Smithsonian.[37]

Airplanes crashed frequently in these experimental years. Ellyson, for example, was seriously injured in a crash on 16 October 1911 that wrecked the A-1. Yet in almost three years of flying, no U.S. Navy aviator had died in a crash. This was an anomaly as aviation fatalities, which totaled thirty-four by the end of 1910, continued to rise. More than two hundred people died in crashes in 1911 and 1912, among them Eugene Ely, several Army aviators, and five of the Wright exhibition team's nine pilots. These fatalities troubled Chambers who worried about his pilots and recognized that the danger of flying discouraged congressional funding. He increasingly emphasized safety, banned most stunt flying, and worked with the aviation community to improve safety. The growing fatalities also affected his pilots. Cunningham stopped flying because his fiancée refused to marry an aviator. Rodgers left aviation shortly after his cousin Cal, a popular civilian stunt pilot, died in a crash.[38]

Whatever the reasons for Navy aviation's luck thus far—and those reasons clearly included Chambers' safety campaign and the quality and training of his pilots—that luck ran out on 20 June 1913. Billingsley, piloting the B-2 with Towers as a passenger, encountered a sudden updraft that tossed the men against the controls. Neither had worn the poorly fitting and uncomfortable safety straps mandated by Chambers. The B-2 stalled and then plunged toward the ground. Billingsley, thrown from the plane, died. Towers managed to cling to the rigging and fell 1,600 feet with the plane. Severely injured, he spent four months recuperating.[39]

Stalls, often described by pilots as "holes in the air," contributed to many crashes in these years. Pilots had yet to develop techniques to recover from them and regain control of their aircraft. Poor control systems, which builders had not standardized, made matters worse. The dual levers of several Wright models were particularly non-intuitive. The left lever moved a plane's nose up and down, while the pilot moved the right lever forward to bank left and backward to bank right. The rudder control was attached to the top of this lever. Wright aircraft were also extremely unstable and placed great demands on their pilots who had to work the controls constantly to keep the plane aloft and prevent stalling. All five Army pilots who died in crashes in these years died in Wright planes. Yet another problem was the pusher configuration of these planes. Mounted in the rear, engines fell forward and crushed pilots in several crashes. This further discouraged them from wearing safety straps. Being thrown from the plane seemed less risky than being trapped in one's seat and crushed to death. Aeronautic research was critical to improve safety.[40]

THE FIGHT FOR A NATIONAL LAB

The Wrights' 1903 success obscured the rather poor state of aeronautic research in the United States. Aeronautic research facilities proliferated across Europe in the first decade of the twentieth century, while the only comparable American operation—a small laboratory with a wind tunnel created by Albert F. Zahm at Catholic University in 1901—soon closed from lack of funds. While European scientists and engineers developed a mature aviation technology for war, Americans remained rooted in an experimental era due to small budgets and the limited vision of senior military and civilian leaders. Towers, who attended the Gordon Bennett air meet in

Chicago in September 1912, complained bitterly about French aircraft, "which were so far ahead of anything in this country that there is no comparison."[41]

Indeed, aircraft improved dramatically between 1909 and 1913 largely due to the work of European inventors who benefited from a generation of experimentation and generous government funding. Inspired by the Wright flights of 1908 and 1909, Louis Blériot, Henry Farman, Gabriel Voison, and others produced a succession of airplanes boasting steadily improved performance. The requirements for the Bennett Prize, for example, increased from 12.4 miles (20 km) to 124 miles (200 km), while the speeds of its entrants more than doubled. In 1913, aviators flying the latest French airplanes swept international awards and set new records in categories ranging from speed (108 mph) and altitude (18,400 feet) to endurance and distance, the latter marked by Roland Garros' 453-mile flight across the Mediterranean Sea. No American manufacturers competed for the Bennett Prize that year. None could match the latest French designs. In fact, Curtiss' 1909 victories in his *Reims Racer* would be the last speed records won by an American plane until 1925 when Jimmy Doolittle would win the Schneider Trophy in another Curtiss plane, the R3C-2 racer.[42]

Making matters worse was a "brain drain": successful American inventors left for Europe. Lawrence Sperry who developed a gyroscopic stabilizer with the help of Glenn Curtiss and several Navy pilots, left for France where he won lucrative prizes and contracts. Riley Scott, a former coast artillery officer, developed a bombsight that achieved a ten-foot accuracy in 1911 tests. After the Army refused to fund further development, Scott left for Paris where he won a $27,500 prize and a government contract. Shortly afterward, the Army also rejected a lightweight, drum-fed machine gun whose inventor, Lieutenant Colonel Isaac Lewis, also departed for Europe where he quickly arranged production contracts.[43]

Long aware of the growing technological gap between American and European aviation and the problems faced by American inventors, Chambers argued for the creation of a national aeronautic laboratory and included recommendations for government prizes for successful inventors in all his official reports. Working with Zahm and Charles D. Walcott, the Secretary of the Smithsonian Institution, Chambers took his campaign for a national lab public in the summer of 1912, and convinced President William Howard Taft to appoint the nineteen-member National Aerodynamic Laboratory Commission. The commission dispatched Zahm and Jerome Hunsaker, a brilliant Navy officer who helped the Massachusetts Institute of Technology (MIT) establish its aeronautics program, to tour European labs; their reports confirmed the inadequacy of American facilities. Unfortunately the Taft administration failed to act before leaving office, forcing Chambers and his supporters to resume the campaign in 1913. Walcott briefly reopened Langley's aeronautical laboratory until Congress and a lack of funds forced him to close it down again. The Navy's Bureau of Construction and Repair began expanding its facilities at the Washington Navy Yard to support aviation research, but these efforts proceeded slowly.

Lack of funds created an absurd situation in which leading advocates of aeronautic research assumed the government would fund only one lab. The Smithsonian and the Bureau of Construction and Repair's Model Basin at the Washington Navy Yard emerged as the leading contenders, though MIT also threw its hat into the ring. Chambers again found himself at odds with the Bureau of Construction and Repair as its Chief, Rear Admiral Richard M. Watt, and his assistant, Captain David W. Taylor, opposed a national aviation research lab, "fearing that it would overlap with the work" of their bureau, which should lead aviation research by focusing on practical issues rather than the theoretical studies favored by Smithsonian scientists. After prolonged lobbying, Chambers and the national lab advocates won their fight in 1915 when Congress created the National Advisory Committee for Aeronautics (NACA). Composed of Army, Navy, and civilian members, it would oversee a national aeronautic lab, placing aviation research outside the squabbling bureaus and inter-Service rivalries. Hunsaker continued to work with MIT, where he built a wind tunnel in 1914. Taylor completed the Navy's wind tunnel the following year. Together, these laid a broad foundation for aeronautic research that came to fruition after World War I.[44]

THE BRISTOL ERA

For his replacement, Chambers suggested Towers or Lieutenant Commander Henry C. Mustin, who assisted Richardson with experimental work and learned to fly on his own. After a prolonged search, Fiske settled on Captain Mark Bristol who assumed charge of Navy aviation on 17 December 1913, though the Navy did not formally establish the Office of Naval Aeronautics until the following July; only in November did it name Bristol its Director. Bristol's prior career had much in common with Chambers'. Both were line officers with substantial ordnance experience, and the two had served together for a time at the Newport Torpedo Station. Assured of Fiske's support, Bristol believed he could build rapidly on the foundation laid by Chambers and perhaps even achieve Chambers' goal of a seaplane on every battleship in the fleet. Stripped of his authority but essential to the program, Chambers remained on duty despite his retirement and continued to guide experimental work into 1919.

To allow year-round flying, Bristol relocated the aviation unit, which then totaled seven aircraft, nine officers, and twenty-three enlisted men, to Pensacola in January. He also secured the obsolete battleship *Mississippi* (BB-23) for aviation training with Mustin as acting Captain. Officially designated a Naval Air Station in November, Pensacola would long remain the center of Navy aviation training. Having just erected their temporary hangars and begun normal operations, most of the aviation unit redeployed to Mexico with the Atlantic Fleet in April after President Woodrow Wilson ordered American intervention in the Mexican Civil War. Towers, Smith, and Chevalier loaded three Curtiss aircraft aboard the *Birmingham* and sailed to Tampico. Shortly afterward, Mustin loaded a Curtiss seaplane and flying boat on to the *Mississippi* and sailed for Vera Cruz with Bellinger and three pilots fresh from training. Rear Admiral Fletcher, commanding at Vera Cruz, used his planes extensively. Bellinger scouted for mines ahead of the fleet and reconnoitered Mexican positions during which he was hit by ground fire, the first combat damage of a Navy aircraft. The fighting was brief, though, and the pilots soon settled into routine operations, often taking reporters and photographers for rides. With little to do off Tampico, the *Birmingham* and her aviators sailed to Vera Cruz, where the combined aviation unit continued daily operations until sailing home in mid-June. Atlantic Fleet Commander Admiral Charles J. Badger praised the aviators, as did Secretary Daniels who declared airplanes "one of the arms of the Fleet, the same as battleships, destroyers, submarines, and cruisers."[45] The government sold the *Mississippi* to Greece on her return, but Bristol obtained the newer and larger *North Carolina* (ACR-12), under Captain Joseph W. Oman with Mustin as his Executive Officer, as a replacement.

Operations at Pensacola had just returned to normal when war broke out in Europe. German troops overran Belgium in August and advanced toward Paris. Assisted by observation aircraft, the French halted the Germans at the Battle of the Marne. As the war entered its static phase, the U.S. government dispatched the *North Carolina*, along with the *Tennessee*, to retrieve Americans trapped by the war. *North Carolina* sailed with Bellinger and other pilots, but without her aircraft, and spent the next thirteen months in European waters. Mustin blamed Bristol for the abandoned aircraft but took advantage of the voyage to gather information on European aviation. The *North Carolina*'s absence disrupted aviation training, and Navy leaders compounded this by assigning its most experienced pilots as attachés to observe the war and gather information. Towers went to Britain, Herbster to Germany, and Smith to France. With hardly any pilots left in Pensacola, aviation operations ebbed and focused on experimental work and practice bomb runs, in which pilots tossed small bombs over the side by hand. Command devolved to Chevalier, until Lieutenant Kenneth Whiting, the last naval aviator trained at the Wright school, arrived in September.[46]

Mustin arranged his transfer to Pensacola in January, and training resumed in July when the first class of ten officers (two of them Marines) arrived along with twenty enlisted personnel to train as ground crew. Lieutenant Richard C. Saufley took a Curtiss seaplane up to 14,500 feet and set a new endurance record of eight hours and twenty minutes in the air. Richardson completed work on Chambers' catapult. Installed on a barge, it successfully launched Bellinger, just returned from Europe, in the AB-2 on 16 April 1915. Transferred to the *North Carolina* after her return from Europe, it launched Mustin, also flying the AB-2, on 5 November.[47]

Chambers had evinced some interest in lighter-than-air craft, but paltry budgets prevented their purchase. By 1915 Towers, Mustin, and most of the other pilots doubted their effectiveness. Bristol, though, became enamored with the craft. After awkwardly comparing dirigibles to aerial battleships in testimony to Congress, he ordered a blimp from the Connecticut Aircraft Company in May. The company lacked experience and the project fell behind. Hunsaker, brought in to save the project, designed a whole a new airship the following year (eventually designated DN-1). Bristol also ordered several balloons, training for which began in June 1916 after the first of them finally arrived at Pensacola.[48]

Like Chambers, Bristol experienced constant problems obtaining funds. Congress remained stingy and appropriated aviation funds to the bureaus, which often withheld some of the money. In 1915, for example, the Bureau of Navigation retained a third of its aviation funds.[49] Rather than the rapid progress he had expected, Bristol found himself repeating Chambers' experience of grueling lobbying to obtain a pittance. Bolstered by the reports of the Chambers Board and overseas naval attachés, he redoubled his lobbying in the last months of 1915, repeating Chambers' previous requests for fifty planes and two planes for each of the fleet's sixteen battleships. The timing was critical since, despite aggressive lobbying and scheming, Fiske did not become Chief of Naval Operations. Instead, Daniels appointed William S. Benson, a relatively junior Captain, to that position on 11 May 1915. Regardless of his personal ambitions and routine dismissal of serious technical issues, Fiske had favored and supported aviation. Benson gave it little thought and considered the *North Carolina* and her few aircraft adequate to the Navy's needs.

While Congress dismissed out of hand Bristol's request for $8 million to convert two merchant ships into aircraft carriers, it authorized $1 million for aviation, marking a tremendous victory for Bristol and the culmination of Chambers' long-delayed hopes. Congress also, however, downgraded Bristol's title to Officer in Charge of Naval Aeronautics. He became an assistant in the Material Division of the Office of Naval Operations, a position not unlike Chambers' when he directed Navy aviation, with his authority reduced to making recommendations on the "type, numbers and general characteristics of aircraft."[50]

Bristol chose not to fight this decision, instead focusing on spending the $1 million appropriation and he accomplished much over the next six months. Working with his Army counterparts, he arranged the standardization of airplane controls systems. He sent Mustin to tour American factories, which employed only 168 workers who manufactured mostly obsolete planes. Only Curtiss, already busy filling orders for his JN seaplanes and larger flying boats, manufactured modern and export-worthy airplanes. Towers buttressed Mustin's report and together they finally convinced Bristol to order modern European aircraft. The war, though, prevented their delivery.[51]

To escape Chambers' fate, Bristol arranged to assume command of the *North Carolina* in March 1916 while retaining his reduced aviation responsibilities. With four planes aboard, *North Carolina* joined the Atlantic Fleet off Guantanamo for maneuvers. Flying planes that differed little from those first ordered by Chambers in 1911, the pilots scouted for the fleet and launched mock attacks on shore targets and the antiquated gunboat *Petrel*. These maneuvers highlighted both the fragility and obsolescence of their equipment, particularly the catapult, which required repair after almost every launching. As Bellinger bitterly noted, the "planes now owned by the Navy are very poor excuses for whatever work may be assigned to them."[52]

Bristol's relations with Mustin, already poor, worsened in these months while Bristol worked to maintain control of all aviation matters despite his reduced authority and command of the *North Carolina*. A skilled pilot, Mustin blamed Bristol for aviation's slow progress and purchase of obsolete pusher aircraft. He routinely derided him for his ignorance of flying and critical technical matters and became particularly irked after Bristol required pilots stationed on the *North Carolina* to stand watches and perform other duties that took them away from flying. In was time, Mustin wrote his wife, for "Bristol to resign from aeronautics and let a real man take his job." Bristol, in turn, accused Mustin of failing to prepare the *North Carolina* for sea and neglecting the development of both the catapult and Pensacola's training programs. Neither officer understood the other's problems. Bristol lacked Chambers' grasp of the technical details of aviation, while Mustin failed to understand the importance of the bureaucratic and political battles that drained Bristol's time and energy as they had Chambers'.[53]

A succession of fatal crashes exacerbated these disputes. On 16 February 1915 Lieutenant (jg) James M. Murray was thrown out of the Burgess D-1 flying boat, a licensed copy of a Wright aircraft, and drowned. The crash reaffirmed Navy suspicions of Wright aircraft, but three months later Lieutenant (jg) Melvin L. Stolz died in a crash after his head was thrown back against the engine. Two more pilots died in crashes the following year, both in pusher aircraft. Bristol blamed Mustin, while Mustin blamed the planes. To keep peace, Benson removed Pensacola and the rest of aviation's shore establishment from Bristol's command on 1 June 1916. The dispute simmered over the next year as Mustin continued to press his case. He blamed the crashes on obsolete and dangerous aircraft and pressed the Navy to modernize. Benson quickly tired of this, and he revoked Mustin's designation as a naval aviator the following year.[54]

Otherwise, Benson allowed Navy aviation to languish. Lieutenant (jg) Clarence K. Bronson assumed Bristol's old Washington duties, representing aviation in the

Office of the Chief of Naval Operations. A personable aviator, he was too junior to challenge his skeptical superiors. His brief tenure ended in November when he died along with Lieutenant Luther Welsh while on a flight to test experimental bombs, which exploded prematurely. Control over aviation matters had already reverted to the bureaus, particularly the Bureau of Construction and Repair. Bristol was detached as Commander of the Air Service on 12 December 1916, and the title ceased to exist as Rear Admiral Albert Gleaves, who commanded the Atlantic Fleet's destroyers, assumed Bristol's remaining responsibilities.[55]

On 24 June 1916, the General Board issued a report that decried Navy aviation's slow progress. It repeated Chambers' and Bristol's requests for three dirigibles to patrol the Atlantic coast and two planes for each battleship and naval district, and asked for $5 million over the next three years to modernize and expand Navy aviation to European standards. Combined with reports on the importance of aircraft in the European war, the General Board's recommendations stimulated a reorganization of the Navy aviation establishment. Recalled from MIT, Hunsaker led a new Aircraft Division at the Bureau of Construction and Repair, which ordered thirty Curtiss N-9 seaplanes, the first Navy plane ordered in quantity. Delivered between November 1916 and February 1917, these tractor biplanes replaced the Navy's obsolete pushers and became its most popular training aircraft during World War I. New orders also separated manufacturing, experimental work, and training at Pensacola, and the base finally began to flourish. After six years of painstaking and often heartbreaking work, damaged and ruined careers, and several fatalities, aviation was emerging as a recognized and important part of the U.S. Navy.[56]

CONCLUSION

When World War I began, the U.S. military had only 23 planes, compared with Russia's 244, Germany's 232, France's 162, and Britain's 113. A number of historians have commented on the relative developmental failure of American military aviation in these years. Tom Crouch, for example, argues that Congress felt no urgency in the matter since the nation faced no pressing military threat. Herbert Johnson blames the Wright-Curtiss patent dispute for stalling innovation and reinforcing the skepticism of politicians and military leaders. Richard Hallion seconds this but casts more blame on Congress, which would fund demonstrations, but would not "build a robust combat-worthy aviation force." As 1914 ended, some members of Congress actually congratulated themselves for not wasting money on aviation. Looking within the Navy, Charles Melhorn, Andrew Krepinevich, and many others blame a so-called gun club of battleship-obsessed senior officers like Admiral Benson, who claimed aviation was "just a lot of noise." They, like many in Congress, lacked vision.[57]

The lack of an immediate threat, though, had not significantly hindered the dramatic expansion of the Navy Battle Fleet before World War I. Congress funded a succession of ever-larger battleships, but proved less generous with smaller warships and auxiliaries. Its members often proved more skeptical of new technology than did military leaders, and this skepticism mounted as each new battleship cost more than its predecessor. Congress proved even more reluctant to purchase airplanes, even though they cost only a few thousand dollars. The aggressive lobbying by aviation enthusiasts further irritated members of Congress and hardened their attitudes. Wild predictions about the future of aviation, which Chambers discouraged, served only to reinforce the skepticism of doubters. Still, the obvious weakness of aerial weapons provided a ready and easy argument against aviation funding.[58]

Chambers understood both the reverence for battleships and the skepticism toward new technology. He worked to present aviation as an adjunct to the battleship—not a threat to its existence, but a necessary complement that would enhance its effectiveness. Chambers became a master of this, putting forth arguments to which his successors would return for the next twenty years. He repeatedly insisted that "no airship or collection of airships" would "ever take the place of a battleship in the maintenance of sea power," while simultaneously insisting that future battleships would carry airplanes for both defense and offense in addition to scouting. As airplanes' capabilities improved, battleships would carry ever more planes.[59] Essentially, Chambers preached Mahanian battleship orthodoxy while systematically undermining it and building an aviation constituency within the Navy. This careful campaign mirrored that from the 1880s in which Chambers and other young officers carefully, but systematically, undermined the Navy's adherence to cruiser warfare, paving the way for Alfred Thayer Mahan's opus and the new paradigm of a battleship-centered fleet.[60]

In the absence of a persuasive aerial prophet, Chambers and his successors worked to present aviation within this Mahanian context that accepted the battleship as arbiter of naval supremacy. When they did so, they generally managed to slowly advance Navy aviation. When they overreached, as Bristol and Fiske did when lobbying for aircraft carriers in 1914 and 1915, they found their requests dismissed out of hand. Bristol achieved his greatest lobbying success by emulating Chambers' careful strategy.

In these experimental years, Chambers, Bristol, Ely, Ellyson, Towers, Richardson, Mustin, and a handful of other pilots and engineers overcame obstacles both within and outside the Navy to prove the utility of aviation. Given the paltry resources with which they worked, their accomplishments remain a testament to what steadfast determination and careful planning and strategy can accomplish. The Navy's close relationship with Curtiss lasted another generation as NACA helped put the United States at the forefront of aeronautic research. Seaplanes and the Chambers/

Richardson catapult, much refined and improved, eventually found their way aboard almost every battleship and cruiser in the fleet. Many of Chambers' hand-picked pilots went on to long, successful careers, particularly Towers and Bellinger—both future admirals. While Chambers faded into obscurity, Bristol returned to the fleet and soon hoisted his flag as an Admiral. Ellyson, the Navy's first aviator, crashed at sea on 27 February 1928. His body washed ashore at Willoughby Spit near the site of Ely's triumphant 1910 landing.

NOTES

1. Richard P. Hallion, *Taking Flight: Inventing the Aerial Age from Antiquity through the First World War* (New York and Oxford: Oxford University Press, 2003), pp. 67–68.
2. Archibald D. Turnbull and Clifford L. Lord, *History of United States Naval Aviation* (New Haven, CT: Yale University Press, 1949), pp. 1–3; and Henry Woodhouse, "US Naval Aeronautic Policies 1904–42," *U.S. Naval Institute Proceedings* 62 (February 1942), p. 163.
3. Hallion, *Taking Flight*, pp. 147–57.
4. George W. Melville, "The Engineer and the Problem of Aerial Navigation," *North American Review* 167 (December 1901), pp. 820–21.
5. Hallion, *Taking Flight*, p. 185; and Tom D. Crouch, *The Bishop's Boys* (New York: Norton, 1989), pp. 256–58.
6. For more on Squire see Charles J. Gross, "George Owen Squire and the Origins of American Military Aviation," *Journal of Military History* 54 (1990), pp. 281–305.
7. Tom D. Crouch, *Wings: A History of Aviation from Kites to the Space Age* (New York and London: W. W. Norton, 2003), pp. 95–99; and Turnbull and Lord, *History of United States Naval Aviation*, p. 4.
8. Hallion, *Taking Flight*, p. 257; Turnbull and Lord, *History of United States Naval Aviation*, pp. 4–5; and Charles Melhorn, *Two-Block Fox: The Rise of the Aircraft Carrier, 1911–1929* (Annapolis: Naval Institute Press, 1974), p. 118 footnote 3.
9. Hallion, *Taking Flight*, p. 258; Crouch, *Wings*, pp. 114–18; and Turnbull and Lord, *History of United States Naval Aviation*, pp. 5–6.
10. Crouch, *Wings*, pp. 117–18; Glenn Curtiss and Augustus Post, *The Curtiss Aviation Book* (New York: Frederick A. Strokes, 1912), pp. 105–6; and Turnbull and Lord, *History of United States Naval Aviation*, pp. 6–7.
11. Henry P. Beers, "The Development of the Office of the Chief of Naval Operations," *Military Affairs* 10 (Spring 1946), pp. 59–64; and Secretary of the Navy, *Annual Report*, 1909, 8–11.
12. On Chambers see Stephen K. Stein, *From Torpedoes to Aviation: Washington Irving Chambers and Technological Innovation in the New Navy, 1876–1913* (Tuscaloosa: University of Alabama Press, 2007).
13. Ibid., pp. 158–59.
14. Turnbull and Lord, *History of United States Naval Aviation*, pp. 4–8; and Stein, *Torpedoes to Aviation*, pp. 160–61.
15. Winthrop to R. M. Watt, 12 October 1910, "Letters Sent Concerning the Navy's Early Use of Aircraft," National Archives, Record Group 24; and Stein, *Torpedoes to Aviation*, p. 160.

16. Washington Irving Chambers, "Aviation and Aeroplanes," *U.S. Naval Institute Proceedings* 37 (March 1911), pp. 162–208; and Stein, *Torpedoes to Aviation*, pp. 160–63.

17. Chambers to the Secretary of the Navy, 23 November 1910, Library of Congress Manuscript Division (LCMD), Chambers Papers, Box 4; Meyer to Ely, 17 November 1910, LCMD, Chambers Papers, Box 15; and George van Deurs, *Wings for the Fleet* (Annapolis: Naval Institute Press, 1966), p. 25.

18. Stein, *Torpedoes to Aviation*, pp. 162–63; Hallion, *Taking Flight*, p. 305; and Turnbull and Lord, *History of United States Naval Aviation*, pp. 12–13.

19. Turnbull and Lord, *History of United States Naval Aviation*, pp. 13–14.

20. For more on Ellyson see George van Deurs, *Anchors in the Sky: Spuds Ellyson, the First Naval Aviator* (San Rafael, CA: Presidio Press, 1978).

21. For more on Towers see Clark G. Reynolds, *Admiral John H. Towers: The Struggle of Naval Air Supremacy* (Annapolis: Naval Institute Press, 1991).

22. Ibid., pp. 28–30.

23. Hallion, *Taking Flight*, pp. 304, 397; and van Deurs, *Anchors in the Sky*, pp. 114–20.

24. Herbert A. Johnson, *Wingless Eagle: U.S. Army Aviation through World War I* (Chapel Hill: University of North Carolina Press, 2001), pp. 104–9; Stein, *Torpedoes to Aviation*, pp. 166–67; van Deurs, *Wings for the Fleet*, p. 35; and Crouch, *Wings*, p. 145.

25. Stein, *Torpedoes to Aviation*, p. 167.

26. Ibid., pp. 164–66.

27. Ibid., pp. 161, 165–66; Turnbull and Lord, *History of United States Naval Aviation*, p. 15; and van Deurs, *Wings for the Fleet*, p. 38.

28. Stein, *Torpedoes to Aviation*, pp. 166–67; and Reynolds, *Admiral John H. Towers*, p. 49.

29. Hallion, *Taking Flight*, p. 299; and Stein, *Torpedoes to Aviation*, pp. 170–72.

30. Stein, *Torpedoes to Aviation*, pp. 164–65; Crouch, *Wings*, pp. 134–35; and Gross, "George Owen Squire," pp. 287–88.

31. Reynolds, *Admiral John H. Towers*, pp. 55–62; and Stein, *Torpedoes to Aviation*, pp. 171–75.

32. Stein, *Torpedoes to Aviation*, pp. 171–72; and Turnbull and Lord, *History of United States Naval Aviation*, pp. 19, 23.

33. House of Representatives, Hearings, Committee on Naval Affairs, 9 January 1913, p. 543; Chambers to the Chief of the Bureau of Navigation, 22 May 1912; Chambers to Senator Benjamin Tillman, 23 April 1913; and Chambers to George Perkins (Chair of the House Naval Affairs Committee), 24 May 1912, all in Chambers Papers, LCMD, Boxes 5 and 6; and Melhorn, *Two-Block Fox*, p. 12.

34. Bradley A. Fiske, *From Midshipman to Rear Admiral* (New York: Century, 1919), pp. 531–32.

35. Stein, *Torpedoes to Aviation*, pp. 182–87.

36. Fiske, *Midshipman to Rear Admiral*, p. 538; Stein, *Torpedoes to Aviation*, pp. 184–90; and van Deurs, *Wings for the Fleet*, pp. 9, 123.

37. House Naval Affairs Committee, 53rd Congress (1914), Hearings, 1794–1803; Turnbull and Lord, *History of United States Naval Aviation*, pp. 33–34; Alex Roland, *Model Research: The National Advisory Committee for Aeronautics, 1915–1958* (Washington, DC: GPO, 1985), pp. 6–20; and Stein, *Torpedoes to Aviation*, pp. 190–91.

38. Crouch, *Wings*, p. 132.

39. Van Deurs, *Anchors in the Sky*, pp. 117–24; Reynolds, *Admiral John H. Towers*, pp. 49, 55; and Stein, *Torpedoes to Aviation*, pp. 181–84.

40. Hallion, *Taking Flight*, pp. xvii, 189–90; Stein, *Torpedoes to Aviation*, pp. 168–70; and van Deurs, *Wings for the Fleet*, p. 47.

41. Hallion, *Taking Flight*, pp. 245, 391; and Reynolds, *Admiral John H. Towers*, p. 54.

42. Hallion, *Taking Flight*, pp. 261–62, 317, 323–25.

43. Ibid., pp. 301–3, 326–27.

44. Roland, *Model Research*, pp. 5–6; Stein, *Torpedoes to Aviation*, pp. 178–79, 189; William F. Trimble, *Jerome C. Hunsaker and the Rise of American Aeronautics* (Washington, DC, and London: Smithsonian Institution Press, 2003), pp. 26–27; and Hallion, *Taking Flight*, pp. 391–92.

45. Reynolds, *Admiral John H. Towers*, pp. 77–80; and van Deurs, *Wings for the Fleet*, pp. 109–10.

46. Reynolds, *Admiral John H. Towers*, p. 84; John Fass Morton, *Mustin: A Naval Family of the Twentieth Century* (Annapolis: Naval Institute Press, 2003), pp. 97–98; and Turnbull and Lord, *History of United States Naval Aviation*, pp. 43–44.

47. Turnbull and Lord, *History of United States Naval Aviation*, pp. 49, 53; and van Deurs, *Wings for the Fleet*, pp. 134–35

48. William R. Braisted, "Mark Lambert Bristol: Naval Diplomat Extraordinary of the Battleship Age," in James C. Bradford (ed.), *Admirals of the New Steel Navy: Makers of the American Naval Tradition, 1880–1930* (Annapolis: Naval Institute Press, 1990), p. 336; Turnbull and Lord, *History of United States Naval Aviation*, pp. 50–51; Reynolds, *Admiral John H. Towers*, p. 92.

49. Turnbull and Lord, *History of United States Naval Aviation*, p. 46–47.

50. Ibid., p. 55

51. Braisted, "Mark Lambert Bristol," p. 336; Hallion, *Taking Flight*, p. 388; and Turnbull and Lord, *History of United States Naval Aviation*, p. 41.

52. Turnbull and Lord, *History of United States Naval Aviation*, p. 60; and van Deurs, *Wings for the Fleet*, pp. 137–39.

53. Morton, *Mustin*, p. 99.

54. Reynolds, *Admiral John H. Towers*, pp. 73–74; van Deurs, *Wings for the Fleet*, pp. 147–53; and Morton, *Mustin*, pp. 105–6, 108–9.

55. Braisted, "Mark Lambert Bristol," p. 339.

56. Turnbull and Lord, *History of United States Naval Aviation*, pp. 52–53, 63–64, 67.

57. Crouch, *Wings*, pp. 145–48; Herbert A. Johnson, *Wingless Eagle: U.S. Army Aviation through World War I* (Chapel Hill: University of North Carolina Press, 2001), pp. 2–10; Hallion, *Taking Flight*, pp. 289, 383–84; Andrew Krepinevich, *Transforming to Victory: The U.S. Navy, Carrier Aviation, and Preparing for War in the Pacific* (Cambridge, MA: Harvard University, John M. Olin Institute for Strategic Studies, 2000); Melhorn, *Two-Block Fox;* William F. Trimble, *Admiral William F. Moffett: Architect of Naval Aviation* (Washington, DC: Smithsonian Institution, 1994), p. 71.

58. Johnson, *Wingless Eagle*, pp. 23–28, 87–89, 173–75; and Stein, *Torpedoes to Aviation*, pp. 206–8.

59. Chambers, "Airships and Naval Policy," unpublished manuscript, Chambers Papers, Box 12.

60. Robert Seager, "Ten Years before Mahan: The Unofficial Case for the New Navy, 1880–1890." *Mississippi Valley Historical Review* 40 (1953), pp. 491–512.

CHAPTER 3

Eyes of the Fleet:
How Flying Boats Transformed War Plan Orange

Edward S. Miller

B etween 1906 and 1941 the U.S. Navy developed War Plan Orange, an offensive strategy to defeat Japan in an all-out war. It was one of history's most successful war plans, belying the adage that no plan survives the opening guns. It was successfully deployed in its grand themes and many details in World War II. Planners believed carrier aviation would play a key role when war came. This essay, however, will focus on a critical period of the 1930s when Plan Orange was salvaged from doubt and defeatism by arrival of the most successful aircraft type of the era, the long-range, multi-engine flying boat.[1]

The Captains and Admirals who adapted Plan Orange to air power were among the brightest of the Service. Plucked from seagoing careers, they served two years in a small War Plans Division (WPD), also known as Op-12, under the Chief of Naval Operations. Earlier planners at the Naval War College and on the staff of the General Board had outlined the fundamental strategic themes. Japan's desire to dominate China would be frustrated by the American Open Door policy to protect China's integrity and its open markets. Someday Japan would pounce, seize the Philippines and Guam, and eliminate U.S. interference from its ocean flanks. Blue planners, noting the huge disparity in warmaking strength, adopted a goal of completely subjugating Japan (although "unconditional surrender" was not named until World War II). Aware that Japan's vigorous army had defeated Imperial Russia, planners projected victory through capital-intensive sea power, and eventually air power.

Their strategic dilemma was the geography of the Pacific. Vast distances separated the belligerents. There were no developed harbors in the five thousand miles between Hawaii and Manila. Therefore the planners envisioned a three-phase war.

In Phase I Japan would swiftly seize America's Western Pacific islands. In Phase II, the longest of the war, the U.S. Navy with support from the Army would counter-attack across the ocean to capture island bases in the Western Pacific. The two fleets would clash in a titanic battle that Blue's superior numbers would win decisively. Thereafter the enemy would be subdued by a Phase III siege of blockade and bombardment by sea and air forces operating from bases on Japan's doorstep.

For thirty years the planning staffs divided into two schools of thought about the Phase II offensive. The "thrusters," as I have named them, were elders steeped in an ethos of offensive audacity, disciples of two Admirals, Alfred Thayer Mahan and George Dewey. They demanded instantaneous mobilization and a naval dash to the Philippines, known as "The Through Ticket to Manila," to rescue the beleaguered Blue garrison and challenge the Imperial Japanese Navy before Japan could fortify its conquests. The impossibly long cruise from the East Coast to the Philippines, 20,000 miles via Cape Horn, was shortened by the Panama Canal in 1914 and relocation of the fleet to California in 1919. Development of Pearl Harbor, to which the fleet moved in 1940, cut the journey to a still burdensome 5,000 miles. Concerned that the American people would weary of a long war, their plan offered hope of a quick and cheap victory. Its fatal flaw was to risk the entire Navy on one roll of the dice against a potent enemy near its home waters. To reduce the risk, thrusters lobbied to build a grand western base, at Luzon or later at Guam, until the Washington Conference of 1922 forbade bases west of Hawaii. Undaunted, Commander in Chief of the U.S. Fleet (CinCUS) Robert L. Coontz projected a cavalry-like charge of a 551-ship convoy nonstop to Luzon, harassed by the Japanese all the way, to an impromptu base vulnerable to air attack from Formosa (Taiwan). At the end of the decade chief war planner Frank M. Schofield conceded the air threat by adapting a slightly saner policy of steaming to southern Mindanao, to improvise a base screened by narrow straits and Army airfields in the central Philippines. Nevertheless by 1934 the menace of Orange aviation was rising while Blue naval power languished below treaty limits during the Depression, which led Army war planner Brigadier General Stanley D. Embick to call the thrusting strategy "literally an act of madness."

The alternative planning school, which I labeled "cautionaries," consisted of younger officers attuned to modern weapons like aircraft and submarines and especially to the tedious study of logistics. Confident that the public would support a long but safer war, they proposed a deliberate step-by-step island-hopping advance to the Far East. Their studies remained curiosities, however, for lack of suitable stepping-stones until 1919. During World War I Japan, siding with the Allies, seized the undefended German islands of the Caroline, Marshall, and Marianas groups. The peace conference awarded them to Japan as demilitarized mandated territories under League of Nations auspices. Thrusters were appalled at Japan's barricade athwart the Blue attack path. Cautionaries, however, applauded the Mandate as a windfall. Excellent atoll lagoons awaited a stepwise Blue advance, step by step, punctuated with pauses to develop proper oceanic bases. Their moment in the sun arose in 1922 when Article XIX of the Washington Treaty outlawed a prepared western base. Rear Admiral Clarence S. Williams, one of the most astute prewar planners, laid out an attack through the Marshall Islands—specifically via Eniwetok—to Truk in the Caroline Islands, the grandest lagoon in the Central Pacific. There, Blue would pause for eighteen months to build a second Pearl Harbor, then resume the advance toward the Philippines or to islands closer to Japan itself. The gradual movement, gaining strength as it went, reduced the risk of catastrophe. It would ensure victory, albeit at the cost of a longer war. New technologies encouraged the advocates of a mid-ocean campaign. The oil-burning fleet had markedly extended its combat range. A vast fleet train of auxiliaries was under design. Within a few years planes from newly launched aircraft carriers would be striking over the horizon.

When Williams departed, the thrusters scrapped his plan and reinstalled the Through Ticket. His cautionary plan also had a fatal flaw: the blindness of a massive Blue fleet based in the vast mid-Pacific. The Navy lacked the means of intelligence of enemy naval whereabouts in a theater where island bases were vulnerable to attack from any point of the compass. Security would depend on aircraft that could search a thousand miles in all directions. Such long-range scouts would also be critical for battle operations in open seas where hostile armadas might close upon each other by five hundred miles overnight. The aircraft carrier had introduced the "frightening possibility" of a superior fleet lost through inferior reconnaissance. The side that remained hidden and launched its planes first might destroy the enemy carriers by an "unanswered salvo" and dominate the skies altogether. Studies of the 1930s indicated that a fleet of two-thirds the opponent's strength could win a decisive sea-air battle. Victory would depend on the earliest information found by long-range aircraft. The United States needed planes that could fly to Hawaii and concentrate rapidly in the Mandate. No such planes were available in the 1920s. Renaissance of the cautionary strategy had to await a technological breakthrough.

Aircraft speed, altitude, ruggedness, and armament were important, but for ocean reconnaissance the vital characteristic was range. A thousand-mile-radius plane could survey ten to twenty times the area of a small shipborne type. The only aircraft suited to the task were flying boats, known in the Navy as VPs—V for heavier than air, P for patrol—formed in 12-plane squadrons called VProns. The flying boat had been pioneered before World War I by the American genius Glenn H. Curtiss whose twin-engine biplanes with notched wooden hulls outperformed pontooned seaplanes. During the war the United States and Great Britain flew hundreds of Curtiss F-5Ls on anti–U-boat patrols out to four hundred miles (larger NC boats that crossed the Atlantic in 1919 proved too fragile for naval service). The sturdiness of the Curtiss boats retarded innovation until they wore out, grew waterlogged,

The Consolidated PBY or Catalina had a 1,000-mile range. By 1941, the U.S. Navy had 330 in service.

and wore out in the mid-1920s. With progress stagnant the Joint Army-Navy Board in 1923 recommended a force of only 84 VPs (414 in wartime), just 4 percent of all military planes. In 1925 the scouting fleet had 14.

A craving for aerial scouts escalated when arms treaties limited cruiser construction. The Navy yearned for VPs that could accompany the fleet "in all waters of the globe," especially in the Pacific where airfield sites were scarce. In the second half of the decade the Naval Aircraft Factory in Philadelphia tinkered with improved types with air-cooled radial engines and hulls of the alloy duralumin. The "flying forest" of struts between the biplane wings was thinned out. Yet each model disappointed and few were put into service. VPs of the late 1920s, supposedly capable of surveillance flights of six hundred to eight hundred miles' radius at one hundred knots, actually covered four hundred miles in maneuvers, scarcely better than the boats of 1918. To fight in the mid-Pacific the Navy needed a plane of twenty-four-hour endurance that could take off at midnight and begin searching at dawn halfway along a thousand-mile radial line. It would need a large crew and autopilots for relief, and of course reliable radios. Engineers of the Bureau of Aeronautics (BuAer) tried again with the P2Y design of 1932–1933, sesquiplanes with stubby underside wings. They were able to exercise at U.S. atolls up to seven hundred miles from Oahu but they still suffered the "eternal problems" of poor performance and short range that constrained operations with a long-legged fleet.

Landplanes, in contrast, were booming ahead in performance and range, dramatized by Lindbergh's flight of 1927. Not surprisingly, the Army's coast artillery function expanded to overwater flights for defense of U.S. shores including naval bases. In 1931 Chief Naval Officer (CNO) William V. Pratt signed a pact with Army Chief of Staff Douglas MacArthur that barred the Navy from acquiring large-wheeled aircraft. Naval aviation was to be based on the fleet and move with it, "confining it to single-engine planes for carriers and the Marines, and to seaplanes and flying boats." On 1 April 1933 Pratt detached the feeble VProns from the Battle and Scouting forces, the power centers of the fleet, and banished them to a new command, Aircraft, Base Force, for stodgy defensive patrolling. Beyond their shriveled search arcs the carriers and catapulted floatplanes would have to cover the fleet. The disgrace of the lumbering geese was reflected in the Vinson-Trammel Act of 1934, which funded most naval aircraft generously but authorized only thirty VP aircraft a year through 1941.

To some desperate airmen dirigibles seemed a credible alternative. In the 1920s the Navy experimented with airships that had ten times the range of VPs at triple the speed of cruisers. Their backers, including Rear Admiral William A. Moffett, the Chief of BuAer, argued that they could reconnoiter far out at sea beyond range of Orange planes, observe ships while hovering beyond gunfire range, and peek at the supposedly unarmed Pacific Mandate Islands. At worst, a timely sighting of the enemy fleet would justify loss of a machine costing no more than a destroyer. Two great dirigibles commissioned in the early 1930s were capable of seven-thousand-mile round-trips carrying small planes launched and recovered from a trapeze slung beneath the mother airship. Each unit could sweep a wider swath than four cruisers. Op-12 wished to base them in Hawaii but they were unstable in bad weather and were frequently "shot down" in maneuvers. The fleet refused to have them. In 1933 the *Akron* crashed, with Moffett among the dead. In 1935 the *Macon* fell. By then the Navy could buy twenty-six VP aircraft for the price of a dirigible. The "Flying Aircraft Carriers" were finished.

Reappraisals of War Plan Orange in the second half of 1933 brought to a head the destiny of the flying boat. Rear Admiral Joseph "Bull" Reeves, a faithful believer in the type, insisted that the fleet could not enter Philippine waters nor even loiter in the Marshalls without a security umbrella of five to seven VProns. Op-12 dutifully incorporated them in the first attack wave. They could fly to the Marshalls via Johnston Island but would have to travel onward to Mindanao as deck cargo. Mobilization tables reserved space aboard all ship classes, yet many of the big planes were to be lashed precariously on minesweepers under tow. The absurdity of the "eyes of the Fleet" wallowing blindly along the dangerous passage helped discredit the "Through Ticket" once and for all.

In October 1933 the credibility of a mid-ocean campaign suddenly brightened. An excellent VP prototype had emerged from successful commercial types "flying down to Rio." The Navy placed orders for the plane that evolved into the most-produced flying boat of all time, the Consolidated PBY, later dubbed Catalina for an island near the factory in California—a British practice of naming planes. The aerodynamically clean, high-winged monoplane soon achieved the long-sought 1,000-mile range—1,500 in some wartime models. War planners could look forward to delivery within three years of flocks of far-winging scouts for an ocean offensive.

Rebirth of the cautionary campaign plan after 1933 owed much to enchantment with the graceful Catalinas. Yet their arrival touched off four disputes among the war planners, operating commanders, and the naval bureaus as to their roles. Three of the disputes were decisively settled before war in the Pacific erupted. Confusion over the fourth had much to do with the tragedy of 7 December 1941.

The Honorable Frank Knox, Secretary of the Navy (right), with Rear Admiral C. C. Bloch, Naval Air Station, Pearl Harbor, Hawaii, September 1940.

The first dispute concerned whether the Navy should acquire as many Catalinas as possible as the workhorses of the fleet, or strive for even larger, more proficient aircraft. Projected numbers of flying boats for a Treaty Navy were modest: 184 operating with the fleet in 1935, with 30 added per year to reach a peak of 330 in 1941. But aeronautical science was advancing rapidly. The Navy funded design studies of what became the two-engine Martin Mariner, which surpassed the Catalinas in speed and altitude and usurped the key scouting role midway through the war. Giant Sikorsky and Martin civilian flying boats operated by Pan Air, and German and British models inspired the four-engine PB2Y Coronado, ultimately built in smaller numbers. In the extreme, the monstrous Martin Mars, an eight-thousand-mile range "flying dreadnought" was supposedly capable of a Hawaii-Tokyo round-trip. Only a handful were built late in the war.

In 1935 the CNO skeptically inquired whether planes of, say, five- to six-thousand-mile ranges were needed. They required long, smooth waters for takeoffs. They consumed much more fuel. They could not be carried aboard ship and cost was a major consideration. He preferred "mid-sized" Catalinas capable of haul-out on primitive shores on their own beaching gear, for service by small tenders, or carried as deck cargo or disassembled to Mandate's lagoons beyond their range. The Commander of Aircraft Base Force thought the ideal to be a two-engine craft of 3,000 nautical miles range at 175 knots, 20,000-foot ceiling, takeoff in less than 2.5 miles of taxi lane. CinCUS Reeves and Chief war planner, Rear Adm. William S. Pye, hoped for 3,500-mile range and thirty-hour endurance. Rear Admiral Ernest J. King, Chief of BuAer, who usually championed the most excellent aircraft, agreed quantity over "utmost" quality in this case. Why was extra range needed when no naval battle had ever been fought more than a thousand miles from land? Besides, bigger planes would not be available in masses for three or four years.

There the matter rested until 1940. In February 1941 PBYs were in service (all earlier types having been retired) with 200 PBY-5s on order for rapid delivery. Only 21 PBM Mariners were on order. The General Board declared for only a few giant boats for a few extraordinary missions. Rear Admiral John Towers felt that a dozen four-engine giants would suffice; at a cost of $926,000 the Navy could procure 9 Catalinas or 4 Mariners (albeit the newer planes had not achieved cost benefits of volume production). The final prewar word was pronounced by Rear Admiral Richmond K. Turner, Chief of the WPD, in November 1941. The war in Europe showed that seaplanes could not match landplanes in range, ceiling, maneuverability, speed, or self-defense. For long-range patrolling the Navy needed big landplane bombers, 25 percent immediately and 50 percent ultimately.

In a second debate, enthusiasts of the wondrous Catalinas envisioned them as a striking force hurling bombs and torpedoes at Japanese fleets and bases. The planes were performing splendidly in exercises out to U.S. atolls. Navy leaders' enthusiasm may seem odd but in the mid- to late 1930s nobody knew how a future air war would unfold. Leading the battle cry was Ernest J. King, an air power devotee who attended flight school in middle age and then commanded the carrier *Lexington*. Moffett's death brought King to the top of the Bureau of Aeronautics. In 1935 King warned against discounting the attack role. A modern VPron could drop twenty-four tons of bombs, almost as much as the thirty tons of all planes on the two largest carriers, the *Lexington* and *Saratoga*. Such planes were "distinctly a naval weapon for use over the sea against a naval objective." Here was an opportunity "just as positive and clear" as Army bombers over land. Like cruisers that also scouted, flying boats could also fight. Any Commander in Chief would welcome them, any enemy would fear them. To ignore such a mission would cede to the Army the most promising development in aviation.

A chorus of skeptics greeted King. The CinCUS considered combat a distinctly secondary role. WPD Director Captain G. J. Meyers noted that VP scouting released carrier planes for combat. The commander of the fleet squadrons imagined Catalinas carrying four 500-pound bombs as a secondary role, but Rear Admiral Frederick J. Horne, commander of the VP squadrons, retorted that loading bombs from rafts onto wing racks was so time-consuming as to render the force impotent for attack. Pye, the next Director of the WPD, said that aerial torpedoes were too big, costly, and delicate. The naysayers conceded only peripheral missions such as attacking submarines while on patrol, mining, or night attacks on poorly defended islands, albeit sacrificing range for ordnance. Nevertheless, when King returned to the fleet to command the VProns he soon was exercising them as bombers and asking for torpedoes. Claude Bloch, the next CinCUS, continued attack training. King was apparently vindicated when the Navy redesignated the Catalina "PBY," the first seaplane to sport a "B" for bomber along with "P" for patrol. Commander in Chief Arthur Hepburn transferred them in 1937 from the defensive Base Force to a new offensive command, Aircraft, Scouting Force.

By early 1940, however, opinion turned negative and soon jelled into hostility. Flying boats were inherently vulnerable. Orange Plan studies had assumed attrition of 10 percent per month, even in the scouting role. Combat raids were not worth the additional sacrifice of essential scouts. Commander of the VProns, A. B. Cook, after exercises, declared that "use as an attack forces is questionable except as a last resort," while torpedo attacks on defended ships "should not be attempted except under desperate circumstances." Captain Russell Crenshaw, Chief of the WPD, concurred. Richmond Kelly Turner delivered the death knell in November 1941 with his plea for long-range landplanes for the attack role as well as for scouting.

A third quandary of operating VP aircraft in a Blue-Orange war involved how and where to base them far beyond the harbors of California, Panama, and Oahu. In the early stages of flying boat development some Navy officers believed they could operate effectively under the most extraordinary conditions. A few thought they might operate en masse from the open ocean, or at least in the lee of islands, if only in circumstances of utmost urgency. Experiments of refueling at sea from the specially configured tanker submarine *Nautilus* proved barely practicable for one or two planes at a time. An ill-advised notion to lift a VP airplane for servicing onto a cradle on the deck of a submarine that would rise to the surface beneath it was wisely squelched by acting CNO Richardson. Further experiments proved open-sea operations dangerous and impracticable (although "Dumbo" VP aircraft rescued many a downed aviator at sea during World War II). Other ideas met similar dead ends. Designs for a ship with stern gates and a ramp for hauling aboard planes with folding wings were shelved. Takeoffs were conducted using catapults mounted on towed barges that could feather into the wind, with some success in calm waters, although this left open the question of where to land on return. One outlandish scheme envisioned VP aircraft packed with Marines landing in lightly defended enemy lagoons, to defend the toehold with hand weapons until reinforcements arrived by ship.

The most successful basing idea in the late 1920s and 1930s was the seaplane tender. The VProns needed sheltered harbors for flights and for ministrations by mother ships that were hybrids of fuel, repair, and barracks vessels. The Navy considered adapting merchantmen and even yachts, but settled on converting several small, slow minesweepers with lyrical names like *Swan, Thrush,* and *Pelican.* The shallow twelve-foot draft "Bird"-class tenders were well suited for uncharted lagoons. Crews could assist in hauling out VP aircraft on beaching wheels for light repairs. However, tenders were so defenseless that they might have to be evacuated during daylight hours and return after dark. Furthermore, their sluggish speed retarded fleet mobility. Working in pairs, one tender would sail off to lay moorings at an advance base while the other stood by until takeoff, then chugged gamely after. The net rate of advance was one-third that of the surface fleet.

During the Depression so many tenders were laid up that movement with a war expedition was virtually precluded. By 1935, however, one large and five small tenders were serving the squadrons, with gasoline enough for thirty hours of flying. Throughout the 1930s CinCUS and General Board reports urged the development of large tenders as semipermanent homes for three squadrons, with far more fuel and berthing capacity and with cranes to lift a VP plane aboard for major repairs by its well-equipped machine shops. After every "fleet problem," that is, massed annual maneuvers, the Commander in Chief and his aviation subordinate identified the "urgent necessity" of more and better tenders as their most important deficiency. CinCUS Reeves demanded that tenders receive highest priority. The Ship Movements Division called for four large and seven small tenders for the squadrons already in service. In 1939 the Greenslade Board's "Are We Ready" studies again listed tenders as the fleet's number one deficiency. The minesweeper types were slow, lacked stowage, and could handle only a half squadron. The converted destroyers cured only the speed problem. The larger types took three years to build.

A new solution for both defensive and offensive VP basing early in a war appeared shortly before the actual war. For mid-Pacific operations the United States possessed a few scattered atolls west of Hawaii. Beginning in 1935 some were developed, with naval encouragement, by Pan Air for its "Flying Clipper" service to the Orient. Three atolls—Midway 1,000 nautical miles northwest of Oahu, Johnston 720 miles southwest, and Palmyra 960 miles south—were envisioned as defensive bases for Pearl Harbor. Squadrons and tenders exercised at Johnston and at French Frigate Shoals halfway to Midway. VProns made record-breaking massed flights to Midway during 1935 maneuvers. In 1938, with world tensions mounting, Congress approved a huge appropriation to develop the defensive atolls as seaplane bases— and at Midway a submarine base as well—by dredging channels through rock-hard reefs and erecting shore facilities, contracted to civilian firms that had built Hoover Dam. In 1941 ground and air defense units were emplaced on the islands. With advanced island bases in the offing the Navy ordered the PBY-5A, an amphibious version of the Catalina, to fly from airstrips as well as lagoons. By 7 December 1941 Midway housed a squadron periodically rotated, and Johnston a half squadron (six planes) from time to time.

Wake Island was a different story. Situated two thousand nautical miles west of Oahu and only a few hundred miles north of the Japanese Marshalls, it was hardly a defensive outpost. In fact, the evolving Orange Plans noted Wake's unique value for the Blue descent on Eniwetok in the northwest Marshalls, the first objective of the offensive, to be occupied six months after the start of the war. VP aircraft could cover the fleet operating nearly a thousand miles beyond Wake. They could scout and might even bomb the Mandate Islands. B-17 bombers, staging through Midway and Wake, could certainly bomb the enemy islands. In 1940 Congress belatedly approved the funding of Wake. Meanwhile VP planes visited Wake on a few training missions by using the Pan Air channel facilities. A permanent deployment was expected in 1942. The fleet now had an advanced base from which VP aircraft could cover it as it moved into the Mandate.

The hurried construction at Wake brought to a head the final, and perhaps most important, debate about the flying boats. Was their primary function defensive scouting, that is, patrolling naval bases against surprise attack? Or was it supporting the offensive as scouts fanning out ahead of the fleet's advance across the Pacific? In the Orange Plans of the 1920s and early 1930s the defensive mission was deemed paramount because Japanese Micronesia lay undefended. U.S. forces could occupy the Marshalls and probably Truk before Japan could fortify them. The VProns' job was to warn of a surprise Japanese counterattack on Blue ships anchored there. Security demanded continuous long-range patrols, round the clock, covering 360 degrees. The war planners expressed confidence in the protective surveillance umbrella.

Offensive scouting, serving as the eyes of the fleet as it advanced, was more problematic. Carrier planes could scout ahead two hundred miles or so, and not at night. Floatplanes of battleships and cruisers could reach somewhat farther. But fleets could close on each other by five hundred miles overnight. Only flying boats could provide information of the enemy's whereabouts a thousand miles out to sea.

Unlike the clear solutions of the other quandaries before the war, planners deemed both defensive and offensive scouting vital. But in 1941 the number of VProns available to the Pacific Fleet was still small, and dwindled as some were sent to neutrality patrol in the Philippines and the Atlantic. Nearly 1,000 more aircraft were on order but were not expected in service until 1943 at the earliest. In an emergency, a Commander in Chief might have to decide which of his scouting functions, offensive or defensive, was most critical. As war loomed, Admiral Husband E. Kimmel, Commander in Chief of the Pacific Fleet, chose the wrong option.

In May 1941 War Plan Orange morphed into the Pacific half of Rainbow Five, a plan for a two-ocean war against Germany and Japan adopted jointly by the U.S. and British governments. President Franklin D. Roosevelt had transferred most of the U.S. Fleet to Hawaii in May 1940 as a deterrent to Japan grabbing U.S. and Allied colonies in the Far East. In February 1941 he promoted Kimmel to command the newly named Pacific Fleet. Kimmel's primary mission under Rainbow Five was to divert the Imperial Japanese Navy for seventy days from attacking the great British naval base at Singapore, long enough for King's Atlantic Fleet to relieve portions of the Royal Navy so they could steam to the rescue of Singapore. However, to ensure that the offensive-minded Kimmel did not thrust too far out into the Pacific during an emergency, say, the collapse of Great Britain, thus requiring a recall to the Atlantic, CNO Harold Stark directed Richmond Kelly Turner's War Plans Division to tether Kimmel's range of action. His ships must not operate west of 166° 39′ E, the longitude of the Marshall Islands and Wake (although some units could cruise in the South Pacific as far as Australia). Kimmel's planning dilemma was how to support Singapore without cruising within 4,500 miles of it! In July 1941 his brilliant war planner, Captain Charles H. "Soc" (for Socrates, his nickname because he was considered an extremely wise man) McMorris, provided the answer in Fleet Plan WPPac-46. When Japan attacked the Far East the fleet would sortie from Pearl Harbor immediately. Several flying boat squadrons would wing ahead to Midway, Johnston, and Wake to cover it. Vice Admiral William F. Halsey's three fast aircraft carriers would steam through the Marshalls twice, first to reconnoiter and then to bomb. Meanwhile Kimmel's eight powerful battleships would rendezvous at Point Tare, the point of maximum cover equidistant between the three atoll VP bases, then take up position between Wake and Midway. In my analysis of Kimmel's strategy the naval ballet made sense only as an elaborate ambush of Admiral Yamamoto's Combined Fleet, presumably enticed by Halsey's gambits to a fight in the Central Pacific. Kimmel, who "wanted to be the American Nelson," almost certainly hoped for a gunnery slugfest about the third week of war, in waters densely patrolled by flying boats from Wake and Midway but far beyond reach of Yamamoto's long-range scouting planes. VProns were the key to Kimmel's grandiose plan. Plan WPPac-46 was no mere school exercise; CNO and Secretary of the Navy Frank Knox approved it in September 1941 and it was not materially amended before 7 December.

Aware that the Catalinas could operate at still-primitive advanced bases for only a few weeks before engine overhauls, Kimmel opted to horde most of them on Oahu in tip-top shape for the surge forward rather than wear them out patrolling in defense of Oahu, knowing the Army Air Corps lacked long-range planes for the job. He had received a war warning. At dusk on 6 December Commander Nagumo's carriers were about 275 miles to the north-northeast, well within the normal radius of flying boats. Kimmel had sixty-eight Catalinas in six VP Squadrons afloat and ashore at Oahu that morning, but only one was airborne guarding the harbor mouth against submarines. The Japanese attack destroyed all but one of the Catalinas. None got airborne. Assigned a nearly impossible mission, Kimmel chose to ignore base defense, the original mission for which the great planes were designed, for the more glamorous role of "eyes of the Fleet" as it steamed to the attack. He made the worst choice.

NOTES

Almost all information in this essay was extracted from Edward S. Miller, *War Plan Orange: The U.S. Strategy to Defeat Japan, 1897–1945* (Annapolis: Naval Institute Press, 1991). The book cites documentary sources such as war plans and related correspondence found mainly in the U.S. National Archives, the Naval Operational Archives Branch, and the Naval War College. Information on flying boats is found under "Flying Boats" in the book's index, under these subcategories: bases for; in blockade; characteristics and numbers; civilian; flights, notable; in phase II; as scouts; as striking force; in WWII; and under "Seaplane tenders."

1. In the "color" plans of the Joint Army-Navy Board Japan was designated "Orange" and the United States "Blue." Until 1940 the plan envisioned a war without allies on either side and a war theater limited to the Pacific north of the equator.

CHAPTER 4

Ships in the Sky

John E. Jackson

FIGHTING WORDS

Whenever fliers gather around a frosted mug there is an immediate and inevitable separation into distinct categories for bragging rights about which group is best in the air: fixed-wing versus rotary wing; fighter jocks versus bomber aces, Maritime Patrol practitioners versus multi-engine bomb and cargo haulers; and in recent years, manned versus unmanned aircraft! But a century ago, the biggest division would have been between lighter-than-air (LTA) proponents and heavier-than-air (HTA) advocates. And as strange as it may now seem through the lens of history, in the early years of aviation the smart money was riding on airships as the platforms that would rule the skies for long-range and heavy-lift missions.

In 1911, at the same time Eugene Ely was barely able to keep his wood-and-wire-powered "box-kite" in the air for periods measured in minutes, the German Airship Transport Company, Ltd., established the world's first airline. Its airship *Deutschland* completed a powered flight of two hours and thirty minutes, with thirty-two people on board.[1] A Schutte-Lanz airship of the period was 420 feet long, 59 feet in diameter, with two engines producing 540 horsepower that could push the airship through the sky at over thirty-eight miles per hour.[2]

Between 1911 and the opening of World War I in 1914, commercial airships in Europe carried more than 34,000 passengers, flying more than 100,000 miles.[3] There were plenty of growing pains for these monsters-in-the-sky, and crashes were frequent (if not fatal), but their potential was clearly evident. Military observers were quick to see the possibilities for airships to meet a wide range of military missions.

A WORD ABOUT TERMINOLOGY

Perhaps the arcane terminology used in discussing lighter-than-air craft has contributed to the mystique and misunderstanding of these "ships in the sky". For purposes of this chapter, let's just say the following: Any steerable flying machine that relies on the buoyant lift from a gas that is lighter than the air in which it flies is an "airship." If it has an internal framework to maintain its aerodynamic shape, it is a "rigid airship." If it is a rigid airship built by the Germans in the 1920s–1930s, it is a "Zeppelin." And if it uses only internal gas pressure to maintain its shape, it is a "blimp." The term "dirigible" means "steer-able," and has nothing to do with rigid or non-rigid status, though the term is often erroneously used to describe rigid airships. Finally, manned balloons, lifted by gas or by hot air, cannot be controlled directionally, and thus had little practical application beyond flight training for airship crewmen.

IN THE BEGINNING

Even with only a cursory look, the attraction of airships for naval operations becomes readily apparent. In the decades of the 1920s and 1930s, blimps, and their larger and more capable rigid airship "cousins," offered the ability to carry heavy loads for long distances. They could virtually hover for days in one location, or travel at low speeds to match the progress of surface ships and merchant convoys. They could then sprint at close to one hundred miles per hour to reposition themselves to inspect a new target or to escape a gathering storm. They held great promise as the ultimate airborne observation platforms, capable of covering thousands of miles of ocean in a single mission. Realizing these potential capabilities, however, demanded state-of-the-art aeronautical engineering, a host of technological breakthroughs, and superb airmanship. The history of Navy LTA flight is filled with triumphs and tragedies as men of courage sought to deliver on the promises made by LTA advocates around the world.

The U.S. Navy's first blimp was the DN-1, delivered to Pensacola, Florida, in the spring of 1917. It was followed by sixteen B-type non-rigid airships, which were little more than an airplane fuselage suspended under an 84,000-cubic-foot helium-filled envelope. The mission was to patrol the East Coast of the United States in search of German submarines. Refinement in airframes and engines continued over the ensuing decades, and Navy blimps grew in size and complexity, ultimately serving with great success during World War II, and into the Cold War.

But the real technological leap forward came with the design and construction of rigid airships, such as the German Zeppelins that had proved formidable scouts and bombers in World War I.

RIGID AIRSHIPS

The 1920 naval appropriations bill authorized the expenditure of $4 million to obtain two rigid airships. The visionary often called the "architect of Naval Aviation," Admiral William A. Moffett, wrote to the Chief of Naval Operations shortly after becoming head of the Bureau of Aeronautics: "In the rigid airship we have a scout, capable of patrolling the Pacific in the service of information for our fleet. . . . The use and development of rigid airships is a naval necessity."[4]

The first American-built ship would be designated ZR-1 and construction began in a newly erected hangar in Lakehurst, New Jersey, in April 1922. Anxious to get into the air as soon as possible with a blue-and-gold behemoth, the U.S. Navy simultaneously sought to purchase a flight-ready rigid airship from the British builder Short Brothers. Upon the planned transfer to the United States, the British R-38 airship would have been re-designated as ZR-2, but fundamental design flaws led to catastrophic failure of the ship over the city of Hull, England, in 1921, and the death of forty-four crewmen, including sixteen Americans who were aboard preparing to accept the ship.

Attention then turned to the construction of the huge rigid-framed ZR-1, the USS *Shenandoah*, which was closely modeled after a German Zeppelin that crashed in England during World War I. First flown in September 1923, the ZR-1 measured 680 feet in length and 79 feet in diameter. She was lifted by 2,100,000 cubic feet of helium, had a top speed of sixty knots and a crew of forty-three. It truly was a ship in the sky, which Navy leaders envisioned as the ideal long-range ocean reconnaissance platform, with extraordinary lift, range, and endurance. It proved to be an inferior design, however, and after two years of flight-testing (and public relations flights) it encountered a massive thunderstorm near Ava, Ohio. It broke up in flight and crashed in September 1925 with the loss of fourteen lives. Shaken by the two losses, the Navy designers redoubled their efforts.

Over the course of the decade that followed, millions of dollars and scores of lives would be consumed in the quest to develop the technology and operational doctrine necessary to achieve the ambitious potential promised by rigid airships. The designers sought to arrive at an elusive formula: a ship large enough to carry the aircrew, food, fuel, and equipment to do the job, yet light enough to be lifted aloft by its helium-filled gas bags. The spiderweb of duralumin girders that formed the hull had to be light enough to fly, yet strong enough to handle the incredible aerodynamic loads and stresses experienced by what was fundamentally a fragile 700-foot-long cylinder suspended in mid-air. Looking back across nine decades of history, it can be argued that it was simply beyond the capabilities of the engineers of the early twentieth century to divine a workable formula. But the potential benefits of LTA flight were so great that courageous pioneers continued to risk reputations, careers, and even lives in their pursuit. Their quest culminated in two of the most remarkable flying machines ever to take to the sky under the command of Navy aviators.

FLEET SCOUTS AND FLYING AIRCRAFT CARRIERS

In the 1920s, American statesmen and military experts viewed the growing power of the Empire of Japan with concern, and recognized that the small and ill-equipped U.S. fleet was wholly inadequate to patrol the vast reaches of the Pacific Ocean. In 1919, Captain (later Fleet Admiral) Ernest J. King reported to the Navy's General Board: "I don't see how the long distance reconnaissance is going to be carried out without using dirigibles."[5] After World War I, U.S. Naval Forces-Europe Commander Admiral William S. Sims stated: "I am thoroughly convinced by my observance of the naval lessons of this war that in the future rigid airships will be part of the fleet of every first-rate naval power."[6] The Navy had learned in the most painful way possible that neither the captured German design of ZR-1 nor the British design of ZR-2 resulted in a successful naval rigid airship. (In 1924 the Navy received a German-built Zeppelin airship, designated ZR-3 and named the USS *Los Angeles*, as a war reparations payment, but by treaty agreement it was to be used solely for "civil purposes." It was a variant of a commercial Zeppelin design that had little application for the intended long-range scouting mission). In 1928 the Navy called for proposals to build a rigid-frame fleet reconnaissance airship, capable of launching and recovering fixed-wing scouting aircraft while in flight. Three companies submitted proposals, and the contract to build two airships (ZRS-4 and -5) was awarded in October 1928 to the Goodyear-Zeppelin Corporation, a partnership created in 1924 to share rigid airship technology. Executing the contract was another matter.

> The construction of the ZRS-4, the Akron, stands as one of the most remarkable performances in the history of American industry. In the two years, eleven months and 2 days between the moment the ink dried on the airship contracts in Washington and when the Akron was cast off from her mooring mast at Akron, Ohio, not only did a hangar to house the erection work have to be built, but a corps of technicians and production personnel had to be developed around a cadre of German engineers; hundreds of workers had to be trained to an art almost unknown in America; and thousands of drawings had to be translated into patterns and jigs for what was to be the largest airship in the world. In order to build these two airships Goodyear was obliged, in one leap, to create an industrial plant of a magnitude which the airplane industry required almost a quarter century to develop.[7]

The statistics of the *Akron* and her sister ship *Macon* were remarkable:

Total Gas Volume	6,850,000 cubic feet
Length	785 feet
Diameter	133 feet
Fuel capacity	126,000 pounds
Envelope covering	33,000 square yards
Total horsepower (8 engines)	4,480 horsepower
Maximum speed	75 knots
Range at cruise speed	7,268 nautical miles
Flight crew	60 officers and men
HTA aircraft	4 Curtiss F9C biplanes

Source: Richard K. Smith, *Airships* Akron *and* Macon (Annapolis: Naval Institute Press, 1965).

On 8 August 1931, First Lady Lou Hoover christened the USS *Akron*, named for the city in which it was built, then considered the "LTA Capital of the World." The Navy now had the prototype of the fleet airship it wanted, but rather than being subjected to the type of slow and deliberate flight-testing one would expect for a totally new aircraft design, *Akron* was pushed to demonstrate her value to skeptical observers both inside the Navy and in the media. In fleet exercises, during a transcontinental flight to San Diego and Sunnyvale, California, and through numerous operations

The U.S. Navy's largest non-rigid airships, the ZPG-3W class, flew until 1962.

where her scouting aircraft were launched and recovered, the *Akron* demonstrated that she had the potential to provide the fleet with unprecedented intelligence-gathering capability.

But, as noted LTA historian Richard K. Smith has written "The *Akron* had been pushed unreasonably hard, with unrealistic expectations, and her inability to score a smash hit which corresponded to the airship propaganda of 1926–1931 made her performance appear as something of a failure."[8] In the fall and winter of 1932 she flew practice missions in which the Sparrowhawk airplanes left the hangar in the belly of the airship using a unique trapeze system to launch and recover while the airship maintained a steady course. The envisioned concept of operations was for the airship to drop two scout planes from the trapeze, and then proceed at sixty knots for up to twelve hours of daylight, recovering the airplanes 720 miles from the drop-off point. The LTA/HTA team could theoretically sweep a path 200 miles wide, covering over 140,000 square miles of ocean. The HTA detachments on both *Akron* and *Macon* became very proficient on the trapeze, so much so that landing gear was removed on some planes, to be replaced with supplemental gas tanks under the fuselage. The concept of the "flying aircraft carrier" was hampered by poor radio communications and direction-finding equipment on the aircraft, but the "wing-hookers" performed with great dexterity, much like their "tail-hooking" colleagues on traditional aircraft carriers. The *Akron*'s continued development of these concepts was abruptly halted on 3 April 1933 when the ship encountered one of the most violent storm fronts to hit the east coast of the United States in a decade. The ship was forced into the sea, with the loss of seventy-three of the seventy-six crewmen aboard. Included in the death toll was Rear Admiral William A. Moffett, Chief of the Navy Bureau of Aeronautics, who had been a strong supporter of airships. The crash shocked the nation and rocked the Navy, particularly the crew of USS *Macon*, the sister ship that had been commissioned only weeks earlier on 11 March 1933. The fate of the Navy's rigid airship program now rested entirely on the untested *Macon*.

The *Macon* proved to be a strong and capable ship, and her move to her new base in Sunnyvale, California (rapidly named Moffett Field in honor of the deceased Admiral), enabled her to work directly with the ships of the Pacific Fleet. *Macon*'s performance proved that large rigid airships could perform many of the missions expected of them, but on 12 February 1935, an unexpectedly strong gust of wind caused a failure in the rear upper fin area. As the stern dropped, ballast was released causing the ship to rise well above its maximum pressure height to over 4,800 feet. Automatic pressure relief valves opened to prevent the gas cells from exploding, and the large quantity of gas vented off made the ship too heavy to remain in the air. It touched down relatively gently on the ocean surface and eighty-one of the eighty-three crewmembers survived as the ship was abandoned. The days of Navy rigid airships immediately came to a close. Three of the U.S.-built rigids had crashed, and

ZPG-2s in hangar.

the Navy walked away from the huge potential these ships held. Decades later, literally thousands of aircraft would be lost to accidents as the Navy transitioned from propeller aircraft to jet-propelled planes, yet development continued because of the great potential seen in the new technology. Perhaps the decision to end experimentation with rigid airships after three crashes was an ill-advised rush to judgment. Some historians have speculated that the surprise attack on Pearl Harbor could have been detected had a "flying aircraft carrier" and her scouting planes been on station.

BLIMPS . . . "THEY WERE DEPENDABLE"

While the Navy abandoned rigid airships in 1935 after the loss of *Macon*, it continued to operate small blimps into the 1940s. The smaller and less expensive blimps were seen as good observation platforms for coastal defense and as a potential partial answer to the threat of enemy submarines. As war clouds gathered in the Atlantic and Pacific, the nation prepared by ordering the procurement of forty-eight nonrigid blimps as part of the "10,000 Plane Program" passed by Congress in June 1940. Growth would continue as America entered the war, and by 1945, 168 blimps would be in service, 134 being the modern K-class airships, which were 240 feet in length, with an envelope carrying 425,000 cubic feet of helium and a crew of 10. Over the course of the war, they would log 55,900 operational flights and accumulate 550,000 hours in the air. Blimps escorted 89,000 ships, and no ship under blimp coverage was sunk during the war. They maintained an 87 percent readiness rating, and flew when bad weather grounded HTA aircraft. They conducted rescues of pilots down at sea, searched for mines, helped route convoys, and delivered packages and personnel onto the decks of ships at sea. Nearly 12,000 officers and men crewed the airships and support stations, which ranged along both coasts in the United States, into South America, and even to French Morocco. The airships of Squadron 14 made the first transoceanic flight from the United States to Morocco in 1944. One measure of the airship's impact can be found in the words of Nazi Grand Admiral Karl Donitz who wrote after the war that "the American blimps were very disturbing to German U-boat activity."[9]

THE LAST HURRAH

Just as with every other type of aircraft, huge numbers of airships were decommissioned at war's end, with one company buying twenty-nine airships as flying billboards. Navy interest continued at a slow but steady pace, and in 1954 a ZPG-2–class airship set a world record for unrefueled flight by logging two hundred hours (eight days) in the air. The last airship design to actually be produced and serve with the fleet was the ZPG-3W Airborne Early Warning blimp. It remains as the largest non-rigid to ever fly, measuring 403 feet long, with an envelope containing 1.5 million cubic feet of helium. It flew from 1958 until August 1962 when the Navy terminated all airship operations, primarily as a budget-cutting measure. Thus ended four decades of Navy LTA flight, filled with triumphs and tragedies. The airships are gone, but their accomplishments should not be forgotten.

POST SCRIPT

Navy aviators have soared into the air to defend the nation for a century. For nearly 40 percent of that time, a small but determined branch of intrepid airmen labored with distinction in an effort to master the technology of buoyant flight. Their aircraft harnessed the lifting power of lighter-than-air gases that enabled them to sail the skies for periods measured in days, not hours. They flew in peace and in war, and hundreds of aviators gave the full measure of devotion at the hands of enemy fire and of hostile winds. In the course of building and flying airships, pioneering work was done in aeronautical engineering, meteorology, metallurgy, electronics, and command and control. Airships contributed to victory in World War II through convoy protection, search and rescue, and anti-submarine and anti-mine warfare. They also contributed to the security of the nation during the Cold War, as they patrolled the coast to detect potential submarines, enemy bombers, and missiles. It is indeed appropriate to recall and respect the accomplishments of the Navy aviators who flew low, and slow, but with dedication and distinction!

NOTES

1. Robert Jackson, *Airship* (Garden City, NY: Doubleday, 1973), p. 61.
2. Ibid., p. 64.
3. Rick Archbold, *Hindenburg: An Illustrated History* (Toronto, Canada: Madison Press Books, 1994), p. 35.
4. William F. Trimble, *Admiral William A. Moffett* (Washington, DC: Smithsonian Institution Press, 1994), p. 125.
5. Richard K. Smith, *The Airships* Akron *and* Macon (Annapolis: Naval Institute Press, 1965), p. xxi.
6. Ibid.
7. Ibid., p. 31.
8. Ibid., p. 62.
9. J. Gordon Vaeth, *Blimps and U-Boats* (Annapolis: Naval Institute Press, 1992), p. 172.

CHAPTER 5

Big Guns versus Wooden Decks:
Naval Aviation Officer Personnel, 1911–1941

Donald Chisholm

Cold steel is not worth a damn in an emergency. You need men to direct it.

—FRED BRITTEN, on the floor of the
U.S. House of Representatives, 15 May 1934

You were selected because you were not regarded as a crank, but as a well-balanced man who should be able to assist in building up a system of aviation training in the Navy. I've no doubt you see the importance of avoiding the hippodrome part of the business and will not do stunts just for the sake of notoriety or to thrill the crowd.

—CAPTAIN WASHINGTON I. CHAMBERS to
Lieutenant Theodore Gordon "Spuds" Ellyson
on his orders to work with Glenn Curtiss,
January 1911[1]

Aviation came to the U.S. Navy at a little more than one hundred years into the latter's existence. At its nascence, it was obvious to no one how naval aviation would turn out. How quickly and in what directions would its technology develop? What specific forms would it take? How potent would be its capabilities? To what purposes would it be put? What doctrine would be devised to orchestrate its employment? What would be its relationship to the Navy's existing ways and means of executing its traditional missions and roles? No matter the specific answers to these questions, aviation, like all such profound innovations, also substantially disrupted the equilibrium of the organization into which it was introduced and its preferred ways of doing business.[2]

Now, at its one-hundredth anniversary, we have a pretty fair idea of how Navy aviation turned out.

Although now many years distant, Navy aviation's three first decades made up the critical period for setting the foundation and parameters for its future development and created the possibility of its present status. The answers to the questions posed above were limned out: carrier-borne fixed-wing aircraft would become aviation's central focus, while long-range patrol aviation would play a supporting role; battleship and cruiser scout aircraft would first be relegated to secondary status and then disappear entirely (with some of their functions taken up by helicopters), as would dirigible lighter-than-air craft. Carrier aviation would supplant the surface capital ship as the Navy's principal offensive weapon for fleet actions and land attack, with spectacular effectiveness in the World War II Pacific Theater, thereafter rendering the United States the world's dominant maritime power and, in turn, making possible the free use by all nations of the earth's ocean commons.

Successive technological innovations—jet power, nuclear-powered carriers, rockets and missiles, sophisticated avionics, stunningly precise navigational and targeting capabilities, precision-guided munitions—have all made Navy aviation more effective than even its most visionary early proponents imagined. But these are the shiny baubles. As Representative Fred Britten wisely observed more than eighty years ago, in the end what renders militaries (and all other organizations, for that matter) effective are their personnel. The problem of aviation personnel, however, has scarcely enjoyed among naval historians the attention it warrants.[3] Here, I refer not to individuals, but the organization's *system* of personnel. Military personnel systems address, broadly speaking, specialization, numbers required, a system of grades and distribution into them, acquisition, education and training, career path, incentives (including pay and other emoluments), promotion, assignment to duty, and retirement.

This chapter provides in broad brushstrokes the essential structure and components of the officer personnel problem as they were understood by the principal actors in the first three decades of Navy aviation, and sketches the solutions to that problem—solutions that shaped Navy aviation then and continue to shape it today. Specifically, addressed here are the interrelated matters of specialization, numbers, and promotion. The Navy's endeavors to address its officer personnel issues more generally provide the background for the issues considered here.[4] Such endeavors formed a virtually unbroken chain punctuated by episodic enactment of law and issuance of administrative direction and policy. This chapter concentrates on those outcomes, leaving discussion of the processes for consideration elsewhere.

TIMING

The particular historical moment of aviation's arrival significantly affected its reception by the Navy's officers, the resources made available to it, how it would be organized, and the status of its personnel within the Navy. The principal factors affecting aviation personnel during its first thirty years included: (1) an established Navy officer personnel system; (2) emphasis on the all-big-gun battleship and gunnery as the Navy's main source of strength; (3) World War I; (4) the Washington Naval Treaty; (5) the Great Depression; and (6) the darkening clouds leading to World War II—in particular the Navy's decades-old focus on Japan as its next main opponent, manifested in its development of War Plan Orange.

Aviation's formal arrival in 1911 inserted it into an ongoing stream of personnel transactions. From aviation's beginning as a "temporary naval armament" in 1893 the Navy had, through a long series of incremental steps, developed an officer personnel system reasonably well adapted to its purposes. The modern Navy officer grades and their duties had all been established, career paths had been devised, the line and engineers had been amalgamated in 1899, a retirement system was in place, and shortly in 1916 promotion by selection up to Commander, Captain, and Rear Admiral would be made into law.

As is often the case with the arrival of new technologies into organizations, the Navy's initial responses to aviation were relatively informal and ad hoc. U.S. entry into World War I only six years after Navy aviation began required rapid expansion for the duration, including acquisition and training, organization into operational units, deployment, and the execution of operations. Consolidating and formalizing aviation's status, organization, and procedures would have to wait until after the war.

SPECIALIZATION

The place of the naval aviator in the officer corps was the central question of the time. Some aviators greatly favored a separate aviation corps, asserting that such a high degree of specialized knowledge was required that only those who spent their entire careers in it could hope to master it; others, including most non-aviators, strongly preferred that aviators remain integrated within the line officer corps.[5] This, in turn, required readdressing the question of what it meant to be a Navy officer. Central to the problem were the criteria for promotion by selection up (which hinged on what it meant to be a Navy officer), reconciliation of the trade-off between proficiency in aviation and expertise in general line duties, and control of aviation by non-aviators.[6]

In testimony before the Morrow Board in autumn 1925, some aviators asserted that most (70 percent) of their brothers favored a separate naval aviation corps because of the "unsympathetic attitude of other branches, flight pay, control and command by non-flying Officers, assignment to aviation of Officers without regard to rank, uniforms." However, to other aviators, because the "introduction of a corps aboard ship has always caused jealousy and heartburnings [*sic*]," a separate corps was to be avoided.

Indeed the Navy had only recently resolved a six-decade conflict between the line and the engineers by merging the two and redefining what it meant to be a Navy officer.[7] Navy engineers had been civilian contractors from 1836 to 1842. Thereafter, until 1899 they constituted a separate corps, with its own set of grades, each ranking with but behind its equivalent in the line. This allowed the line to gain access to engineering expertise without redefining what it meant to be an officer (navigator, handler of a ship under sail, accurate gunner, maintainer of the ship, and manager of her crew) and without ceding much power to the engineers. The staff corps had been the time-honored method (following the model of the Royal Navy) of absorbing any newly required expertise while retaining the purity and power of the line. However well this solution had worked for surgeons, paymasters, and naval constructors, their expertise was not integral to actually fighting the ship, while engineers were very necessary.

Aboard ship, engineers could command only their own personnel within their own spaces. Ambiguity about their status with regard to the Executive Officer and the Officer of the Deck led to more than one court-martial. By the 1890s, however, it had become clear that no Commanding Officer could fight his ship without a keen knowledge of its engineering. From 1899, to adapt to the changed requirements

Early naval aviators pose at the Naval Aeronautic Station, Pensacola, Florida, spring 1914.

of modern warships, the two officer corps were amalgamated and the line officer, in addition to his earlier duties, was now expected to perform as an engineer. Additionally, following the British model, enlisted ratings were assigned a range of duties that were formerly the province of engineers.

Aviation posed a more extreme version of the specialization problem—where the engineers had been necessary to the fighting ship, aviation aspired to complement and ultimately supplant the centuries-old gunned ship, only recently incarnated as the all-big-gun battleship. Destroyers were deemed analogous to the capital ships, and even submarines, given their limited capabilities at the time, were not considered a threat to the battleship's dominance.

The unpleasant experience of the line–engineer conflict thus rendered a separate aviation corps entirely improbable. As a 1925 Bureau of Navigation report commented,

> Aviation is no more specialized as to knowledge required than is submarine or destroyers, and BuNav does not believe that aviation demands of an Officer more skill or technical knowledge than is required of a chief engineer or a gunnery Officer. . . . The manipulative skill required for flying is of no consequence in determining that the Officer is fit to hold a higher command in aviation or general line duties, nor does the possession of the naval aviator designation by a group of men carry the argument for its perpetuation by medium of a corps.[8]

Non-aviator officers saw no reason to populate aviation with a high proportion of officers. Chief of Naval Operations Edward Eberle believed that additional aviators could only be secured by a higher proportion of enlisted men. He proposed a fifty-fifty split between officers and enlisted personnel, depending on the task.[9]

In its final report, the Morrow Board noted the justifiable "unrest and dissatisfaction among the aviation personnel" and recommended sundry changes in personnel policies, including:

1. carrying as extra numbers aviators who had specialized in aviation so long as to jeopardize their chances for promotion by selection to Commander, Captain, or Rear Admiral;

2. granting temporary higher rank to junior Officers assigned to aviation duty whenever the higher rank was appropriate;

3. maintaining flight pay as then provided, while investigating a scheme of insurance;

4. confining selections for command of aviation activities to Officers who while otherwise qualified were also naval aviators;

5. dissociating from naval aviation aviators assigned to general line duty for purposes of qualification for command to the minimum extent;

6. ensuring that junior Officers who had not had the required sea duty have that duty before being examined for promotion; and

7. studying the desirability of increasing the number of enlisted pilots in naval aviation.[10]

But this was by no means the last word on the matter, for both legislation and administrative rules were necessary.

The House Naval Affairs Committee quickly responded to the board's recommendations, notably proposing the first legal definition of "naval aviator"[11]:

> Any commissioned Officer or Warrant line Officer in the Navy or Marine Corps who has successfully completed the course prescribed by competent authority for naval aviators and who has been or may hereafter be designated or appointed a naval aviator by competent authority and who has flown alone in a heavier-than-air craft not less than seventy-five hours and who has flown in heavier-than-air craft not less than 200 hours or who has been in the air, under training in rigid airships not less than 150 hours and successfully completed the course prescribed by competent authority.[12]

"Naval aviation pilot" would refer to any Navy or Marine enlisted man who completed the same course and met the same hours requirement. "Pilot" would be construed to encompass both naval aviator and naval aviation pilot. At the same time, the bill would create a cadre of "naval aviation observers," those officers who completed a prescribed course and had not fewer than one hundred hours in the air. This last designation was intended to "grandfather" into aviation those senior officers who supported naval aviation but were not physically qualified (because of age) to fly as naval aviators.[13]

Of course, these criteria were supplied by the naval aviators, and like all such definitions, would serve both to maintain professional standards and exclude unwanted others. The criteria had no real teeth on their own, however. Complementary provisions in the bill established eligibility for aviation commands. Officers detailed to command aviation schools, air stations, or tactical air units would have to be naval aviators. This would ensure that immediate control of air operations would be in the hands of line officers who had qualified and spent time as naval aviators—which had not been the practice to date. While command of "aircraft vessels" (aircraft carriers and seaplane tenders) could be given to officers who were "skilled executives," it was "also necessary that they have a dual capacity and be skilled in the operation of aircraft."[14] Thus, command of such vessels would be restricted to naval aviators and naval aviation observers. Both creating in law naval aviation observers and allowing them to command carriers and tenders would give the aviators breathing room to see sufficient aviators advanced to Commander and Captain, so that in time all such ships would be in charge of naval aviators. They much preferred this mechanism to temporarily advancing aviators to the grades appropriate for the command billet (which had been done) or worse, detailing non-aviators to such commands. Simultaneously, this provision would create a restricted list of sea commands that would ensure that aviators would achieve the requisites for promotion by selection. The Act of 3 July 1926 rendered these mechanisms into law.

Navy aviators would enjoy henceforth a special status within the Navy. They would remain an integral component of the unrestricted line, be expected to serve and command in ships, and be subject to the same requirements for promotion as other officers while retaining the power to define who qualified as a naval aviator and the criteria for eligibility to command aviation units.

NUMBERS

Direction and command of naval aviation, of necessity, devolved upon commissioned line officers. However, whether the bulk of the pilots should be commissioned or enlisted was a separate question. Greater numbers of enlisted pilots could more readily be accessed than commissioned officers, but that would attenuate the power of naval aviation within the Navy when it came to claims on scarce resources. Not surprisingly, non-aviator officers preferred that most pilots come from the enlisted ranks; aviators took the antipodal position. In practice, in its early decades naval aviation comprised about 75 percent officers and 25 percent enlisted men, a ratio of officers to enlisted effectively the opposite of that which obtained aboard ship.

Another approach was to rely on Naval Reserve officers to supply the bulk of commissioned pilots, with a small number of regular officers to fill the key command billets and to provide organizational continuity. This method carried risks similar to relying primarily on enlisted men for pilots—Reserve officers carried no weight on important issues facing the Navy. Yet another means would be to obtain regular commissions for officers accessed from sources other than the Naval Academy. Once again, this posed certain risks to aviation because at the time non-academy officers were informally accorded little more than second-class citizenship. Ultimately, pilots for Navy aviation would be drawn from a complex mix of these sources, an olio that changed over time to adapt to new circumstances.

Initially, officers for aviation were simply taken out of hide—volunteers from the regular line—for the numbers were very small. However, the dramatic Navy expansion occasioned by U.S. entry into World War I necessitated other measures. The Act of 29 August 1916 established the largest naval construction program for any nation to that date.[15] The sole source of commissioned officers was still the Naval Academy, which even with an expanded brigade and a truncated curriculum could hardly supply enough officers in a timely manner to meet both fleet and aviation requirements for wartime.

During the four preceding decades, the Navy had worked out an algorithm for establishing the required number of enlisted personnel based on tonnage of capital ships in commission. The Act of 29 August 1916 established the number of officers in turn as a ratio (4 percent) of enlisted personnel. However, just as changes in the types of ships in the fleet affected the appropriate distribution into the several grades and specialties, so the arrival and expansion of aviation called into question the existing algorithm, by requiring a much higher proportion of officers.

The Act also contained personnel provisions to support the dramatic fleet expansion. It authorized increasing enlisted personnel and slightly increased annual appointments to the Naval Academy, provided for temporary officers (to be commissioned from senior enlisted and warranted personnel), and created a Naval Reserve Force with several classes of officers and men within. The Act specifically established a Naval Flying Corps in addition to those officers and men already provided for in law.

Complementary to the Naval Flying Corps was a Naval *Reserve* Flying Corps, part of the larger Naval Reserve Force, which would be developed through transfers of officers and enlisted men from the former, from "surplus" graduates of aeronautics schools, and from other Naval Reserve Force members who already had aviation experience.[16] The reserves proved essential to the war effort: when the United States entered the war in April 1917, the sum of regular personnel assigned to naval aviation still totaled only 48 officers (including 6 Marines) and 239 enlisted men.

In practice, volunteer aviation units were initially formed at several universities (including Yale) from which came a core of Reserve aviator officers. The few regular aviators, such as Marc Mitscher, were detailed to command the training stations that in nineteen months produced about 2,000 aviators and 30,000 enlisted personnel, which then were deployed to twenty bases overseas, flying more than two million miles of coastal anti-submarine patrols, damaging or sinking twelve German submarines before the end of the war, bombing German submarine bases, and beginning to support the Allied strategic air attacks on German land targets. By the Armistice, naval aviation had peaked at 37,407 officers and men, 82 percent of whom were reservists.[17]

With the 11 November 1918 Armistice, however, came the need simultaneously to reverse the temporary wartime expansion and to maintain a permanent increase of the regular officer corps—in good measure to support a larger naval aviation component. However, any additional officer aviators would come at the expense of filling shipboard billets. The increasing technological complexity of ships also demanded more officers.[18] Unfortunately, although the fleet grew over the next decade, authorized officer strength remained essentially static. BuNav was compelled to strip shore installations of officers for the ships, especially the new destroyers. By the end of 1920, only a comparatively small number of Reserve officers remained on active duty. By 1922 the Naval Reserve Flying Corps was rendered inactive.[19] Under these conditions it proved very difficult for Navy aviation to grow, absent new institutional mechanisms for providing officers.

The 4 June 1920 Naval Appropriations Act authorized 500 Reserve officers for active duty in naval aviation and extended temporary commissions—combined with regulars and reserves—not to exceed the total authorized officers, or 5,499 (4 percent of regular, authorized, enlisted personnel), until the end of 1921.[20]

> More important to the aviators, this same act provided that Officers holding temporary commissions and Warrant ranks in the Navy and members of the Naval Reserve Force of commissioned and Warrant ranks shall be eligible for transfer to an appointment in the permanent grades or ranks in the Navy for which they may be found qualified not above that held by them on the date of transfer, but not exceed a total of one thousand two hundred commissioned Officers of the line, of which five hundred may be appointed from class five, Naval Reserve Flying Corps.[21]

No transfers would be made above the grade of Lieutenant. Aviation was assured of at least some new permanent officers. However, bringing into a corps of fewer than 3,000 officers—virtually all of whom were Naval Academy graduates—another 1,200 officers, none of whom were Academy graduates and many of whom were aviators (most of the Reserve aviators still on duty applied for and were accepted into the regular line), could not fail to cause heartburn among the former.[22] Transferred officers took lineal precedence between the Naval Academy classes of 1919 and 1920, creating an enormous "hump" that blocked promotion for officers commissioned thereafter, and as we shall see, shortly precipitated extension of promotion by selection up.

By early 1921, of the ships authorized by the Act of 1916, ten scout cruisers and more than sixty submarines were nearly complete and fifty destroyers had been commissioned, while ten battleships and six battle cruisers remained incomplete. Congressional wartime largess turned to peacetime unwillingness to spend on armaments. Faced with strong congressional sentiment, President Warren G. Harding organized the Washington Naval Conference, which resulted in drastic formal limitations on capital warships among the great naval powers. In the United States, this also translated into severe limits on enlisted personnel and commissioned officers. Although the Act of 1916 authorized 160,000 peacetime enlisted personnel, Congress ultimately only appropriated for 86,000 men and 4,500 line officers.

In June 1921 there were 5,295 regulars and reserves on active duty. All temporary commissions terminated at the end of 1921, the remaining 1,011 temporary officers reverted to their permanent status, while 1,059 regular officers serving temporarily in higher ranks reverted to their permanent ranks. Through dismissal or resignation, 174 permanent officers had left the service.[23]

These terminations left a regular line officer strength of 4,436 officers by June 1922. Congress refused to appropriate additional pay for reservists, and by mid-1923 the regulars and reserves combined totaled only 4,596 (of which 41 percent were Ensigns or junior Lieutenants). It became exceedingly difficult to officer ships in commission, let alone those still building. Fleet operations were continually short of officers. Ships operated with 85–90 percent of normal officer complements, while destroyers were rotated in and out of commission. Inexperienced Ensigns performed duties usually reserved for more experienced seniors. Although the Naval Academy classes were now the largest ever, and contributed to the "hump," they remained insufficient to replenish the line and to bring it up to its authorized strength. The 1923–1924 appropriations act returned the number of Academy appointments to pre-war levels. Naval aviators occupied almost exclusively the three lowest officer grades. None of this was auspicious for naval aviation, which was bent on growing.

At this time, attention again focused on an effective Naval Reserve, culminating in the Naval Reserve Act of 4 March 1925. At Rear Admiral William Moffett's urging, the Chief of Naval Operations had published a Naval Aviation Reserve Policy in November 1923, providing for one aviation unit in each naval district, which mission was to enroll and train "new members who were suitable officer material in order to insure a supply of new blood, and to maintain the efficiency of members already qualified."[24] The practical challenge was to secure adequate funding from an increasingly penurious Congress. Even if appropriations were secured and more officers commissioned, these naval aviators still lacked the requisite education and experience to make them effective naval line officers. As such they would be relegated, if only informally, to second-tier status in the officer corps.[25]

The 1925 law disestablished the Naval Reserve Force created by the Act 29 August 1916 and in its stead, using the Army's Reserve Officer Training Corps as a model, created a *Naval* Reserve Officer Training Corps (NROTC), organized at six universities, at a maximum overall strength of 1,200 members.[26] This would supplement the Naval Academy's output of college graduate officers. The first 130 NROTC graduates were commissioned in spring 1930. They would comprise an elite cadre of Reserve officers.[27] Naval aviation would gain a portion of those newly commissioned officers.

Problems of stagnation in promotion resulted in officers old for their grades and the inevitable discouragement this engendered. In response, the Act of 3 March 1931 permanently established length of service as the mechanism for retirement of officers, irrespective of commissioning source, which was directed principally toward expediting promotion, evening chances for promotion, and regularizing the promotion process. It also laid the foundation for retirement of non-Academy officers, mostly naval aviators, not promoted.[28]

Naval Reserve Freshmen, class of 1930, University of California.

The simultaneous continued differentiation of the fleet into different types of ships and the continued commissioning of new ships occasioned a requirement for more-junior officers, but Congress would not fund the authorized five appointment regimen for the Naval Academy, nor would it authorize an increase in the total number of officers. This meant no accommodation for the long-term growth of naval aviation, especially given the policy that 75 percent of pilots would be officers.

In 1933 the authorized strength of the line remained below that required for the peacetime treaty-strength Navy (let alone wartime), especially given vessels then under construction and the continued expansion of Navy aviation. Graduating Naval Academy classes exceeded annual attrition of officers, leaving the problem of what to do with the surplus. The "hump" created by the accession of officers under the Act of 4 June 1920 had not gone away and stagnation in promotion was intensifying: Academy graduates would have to retire for service in grade before being promoted because non-Academy officers were ahead of and blocking them.

The immediate solution for Navy aviation was another new mechanism for accession. The Act of 27 March 1934 authorized a 1,910-aircraft program for Navy aviation, but there were only 806 naval aviators. The Act of 15 April 1935 redressed some of this shortfall, and in a novel manner. Based on an analysis of officer personnel problems prepared by Commander John S. "Slew" McCain and drafted in the Bureau of Aeronautics, it authorized the Secretary to appoint an unspecified number of aviation cadets to the Naval Reserve (Swanson intended to train 498 cadets in fiscal 1935 and 1936). The cadets were intended both as a temporary palliative to quickly bring active duty naval aviation personnel up to peacetime requirements until the grades could be filled with regular officers and to create an experienced cadre of aviators in the Naval Reserve.

Cadets were obligated to four years of active service, the first in pilot training, the next three in active flying duty. They were then to be commissioned as Reserve Ensigns (or Reserve Marine second Lieutenants), and subject to recall to active duty as skilled aviators in a national emergency. Naval aviation cadets were neither commissioned nor warranted officers nor enlisted personnel; they ranked immediately below Ensigns and above warrant officers. From the aviators' perspective, this mechanism provided for the numbers required for the treaty-strength Navy. From the non-aviators' point of view, this was attractive: it reduced the strain on future Naval Academy classes, did not increase aviation officers in the regular line (hence, did not intensify competition for and speed of promotion), and cadets would be in and out of active duty in four years.

A frugal Congress found the Act appealing as it required no increase in authorized officer strength and cadets were paid less than Ensigns: $75 per month when training or not flying, and $150 monthly when on flying duty. Cadets completing their four-year obligation received a $1,500 lump-sum bonus, and, notably, they were afforded $10,000 in life insurance. Congress also liked that applicants for aviation cadet would apply at the thirteen naval air stations "from the east coast to the west coast and from the north to the south and adjacent to our populous cities."[29] What member of Congress could oppose a bill to provide jobs, especially when his constituents would have a shot at them?

The Bureau of Aeronautics wasted no time:

> The first class of fifty-five cadets reported to Pensacola on July 20, 1935, and by September, there were 192 aviation cadets undergoing training, with an additional 201 potential cadets undergoing elimination training to determine their adaptability to flight before going to Pensacola.
>
> By September 1936, the first cadets were at sea, and, two years later, 614 aviation cadets were on active Naval Aviator duty.[30]

Notwithstanding initial ambivalence about the aviation cadets, they soon became integral to fleet operations, and by 1939, when the first cadets were due to leave active duty for commissions as Ensigns in the Naval Reserve, at least some senior officers recognized that their release would seriously hamper fleet operations.[31]

Throughout the mid-1930s the problem of numbers was accompanied by the persistent difficulty of maintaining sufficient training time for Reserve aviators. As part of broader cost-cutting policies, all Reserve training was reduced. For the 1934 fiscal year, annual flying hours for the reservists were reduced from forty-five to thirty and drills from forty-eight to twenty-four, while flying hours for the Volunteer Reserve were entirely eliminated.[32] The Bureau of Aeronautics contended that fewer than forty-eight flying hours per aviator annually raised the probability of accidents due to poor flying proficiency to an unacceptable level. It pointed out that if aviators in the Volunteer Reserve were "not provided with flight training from time to time, they would soon cease to be Naval Aviators."[33] The problem of training time also affected surface and submarine Reserve officers, but the relatively greater combined complexity and perishability of flying skills rendered the problem more acute for naval aviation.[34]

The Act of 22 July 1935 partially redressed the problem of numbers by increasing the number of officers as a percentage of enlisted personnel from 4 percent to 4.75 percent. This translated to increasing the authorized strength to 6,531 officers, well short of the 7,102 officers required to maintain the fleet in readiness for war, and the 7,941 officers required for the treaty-strength Navy that was authorized and building. It capped the numbers of Rear Admirals, Captains, and Commanders, except in wartime, and specified that the Lieutenant Commanders could be increased up to 15 percent when required. Lengths of service for Lieutenants and junior Lieutenants were extended, while lifting restrictions on involuntary retirements of officers in those grades. These provisions aimed to supply the minimum officer needs while eliminating overage officers who clearly were not going to be promoted. Meanwhile, Naval Academy appointments had been reduced to three per member of Congress annually, which would not even cover normal attrition let alone any increase in strength.

Three years later, the Act of 22 June 1938 increased authorized strength of the line to 5.5 percent of enlisted strength along with reorganizing the system of promotion more extensively than any time since the Act of 29 August 1916 (discussed below). But authorized and actual strength remained two different numbers. With the graduation of the Naval Academy class of 1938, the actual strength increased to 6,565 officers, still well short of the 7,211 (excluding 730 naval aviation cadets) required for the treaty Navy and short of the additional 1,200 officers necessary for the expansion Congress had just provided. At about the same time, Congress was working through what would become the Act of 22 June 1938, which fundamentally reorganized the Naval Reserve as it had been established by the Act of 1925.

With the clouds of war gathering, President Roosevelt signed the Naval Aviation Reserve Act on 13 June 1939. This law amended the Act of 15 April 1935 that had created naval aviation cadets. They were no longer to dwell in the nether world between enlisted and commissioned status, and the Navy would gain their services for longer periods, relieving pressure on the line from fleet expansion and aviation's growth. Once graduated from Pensacola, they would immediately be commissioned Reserve Ensigns, and after three years' active service become eligible for promotion to Reserve junior Lieutenants. They might be required to perform active duty for up to four years; they were allowed to serve up to seven years. Meanwhile Congress again increased the authorized strength of the line to 7,562 officers, but this remained short of the 8,671 needed to man the fleet to peacetime complements, and in any case the actual number of active list officers amounted to only 6,877 on 30 June 1939. The September 1939 German invasion of Poland had a positive effect on the Navy— President Franklin D. Roosevelt immediately issued an executive order increasing the actual enlisted strength and authorizing active duty for retired and Reserve officers. By June 1940, 539 retired and 1,806 Reserve officers were on active duty.

In August, September, and October 1940, three more laws aimed to increase the numbers of officers in order to accommodate the vastly increased requirements created by laws signed in June and July (following the fall of France to the Nazis). These acts expanded the fleet by 1,325,000 tons of combatants and boosted naval aviation to an unbelievable *15,000 aircraft*. They alone augmented ships and aircraft by more than 80 percent; the fleet expansion acts called for 2,200 additional short-term naval aviators. That magnitude of increase rendered previous mechanisms for accessing officers, especially aviators, inadequate and incomplete.

To quickly address these vast new requirements, the Act of 27 August 1940 "Naval Aviation Personnel Act," based largely on the recommendations of the Horne Board, whose establishment had been mandated by the Act of 13 June 1939, authorized appointment of as many Naval Reserve aviators (essentially, those officers commissioned from the naval aviation cadet program) to the regular line as necessary.[35] Authorized officers would be increased automatically.[36] Almost incidentally, one week later, the Act of 4 September 1940 authorized the president to commission Naval Academy graduates who were qualified but had not been previously commissioned (due to earlier limits on authorized strengths).

The Act of 8 October 1940 provided still more officers for the regular line by mechanisms that would admit NROTC commissioned Reserve officers. Since the first NROTC class in 1930, 2,154 students had graduated and been commissioned, making a large pool of college-educated officers deemed the next best source after Naval Academy graduates for regular officers. The numbers to be so transferred were left to presidential discretion. The law did not increase authorized officers because the actual number remained so far below existing authorized strength.

Rapidly changing conditions soon made it obvious that even these novel methods for increasing the line were inadequate. The earlier Horne Board was reprised, and it recommended reducing the Naval Academy course to three years (the Navy had already graduated the 1940 and 1941 classes after completing three and one-half years—by interpreting the law to mean four *academic* years) on the five-appointment regimen. This was the same mechanism employed during World War I. The recommendation became law on 3 June 1941. This avenue was soon supplemented on 11 July 1941 by a law providing for the appointment of temporary officers and for the temporary promotion of officers as required, but not more than six months after the termination of war.

Thus, by the time of U.S. entry into the war, the Navy had adopted a solution to securing officers, one that institutionalized a two-tier personnel system in which there were, first, officers of the regular line, and, second, everyone else. Expansion of the officer corps had been transformed from gaining approval for an increase in the regular line to devising methods to enlarge it temporarily, and to populate it, even during peacetime, with second-class citizens in the form of Reserve officers, reactivated retired officers, and retained fitted officers no longer in the running for promotion.[37] The problem of distribution was addressed by temporary promotions of both regular and Reserve officers. These personnel policies especially helped to supply the vast number of junior officers necessary to fly the Navy's burgeoning fleet of aircraft. Of course, the realities of the war's requirements soon also outstripped these several devices for expanding the line. However, these mechanisms had established a solid institutional foundation for growing the line, and the subsequent wartime commissioning programs were extensions of and variants upon them. Naval aviation would have its own versions of wartime Reserve commissioning programs.

PROMOTION

Although necessary, an adequate number of aviator officers was not in itself sufficient to put naval aviation on the right track: such required the proper distribution of officers into the several grades. In all organizations, but especially the military, rank is the currency of the realm. With it, all things are possible, without, very little. This was another principal lesson of the conflict between the engineers and the line. Unlike most large organizations, in closed institutions such as the military, entry into executive positions is secured only through advancement from one grade to another, after having been commissioned at the lowest grade. There are, with few exceptions, no lateral entries into the higher grades from without. This renders technological innovation, such as the introduction of aviation into the Navy, profoundly difficult.

Closely tied to promotion is the matter of specialization and defining what it means to be an officer. This is of lesser moment in a Service in which promotion is decided strictly through seniority. Promotion by seniority had been virtually sacrosanct in the Navy until 1899.[38] Promotion by selection up, based on comparative fitness of an officer for the duties of the next higher grade—to Rear Admiral, Captain, and Commander—was established by the Act of 29 August 1916. Thus it was that aviation arrived just as the Navy shifted to a promotion mechanism that (1) did not assume that competence in the junior grades necessarily meant competence in the duties of the senior grades and (2) required a formal complex representation of each grade's duties and the skills required to perform them.

Because its officers would not be organized into a separate corps, but remain within the line, the practical challenge for Navy aviation was to obtain the inclusion of promotion criteria that managed to balance the competing demands of the specialized duties of aviation with the duties of a general line officer. Having redefined line officer to include engineering expertise only a short while before, line officers (read: "battleship sailors") were loath to alter it again so soon. Moreover, maintaining the existing definition of officer served the purposes of non-aviators in fending off what they perceived as the threat of aviation to the battle line's dominance. However, selection boards were unlikely to entertain multiple concepts of career paths as legitimate for promotion.[39]

Compounding these difficulties was the initial absence of aviators in the flag grades. For the first decade or so, Navy aviation would have to rely on selection boards composed of battleship admirals, some of whom were actively opposed to any significant role for aviation in the Navy, to promote aviators whose career paths did not look familiar to them. Two methods were adopted to address this problem. Aviators worked to insert language by law and administrative direction in the instructions to selection boards about criteria for evaluating officers. Simultaneously, as noted above, aviators sought sympathetic battleship officers who might be formally grandfathered in as naval aviation observers. In turn, aviators lobbied within the Navy to see that at least one such formally designated officer (and subsequently naval aviators) would be included on every selection board.

Analysis of line selection board membership over the 1916–1941 period reveals that their efforts were successful. Although never part of administrative regulations, let alone law during this period, aviators appear to have gained an informal "quota" for selection board membership. Beginning with the June 1926 board, at least one aviator (and occasionally two) was included among the nine members. This started with the senior officers qualified as naval aviation observers and continued until enough naval aviators had reached flag rank to serve. The overwhelming majority of non-aviator board members were drawn from officers stationed in or near Washington, D.C.; for example, Boston, Brooklyn Navy Yard, Philadelphia. By contrast, the aviator members came a great distance to serve on the boards.[40]

Support for extending promotion by selection to Lieutenant Commander and Lieutenant grew as a way to address the "hump," as we saw above. Although ostensibly a neutral mechanism functioning solely to promote the officers comparatively best fitted for the duties of the next higher grade, another agenda was also at work, namely, the place of aviation officers and the larger problem of generalists versus specialists. The comments of Rear Admiral J. Raby, following his tenure on the December 1932 selection board, are instructive:

> If you look over the list today you will find that there are a good many men who are able to pass their examinations, *not necessarily Naval Academy graduates, but men who came up from the ranks or temporary Officers during the war and*

many who are aviators. They followed one line all their lives and it does not look to me that they are qualified to perform their duty as Lieutenant Commander aboard ship, and for that reason . . . we ought to have some way of eliminating those men that would probably be a drag on that grade. They eventually . . . will fail in selection when they get to the next higher grade.[41]

It was the boldest declaration to date of the lack of confidence of senior officers in the non-Academy officers in the "hump" and the most direct linkage of the "hump" and naval aviation.

The Act of 29 May 1934, conceived in the Bureau of Navigation and introduced and passed in the Congress in a mere six weeks (while most officers were at sea on a fleet problem), extended promotion by selection to Lieutenant Commander and Lieutenant as a means, not so much to secure more effective officers, but to eliminate stagnation in promotion for Academy officers, and along the way to reduce if not completely purge the non-Academy officers, many of whom happened to be aviators.[42]

A key element in selection for promotion would be how sea service was defined. When promotion by selection was established in 1916, eligibility for selection was tied to four years' service in grade, two of which had to be at sea; this, to forestall promotion of officers who navigated only their desks ashore. At the time, the specialized duties of aviators had not become entirely clear and their numbers were small. With the extension of selection up to the junior line grades, this provision became an obstacle to the aviators. More generally, it is indicative of the challenge aviation and its requirements posed to the prevailing understanding of what it meant to be a Navy officer.

Shortly before the first selection boards were to consider officers for promotion to Lieutenant Commander and Lieutenant, Rear Admiral William Leahy, Chief of the Bureau of Navigation, issued a circular letter defining sea duty as "service on board sea going ships of the Fleet and special services considered sea service." He laid out specific duties and ships that were *not* considered sea duty.[43]

Consequently, Chief of the Bureau of Aeronautics, Rear Admiral Ernest King, on the belief that this interpretation of sea duty was strongly prejudicial to aviation interests, wrote to Leahy recommending that language governing Marine Corps promotion be inserted in junior selection board precepts, to wit: "in determining an Officer's fitness for promotion, administrative staff duty performed by him under appointment or detail, and duty in aviation, or in any technical specialty, shall be given weight by the Board equal to that given line duty equally well performed."[44] King argued such was necessary both to protect equity for individual officers, who, through no fault of their own, had not been to sea, and to ensure that an adequate number of aviators would be retained in the Navy.

Leahy was willing only to provide the language proposed by King in a composite of laws regularly furnished to selection boards—no special attention would be given to it. Not one to concede defeat readily, King appealed directly to Secretary of the Navy Claude Swanson. Shortly thereafter the latter clarified Navy promotion policy in a January 1935 instruction to Leahy. Notably, the instruction was couched in general terms, but its most important outcome was intended to be the protection of junior naval aviators:

> The repeated assignment of many Officers to special types of duty, for which they have been fitted by postgraduate instruction or special training, is highly essential to the efficiency of the Fleet . . . and that the assignment of Officers below the rank of Commander to other general service for the sole purpose of "rotation" or "rounding out the record" of an individual at the expense of the Service is, at the present time, considered neither necessary nor desirable.
>
> The Secretary considers it necessary to Naval efficiency and to the best interests of the Service that extended devotion to duty in all Naval specialties and the successful performance of specialist duty be given full consideration in determining an Officer's fitness for promotion, equal to that given other general line duties equally well performed. Continued employment on specialist duty of Officers below the rank of Commander should not adversely affect their prospects for selection and promotion.[45]

Although the issues of specialization and the equivalence for purposes of promotion of broadly different types of duty within a single unrestricted line officer corps were not now entirely laid to rest, the foundational concept had been established. As officer career paths were increasingly formalized in succeeding decades, greater precision was achieved in assessing the equivalence of different kinds of duty. Inevitably, and appropriately, some duties would be more equal than others in selecting officers for promotion.

In the event, junior line selection boards passed over 247 of 292 Lieutenants who were not Naval Academy graduates while the overall promotion rate from Lieutenant to Lieutenant Commander was nearly 70 percent. Lieutenant W. J. Slattery testified before the House Naval Affairs Committee that Academy graduates were promoted who "were in high school when I was standing watch on a warship in the World War. I am in command of a squadron from which two Lieutenants have just been selected over my head."[46] Some in Congress, focused on equity for the non-Academy officers, responded sympathetically. Others, most concerned with naval efficiency, noted that promotion was not so much a matter of individual merit as it was usefulness to the Service.

The Act of 22 June 1938 approached a comprehensive reorganization of the line officer corps. Notably, it created the category of "fitted Officer" (vice "best fitted"), to which a selection board might assign an officer—an officer who might be continued on active duty and remain eligible for consideration by the next selection board or who could be retired in his existing grade at the discretion of the board. The law's provisions also institutionalized administrative practices, established specific new procedural protections for officers in selection, and clarified areas that contained significant ambiguities. Referring to the difference between fitted and best fitted officers, a subsequent Bureau of Navigation memorandum to flag officers noted that "the law fixes no standards for this adjudgment; the selection boards must, in their collective experience and judgment, develop them for their own guidance."[47]

The Act of 13 June 1939 called for the Navy to appoint a board to consider the regular and Reserve personnel of naval aviation, which board was to render its report by 1 December of that year. The Horne Board (discussed earlier) proceeded from the principle that "no solution proposed at this time can be lasting. It is, therefore, of first importance to emphasize the most effective method of obtaining the desired result." This included permitting the Navy the maximum administrative discretion possible in reshaping the officer personnel for wartime.

> Indicating how far understanding of the place of aviation within the Navy had come since its 1911 inception, the Board had constantly kept in mind the fact that naval aviation is inseparably woven into the very warp and woof of the entire naval establishment. Therefore the board has given the most mature thought to the question of the relation of aviation personnel to the Navy as a whole. One element cannot be separated from the other elements and treated independently without gravely jeopardizing the strength and stability of the whole structure.[48]

It was a mature reflection on what it meant to be a naval officer.

The board recommended, among many things, that regular officers for aviation be secured based on (1) their completing two years' sea service; (2) being under age 32; and (3) volunteering. Because it believed that "intensive aviation activity required in carrier-based aircraft squadrons tend[ed] to the early development of individual responsibility and piloting ability," officers—after completing the aviation course—would perform two years' duty with fleet aircraft squadrons before becoming eligible for other duty.

Its conclusions are worth noting in detail:

1. Officers should be rotated through all aspects of aviation duty to acquire a well-rounded knowledge;
2. assignment of line Officers . . . to aviation duty permits such diversification of duty from junior to senior billets that the designation "naval aviator" should be *considered an added qualification and not a specialty tending in any way to divorce those Officers from the line* [my emphasis];

3. aviation is an integral part of the Navy and continuous assignment to aviation should not prejudice an Officer's career;

4. aviators should be required to maintain qualification for general line duty;

5. aviators on duty in aviation from junior to command grades should be considered eligible for assignment to command based on relative professional fitness with other line Officers;

6. aviators should be available for assignment to any line duty commensurate with their grade, without prejudice to reassignment to aviation duty or to future advancement;

7. as required by law, Commanding Officers of aircraft carriers or seaplane tenders should be naval aviators or naval aviation observers; Commanders of naval aviation schools, naval air stations, or naval aviation units for flight tactical purposes should be naval aviators; and

8. only naval aviators who were regular line should be assigned duty commanding a group or wing of aircraft.[49]

Thus, the board came down strongly on maintaining regular aviators, notwithstanding their need to develop certain specialized skills and abilities, as integral members of the unrestricted line. It specified certain career milestones and requirements that it believed would facilitate the appropriate probability of promotion for aviators.

However, as noted above, the board also recognized that all military organizations had to maintain large foundations of junior officers, with "successive groups of increasing responsibility and authority leading up to a small group in highest authority." Expansion required principally increases in the numbers of junior officers and relatively fewer in the senior grades. Sufficient numbers of aviators would never be accessed through the regular line. Thus, the long-term solution was to have some officers pursue a naval career, while others would stay a short while and return to civilian life. In its view, the permanent number was to be 45 percent.

Reserve officers would continue to play an essential and expanding role (especially in wartime) in naval aviation. It devised a series of milestones for the development of Reserve officers following their accession through existing NROTC programs, from among graduates of aeronautical engineering courses at recognized universities, among other university graduates and those who had completed at least one-half of the courses required for graduation. The board proposed retaining Reserve aviators on active duty for up to twenty years, with some few annually permitted to commission into the regular line.

The board's report was forwarded to Congress in January 1940. Most of its recommendations were incorporated into the Naval Aviation Personnel Act of 1940, signed into law by President Roosevelt on 27 August 1940. The Horne Board had laid out much of the foundation for conceptualizing and operating the officer personnel system for the next decades, especially the place of naval aviator officers within the larger regular line. Notably, regular aviators would have to meet the same requirements as any other line officer; they could not simply fly aircraft. Conversely, naval aviators would not be precluded from promotion and higher command on account of their "additional qualification."

The problem of supplying the very large numbers of officers to fly in aviation units would be solved by acquiring Reserve officers, most all of whom would serve only in the junior grades, but could compete for a small number of regular commissions annually. Naval aviation would thereby have enough regular officers to provide organizational continuity and greater levels of expertise, *and* to compete for promotion to the higher grades and positions of greatest responsibility in the Navy with non-aviator regular line officers. In reality, there was no other mechanism by which the Navy might afford a peacetime naval aviation establishment that could greatly expand temporarily as required in the event of war.

CONCLUDING THOUGHTS

The introduction of aviation in 1911 triggered a set of organizational dynamics within the Navy resembling those occasioned by previous requirements for new kinds of expertise afloat, especially that of steam engineering in the mid-nineteenth century. Aviation called for a significant readjustment of thinking within the Navy about how "line officer" was defined, and, predictably, a three-decade tussle over the place of aviation within the Navy ensued over that meaning, resolved only on the eve of World War II. In that resolution were contained mechanisms to address three intertwined primary officer personnel problems: how specialization in aviation would be treated, how the appropriate numbers of officers would be acquired for aviation, and how naval aviators would fair in the rigorous process of promotion to the higher grades. The solutions adopted for these problems broadly defined naval aviation and still condition its place and performance in the Navy today.

Throughout these first three decades of naval aviation, the technology of aircraft and ships advanced rapidly, and the concept of operations for and aviation's role in the fleet matured greatly. However, the underlying environmental conditions during this period were mostly not conducive to the development of aviation's organization and personnel: the practical necessity of tremendous expansion of aviation for World War I, followed by its dramatic contraction in the immediate postwar period, the sore limitations imposed by the Washington Naval Treaty and the penuriousness of Congress in the 1920s, effects of the Great Depression, and then the threat of war. And, as naval aviation was attempting to find its place, the Navy was engaged in attempting to structure and solve its larger officer personnel problems.

That from these early decades naval aviation emerged poised to make its contribution as the fleet's principal striking force in the great campaigns of World War II's Pacific Theater is all the more remarkable, therefore. Out of a combination of sustained, systematic problem solving and internal political conflict came the personnel system that produced the officers necessary to plan and execute that wartime contribution, for, as Representative Fred Britten observed in 1934, "Cold steel isn't worth a damn in an emergency. You need men to direct it." We know well the most senior officers who led aviation during the war—Ernest King, William Halsey, Marc Mitscher, John S. McCain, John Towers; but for every one of these flag officers there were thousands of junior to command grade naval aviators, regular and reserve, who made it possible to execute the high-level plans and accomplish the strategic objectives. Although it is the ships and especially the aircraft that most often capture our attention and imagination, the presence in the Navy of a vast cadre of aviators and their performance in combat was rendered possible by the often invisible, sometimes arcane, and typically not very interesting officer personnel system.

NOTES

This chapter is based, in part, upon material contained in, and the research conducted for, Donald Chisholm, *Waiting for Dead Men's Shoes: Origins and Development of the U.S. Navy's Officer Personnel System, 1793–1941* (Stanford, CA: Stanford University Press, 2001).

1. George van Deurs, *Anchors in the Sky: Spuds Ellyson, The First Naval Aviator* (San Rafael, CA: Presidio Press, 1978), p. 59.
2. Ibid.
3. The administrative place, standing, and organization of naval aviation are matters complementary to that of personnel. Significant administrative developments parallel those of personnel in the first three decades of naval aviation. Fortunately, they have received more attention than the personnel problem.
4. Marine officers and enlisted personnel were (and still are) included under the rubric of "naval aviation." This chapter focuses on the Navy's side of naval aviation.
5. See Thomas C. Hone, Norman Friedman, and Mark D. Mandeles, *American and British Aircraft Carrier Development, 1919–1941* (Annapolis: U.S. Naval Institute Press, 1999), for a discussion of the different paths by which the United States and Great Britain chose to organize their respective naval aviation forces and the practical consequences of those choices.
6. The Act of 29 August 1916 established selection up as the mechanism for promotion to Rear Admiral, Captain, and Commander. Selection up was extended to promotion to Lieutenant Commander and Lieutenant by the Act of 29 May 1934. Prior to these acts, promotion was accomplished by attrition and seniority, tempered only marginally by passing promotion examinations.
7. See Chisholm, *Waiting* (2001), chapters 18 and 19.
8. NAV-DMS, 29 August 1925, 7. Records of the Bureau of Navigation, National Archives.
9. See text later in this chapter for a discussion of the question of the appropriate distribution of pilots between commissioned officers and enlisted personnel.
10. *Senate Document No. 18*, 69th Congress, 1st Session, 10 December 1925, p. 3.

11. Qualifications for "Navy Air Pilot" had been established by administrative order of the Secretary of the Navy in April 1913, but these had no standing in law. In March 1915, "Naval Aviator" replaced "Navy Air Pilot" as the designation for naval officers qualified as aviators.

12. *Congressional Record*, 3 June 1926, 10586.

13. First used in March 1922 to comply with the law creating the Bureau of Aeronautics that required that the Chief of the Bureau and 70 percent of its officers be either aviators or observers, the "naval aviation observer" designation as established in law in 1925 had no relationship to usages of the same term in later decades. In this incarnation it was a practical success. Notable among the small initial cadre of naval aviation observers were William A. Moffett, Emory S. Land, and Joseph Mason Reeves. Moffett qualified as the first naval aviation observer in June 1922 in order to become the first Chief of the Bureau. An officer of many parts, Reeves began his commissioned service as an assistant engineer, became a line officer following the 1899 amalgamation of engineers with line, qualified as a naval aviation observer in 1925, and rose to become Commander in Chief of the U.S. Fleet in 1934. His contributions to the development of aviation and its effective integration into fleet operations cannot be overstated. See chapter six in Thomas Wildenberg, *All the Factors of Victory: Admiral Joseph Mason Reeves and the Origins of Carrier Air Power* (Washington, DC: Potomac Books, 2005).

14. *House Report No. 389*, 69th Congress, 1st Session, 26 February 1926, p. 7.

15. The Act of 29 August 1916 appropriated $313 million for the Navy. It called for constructing sixteen capital ships, with eight to be built immediately, and 157 other warships during the following three years. *House Report No. 1155*, 64th Congress, 1st Session, 18 August 1916, p. 4.

16. For all states, a fundamental problem is to build institutional mechanisms that allow rapid military expansion during wartime and an affordable military in more peaceful times. There was at this time no "naval reserve" as organized from the 1930s to the present. President Thomas Jefferson's proposal for a naval militia failed. During the Civil War additional officers were procured by commissioning former naval officers and merchant marine officers, some few of whom were augmented into the regular line following the war. See Chisholm, *Waiting* (2001), chapters 12–14. A number of coastal states organized naval militias, mirroring their land militias, beginning in 1889. Although organization and training of these militias was haphazard at best, the total personnel, officers and men numbered over 4,000 by the Spanish-American War in 1898. Some 2,600 were mustered into the Navy as individuals, while 1,600 others joined the short-lived Auxiliary Naval Force and the Coast Signal Service. Support for any sort of Naval Reserve faded, not to revive until the 1914 onset of World War I. The 1914 Naval Militia Act authorized the president to mobilize the Naval Militia and Naval Reserve, but as there existed no Naval Reserve, in practice this meant calling out the militias (which by then added to 10,000 officers and men in twenty-two states). The Act of 3 March 1915 established the first U.S. Naval Reserve, to be composed of persons previously honorably discharged from naval service. This proved grossly inadequate. In consequence, following the National Defense Act of 1916, the Act of 29 August 1916 established a U.S. Naval Reserve comprising six classes, with the intent of quickly organizing a reserve of 10,000–15,000 officers and men. In September 1917, from the militias, 850 officers and 16,000 men were serving on active duty in the Naval Reserve Force in the class National Naval Volunteers, while the new Naval Reserve force itself provided 10,000 officers and men. The Act of 1 July 1918 transferred en masse the National Naval Volunteers to the Naval Reserve. With the Armistice, weighed down by an overly complicated set of laws and administrative rules, and congressional unwillingness to fund necessary training, the reserves, including the

aviation reserve, fell into a state of desuetude. This brief narrative is drawn from the excellent account contained in Kenmore M. McManes, "Development of the Naval Reserve," *Military Affairs* 17 (Spring 1953): 8–11.

17. See Peter Mersky, ed., "U.S. Naval Air Reserve" (Washington, DC: Deputy Chief of Naval Operations and [Air Warfare] and the Commander, Naval Air Systems Command, 1987) for a detailed narrative and chronology of the development of naval aviation.

18. See Gerald E. Wheeler, "Edwin Denby," in Paolo E. Coletta, ed., *American Secretaries of the Navy, Volume II* (Annapolis: U.S. Naval Institute Press, 1980), pp. 583–84.

19. Mersky notes that "funds were provided in 1920 for 15[-]day training periods at Rockaway Beach, N.Y., for a limited number of Officers of Class Five. However, due to lack of funds, this opportunity was not offered again to Reserve aviators and, subsequently, all Class Five students were transferred to Class Six of the Volunteer Naval Reserve Force. Due to the fact that provision for actual flying was no longer made in the Naval Reserve, hundreds of aviation officers failed to reenroll at the completion of their first four years and left the Naval Reserve Force," "U.S. Naval Air Reserve" (1987), p. 4.

20. Note that authorized and actual numbers of officers were inevitably different in the event. Congress did not always appropriate enough monies to support the authorized strength and, when it did so, the Navy was not always able to commission enough officers annually to compensate for the attrition of officers, let alone to grow the officer corps to authorized strength. Usually the actual number of regular officers on active duty was less than that authorized.

21. U.S. Statutes, 66th Congress, Session II, Chapter 228, pp. 834–35.

22. Applications for transfer to the regular line totaled 1,461: 654 of 749 temporary Lieutenants, 382 of 576 Junior Lieutenants, and 425 of 591 Ensigns. Of this total number, 585 were Chief Warrant Officers, 399 Reserve officers, 474 enlisted men, and 3 Ensigns. Naval Academy officers were then retired on the basis of age-in-grade. Consequently, among the specific factors causing heartburn among the Naval Academy–educated officers was the length of service retirement mechanism accorded the transferred officers because they entered the Navy across a wide range of ages.

23. In the early 1920s, the officer corps averaged about twenty resignations per month.

24. Mersky, "U.S. Naval Air Reserve" (1987), p. 6.

25. At this time, about 25 percent of the Navy's pilots were in enlisted status as naval aviation pilots.

26. In the event, only six universities organized and executed NROTC programs: University of California, University of Washington, Northwestern University, Georgia Tech, Harvard, and Yale. The Navy had run a Volunteer Naval Reserve unit at St. John's College commencing in fall 1924 (with a second class beginning fall 1925) as a proof of concept for the benefit of Congress. See Gerald E. Wheeler, "Origins of the Naval Reserve Officer Corps," *Military Affairs* 20 (Autumn 1956): 170–74.

27. An examination of World War II ships' logs reveals that as Reserve officers reported aboard and departed ship, their commissioning source was indicated following their name and rank. Not all such officers were created equal. By mid-1943, NROTC line officers who went on active duty before the war started had been promoted to temporary Lieutenant Commanders, while Reserve officers from other sources rose no higher than Lieutenant.

28. Section Five of the Act provided that officers not promoted and who, by length of service had become ineligible for further consideration for promotion, or who had been selected for promotion but found professionally unqualified on being examined, would be retired. Lieutenants age *forty-five* or more, or who had completed twenty years or more service and had failed the promotion examination for Lieutenant Commander, would be retired

[my emphasis]. If they had been permanently appointed Ensign or above while holding permanent Warrant rank, they could revert to that rank rather than retire. These provisions disproportionately affected naval aviators.

29. Comments of Representative John Delaney (D-NY) on the House floor. *Congressional Record*, 27 March 1935, 4541.

30. Mersky, "U.S. Naval Air Reserve" (1987), p. 10.

31. The Bureau of Aeronautics had projected that naval aviation's requirements for 1941 would be met by the more than seven hundred aviation cadets expected to be on active duty by then. After that, their numbers would decrease gradually "until they eventually disappeared." Ibid., p. 11. Some in naval aviation, however, believed that "there is little prospect of meeting Naval Aviator requirements from regular service sources, and that we must accept the Aviation Cadet as a permanent fixture and expect them to compose forty-five percent of the Naval Aviators, unless some remedial action can be taken," ibid.

32. Naval aviators in the Volunteer Reserve were largely "Pensacola graduates who were not attached to a Fleet Reserve squadron, largely because of their place of residence," ibid.

33. Ibid.

34. Initial appropriations for fiscal 1935 partially restored the number of annual drills for aviators to thirty-six from the twenty-two that had been held the year previous. Supplementary funds allowed forty-eight drills to be held by the end of the year. More important, flight training was returned to forty-five hours (although still none for the Volunteer Reserve), ibid.

35. The Horne Board comprised Rear Admiral Frederick J. Horne (then on the General Board) as senior member, and Captain George D. Murray, Commander Edwin T. Short, Lieutenant Colonel Lewie G. Merritt (USMC), and Lieutenant Commander Walton W. Smith as members. It operated according to the regulations governing Navy courts and boards. See Chisholm, *Waiting* (2001), pp. 736–41.

36. Transferred officers would be carried as additional numbers in the grades to which they were transferred and in any grades to which they might subsequently be promoted. To be eligible for transfer, officers must have completed eighteen months active duty since completing naval aviation cadet duty. Sea service requirements would not apply to transferred officers while in the grade to which they were originally appointed. Reserve naval aviators would be paid a lump sum ($500) when released from active duty. When mobilized, reservists would take precedence after the regular officers whose active service was one-half of theirs. To appoint up to 370 Reserve naval aviators to the regular line, a board of officers was established, the Leary Board, which in October 1940 recommended 3 Lieutenant Commanders, 20 Lieutenants, 56 Junior Lieutenants, and 284 Ensigns for the regular line. This constituted the largest such appointment of non–Naval Academy officers to the regular line since the Act of 4 June 1920.

37. The two-tier system meant that only some junior officers would be on the track to the higher grades; the remainder would be in and out, with some happy few given the opportunity to become regulars and the rest taken care of equitably by bonuses on separation.

38. From 1899 through 1915, in order to reduce the age of officers in the senior grades—if insufficient natural attrition (death, disability, dismissal, or resignation) occurred to provide the specified annual flow—a board of senior officers was constituted to "pluck" those officers deemed inefficient. Out of equity concerns, Congress rescinded approval of this mechanism in 1915. During the regime of promotion by seniority, officers were required to pass examinations before being promoted. However, these examinations were of insufficient rigor to weed out officers incompetent to the duties of the next higher grade. Rear Admiral G. T. Pettingill observed in 1933 that "examining boards have always been chick-

enhearted about handling cases drastically because the penalty is so great." Hearings before the General Board, Naval War College Microfilm Collection, 15 February 1933, p. 28.

39. Integration into the line did not, of course, mean that naval aviator officers appeared no different than their battleship brethren. To mark their additional qualification as a naval aviator, officers quickly sought a distinguishing badge (perhaps stimulated by Army aviators, who began wearing special badges in 1913). John Towers recollected in 1948 that when he took over the aviation desk in the office of the Chief of Naval Operations in autumn 1916, he recommended that naval aviators be authorized to wear an insignia. He submitted a design for same based on work by the naval artist Henry Reuterdahl, which was in turn modified by the manufacturer Bailey, Banks, and Biddle. "Origin of Navy Pilot Wings: Adm. Towers Recalls Artist-Designer," *Naval Aviation News* (Autumn 1948): 21. Based on Towers' proposal, the Chief of Naval Operations wrote to the Bureau of Navigation in July 1917 that since the Army and foreign services already had aviation devices, naval aviators should be given comparable recognition. Secretary of the Navy Josephus Daniels approved an amendment to the Navy's Uniform Regulations in September 1917, establishing official recognition of the "wings of gold": "A Naval Aviator's device, a winged fouled anchor with the letters 'U.S.', is hereby adopted to be worn by qualified Naval Aviators. This device will be issued by the Bureau of Navigation to Officers and Men of the Navy and Marine Corps who qualify as Naval Aviators, and will be worn on the left breast." The first gold wings were evidently delivered two months later. No other line officers had such a distinguishing badge at the time. Submariners would not have their "dolphins" until 1924 (at Ernest King's recommendation), and it would be several decades more before the Navy's other communities developed their own distinguishing marks. In addition to the "wings of gold," the same month Secretary Daniels approved the "aviation working greens" uniform (based on the Marine Corps' green uniform) for naval aviators, prompted by a desire that the aviators would have a practical uniform they would actually wear (aviators were already notorious for disregarding uniform requirements, in part because existing uniforms were poorly adapted to the conditions of flying). Add to the wings and the greens the aviators' brown shoes (worn with the greens and with khakis) and leather flight jackets—none of which were authorized for non-aviators—and it is not difficult to grasp the heartburn, if not outright hostility, aviators occasioned among the latter, particularly senior officers. Naval aviators might be part of the line but they made no bones about what was in their view, their special status.

40. At a time when long-distance travel, even for naval aviators, was mostly accomplished by means of rail, this required a greater investment of time for aviators than that expended by their battleship brethren. Of course, naval air stations were largely at substantial remove from the northeastern United States. The implication is that special efforts were made to ensure that naval aviators would serve on the selection boards.

41. Hearings before the General Board, Naval War College Microfilm Collection, 15 February 1933, p. 28.

42. In testimony before the House Naval Affairs Committee, Admiral William Leahy, Chief of the Bureau of Navigation, estimated that of the 1,219 officers commissioned under the Act of 4 June 1920, the law would remove 787 by 1942. Most of those would be aviators. To be sure, there was a genuine problem of stagnation in promotion, and existing length-of-service retirement provisions meant than many officers would be retired before being promoted. For example, by early 1934, 250 officers had accumulated on the Lieutenant Commanders' promotion list, but only eighty vacancies occurred annually. The law established the junior selection boards with one rear admiral as president and eight captains as members.

43. *Army and Navy Register*, 30 June 1934, pp. 501, 517.

44. The Act of 11 May 1928 had already specified that "when Officers are assigned to airships on duty requiring them to participate regularly and frequently in aerial flights, the Secretary . . . shall determine and certify whether or not, in his judgment, the service to be performed is equivalent to sea duty. If such service as this is considered to be the equivalent of sea duty, it shall be considered to be actual sea service on sea-going ships for all purposes." King also proposed that this language be made known to the selection boards. Memorandum, Chief of the Bureau of Aeronautics to the Chief of the Bureau of Navigation and the Judge Advocate General, 25 July 1934, Aer-F-3-HAD (OL P16-3), pp. 1–2. Records of the Bureau of Navigation, National Archives.

45. Leahy could only respond, weakly, that "repeated assignment to specialist duties of Officers below the grade of Commander has not had any adverse effect on these Officers' prospects of promotion and it is particularly important that it should not in the future have an adverse effect in view of the present policy of the Department to utilize young line Officers for the duties of the staff corps." *Army and Navy Register,* 19 January 1935, p. 41.

46. *Army and Navy Register,* 2 April 1938, p. 20.

47. Memorandum, Chief of Bureau of Navigation to All Flag Officers, 9 August 1938, Nav-en. Records of the Bureau of Navigation, National Archives.

48. *House Document No. 566,* 76th Congress, 3rd Session, 16 January 1940, p. 4.

49. Ibid., pp. 19–20.

CHAPTER 6

Admiral Joseph Mason "Bull" Reeves, Father of Navy Carrier Aviation

Douglas V. Smith

Admiral Joseph Mason "Bull" Reeves.

War at sea in the twenty-first century was dominated in all its aspects by the advent and evolution of carrier aviation. More than any other single individual, Admiral Joseph Mason "Bull" Reeves left his mark indelibly on the mating of the aircraft carrier and her embarked aircraft as the centerpiece of American seaborne offensive lethality. Moreover, Reeves deserves significant credit for America's victory against the Japanese in World War II.

EARLY STAGES OF NAVAL AND CARRIER AVIATION

As early as April 1917 the Navy had 54 aircraft, and by November 1918 it had 2,107—yet the Navy's first carrier, the experimental USS *Langley* (CV-1), was not recommissioned from the old collier *Jupiter* until late March 1922, well prior to entering the fleet.[1] General Billy Mitchell lamented during his trial by courts-martial in 1925 that the Navy had estimated a requirement of $37,360,248 for aircraft procurement while the Army Air Corps—"entrusted by law with the serial defense over the land areas of the United States and its possessions, including protection of navy yards"—asked for only $24,582,000.[2] Mitchell found the Navy's obvious intent of building a huge land-based air fleet outrageous because the Navy had only one aircraft carrier, the *Langley,* an obsolete collier converted to a carrier capable of holding only thirty-six small airplanes (at that point in time) and with extremely limited speed—15.5 knots, half that of a battleship—and was building two more aircraft carriers, the *Lexington* and *Saratoga,* which were "practically obsolete before they were completed."[3] He and others wondered why the Navy was intent on investing so heavily in aircraft that had questionable ability to support its congressionally mandated role of gaining and if necessary maintaining control over lines of American communications or intended battle areas at sea.

Thus the U.S. Navy found itself in the position of having to devise operational concepts, tactics, and doctrine for aircraft carriers that were not purpose-built and had not even reached operational status. What resulted, however, was not the disarray and lack of focus and purpose that one might expect. Detailed planning, gaming, and concept generation were completed at the Naval War College in Newport, Rhode Island, well prior to USS *Langley* joining the fleet. Commissioned in March and launched in November 1922, she did not enter active fleet service until 1924 when she was transferred to the Pacific Fleet. She lacked any real operational potential until then Captain Joseph Mason Reeves assumed his position as Commander, Aircraft Squadrons, Battle Fleet, aboard her on 12 October 1925.

Most of the early Navy carrier tactics were formulated during the presidency of Admiral William Sowden Sims at the Naval War College, 1919–1922, before the first carrier, USS *Langley,* entered the fleet.[4] Thus tactics were developed to large extent before there was even a carrier with which to test the ideas on which they were based.

Originally *Langley* had been USS *Jupiter* (Collier #3), from 1913 to 1920. *Langley* displaced 13,990 tons empty and 15,150 with a full load, was 523 feet in length and 65 feet 3 inches wide, with an above-water height of 22 feet 1 inch fully loaded and a speed of 15.5 knots. She could ultimately carry forty-eight aircraft and had one elevator and one catapult (with a second catapult added soon after she was launched).

Interestingly, three of the most important players in the formulation of the aviation Navy received their groundings in very similar fashion at about the same time just shortly after Admiral Sims started consideration of naval carrier aviation in earnest at Newport. Fleet Admiral Chester Nimitz graduated with the Naval War College class of 1923—before entry of aircraft carriers into general fleet usage. He credits Captain R. C. MacFall, his classmate in both the U.S. Naval Academy class of 1905 and Naval War College class of 1923, with "devising the circular tactical formations used so successfully in World War II."[5] Reeves, a 1884 graduate of Annapolis, was in the class immediately following Nimitz and MacFall—the War College class of 1924.[6]

Under Admiral Sims, war games were conducted to determine the utility of the aircraft carrier and her embarked aircraft in various roles at sea. While most of the senior officers in the Navy envisioned the carrier as best suited to provide surveillance and target locations, to serve as spotters for directing naval gunfire from battleships, to locate and attack surfaced enemy submarines, and possibly to screen ships for enemy battleship formations, Sims was among the first to envision the carrier as the new centerpiece of offensive naval weaponry. Thus he emphasized the carrier in the attack role and was responsible for many of the tactics for carrier operations. Two of the main elements of tactical operation emanated from this pre-carrier period. First and foremost, gaming at Newport led to the conclusion that the carrier that first laid ordnance on the enemy's deck was invariably the victor—especially if the enemy carrier was hit while its aircraft were still on the deck. Second, the carrier that was able to get the most aircraft airborne in the shortest amount of time was normally victorious. This led to the refinement of sequencing the launch of aircraft of different types. Sims, his instructors, and students also addressed the three competing requirements for embarked air wings that were central to carrier operations: to defend the carrier(s) and screening ships in the formation against enemy attack; to apportion aircraft to search out and locate the enemy's carriers; and to attack the enemy's carrier(s) and other supporting ships.

At the Naval War College, war games were played by the students to refine and hone their abilities to know the battle parameters of their weapons systems and to employ those systems in a combat environment, as well as to coordinate strategy and "tactics." (Please note that we now refer to what was at that time called "tactics" as "operations.")

Opposing fleets were arrayed as miniature ship models on the checkerboard tiles of Luce (and later Pringle) Hall, and these fleets were concealed behind curtains so that the moves of the opposition were invisible to the students composing the opposing fleet. Tables were constructed to indicate the percentage of shell and bomb hits that could be reasonably expected at a given range from the enemy, based on real-world observations of the weapons systems they were constructed for. Similarly, tables presenting the expected lethality of these weapons systems were constructed so that faculty "umpires" could assess the amount of damage done under various conditions and ranges.[7]

Though a good number of war games were played by each class at the War College during the eleven-month course of study, the most complex and challenging of these was probably the annual "Battle of Sable Island." This battle, "constructively" played off Nova Scotia, was essentially an engagement based on the Battle of Jutland of World War I. However, east and west were inverted so that the U.S. fleet was in the British position and the British fleet was in the German position of that earlier battle. Also, the Canadian fleet was made available to the current British fleet composition for their conduct of "operations."[8]

It is interesting to note that extensive blueprints were made of the "Battle of Sable Island" game for later consideration. Recently uncovered in the War College Archives is a sample blueprint that consists of 128 pages of two-foot by three-foot detailed diagrams.[9]

As with all games, the "Battle of Sable Island" stressed problem solving and development of a sound decision process that involved four essential steps:

1. Estimating the situation at hand;
2. Formulating orders for the actions of units of the fleet;
3. Maneuvering the fleet to engage the enemy;
4. Critiquing the three items above.[10]

Captain Harris Laning, Head of the Tactics Department from 1922, when he graduated from the War College, to the graduation of the class of 1924, provided a pamphlet, "The Naval Battle," that was a useful study of modern naval tactics including the rudiments of aviation tactics.[11]

One of the most significant conclusions to emerge from the game board concerning the use of aircraft during that first year (1923) was the need for the fleet's aircraft carriers to strike their counterparts in the enemy fleet as soon as they came within range. It was essential that they immediately strike the enemy carriers with as many attackers as possible in order to gain air superiority over the enemy fleet.[12]

As Laning put it, "The first step of any air plan should be to get control of the air."

Captain Reeves had so impressed Laning and Rear Admiral Clarence S. Williams, the serving President of the Naval War College (3 November 1922–5 September 1925), that while Reeves was a student they selected him as Laning's successor as Head of the Tactics Department. Reeves, who had learned that concentration of force was essential during his studies, applied what he had learned to the aviation asset of the Battle Fleet. In doing so, he rightfully established himself as the "Father of Carrier Aviation."

During his war gaming as a student, Reeves came to understand that the British battleships opposing his American force had superior lethality: the guns on the U.S. battleships lacked the ability to be elevated sufficiently to match the British in plunging fire. While a member of the faculty, he strove to make his superiors aware of this problem. Ultimately, he was tasked to testify before Congress on the matter, where he produced a graphic that vividly depicted the problem.

Though Congress nevertheless failed immediately to allocate funding to modify the fleet's existing battleships, Reeves had established himself as an expert on ordnance and gunnery.[13] His concentration on the aircraft carrier as a means of striking the capital ships of the enemy, thus nullifying their superior firepower, resulted in the refinement of carrier and air-strike tactics during his tenure as Head of the Tactics Department. All advances in aviation theory and tactics while Reeves was in this position, it should be remembered, took place before the first American carrier entered the fleet in 1924.

COMMANDER, AIRCRAFT SQUADRONS, BATTLE FLEET

At the completion of his instructor tour at the Naval War College, Reeves was detailed to proceed, via the Bureau of Aeronautics—of which Admiral William A. Moffett was the chief—in Washington, D.C., to Pensacola for training as a Naval Aviation Observer. Since by law all aviation squadrons had to be commanded by aviation officers, and since only one aviation-trained officer had as yet risen to the rank of captain, the Naval Aviation Observer course was a way to get Reeves and other more senior officers indoctrinated in aviation matters so they could be assigned to command. Reeves graduated from the Naval Aviation Observer course on 3 September 1925 and received orders from the Bureau of Navigation (which then issued all officer orders for duty) to assume command as Commander Aircraft Squadrons, Battle Fleet. He proceeded to Mare Island, California, to board his flagship—the carrier *Langley*—which he had commanded before it was converted from the collier USS *Jupiter*—and then proceeded to North Island in San Diego where the two squadrons of observation planes (VO-1 and VO-2), two squadrons of fighter aircraft (VF-1 and VF-2), and a single squadron of torpedo planes (VT-2) were located.

It was as Commander, Aircraft Squadrons, Battle Fleet, from 12 October 1925 until 3 May 1929 that Reeves defined carrier aviation.

Reeves' first observation was that "[this command] lacks a coordinated set of fleet-plane tactics and has no conception of the capabilities and limitations of the air force."[14] Reeves immediately set out to change that. When he took command, Reeves was appalled to learn that USS *Langley* could put only six aircraft in the air at one time. Because, while a student and instructor at the Naval War College, he had helped to establish that the only way to defend a carrier successfully against air attack

DT-2 taking off from USS Langley, *circa 1925.*

was to put as many fighter aircraft in the air as possible in the shortest time, Reeves' first challenge was to increase *Langley's* sortie rate and decrease the time interval between takeoffs. The limiting factor in doing so was that only seven aircraft could be placed on deck at a time with the current procedures for launching them, and others had to be brought up from the hangar deck and readied for takeoff—a time-consuming process—before launching more. Moreover, with both arresting wires and longitudinal cables to keep the planes in line with the carrier's deck (planes had no steering or brakes), landing of the two groups of aircraft launched took almost an hour. Reeves and his senior pilots decided to have all launched aircraft make right turns immediately after leaving the carrier's deck to eliminate the prop vortex, and came up with the oval pattern for aircraft arriving for landing so as to have a continuous flow as soon as the last plane to touch down had been moved out of the way.

Here too Reeves improved procedures by modifying equipment so that planes would not have to be individually lowered by elevator below decks before the next plane could land. He accomplished this by adding additional arresting wires, doing away with the longitudinal aircraft directing wires, and inventing a safe but flexible barrier so that arrested aircraft could be moved in front of it and others could land behind it without fear that they would collide with those already safely on deck. By the time of "Fleet Problem VI" (the sixth of twenty-two Fleet Problems that were scheduled between 1919 and 1941)—February 1926—Reeves had enabled ten aircraft to be launched in a single sortie.[15]

Another major advance was the way in which Reeves and the *Langley*'s Executive Officer, Commander John H. Towers, organized deck operations. Special "crews" of men, distinguished by shirts or vests of several identifiable colors, were assembled to handle such things as spotting (yellow) and moving aircraft (blue), handling fueling (purple) and arresting gear (green), ordnance (red), and serving as plane captains (brown). Thus confusion was greatly reduced and safety enhanced. Also, a sense of pride developed that enhanced morale, and the better coordination and sense of competition engendered led to a faster tempo of flight-deck operations. A flight control officer was tasked to launch aircraft at safe intervals, and hand signals were devised to expedite movements and actions because noise precluded audible cues. By early August 1926, Reeves had set a new record of 127 launches and landings in a single day. By September Reeves and his crews had reduced landing intervals to just one minute and seventeen seconds. The records would continue as time progressed.

AVIATION TACTICS AND DOCTRINE

Just as with deck operations, Reeves schooled his pilots in aerial maneuvers and tactics. He made great use of extended periods—that he called "concentration periods"—at North Island and the surrounding San Diego area to work out details of operations and doctrine that would be necessary to have the right answers to and execute correctly in combat.

> With his strategy [for developing aircraft tactics and doctrine] decided on, [Reeves] filled the San Diego auditorium with the officers of his command, and gave them a lecture that is still remembered; it was, in effect, a statement of the principles on which the air force was to be developed.
>
> First of all, Reeves declared that what he had seen in the last six weeks had proved the complete lack of coordinated fleet-plane tactics, and had shown as well that there was no conception of either the capabilities or limitations of the air force. There followed a formidable series of questions. "What is the most efficient method of launching planes from the 'Langley', and of handling them after they have landed?" . . . "How should our fighters attack other aircraft?" . . . "What formations should be used in aerial spotting, and what position should these spotters take?" . . . "How should an aircraft torpedo attack be made, and how can it be most effectively repelled?" . . . "What is the maximum interval to be taken between the planes in a scouting screen; what is the best method of procedure in such scouting?"
>
> After a score of such problems, Reeves startled his audience with a bold and unexpected declaration: "I do not know the answers to these questions and dozens like them any more than you do, but until we can answer them, we will be of very little use to the fleet. That means that we must become a school before we can become an air force."[16]

Reeves set out during his "concentration periods" to test in the air the theoretical answers to practical questions in his mimeographed pamphlet that he called his "One Thousand and One Questions." It contained a list of the information that Reeves had decided must be gathered before his command could function effectively.[17]

In the air his pilots would attack such problems as tactics and doctrine for dealing with air contacts. Specific task areas were assigned in Reeves' "Employment Schedule, for Study and Practical Development of Aircraft Tactics," such as the one promulgated for the 12 June–11 September 1926 "concentration period":

1. When should "Control of the Air" be undertaken?

2. How far and in what manner should efforts to gain control of the air extend?

3. How proceed [*sic*] if "Control of the Air" is gained? If not gained?

4. Considering the vital importance of "Control of the Air," does our present Basic Air Organization provide sufficient fighting planes?

5. Can we deny enemy planes Tactical Scouting?

6. How can aircraft best aid surface craft during this phase?[18]

Other major obstacles to operational success had to be overcome through innovation. Concerned that their extended time over target would make his bombers vulnerable to anti-aircraft fire, Reeves and Lieutenant Commander Frank D. Wagner, the Commanding Officer of his fighter wing, devised what subsequently came to be known as "dive-bombing."[19]

> Reeves knew from his own experience at Pensacola that high-altitude bombing could be effective only under ideal conditions and over a defenseless target. In his pamphlet of questions, he had pointed out the inadequacy of the bombsight, the difficulty of estimating air currents and density, and had asked, "How can we bomb more effectively?"
>
> It was not an easy problem, but Lieutenant [Commander] Frank Wagner, Commander of the fighter squadron, finally solved it. If the bomber could get close enough to its target, he reasoned, there would be no room for errors— yet how could this be done before the plane itself was destroyed? For months Wagner struggled with the problem, while Reeves gave encouragement and advice. At first the pilots tried gliding down on their targets, with engines idling, and later on, with full power. Then in March [1926], Wagner quietly added a little more piano wire to the rigging of his plane, placed a 100-pound bomb under each wing, and started out on what was supposed to be a routine flight. Instead, he climbed to seven thousand feet in easy spirals, opened his throttle as far as it would go, and nosed over into a vertical dive at the field below. The airport crew watched, horrified as the plane rocketed toward them, and then scattered wildly. Somehow Wagner pulled out at the last moment, brushed over a hangar, and landed; he had risked his life, but found the answer.[20]

By also adopting a tactic of coming in toward the target from out of the sun, the bombers' steep vertical dive made them almost impossible to hit as they neared their targets. Moreover, the accuracy of 311 bombs dropped in the initial testing of these tactics in October 1926 was an astounding 44.5 percent on a target only one-third the length and ten feet shy the width of a typical cruiser.[21] When further refined, and with the entrance of the Dauntless dive-bomber into the fleet inventory, this combination of tactics resulted in one of the most lethal weapons systems of World War II.

One of the major challenges that confronted Reeves was gaining insights on and formulating a plan for the most appropriate types of aircraft composing the air wings. Controversies arose regarding such things as whether a single- or two-seat fighter was most appropriate; whether a future fighter should serve the dual purpose of being able to drop bombs as well as defend the carrier(s); the proper ordnance load for a bomber; and what type of engines and landing gear would best serve the purpose of a particular type of plane. Noting that *Langley* was at first equipped with biplanes and that the age of monoplanes had arrived, the design tradeoffs required a lot of speculation. Yet Reeves and his officers in Aircraft Squadrons, Battle Fleet managed to keep abreast of design advances and provide timely and useful recommendations to the Bureau of Aeronautics. This ultimately led, by the start of World War II, to the inclusion of one squadron each of F4F-3 Wildcat fighters and TBD-1 Devastator torpedo planes and two squadrons of SBD-3 Dauntless dive-bombers on U.S. carriers each of eighteen aircraft. Though the two squadrons of Dauntlesses were in reality interchangeable, one was given the "VB" designation of bomber aircraft and the other the "VS" designation of scout aircraft. Thus the men of Aircraft Squadrons, Battle Fleet—even with primitive aircraft and a carrier of extremely limited space and capability in *Langley*—made a major contribution to the carrier air wing structure that proved so successful in the initial stages of the coming war.

Reeves was equally adept at manipulating the local population and the media to best advantage. During his time in command of Aircraft Squadrons, Battle Fleet he orchestrated a good number of "parades" of ultimately over 150 aircraft in a single formation and nurtured an aerial exhibition team of three pilots and their planes— against Navy regulations—that were unrivaled by the Army Air Corps. At almost every opportunity, particularly when a dignitary such as the Secretary of the Navy was present, Reeves unveiled his "air show" to demonstrate the capabilities of his pilots and their aircraft. Such shows usually concluded with a stellar performance by his de facto flight demonstration team and an exhibition of the dive-bombing techniques he had developed immediately overhead the observers. Similarly, Reeves employed the tactics developed by the *Langley* Air Wing at every opportunity to demonstrate the utility of both the carrier and its aircraft. Gradually those at the highest levels of leadership in the Navy began to take notice of the potential of the carrier and it's Air Wing. Thus Reeves was at once a publicist for Navy aviation and its most powerful advocate.

An example of Reeves' acumen in driving home the utility of the carrier came in late 1928 when Vice Admiral Sir Cyril T. M. Fuller, Commander of the Royal Navy's American and West Indies Squadron, arrived in San Diego aboard his flagship, HMS *Despatch*, to discuss carrier developments. Fuller was truly impressed when Reeves told him, erroneously, that *Langley*—now fitted with a thirty-six-foot extension to the aft of her flight deck—could operate twenty-four aircraft, significantly more than the British under current practices.[22] Reeves refused Admiral Fuller's request to walk *Langley*'s flight deck and view the arresting gear that had been modified to do this and purposely withheld the true number of planes *Langley* could operate, stating to Admiral Moffett, Chief of the Bureau of Aeronautics later: "I did not tell Admiral Fuller that we operated not twenty-four, but thirty-six, and could operate forty-two and possibly forty-eight airplanes from the *Langley*."[23] This was made possible by an earlier push by Reeves to increase the number of aircraft onboard *Langley* in preparation for Fleet Problem VII by loading an almost impossible thirty-six aircraft on her deck in addition to those on her hangar deck. Again, this was a major innovation.[24]

The requirement to load a large number of aircraft on *Langley*'s flight deck because of her small size ultimately led to the practice of "deck park," which enabled newer and larger carriers such as USS *Lexington* and USS *Saratoga* to embark more aircraft than Japanese carriers of similar tonnage while still keeping space open on their hangar decks for aircraft maintenance functions.

Admiral Joseph Reeves' contributions to carrier aviation—as well as those to surface gunnery and design practices—are too numerous to chronicle here. They continued when USS *Lexington* and USS *Saratoga* were commissioned in 1927 and entered fleet service shortly thereafter.

By the time Reeves relinquished command of Aircraft Squadrons, Battle Fleet on 3 May 1929 the pilots and planes he had commanded on USS *Langley*, USS *Lexington*, and USS *Saratoga* had flown for 5,700 hours and covered 436,000 miles without incurring a single fatal injury to any of his flying personnel.[25] Considering the primitive state of the aircraft flown, the small size and sizeable air wing of USS *Langley*, the pace of operations, and the danger inherent in experimenting with tactical innovations, this safety record was a phenomenal accomplishment. Moreover, perhaps more than any other aspect of Reeves' demonstration of the advantages of carrier aviation, this outstanding record of safety impressed those in decision-making positions of the viability of naval aviation as a primary aspect of the Navy's offensive lethality.

While Admiral Reeves was pioneering carrier aviation, others were at work too. Though advocacy for the carrier in an offensive mode saw ebbs and advances through the prewar years, the Naval War College continued to establish operational methods, doctrine, and tactics for carriers and their Air Wings that emanated in large part from experience gained from the war games held there. Foremost among these were:

1. Having two staffs for the Pacific Fleet—one of these would do the planning for the next major operation while the other was at sea executing the current operation. This shifting of staffs ensured that those executing the plan of action thoroughly understood every aspect of it.

2. Advancing the notion that future generations of battleships and cruisers needed increased anti-aircraft capability. This was hugely important when USS *North Carolina* (BB-55) entered the Pacific Fleet in June 1942 because her vastly superior anti-aircraft gunnery preserved major fleet assets, including carriers, through the remainder of the war.[26]

3. Settling on the characteristics of carriers to be constructed during the war. After *Lexington* and *Saratoga* were commissioned, a battle raged over the size of new carriers. Since available tonnage for new carriers was limited as a result of the Washington Naval Treaty, many advocated building smaller carriers. The result was the USS *Ranger,* which proved to be too small to be of any real use. Since *Lexington* and *Saratoga* weren't ready to participate in Fleet Problems until 1929, the debate continued until empirical evidence could be gathered. Thus the theoretical debate was conducted mainly at the Naval War College. The result was ultimately the greatly improved fighting characteristics of the *Essex*-class of carrier.

4. Operating carriers independently rather than as an integral group in battle. This doctrine, which proved to be in error, was conceived so that carriers could take advantage of weather and cloud cover during battle for concealment. Admiral Jimmy Thach, who maintained until his dying day (as chronicled in the Naval Institute Press "oral history" manuscript he provided) that USS *Yorktown* would not have been sunk in the Battle of Midway if she had been operating in close company with *Enterprise* and *Hornet.*

So also were doctrine, operational procedures, and tactics advanced while conducting the twenty-one Fleet Problems and less frequent Grand Joint Exercises (GJE) during the interwar period in which the Navy tested, under real-world conditions, the theoretical doctrines and tactics generated at the War College.[27] Much has already been said of how Admiral Joseph Reeves profited from ideas he tested in war games. Almost every aspect of carrier warfare was enhanced as a result of lessons learned in the Fleet Problems and Grand Joint Exercises pioneered by Commander, Aircraft Squadrons, Battle Fleet, Admiral Joseph Mason "Bull" Reeves.

Reeves' impact on carrier aviation didn't stop there. After leaving duty as Commander, Aircraft Squadrons, Battle Fleet, Reeves was assigned to the General Board where his impact on Navy aviation continued. He was selected for this assignment specifically by Secretary of the Navy Charles F. Adams, a selection emanating from the secretary's favorable impression of a sixteen-page position paper Reeves had written in December 1928 rejecting Congress' fascination with the prospect of creating a single Department of Defense and a single American air arm, thus subjugating U.S. Navy aviation to another Service as had been done by the British. Though this idea died from lack of momentum in 1929, Reeves had significant impact on fleet issues in general—but particularly on Navy cruiser design requirements and aviation matters—throughout his assignment to the General Board.[28]

At the completion of his tour on the General Board, Reeves was offered his choice of duty as President of the Naval War College—a position he truly wanted after stepping down as Commander, Aircraft Squadrons, Battle Fleet—or duty at sea returning to his old job as Commander Aircraft Squadrons, Battle Fleet. He chose the latter without hesitation and on 12 May 1930 was designated to relieve Rear Admiral Henry V. Butler as Commander Aircraft Squadrons, Battle Fleet.[29] There he further refined aviation tactics and doctrine, primarily during the continuing interwar Fleet Problems.

On 27 June 1931, Rear Admiral Joseph Reeves' flag was lowered aboard USS *Saratoga,* in his mind ending his days at sea. He was posted to the Pacific Coast Section of the Board of Inspection and Survey, a sure sign that a dreary succession of desk jobs was in his future until retirement.[30] This, though, was not to be the case. Having impressed CNO William V. Pratt, Reeves was selected for an interim assignment. Only three months and a few days after Franklin Delano Roosevelt became president in March 1933, Reeves received a most unexpected letter from him designating Reeves as "Commander of the Battleships, Battle Force with additional duty as Commander Battleships, United States Fleet." This was an expedient way for Reeves to be promoted to Vice Admiral in Admiral Pratt's plan to subsequently assign an aviator to a position of even higher importance—the four-star rank of Commander, Battle Force.[31]

That promotion and assignment commenced when Reeves became Commander-in-Chief of the United States Fleet the morning of 15 June 1934—the first aviator to become Commander in Chief of the U.S. Fleet.[32] Admiral Reeves' flag was hauled down for the last time aboard USS *Pennsylvania* (BB-38) on 24 June 1936. His final posting for five months before retiring was to be again on the General Board, where he went about ensuring that the Navy's newest battleship, USS *North Carolina* (BB-55)—which was to reach Pearl Harbor four days after the Battle of Midway and was to be so crucial in her anti-aircraft role protecting carriers in the

Battle of the Eastern Solomons and thereafter—met the Navy's needs for impending war with Japan.[33]

The end to Reeves' career in the Navy on 30 November 1936, however, was to be short lived. So important had Admiral Reeves' contribution been to all aspects of carrier aviation that he was recalled to active duty on 20 May 1940 and made one of two members of the Compton Board to consider "the distribution, promotion, and retirement of naval officers assigned to the Staff Corp as well as officers designated for engineering and aeronautical engineering only duty."[34] When war broke out in Europe in 1939, the Lend-Lease Act was passed on 11 March 1941. The Secretary of the Navy was responsible for all decisions on requests for naval material under its provisions. In April 1941 Secretary Frank Knox delegated his authority under the Act to Admiral Reeves, who exercised it through the remainder of the war.[35] Reeves was assigned to be one of the five members—and one of only two aviators—to be part of the Roberts Commission that was charged with investigating the debacle at Pearl Harbor. Reeves was a vehement critic of both Admiral Husband E. Kimmel and Major General Walter C. Short.

Reeves received the Distinguished Service Medal for his wartime service, during which he was advanced to Vice Admiral and then Admiral on the retired list. He retired a second time on 2 April 1947 and died shortly afterward in March of the next year.

From his earliest days at the Naval War College through the toughest days of World War II, it can honestly be said that Admiral Joseph Mason "Bull" Reeves was the mastermind behind U.S. Navy carrier aviation—the father of carrier aviation.

NOTES

1. Thomas C. Hone, Norman Friedman, and Mark D. Mandeles, *American and British Aircraft Carrier Developments 1919–1941* (Annapolis: Naval Institute Press, 1999), pp. 20, 31.

2. Mitchell had been returned to his permanent rank of Colonel in 1925 prior to his trial.

3. *United States v. War Department: Trial by General Courts Martial in the Case of Colonel William Mitchell, Air Service,* "Opinion of the Board of Review, Taylor, Abbott and Korn, Judge Advocates," dated 20 January 1926, pp. 9–10. Record Group (hereafter RG) 153, Records of the Office of the Judge Advocate General (Army), Box No. 9214-2, Folder 1, p. 1. National Archives of the United States of America, NA-2, College Park, MD.

4. Admiral William Sowden Sims, USN, had been commander of all U.S. naval forces in European waters after American entry in World War I. He returned from Europe to become the sixteenth President of the U.S. Naval War College from 11 April 1919 to 14 October 1922.

5. Chester W. Nimitz, Fleet Admiral, U.S. Navy. Letter to Vice Admiral Charles Melson, President of the United States Naval War College, dated 19 September 1965, on display in McCarty-Little Hall at the U.S. Naval War College, Newport, Rhode Island.

6. *Register of the Alumni, Graduates and Former Naval Cadets and Midshipmen, United States Naval Academy Alumni Association. Inc., 1845–1985,* 1985 edition. Published by the United States Naval Academy Alumni Association. Also *The Register,* manuscript listing of the U.S. Naval War College Faculty and Graduates, provided by Dr. Evelyn Cherpak, Archivist, U.S. Naval War College. Please note that all listings of graduation dates from the Naval Academy and Naval War College are drawn from these two publications.

7. Joseph M. Reeves, class of 1924 thesis, "Tactics," Submitted by Captain J. M. Reeves, U.S. Navy, room no. E-11, U.S. Naval War College, Newport, RI, 1 May 1924. United States Naval War College Archives (hereafter USNWCA), RG 13.

8. Battle of Sable Island Manuscript, Serial No. 71, dated October–November 1923. USNWCA: RG-14/15, 128 pages including accompanying diagrams.

9. Ibid.

10. Gerald J. Kennedy, *United States Naval War College, 1919–1941: An Institutional Response to Naval Preparedness.* U.S. Naval War College Archives. Unpublished manuscript, pp. 57–59. This manuscript provides an excellent narrative of the development of and changes in the curriculum at the Naval War College during the interwar period, as well as of the imprint made by each President of the War College during that period.

11. Harris Laning, Captain, U.S. Navy. *The Naval Battle.* Tactics, Section I, June 1923. USNWCA: RG-4.

12. Thomas Wildenberg, *All the Factors of Victory: Admiral Joseph Mason Reeves and the Origins of Carrier Airpower* (Washington, DC: Brassey's, 2003), p. 109.

13. Joseph M. Reeves, Captain, U.S. Navy. *Comparison of Blue-Red [U.S.-British] Capital Ship Strength.* 1491/9-24 XTYG 1924 160, Blue-Red Tactical Exercise I, Capital Ships Major Gunfire Only (DECL IAW DOD Memo of 3 May 1972, Subj.: DECL of WW II Records), USNWC Newport, RI, September 1924, p. 8. USNWCA: RG-13.

14. Adolphus Andrews Jr., "Admiral with Wings: The Career of Joseph Mason Reeves." Unpublished bachelor's thesis, Princeton, NJ, Princeton University, 1943, U.S. Naval Academy Nimitz Library microfilm collection, p. 55.

15. Ibid., p.58.

16. Ibid., p. 55.

17. Ibid, pp. 55–56.

18. Joseph M. Reeves, Rear Admiral, U.S. Navy, "Commander Aircraft Squadrons battle fleet letter dated April 7, 1926, to Aircraft Squadrons battle fleet, subject employment schedule, For Study and Practical Development of Aircraft Tactics, during Concentration Period from 12 June to 11 September 1926, serial 1199," p. 3.

19. Wildenberg, *All the Factors of Victory,* p. 142.

20. Adolphus, "Admiral with Wings," pp. 57–58.

21. Wildenberg, *All the Factors of Victory,* pp. 142–43.

22. Andrews, "Admiral with Wings," pp 76–77.

23. Ibid.

24. For more information on Fleet Problem VII and other Fleet Problems, consult chapter 7, this volume, by Dr. Al Nofi.

25. Wildenberg, *All the Factors of Victory,* p. 200.

26. Ibid., p. 258. Admiral Reeves worked primarily on improvement of battleships while assigned to the General Board for the last five months of his first term of active service prior to his retirement. During this time his main focus was on improvements to USS *Pennsylvania* (BB-55).

27. For more information on Fleet Problem VII and other Fleet Problems, consult chapter 7, this volume, by Dr. Al Nofi. While twenty-two Fleet Problems were initially scheduled, the twenty-second and last Fleet Problem was cancelled due to the outbreak of World War II in Europe.

28. Wildenberg, *All the Factors of Victory*, p. 200–201. This book by Wildenberg is an outstanding consideration of the entire career of Admiral Joseph Mason Reeves.

29. Ibid., p. 212.

30. Ibid., p. 224.

31. Ibid., pp. 224–26.

32. Ibid., pp. 230, 235.

33. Ibid., pp. 224–25.

34. Ibid., p. 259.

35. Ibid., p. 261.

CHAPTER 7

Aviation in the Interwar Fleet Maneuvers, 1919–1940

Albert A. Nofi

etween the world wars, the U.S. Navy conducted twenty-one "Fleet Problems,"
free maneuvers in which enormous forces "fought" on an oceanic scale to
secure specific tactical, operational, and even strategic objectives.[1] Together
with occasional Grand Joint Army and Navy Exercises (GJE) and many smaller
maneuvers, the Fleet Problems shaped the Navy's understanding of the complexities
of transoceanic operations and refined its mastery of the tools of sea power, while
introducing innovative technologies and doctrines and honing the skills of those
who would command and staff the fleet in wartime—creating the integrated "naval
force" that successfully prosecuted the Pacific War.[2]

The Fleet Problems were critical to new developments in all naval warfare
areas—offensive and defense operations, amphibious warfare, coast defense, surface tactics, convoying, mine warfare, submarine and anti-submarine operations,
communications, intelligence, underway replenishment, cryptology, special operations, and more, even fleet postal services—but it was the evolution of naval aviation from a minor auxiliary to the backbone of the naval force that was the most
important legacy.

The Fleet Problems provided experience in all types of naval air operations
under more or less wartime conditions, helping aviators and the fleet's senior leadership better understand the capabilities and limitations of naval aviation in all types
of missions, strike, reconnaissance and patrol, land attack, fleet defense, and more.
The simple need to operate under realistic warlike conditions provided invaluable
experience to the aviators and the leadership of the fleet. Perhaps equally important,
however, was the careful management of aviation's role in the problems by the more

air-minded officers so that they were able to instill across the Navy an appreciation and understanding of the capabilities and limitations of air power as an instrument of naval warfare as it evolved over the years.

While not neglecting other forms of naval aviation—battleship and cruiser floatplanes, flying boats, land-based aircraft, rigid airships—this essay will focus on the Fleet Problems and the evolution of carrier aviation, the backbone of naval air power.

PATTERNS, 1923–1941

In an invaluable analysis of air power and the development of the fleet battle doctrine between the world wars, Mark Allen Campbell observed that the participation of carriers in the Fleet Problems unfolded in four phases.[3]

- Fleet Problems I–II (1923–1924). Surrogates provided some useful ideas about the potential of carrier operations.
- Fleet Problems III–VIII (1924–1928). USS *Langley* (CV-1) permitted more realistic experimentation and provided experience in carrier operations, despite limitations as an improvised experimental vessel.
- Fleet Problems IX–XV (1929–1934). USS *Lexington* (CV-2) and USS *Saratoga* (CV-3) permitted more realistic experimentation, leading to the evolution of the independent Carrier Task Force.
- Fleet Problems XVI–XXI (1935–1940). As more carriers joined the fleet, increasingly complex experiments helped refine carrier doctrine.

GETTING STARTED: FROM EUGENE ELY
TO FLEET PROBLEM II, 1910–1924

Eugene Ely's 1910–1911 experimental operation of airplanes from ships led the Navy to procure several aircraft and arrange flight training for some officers. In January 1913, a half-dozen seaplanes and flying boats took part in the Caribbean maneuvers, garnering useful experience in operating in support of the fleet under realistic conditions, lessons put to good use the following year during the occupation of Vera Cruz. Aircraft took part in subsequent maneuvers until 1917, by which time the armored cruiser USS *North Carolina* (CA-12) had been fitted with a catapult and become the first ship in the fleet to regularly operate airplanes.

World War I (1917–1918) put an end to large-scale maneuvers, but also led to an enormous expansion of naval aviation. By war's end the Sea Services had some two thousand airplanes of various types and a handful of lighter-than-air craft, with a half-dozen ships adapted to serve as aircraft tenders, and several battleships had been fitted with flying-off platforms for seaplanes while serving with the Royal Navy.

War's end brought drastic reductions in the fleet and its aircraft inventory, but also a resumption of maneuvers on a small scale, involving some air operations.[4] In January and February 1921 the Navy resumed full-scale maneuvers, bringing both the Atlantic Fleet and Pacific Fleet to the Gulf of Panama for exercises in which aircraft played a small role.

In 1922, reductions by the Washington Naval Arms Limitation Treaty caused the operating forces of the Navy to be organized into a single "United States Fleet" under the "Commander-in-Chief, U.S. Fleet" (CinCUS), with a "Battle Fleet" based in Southern California and a smaller "Scouting Fleet" in Virginia. This set the stage for the Fleet Problems.

In concept, procedure, and execution, the Fleet Problems were similar to the annual maneuvers that the Navy had conducted since 1903. But whereas in the pre-war period major elements of the fleet were often diverted to support American

USS Langley *in Pearl Harbor in 1928.*

diplomatic goals, after the Great War "real-world" problems rarely intruded on the fleet's routine, making it "a giant training center and laboratory, and its operations giant training drills and fleet battle experiments."[5] Aviation—particularly carrier aviation—played an increasingly important role in these maneuvers and in the overall life of the fleet.[6]

The Navy had initiated the conversion of the collier *Jupiter* (AC-3) into an aircraft carrier in 1920. Commissioned in 1922, the USS *Langley* (CV-1) did not take part in the first of the Fleet Problems, requiring nearly two years to become fully operational. In her absence, surrogates were used, to surprising effect.

During Fleet Problem I (FP I) (February 1923), a small American force ("Blue") had to defend the Pacific side of the Panama Canal from a major attack, to gain time for the Atlantic Fleet to make a transit.[7] Two battleships were designated surrogate aircraft carriers on the *Langley* model and assigned to "Black," the attacking force. By 22 February skirmishes were taking place between destroyers as Black reached a position about four hundred air miles northwest of the canal entrance. That morning the Black "carrier" USS *Oklahoma* (BB-37) catapulted a single airplane, representing a squadron of fifteen aircraft. The attack achieved total surprise, "destroying" the locks on the Pacific side, preventing the Blue movement into the Gulf of Panama. Black then conducted a mock assault on the canal, securing an advanced base. CinCUS Hillary P. Jones praised the performance of the fleet, and was particularly complimentary to its airmen.[8] Some officers criticized Black's decision to use its aircraft offensively, arguing that it left the fleet without air cover, but Jones noted that Blue had no aircraft suitable for use as bombers, and thus Black was not at risk from air attack. Jones, however, criticized Blue for neglecting to use its superiority in aircraft (over thirty airplanes) to conduct patrols that might have detected Black's approach. He called for more aircraft carriers, more observation planes for battleships, and improved air defense of the canal. Captain John F. Hines of USS *Pennsylvania* (BB-38) provided a very perceptive critique of Black's air tactics, arguing that waiting until daylight to launch *Oklahoma*'s "air strike" was an error, since "both plane carriers might be lost without any planes getting off" in the event of an enemy surface attack; moreover, launching the strike at 0200 would have permitted an approach to the canal under cover of darkness, and a dawn attack, with greater chances for successes.[9]

The three Fleet Problems held in January 1924 represented linked phases of an ongoing naval campaign. FP II involved the movement of the Battle Fleet from the West Coast to Panama, as the initial phase of an advance across the Pacific from Hawaii. Although a surrogate carrier was assigned to the fleet, air operations played only a marginal role in the problem. This set the stage for the debut of *Langley*.

LANGLEY POINTS THE WAY:
FLEET PROBLEMS III–VIII, 1924–1928

The first Fleet Problem in which *Langley* took part, FP III (4–18 January 1924) incorporated GJE No. 2, a test of the defenses of the Panama Canal against attack from the Caribbean. Blue (U.S.) with light naval forces, including an aircraft tender, on the Caribbean side, was supported by some Army aircraft. The attacking Black (European) fleet was accompanied by *Langley,* constructively assigned seventy-five aircraft, making her a surrogate for *Lexington*-class ships, then under conversion from incomplete battle cruisers. While *Langley*'s efforts to bomb the locks were effectively blocked by Blue Army pursuit planes, her aircraft were ruled to have beaten off an attack on the Black fleet by Blue Army bombers, providing excellent air cover while the battleships bombarded the locks with the help of their spotter aircraft, and then covered the landing of a notional expeditionary force.

FP IV (23 January–1 February) required Blue to conduct an offensive across the Caribbean (representing the China Seas) from Panama (the Philippines) to Vieques (Okinawa).[10] Although assigned *Langley* and greatly superior overall, Blue was inferior in aviation assets, having fewer than sixty airplanes, against nearly one hundred for Black, most of them Army aircraft. Nevertheless, when Blue arrived off Vieques, energetic efforts by Army aircraft to inflict damage on the attacking fleet were effectively countered by the fleet's anti-aircraft fire and *Langley*'s fighters.[11]

Critiquing the three 1924 problems, Black commander Vice Admiral Newton A. McCully praised *Langley*'s performance, writing, "Great credit is due her aviators for their effective work against so much [*sic*] superior air forces, and it indicates the power of the air attack even when the forces may appear insignificant, and the enemy greatly superior."[12] CinCUS Robert E. Coontz, Chief Umpire for the problems, noted the need for more aircraft and urged the swift completion of *Lexington* and *Saratoga*.[13]

FP V (February–March 1925) required Black (Japan) to capture an advanced base on Guadalupe Island (about 250 miles south of San Diego) and then attack the Panama Canal, opposed by a small Blue (U.S.) force trying to buy time for reinforcements to arrive from the Atlantic. Black was superior in air power, with some eighty real and constructive aircraft, about half assigned to *Langley* and two surrogate carriers, plus battleship and cruiser spotter aircraft as well as patrol bombers and their tender; Blue had only about thirty floatplanes, roughly half notional. Black advanced behind a cruiser screen supplemented by *Langley* aircraft, often as many as ten planes simultaneously, on missions lasting as long as two hours. "Capturing" Guadalupe, Black advanced toward Panama. Surprisingly, despite energetic scouting, the two fleets never actually encountered each other before the problem ended. Nevertheless, CinCUS Coontz complimented *Langley*'s aircraft, again urged the swift completion of *Saratoga* and *Lexington*, and noted the need for more capable aircraft and better aircraft handling facilities on battleships and cruisers.[14]

A few weeks later, the fleet took part in GJE No. 3 (14–27 April), testing the defenses of Hawaii and the fleet's ability to conduct expeditionary operations. Blue, tasked with "recapturing" Hawaii from Black, included *Langley* (notionally eighty-four aircraft) as a surrogate for *Lexington*, while Black had about sixty Army and thirty Navy airplanes but lacked unified air command. Blue achieved complete surprise, "capturing" Molokai Island in a swift amphibious landing on 25 April. Black aircraft intervened, but Army-Navy squabbling caused the attacks to be conducted in a piecemeal fashion, and they were ruled largely ineffective, though Army umpires declared *Langley* out of action by air attack even before she could launch any aircraft, which the Navy protested. While this ended carrier operations, spotter aircraft did an excellent job supporting the "bombardment" of beaches during subsequent landings on Oahu. The joint critique revealed a deep rift between Army and the naval Services over air power. The issues included "jurisdictional disputes" over whether the Navy could operate land-based aircraft and how far over the sea the Army could operate aircraft. In addition, Army airmen were more optimistic about their ability to hit maneuvering vessels than were Navy airmen, who actually had experience in the matter. Both sides agreed that joint operations required unified air command, but naturally disagreed as to which service should be in charge.

Over the next three years, aircraft, including those on *Langley*, continued to participate in Fleet Problems and other maneuvers. The fleet experimented with ways to incorporate the carrier into cruising formations, while carrier aircraft clearly proved easier to operate than battleship and cruiser floatplanes. Moreover, as aviation missions continued to be explored and expanded, to include reconnaissance, fleet air defense, spotting, supporting amphibious operations, anti-submarine patrol, and land attack, the need to balance demands on aviation assets soon arose. In a Joint Army-Navy maneuver in March 1927, a series of air strikes by flying boats and *Langley* aircraft against the Pacific end of the Panama Canal reduced fighter protection for observation planes supporting the battleships bombarding the coast defenses, causing many to be "lost" to enemy fighters, reducing the effectiveness of the bombardment, an indication of the extent to which battleships had come to rely on aerial spotting.[15] A few days later, on 13 March, during FP VII a similar situation arose when Blue fighters were sent to attack an enemy destroyer squadron, and while so engaged the Blue fleet was hit by two dozen Black Army bombers with marked success, due largely to the absence of fighter opposition.[16]

Meanwhile, progressive thinkers such as Commander Aircraft Squadrons (ComAirRons) Joseph M. Reeves urged more aggressive use of aviation. By mid-1927 Reeves proposed having aircraft carriers conduct "scouting and offensive operations at a distance from the battle line," arguing that there should be "complete freedom of action in employing carrier aircraft," a position with which CinCUS Charles F. Hughes concurred.[17] During FP VIII (April 1928) poor weather limited *Langley* to only four days of operations, but on those days her aircraft reconnoitered as far as seventy-five miles from the fleet.

A few weeks later, *Langley* gave a spectacular demonstration of what an autonomously operated aircraft carrier could do, during a joint Army-Navy exercise testing the defenses of Hawaii against a surprise air-sea attack. The fleet, organized into a small task force built around *Langley*, commanded by Rear Admiral Reeves, and two battleship task forces, approached Oahu from the south on the night of 16–17 May. By 0430 on the 17th *Langley* was ten miles south of Diamond Head, with the battleship task forces some distance to her east and west. While coast defense searchlights probed the sea and sky, *Langley* launched thirty-five aircraft. At dawn, what the press described as "swarms" of planes achieved complete surprise in simulated raids on various installations. *Langley* fighters then kept Army aircraft away from the battleships as they engaged coast defense installations.[18]

Shortly after this impressive performance, the fleet's new aircraft carriers, *Lexington* (CV-2) and *Saratoga* (CV-3), arrived in Hawaiian waters. ComAirRons Reeves transferred his flag to *Lexington*, and over the next few weeks the two big carriers engaged in daily training in the conduct of flight operations and in a series of exercises testing how carriers could operate together, becoming the first operational carrier division in the fleet.[19]

EMERGENCE OF THE FAST CARRIER TASK FORCE: FLEET PROBLEMS IX–XV, 1929–1934

The Fleet Problems of 1929–1934 were the most critical in the development of the autonomous Carrier Task Force.[20] Of these, FP IX (1929), the first in which *Lexington* and *Saratoga* took part, was certainly the most important.[21]

Held in January, the scenario was familiar: the defense of the Panama Canal by a smaller force against a major attack from the Pacific side. Admiral William V. Pratt, commanding Black (Japan), had originally intended to proceed to the Galapagos and approach Panama from the southwest, but financial considerations led to the plan being changed to a direct approach from the northwest. Based on a suggestion by ComAirRons Joseph M. Reeves, as the forces were still taking up their initial positions, Pratt dispatched *Saratoga* at high speed to the Galapagos, to approach the canal from the southwest, while the main body approached more directly.

Escorted by one light cruiser, *Saratoga* proceeded to the Galapagos, and then turned northward for a fast approach to Panama. At 0548 on 26 January, when about 140 miles south of the canal, she began launching seventy aircraft: seventeen bombers, forty-nine fighters, three scouts, and a "communications relay" plane.[22]

Blue was aware of a possible carrier strike from the southwest, but the raid neverthe-less achieved complete surprise. Beginning about 0700 *Saratoga*'s planes "destroyed" the Miraflores and Pedro Miguel Locks, before hitting military installations. Army fighters attempted to intercept, but the attackers escaped without loss. *Saratoga* followed this strike with two more, at one point maintaining eighty-three aircraft in the air simultaneously. Compounding this success, aircraft tender *Aroostook* (CM-3), standing in for *Langley*, with the Black main body, launched a single amphibian representing a notional twenty-four aircraft, which "destroyed" the Gatun Locks, on the Atlantic side of the canal. Unfortunately, shortly after this, *Saratoga*, operating in foggy weather, was located by Blue battlewagons making a sweep of the Gulf of Panama and ruled "sunk."

Half of CinCUS Henry A. Wiley's thirty-six page critique of the problem dealt with air operations.[23] Praising the quality of Navy aircraft and aviators over those of the Army, he went on to stress "the great usefulness of aircraft carriers," recommend-ing that more be procured, though noting the difficulty of protecting them. In the process, stressing a point first made by Blue commander Vice Admiral Montgomery Meigs Taylor during planning for the problem, Wiley concluded that the primary objective in carrier operations was the defeat of the enemy carriers.

Given her thirty-three knot speed, it may seem curious that *Saratoga* was "sunk" by enemy battleships, but this was in fact the first of many such incidents. Carriers would be "sunk" or "damaged" by surface ships during virtually every problem between 1929 and 1937, and would come under "gunfire" on numerous other occa-sions.[24] The fleet's aircraft lacked the range to conduct effective operations at long distances, forcing carriers to get close to their objectives to launch and recover strikes, putting them at risk from slower surface combatants. Not until mid-1941 would the U.S. Navy have aircraft capable of long-range operations, a year after the Japanese navy. This vulnerability, as much as any hostility to aviation, led some Admirals to be wary of independent aircraft carrier operations.

FP X (March 1930) required Blue (U.S.) to conduct an offensive across the Caribbean to oust Black (a European power) from a lodgment in the Antilles. Inspired by *Saratoga*'s performance in 1929, Black's Admiral William C. Cole formed an independent strike group around *Lexington*. As Blue, with both *Saratoga* and *Langley*, drove across the Caribbean from Panama, Black concentrated north of Haiti. On 10 March, with destroyers and cruisers forming a scouting line ahead of her, *Lexington* proceeded at high speed into the Caribbean south of Guantanamo, as the Black main body followed, covered by flying boat patrols. Scouts from the two fleets began making contact on the 13th.

Early on the 14th, with the fleets about seventy-five miles apart, south and south-west of Haiti, the two Blue carriers were on a northwesterly course some two dozen miles east of Navassa Island. Some *Langley* fighters were on reconnaissance, and

The USS Lexington *with Martin bombers on deck.*

both carriers had aircraft spotted on deck and others below being serviced. Shortly after 0800 three *Lexington* scout bombers spotted the Blue carriers. Calling for support, at 0815 the scouts dive-bombed *Saratoga,* putting several bombs into her flight deck, inflicting serious damage. *Saratoga*'s crew began to put out notional fires and haul aircraft out of danger, but fourteen minutes later five waves of *Lexington* dive-bombers began arriving, forty-two aircraft in all, to shower the ship with bombs. Aircraft aboard *Saratoga* began "exploding" and she was ruled out of action. Four minutes after that, fifteen *Lexington* fighter bombers struck *Langley,* followed two minutes later by a dozen more, and soon she too was ruled to be in flames. Blue aircraft returning from patrol interfered, but were ineffective. In less than twenty minutes both Blue carriers had been put out of action, and Black surface forces shortly arrived to sink *Langley.*

In his critique, CinCUS William V. Pratt noted how the "suddenness with which Black gained complete control of the air" had decided the outcome of the problem.[25] Inspired by the "Battle of Navassa Island," most observers agreed on the importance of getting in the first blow, urged the acquisition of more carriers, and recommended procurement of better scout aircraft, to increase the carrier's reconnaissance reach and ability to make preliminary strikes. Aviation officers stressed the value of operating carriers in independent strike forces, while the Chief of Staff of the Battle

Fleet recommended carriers conduct continuous scouting and maintain an offensive reserve always ready to strike the enemy.[26]

During FP XI (April 1930), held in the same waters, both sides tasked their aircraft carriers with eliminating their opposite numbers. Inclement weather and a number of command and staff errors hampered the effectiveness of air operations, though *Saratoga* did eventually inflict extensive damage on *Lexington,* confirming the value of hitting the enemy's aircraft carriers first. During the problem, Vice Admiral William C. Cole, commanding Blue, had formed a task force around *Lexington,* and in his critique he proposed that permanent Carrier Task Forces be established—of one carrier, heavy cruisers, and destroyers—to train and operate together: an idea that would be extensively tested for the rest of the decade, be formally implemented in early 1941, and prove highly effective during the first year of the Pacific War.[27]

Cole's proposal was first tested in FP XII (February 1931), a trial of the effectiveness of an aircraft-heavy force against a conventional Battle Fleet with limited air assets, during a hostile attack on the Pacific side of the Panama Canal.[28] Blue's Vice Admiral Arthur L. Willard, although inferior in most assets, was given *Lexington* and *Saratoga,* several aircraft tenders, and the airship *Los Angeles* (ZR-3). He formed a "Striking Force" under Rear Admiral Joseph M. Reeves, who organized two task forces, each of one carrier, two cruisers, and four destroyers. Directly under Reeves, the *Saratoga* Task Force was to cover the approaches to Panama from the northwest and west, while the *Lexington* Task Force, commanded by the carrier's skipper, Captain Ernest J. King, provided cover from the south and southwest. Airship *Los Angeles* was assigned to patrol along the demarcation line between the carrier operating areas, while aircraft based on tenders conducted reconnaissance and patrols in support of the carriers and their scouting lines. The Black fleet commenced the maneuvers about 850 miles southwest of the Panama Canal, a few degrees above the equator, divided into two expeditionary forces and supporting task forces.

Blue's task organization proved quite effective. Flying boats from Panama located elements of the Black fleet on 18 February, the second day of operations. On the 19th, both Blue carriers located the Black expeditionary convoys, with some help from the airship *Los Angeles,* which was promptly lost to an enemy airplane. Extensive carrier air strikes on Black caused heavy damage, but not enough to prevent both Black convoys from effecting notional landings, though the beachheads came under sustained air attack until the problem ended on the fifth day.

Although not decisive, the performance of naval aviation during the problem had again demonstrated that aircraft, and particularly carrier aircraft, could serve as an offensive arm. Nevertheless, carrier operations had been hampered by the short range of their aircraft, which forced them to approach close to their objectives, leading to several close encounters with Black surface forces.

Los Angeles received mixed reviews. While Black's Admiral Frank H. Schofield concluded that their cost was "out of all proportion to their probable usefulness," noting that "they had an appeal to the imagination that is not sustained by their military usefulness," Blue's Vice Admiral Willard, endorsed their use.[29]

Perhaps the most important result of this problem was that it first revealed the serious logistical demands of carrier operations. The high speed and operational tempo that the carriers maintained resulted in both running very low on fuel, avgas, ordnance, and aircraft—about half of which were "lost" in combat or to mechanical problems. At the time, these logistical difficulties were viewed as limitations of carrier aviation, but they underscored the need for an effective underway replenishment system, already under experimentation.

After routine exercises around Panama, the Battle Fleet departed for California in March, leaving behind the carriers, which entered the Caribbean with the Scouting Fleet for a series special maneuvers (21–30 March). The most important of these was the first, essentially a duel between two carrier task forces, each of one carrier, four light cruisers, and two destroyers, with Rear Admiral Reeves in *Saratoga* defending the canal from an attack by Captain King's *Lexington*.[30]

After *Lexington* had a day's head start to "lose" herself in the Caribbean, the maneuvers began well before dawn on 22 March. With *Saratoga* about 150 miles east of Colon, Reeves, considering King's options, concluded that *Lexington* was most likely northeast of Colon and sent a destroyer in that direction, calculating that the aggressive King would be unable to resist the "bait." He then positioned *Saratoga* in echelon behind the destroyer. Reeves' estimate was exactly correct. *Lexington* scouts found the destroyer soon after dawn on the 22nd. King ordered a major air strike to trace the destroyer's course back to *Saratoga*. Meanwhile, a *Saratoga* scout had already located *Lexington*. Reeves put a large strike in the air and ordered some cruisers toward the enemy carrier. As *Lexington*'s aircraft looked for *Saratoga*, seventy *Saratoga* aircraft "sank" their carrier, aided by the cruisers that arrived during the action; from the time *Saratoga*'s strike was launched until *Lexington* was "sunk" little more than an hour had passed. While this underscored the importance of getting in the first blow, the "loss" of *Lexington* led to some calls for "small carriers and flying deck cruisers" to avoid losing too many aircraft with a single ship, a recommendation that went nowhere.[31]

Early 1932 saw one of the most dramatic events in the evolution of carrier aviation. For GJE No. 4, Blue (U.S.), with most of the Battle Force, including *Lexington* and *Saratoga* plus a constructive expeditionary force, had to recapture Hawaii from Black (Japan), which had taken it earlier.[32] Blue's Admiral Richard H. Leigh adopted a proposal by veteran airmen Rear Admiral Harry E. Yarnell and Captain John H. Towers for a surprise attack on Oahu by an "Advance Raiding Force" of the carriers and some escorts.[33] Departing the West Coast with the main body, on 5 February the Advance Raiding Force separated from the fleet and proceeded to Hawaii independently. After a final twenty-five-knot run to about one hundred miles north of Oahu, the carriers began launching 150 aircraft in two waves before dawn on Sunday, 7 February. Achieving total surprise, the first wave hit Army air fields across Oahu and then went after the fleet and installations at Pearl Harbor. Army aircraft intervened, to little effect, and were themselves intercepted while returning to their bases by the Blue second wave, which inflicted heavy losses on the defenders.

Recovering their aircraft, the Blue carriers took evasive action, heading southwest of Oahu. At dawn on the 9th, *Saratoga* again raided Oahu while reconnoitering landing sites, once more with considerable success, though losing ten of the sixty-six aircraft engaged. Heading south, she linked up with *Lexington* overnight. By 11 February, Blue had effected landings on Oahu covered by aircraft from the carriers, though by then both were low on aircraft and *Lexington* was out of action due to enemy attack.

The critique of GJE No. 4 was acrimonious, as Army and Navy personnel disagreed on many issues. Nevertheless it was clear that the carrier raid on Oahu on Sunday morning, 7 February—termed by historian Thomas Fleming "a date that would live in amnesia"—had thrown the defenders off balance, and they were never able to gain the initiative. Less than a decade later, the Japanese would open the Pacific War with precisely the same attack.

A month later FP XIII postulated that Blue (U.S.) was preparing a major offensive from Hawaii against the outer fringe of the Black (Japan) empire, a series of "atolls" at Puget Sound, San Francisco, San Diego–San Pedro, and Magdalena Bay, Mexico.[34] Blue's Admiral Leigh again had the bulk of the fleet, plus *Saratoga* (seventy-two aircraft), commanded by the aggressive Captain Frank R. McCrary, as well as thirty-six patrol planes and torpedo bombers based at Pearl Harbor and thirty-five battleship and cruiser floatplanes, plus a notional expeditionary force. Black's Vice Admiral Willard had *Langley* and Captain Ernest J. King's *Lexington*, with a total of ninety-eight aircraft, plus four aircraft tenders with thirty-six flying boats, and the airship *Los Angeles,* plus some surface forces.

Blue formed two principal task forces, a convoy and escort, and an offensive force composed of *Saratoga*, three battleships, and ten destroyers, to attack Puget Sound. Black, operating from the San Pedro–San Diego area, formed four task forces and a train. The "Striking Group," *Lexington* with some cruisers and destroyers, was to intercept Blue at the earliest opportunity and inflict maximum damage to his forces, supported by submarine attacks to erode his strength in preparation for a surface action.

The maneuvers began on 10 March, with both fleets moving cautiously. Black submarines ascertained Blue's course, which suggested San Francisco was its objective. On the morning of the 13th, however, Blue altered course for Puget Sound while the *Saratoga* Task Force remained on course for San Francisco, both as a deception and to provide cover for the rest of the main body. By morning on the 14th, the opposing carrier groups were hardly two hundred miles apart on a collision course, and scouts from *Saratoga* detected three Black cruisers. Alerted to each other's presence, the carriers launched air strikes against each other as the range closed early that afternoon. *Saratoga* aircraft inflicted 38 percent damage on Black's *Lexington*, but received 25 percent damage from enemy aircraft.

Captain King now convinced Willard to operate Black's *Lexington* independently against Blue's carrier, to reduce the enemy air threat. He moved *Lexington* out of range of *Saratoga* under cover of darkness, to gain sea room. During the 15th, clashes between surface forces began to develop as Black cruisers probed the outer perimeter of Blue's screen, though *Saratoga* aircraft sank two Black cruisers and heavily damaged a third. These strikes betrayed her position. Calculating that *Saratoga* would be recovering aircraft just before dusk, King moved *Lexington* in at high speed and launched a forty-nine-plane strike that hit *Saratoga* just as he had figured; the Blue carrier was ruled to have taken 49 percent damage, rendering her incapable of operating aircraft. The following day, Black destroyers "sank" *Saratoga*, rendering Blue bereft of carrier support. Although the maneuvers continued, the fleets lost contact on the 17th and the problem was ended.

The 1932 maneuvers reaffirmed the lesson that in carrier warfare, the first strike is the most important. Blue air commander Harry Yarnell concluded his critique by noting that *Lexington* and *Saratoga* were inadequate to the needs of a Pacific war, suggesting a minimum of six, if not eight, as a basic operational necessity, while Captain King argued that the Fleet Problem had demonstrated that carriers should be operated by divisions.

The Fleet Problem also added further evidence that the airship was of doubtful value as *Los Angles* had done nothing useful. Airship proponents brushed this aside, touting the merits of the new "flying aircraft carriers," *Akron* (ZRS-4) and her sister *Macon* (ZRS-5), neither of which had taken part in the maneuvers. Nevertheless, in a prescient comment to CNO William V. Pratt, CinCUS Frank Schofield said "the need for aircraft is not more *Akron*s, but more carriers," which seems to have summed up the fleet's opinion as well.[35]

FP XIII brought to a head the contentious issue of the effectiveness of air attacks against ships. Neither World War I nor the events that followed provided any useful guidance, and an acrimonious debate had developed in the Service—and between the Navy and the Army—over this question.[36] Rules for horizontal bombing and dive-bombing had been developed based on trials held during the late 1920s using dummy bombs against various targets. Following FP XIII, Commander, Battle Force (ComBatFor) Admiral Luke McNamee, considering the existing rules too optimistic, proposed some revisions, while Rear Admiral William A. Moffett Jr., formidable Chief of the Bureau of Aeronautics, proposed even more generous guidelines.

About this time the target ship *Utah* (AG-16, ex-B-31) entered service. Trials with *Utah* produced figures even less optimistic than those proposed by McNamee, and new guidelines were issued for FP XIV (1933) over protests from aviation enthusiasts. In 1934 more optimistic rules were introduced, only to be rescinded in 1938. Wartime experience would prove that even the most pessimistic prewar guidelines were rather generous.[37]

The Rules Debate: How Accurate in Terms of Bombs on Target Are Air Attacks against Maneuvering Capital Ships?

Type of Attack	Horizontal	Dive
FP XIII Rules—1932	20 %	20 %
McNamee Proposal	15	30
Moffett Proposal	22	35
Utah Trials—1932	c. 6	18
FP XIV Rules—1933	8	16
WW II Experience	~ 0	c. 15

FP XIV was intended to test the fleet's ability to defend its bases from carrier raids and the effectiveness of carriers operating independently. Black (Japan) had to conduct a series of carrier raids against Blue (U.S.) bases on the West Coast in order to disrupt preparations for offensive operations. Black's Vice Admiral Frank H. Clark had *Saratoga* and *Lexington* and seven heavy cruisers, together the fastest ships in the fleet, plus some old destroyers and two oilers. Blue's Admiral Luke McNamee had virtually everything else in the fleet.

Since Black was to begin operations near Hawaii, the arrival of the carriers in the islands permitted a joint exercise with the Army's Hawaiian Department supported by local naval forces (27 January–1 February).[38] The defenders went on full alert on the 27th, when the carriers were still well to sea, as destroyers and some other vessels were dispatched to patrol northeastward of the islands. On the 29th the defenders initiated a twenty-four-hour air patrol out to 150 miles. Clark, not an aviator, adopted a plan devised by his airmen. Avoiding enemy air patrols, the carriers and some escorts arrived north of Molokai around midnight on 30–31 January, while a task group of heavy cruisers approached Oahu from the south. About two hours before dawn on the 31st the carriers put some ninety aircraft in the air, reserving about forty for fleet defense. The strike force attained complete surprise, arriving over Pearl Harbor around dawn, and was ruled to have inflicted serious damage.

While the carriers proceeded to Hawaii and maneuvered with the Army, Blue prepared for the enemy raid.[39] Admiral McNamee concluded that Black was most likely to operate its carriers individually and conduct a series of simultaneous raids. Since the most critical Black targets were around San Francisco and San Pedro–San Diego, and knowing the range of the attacking aircraft, he formed two large task forces. The Northern Group's patrol area reached 100 miles from San Francisco, while the Southern Group reached 125 miles from San Diego–San Pedro. Each patrol area consisted of an outer perimeter of destroyers, submarines, and other vessels picketed more or less within sight of each other, supported by cruisers some miles to their rear, and battleships still further back, while flying boats patrolled beyond the outer edges.

As McNamee had calculated, Black's Clark decided to use his carriers individually to conduct two pairs of strikes on two successive days, hitting San Francisco twice and San Pedro and Puget Sound once each. Each carrier had three heavy cruisers as escorts, while his destroyers and oilers, unable to keep up with the carriers, formed a support group. The Carrier task forces began the problem roughly five hundred nautical miles south-southeast of Oahu on 10 February. The results were not impressive. Attempting to raid San Francisco on the morning of the 16th, the *Lexington* Task Force ran into fog, became lost, and was shortly intercepted by battleships and quickly dispatched. *Saratoga* had better luck, conducting extensive raids in the San Pedro area that morning, but she was also intercepted by enemy surface forces, barely escaping with some damage to her escorts—an experience repeated the following day when she undertook raids in the San Francisco area, once again barely escaping enemy battleships.

Critics of naval aviation argued that the outcome demonstrated the vulnerability of carriers operating independently, but carrier advocates rightly observed that the results were due to faulty planning and tactics, and to the limitations of training and equipment rather than to a flawed concept, noting that had the carriers operated together, they would have benefited from mutual support and the attacks could have been delivered with maximum possible force. Moreover, had the carriers and their personnel been equipped and trained for night operations, their effectiveness would have been greatly enhanced. Most importantly, however, they pointed to the need for longer-range aircraft, so that carriers could stand well away from their objectives; McNamee's 100–125-mile patrol areas around the critical ports had been dictated by the range of the existing carrier aircraft.[40]

Vice Admiral Yarnell, commander of the *Saratoga* Task Force, observed that had the Black attack been made with six or eight carriers, it would likely have been devastating, and he called for more carriers—a goal already well in hand with USS *Ranger*

(CV-4) about to be launched, USS *Yorktown* (CV-5) and USS *Enterprise* CV-6) about to be laid down, and USS *Wasp* (CV-7) soon to be ordered.

Some naval aviators believed that the outcome of the Fleet Problem had a major effect on command arrangements in the Navy. Apparently Vice Admiral Clark had been widely expected to be appointed Commander in Chief, U.S. Fleet in 1934, but the post went to Joseph M. Reeves, the highest ranking aviator in the fleet. The aviators attributed this development to Clark's performance in the Fleet Problem.[41]

The following year, FP XV (April–May 1934) was a series of loosely connected tactical and operational exercises in the Pacific and the Caribbean, representing phases of a war with a European-Asian coalition.[42] The initial movement of the fleet to Central American waters was "harassed" by Brown (Japan) light forces, during which Blue's three carriers, *Lexington, Saratoga*, and *Langley* (a surrogate for *Ranger*), proved effective in providing anti-submarine protection to the fleet, while cruiser and battleship floatplanes proved useful for patrols and reconnaissance.

A mock attack on the Canal Zone followed, against some submarines, cruisers, and Army coast defense and air forces. While the Navy claimed to have wrought great destruction on the canal's defenses, and the Army claimed to have sunk two aircraft carriers, no umpiring rules had been agreed upon, and the results were tactfully declared a "draw."[43]

The main event of the Fleet Problem, "Exercise M" (5–10 May), presumed that Gray (a "European coalition") had captured the Virgin Islands and parts of Puerto Rico, and thus Blue (U.S.) had to undertake an offensive from Panama to recover these territories before enemy reinforcements arrived. Blue's Admiral Joseph M. Reeves had *Saratoga*, representing herself and another carrier, *Langley* (as *Ranger*); five aircraft tenders and "aerial cruiser" *Macon* (ZRS-5); a large fleet consisting of numerous battleships, cruisers, and destroyers, about half notional, plus notional submarine and expeditionary forces based in Panama and some forces at Guantanamo Bay. Gray's Vice Admiral Frank H. Brumby was given *Lexington* (representing three carriers); a smaller fleet of five battleships (one notional); many cruisers, destroyers, and submarines (mostly notional); plus a garrison in the captured territories.

Exercise M was a knock-down, drag-out fight greatly resembling the protracted air-sea-land Battle of Guadalcanal, 12–15 November 1942. Contact between the fleets began early on 5 May and didn't end until the maneuvers were over. From the afternoon of the 5th through the 9th, there were thirty-one separate engagements; fifteen surface actions, including five massed night destroyer torpedo attacks and a very successful Gray cruiser raid that wiped out Blue's aircraft tenders in a Haitian bay; nine submarine attacks; and seven air attacks, including one by the new Consolidated P2Y flying boats.[44] Early on the 10th the maneuvers culminated in a complex general action off Culebra characterized by coordinated air-surface combats, leaving Blue once more in possession of the island.

The carriers were busy during Exercise M, and CinCUS David Foote Sellers wrote, "It is generally accepted in the Fleet that our carriers, accompanied by strong cruiser forces, should be used offensively," and called for better aircraft, specifying that carrier bombers be able to carry 500- and 1,000-pound bombs long distances, recommended larger aircraft tenders, and noted problems operating and recovering cruiser scout planes.[45] The call for heavier bombs, and thus aircraft capable of carrying them, had been made before, but it seems that the FP XV finally drove the point home to the fleet's senior leadership.

The extensive trials of coordinated air-surface-undersea actions—that is, surface combats in which air and submarine forces took part—were ruled quite successful and became a common feature of subsequent maneuvers. Despite much optimism about such tactics, there were not many occasions during World War II when they were used.[46]

The problem finally settled the question of the value of airships. *Macon* had mostly been unable to operate due to contrary winds, and although on 6 May she had spotted the "enemy" main body, she was promptly shot down by fighters. This was the last problem in which an airship participated, for *Macon* crashed early the following year, after which reconnaissance and patrol mission was assigned to more reliable flying boats.[47]

CinCUS Sellers' comment, "It is generally accepted in the Fleet that our carriers . . . should be used offensively," was not merely an opinion.[48] Although most of the fleet's senior leaders still believed in the primacy of the battleship, by the mid-1930s they had also come to realize the extraordinary value of carrier aviation.[49] This trend was strengthened when Joseph M. Reeves, the fleet's premier carrierman, became Commander in Chief, U.S. Fleet on 15 June 1934, just eleven days after *Ranger* was commissioned, developments that were reflected in subsequent Fleet Problems.

CREATING THE "NAVAL FORCE": FLEET PROBLEMS XVI–XXI, 1935–1940

The largest maneuvers yet held in the Pacific FP XVI were the first to be truly strategic in scope, with multiple operations across a theater encompassing five million square miles from the West Coast to Hawaii to the Aleutians.[50] It was also the first problem to include four carriers (*Langley, Lexington, Saratoga,* and *Ranger*) with nearly 500 aircraft, almost 50 percent more than in any previous problem. It assumed that Black (Japan), operating from the Aleutians, had established a strong advanced base at Midway and was threatening Hawaii, requiring White (U.S.), based on the West Coast and Hawaii, to recover Midway.

In the first phase of the problem White was directly commanded by CinCUS Reeves, with virtually the entire U.S. Fleet, operating from the West Coast. Formed into five task forces, including one bound for Alaska and the Aleutians, White put to sea on 3 May 1935. White's movement was uneventful, aggressive patrolling keeping Black's many submarines at bay. By the 11th White's task forces had reached the vicinity of Hawaii or of Alaska.

The "main event" of the problem began on 15 May, with reorganized fleets. White, now commanded by Vice Admiral Harris Laning, had *Saratoga, Ranger,* and *Langley,* most of the battleships, plus some cruisers, destroyers, and submarines, as well as the Fleet Marine Force, with some support from the Army's Hawaiian Department. Black's Vice Admiral Arthur J. Hepburn had *Lexington,* with a roughly equal force of surface combatants and submarines, plus 2 cruisers acting as battle-cruisers, some minelayers, and 45 flying boats and their tenders at Midway. White was superior in air forces, especially combat aircraft, with 173 carrier airplanes and 62 ship-borne floatplanes against Black's 74 carrier aircraft, 42 floatplanes, and 45 tender-based patrol bombers, though the latter had more patrol aircraft.

On 15 May, most of White lay at Pearl Harbor, but Rear Admiral Thomas C. Hart had three heavy cruisers at sea 230 miles northeast of Midway. Black had three task forces; *Lexington* and her escorts, about 165 miles north-northwest of Midway (about 250 miles west of Hart); the battleships and their escorts some 560 miles north of *Lexington*; and the "battlecruisers" and some light cruisers in Alaskan waters, while strong submarine forces were deployed in and around Hawaii.

Rather than push directly up the Hawaiian chain to Midway, Laning opted for an indirect approach. The fleet sortied from Pearl Harbor in two echelons on the 15th and 16th, covered by air anti-submarine warfare (ASW) patrols, and initially steamed as if bound directly for Midway, while Laning dispatched *Ranger* and some escorts northward to support Hart. After dark on the 16th, however, Laning altered course westward. Late on 17 May, while Laning was hiding his fleet in the ocean west of Oahu, Hart's cruisers ran in toward Midway. By about midnight they were about ten miles off the atoll. Shortly afterward, with a full moon rising, the cruisers catapulted a dozen Vought O3U-1 floatplanes into the air, before heading directly away from Midway. The floatplanes hit Midway at 0150 on the 18th in two waves, strafing the forty-five Black flying boats clearly visible at anchor in the lagoon, destroying or damaging more than half of them, with three casualties to themselves. The floatplanes then followed the track of the cruisers for a dawn rendezvous, after which the ships headed eastward at high speed. Later that afternoon Hart made contact with *Ranger* and her escorts. His task force then began a series of diversionary maneuvers, to draw Black's attention eastward.

Meanwhile the White main body, having steamed west for about forty-eight hours, turned north toward Midway. At the same time, Black's main body, proceeding south from Alaska, had reached the vicinity of Midway. The opposing fleets were thus only a few hundred miles apart. On the 22nd, opposing scout cruisers began to clash about two hundred miles south of Midway. As the fleets closed for a major surface action, a flying boat went missing. All air assets were diverted to the search as were some destroyers and light cruisers.[51] The remaining elements of the two fleets resumed their surface engagement, the umpires ruling that both could assume they had observation planes to help spot targets. Through a staff error, however, White commander Laning was not informed of this decision. As a result when Black opened fire at very long range, taking advantage of the constructive spotting aircraft, Laning believed they were just "wasting ammunition," while in fact the umpires were assessing hits against him. He did not learn of the communications error until the end of the Fleet Problem, by which time he had been "soundly defeated, a telling commentary on the extent to which the battle fleet had come to rely upon the use of spotter aircraft."[52]

Although this was the first—and as it turned out, only—problem in which opposing carriers neither attacked nor even detected each other, the problem was extremely important in the development of the Carrier Task Torce.[53] During the advance from the West Coast toward Hawaii, *Lexington,* operating at high speed for five days while conducting ASW and reconnaissance patrols, ran critically low on fuel. This potentially disastrous development led to a call for experiments in the underway refueling of carriers and other heavier ships, which was crucial if carriers were to operate freely. The problem also helped develop procedures for large-scale coordinated operations by patrol bombers.

Set in Central American waters, FP XVII (April–June 1936) assumed that White (Japan) had undertaken an offensive war against Blue (U.S.) at a time when conflict in Europe was occupying the latter's attention, so that major portions of the Blue fleet were in the Atlantic or otherwise unavailable in the Pacific.[54] So while White overran the Far East, the Blue main body, harassed by White light forces, had to proceed to Panama to unite with the Atlantic squadron and other dispersed forces, before undertaking operations against the enemy. The fleets were organized and commanded somewhat differently in each of the problem's five parts. For naval aviation the most important part was a test of fleet carrier tactics on 21 May 1936, held south and west of Panama.[55]

Brown (Japan), under Admiral William D. Leahy, had *Saratoga* and some patrol bombers and their tenders plus some battleships, cruisers, and destroyers with which to attack Balboa. Black (U.S.), under Vice Admiral Clarence S. Kempff, had to defend Balboa and the canal with *Ranger* and *Lexington,* plus a number of battleships, cruisers, and destroyers.

At the start of the maneuvers, Black lay about 100–150 miles south of Balboa, while the outer edge of the Brown fleet was roughly 170 miles almost directly to its west. Black adopted a fairly standard disposition, with battleships in the center, surrounded by cruiser-destroyer screens, with a carrier and two destroyers about

60 miles on either flank, linked to the main body by a chain of two or three cruisers. The carriers were to "locate and bomb Brown battleline and carriers. Time is of the essence."[56] Brown's sole carrier, Captain William S. Halsey's *Saratoga,* and two destroyers were south of the Brown main body, while patrol bombers based in Panama provided air cover to the north.

No detailed narrative of the operations appears to exist, but the course of events is roughly clear. Scouts off Black's *Ranger* and Brown's *Saratoga* each spotted the opposing carrier. Although the weather was poor, Halsey launched a strike, which failed to locate *Ranger* due to meteorological conditions. In contrast, *Ranger's* Captain Patrick Bellinger acted with greater caution, launching a strike as the weather cleared. This caught *Saratoga* and inflicted heavy damage. Although getting in the first blow was normally best in carrier operations, in this instance Halsey's aggressiveness in risky circumstances had not paid off, while Bellinger's caution had. Shortly afterward, *Ranger* was caught by a succession of attacks from a flight of Brown patrol bombers, followed by torpedo bombers and then another group of flying boats, and was ruled 48 percent damaged. In a surface action later that day, *Saratoga* was sunk by notional Black "battlecruisers," underscoring the continuing need for longer ranged aircraft.

Although the problem shed little new light on the employment of carriers, during several phases *Saratoga* had maintained such high rates of speed—twenty-five knots was required to operate aircraft—for such long periods that her fuel consumption averaged 10 percent of bunkerage per day, similar to *Lexington's* experience the previous year—a development that strengthened calls for the adoption of underway refueling for carriers. The problem was also a fairly vigorous test of various types of flying boats, reflecting the Navy's belief that they could compete with the Army's B-17s in long-range maritime patrol and reconnaissance and as strike aircraft. The Douglas P2D1s, Consolidated P2Ys, and Martin PMs and PM-2s, some capable of staying aloft for nearly twenty-four hours, performed well, particularly those equipped with an experimental autopilot, which eased the strain on their crews. Of these aircraft, however, only the P2Y was considered fully suited to the needs of the fleet, which led directly to the adoption of Consolidated's follow-on patrol bomber, the PBY Catalina.[57]

A test of the fleet's ability to conduct advanced base operations, FP XVIII (April–May 1937) required Black (U.S.) to recapture the Hawaiian Islands and Johnston Island from White (Japan) as the initial phase of an offensive across the Pacific.[58] Although naval aviation played a role in all of the problem's six "periods," it was particularly important in two.

Period 2 (23–25 April), a joint Army-Navy exercise, tested the defenses of Hawaii and the effectiveness of independent carrier operations. On the 23rd, fleet aircraft conducted surprise reconnaissance and attacks across Oahu, while a strong task force subjected the island of Hawaii to a combined air-surface bombardment, followed by a successful simulated landing. Meanwhile, defending patrol bombers attempted to locate the main body of the attacking fleet, while the Air Corps responded vigorously to the air attacks. As, once again, no agreement had been made on how to assess casualties during air combats, no results were declared. The following day, defending reconnaissance aircraft located the fleet as it approached Oahu. A series of air attacks on the fleet followed, during which Army airmen claimed considerable success, but did not prevent the fleet from executing major raids across Oahu by carrier aircraft and battleship-cruiser floatplanes, providing cover for the approach of a simulated landing force and its escorts. The maneuvers ended before a "landing" could take place. Both Army and Navy commanders expressed their satisfaction with the exercises, but no major recommendations resulted and no formal report seems to have been made.

The most important phase of the problem was Period 4 (4–9 May), a Black offensive against White bases in the Hawaiian chain. White's Vice Admiral William T. Tarrant had *Ranger* (74 aircraft), two seaplane tenders, plus battleships, cruisers, destroyers, and submarines, while Black's Admiral Claude C. Bloch, among the least imaginative of the Navy's senior officers, had *Lexington* and *Saratoga* (162 aircraft) and three aircraft tenders, and was roughly equal to White in other combatants.

ComAirRons Vice Admiral Frederick J. Horne urged Bloch to use his carriers to build two fast task forces, to seek the enemy's carrier, arguing that "once an enemy carrier is within striking distance of our Fleet no security remains until it, its squadrons, or both, are destroyed, and our carriers, if with the main body, are at a tremendous initial disadvantage in conducting necessary operations."[59] Bloch, wishing to provide air cover for his main body and believing carriers highly vulnerable to air attack, disregarded Horne, limiting the carriers to reconnaissance, screening, and fleet defense, thus losing the benefit of their very high speed. In contrast, although not an aviator, Vice Admiral Tarrant, acting on the advice of his air chief, Rear Admiral Ernest J. King, decided to operate *Ranger* autonomously.

On 4 May White was spread throughout the Hawaiian chain, with seaplane tenders stationed at several islands from Midway to Hawaii. Black was concentrated about one hundred miles southwest of Midway, near the 180th meridian, formed into two task forces, a main body with *Lexington* and the bulk of the fleet, and an expeditionary force, including *Saratoga,* carrying Marines to capture Midway. Both sides initiated aggressive air patrols.

White flying boats detected the Black main body very early on the 4th, ascertaining its speed and course. Meanwhile, the Black expeditionary force reached Midway, conducted air and gunnery attacks, landed Marines, and on the 5th an aircraft tender began operations. On the 6th, Bloch dispatched *Lexington,* an aircraft tender, and a small force to capture French Frigate Shoals. White's aggressive air patrolling paid off, and by mid-morning Tarrant had a clear picture of the location and strength of the Black main body and began to make movements accordingly. Meanwhile, around noon, Black's *Lexington* Task Force captured French Frigate Shoals, though White resistance resulted in serious damage to the carrier.

By mid-morning on the 7th, as the *Lexington* Task Force rejoined the Black main body, reconnaissance contacts between the two fleets became more frequent. By 1320 the two fleets were close enough for Black battleships to open fire on White heavy cruisers, initiating a long-range skirmish that lasted several hours. White's carrier *Ranger,* operating autonomously, provided support to the surface forces, heavily damaging *Saratoga* and some of Black's transports. Overnight, White essayed several well-executed cruiser-destroyer attacks, with patrol bombers taking advantage of moonrise to make low altitude strike. Black's losses were heavy, with an aircraft tender and eight other vessels "sunk" and both carriers, two battleships, and four other ships taking varying degrees of damage, while White suffered several heavy cruisers and destroyers damaged.

At 0441 on the 8th, a general battleline action began, lasting for about an hour. As the battleships exchanged fire, White patrol bombers attempted several attacks, but were badly handled by Black carrier fighters. Though White inflicted heavy damage on Black, leaving *Lexington* in almost sinking condition, it suffered in turn, "losing" the surface action. Breaking off, White retired on Lahaina Roads, while conducting patrol bomber attacks against the new Black base at French Frigate Shoals. The problem was declared at an end at noon.

Critiquing the exercise, Admiral Bloch praised the work of carrier aircraft in scouting and defending against White patrol bombers and submarines, but made scant mention of their offensive potential.[60] Defending his decision to keep the carriers close to the battleline, he asserted that by being with the main body they benefited from "mutual support," noting that "75% of the damaged assessed on *Lexington* was due to gun and torpedo fire," which hardly proves his point. Discussing Admiral Horne's proposal to use the carriers independently, drawing their security from their high speed, evasive tactics, and offensive ability, he asserted that "evasive tactics" would result "in a private war between the opposing air forces, often with complete disregard of the part of the air forces were intended to play in the furtherance of the plans" of the Fleet Commander. He further claimed that "evasive tactics were fallacious and untenable" against tender-based or shore-based long-range aircraft, an odd assertion given that he had just praised the performance of his carrier aircraft for their role in the defense of the fleet against those threats. While Bloch was right about the vulnerability of carriers to air attack, he failed to recognize that the best way to secure the fleet—and one's own carriers—from air attack was to ensure the loss of the enemy's carriers.

Horne made some valuable recommendations on the need for all-weather carrier aircraft, increased training in night air operations, improved availability of aviation fuel, and, naturally, greater autonomy for carriers.[61] Other observers noted that the new PBY patrol bombers had been less effective than expected in long-range mass attacks, but excellent for reconnaissance.

This Fleet Problem is the only one for which there is a hint of command interference in a dissenting opinion. Aviation officers later claimed that "after the exercise, when Vice Admiral Frederick J. Horne . . . circulated a paper calling for independent carrier operations, Admiral Bloch had him recall all copies." This assertion cannot be proven, but suggests a high degree of dissatisfaction with Bloch's handling of the critique.[62] Certainly, Bloch's appointment as Commander in Chief, U.S. Fleet in January 1938 probably came as a shock to naval airmen.

FP XIX (March–April 1938) was a general test of the fleet's abilities, held in several parts.[63] For Part II, Black had to concentrate off Southern California, defended by White. Black, commanded by Vice Admiral Edward C. Kalbfus, had *Lexington* and *Saratoga*, six battleships, and various other vessels. Kalbfus spurned the advice of his friend Rear Admiral Ernest J. King, who commanded the two carriers, and formed two task forces, each of a carrier, three battleships, and some cruisers and destroyers, approaching Southern California from the northwest and south, respectively. In contrast White's Vice Admiral Tarrant, as he had done the previous year, built a task force around *Ranger*, put his four battleships in a supporting role, and reserved his strong contingent of PBYs for offensive operations.

The outcome was decidedly in White's favor. At the start of the maneuvers, on 16 March, Tarrant sent the *Ranger* Task Force northwest from San Diego–San Pedro, following with his slower battleships. Contact occurred on the 17th, and aircraft from *Ranger* promptly hit *Lexington,* an attack followed immediately with a mass strike by thirty-six PBYs, which put the Black carrier out of action. Soon afterward, White's battleships caught *Saratoga* and, despite her much greater speed, promptly sank her.

The sides were reorganized for Part V (25–30 March), which postulated that after a major defeat by Blue (Japan), Red (U.S.) had regrouped to defend Hawaii. Blue, under Kalbfus, had most of the fleet, three carriers, nine battleships, and so forth. In contrast, Red had only four cruisers, some two dozen destroyers, fourteen submarines, and about seventy-two PBYs, including those assigned to the 14th Naval District, and, on paper, Army aircraft based in Hawaii. Having learned from his experience in Part II, Blue commander Kalbfus listened to King, who planned a surprise air raid on Pearl Harbor. King directed *Saratoga* to the northwest of Hawaii, and then, running in behind a convenient weather front, the carrier launched an attack very early on 29 March from one hundred miles north of the island, hitting local air bases with devastating effect.[64] While the air attacks were under way, *Saratoga* ran in closer to shore, to facilitate recovery of the aircraft, which was completed by 0835. Quickly refueling and rearming his fighters, King had enough of them airborne in time to beat off a counterattack by PBYs from Oahu, which suffered heavily.[65] This set the stage for successful Blue landings on Oahu.

Part IX (25–28 April), postulated a Purple (Japan) offensive bypassing Hawaii to hit the Green (U.S.) West Coast, at a time when the bulk of Green's fleet was otherwise occupied; although the attacking fleet was larger, the scenario was similar to that of FP XIV, though with decidedly different results. Purple, under Kalbfus, had *Saratoga, Lexington,* and *Ranger,* plus battleships and some surrogate battle cruisers, cruisers, and destroyers. Including surrogates, Green was somewhat stronger in surface combatants and had some submarines, all based primarily at San Pedro and Mare Island, plus fifty-four flying boats on the West Coast and seventy-two in Hawaii, and a constructive "main body" near the southern end of Baja California.

Kalbfus again released the carriers to King for independent operations, and before dawn on 28 April they "raided" Mare Island, and then eluded pursuing Green destroyers, taking little damage. The raid drew the Green battle fleet northward from the San Pedro area, into an ambush by Purple's surface forces, supported by the carriers that had moved south at high speed, bringing the problem to an end.

Twice during FP XIX fast carrier task forces had executed surprise raids on major bases, Pearl Harbor and Mare Island, providing "excellent experience . . . in planning and executing a fast carrier task force attack against shore objectives."[66]

FP XX (20–27 February 1939) assumed that White, a European fascist power, had secured a foothold in the Lesser Antilles, sparking a response from Black (U.S.).[67] The problem was the first to involve four carriers, *Lexington, Ranger, Yorktown,* and *Enterprise.* As a result, while the fleet was concentrating in the Caribbean, Vice Admiral Ernest J. King conducted special maneuvers in the use of large carrier task forces; this was the largest concentration of American carriers to operate together until October 1943.[68]

For the Fleet Problem, Black's Vice Admiral Adolphus Andrews, an aviator, had *Ranger* plus five aircraft tenders as well as several battleships and cruisers, and numerous destroyers, auxiliaries, and a contingent of Marines; White's Admiral Edward C. Kalbfus had *Lexington, Yorktown,* and *Enterprise* plus about the same proportion of surface combatants, as well as numerous submarines, and target ship *Utah,* a surrogate for a troop convoy, with the mission of reinforcing the White foothold in the Lesser Antilles. In the air, White was stronger in attack aircraft, with some 220 carrier planes plus some 48 battleship and cruiser floatplanes, but Black had more aircraft overall—72 carrier planes, nearly 60 floatplanes, 102 PBYs, and 62 land-based Marine aircraft.

Both Admirals made air power the central focus of their plans, each in his own way. Andrews, an aviator, deciding that his objective was the destruction of the

White fleet, held the bulk of his fleet southwest of Puerto Rico, covered by patrol bombers based there, in Haiti, and the Virgin Islands, and formed a cruiser scouting line, backed by *Ranger*, to probe for the enemy planning to bring about a day surface action within range of his carrier and patrol bombers. In contrast, Kalbfus planned to keep out of reach of Black's air force, to concentrate on getting his convoy through, but was willing to use it as "bait" to entice enemy action. He placed the convoy and *Lexington* ahead of his battle fleet, with his second carrier between the battleships and the bait, and his third carrier covering the exposed right flank of the fleet as it advanced into the Caribbean. He reasoned that if Black committed its air power against the convoy, his carriers would be able to protect it, while reducing enemy air resources; and should Black surface forces intervene, his air forces would punish them while he brought up his battleships. Although relatively creative, Kalbfus' plan elicited objections from Vice Admiral Ernest J. King, overall air commander, who wanted to use the carriers more aggressively.

The fleets began feeling for each other on 20 February. Despite rough seas, both sides were able to put floatplanes in the air and began spotting each other's cruiser scouts on the 21st. Since King had instructed his airmen that *Ranger* was their primary target, they obediently refrained from attacking Black's cruisers. As a result, some Black cruisers encountered and began exchanging fire with some of the White convoy's escorts. During this exchange, *Yorktown*'s Air Group, returning after failing to locate *Ranger*, arrived on the scene and all seventy-two aircraft promptly attacked and sank two of the Black cruisers, while the third was dispatched by White surface ships. Meanwhile, *Enterprise* and *Lexington* aircraft spotted other Black scouts, sinking two cruisers and damaging two more. In one afternoon Black had lost half its cruisers sunk or damaged, though White lost thirty-nine aircraft, plus damage to three heavy cruisers.

Overnight on 22–23 February, Kalbfus attempted to destroy Black's reconnaissance assets by nocturnal destroyer raids on enemy aircraft tenders at San Juan, Culebra, and St. Thomas, followed by carrier air strikes at dawn. The attacks had mixed results; two tenders were sunk, for the loss of several of the attacking destroyers. As a result, around dawn on the 23rd, reserving *Yorktown* to cover the main body, Kalbfus released King with *Lexington* and *Enterprise* and some escorts to finish the job. King took this task force eastward around Puerto Rico, to approach his objectives from the north, and on the following morning, assigned *Enterprise* to strike the Black air bases and aircraft tenders, and *Lexington* to search for *Ranger*. To improve the carriers' chances, he switched *Lexington*'s scout bomber squadron with *Enterprise*'s fighter squadron, thereby giving each carrier a rather specialized air group. Before the carriers could complete their missions, however, Black PBYs from Culebra spotted them and, soon joined by PBYs from San Juan and Samana Bay, began a series of attacks against *Enterprise* and *Lexington* that lasted from mid-morning into the late afternoon. Although Black PBY commander, Captain Marc Mitscher, claimed great success, the umpires ruled that *Lexington* had taken only light damage, while his aircraft had lost heavily to anti-aircraft fire. The PBY attacks did, however, delay King's strikes on their tenders for a day. Finally, early on the 25th, *Enterprise* launched her aircraft against Black's air bases and aircraft tenders from a point about 120 miles north of San Juan, which resulted in two aircraft tenders and two oilers being sunk, as well as many aircraft destroyed. During its flight to Samana Bay, *Enterprise's* Torpedo Squadron 6 spotted the Black main body and was immediately ordered to search for *Ranger,* actually about a hundred miles to the north. *Ranger,* however, had by this time located *Enterprise* northwest of Puerto Rico by using an experimental high-frequency direction-finding system. Between 0845 and 1040 *Ranger* aircraft subjected *Enterprise* to a series of bomb and torpedo attacks; lacking fighters, *Enterprise* was sunk. Shortly after this, *Ranger* was spotted by White reconnaissance aircraft, and she took some damage. By the afternoon of the 25th, Black had lost four aircraft tenders and two oilers sunk, plus at least fourteen PBYs destroyed and a further forty-seven damaged with little possibility of repair, while White had lost one carrier and seen another damaged. Late that afternoon, Black PBYs from San Juan (where the elusive fifth Black aircraft tender had just arrived) began two days of attacks against White. Part I was declared over on the 26th, a day earlier than planned due to the enormous "loss" of aircraft by both sides; Black had only forty PBYs operational, with limited facilities to repair or maintain them, plus fifty-seven aircraft on the lightly damaged *Ranger,* while White had eighty-six operational aircraft on its two remaining carriers, *Yorktown* and the damaged *Lexington.* Officially no "winner" was declared, but there was widespread opinion to the effect that White had done well.

The Fleet Problem, although short, demonstrated a high degree of sophistication in carrier operations. Both commanders had handled their air forces rather well, each concentrating his efforts at destroying his enemy's air power before attempting to go after his battle fleet, by making carriers the centerpiece of independent task forces. The problem led to many recommendations. Perhaps the most important criticism, though most neglected, was that Carrier Air Wings lacked sufficient fighters to both defend the ship and escort strike forces; the proposal would languish until well into the Pacific War, with serious consequences. The problem offered further evidence, if any was needed, that horizontal bombers were ineffective against maneuvering warships, in contrast to dive-bombers and torpedo bombers, which proved quite potent. The PBY again won praise for its effectiveness at long-endurance reconnaissance and patrol, though its use as an attack bomber received mixed reviews.

Held in the Pacific, FP XXI (April–May 1940), the last in the series, addressed various aspects of a Pacific war. Two parts were significant for carrier aviation, II and VI, in both of which commanders—even confirmed "Gun Club" members—demonstrated considerable facility in the operation of carrier task forces and also remarkable organizational flexibility. [69]

For Part II (3–5 April), the West Coast was constructively taken to be a chain of atolls, controlled by Black (Japan) to the northeast, with a major base at San Francisco (standing in for the Marshall Islands), while White (U.S.), with its homeland off Central America, controlled Hawaii and San Diego (Guam). Black's Admiral Charles P. Snyder had to effect a rendezvous between a task force returning from a strike on Hawaii, and a covering force based at San Francisco, while White's Vice Admiral William S. Pye, coming up from San Diego, had to try to stop him. Black's raiding force, having lost a carrier during the attack on Hawaii, consisted of cruisers and destroyers, while the covering force had *Yorktown*, with some battleships, cruisers, and destroyers. White had *Lexington* and *Saratoga*, battleships, cruisers, and destroyers, plus patrol bombers based at San Diego.

Beginning the problem at sea about 350 nautical miles southwest of San Diego, White's Pye decided to use his superiority in air power to defeat the Black covering force before it could rendezvous with the raiding force, and formed three task forces, one of *Lexington* and *Saratoga* with four heavy cruisers and four destroyers; the second of light cruisers and destroyers; and the third, a main body of battleships, cruisers, and destroyers.

Black's Snyder, calculating that seasonally foul weather would impede White's air operations, decided to postpone combat as long as possible, to increase the chances of joining his task forces, set their rendezvous for noon on 5 April at a point roughly seven hundred miles southwest of San Francisco, north of the direct route from Hawaii. He planned to keep *Yorktown* fifty to seventy-five miles to the north of his main body, and use her offensively, closing to launch air strikes over the battleships, and then heading back a safe distance upon recovery of her aircraft.

Snyder's plans were disrupted by a streak of bad luck. The weather turned out to be unseasonably good, and shortly after the problem began the umpires informed White that Black's code had been broken. As a result of these strokes of fortune, Vice Admiral Pye's plans unfolded more or less as expected. His reconnaissance aircraft spotted Black's covering force in mid-morning on the 4th, only about two hundred miles east-of-north of his own main body About an hour after noon, *Lexington*'s aircraft began a series of attacks against Black, shortly joined by *Saratoga*'s planes. Black's combat air patrol beat off the initial attacks, but from 1350 to 1458 *Yorktown* suffered 40 percent damage, with her speed cut to sixteen knots, while the battleships averaged 9 percent damage, with fleet speed down to fourteen knots. White's losses in aircraft were heavy, twenty of the forty-six attackers being shot down, which led Pye to protest "unrealistically optimistic assessments of AA fire effectiveness" in his after action report. Toward the end of the air attacks, Black's raiding force came within sighting distance of the White carriers, and there was some exchange of fire before the two groups lost track of each other due to poor visibility and high-speed maneuvering. There followed "a confused night battle" between White destroyers and the Black fleet, raising damage to Black battleships to an average of 30 percent and reducing fleet speed to just nine knots, though over 60 percent of the attacking destroyers were sunk. A bit after dawn on the 5th, *Yorktown* managed to get off her only strike of the maneuvers, but Black's bad luck held; only one *Yorktown* squadron located the White main body, and it did little harm. Later that morning, the White carriers conducted two more strikes on Black, inflicting more damage, though losing thirty-four of the nearly one hundred attacking aircraft. By then, however, Vice Admiral Snyder had managed to interpose his main body between the two Black task forces. With the weather deteriorating, CinCUS James O. Richardson, acting as Chief Umpire, declared this phase of the problem over.

For Part VI (19–23 April 1940), Vice Admiral Adolphus Andrews' Maroon (U.S.) fleet controlled Hawaii, Johnston Island, Midway, the Aleutians, and some other areas, including Balboa, in Panama; Purple (Japan), under Admiral Snyder, having captured Samoa, Guam, and Wake, was preparing to take Hawaii by landings at Lahaina Roads.[70]

Snyder formed a main body around *Saratoga* with battleships, cruisers, and destroyers, escorting a landing force, and a "Raiding Force" of *Lexington,* with a smaller number of battleships, cruisers, and destroyers plus a patrol force of twenty-four PBYs and two aircraft tenders, subordinated to Raiding Force, thus dividing the carriers and tying them the much slower battleships and violating the principle that carriers should operate in fast, autonomous task forces. Oddly, although an aviator, Maroon's Andrews made the same mistake, forming three task forces, a northern group of battleships, cruisers, and destroyers; a southern one of *Yorktown*, battleships, cruisers, and destroyers; and an "Island Force" of a light cruiser, a destroyer, submarines, and thirty-eight PBYs with three aircraft tenders, plus an oiler and mine layers, to secure French Frigate Shoals, Lahaina Roads, and other places in the Hawaiian chain.

Purple began the maneuvers widely dispersed: the main body was about 300 miles south of Midway, the Raiding Force 700 miles south-by-southwest (about 360 miles south of Johnston Island), and the aircraft tenders about 50 miles southwest of French Frigate Shoals. Snyder planned to establish a Purple PBY base at French Frigate Shoals, while using carrier air strikes to deny Maroon the use of Johnston Island for their flying boats. Maroon was also widely dispersed, the northern force nearly 450 miles north of Oahu, as if coming from Dutch Harbor, the southern force about 350 miles directly south of Oahu, and the Island Force had an aircraft tender with some patrol bombers plus several submarines at both Johnston Island and French Frigate Shoals, with the rest of its forces spread through the Hawaiian Islands.

The problem began early on the 19th, in adverse weather. Maroon patrol bombers from French Frigate Shoals and Johnston Island were able to conduct reconnaissance, but Purple's *Saratoga* was unable to put scouts up until about noon, though *Lexington,* hundreds of miles farther south, conducted routine reconnaissance. Purple's Admiral Snyder dispatched small task groups of cruisers, destroyers, and transports from his main body to attack French Frigate Shoals and Johnston Island. Both fleets probed for each other through the 19th and into the 20th. To facilitate this mission, Andrews detached *Yorktown* from his southern group and formed a scouting force with some cruisers and destroyers, demonstrating considerable organizational flexibility. Meanwhile, his patrol bombers from French Frigate Shoals spotted the Purple main body in mid-morning on the 20th, and he ordered his southern force to intercept.

Meanwhile, Johnston had already fallen to Snyder's small task force, sinking a Maroon aircraft tender and two submarines in the process, but the Purple task force assigned to capture French Frigate Shoals was beaten off with heavy losses.

On the evening of the 20th, Snyder dissolved the Purple "Raiding Force," adding the bulk of its ships to the main body, while forming an "Advance Detachment" of *Lexington* and some cruisers and destroyers to scout to 125 miles ahead of the fleet, another demonstration of the fleet's organizational flexibility.

Purple's Advance Detachment had many contacts with Maroon submarines on 21–22 April, sinking several while suffering no harm. On the 22nd, *Lexington*'s aggressive air patrols paid off when at a little over ninety minutes after sunrise they spotted Maroon's *Yorktown* Task Group. *Lexington* launched a series of large strikes, as *Saratoga* closed rapidly with the rest of the main body. *Yorktown* hit back, inflicting 26 percent damage on *Lexington* before being overwhelmed and sunk. With her flight deck ruled damaged beyond repair, *Lexington* "lost" most of her aircraft, "ditched" in the sea. By late afternoon on the 23rd, Purple's main body had come up to support the Advance Detachment, while Maroon's scouting group with *Yorktown* lost, broke off contact, retiring at high speed. Purple was by then less than three hundred miles south-southwest of Lahaina Roads, and *Saratoga*'s scouts were able to hit Maroon patrol bombers at anchor in Pearl Harbor and elsewhere in Hawaii. After dark on the 24th surface forces began clashing in Hawaiian waters and a major battleline action began to develop. Part VI was declared over by CinCUS James O. Richardson at 0330.

Despite the relative ease with which both Snyder and Pye had operated carrier task forces, not all "Gun Club" members were equally comfortable with the notion of autonomous carrier operations. CinCUS Richardson argued that operating *Yorktown* independently had led to her loss, demonstrating "the folly of stationing a carrier where it would not receive maximum protection from the antiaircraft gun resources of the Task Force of which it was part."[71] Richardson was wrong, of course, ignoring both the fact that the instrument of *Yorktown*'s loss was *Lexington*, also operating independently, as well as the experience in Carrier Task Force operations since *Saratoga*'s Panama raid eleven years earlier during FP IX.

CONCLUSIONS

By 1941 the Fleet Problems had contributed to a broad consensus in the Navy as to the value of naval aviation.

- The aircraft carrier had become a partner with the battleship as an arbiter of sea power.
- High-speed, autonomous carrier task forces possessed enormous ability to project naval air power over great distances.
- Aircraft carriers were extraordinarily vulnerable to air attack, mandating a "carrier first" strike doctrine.
- Carriers were extremely vulnerable when in proximity to enemy surface forces.
- Carrier operations demanded extensive logistical support.
- Air search was superior to surface search.
- Dive-bombing was far superior against ships than horizontal bombing.
- Patrol bombers were relatively ineffective as attack aircraft, but excellent for long-range reconnaissance and patrol.
- Ship-borne floatplanes were of limited value for attack or reconnaissance, but highly useful for gunnery spotting.
- Airships were ineffective as fleet scouts.

The Fleet Problems also helped naval aviators and aviation personnel acquire much-needed practical experience. During a Fleet Problem it was not unusual for aviators to double their monthly flight time, from a normal Depression-era 20 to 25 hours to 50 or more. In the ten days of FP XIII (8–18 March 1932), *Lexington* generated 310 sorties for a total of 748 flying hours, while *Saratoga* did 423 sorties for 1,035 hours, aircraft averaging about 2.4 hours per sortie. This high sortie rate not only provided airmen and plane crews with invaluable experience, but also resulted in a more realistic understanding of the maintenance and logistical requirements demanded by a high operating tempo.[72]

Several developments were essential to the success of the autonomous fast Carrier Task Force.

- Large, fast carriers—achieved by 1928, though few in number until 1940
- Task force concept—proposed in 1930
- Radar—experimentally available from 1936

- Underway replenishment—achieved by 1940
- Long-range aircraft—achieved 1940–1941

The Fleet Problems played a major role in the development of these capabilities. As a result, by about 1937, most senior officers in the U.S. Navy disagreed not so much as to *whether* naval aviation—specifically carrier aviation—would probably supplant the battleship, but as to *when* this was likely to take place, conservative thinkers believing it was still some time in the future, while the more optimistic thought it would be soon, if it had not already happened.

Certainly carrier operations during Fleet Problems in 1938–1940 very closely resembled what actually transpired in the Pacific in 1942, when such non-aviators as Frank J. Fletcher, Wilson Brown, and Raymond Spruance turned in often outstanding performances commanding carrier task forces.[73]

NOTES

1. On the Fleet Problems, see my "*To Train the Fleet For War*": *The U.S. Navy Fleet Problems, 1923–1940* (Newport, RI: Naval War College Press, 2010), which looks at the process that underpinned the evolution of the Navy's vision of what a future war would look like; and Craig C. Felker, *Testing American Sea Power: U.S. Navy Strategic Exercises, 1923–1940* (College Station: Texas A&M Press, 2007), on how the problems affected the ways in which specific technological and doctrinal developments (e.g., submarines, amphibious operations, aviation, etc.) were integrated into the Navy's toolbox.

2. The very apt term "naval force" is borrowed from Thomas C. Hone, e-mail, 2 September 2002.

3. Mark Allen Campbell, "The Influence of Air Power Upon the Evolution of Battle Doctrine in the U.S. Navy, 1922–1941" (master's thesis, University of Massachusetts at Boston, 1992), pp. 147–79, provides a very detailed analysis of lessons learned in aviation. This is a work in need of wider circulation.

4. During such an exercise off Cuba in March 1919 *Texas* (BB-35) successfully used a catapulted floatplane to spot for her main battery, leading some officers to conclude that aerial spotting could result in a 200 percent increase in gunnery accuracy; see Thomas C. Hone and Trent Hone, *Battleline: The United States Navy, 1919–1939* (Annapolis: Naval Institute Press, 2006), p. 81.

5. Peter M. Swartz, *Sea Changes: Transforming U.S. Navy Deployment Strategy, 1775–2002* (Alexandria, VA: The CNA Corporation, unpublished study, 2002), p. 39. From 1904 to 1917, major elements of the fleet—including whole battle squadrons—were diverted from peacetime routine to Morocco during the Perdicaris Affair (1904) and Tangier Crisis (1905–6), to address problems in Cuba (1906–9 and 1912), Nicaragua (1912–13), Mexico (1914), and Haiti (1915), and to the Mediterranean during the Balkan Wars (1913–14), while smaller contingents responded to lesser crises on a regular basis, and there were also a half-dozen major transoceanic "show the flag" cruises, of which the "Great White Fleet" (1907–9) was the largest. In contrast, the interwar period saw only two modest diversions of fleet units—in 1924 when the Special Service Force (the Caribbean Squadron), two light cruisers, and a destroyer squadron were diverted from FP II due to tensions with Mexico, and during FP VII (1927) when two light cruisers were diverted to Nicaragua and four to the Far East, during the Chinese government's "Northern Expedition"; and there

was only one major transoceanic cruise, when the fleet visited Australia and New Zealand in 1925.

6. Aviation-rated officers and enlisted personnel increased steadily during the interwar period, even during the years (1924–33) when overall manpower fell, rising from about 2 percent of manpower in the early 1920s to 20.4 percent in 1939.

7. Naval War College Archives (hereafter NWCA), Carton 60, "Report on United States Fleet Problem Number One."

8. Ibid., especially pp. 131–34; and "Admiral Sums Up Canal Maneuvers," *New York Times*, 8 April 1923.

9. NWCA, Carton 60, "Report on United States Fleet Problem Number One," pp. 89–90.

10. Colon is about as far from Culebra as Manila is from Okinawa, some 1,100 miles, so the Caribbean was a good substitute for the China Seas.

11. National Archives and Records Administration, Microfilm Series M964, *Records Relating to United States Navy Fleet Problems I to XXI, 1923–1940* (Washington: NARA, 1975), 36 rolls, M964-3, 1, COMSCOFLT to CINCUS, "Fleet Problem No. 4—History of Operations," p. 7 (NARA Microfilm Series M964 sources are cited hereafter as "M964-X,Y" to indicate roll and target, where appropriate, followed by document title).

12. M964-2, 1, "Talk on Operations of Black Forces Delivered by Vice Admiral McCully, before Conference on Problem No. 3, 21 January 1924," p. 5.

13. NWCA, Carton 61, CINCUS, "Material Effectiveness, Fleet Problems II, III, and IV."

14. Coontz felt so strongly about aviation that he included these recommendations in his *From the Mississippi to the Sea* (Philadelphia: Dorrance, 1930), p. 446.

15. James M. Grimes, *Aviation in the Fleet Exercises, 1911–1939, U.S. Naval Administrative Histories of World War II*. Vol. 16 (Washington: United States Navy, n.d.), pp. 14–15; Thomas Wildenberg, *All the Factors of Victory: Adm. Joseph Mason Reeves and the Origins of Carrier Air Power* (Dulles, VA: Brassey's, 2003), pp. 146–47.

16. M964-8, 1, CINCUS to CNO, 4 May 1927, "U.S. Fleet Problem Seven—Report on," pp. 2–3; Wildenberg, *All the Factors*, pp. 147–48.

17. NWCA, Carton 61, CINCUS, Report of U.S. Fleet Problem Seven (4 May 1927), p. 2.

18. "100 Planes Concentrate to Defend Hawaii in Manoeuvres," *New York Times*, 16 May 1928; "'Attackers' Subdue Oahu in War Games," *New York Times*, 18 May 1928; Norman Polmar, "Bombing Pearl Harbor," *Naval History*, XVI, 3 (June 2002), pp. 14, 16; Wildenberg, *All the Factors*, p. 162.

19. NWCA, Carton 64, White Task Force OpOrd No. 1, Task Organization, 18 May 1928; Wildenberg, *All the Factors*, pp. 162–64.

20. For a good analysis of developments between 1931 and 1934, see Francis Lovell Keith, "United States Navy Task Force Evolution: An Analysis of United States Fleet Problems, 1931–1934" (master's thesis, University of Maryland, 1974), pp. 281ff.

21. More has been written about FP IX than any other. Among the more valuable analyses, comments, and observations are Eugene E. Wilson, "The Navy's First Carrier Task Force," *Proceedings*, February 1950, pp. 163–66; Wildenberg, *All the Factors*, pp. 1–10, 188–91; Grimes, *Aviation in the Fleet Exercises*, pp. 23–53; Gerald E. Wheeler, *Admiral William Veazie Pratt, U.S. Navy: A Sailor's Life* (Washington, DC: Naval History Division, 1974), pp. 268–75. Press coverage was extensive, e.g., Lewis Freeman, "*Saratoga*'s Raid Left Fleet Behind," *New York Times*, 18 February 1929; Lewis Freeman, "Commander's Story of Saratoga's Raid," *New York Times*, 19 February 1929.

22. The "communications relay" aircraft was necessary because, due to their weight, radios were not routinely fitted to all aircraft.

23. M964-12, 1, "United States Fleet Problem IX, 1929, Report of the Commander in Chief, United States Fleet, Admiral H. A. Wiley, U.S.N."

24. Campbell, "The Influence of Air Power," summarizes these, pp. 158–65, 174–75. Even during World War II there were several occasions on which carriers came under enemy surface fire or were within easy steaming distance of enemy surface combatants: the loss of HMS *Glorious*, June 1940; the *"Bismarck* Chase," May 1941; Coral Sea, May 1942; Midway, June 1942; and most famously off Samar, 25 October 1944.

25. M964-23, 1, "United States Fleet Problem X, 1930, Report of the Commander in Chief, United States Fleet, Admiral W. V. Pratt, U.S.N.," pp. 40ff; Grimes, *Aviation in the Fleet Exercises*, p. 62.

26. M964-23, 1, "United States Fleet Problem X, 1930, Report of the Commander in Chief, United States Fleet, Admiral W. V. Pratt, U.S.N.," pp. 59ff includes comments by many officers.

27. M964-13, 7, "United State Fleet Problem XI, 1930, Report of the Commander in Chief, United States Fleet, Admiral W. V. Pratt, U.S.N.," esp. pp. 50–53.

28. For FP XII, see M964-13, 13, "U.S. Fleet Problem XII, 1931, Report of the Commander in Chief, United States Fleet, Admiral J. V. Chase, U.S.N."; NWCA, Carton 62, Comments of Adm. Frank H. Schofield, U.S.N., C-in-C Black Fleet, on Problem XII . . . (2 March 1931); Keith, "United States Navy Task Force Evolution," pp. 22–57; Grimes, *Aviation in the Fleet Exercises*, pp. 81–96. The scenario postulated a notional Nicaraguan Canal as well, though this did not figure much in the way the problem unfolded.

29. *Los Angeles'* role in locating Black on the 18th appears to have been one of only two occasions during any of the fleet maneuvers that an airship did anything useful, the other being during FP XV (1934), when *Macon* (ZRS 5) had a very similar experience. Paolo E. Coletta, "Dirigibles in the U.S. Navy," *New Interpretations in Naval History: Selected Papers from the Tenth Naval History Symposium*, ed. Jack Sweetman et al. (Annapolis: Naval Institute Press, 1993), pp. 213–29, is a concise overview of the use of airships by the fleet.

30. "227 Planes to Fight in Caribbean 'War,'" *New York Times*, 22 March 1931; "Navy Fliers Aloft this Week in Test over Caribbean Sea," *Washington Post*, 22 March 1931; "Says Navy Must Get Small Plane Carriers," *New York Times*, 28 March 1931; "Naval Planes Show Power in War Game," *New York Times*, 29 March 1931; "A Lesson of the War Game," *New York Times*, 30 March 1931.

31. "Says Navy Must Get Small Plane Carriers," *New York Times*, 28 March 1931. On "flying deck cruiser" see Norman Friedman, *U.S. Aircraft Carriers: An Illustrated Design History* (Annapolis: Naval Institute Press, 1983), pp. 89ff.

32. Thomas Fleming, "February 7, 1932—A Date that Would Live in Amnesia," *Kazine* No. 27; Clark G. Reynolds, *On the Warpath in the Pacific: Admiral Jocko Clark and the Fast Carriers* (Annapolis, MD: Naval Institute Press, 2005), pp. 96–99; Wadle, "United States Navy Fleet Problems," pp. 78–84; "Grand Joint Exercise No. 4," *Time*, 15 February 1932; Charles M. Austin, "Victory for 'Blues,'" *New York Times*, 15 February 1932; "Blue Forces Seize Hawaii in Darkness," *Washington Post*, 14 February 1932; "Manoeuvers Close with 'Blue' Ahead," *New York Times*, 14 February 1932; "Joint Exercise Highly Successful," *Washington Post*, 21 February 1932.

33. In an interesting experiment, acting on a suggestion made after FP X (1930), the carriers swapped aircraft, forming two specialized air groups. *Saratoga* ended up with ninety-seven aircraft, mostly fighters, while *Lexington* had only fifty-eight aircraft, mostly bombers and scouts, in the hope that a higher operational tempo might be attained. The experiment was repeated during FP XX (1939), when Ernest J. King swapped *Lexington's*

scout bomber squadron for *Enterprise*'s fighter squadron, but the results were not impressive. In spring 1943, the two Allied carriers in the Pacific, *Saratoga* and HMS *Victorious*, pooled their air groups, both of which consisted of American-built aircraft, the former ending up with seventy-two TBF bombers, but only twelve fighters, and the latter thirty-six fighters but only twelve bombers, which seems to have yielded no useful advantage.

34. M964-14, 1, "U.S. Fleet Problem XIII, Report of the Commander-in-Chief, Admiral Frederick H. Schofield"; Keith, "United States Navy Task Force Evolution," pp. 58–118; Grimes, *Aviation in the Fleet Exercises*, pp. 97–107. Some newspaper accounts are of interest: Charles M. Austin, "Action Off California in March," *New York Times,*16 February 1932; Hanson W. Baldwin, "The Admirals Play Their Game of War," *New York Times*, 13 March 1932; Hanson W. Baldwin, "Fleets, Far at Sea, Play Hide-and-Seek," *New York Times*, 13 March 1932; Hanson W. Baldwin, "Black Planes 'Sink' Carrier Saratoga," *New York Times*, 18 March 1932; Hanson W. Baldwin, "Aviation Triumphant in Naval War Games," *New York Times*, 27 March 1932.

35. Cited in Coletta, "Dirigibles," p. 224.

36. Campbell, "The Influence of Air Power," pp. 133–36, has an excellent analysis of the debate over the revision of the air attack rules.

37. NWCA, Carton 56, L. McNamee, U.S. Fleet Umpire Instructions, 1932: Suggested Changes, and Carton 56, William A. Moffett, Chief, BuAir, p. 2; Naval Historical Collection Box 270, Change # 3, USF 10, 5 October 1934, and Box 270, CINCUS to Holders of USF 10, Change #12, USF 10, 24 January 1938. For *Utah* see R. S. S. Howman-Meedk, Harold Johnson, K. D. McBride, and Christopher C. Wright, "Target Ships," *Warship International*, 2002, No. 1, pp. 24–36.

38. "Honolulu Awaits 'Attack' from Sea," *Washington Post*, 30 January 1933; "Hawaii Guns Await 'Foe' in War Games," *New York Times*, 30 January 1933; "Air Assault Opens Hawaii War Game," *Washington Post*, 1 February 1933.

39. M964-15, 1, United States Fleet, Problem XIV, Report of the Commander-in-Chief, United States Fleet, Admiral R. H. Leigh, 20 April 1933; NWCA, Carton 62, U.S. Fleet Problem XIV, Report of the CINCUS, Adm. R. H. Leigh, 20 May 1933; Keith, "United States Navy Task Force Evolution," pp. 119–86, provides some excellent analysis.

40. NWCA, Carton 62, U.S. Fleet Problem XIV, Report of the CINCUS, Adm. R. H. Leigh, 20 May 1933, Section 4, p. 2.

41. Clark G. Reynolds, *John H. Towers: The Struggle for Naval Air Supremacy* (Annapolis: Naval Institute Press, 1991), pp. 245–47, 268.

42. M964-16, 1, "Report of Fleet Problem XV, CINCUS, 1 June 1934." There is a good analysis in Keith, "United States Navy Task Force Evolution," pp. 187–276, and Grimes, *Aviation in the Fleet Exercises*, pp. 120–42; Harris Laning, *An Admiral's Yarn*, ed. Mark Russell Shulman et al. (Newport, RI: Naval War College Press, 1999), pp. 362–69; Wildenberg, *All the Factors*, pp. 231–35. Press coverage was extensive; e.g., "102 Navy Vessels Open '30-Day War,'" *New York Times*, 11 April 1934; "Submarines Aid in Fleet 'Battle',"" *New York Times*, 12 April 1934; "Fleet Begins Trip Through Panama Canal," *Washington Post*, 22 April 1934; Hanson W. Baldwin, "4 Caribbean Bases Await Fleet War," *New York Times*, 5 May 1934; Hanson W. Baldwin, "Gray Fleet Seizes Culebra Island," *New York Times*, 11 May 1934; Hanson W. Baldwin, "Final 'Battle' Ends Fleet Manoeuvres," *New York Times*, 18 May 1934.

43. "Canal Defenses Trained on Fleet," *New York Times*, 20 April 1934; "Submarines Give Test," *New York Times*, 20 April 1934; "Great Fleet Heads for Canal Attack," *New York Times*, 21 April 1934; "Warships Mass in Pacific," *New York Times*, 21 April 1934; "Battle for Canal results in a Draw," *New York Times*, 20 April 1934.

44. M964-16, 1, Report of Fleet Problem XV, CINCUS, 1 June 1934, pp. 71ff.

45. Ibid., p. 36.

46. Trent Hone, "The Evolution of Fleet Tactical Doctrine in the U.S. Navy, 1922–1941," *The Journal of Military History* 67 (October 2003), pp. 1139–41, has a short analysis of these tactics. Arguably, the most notable occasion on which the U.S. Navy used such tactics was in the desperate Battle off Samar, 25 October 1944.

47. M964-16, 1, Report of Fleet Problem XV, CINCUS, 1 June 1934, p. 54; Grimes, *Aviation in the Fleet Exercises*, pp. 127–28; "Macon Fails in Fleet Test," *Washington Post,* 10 May 1934, p. 1; "Airship Building Will Come to Halt," *New York Times,* 14 February 1935.

48. M964-16, 1, Report of Fleet Problem XV, CINCUS, 1 June 1934, p. 36.

49. Campbell, "The Influence of Air Power," p. 183ff, summarizes the evolving view of the role of the carrier in the fleet.

50. M964-18, 1, Fleet Problem XVI, Report of the Commander-in-Chief, United States Fleet [15 September 1935]; NWCA, Carton 63, Operations of the U.S. Fleet, Fleet Problem Sixteen, Enclosure "V"; U.S. Fleet OpPlan 1–35, Task Organization, 1 March 1935. See also, Grimes, *Aviation in the Fleet Exercises*, pp. 143–50. Harris Laning, then ComBatFor, included some interesting commentary on the problem in his memoirs, *An Admiral's Yarn*, pp. 372ff. The problem was heavily covered by the press, the *New York Times* alone carrying dozens of stories.

51. In addition to the flying boat and its crew of six, lost with all hands, four other aircraft were lost to accidents during the problem, though there was only one additional fatality; Grimes, *Aviation in the Fleet Exercises*, p. 145.

52. Hone, "Evolution of Fleet Tactical Doctrine," pp. 1135–37. Laning does not mention this incident in his memoirs.

53. M964-18, 1, Fleet Problem XVI, Report of the Commander-in-Chief, United States Fleet [15 September 1935], p. 32.

54. Despite extensive surviving documents for this problem, this writer was unable to find either a detailed narrative or anecdotal chronology. See, however, M964-21, 2, CINCUS to CNO, 26 November 1935, "Fleet Problem XVII," with Enclosures; M964-21, 2, CNO to CINCUS, 23 December 1935, "Fleet Problem XVII, Concept of"; M964-21, 6, United States Fleet, Operation Plan No. 3-36, 20 January 1936, "Task Organization"; NWCA, Carton 64, "Fleet Problem Seventeen, Report of CINCUS," 6 June 1936; NWCA, Carton 64, "Critique, Phase II, Fleet Problem Seventeen, United States Fleet," 15 May 1936. Grimes, *Aviation in the Fleet Exercises*, pp. 151–56, has some useful observations. This was the first Fleet Problem for a virtual complete ban was imposed on the press, so tight that even honors to Neptunus Rex were not reported until months later; see Hanson W. Baldwin, "Navy Sails Far South in Secret War Games," *New York Times,* 24 May 1936; Windsor Booth, "Roosevelt's Crossing of Equator Recalls Mass Polliwog Initiation at Fleet Maneuvers," *Washington Post,* 29 November 1936.

55. M964-21, 6, Black Fleet Operation Order No. 5-36, 13 May 1936; M964-21, 6, Black Fleet Carrier Group OpOrd 236 (14 May 1936). Unfortunately, no similar document was found for Brown. See also Paolo E. Coletta, *Patrick N. L. Bellinger and U.S. Naval Aviation* (Lanham, MD: University Press of America, 1987), pp. 189–93.

56. M964-21, 6, Black Fleet Operation Order No. 5-36, 13 May 1936, p. 2. Although lack of documentation makes it difficult to determine Brown's organization and plans, these appear to have been quite similar to those adopted by Black based on occasional comments in NWCA, Carton 64, Fleet Problem Seventeen, Report of CINCUS, 6 June 1936.

57. Shortly after Fleet Problem XVII, *Langley* was taken in hand for conversion to an aircraft tender, to free tonnage for the construction of newer carriers, leaving the fleet with only three carriers until *Yorktown* (CV-5) entered service in late 1937.

58. NWCA, Carton 64, CINCUS to Fleet, U.S. Fleet OpOrd No. 7-37 (1 May 1937); M964-22, 3, Commander Battle Force (Commander Black Fleet) to CINCUS, 11 May 1937, "FPXVIII—Narrative of Events and Track Chart"; M964-23, 1, Commander Scouting Force (Commander White Fleet) to CINCUS, 10 May 1937, "Fleet Problem XVIII, Narrative of Events"; M964-23, 1, Commander Aircraft, Battle Force, to CINCUS, 4 June 1937, "Comments and Recommendations—Fleet Problem XVIII." See also, Reynolds, *On the Warpath*, pp. 121ff. Press coverage was restricted, but some useful stories did appear: "Air and Sea Drive Besets Honolulu," *New York Times*, 25 April 1937; "Fleet Attacking Oahu In Pacific War Game," *Washington Post*, 26 April 1937; "Fleet 'Attack' Ends, Ships at Honolulu, *New York Times*, 26 April 1937. For the problem, the entire geography of the Pacific was notionally rearranged; White's homeland was in the Aleutians, the Alaska Peninsula, and Kodiak Island, while Black lay somewhere in the southwestern Pacific, and Hawaii and Johnston Island were stand-ins for Micronesia.

59. M964-23, 1, Commander Aircraft, Battle Force, to CINCUS, 4 June 1937, "Comments and Recommendations—Fleet Problem XVIII," p. 7.

60. M964-23, 1, Commander Battle Force (Commander Black Fleet, Fleet Problem XVIII), to CINCUS, 23 June 1937, "Comments and Recommendations on Fleet Problem XVII," pp. 7–11, 18–19.

61. Joseph J. "Jocko" Clark, Capt., USN. "Comments and Recommendations–Fleet Problem XVIII," M964-23, 1, Commander Aircraft, Battle Force, to CINCUS, 4 June 1937, p. 65.

62. Reynolds, *John H. Towers*, p. 272. If true, this suggests that Horne's available final report, M964-23, 1, Commander Aircraft, Battle Force, to CINCUS, 4 June 1937, "Comments and Recommendations—Fleet Problem XVIII," is a much toned-down document.

63. M964-24, 1, United States Fleet, 3 January 1938, Operation Order No. 3-38, Task Organization, with annexes; NWCA, Carton 65, U.S. Fleet, General Instructions and Information (12 January 1938), and U.S. Fleet OpPlan 3-38 (6 January 1938), with annexes.

64. Captain John Towers commanded *Saratoga*, the first of the Navy's pioneer airmen to command a carrier, having earned his wings in 1911. *Lexington* did not take part because food poisoning had incapacitated 450 of her crew. For a brief treatment, see "*Lexington*, CV-2, March 29, 1938, Hawaiian Flu Felled 450 Sailors," *Carrier Capsules* 151 (31 March 2000), www.carriersg.org/151.htm.

65. Very tight security resulted in King's "surprise attack" on Pearl Harbor receiving no press coverage at the time, but word eventually leaked out; see Lieutenant Stephen Jurika Jr., "Pilots, Man Your Planes," *The Saturday Evening Post*, 7 January 1939, pp. 33ff.

66. Grimes, *Aviation in the Fleet Exercises*, p. 184.

67. M964-25, 1, CNO to CINCUS, n.d., "Fleet Problem XX—Concept of"; NWCA, Carton 65, U.S. Fleet OpOrd No. 13-38 (4 November 1938), Task Organization; M964-25, 4, U.S. Fleet Operation Order 3 November 1938; E. C. Kalbfus, "Fleet Problem XX: White Fleet Estimate of the Situation"; Black Fleet, "Fleet Problem XX Estimate of the Situation," 18 January 1939; Commander Battle Force to CINCUS, 20 March 1939, Critique Fleet Problem XX—Remarks of Commander WHITE Fleet; Commander, Black Fleet (Commander, Scouting Force) to CINCUS, Fleet Problem XX—Comment and Recommendation. Patrick Abbazia, *Mr. Roosevelt's Navy: The Private War of the U.S. Atlantic Fleet, 1939–1942* (Annapolis: Naval Institute Press, 1975), pp. 33–50, has an excellent treatment. The scenario assumed that a coup in Green (notionally comprising north-

ern Brazil, the Guianas, half of Venezuela, and most of the Lesser Antilles) had secured Italo-German support. It reflected the events of the Spanish Civil War and was hardly fanciful, given pro-fascist movements in several Latin American countries. A commentator in *Time* flatly stated that the problem was intended to "remind Europe's fascists that the U.S. is still a major power in the Atlantic," see "Fleet Problem XX," *Time*, 9 January 1939.

68. *Saratoga* remained in the Pacific with a small task force showing the flag and conducting exercises in underway replenishment. As carriers required about two years to become fully operational, *Yorktown* (CV-5) and *Enterprise* (CV-6), commissioned in September 1937 and May 1938, respectively, were limited to operating aircraft in good weather during daylight hours only. Minoru Genda later claimed that watching a newsreel of the four American carriers operating together during King's maneuvers led him to propose creation of the "First Air Fleet," which opened the Pacific War for Japan in spectacular fashion. See Minoru Genda, "Evolution of Aircraft Carrier Tactics in the Imperial Japanese Navy," *Air Raid: Pearl Harbor! Recollections of a Day of Infamy*, ed. Paul Stillwell (Annapolis: Naval Institute Press, 1981), p. 24. In October 1943 three fleet carriers and three light carriers conducted a series of raids on Wake Island.

69. M964-32, 1, United States Fleet, 16 February 1940, Change No. 1 to U.S. Fleet Operation Order No. 2-40; NWCA, Carton 66, U.S. Fleet OpOrd 2-40, Task Organization, 15 January 1940, with Annex B, "General Plan for Fleet Problem XXI and Annual Fleet Exercises, 1 April–17 May 1940." Of particular interest is James O. Richardson, *On the Treadmill to Pearl Harbor: The Memoirs of Admiral James O. Richardson, U.S.N. (Ret.)*, as told to George C. Dyer (Washington, DC: Naval History Division, 1973), pp. 236–50, the only published critique of a problem by a CinCUS. See also, John F. Wukovits, *Devotion to Duty: A Biography of Admiral Clifton A. F. Sprague* (Annapolis: Naval Institute Press, 1995), pp. 49–56.

70. M964-33, 4, COMSCOFOR (Commander Maroon Fleet), to CINCUS, "Maroon Report of Part VI, Fleet Problem XXI," with COMSCOFOR to CINCUS, 26 April 1940, "Fleet Problem XXI, Part VI, Narrative," attached; M964-35, 1, COMBATFOR to CINCUS, 15 May 1940, "Part VI, Fleet Problem XXI—Report of Commander Purple Fleet."

71. Richardson, *Treadmill*, p. 246. Campbell, "The Influence of Air Power," pp. 177–79.

72. M964-14, 1, "U.S. Fleet Problem XIII, Report of the Commander-in-Chief, Adm. Frederick H. Schofield," pp. 16, 32. The higher operating tempo was particularly important during the years of Depression budgets (FYs 1930–1933), when flying hours appear to have fallen as low as fifteen a month; for some comment, see Steve Ewing, *Thach Weave: The Life of Jimmie Thach* (Annapolis: Naval Institute Press, 2004), pp. 15ff.

73. Two of these officers have good biographies: Thomas B. Buell, *The Quiet Warrior: A Biography of Admiral Raymond A. Spruance* (Boston: Little, Brown, 1974); and John B. Lundstrom, *Black Shoe Carrier Admiral: Frank Jack Fletcher at Coral Sea, Midway, and Guadalcanal* (Annapolis: Naval Institute Press, 2006). But Wilson Brown, and most of the other officers mentioned in this essay, still await one.

CHAPTER 8

The Two-Ocean Navy Act of 1940: The Impact on American Preparedness for World War II

Timothy H. Jackson and Stanley D. M. Carpenter

Commander of the Asiatic Fleet, Rear Admiral William F. Fullam, observing a display of naval aviation on Armistice Day, 11 November 1918, stated: "They came in waves, until they stretched almost from horizon to horizon, row upon row of these flying machines. What chance, I thought, would any ship, any fleet have against an aggregate such as this? You could shoot them from the skies like passenger pigeons, and still there would be more than enough to sink you. Now I loved the battleship, devoted my whole career to it, but at that moment I knew the battleship was through."[1]

Common perception has long held that the advocates of the large, dreadnought, big-gun capital ship actively frustrated and obfuscated aircraft carrier and general naval aviation development in the interwar period. While the battleship advocates, especially those associated with the Bureau of Naval Ordnance (aka the "Gun Club") refused to view the aircraft carrier as the key capital ship of the future, many primary players of the period nevertheless did not discourage the development of naval aviation. Rather, most battleship advocates viewed the carrier as an adjunct to the battle line, performing fleet support roles such as scouting, reconnaissance, and gunfire spotting. Key leaders such as Rear Admiral William A. Moffett, Chief of the Bureau of Aeronautics (BuAer) from 1921 until his untimely death in an airship accident in 1933, pushed naval aviation development with great vigor and positive results. In Congress, naval aviation advocates such as Representative Carl Vinson (D-GA), formed a corps of powerful advocates who ensured that the legislative and budgetary process supported naval aviation through the fiscally challenging 1930s. The ultimate expression of naval expansion following the lean interwar years, as characterized by ship and personnel drawdowns in accordance with naval armament treaties (1922 and 1930), came in the summer of 1940 with the two-ocean naval legislation (Vinson-Walsh Act). That legislation, the result of which was the massive United States Navy of World War II, will be examined in light of the impact on the evolution and development of naval aviation that rapidly replaced the battleship as the ultimate capital ship in the immediate post–Pearl Harbor era.

Left to right: *Representative Carl Vinson (D-GA); Secretary of Navy Francis P. Matthews; Admiral Louis E. Denfeld, Chief of Naval Operations; and Admiral Arthur W. Radford, Commander, Pacific Fleet, 6 October 1949.*

While many directions might be taken, this chapter examines three essential topics. Part I addresses the contextual background to the evolution of aircraft carriers and naval aviation in the interwar period of 1919–1939. Part II examines the legislative process, particularly the actions of Representative Vinson, the major political champion of naval expansion and aviation. Finally, part III looks at the results of the 1940 legislation in practical terms and how it put to sea the fleet of 1943–1945 that won the war in the Pacific and ensured Allied domination of the Atlantic against the

German Kriegsmarine. While other ship types resulting from the 1940 legislation will be mentioned, this chapter focuses on aircraft carriers and naval aviation.

PART I—THE INTERWAR CONTEXT: CARRIERS IN THE WINGS

In the interwar period, several prominent admirals and decision makers publicly stated the importance of naval aviation to fleet operations. While not yet proclaiming aviation as the essential core of the fleet supplanting the battleship, many senior officers nonetheless captured the essence of the new aviation thinking. Two examples illustrate this dynamic. In 1933, British Royal Navy First Sea Lord Admiral of the Fleet Alfred Chatfield commented: "The air side is an integral part of our naval operation . . . not something which is added on like the submarine, but something which is an integral part of the navy itself, closely woven into the naval fabric. Whether our air weapon is present or not will make the whole difference to the nature of the fighting of the fleet and our strategical dispositions. That is a fact which will increase more and more, year by year."[2]

Of great importance to the acceptance of Navy aviation in the United States was the attitude of Admiral William S. Sims. Sims had commanded U.S. naval forces in Europe during World War I and had a keen appreciation of naval aviation as pioneered by the Royal Navy. As President of the Naval War College in Newport, Rhode Island, from 1919 to 1922, he encouraged war game simulations to validate the concept of aviation not only as a fleet support adjunct, but also as an offensive weapon. Sims argued against the "unreasoning effect of deadly conservatism" on the part of those senior officers unable or unwilling to recognize naval aviation's potential.[3] In testimony before Congress in 1925, the Admiral, then retired, concluded decisively that the fast carrier was the capital ship of the future and that it carried far more offensive capability than a battleship.[4] With a supporter of Sims' stature, naval aviation could only prosper in the long haul.

In truth, few top officials argued against naval aviation. Rather, it was the role played by aircraft that generated controversy. Immediately following World War I, even later aviation advocates doubted that aircraft carriers would ever play more than a supporting role in fleet operations. Then-Commander John H. Towers, Naval Aviator #3 and eventual Commander in Chief, Pacific Fleet, testified to the Navy General Board in 1919 that he doubted that aircraft operating from an airplane carrier would "last very long."[5] Despite doubts about the utility of shipboard-based aircraft, the General Board reported to Secretary of the Navy Josephus Daniels that the United States should ensure air supremacy or at least meet on equal terms any potential adversary. Not only did the General Board assert that aviation had become an "essential arm of the fleet," but that "fleet aviation must be developed to the fullest extent."[6] The real argument in those days of limited defense budgets was not over whether the airplane was needed, rather it was over aviation's role as an adjunct for fleet support or as an offensive weapon based on its own lethality. Indicative of Navy aviation's rise to prominence was the creation of the Bureau of Aeronautics in August 1921 under Rear Admiral Moffett. Answering only to the Secretary of the Navy (as was common to all Navy bureaus), the creation helped insulate early aviation from those officers most adamantly opposed to Navy air power.

Technology and geography also played a role in the evolution of carrier-based aviation. Various techniques for launching and recovering aircraft from a deck underway had been conducted by the Royal Navy during World War I; however, due to the creation of an independent air arm with the establishment of the Royal Air Force in April 1918, British navy aviation lost momentum and control of its own destiny. Thus, by the mid-1920s, the U.S. Navy surged ahead of Britain in carrier development. The modification of the collier *Jupiter* into the USS *Langley* (CV-1) by 1922 provided the platform for testing and perfecting carrier operations, including tail hooks for landing traps. Eventually, wheeled aircraft replaced floats in frontline aircraft. By the time the first operational fleet carriers arrived in 1927 (*Saratoga* and *Lexington*), technology and doctrinal changes had moved the aircraft carrier into an offensive rather than simply a fleet support mode.

By the 1920s, Navy planners assumed that a maritime conflict with Japan in the Pacific loomed inevitable and that Navy aviation would play a great part in supporting fleet operations, both as support for the battle line (reconnaissance, scouting, and gunfire spotting) and in actual offensive operations. Fleet battle problems using carriers in an offensive role showed the potential for carrier-delivered air raid operations. In the 1930s, the Navy perfected effective dive-bombing techniques, making the airplane a potentially deadly weapons system even against maneuvering vessels. And the Navy realized that forward naval operations in the Western Pacific against Imperial Japan far from land-based stations such as the Hawaiian Islands (assuming the initial loss of the Philippine Islands) could only be conducted with robust air support; only dedicated carriers could transport, support, launch, and recover aircraft on a routine, sustained basis. Geography thus aided in the evolution of pro-aviation thinking, technology, and—gradually—war-fighting doctrine.

Another milestone in Navy aviation development occurred in 1925 with the Morrow Report. Appointed in 1925 by President Calvin Coolidge as a study group composed of nine members drawn from Congress, the Army, the Navy, and the private aviation industry to examine both military and commercial aviation policy, the Morrow Board conducted four weeks of hearings, interviewed almost a hundred expert witnesses, including the Secretaries of War, Navy and Commerce as well as representatives of the fledgling aircraft industry. Headed by Dwight Morrow, the recommendations of the board set the standards for Navy aviation for decades and led to critical congressional legislation in 1926. Among the most far-reaching results were the creation of the Office of Assistant Secretary of the Navy (Aeronautics) and the requirement that all commanding officers of aircraft carriers, seaplane tenders, and naval air stations must be qualified naval aviators. While the Assistant Secretary position was eventually left vacant by the 1930s, the command requirement ensured a career track for Navy aviators that appealed to those interested in professional progression and major command opportunities.[7]

The board advocated that a "strong air force was vital to national security and there must be a strong private industry and long-term continuing program of procurement which was essential to the creation of adequate engineering staffs and the acceleration of new developments." In this regard, the board concluded that the private aircraft industry represented a vital component of national defense and that "government competition with civil industry should be eliminated."[8] In other words, the government appropriated the funds and specified the technical objectives and requirements for military aircraft, but the private sector executed the design and manufacture of military aircraft. It is important to note that a key board member was the young congressman from Georgia, Carl Vinson.

PART II—THE LEGISLATIVE IMPERATIVE

With the changes in the international climate by the early 1930s and the presidency of Franklin D. Roosevelt, a former Assistant Secretary of the Navy and ardent Navy supporter, carrier aviation accelerated. The political will for naval expansion had finally returned after fifteen years in hibernation. Representative Vinson, who became Chairman of the House Naval Affairs Committee with the Democrats taking the majority in 1931, immediately set about the legislative process. Vinson served in the House of Representatives for fifty years, much of which as Chairman of the House Naval Affairs Committee and later Armed Services Committee. From the Service side, the new Commander in Chief, US Fleet (CinCUS) Admiral Joseph Mason Reeves, a qualified naval observer, encouraged Navy aviation, thus setting the stage for the necessary legislative, budgetary, and senior leadership support required for dramatic aviation expansion.

Beginning in December 1931, Vinson met with various Republican and Democratic lawmakers as well as Secretary of the Navy Charles Francis Adams, to lay the legislative foundations for accelerated naval shipbuilding.[9] Funded by the National Industrial Recovery Act (NRA) of 1933, USS *Yorktown* (CV-5) and USS *Enterprise* (CV-6), both laid down in 1934 and commissioned in 1937 and 1938, respectively, formed the backbone of carrier forces in the early months of the coming Pacific War.[10] In January 1934, flush with the first funding success for fleet modernization and capital ship construction, Vinson announced that he intended to push for millions of dollars in additional public works funds in the 1935–1936 fiscal years.[11] From the start of the Roosevelt administration, Vinson championed naval rearmament. While others dithered and hoped for peace in the world through disarmament, treaties, and downsizing, Vinson understood the dangers of military unpreparedness and more importantly, the effort, funding, and lead time required to ensure preparedness. Just after the 1932 election that swept the Democrats back into the White House and into the congressional majority, Vinson began his crusade for rearmament, stating, for example, that "our national defense in time of peace is allowed to decline and to grow weak, and when war comes, as unhappily it does, billions of dollars are poured out in the vain effort to build up our Navy and to create an Army to meet an emergency that we find upon us. Again and again we must be taught that soldiers cannot be made in a day and that it takes years to create ships."[12]

In conjunction with Senator Park Trammell of Massachusetts, Chairman of the Senate Naval Affairs Committee, Vinson achieved the next great legislative success in 1934—the Vinson-Trammell Act. Objections to the bill emanated from two quarters: those who saw the bill as unnecessary government spending in the midst of the Great Depression and isolationists. Vinson argued that the stimulus aided economic recovery, especially in hard-hit industrial areas such as steel and shipbuilding. Additionally, he pointed out that the United States had not even built up the Navy to the treaty limitation displacement tonnages imposed by the 1922 Washington and 1930 London naval agreements. Thus, American national security relative to the two potential maritime adversaries—Great Britain and Japan—suffered serious deficiencies.[13] He won the argument. The bill passed, authorizing over $5 million for new ship construction to bring the Navy up to treaty strength with over 100 new warships and over 1,200 aircraft.[14] However, the bill did not actually appropriate any specific money; rather, it authorized funding for future appropriations. Despite the political opposition, President Roosevelt signed the bill on 28 March 1934. Navy aviation, which had expanded little in the interwar years with only three operational carriers, benefited greatly from the legislation, prompting Admiral Jonas Ingram to comment that the legislation represented a seminal event "looking toward the continued operating efficiency and future expansion of naval aviation."[15] In truth, the Vinson-Trammel Act broke the logjam of dithering, complacency, and calculated inattention to Navy aviation that characterized the first decade and a half of the interwar period. As the treaty limitations expired at the end of 1936, the United States now clearly had set a new course in naval rearmament. The authorizations and appropriations of the 1930s based on Vinson's efforts set the stage for the 1940 Two-Ocean Navy Act and the dramatic expansion of U.S. naval forces.

By the late 1930s, events in Europe and Asia took an ominous direction. With the refusal of key nations to continue naval arms limits, even the appropriations resulting from the 1934 Act seemed inadequate for national security. New Chief of Naval Operations Admiral William D. Leahy recommended an authorization to

exceed the limits of the earlier Vinson-Trammel Act.[16] Congress responded positively. For example, legislation in 1935 authorized commissioning six hundred
new Naval Reserve pilots.[17] Thus, the foundations of the 1940 Act were laid. In the
interim, however, incremental authorizations and appropriations boosted Navy
shipbuilding. On 3 March 1938, the Naval Affairs Committee recommended a massive increase in the building program even beyond Roosevelt's recommendations.
The appropriation passed the House of Representatives as H.R. 9218 by a vote of
294 to 100 and on 17 May 1938, the president signed what came to be called the
"2nd Vinson Act." The result—a 20 percent expansion of the fleet beyond the projected treaty size of just two years earlier and the authorization for acquisition or
construction of Navy aircraft up to three thousand airframes.[18] While isolationists
railed against the increased appropriations, the argument that defending the United
States well out to sea versus at the shoreline won the day. Indications that Japan had
almost 300,000 displacement tons of new naval vessels already under construction
certainly charged the debate in favor of naval expansion. As in the heady days of
U.S. naval expansion forty years earlier, the influence of Rear Admiral Alfred Thayer
Mahan's admonition that national security lay in decisive battle for command of the
sea through great battle fleets overwhelmed arguments for isolationism or govern-
mental economy.[19]

The 1939 naval appropriation bill included the laying down of two new battleships of the *South Dakota* class. Within a week of signing the 1939 appropriation, still
based on the original 1934 authorization, President Roosevelt recommended constructing an additional two battleships.[20] For the future of Navy aviation, the president called for two additional aircraft carriers, which would become USS *Hornet*
(CV-8, third ship of the *Yorktown* class that reached the fleet in 1941), and ultimately, the main fleet carrier–class leader of the last two years of the war, USS *Essex*
(CV-9). Eventually, twenty-six *Essex*-class carriers were ordered and twenty-four
completed.[21] Additionally, the 20 percent increase appropriated funds for 950 more
aircraft. The USS *Wasp* (CV-7) and USS *Ranger* (CV-4), both launched in the 1930s
and smaller designs than the *Yorktown* class, rounded out the carriers as war erupted
in the Pacific. The need for shore air facilities drove further congressional legislation
in 1939, resulting in an appropriation for naval aviation facilities at Kaneohe and
Pearl Harbor, Hawaii; Midway Islands; Wake, Johnston, and Palmyra Islands in the
Central Pacific; Kodiak and Sitka, Alaska; San Juan, Puerto Rico; Pensacola, Florida;
Norfolk, Virginia; Quonset Point, Rhode Island; and Tongue Point, Oregon.[22]

Disregarding objections from many prominent legislators, in March 1940,
Vinson set the stage for the most critical of all the Vinson bills, the Two-Ocean Navy
Act in June. He announced as early as November 1939 that he intended to propose
mammoth Navy authorization legislation in 1940 calling for three additional carriers as well as other ship types and to allow for long-term, low-interest government

loans to aid shipbuilders. Additionally, Vinson's proposed legislation sought to lift the requirement that a minimum of half of all construction must occur in government yards such as the Philadelphia Navy Yard, Brooklyn Navy Yard, Norfolk Navy Yard, Puget Sound Navy Yard, and so forth, and grant the Navy Department authorization to award noncompetitive bid contracts. Beginning in January 1940, Vinson's Naval Affairs Committee conducted hearings on H.R. 8026, known as the Vinson Naval Expansion Act of 1940. Arguing that Japan had embarked on a massive carrier-building program beginning in March, he shepherded through Congress an additional appropriation for three new carriers as part of a two-year authorization program leading to an 11 percent fleet expansion.[23] The bill passed the House by a striking 305 to 37 vote. With quick Senate passage, the law became effective on 14 June 1940. The carriers USS *Yorktown* (CV-10) (formerly *Bon Homme Richard*), USS *Intrepid* (CV-11), and USS *Hornet* (CV-12) (formerly USS *Kearsarge*) resulted from the legislation; CNO Directive of 20 May 1940 initiated the contracting process.

Vinson had many allies in the Navy for his expansive proposals, especially for naval aviation. As BuAer Chief beginning in 1939, Rear Admiral John Towers had an immense impact on the shape of the new Vinson Navy particularly in providing the professional expertise required to shape the legislation. Vinson frequently consulted Towers on aviation matters. Towers had direct access to the president, Chief of the Army Air Corps, and the senior executives of the aircraft industry, thus he played a pivotal role in the events of March to June 1940 in terms of ship and aircraft acquisition. The Chairman of the Naval Affairs Committee frequently tasked the admiral to draft the legislation for fleet expansion even though that task lay clearly beyond the scope of his authority and responsibilities at BuAer. The crucial day of deliberations between Towers, Vinson, and members of the committee, 22 May 1940, shaped the course of legislative events into June as Vinson pushed his agenda through Congress with great alacrity. The noted naval air historian, Clark G. Reynolds, asserts that "it is no exaggeration to say that more was done toward creating the modern air-centered wartime and postwar U.S. Navy on the twenty-second of May 1940 than had been in years of struggling by BuAer and the fleet's aviators, Towers foremost among them." In short, the process that led to the Two-Ocean legislation in June 1940 represented a symbiosis of professional and legislative leaders of incredible energy, expertise, and influence at a critical moment in the evolution of U.S. Navy air power.[24]

Thus, on the eve of the Battle of France in May–June 1940, the various appropriations came to a total of five new aircraft carriers. But, illustrating the continued dominance of the battleship as the main capital ship type, the same legislation called for twenty-one new dreadnoughts. By 1940, however, only the two *North Carolina*–class battleships had been launched, with all other existing battleships rapidly nearing the end of usable service life. However, the fleet had in commission five carriers of relative youth, though of more or less capability. A far-sighted observer in spring

1940, aware of the Japanese carrier-building program, might easily conclude that the ascendancy of the aircraft carrier and power projection through the air was at hand.

On 19 May 1940, the headline in the *Washington Post* announced the German capture of Antwerp, Belgium, one of Europe's busiest ports.[25] With the collapse and surrender of France and evacuation of the British Expeditionary Force from Dunkirk, it became clear that the United States' future security relied upon an immediate and profound armed forces expansion. In a classified memorandum dated 22 May 1940, Major Matthew B. Ridgeway, future United Nations commander in Korea, analyzed in stark language the dangerous security situation facing the country: "It is not practicable to send forces to the Far East, to Europe, and to South America all at once, nor can we do so to a combination of any two of these areas without dangerous dispersion of force . . . we cannot conduct major operations either in the Far East or in Europe due . . . to a lack of means at present." Copies of the memorandum went to the president, the Chief of Naval Operations, the Secretary of the Navy, and to the Chief of Staff of the Army who expressed his "complete agreement with every word of it," according to an annotation added 23 May 1940 as a NOTE FOR RECORD.[26] The fall of France and the realization that the United States lacked the means and resources to fight a multi-front war against the fascist powers jolted Congress and the administration into action, with Vinson leading the charge.

On 2 May, Vinson introduced a bill calling for increasing Navy aircraft from 3,000 to 10,000 air frames and pilots from 2,602 to 16,000 along with the required training facilities as well as a further 11 percent increase in hulls, which included an additional carrier.[27] In early June, he ramrodded the bill through Congress (known as the 3rd Vinson Act).[28] Events moved swiftly as German *Wehrmacht* panzers charged across a hapless France; the new Navy authorization became law on 14 June, the day following the fall of Paris.[29]

After the success of the June bill, the new CNO, Admiral Harold Stark, testified before Vinson's committee that the Navy required a 70 percent increase in fleet assets to meet the two-ocean challenge. In dramatic but understated fashion, the chairman asked the CNO: "In view of world conditions, you regard this expansion as necessary?" Stark responded directly and crisply: "I do, Sir, emphatically."[30] Vinson upped the ante with an increase of a previous proposal for a $1.2 billion authorization to an over $4 billion bill to meet the 70 percent expansion goal. Although it bore the name of Senator David I. Walsh (D-MA), Chairman of the Senate Naval Affairs Committee, the key instigator of what came to be called the Vinson-Walsh Act or Two-Ocean Naval Expansion Act was the Georgia congressman. Recognizing that the threat lay in two seaward directions, the bill proposed a massive naval building program that allowed the United States to fight a two-ocean maritime struggle against Germany and Italy in the Atlantic and Japan in the Pacific. Admiral Mahan had argued for a concentration of forces. The Two-Ocean Navy Act sought to create such an overwhelming force that the U.S. Navy could bring to bear Mahan's concept of decisive concentration in both theaters simultaneously—a bold move. Admiral Stark, at an executive session of the Naval Affairs Committee, argued for 439,000 tons of new construction, but Representative Vinson pushed the amount further to 1,250,000 tons. The proposed bill grew larger by the hour. The committee added a further 75,000 tons for additional aircraft carriers, patrol boats, shipbuilding facilities, and improvements to the factories and foundries that manufactured armor plate and naval artillery. The committee unanimously approved the bill and it moved quickly to the House floor. The Vinson-Walsh Act (H.R. 10100) passed with only two hours of debate in the House of Representatives on 22 June and an hour in the Senate on 11 July without a single "nay" vote.[31] On 22 June, the government of France signed an armistice amounting to a complete capitulation to Hitler's Germany, underscoring the dramatic change in U.S. security needs.

H.R. 10100 provided for 385,000 tons in new battleship construction, but only 200,000 tons in aircraft carriers. But, in the post–Pearl Harbor environment, as it became obvious that the maritime struggle in the Pacific would be an airman's war, the battleship appropriation over time transferred to carrier construction. A single-line memorandum from Navy Budget Officer Captain E. G. Allen, of 20 July 1940 to all Navy bureaus and offices, the Navy Department, and Headquarters, U.S. Marine Corps, announced in dry and understated comment the most overarching and dramatic expansion of the United States Navy in history. Captain Allen simply stated that "Bill H.R. 10100 (the 70 percent Naval Expansion Bill) was approved by the President on 19 July 1940."[32] The impact of that statement on the Navy, the United States, and the world's future would be dramatic. On the 30th, Admiral Stark advised the Secretary of the Navy that based on a meeting on the evening of 25 July with the president, negotiations for contracts for two battleships, six large-gun heavy cruisers, ten light cruisers, and three fleet carriers of the *Essex* class could begin. Interestingly, the remaining five battleships included in the 70 percent bill were "not cleared and no contracts are to be negotiated for them."[33] The statement could be interpreted as indicating that as early as a year and a half prior to Pearl Harbor, the Navy realized that the carrier had arrived as the primary fleet capital ship. However, despite the advancements in aviation and carrier technology as pioneered in the interwar period, most senior officers in 1940 still viewed the airplane as an adjunct to the battleship. Pearl Harbor would change all of that.

PART III—THE NEW VINSON NAVY

Based on the legislation from early June (11 percent expansion) and H.R. 9822, which streamlined the contracting process, the Navy proceeded without hesitation to order new construction at the beginning of July. Within two hours of the president signing the legislation, the Navy Department let contracts for forty-five warships.[34] Pursuant to the Two-Ocean Navy Act, the Navy contracted for seven additional carriers, all of which eventually reached the fleet for war service in the Pacific.[35] Construction numbers starkly illustrate the power of the naval appropriations legislation. By early September 1940, American shipyards had 201 naval vessels under construction.[36] In January 1941, multiple shipyards had under construction 17 battleships, 12 carriers, 54 cruisers, 80 submarines, and 205 destroyers.[37] Despite this rapid increase in ship-building activity, Navy leaders worried that the potential Axis threat could not be met based on the established two-ocean timetable. Then Commander of the Atlantic Fleet Admiral Ernest J. King, in a 30 July 1941 letter to the Navy Board chairman pointed out that while *Hornet* was due to be completed by the end of 1941, follow-on CVs would not be commissioned until early 1944 based on the thirty-six-month construction cycle. King further and forcefully advised that the "current sched-uled rate [of construction] is wholly inadequate and requires to be expedited . . . [and] considering the accelerating importance of air power, the conversion of suit-able and available ships to carriers should be undertaken at once."[38] Not only did American shipyards respond with an expedited schedule, but accelerated hull con-version programs spurred further acquisition of two critically important carrier types, the *Independence*-class light carriers and multiple escort carrier classes.

Carrier construction contracts went out to major shipyards, including Bethlehem Steel's Quincy, Massachusetts, shipyard, Newport News Shipbuilding in Virginia, and the New York Navy Yard in Brooklyn, New York. For example, on 1 October 1940, Bethlehem Steel accepted the contract offered by the Navy on 9 September 1940 for carriers CV-16, CV-17, CV-18, and CV-19 (USS *Lexington*, USS *Bunker Hill*, USS *Wasp*, and USS *Hancock*)—all to be built at the company's Fore River Yard in Quincy, Massachusetts, for a price of $191,200,000, or $47,800,000 per ship. All four carriers eventually saw Pacific service. USS *Lexington*, the first of the group when launched in September 1942, saw action beginning with the Gilbert Islands Campaign that initiated the Central Pacific thrust of the overall multipronged strat-egy against Japan (other prongs included the Southwest Pacific (SOWPAC) thrust under General Douglas MacArthur, the South Pacific (SOPAC) prong under Admiral Chester Nimitz, the B-29 strategic bombing campaign, the unrestricted submarine maritime interdiction campaign, and the China-Burma-India (CBI) Campaign under Lord Louis Mountbatten with U.S. forces in a supporting role). USS *Hancock*, launched in January 1944, reached Pacific Fleet in time for the Philippines and Iwo Jima campaigns.[39]

In 1940 the American shipbuilding industry, buffeted by a decade of economic depression, stood ready, able, and willing to ramp up on a massive scale. As a further inducement to speed construction, Congress suspended the profit-limiting provi-sions of the Vinson-Trammell Act in legislative action on 8 October 1940, a feature that had roiled relations between the Roosevelt administration and the manufacturers to the point that no company would agree to begin construction or manufacture of ships or aircraft until the restriction had been modified.[40] In the contract acceptance letter from Bethlehem Steel, Vice President A. B. Homer pointed out to the Secretary of the Navy that "execution of the contracts in question will be postponed until that Act [profit limitations clause included in the 1934 Vinson-Trammel Act] shall have been repealed."[41] Additionally, the issue of new plant facilities required by Bethlehem Steel to accommodate not only the four new carriers, but the additional cruisers included in the contract, became a source of contention. The company required over $10 million to construct these facilities within the specified time frame; without these upgrades at Fore River, the ships could not be started. A new welding building; transportation equipment; cranes; sheet metal, paint, and machine shops as well as an additional wet basin and so forth all had to be constructed to accommodate the rapid shipyard expansion. For accelerated wartime construction, the normal amortization and depreciation of new facilities and plant expansion over an extended period could not be relied upon. Clearly, Congress needed to grant protection to manufacturers from rapid postwar drawdowns and other costs that would not be part of the normal, peacetime business cycle. Indeed, Admiral Towers had been able to let only a single contract with the Stearman Company for training biplanes, such was the reticence of companies to accept contracts without financial protections. With German forces occupying Paris and Great Britain under air siege in autumn 1940, no one in Congress, the Roosevelt administration, or the Navy desired any delays. An old saying in naval aviation goes, "maximum speed, minimum drag, speed is life." Clearly, Congress understood this imperative with war imminent and responded accordingly with the Internal Revenue Act of 1940, passed on 8 October, that repealed the profit ceilings on ships and aircraft, established a five-year plant amortization schedule, and set up a tax structure to guarantee sufficient manufacturer profits.[42]

The contract for the Newport News Shipbuilding and Drydock Company of Newport News, Virginia, went out from the Secretary of the Navy on 11 September. Similar to that awarded to Bethlehem Steel, the contract called for the construction of CVs 12–15 (USS *Hornet* [originally *Kearsarge*, but renamed *Hornet* after the loss in action of the original *Hornet* (CV-8) at the Battle of Santa Cruz on 27 October 1942], USS *Franklin*, USS *Ticonderoga*, and USS *Randolph*). The contract award also specified that each ship had to "conform substantially to the contract plans and specifications to be furnished by the Navy Department for Aircraft carrier CV-9." Since USS *Essex* (CV-9, launched in July 1942) and USS *Yorktown* (launched January 1943 and originally USS *Bon Homme Richard*, but renamed *Yorktown* following the loss of the original *Yorktown* (CV-5) at Midway in June 1942) were then under construction at Newport News, the shipyard stood ready from a technical viewpoint to construct the new class of carriers. In fact, Newport News had constructed the earlier *Yorktown* and *Enterprise*, both launched in 1936 and *Hornet*, which would be launched in December of that year. Thus, their expertise in large-carrier construction stood at a pinnacle by late 1940. It is interesting to note that the cost per unit for the Newport News carriers came in at $42,090,060, a substantial reduction compared to the Bethlehem Steel price. However, considering that the cost of living in 1940 in Hampton Roads/Tidewater, Virginia, compared to that in the Boston, Massachusetts, area probably was considerably less, the relative costs per ship seem reasonable. Additionally, the more heavily unionized Boston area might also explain a higher per unit cost. Keeping in accordance with the need for rapid delivery, the Navy offered the shipyard an incentive bonus of $3,000 per day under the contractual time of delivery. The Navy also allowed $7 million for acquisition of additional plant facilities required to upgrade the Quincy yard. From a cost and budgetary viewpoint, clearly the carriers built in Virginia made better economic sense. However, the need to build as rapidly as possible to the 70 percent fleet expansion as called for in the Two-Ocean legislation meant that the Navy could not rely upon a single company or yard. Bethlehem Steel did have considerable large-hull construction capability and experience. For example, that yard had built the carrier USS *Lexington* (CV-2) in the 1920s, USS *Wasp* (CV-7) launched in April 1939, and also the battleship USS *Massachusetts* (BB-59) laid down in July 1939. The same dynamic justified the higher costs of building ships in New York at the New York Naval Shipyard in Brooklyn or New York Shipbuilding in Camden, New Jersey, which constructed the USS *Saratoga* (CV-3) and eventually all nine of the *Independence*-class light carriers (CVL 22–30). The New York Naval Shipyard, better known as the Brooklyn Navy Yard, constructed the later *Essex*-class carriers *Bennington* (CV-20), *Bon Homme Richard* (CV-31), *Kearsarge* (CV-33), *Oriskany* (CV-34), and the late-war USS *Franklin D. Roosevelt* (CVB-42) of the *Midway* class launched in April 1945.

Wartime exigency thus played a vital role in carrier construction. With the loss of the battleships USS *Arizona* (BB-39) and USS *Oklahoma* (BB-37) at Pearl Harbor, with the time required to repair and refit the remaining damaged dreadnoughts, and with the attrition of the prewar carriers in combat through 1942, the Navy needed the new capital ships as rapidly as possible. While the older carriers, cruisers, and destroyers of the Pacific Fleet had been able to blunt the Japanese Pacific advance through the various naval engagements in 1942—including the battles of the Coral Sea in May, Midway in June, Eastern Solomons in September, Santa Cruz in October, and the multiple actions in the Solomon Islands in support of the Guadalcanal Campaign—by early 1943, the Pacific Fleet had been reduced to two operational carriers: USS *Enterprise* (CV-6) and USS *Saratoga* (CV-3). Any hope of initiating the Central Pacific prong, which reflected the long-standing War Plan Orange calling for a rollback offensive in the Central Pacific leading to a decisive,

Mahanian-style great battle fleet engagement against the Imperial Japanese Navy (IJN) in the Philippine Sea followed by maritime interdiction and bombardment of the Japanese home islands, depended on the arrival of the new Vinson Navy. By March 1943, the Joint Chiefs of Staff contemplated the strategic plans for the war against Japan. MacArthur argued for the SOWPAC campaign aimed at retaking the Philippine Islands. Admiral Chester Nimitz, Commander in Chief of the Pacific Fleet, as supported ably by his new chief of staff, Admiral Raymond Spruance, the hero of Midway, argued for the Central Pacific advance. In a compromise solution in June 1943, the Joint Chiefs of Staff agreed upon a dual-pronged advance with the Navy–Marine Corps leading through the Central Pacific island archipelagoes and the Army and Army Air Force with Navy support thrust through the Southwest Pacific (primarily the northern New Guinea coast) toward Rabaul and eventually the Philippines. But a potential problem loomed. The SOPAC campaign had moved along briskly and by early 1943 Guadalcanal had been secured as American forces advanced rapidly up the Solomons chain. In the SOWPAC, MacArthur had initiated operations in New Guinea with Operation Cartwheel in June. So long as the Central Pacific thrust remained a strategy in waiting, the Japanese ability to outflank American and Allied forces from the north, even to the point of cutting off the communications route to Hawaii and the United States, remained an issue. With a robust campaign aimed at the center, Japan would have to defend on many fronts and in many spots to maintain its defensive perimeter, which would of necessity prevent enough concentration of forces so as to threaten the SOWPAC and SOPAC theaters. In other words, the sooner the Vinson Navy could be on station, operational, and ready to fight with new carriers and improved combat aircraft, the better.

American industry answered the call. For example, the contract with Newport News required completion of USS *Lexington* within fifty-seven months of contract award. For the fourth carrier, USS *Randolph*, the contract stipulated seventy months from award to delivery. The date of the contract award letter from the Secretary of the Navy to Newport News was 11 September. *Lexington* was launched on 30 August 1943 and commissioned on 29 November 1943, merely thirty-seven months rather than the contractually required fifty-seven. Similarly, *Randolph*'s time to delivery was only forty-eight months rather than the mandated seventy (commissioned 9 October 1944). In like manner, contract deliveries for the Bethlehem Steel Quincy Yard for *Lexington* from time of contract award to delivery took only twenty-nine rather than the prescribed forty-three months, and *Hancock*'s delivery in only forty-three months beat the contractual time by twenty-three months.[43] Armed with the new construction ships and airplanes, a testament to the incredible industrial capacity of American industry and the productivity of American workers, the Navy initiated the Central Pacific thrust against the Gilbert Islands with the amphibious assault against Tarawa Atoll on 20 November 1943, an operation that could not

USS Essex *(CV-9), circa 1945.*

have been even contemplated had not the shipbuilders delivered the new carriers and other ships funded by the Two-Ocean legislation well ahead of schedule. Few archives so vividly illustrate the scope of this economic and industrial power than the 1 January 1943 message to the Commander in Chief (COMINCH), Navy from Captain Donald B. Duncan, USN, Commanding Officer, succinctly stating that "USS ESSEX, CV-9, PLACED IN FULL COMMISSION AT 1700 THIS DATE." Only thirteen months after the destruction of the Pacific Fleet battleships at Pearl Harbor, the first of the new class of aircraft carriers intended for the destruction of the Japanese Empire, became operational.[44]

An additional issue complicated the construction plan. Did the Navy require carriers quicker or a newer, more robust design? The Bureau of Construction and Repair and the Bureau of Engineering (merged in 1940 into Bureau of Ships or BuShips) pointed out in early July, after passage of the legislation, but prior to the president's signature, that to build CVs of the newer design would require additional months compared to using the current *Hornet*-class design. If the first four newly appropriated ships, starting with CV-9, were built to the *Yorktown/Hornet* design, then the estimated time to delivery would be thirty months versus the newer design requiring forty-four months. Total tonnage did not present a problem with either class design. To build five at 19,800 tons each would bring the program well under the budgeted tonnage. To build four *Yorktown/Hornet* designs and one new design of 26,500 tons came to 105,700 tons or just under the limit.[45] Such were the design decisions facing the Navy as Vinson pushed through ever-greater naval legislation. However, the events of 1940 in Europe had the effect of removing qualms about building the best carrier design available in the most expeditious manner. Accordingly, the Navy decided on the new design beginning with USS *Essex*.

Essex's design dated to 1939 when the Navy still operated under the terms of the treaty imitations (20,000 tons gross displacement). From a practical standpoint, she appeared much like an improved *Yorktown* class. But, with the outbreak of war and the subsequent renunciation of treaty tonnage limits, the United States removed all restrictions, resulting in the eventual, more robust *Essex* design. An increase in armor and flight deck area gave improved survivability and space for aircraft deck parking. For air defense, the 5-inch guns, mounted in singles on the *Yorktown*s, became twin mounts—two turrets forward and two aft of the island superstructure. Engineering space improvements with an alternating boiler room/machinery room design gave better damage control capability. At 872 feet and with a 33,000-ton displacement, the new *Essex* far outstripped the older *Yorktown*-class design. Changes in 1942 included a deck-edge elevator, air and surface search radar, and an increase in anti-aircraft defenses built around the Swedish Bofers model 20-mm and 40-mm rapid-fire guns mounted primarily in rows (20 mm) and quad configurations (40 mm) on platforms and catwalks just below the flight deck. As a result of the decision to proceed with the larger, more capable design, shipyards constructed twenty-four *Essex*-class fleet carriers by war's end with the bulk of the hulls in service by late 1943 to mid-1944, a truly remarkable achievement. From the June 1940 legislation, ten *Essex*-class carriers resulted, all of which saw significant action in the Pacific. Arguably, the single most important American warship of the war, *Essex* slid down the ways on 31 July 1942.[46]

Additionally, smaller ship types such as the *Independence*-class (CVL-22) light carrier (launched 22 August 1942) and escort carrier (CVE) emerged from the early war experience. Admiral Stark advised BuShips that a *Cleveland*-class light cruiser originally authorized in the 1934 bill and ordered in 1940 (USS *Amsterdam*, CL-59) would be converted to the new *Independence*-class light carrier as funded by the Two-Ocean legislation. Convoy protection in the Atlantic proved to be a critical mission for naval aviation as German submarines, commerce raiders, and *Luftwaffe* aircraft threatened the logistical supply line to Great Britain and the Soviet Union. Nine CVLs saw war service as well as over eighty escort carriers, starting with the USS *Long Island* (CVE-1) launched 2 June 1941.[47] In October 1940, Roosevelt directed that the Navy obtain a merchant hull for conversion to an escort carrier, resulting in the first of a long line of highly capable warships used primarily in the anti-submarine warfare and convoy escort roles. USS *Long Island* (CVE-1), converted from the merchantman *Mormacmail* and completed in June 1941, did service in the Pacific in delivering Marine fighter and bomber squadrons to Guadalcanal before returning to San Diego for duty as a training vessel. Roosevelt's plan to convert merchant ships to small 6,000- to 8,000-ton carriers capable of carrying ten to twelve fighters for convoy escort proved a valid concept with the success of the British escort carrier HMS *Audacity* in the Atlantic. With speeds of eighteen knots and better, the CVEs could travel faster than any convoy and almost as fast as the best German submarines on the surface. Primarily carrying *Wildcat* fighters of twenty or more per ship, the CVEs provided substantial air cover for the Atlantic convoys. In the Pacific, they provided close air support (CAS) to the land forces once an amphibious landing had secured the beachhead. In the Leyte Gulf engagement, USS *St Lo* (CVE-63) and USS *Gambier Bay* (CVE-73) sank under the pounding of Vice Admiral Kurita Takeo's battleship-cruiser force. Many CVEs transferred to the British Royal Navy. The Navy designated thirty-five CVEs, constructed or converted under the Two-Ocean legislation, for assignment to the Royal Navy, including eight of the original hulls from 1942.[48] Of the *Casablanca*-class (CVE-55 through CVE-104), the first purpose-built CVEs from the keel up and constructed in the Kaiser Company's Vancouver, Washington, shipyard, all but two served in the Pacific Theater. The late-war *Commencement Bay*–class ships (CVE-105 through CVE-124), built in the Todd-Pacific and Allis-Chalmers yards in Tacoma, Washington, rounded out the CVEs but only three ships saw combat action. Previous classes had been conversions primarily from merchantmen and oilers. War realities drove the eventual development of designs and capabilities of ships and aircraft, but the funding emanating from the 1940 legislation provided the ability to literally invent new ship types as war exigencies dictated.

These and later ships carried aircraft such as the Grumman F6F Hellcat fighter, Vought F4U Corsair fighter-bomber, TBF Avenger torpedo bomber, and SB2C Helldiver dive-bomber that replaced the prewar design F4F Wildcat, SBD Dauntless, and TBD Devastator types. Funds for the thousands of aircraft of the new types resulted from the Two-Ocean legislation and by 1943–1944, largely replaced the early war models. The legislation increased the number of Navy aircraft to 15,000 as well as the expansion of shore facilities to accommodate the expanded Navy air assets. Forty-two existing naval air stations required substantial upgrades. Many Naval Reserve aviation bases needed modification; seven new reserve bases required establishment.[49] Additionally, the increase in pilot numbers first stimulated by the 1935 appropriation continued as 1940–1942 appropriations dramatically increased the need for aviators. Some characteristics of these new aircraft illustrate the tremendous advances in naval aviation technology—capability and design made possible by the various naval appropriation bills between 1935 and early in the war.

The Vought F4U-4 Corsair first flew on 1 May 1940. With its distinctive gull wing shape and powerful Pratt and Whitney R-2800-18W radial engine that produced 2,100 hp, first production models arrived by September 1942. With a top speed of 446 mph and a 26,200-foot ceiling, the Corsair proved a versatile and deadly fighter and fighter bomber able to engage in air combat and carry both bombs and rocket ordnance. The Curtiss SB2C Helldiver replaced the Dauntless. Designed in 1939, production contracts went out in November 1940, just after the contracts for the *Essex*-class ships. The first combat employment of the airplane occurred in strikes against the Japanese air and naval base at Rabaul on New Britain. The TBF/TBM Avenger first entered combat in 1942 at the Battle of Midway. Designed to replace the unsuccessful Devastator, the large three-man aircraft carried torpedoes, bombs, or depth charges depending on the mission. Despite its durability and survivability, the F4F Wildcat suffered technologically compared to the A6M Zero fighter, and a replacement finally arrived in August 1943. The F6F Hellcat, with a maximum speed of 380 mph at 14,000 feet and a service ceiling of 37,300 feet outclassed and outperformed the Zero in many critical performance characteristics. With a range of close to a thousand miles, the Hellcat gave the carriers an extraordinary combat radius and became the primary naval fighter for the remainder of the war. Aircraft, however, were expensive. A Corsair ranged from $61,000 to almost $70,000 per airplane depending on the acquisition date. A Hellcat fighter ran $54,000. By contrast, the older Dauntless dive-bomber came in at $32,800, while the Wildcat cost $42,000.[50] In the rapid expansion period following the fall of France, the 1940 appropriations provided the funding for the new 15,000-aircraft Navy.

To support the aviation expansion, new bases needed construction and older facilities upgraded. Funding for such public works projects came from the various appropriations. Illustrative of the cost is the estimate provided by Chief of BuAer, Rear Admiral John S. McCain, in May 1943 requesting approval for additional public works projects at naval air stations totaling $16,598,636. For the period from 1 September 1943 to 30 June 1944, the new chief, Rear Admiral D. C. Ramsey, proposed $93,834,500, a stunning figure by contemporary standards.[51] Increased pilot training followed aircraft acquisition, a dynamic also funded in the various appropriations. Illustrating this dynamic, then-Captain Arthur W. Radford reported the status of flight training as of 30 June 1942 showing 6,901students in the training pipeline, including a number of British officers.[52] Fortunately for the Navy, Vinson and Congress accounted for the massive overhead cost of fielding and supporting a robust fleet and air expansion, without which the new force could not be sustained.

Naval expansion and, in particular, the growth of naval aviation, intensified after the Pearl Harbor attack of 7 December 1941; authorization and appropriation bills became common throughout the first three years of the U.S. war effort. Representative Vinson remained the centerpiece of naval legislation until his eventual retirement in 1964. Nonetheless, the single most important legislative and ultimately far-sighted action for America's ability to win the maritime struggle with Japan and sustain the beleaguered British and Soviet allies was the Two-Ocean Navy Act of 1940.[53] The Act provided the forces with which Admiral Nimitz executed the Central Pacific campaign to the Japanese home islands as envisioned in the Navy's War Plan Orange and supported the SOPAC/SOWPAC campaigns with overwhelming carrier-based air power. By the time of Japan's September 1945 surrender, sixteen of the seventeen Pacific Fleet carriers resulted from Vinson-sponsored legislation.[54] And, it allowed the U.S. Navy to fight a two-ocean struggle against the German Kriegsmarine in the vital Atlantic Theater. Finally, the Two-Ocean legislation, when combined with the various other appropriation and authorization bills in the late 1930s and early 1940s, vaulted the United States Navy into the world's pre-eminent maritime force based on command of the sea through command of the air, a continuing dynamic guaranteed by the flourishing of naval aviation since 1940.

NOTES

1. *Proceedings of the Special Board and Records of Evidence* (Eberle Board), United States National Archives (hereafter NA), Record Group (hereafter RG) 80. Rear Admiral Fullam observed over two hundred aircraft based at Rockwell Field near San Diego as they performed fly-bys for over three hours to celebrate the end of World War I.

2. Lord Chatfield, First Sea Lord, Inskip Inquiry, 13 July 1936, London: National Archives of the United Kingdom, CAB 16/151.

3. Admiral Sims made these comments in an address to the Naval War College class of 1921 at the college on 19 November 1921.

4. Clark G. Reynolds, *The Fast Carriers: The Forging of an Air Navy* (Huntington, NY: Robert E. Kreiger, 1978), p. 1; NA, General Records of the Department of the Navy, 1798–1947, Secretary of the Navy General Correspondence (hereafter SECNAV): 1940–42, RG 80, 370/19/27/17, Box 20, Morrow Board Report Summary dated 12 July 1944 and Resume of Report of Morrow Board, Vol. 3, dated 30 November 1925.

5. NA, Department of the Navy, Records of the General Board Transcripts of Hearings, 1917–1950, Vol. 2, 1919, RG 80, Box 4, Vol. i–iii.

6. Letter to SECNAV dated 23 June 1919, Bureau of Aeronautics, General Correspondence (hereafter BuAer), NA, RG 72, Entry #15.

7. Reynolds, *The Fast Carriers*, p. 15. The Morrow Board Report was printed in the USNI *Proceedings* 52 (1926), pp. 196–225. In addition to the personnel requirements, the Board called for the acquisition of a thousand aircraft in the 1926–31 time frame.

8. SECNAV, RG 80, 370/19/27/17, Box 20, Morrow Board Report Summary dated 12 July 1944, and Resume of Report of Morrow Board dated 30 November 1925.

9. *New York Times* (hereafter *NYT*), 3 December 1931, p. 12 and 5 December 1931, p. 2.

10. USS *Ranger* (CV-4), the first purpose-built carrier from the keel up proved inadequate for fleet operations due to size and stability limitations. However, follow-on designs using

the lessons pioneered aboard *Langley* and perfected by *Saratoga* and *Lexington*, came forward beginning with the *Yorktown* class.

11. *Washington Post* (hereafter *TWP*), 9 January 1934, p. 9.

12. *Congressional Record*, 72nd Congress, 2nd Session, in *Congressional Record*, 63rd Congress—88th Congress (Washington, DC: Government Printing Office, 1914–1965) (hereafter *CR*), 22 February 1933, 4720–23.

13. Vinson's OPEDs in *NYT*, 23 January 1934, p. 2; *NYT*, 29 January 1934, p. 4; and *The Atlanta Constitution*, 28 January 1934, p. 7A.

14. *CR*, 74th Congress, 1638.

15. Admiral Jonas Ingram, "15 Years of Naval Development," *Scientific American* (November 1935), p. 234.

16. *NYT*, 5 January 1938, p. 11; *TWP*, 26 January 1938, pp. 1, 7.

17. Many of these Naval Reserve aviators went on to form the core of experienced pilots upon which the huge personnel expansion of 1940 was based. But other capital ships were not overlooked in the 1935 legislation. For example, the *North Carolina*–class battleships *North Carolina* (BB-55) and *Washington* (BB-56), the first U.S. battleships built since World War II, resulted from the naval expansion legislation of 1935.

18. *TWP*, 29 January 1938, pp. 1, 5; *NYT*, 29 January 1938, pp. 1, 4, 5.

19. Alfred Thayer Mahan, *The Influence of Sea Power upon History, 1660–1783*, originally published in 1890 and based on Mahan's Naval War College lectures, profoundly altered naval strategic thinking in not only the United States, but in Europe and Asia as well. Previously non-naval states such as Imperial Germany, Japan, China, Austria-Hungary, and Italy raced to build larger and more capable capital ships in search of the decisive great battleship clash far out to sea.

20. USS *Massachusetts* (BB-59) and USS *Alabama* (BB-60). The original two BBs were USS *South Dakota* (BB-57) and USS *Indiana* (BB-58).

21. The early 1943 aircraft configuration of the *Essex* class consisted of four squadrons— 36 fighters, 36 dive-bombers, and 10 torpedo bombers or 91 total aircraft with 9 planes stored and broken down in reserve. By the war's end, the typical air group complement stood at 36 Hellcat fighters, 36 Corsair fighter-bombers, 15 Helldiver dive-bombers, and 15 Avenger torpedo planes or 102 total aircraft.

22. Many of these new naval air facilities played prominent roles in World War II and beyond. Naval Air Station Pensacola is the basic training activity for naval aviation. Quonset Point became one of the original Naval Construction Battalion (SEABEE) training and headquarters sites and is now a Rhode Island Air National Guard facility. Naval Air Station Norfolk still supports Hampton Roads naval activities.

23. *CR*, 76th Congress, 3rd session, 2731–33, 2750, 2752; *TWP*, 13 March 1940, pp. 5, 6.

24. For the pivotal role played by Rear Admiral Towers in the events of spring 1940 that resulted in the Two-Ocean legislation, see Clark G. Reynolds, *Admiral John H. Towers: The Struggle for Naval Air Supremacy* (Annapolis: Naval Institute Press, 1991), pp. 315–31.

25. *TWP*, 19 May 1940, p. 1.

26. War Department, SECRET MEMORANDUM: Subject: National Strategic Decisions, WPD MBR dated 22 May 1940 (declassified 24 October 1973), NA, Records of the War Department Special and General Staffs, War Plans Division, General Correspondence, RG 165, 270/4175–77.

27. *TWP*, 22 May 1940, p. 4. The 11 percent bill included funding authorization for 21 warships, 22 auxiliaries, and 1,011 aircraft.

28. *CR*, 76th Congress, 3rd session, 2750.

29. The bill authorized the increase in air frames from 3,000 to 10,000, billets for 16,000 pilots and funding for the construction of twenty new naval air stations, both in the continental U.S. (CONUS) and at various outside of continental U.S. (OUTCONUS) locations, particularly in the Pacific.

30. *The Atlanta Journal*, 18 June 1940, p. 1.

31. *The Atlanta Constitution*, 11 July 1940, p. 1; *NYT*, 23 June 1940, p. 1, 14; *CR*, 76th Congress, 3rd session, 9064–65, 9078, 9570. The bill provided for 385,000-tonnage battleships, 200,000-tonnage carriers, 420,000-tonnage cruisers, 250,000-tonnage destroyers, 70,000-tonnage submarines. Within two hours of the signing of the bill, contracts began going out from the Navy Department.

32. MEMORANDUM from Captain E.G. Allen dated 20 July 1940, NA, SECNAV, RG 80, A1-3/A18 (340213-17), 11W3/25/32/2, Box 2.

33. Letter from Chief of Naval Operations to Secretary of the Navy dated 30 JUL 1940, NA, SECNAV, RG 80, 370/19/14/1-2, Box 20 (Declassified IAW NNDD813002 by NARA on 17 September 2009).

34. NA, SECNAV, Aircraft Carrier Awarded, RG 80/11W3/25/32/2, Box 2; CVA Contracts List, RG 80/11W3/25/32/2, Box 2; *NYT*, 2 July 1940.

35. NA, SECNAV, RG80, CV-12/L4-3 Aircraft Carrier, 11W3/26/6/1, Box 324. USS *Franklin* (CV-13), USS *Ticonderoga* (CV-14), USS *Randolph* (CV-15), USS *Lexington* (CV-16), USS *Bunker Hill* (CV-17), USS *Wasp* (CV-18), and USS *Hancock* (CV-19).

36. *CR*, 76th Congress, 3rd session, Appendix, 5721–22.

37. Ibid., 6130ff.

38. SECRET MEMORANDUM from Admiral E. J. King, U.S. Navy to Chairman, General Board dated 30 July 1941, NA, General Board Subject File, 1900–1947, RG 80, GB 420-2, 1941–42, Box 63 (declassified 11 February 1972).

39. For example of a contract award for CV-16/17/18 (*Lexington, Bunker Hill, Wasp*), see NA, SECNAV, CV16/L4-3 Bethlehem Steel, RG 80, 11W3/26/6/1 Box 325.

40. *CR*, 76th Congress, 3rd Session; Letter from Chief of the Bureau of Ships to Judge Advocate General of the Navy dated 24 October 1940, para. 2, NA, SECNAV, CV12/L4-3 Aircraft Carrier, 11W3/26/6/1, Box 324, For example, the Vinson-Trammell Act required that at least 10 percent of all naval aircraft and engines be manufactured at the Naval Aircraft Factory in Philadelphia and restricted the profit margin of shipbuilders and aircraft manufacturers to no more than 10 percent.

41. NA, SECNAV, CV16/L4-3 Bethlehem Steel, RG 80, 11W3/26/6/1 Box 325.

42. Reynolds, *Towers*, p. 330.

43. Letter from Lewis Compton, Acting SECNAV to Bethlehem Steed dated 9 September 1940 and Letter from Lewis Compton, Acting SECNAV to Newport News Shipbuilding and Dry Dock Company, NA, SECNAV, CV16/L4-3 Bethlehem Steel, RG 80, 11W3/26/6/1, Box 325.

44. USS *ESSEX* Naval Message dated 1 January 43, NA, BuAer, RG 72, 470/63/18/05, Box 72 (declassified NND730026 by NARA dated 17 September 2009).

45. MEMORANDUM from Bureau of Construction and Repair and Bureau of Engineering (n.d.), received Navy Department 17 July 1940, NA, SECNAV, CV/L8-3(11), RG 80, 11W3/26/6/1, Box 322.

46. Paul H. Silverstone, *U.S. Warships of World War II* (Garden City, NY: Doubleday 1965), pp. 36–48. *Yorktown* is a memorial/museum ship in Charleston, South Carolina, while *Intrepid* is berthed in New York as a floating naval air museum, a testament to the endur-

ing legacy of these ships. *Lexington* served many decades as a training ship in Pensacola, Florida, for thousands of naval aviators for decades following the war.

47. Ibid., pp. 46–64.

48. CONFIDENTIAL MEMORANDUM FOR MR. GATES dated 10 February 1944, NA, SECNAV, RG 80, 370/19/26, Box 1 (declassified IAW DoD DIR 5200.30 of 23 March 1983 by NARA on 17 September 2009).

49. Letter from Chief of Naval Operations to Various Officials dated 22 July 1940, NA, SECNAV, RG 80, 370/19/14/1-2, Box 20 (declassified IAW NND813002 by NARA on 17 September 2009).

50. Cost Trend of Principal Naval Aircraft dated 10 February 1944, NA, SECNAV, RG 80, 370/19/7/15, Box 9.

51. Letter from Chief BuAer to Secretary of the Navy dated 6 May 1943, BuAer, RG 72, 370/19/27/3, Box 34 (declassified IAW DoD Directive 5200.30 of 23 March 1983 by NARA 17 September 2009).

52. CONFIDENTIAL MEMORANDUM from Captain A.W. Radford to Chief, BuAer dated 30 June 1942, NA, BuAer, RG 72, 370/19/27/3, Box 36 (declassified IAW DoD DIR 5200.30 of 23 March 1983 by NARA on 17 September 2009).

53. The 1940 legislation eventually resulted in the following numbers:
1,325,000 tons new construction
New warships
2 *Iowa*-class battleships
2 *Alaska*-class battle cruisers
18 *Essex*-class carriers
27 *Baltimore*-, *Atlanta*-, *Cleveland*-class cruisers
115 *Bristol*-, *Fletcher*-class destroyers
43 *Gato*-class fleet submarines
15,000 aircraft
Numerous repair/tender/support ships

54. Silverstone, *U.S. Warships*, pp. 36–48. Only USS *Saratoga* (CV-3), which had been laid down as a battle cruiser during World War I and launched in 1925 could be characterized as a non-Vinson carrier. USS *Enterprise* (CV-6) resulted from the 1933 National Recovery Act, but Vinson had been a major influence in that appropriation effort. Thus, sixteen of the seventeen Pacific Fleet carriers at the time of Japan's surrender could be said to have been part of the "Vinson Navy."

CHAPTER 9

U.S. Aircraft Carrier Evolution, 1911–1945

Norman Friedman

U.S. carrier aviation began almost a century ago in November 1910, when, under naval auspices, an intrepid aviator named Eugene Ely landed on the cruiser USS *Birmingham*, whose fantail had been partly covered by a temporary deck equipped with what we would now call arresting gear ropes.[1] In January 1911 Ely landed on and then flew off a similar deck rigged over the bow of the cruiser *Pennsylvania* in San Francisco harbor. The next month Glenn Curtiss landed his "hydroplane" alongside *Pennsylvania*, was hoisted aboard, then hoisted out and flew off, demonstrating a form of fleet aviation that could operate with minimum impact on a surface warship. Senior U.S. officers were impressed; they understood that aircraft could change naval warfare by giving fleet commanders much wider vision. The formal characteristics (staff requirements) for the 1910 battleship (*Texas* class) were amended to include provision for aircraft (although nothing was done in the end). Landing-on and flying-off decks at both ends of a ship would block too much of a ship's main battery; instead work proceeded on a catapult (designed at the Naval Gun Factory [Washington Navy Yard] in 1912) whose fixed track would cover the after guns of a large cruiser. The third catapult built was installed in 1915 on board the armored cruiser *North Carolina*, making the first catapult shot from a moving ship (the pilot was Captain Henry C. Mustin).[2] In 1916 several other armored cruisers were so modified, carrying large seaplanes that could land alongside when they returned. They represented a much greater diversion of frontline warships to aviation than other navies then contemplated.

About 1911 other navies were experimenting with launching aircraft from ships and also with operating aircraft from the shore. The Germans in particular became interested in reconnaissance by Zeppelins; the British were so impressed that they used an aircraft-carrying cruiser, HMS *Hermes*, to simulate enemy airships during their 1913 maneuvers. At the outbreak of war the British converted three Channel steamers to carry floatplanes, and in December 1914 these ships launched the first naval air attack in history, specifically to destroy the German Zeppelin force. Although the attack succeeded, the German force was never completely destroyed, and during the war the Royal Navy began placing fighters on board its battleships and cruisers (they landed either ashore or in the water), specifically to deal with Zeppelin scouts. They had good reason to do so: in August 1916 the British Grand Fleet failed to catch the Germans at sea because a Zeppelin spotted them shortly before the two fleets would have come into contact. The British also became interested in aircraft to scout for their own fleet; a British floatplane (piloted by "Rutland of Jutland") was peripherally involved in the Battle of Jutland, but the main British carrier, HMS *Campania*, did not go to sea with the fleet due to a signaling failure.

The Royal Navy also became interested in torpedo attack, an idea first popularized by U.S. Rear Admiral Bradley Fiske. Conversion of the three Channel steamers was initially motivated by a plan to attack the German fleet in harbor (the aircraft were hardly up to it, however), and in 1915 a British naval floatplane made the first aerial torpedo attack in history, on a Turkish steamer. The British became particularly interested in torpedo strikes after 1916, when it became clear that the German fleet would remain in harbor, tying down the British, preventing them from using their sea power offensively. Airplanes offered a unique way to get at the Germans despite their unwillingness to go to sea. In 1918 the British had enough carrier decks, either ready or in prospect, to plan a recognizably modern carrier raid on the German fleet in harbor. They revived the idea in the 1930s when they faced war against Italy, and they executed just such a raid against the Italian fleet base at Taranto in November 1940. It in turn may have helped inspire the Japanese attack on Pearl Harbor, which had much the same aim. By 1918 the British also saw aerial spotting as a key to future gun battles, particularly when fog limited visibility on the sea. It was not so much that aircraft had been decisive during World War I, but that what they had done pointed to a large future role. In 1924 it was estimated that 150,000 aircraft had been built by various combatants during the war.[3]

All of this mattered to the U.S. Navy because U.S. naval officers joined the British fleet after the United States entered World War I in April 1917. A U.S. battle squadron joined the Grand Fleet, which operated most British carrier aircraft; a U.S. naval staff (under Admiral William S. Sims, who was later President of the Naval War College) was set up in London, with close contact with the Admiralty; and U.S. officers and U.S.-built aircraft became involved in the huge British air anti-submarine warfare (ASW) effort (unlike land planes, in which the British and French had an enormous edge, U.S. flying boats were considered quite modern and were used by the Royal Navy).

The U.S. officers watched the British create the world's first carrier force, and they reported back, both during and after the war, how it worked and what it could do. The U.S. staff in London so absorbed current Admiralty thinking that in 1918 it proposed a U.S. naval building program modeled closely on contemporary British warships. The Royal Navy sent a senior naval constructor, Stanley V. Goodall (later Director of Naval Construction, equivalent to the Chief of the U.S. Bureau of Ships), to work with U.S. warship designers at the Bureau of Construction and Repair (C&R, later part of the Bureau of Ships). Goodall brought with him plans of current British warships, including some of the new carriers *Argus*, *Furious*, and *Hermes* (as they were when he left England in 1917, for example, when *Furious* had only her forward flying-off deck, with a hangar below it; Goodall stated that she had been further modified with a flying-on deck aft, but he had no details). Further plans, which survive in U.S. archives, were supplied as late as 1919–1920, as for a time postwar the British hoped that the United States would become an ally (this idea died when the Senate rejected the League of Nations).

The wartime Royal Navy considered carriers so important that it chose to complete the new battleship HMS *Eagle* as a carrier (her sister ship was the battleship HMS *Canada*). The "large light cruiser" *Furious* received first a flying-off deck forward (in place of one of her two 18-inch guns) and then a flying-on deck aft. She was the scene of the first British carrier landing, in 1917, but the air eddying around her superstructure caused serious problems, including the death of the first carrier-landing pilot. The British also laid down a cruiser-size carrier, HMS *Hermes*. She was the first ship to be designed as a carrier from the outset. The Royal Navy clearly considered her important enough to divert the resources that otherwise could have gone into a heavy cruiser. British capital ships and cruisers were fitted with flying-off platforms for fighters. Among lessons of early British carrier operations was the danger of air currents brushing aside the lightweight aircraft as they tried to land. The first British aviator to land on an operational carrier (*Furious*) was blown over the side and drowned on his second landing. Among the British responses was to lay wires lengthwise on the deck, providing airplanes with T-shaped hooks under their wheels, the idea being that a landing airplane would catch the wires and stay on the deck. The wires were often called arresting gear, but that was not their main function. The U.S. Navy adopted this idea, retaining such wires as late as about 1928. The Royal Navy found that, once airplanes were heavy enough not to be affected fatally by gusts of wind, the lengthwise wires tended to foul; they were abandoned. This experience was one reason the Royal Navy did not adopt arresting gear until the late 1930s. One consequence of not having arresting gear was that the Royal Navy was far more concerned than the U.S. Navy to maintain smooth air flow over its flight decks and around its carriers' islands (which had airfoil-section funnels). Adopting arresting gear and the corresponding style of landings made it much easier for the U.S. Navy to design carriers and also to adopt high-powered aircraft with high approach speeds.

In June 1918 the Division of Naval Aviation (within OpNav) proposed characteristics for a carrier.[4] Goodall provided advice. By fall 1918 carriers figured in proposed U.S. postwar building programs (they were omitted from the 1919 program, prepared in 1918, because they could not possibly be ready in time to fight during World War I).[5] No such ship could enter service for some time, so in 1919 the large collier *Jupiter* was ordered converted into an experimental carrier, a flat deck being built above her hull. She was available because the fleet was being converted from coal to oil fuel. The converted ship was commissioned as USS *Langley* in 1922. She was always considered an interim experimental carrier, hence her low speed and limited hangar capacity were both acceptable.

The U.S. Navy was well aware that not only the British but also the Japanese—considered the next most likely enemy—were interested in carriers; a May 1920 OpNav memo on the subject (written by Aviation Director, Captain T. T. Craven) mentions an Office of Naval Intelligence (ONI) report to that effect. The ship was *Hosho*, and ONI did not know that a British naval aviation mission would soon be providing the Japanese with the fruits of wartime British experience.[6] The memo argued that *Langley* could not by herself teach the necessary lessons. Her sister ship, *Neptune*, should also be converted, and one or more fast carriers obtained in order to learn the important tactical and strategic lessons of naval air power.

As a hint of U.S. naval thinking, in July 1920 the now-familiar system of ship type symbols was introduced. Carriers were placed in the cruiser (i.e., combatant) category, rather than in an auxiliary category, with the symbol CV (C for cruiser, V for fixed-wing—Z was for airships, and much later the symbol H was introduced for helicopters). At the same time symbols were created for fighters (VF) and for torpedo bombers (VT), but not for bombers as such; dive-bombing had not yet been formally introduced, so torpedoes were the principal way in which U.S. naval aircraft could directly attack enemy warships. Symbols were, however, introduced for scouting (VS) and for observation (VO), the latter meaning spotting for heavy gunfire. At this time the Navy's Bureau of Ordnance was much intrigued by the possibility that spotting aircraft could extend battleship gunfire range even beyond the visual horizon, offering the U.S. fleet a battle-winning advantage. Carriers might or might not launch the spotters, but their fighters would make it possible for them to work unmolested. It was assumed that torpedo attack, bombing (level, not dive, which did not yet exist), and scouting functions could all be combined in one type of airplane. Only torpedoes, which had to be launched at close range, could be expected to hit and damage maneuvering ships, but a 1924 report suggested that gas, which had been used to great effect during World War I, might be a useful air weapon, because a cloud of gas did not have to be delivered very precisely. There was a real fear that, once gassed, a ship could not be decontaminated (the Royal Navy of this period seems to have had similar fears). It turned out that gas was the one weapon of this period whose further use was ruled out by deterrence.

By 1920 public support for the expensive naval program was evaporating: if World War I had indeed been fought "to end wars" why should the U.S. Navy be preparing for another? U.S. strategists understood differently: it was unlikely that a war would break out in the near future, but it seemed entirely possible that at some point the United States and Japan would fight over Pacific dominance. Like other navies, the U.S. Navy needed to develop carrier aviation. With no prospect of a carrier in the FY21 program, C&R proposed converting one of the ten *Omaha*-class light cruisers then under construction. The General Board rejected the idea on the grounds that the Navy badly needed light cruisers (it had no modern ones) and that the proposed carrier would be mediocre. It much preferred a new design.[7]

In November 1920, the General Board, responsible for advising the Secretary of the Navy, called not only for two ships in the FY22 program, but for more in subsequent ones, up to a total of six or seven. Congress had already authorized a massive building program in 1916: ten battleships, six huge battle cruisers, ten light cruisers, and many lesser ships, most of them suspended during the war as destroyer construction became the highest priority (to defeat the German U-boats). For a time after the war it seemed that the 1916 program would be completed and further ships laid down to give the United States its desired position as premier sea power. In that context it was perfectly reasonable to assume that Congress would approve the important new carrier.

Looking toward the 1922 program, in the winter of 1920 the General Board drew up characteristics while C&R's preliminary designers developed a pair of alternatives, one displacing 25,000 tons (about thirty knots) and the other 35,000 tons (about thirty-five knots). The larger ship offered a larger flight deck (800 × 100 feet), greater speed, a steadier platform (due to the greater displacement), and ample stowage space, at the cost of greater expense and building time. The board chose the larger design as the basis for characteristics it submitted in February 1921, for a 35,000-ton, 32.75-knot carrier.[8] A model based on the design showed a flush-deck (island-less) carrier, her twin 6-inch guns arranged along the side of the flight deck, with smoke pipes extending to the ship's sides. This was much the pattern the Royal Navy had just followed in its prototype carrier, HMS *Argus* (a converted merchant ship), and what it was pursuing in rebuilding HMS *Furious* as a satisfactory carrier. The U.S. Navy had plans of *Argus* but not of the rebuilt *Furious*. In July 1921, the General Board ruled on several vital design questions, based on studies conducted by C&R. It rejected flush-deck designs because wind tunnel tests had just shown that in a flush-decker, gases were drawn in against the ship's side and across the flight deck, even with a slight crosswind. Moreover, no one had ever tried to dispose of the vast volume of gas associated with high power (for the desired high speed) without using a conventional funnel. The same experiments suggested that a closed stern would be much safer than an open one for the ship—the hangar would therefore be buried in the hull, as in HMS *Hermes*. The flight deck would not be armored, because even 2 inches would add enormous topweight (about 1,800 tons, and another 1,450 for each additional inch), and it would provide little real protection. In contrast to a C&R sketch design, the fore and aft hangar spaces would not be separated, "as the greatest facility of stowage and transportation of planes seems the chief point to be considered." On the basis of wind tunnel tests the General Board rejected earlier arrangements in which defensive guns were mounted along the ship's side. Instead she should have six twin 6-inch mounts and twelve 5-inch anti-aircraft guns, all on the open deck. These decisions shaped the design adopted for the two U.S. battle cruiser conversions, *Lexington* and *Saratoga*, and to some extent subsequent designs.[9]

In 1921, too, the U.S. Navy created a Bureau of Aeronautics (BuAer), which was unique among the bureaus of the Navy in combining administration (e.g., of pilots) and technical functions. The Act that created the bureau decreed that officers commanding aviation units (except for carriers and seaplane tenders) had to be aviators. Because there were not nearly enough senior pilots, BuAer created a course that could train senior officers (typically captains) as aviation observers. Senior officers were encouraged to seek aviation training, even at advanced ages; they included Captain Ernest J. King, who commanded the U.S. Navy during World War II as Chief of Naval Operations, as well as Captain William F. Halsey. The many senior officers who therefore sought aviation training apparently educated non-aviators such as Admiral Chester Nimitz and Admiral Raymond Spruance. For that matter, officers who had already seen a great deal of the rest of the Navy presumably were better at integrating the new naval air arm into it.

By July 1921 the U.S. government was planning an international naval disarmament conference in Washington, which it held in November 1921. Apparently an influential senator (William Borah, R-ID) had demanded that the government seek an international agreement to end new naval construction before asking for money to complete the 1916 ships, and the Harding administration called the conference to forestall him. Many in Congress saw the conference as an opportunity to discard the expensive 1916 program. It seemed at the time that a capital shipbuilding competition was beginning among Britain, Japan, and the United States; it was widely imagined that the pre-1914 competition between Germany and Britain had helped cause the ruinous war recently ended (this idea now seems much less convincing). The main outcome of the conference was that the United States achieved naval parity, at least in capital ships, with Great Britain—in the past by far the dominant naval power. Japan was forced to accept a limit of 60 percent of U.S. or British tonnage, creating the famous 5:5:3 ratio. The Washington Naval Treaty that emerged from the conference dominated warship design—including carrier design—during the interwar period. In July 1921 one senator linked naval disarmament with a proposal to convert two of the incomplete battle cruisers into carriers.[10] They were the closest the Navy could hope to come to the General Board's preferred 35,000-tonner.

Although they were new, the Washington Treaty treated carriers as capital ships, subject to the same 5:5:3 ratio as battleships. With preliminary designs for the converted battle cruisers in hand, the U.S. delegation secured a clause that allowed any of the three main signatories to convert two existing or incomplete capital ships into carriers, displacing up to 33,000 tons (battleships could displace up to 35,000).[11] New carriers could displace up to 27,000 tons, a figure based on a contemporary U.S. design study. The U.S. position was to seek enough tonnage for the two battle cruisers plus *Langley*. The British, who were already using carriers, believed that a fleet needed a substantial number. This position in turn reflected the British belief that no single carrier could operate very many aircraft (see below). The effect of this British concern was to set a much higher total, 135,000 tons, than might have been expected for what many still imagined was an entirely experimental type of ship (the battleship total was set at 525,000 tons). Clauses in the treaty allowed replacement of existing ships after a set lifetime, but the British were allowed an escape clause: their World War I ships were classed as experimental and hence could be replaced much earlier. However post-1918 Royal Navy could never convince the British government to do so.

The U.S. delegation was determined to obtain enough tonnage to complete the two battle cruisers. Chief Constructor David W. Taylor knew that preliminary designs for the huge converted battle cruisers would require about 36,000 tons, and it was impossible to demand more for a carrier than for a battleship (when the U.S. delegation tried, the British demanded that the limit be raised to 45,000 tons, which would have allowed them to complete some entirely new ships that would have outclassed all existing ones). On the other hand, the treaty allowed navies to rebuild existing battleships (to reduce incentives to build new ones) to improve their protection against the threats of bombs and underwater weapons, which had not really been taken into account when most existing ships had been built. Navies were allowed 3,000 tons per ship for this purpose. The U.S. interpretation of the treaty treated the two huge ex–battle cruisers as existing ships that could be so modified (several attempts to redesign them without the extra 3,000 tons showed just how necessary that tonnage was). Like the United States, Japan converted two new capital ships, as yet incomplete, into large carriers. Unfortunately for the Royal Navy, in 1921 it had just ordered new ships, but none had yet been laid down, so it had to make do with conversions of two much smaller "large light cruisers," HMS *Courageous* and HMS *Glorious*, plus further reconstruction of HMS *Furious*.

The treaty provided the U.S. Navy with the two largest carriers in the world, USS *Lexington* and USS *Saratoga*. A distinctive U.S. way of operating carriers (see below) gave the nation the largest Carrier Air Wings in the world, and experience with those air wings showed the U.S. Navy what carriers could do. Second, the generous tonnage allowance encouraged the U.S. Navy to build a substantial carrier force during the interwar period. The designs of this time became the basis for the fleet carriers the U.S. Navy built during World War II.

While U.S. naval aviation developed in the decade after World War I, U.S. naval planners worked out the details of a war against the most likely future enemy, Japan, code-named "Orange." By 1929 it was clear that an Orange war would involve large numbers of airplanes, far beyond what the treaty-limited carrier force could possibly accommodate. The Orange war plan therefore envisaged converting merchant ships into auxiliary carriers (XCV, the X indicating conversion) as well as into numerous other types of auxiliaries. Conversion plans were drawn up for several large U.S. liners. The relatively anemic U.S. Merchant Marine of the time offered too few suitable ships (even the largest liners were relatively slow), and the conversion plan was eventually dropped because the plans envisaged would have taken far too long to carry out. In 1936 a new U.S. Maritime Commission was created to revive the U.S. merchant fleet, and specifically to build fast merchant ships that might be suited to wartime conversion. Within a few years it had designed a passenger ship (P4-P) specifically suited to carrier conversion (it was never built). The Maritime Commission did develop the C3 freighter, which became the basis for World War II escort carriers, and it created the industrial base that built, among many other things, fifty *Casablanca*-class escort carriers during World War II. Merchant ship conversion was considered by the other two carrier navies, the Royal Navy and the Imperial Japanese Navy. Only the Japanese took it really seriously, subsidizing merchant ships specifically intended for wartime conversion—including some that became World War II carriers.

The *Lexington* design was undoubtedly influenced by the British designs for their first two fleet carriers, HMS *Eagle* and HMS *Hermes*. In both ships the flight deck was integral with the hull, the hangar a cavity scooped out of the hull. The hangar was a closed space without side openings. That in itself limited hangar capacity for a hull of a given size (estimated capacity was seventy-two aircraft).[12] Unlike the British ships, the U.S. carrier was given a powerful surface gun battery, eight 8-inch guns in four twin mounts. They were intended to defend her in the event she was caught by cruisers, but they consumed valuable flight-deck space (and the ships' flight decks narrowed forward because they were blended into the hull). These were the most powerful guns allowed on board carriers by the Washington Treaty, and presumably they were considered essential because the treaty encouraged creation of a new kind of 8-inch gun cruiser. The initial sketch showed two turrets forward of the island and two more alongside the flight deck aft, but ultimately the ship had all four turrets on deck, and her flight deck was widened aft. The new Bureau of Aeronautics resisted the idea of this kind of encroachment from the beginning of the new carrier design. No other navy placed heavy guns on the flight deck; the bureau did succeed in killing the proposed torpedo tubes, on the grounds that the ship's own torpedo bombers should suffice, and also succeeded in moving the 5-inch guns down to cuts in the flight deck rather than, as planned, on the flight deck itself. On the eve of World War II modernization plans included removal of the heavy gun battery, which was to be replaced by twin 5-inch dual-purpose guns (*Lexington* was sunk after her 8-inch guns were removed but before new flight-deck guns could be installed). Because the ships were expected to operate not only wheeled aircraft but the floatplanes otherwise launched by cruiser and battleship catapults, the design included a flywheel-powered catapult (one forward and one aft in the original design, only the bow one as built). This catapult was not intended to launch the ship's wheeled aircraft (the British later adopted much the same approach). Catapults became important only later.

The USS Saratoga (CV-3), recovering her aircraft, June 1935.

REEVES' CARRIER REVOLUTION

The U.S. Navy of that era was very fortunate in that it tested its ideas on the game floor of the Naval War College, that is, not only at sea (more generally, the War College acted as the Navy's think tank). Although such experimentation might seem the obvious way to develop new technology, the U.S. Navy seems to have been unusual in emphasizing it. The ships and aircraft involved could adopt whatever characteristics seemed relevant to future warfare. Officers could see what the aircraft of the future (rather than existing relatively primitive ones) might contribute to a naval battle. The games showed how important it was to mass aircraft (and also to launch them quickly, as a carrier might easily be put out of action by enemy attack). Captain (later Admiral) Harris Laning encouraged games involving large numbers of aircraft, far beyond what the existing carrier *Langley* could support, and emphasized the need to put the enemy's carriers out of action at the outset. Captain (later Admiral) Joseph M. Reeves took this lesson with him when he assumed command of the aircraft of the Battle Force, which at the time meant mainly the few assigned to *Langley*.[13] He had attended the War College in 1923–1924, became head of its tactics department in 1924, and on 1 June 1925 was assigned to the Bureau of Aeronautics. A few days later he went to Pensacola for the aviation observer's course, which would fit him to command an air unit. Once graduated, he was assigned in September 1925 to command Battle Fleet Aircraft Squadrons as senior officer aboard the prototype carrier, *Langley*. Reeves saw *Langley* as the essential school in which U.S. naval air doctrine would be created. She first went to sea, with Reeves aboard, in December 1925.

It was assumed that the aircraft capacity of any one carrier was limited because the Royal Navy, the most experienced carrier navy by far, had reached that conclusion after trials in 1918. Just as aircraft landing ashore would taxi off the runway before the next aircraft landed, the British stowed their aircraft in the carrier's hangar upon landing. That made for lengthy intervals between landings. It also meant that a ship's aircraft capacity was set by her hangar capacity, which in early carriers was very limited. Hence the British insistence on a large total carrier tonnage at Washington in 1921.

Coming from the War College, Reeves understood that he had to pack more air power into the small *Langley*. He found that airplanes did not need the whole deck on which to land. Instead of being stowed below upon landing, they could simply be wheeled forward, protected from landing aircraft by a wire barrier. In this way aircraft could be taken on board much more quickly.[14] Once all were aboard, they could be moved aft and be massed at the after end of the flight deck. They could take off again, en masse, to attack. In contrast to the British, in this view the hangar was mainly a workshop; many aircraft would spend very little time under cover. By March 1926 it was understood that an American carrier deck should be divided into three areas, all working simultaneously: a landing-on area aft, equipped with arresting gear; a rearming and servicing area roughly amidships, to prepare a follow-on strike; and a launch area forward. It became clear that launching tempo depended on landing tempo; if the landing interval was too long, aircraft would run out of fuel. Reeves therefore pressed his pilots to fly more precisely so that landings would be much quicker and much safer, with innovations like a circular formation feeding aircraft continuously into the landing area and like the division of the flight deck (aircraft handling) crew into teams with distinctively colored uniforms. As aircraft performance improved, it became impossible to operate the flight deck continuously. Instead, carriers spotted all or most of their strike aircraft aft, launched them, and spotted them forward (in front of the barrier) when they returned. After all had landed, they were all re-spotted back aft for a new strike. This change probably occurred in the mid-1930s.

The use of one end of the ship for landing, the other for taking off, and the area between for parking and servicing, encouraged BuAer to suggest in 1926 that future carriers should be truly double-ended, for greater flexibility, with arresting gear and catapults at both ends. The *Yorktowns* of the late 1930s had arrester wires at both ends, with four barriers between them, but they had only a limited ability to sustain high speed running astern. In theory this made it possible for the ship to launch fighters or scouts even when the bow was full of strike aircraft just recovered and not yet re-spotted. Similarly, scouts might be recovered over the bow when the usual landing area was full of aircraft spotted for a strike. The World War II *Essex* class did have the ability to sustain high astern speed. A few surviving photographs show *Essex*-class carriers recovering aircraft over their bows, running astern. Another means of launching when most aircraft were spotted forward was a hangar deck catapult firing athwartships, a feature of the *Ranger* and later designs (though not installed on board many of these ships).

Langley ultimately operated about four times as many airplanes as she had before Reeves arrived. From a ship design point of view, Reeves' innovation meant that carrier operating capacity depended on the size of the flight deck and the length of deck airplanes needed to take off, rather than on the capacity of the hangar. It took some years for that to become obvious, because at first the assumption was that aircraft would be placed on the flight deck only when they were about to fly, or had landed. Probably the U.S. Navy took time to realize that aircraft could survive prolonged exposure there (it helped that the U.S. Navy operated mainly in temperate climates). Neither the British nor the Japanese (who began their naval air arm with British tutelage) ever understood this use of the flight deck, to the extent that even many decades later a senior British warship designer asked this author how it was that American carriers packed in so many more aircraft with less hangar space than did British carriers. The radical difference in operating practice was why numbers of aircraft at the Battle of Midway were fairly equal, even though the Japanese had six carriers to the U.S. Navy's three.

It may have been key that Reeves was not a pilot (he had trained as an observer); he understood what naval aviation could provide to the fleet, but he was not viscerally aware of just how dangerous carrier operation could be. To a pilot, it must have seemed unnatural to land an airplane into a mass of parked aircraft, relying on arresting gear and a barrier to keep from crashing into them. The British based their own estimates of carrier capacity (and their operating practices) on pilots' views, because from 1 April 1918 on, their naval aircraft were operated by the new Royal Air Force. It is striking that the U.S. Navy often discussed—and accepted— the dangers of carrier operation, to the point that films of the classic era of carrier aviation seem incomplete without numerous crashes, many of them fatal. A memoir of interwar British carrier aviation was titled *It's Really Quite Safe, You Know*. American observers were surprised by how casual British carrier landings seemed. U.S. landings were highly disciplined because they had to be so precise to engage the arresting gear in the right place (for many years the Royal Navy did not even use arresting gear). About 1930 the Royal Navy finally realized that it could operate a lot more aircraft by adopting U.S.-style deck parking. Nothing happened, because by that time the British Air Ministry feared that total British aircraft numbers would be limited by a future disarmament treaty; it did not want the Royal Navy to consume too much of that limited pie.

Reeves' operating technique shaped U.S. carrier aircraft. Carriers had catapults, but they were not considered very effective, so aircraft generally rolled down the flight deck to take off. Carrier capacity was determined by how far aircraft had to roll, because when the carrier launched all her aircraft for a strike the first airplane had to start out from just ahead of a mass of aircraft parked on the after part of the flight deck. Generally the requirement was that the airplane be able to take off in four hundred feet in the twenty-knot wind the ship could generate. It turned out to be quite acceptable until the end of World War II. Among other things, it meant that a ship with a relatively short deck could operate modern carrier aircraft as long as she was assigned a small enough air group that they left the necessary four hundred feet of deck. That became very important during World War II.

Given U.S. operating practice, carrier deck capacity could be set either by the required landing area plus the spotting area used by aircraft once they landed, or by spotting area plus the takeoff space needed by the first airplane. Between 1930 and 1939 takeoff run increased by 93 percent—but average carrier deck length increased by only 7 percent. Higher aircraft performance required higher wing loading, which in turn increased the takeoff run—which was one reason catapults became increasingly important during World War II. They were disliked because they greatly increased the interval between launches, but without catapults the need to match increasingly powerful land-based aircraft would make it more and more difficult to operate enough aircraft on a carrier; ultimately airplanes might need the whole flight deck merely to take off. That is what happened as jets entered service; they became usable only as powerful enough catapults entered service.

Landing space depended on the airplane's stall speed, which rose by about 13.5 percent in 1930–1939. High lift devices were applied from 1935 on, and this reduced stall speed and enabled a slower approach speed. To the landing area had to be added the run-out of the arresting wire, which absorbed the energy of the landing airplane (in 1939 this distance was 40 to 100 feet). The overall length devoted to landing was about 315 feet, including the run-out. If this length were not increased as landing speed increased, then the rate of barrier crashes would rise; the rate for 1937 was 1.11 per 1,000, cut to 0.96 in 1938 but increased to 1.23 in 1939. Since carriers could not grow to keep pace with the higher performance airplanes introduced during and after World War II, it was not surprising that crashes became more common—that the existing form of flight deck was perceived as more and more dangerous. The number of aircraft that could park on deck depended on the area per airplane, which until 1936 fell as biplanes became more compact, with higher wing loading, but then grew as monoplanes entered service.[15]

If a carrier (like *Ranger*) had too small a deck, she could not spot all of her aircraft on deck. Some aircraft had to go into the hangar after landing. U.S. hangar design practice (open hangars) made that more acceptable, as these aircraft could warm up for flight while still in the hangar, then be brought up onto the flight deck ready for launch, after the aircraft already there had been launched (*Lexington* and *Saratoga* struck a few aircraft below deck as they landed, but could not warm them up in their closed hangars; in 1940 plans were under way to improve their ventilation). By 1940 this argument applied to the new *Essex* class, which would almost certainly have to operate multiple generations of higher and higher performance airplanes. If the aircraft operating cycle once again depended on elevators, their speed and location became crucial. The forty-five-second operating cycle in the *Yorktown*s might be too slow, since carriers enjoyed a sixteen-second minimum launch interval. On the other hand, feeding one hangar airplane for every two on deck would make up for the elevator cycle. It turned out that elevator speed could not be increased significantly. Nor could many more elevators be provided in the right places. For example, particularly given the argument that planes from the flight-deck spot should be mixed with those brought up from below, it was essential that at least some elevators obstruct the flight deck to the minimum possible extent. Similarly, the elevators should be brought toward the middle of the ship so as to limit their effect on launching and recovery, and so that two elevators might be usable for either (i.e., both had to be clear of both deck parks). The position amidships (lengthwise) was particularly valuable because it would be just forward of the landing area and just abaft the launch area (if that were possible, given lengthening takeoff runs). It was also preferable, for handling in the hangars, not to place any elevators near the ends of the hangars. Typically U.S. carriers had their hangars divided into thirds by fire curtains, so they had one elevator per hangar bay. In 1940 the U.S. Navy was experimenting with a solution to the elevator problem, a deck-edge device that rose and fell away from the traffic on the flight deck. A simple elevator was tested in USS *Wasp*, and a much larger one was designed into the *Essex* class. The elevator design in the *Essex* class was based on that of the stage of Radio City at Rockefeller Center in New York, which could be raised and lowered as needed.

NAVAL CONTROL VERSUS AIR UNIFICATION

The U.S. Navy watched the creation of the Royal Air Force (RAF) and drew the lesson that it did not want to suffer a similar disaster. Although in theory the RAF was expected to provide air services for the Royal Navy and for the army, in practice it disdained both. For example, it became interested in large flying boats as a substitute for the fleet, a consequence being that the Royal Navy needed long-range carrier reconnaissance aircraft. Because carrier aircraft capacity was so limited, the British became interested in using catapults aboard battleships and cruisers to launch combat aircraft. At first that must have seemed an excellent idea, but as aircraft performance improved, the requirement that, for example, torpedo bombers must be suited to such operation dramatically limited their performance—particularly because they also had to function as long-range fleet scouts. The U.S. Navy managed to retain control of its aircraft, including flying boats. It came to see big sea-based airplanes (most famously the PBY Catalina) as a way around the limits imposed by the Washington Treaty—at the least, as a vital fleet scouting force.[16]

Naval control of naval aviation had other consequences. The U.S. Navy had in-house technical aviation expertise, which could respond to its own needs; the Royal Navy depended on the separate Air Ministry, whose experts might not understand naval warfare at all. Perhaps most important of all, by keeping naval aviation within the U.S. Navy, the United States maintained an organic relationship between flyers and the rest of the Navy. To further encourage air-mindedness in the fleet, a law passed in 1926 extended the aviator-in-command requirement to carriers and seaplane tenders.

Again, the Royal Navy was very different, because after 1918 all pilots held RAF ranks. They could rise to flag rank within the RAF, but they could not achieve high naval rank. Naval officers learned what existing naval aircraft and carriers could do for the fleet, and they certainly became acutely aware of the need for fleet air defense (probably more than in other navies of this period), but without air experience of their own they probably could not imagine more remote possibilities. Without

in-house technical expertise, it was difficult for the Royal Navy to frame requirements effectively. For example, based on its own experience that British naval aircraft had limited performance, the Royal Navy seems to have concluded that all naval
aircraft would be limited in performance—with unfortunate consequences when it
faced the Imperial Japanese Navy in 1941–1942.

Given Reeves' innovation and the understanding that numbers were vital, the
U.S. Navy bought large numbers of aircraft during the interwar period. Numbers
gave the Navy's Bureau of Aeronautics the clout to demand high performance
(roughly like that of contemporary land-based aircraft) and also the rationale to
finance the necessary engine development. During the interwar period, the U.S.
Navy bought about as many aircraft as the U.S. Army Air Corps, in distinct contrast
to the British experience. Moreover, because the Navy incorporated the full range of
technical expertise, it could understand the potential of new aviation technology far
better than could the contemporary British Admiralty.

TREATY CARRIERS

The same Naval War College exercises that motivated Reeves to recast carrier operating practices led U.S. naval thinkers to try to juggle the tonnage left over from the two
ex–battle cruisers to get the greatest possible number of aircraft.[17] In March 1926, in
connection with an abortive proposal for a light carrier (below 10,000 tons, hence
not limited by the Washington Treaty), BuAer pointed out that carrier operating
capacity was not merely a matter of hangar and flight-deck size but also of the rates
at which airplanes could be assembled, brought up to the flight deck, and launched
and also the rate at which they could be recovered and rearmed for a second strike.
A larger number of small carriers might also be less vulnerable than a smaller number of larger ones. The main threat to a carrier lay in the gasoline spread among her
aircraft and in fuel tanks and lines. Given this explosive load, the same weapon could
destroy a carrier of any size, since all it had to do was touch off the gasoline and its
vapor. Size bought little in the way of protection, it seemed. So what was the minimum acceptable size of a carrier? Surely it was set by the needs of the aircraft. Hangar
headroom decided what sort of aircraft the ship could operate; BuAer considered 17
feet a minimum for the largest ones (the torpedo bombers). Hangar width was also
important; the bureau considered 68 feet optimum. The ship should have the largest
possible hangar, which would necessarily extend to the sides of the ship.[18] The desirable minimum deck width was 80 feet; cutting to 70 would be possible, but would
dramatically reduce the area available for aircraft warming up for takeoff (by an
entire fore-and-aft row). That is, the strength of the strike the carrier could launch
would depend on how much parking space was available aft in which to warm up
airplanes. The island particularly blocked the flight deck; without it, aircraft could

be placed outboard until their wheels were in the scuppers at the edges of the flight deck. Thus the island denied the parking space extending abaft it, and even somewhat to the side. The success of the flush-decked *Langley* suggested that it might not really be so difficult to vent smoke over the side of the ship rather than through conventional uptakes. BuAer had C&R sketch three carriers with its new deck and island arrangement, all capable of 32.5 knots: 23,000 tons (sixty-four aircraft in a mixed air group), 13,800 tons (forty-four aircraft), and 10,000 tons (twenty-four aircraft). Another set of studies showed that if the speed of the 13,800-tonner were reduced to twenty-five knots, aircraft capacity would increase to fifty-six.[19] The studies showed that hangar deck area (hence aircraft capacity) shrank more slowly than tonnage, so on a fixed total treaty tonnage it would pay to buy more, smaller carriers rather than a few large ones.

C&R (presumably based on BuAer comments) argued that the rate at which strike aircraft could be rearmed for another strike was the key design consideration. The lengths required to land (about 250 to 400 feet) and to take off (70 feet for fighters, 250 for torpedo bombers) were relatively fixed. The space between the two determined how quickly aircraft could be rearmed, and even whether they could be parked at all after landing. In other ships, length was chosen to achieve the desired speed for a given power plant. For a carrier, length came first, and an unusually long hull might achieve high speed even with limited power. Minimum length was clearly 600 to 650 feet, but anything longer would be highly desirable. Conversely, anything that made for slow landings would ultimately limit carrier operation. A 10,000-ton carrier could not have a deck more than about 600 feet long, which ruled it out from this point of view. It seemed that, beyond a point, any carrier would launch aircraft at about the same rate. On this basis a larger number of smaller carriers would put aircraft into the air, for a maximum air effort, more quickly than a smaller number of larger carriers.

For the first post–battle cruiser carrier, then, the General Board chose the smallest acceptable ship (13,800 tons), because it could get five such ships (the maximum number of aircraft) on the available tonnage: USS *Ranger* (CV-4).[20] One advantage of minimum size was that it would be associated with the minimum power plant, whose smoke might be easiest to vent through the desired side pipes. BuAer's arguments were taken so seriously that many in the Navy considered the two ex–battle cruisers white elephants, before either had been completed. In line with the BuAer arguments, *Ranger* was designed with a flush deck and no island at all, venting her smoke from deck-edge pipes, which could fold down for air operations. Her flight deck was built as a light superstructure atop the hull. The large openings in the sides of the hangar were closed by sliding doors. Aircraft of this era had to warm up their engines before flight. Those stowed in an open hangar could do so before being lifted up to the flight deck, so a second strike could be launched soon after the aircraft spotted aft had taken off. This arrangement also made it relatively easy to cut large holes in the flight deck for elevators. The big open hangar accommodated growth in the aircraft themselves. The ship was designed with two catapults but completed with none.[21] Speed was cut to 29.5 knots and the number of aircraft carried was increased (108 aircraft as compared to 91 that would normally be carried on a 32.5-knot designated ship). The lower speed of 29.5 knots simplified the smoke problem. The demand for a flush deck precluded anything like the 8-inch battery of the big carriers, so *Ranger* was assigned a combination of their twelve 5-inch anti-aircraft guns and machine guns, all mounted alongside her flight deck (she had eight 5-inch as completed). While *Ranger* was being built, experience with the big carriers showed just how valuable an island could be, and she was redesigned while under construction. It was too late to change the run of her smoke pipes. They gave considerable trouble in service.

As *Ranger* was being designed, in 1926, U.S. naval aviators first demonstrated dive-bombing. This revolutionary means of attack made it possible to hit maneuvering ships, and it was far more difficult to defend against. In his FY28 report (September 1928), the fleet commander recommended abandoning torpedo bombers (which were large and heavy and had limited performance) in favor of the much more agile dive-bombers, which could be made so fast that fighters could effectively escort them. On the other hand, bombs from dive-bombers could not accelerate sufficiently to penetrate heavy armored decks; without torpedo bombers U.S. carriers would pose threats to enemy carriers and cruisers, but not to enemy battleships. As a member of the General Board later put it, the question was not whether carriers would ultimately supersede battleships, but when. When that would happen depended on when carriers could wield a battleship-killing weapon, a torpedo bomber with sufficient performance to survive in the face of enemy fighters and anti-aircraft guns. Given very limited funds, *Ranger* was not ordered until 1930 and not completed until 1934.

Initial experience with the two big new carriers, *Lexington* and *Saratoga*, completed in 1927, was a surprise. Each could accommodate about a hundred aircraft. War games (with the ships rather than on a game floor) showed that they derived considerable advantages from their speed coupled with their large air groups. It seemed clear that *Ranger* had been a mistake, but she could not be cancelled and reordered. To hold down her size, she had been made much slower than the two big carriers, and she lacked their protection, particularly against underwater hits. One factor in the preference for large carriers was the conclusion, based on operations, that carriers would have to operate individually. Ironically, the Japanese operated their carriers together at Pearl Harbor and Midway after having seen a film of four U.S. carriers proceeding together (on their return from a fleet exercise, not during it).

With the two ex–battle cruisers and *Ranger* built, around 1930 the U.S. Navy had about 55,000 tons of carriers left to build (not counting the obsolete *Langley*, which could be replaced at any time). The choice lay between three 18,400-ton carriers or two 20,000-ton and one 15,200-ton carriers. Given experience with the big, fast ex–battle cruisers (34 knots), speed was set at 32.5 knots, a figure that became standard.[22] According to a paper justifying the new design, *Ranger* corresponded to theoretical analysis of carrier requirements made before it was clear just how versatile such ships would be—and how often they might have to operate with few or no escorts. High speed was essential. After considering a 15,200-ton design, about October 1931 the General Board chose the 20,000-tonner, which could be armored to some extent, provided with underwater protection, and also be faster than *Ranger*. It seemed that no carrier short of 18,000 tons could have sufficient speed and protection, and also that no power plant sufficient for 32.5 knots could be compatible with a flush-deck design (i.e., could rely on side exhausts). Experience with the two big carriers showed that the island seemed not to be any problem in air operations, and it certainly simplified ship and anti-aircraft fire control and also provided a valuable flight-deck control position. There was also a suspicion, which turned out to be justified, that too much freeboard had been sacrificed to make the *Ranger* design practicable; she was too wet. Elevators were again entirely rearranged, with one in the bow, one in the stern, and one amidships, corresponding to the evolving practice of spotting all aircraft either forward or aft. The midships elevator could serve aircraft massed either in the bow or the stern. Both the 15,000- and the 20,000-ton designs showed large islands to serve their considerable power plants. General Board characteristics required provision for hangar deck catapults, to be installed if the *Ranger* installation proved successful, but the sketch design showed no catapults at all. The ships were to carry 90 aircraft, 40 percent of them of the largest type (i.e., torpedo bombers), compared to 110 for *Saratoga* and 70 for the projected 15,200-tonner.

BuAer justified the *Ranger* design (perhaps retroactively) on the grounds that the U.S. Navy needed at least seven carriers (two *Lexington*s and five *Ranger*s). The flight-deck cruiser idea offered a real possibility that the U.S. Navy could gain up to eight cruiser-carriers, in which case (according to BuAer) the seven-carrier requirement could be foregone, and the 20,000-tonner adopted (which, according to a 12 November 1931 BuAer letter, had been shown some years earlier to be the ideal carrier size). BuAer's position did not, however, change with the demise of the flight-deck cruiser shortly afterward. Meanwhile war planning studies suggested that at least fourteen carriers would be needed to fight Japan. Few existing American merchant ships were suitable for conversion, and that would take nearly a year in any case. The U.S. Navy would have to fight with what it had, and each carrier would have to provide maximum air effort. These arguments were used to defeat a suggestion to build a pair of 25,000-tonners armed with centerline 8-inch guns (at the expense of flight-deck length), with about a third fewer aircraft than the 20,000-ton "pure" carrier (the Japanese tried much the same idea at about this time). BuAer did point out that with five *Rangers* it could operate 635 aircraft, but with the planned two 20,000-tonners and the 15,000-tonner that would be reduced to 553; if only two 25,000-tonners were built, the total would fall once more, to 429, and there would be only five carriers instead of six or seven.

Although a sketch design was prepared in 1931, there was no money for new construction until the Roosevelt administration passed the National Industrial Recovery Act in 1933. It provided money to build two ships: *Yorktown* and *Enterprise*, completed in 1937 and 1938, respectively. Meanwhile the hangar deck powder catapults were abandoned, although interest in hangar deck catapults survived. BuAer meanwhile developed a successful hydraulic catapult that could be mounted flush on the fore end of the flight deck. It was so attractive that special measures were taken to save enough weight to fit it within the 20,000-ton displacement limit. The new ships had three such catapults, two on the flight deck and one (athwartships) on the hangar deck.

Initially (1933) the new carriers were designed to operate ninety-four aircraft: eighteen fighters, thirty-six scout bombers, eighteen torpedo bombers, eighteen bombers (heavy dive-bombers—a category soon to be filled by the Northrop BT, predecessor of the Douglas SBD Dauntless), and four utility aircraft. The scout bombers were capable of dive-bombing with light bombs (500 pounds), but they were primarily scouts. The flight-deck spot could not accommodate all of them; typically nine torpedo bombers had to remain in the hangar when all the others were on deck. Even then operation was marginal; the first fighter in line had only 116 feet of deck in which to take off, but in a twenty-five knot wind the most efficient such airplane (XF3U, with a controllable-pitch propeller) needed 143 feet, not including the usual 25 percent safety margin. BuAer strongly argued for a deck extension. It was clear by 1934 that with their full air complement the ships could not employ the standard spot in which the after arresting gear was clear for landings and the forward length clear for takeoff. Worse, there was not sufficient hangar deck space for those that could not fit on the flight deck. By World War II the bomber (heavy dive-bomber) and scout bomber categories had merged, and airplanes were considerably larger, so the ships were expected to operate four eighteen-airplane squadrons: fighters, scouts, dive-bombers, and torpedo bombers, for a total of seventy-two combat aircraft. Because they carried the heaviest weapons, the torpedo bombers were also considered suitable for level bombing (mainly for land attack) with heavy bombs.[23]

With the *Yorktown* design BuAer accepted that an island structure was not merely a necessary evil, but that it presented a vital means of controlling the flight deck. By 1932, with *Ranger* nearly complete, the bureau badly wanted her modified to incorporate an island. It was far too late to lead smoke pipes up through the small new island, but the structure did provide a conventional bridge (that incidentally reduced congestion in the forward part of the hangar) as well as positions for two directors, which made the ship's 5-inch guns far more effective. The *Ranger* island was in effect the island structure planned for the *Yorktown*s less their massive funnels.[24]

In effect these ships were pre-prototypes of the mass-produced *Essex* class of World War II. Investing in them showed just how important naval aviation was to the interwar Navy. They proved extremely tough. *Enterprise* fought in nearly every Pacific battle and survived the war. *Yorktown* was sunk at Midway.

There was not enough tonnage for a third ship, so the General Board suggested a 15,200-tonner (32.5 knots, like the 20,000-tonner) for the next (1934) program. Construction was delayed because the tonnage involved was absorbed by the obsolescent *Langley*. In 1937 she was de-rated to seaplane tender status, hence removed from carrier tonnage. A much-improved *Ranger*, USS *Wasp*, was built (by this time available tonnage had dropped to 14,500). Like the *Yorktown*s, she had a massive island. Again, limited tonnage meant limited speed and also limited survivability. In *Wasp* as in earlier carriers, there was interest in flying aircraft from the hangar deck to increase the rate at which they could be launched. She was completed with two hangar deck catapults in addition to two flight-deck catapults. As with other carriers, *Wasp* was given an enlarged fighter squadron (twenty-seven aircraft) in 1940. For the rest she had a standard air group at the beginning of World War II: a scout squadron, a scout bomber squadron (dive-bombers), and a torpedo squadron, but by 1942 the torpedo squadron was twelve rather than the usual eighteen aircraft. The scouts and dive-bombers were the same SBD airplane, but their roles were quite different. Although the 15,200-tonner conceived in 1931 would have had the power and speed of the *Yorktown*s, *Wasp* was laid down with a 70,000 rather than 120,000 SHP) plant and a designed speed of 29.5 knots (*Ranger* produced only 57,000 SHP.

Toughness meant the carriers were difficult to sink, but it was widely understood, in the 1930s, that their flimsy flight decks could easily be destroyed by light bombs. Although the phrase "eggshells wielding hammers" was coined to describe contemporary heavy cruisers, carriers were best described in this way, particularly as their offensive power grew during the 1930s. It was assumed that whichever side found the enemy's carriers first would put them out of action. After a war game, for example, Admiral King, commanding the Battle Fleet Aircraft, was asked by battleship officers why his ships were not providing them with air services (such as protection for their spotting aircraft). They seemed to fight a private carrier versus carrier war in every fleet exercise. King replied that unless his carriers defeated the enemy's at the outset, the battleships would never have any air services at all. Given this perception, through the 1930s U.S. carrier officers asked why future carriers could not be provided with at least lightly armored flight decks.

The answer says a great deal about contemporary U.S. thinking. An armored flight deck would represent considerable topweight, even with thin armor. On a given displacement (limited by treaty), that topweight could be accommodated on a smaller hull with a smaller air wing. The alternative, unavailable at the time, would be to provide much the same air group by growing the hull to balance off the top-weight involved. The smaller-carrier solution was regularly rejected because it was so important both to find and to kill enemy carriers. U.S. carriers were expected to operate alone, so each carrier had to be able to conduct all these functions. Finding an enemy required a squadron of dedicated scouts. Killing an enemy required a squadron of dive-bombers, preferably accompanied by a squadron of torpedo bombers—and by fighters. Four squadrons—more than eighty aircraft—required a large flight deck, hence a large carrier. The scouting (S) and dive-bombing (B) roles were combined in single airplanes by the late 1930s, but they were still separate functions and they still required separate squadrons. Thus by the outbreak of World War II, U.S. carriers typically accommodated two squadrons of scout bombers, such as the Douglas SBD Dauntless.

In the late 1930s the big Fleet Problem exercises awakened the fleet to the desperate need for direct fighter protection; there was only limited faith in anti-aircraft guns, and it seemed that only fighters (if anything) could deal with the dive-bombing attacks the U.S. Navy itself favored. Yet the single squadron of fighters aboard each carrier was considered part of that ship's own anti-aircraft screen, or as protection for the ship's own striking force (both the war in China and the Spanish Civil War seemed to show that such protection was essential). The standard carrier squadron of eighteen fighters already included nine spare aircraft to allow for attrition and to maintain full operating strength when some aircraft were being overhauled. Up to three of these "operating spares" were normally used that way. Commander, Aircraft Squadrons Battle Force Rear Admiral Ernest J. King (later the wartime CNO) proposed using spares to strengthen fighter squadrons on board the large carriers to twenty-four active aircraft. The Scouting and Battle Force commanders wanted a lot more. Ultimately the recommendation was to give the two slow carriers (*Ranger* and *Wasp*), which would probably work with the battle fleet, fighter-heavy air groups, leaving the big fast carriers, which would probably operate as independent striking forces, with their original air groups, tilted toward attack rather than defense. After all, if it was accepted that an air attack once launched could not be stopped, the only real fleet air defense against enemy carrier aircraft was to destroy them at source—at the enemy carrier. As for the strike carrier's own fighters, normally they would form a continuous combat air patrol. Maintaining it would exhaust the pilots, who would be unable to escort the carrier's bombers once the enemy fleet was found. Note that search radar could change this situation; the carrier might have to mount a combat air patrol only after enemy aircraft were detected.

Ships already had the capacity for twenty-seven fighters; they just normally did not carry enough pilots. In June 1940 BuAer proposed that the fighter squadrons be boosted to twenty-seven airplane strength, and OpNav agreed. By that time the agreed characteristics for the next carrier class (*Essex*) already incorporated an interesting twist: they should have the usual four eighteen-airplane squadrons, but also space to accommodate a fifth (fighter) squadron of eighteen aircraft. Given pressure for more fighters, the bureaus interpreted this to mean five squadrons of planes with their personnel, stores, guns, and ammunition rather than the spare planes previously imagined. This new interpretation certainly comported with the twenty-seven fighter concept approved in June 1940; the new *Essex* had sufficient capacity for a double fighter squadron (thirty-six aircraft).

Surviving papers do not mention radar as a factor in these changes, but it is difficult to discount, because it solved a serious problem. Through the 1930s hopes that the carrier's own fighters could protect her against enemy attack had declined. About 1930, U.S. thinking envisaged a circular formation in which destroyers many miles from the carrier could spot approaching enemy aircraft in time for carrier fighters to take off and deal with them. Through the 1930s aircraft performance improved dramatically, to the point that it was no longer possible to set up a satisfactory screen (that proved difficult enough even *with* radar). Some suggested abandoning carrier fighters altogether. They survived mainly as a means of supporting strike aircraft (with light strike capability) and also as a means of supporting the Marines should they have to land on enemy islands (a role already being taken very seriously). The advent of radar in 1937–1939 changed the situation completely. Suddenly it became possible to provide effective warning, even against fast aircraft. Radar was first tested in the January 1939 maneuvers, aboard the battleship *Texas*. It did take considerable time for the U.S. Navy to turn this raw technology into an ability to control fighters. At Midway a carrier versus carrier battle developed much as had been predicted. U.S. strike aircraft found three Japanese carriers before the Japanese found the Americans and inflicted fatal damage. Then the surviving Japanese carrier found an American carrier, USS *Yorktown*. Her aircraft managed to damage *Yorktown* fatally (she sank due to loss of power and inability to de-water after numberous Japanese hits). The U.S. ships had radar, but they also had only very primitive fighter control arrangements. Two years later, at the Philippine Sea, the Japanese found the American carriers first. However, the U.S. ships had highly developed fighter control based on the new technology of the Combat Information Center (CIC). The Japanese air striking force was massacred in the "Turkey Shoot." It happened that most Japanese carriers themselves survived. One irony of the battle was that the U.S. aircrews thought they had done poorly; Samuel Eliot Morrison reports a feeling of depression on the hangar decks. In fact they had ended the Japanese naval air arm, because the Japanese could never train replacement aircrew—a fact not appreciated a few months later at

Leyte Gulf. The core issue was aircrew more than carriers: the great strength of the U.S. Navy lay not only in its ability to multiply carriers and their aircraft but even more in its ability to multiply aircrew.

The Washington Treaty (and its successor, the London Treaty of 1930) affected the U.S. Navy in a subtle way. Until 1934 U.S. warships were individually authorized by Congress. That year Japan withdrew from the treaty system, and a few in the United States realized that war might be coming. Congress passed the Vinson-Trammell Act, which authorized a "modern Treaty Navy." This phrase avoided the appearance of expansion, but allowed considerable new construction, because the United States was well below the allowable tonnage. (Congress still decided how much money to appropriate, thus still controlled new construction.) By 1936 it was clear that Japan was no longer interested in any kind of limitation, but there was still hope that a treaty system might limit naval spending and indirectly avoid war. To that end the replacement London Treaty eliminated the tonnage totals on battleships and carriers, but it retained limits on individual ship size (the carrier limit was reduced to 23,000 tons, at British insistence). Signatories had to announce their naval building plans well ahead of construction, the idea being that they would restrain themselves to avoid touching off a building race. Given the form of the Vinson-Trammell Act, as the international situation worsened Congress authorized a percentage increase in various categories of treaty-limited warships in the Second Vinson Trammell Act (1938).[25] Because battleship and carrier tonnages were tied back to the Washington Treaty, the Act implicitly maintained much the same ratio between the two types—which had reflected the much earlier experience of World War I. The phrase "modern Treaty Navy" meant that new construction was approved to replace existing overage ships, replacement age having been set by treaty. In 1936 the only over-age U.S. capital ships were battleships. U.S. carriers were all far too young to replace in the near term.

Particularly if carriers did not use torpedo bombers, it was not clear how effective they could be against other ships. An American attempt to multiply naval aircraft within the treaty limit shows how tricky this question could be. In the run-up to the 1930 London Naval Conference, Admiral William A. Moffet of the Bureau of Aeronautics suggested building a flight-deck cruiser, which could add to the fleet's air strength without counting against carrier tonnage. At the conference, the chief American naval adviser, CNO Admiral William V. Pratt, managed to get the flight-deck cruiser into the newly limited total cruiser tonnage, of which the United States had a great deal available (the British, with whom the United States had parity, had a far larger cruiser fleet). However, when the flight-deck cruiser was tested at Newport, it failed. Its aircraft just did not have enough offensive power to balance off the reduction in cruiser guns; in duels the flight-deck cruiser was generally sunk. The design effort, which had gone to the point of preparing plans for bids by shipbuilders, was abandoned.

The Second Vinson-Trammell Act provided enough tonnage to build a slightly improved *Yorktown* (USS *Hornet*). Her construction seems to have been pushed through by Congress against some naval staff opposition; the General Board felt that it was more urgent to build modern battleships. That did not necessarily mean that the senior navy was against carriers: one role of modern fast battleships was as escorts for carriers. Existing battleships could not keep up with carriers, and in a pre-radar era there was a real possibility that enemy capital ships would catch carriers—as actually happened in 1940, when the German *Scharnhorst* and *Gniesenau* sank HMS *Glorious*.

In the late 1930s there was also a fear, at least on the General Board, that the best land-based aircraft grossly outperformed modern naval aircraft, hence that carriers might be moving toward obsolescence.[26] That turned out to be a temporary consequence of the level of engine development. The most powerful engines suited to fighters produced about a thousand horsepower. The British and the Germans achieved high performance effectively by wrapping airplanes like the Spitfire around these engines, providing far too little fuel for naval purposes as then understood. The U.S. Navy found that similar power applied to a fully navalized airplane like the Wildcat (F4F) produced much less performance (the Japanese solved the performance problem in the A6M Zero by adopting a very light structure, limited armament, and no armor at all). Spitfire speed was limited more by what a propeller could handle than by engine output. By 1938 the Bureau of Aeronautics understood that the coming generation of two-thousand-horsepower engines would solve the problem. Aircraft could not gain much more speed, but they could achieve maximum speed with acceptable range and other features. The resulting fighters, like the Hellcat and Corsair, were quite the equal of their land-based contemporaries. It is not clear how quickly the conclusions reached at the technical end of the Navy reached the policymakers.

U.S. naval exercises show how current fears played out. In the early 1930s, U.S. carriers regularly practiced attacking land targets, raiding Los Angeles and Pearl Harbor. In the mid-1930s the U.S. Navy adopted the high-performance (for the time) Catalina (PBY) flying boat. In line with the policy of using large numbers of flying boats (not limited by treaty) to provide an important component of naval air power, the Navy hoped that the Catalina could function not only as a scout but also as a bomber (hence the B in its designation). It seemed that Catalinas or their equivalents patrolling from Pearl Harbor could find an enemy carrier force before it got within attack range. The comment that land-based aircraft were reaching superiority meant that such detection would be fatal; the U.S. carriers stopped raiding Pearl Harbor in their exercises. This shift may have played into disbelief, in 1941, that

Japanese carriers (presumably operating under the same limitations as U.S. ships) would attack Pearl Harbor. It turned out that scouting was far more difficult than had been imagined prewar, and that carrier attacks on land targets were generally entirely practicable; but that took time to learn. Again, the perceived vulnerability of carriers was key to U.S. naval thinking.

CARRIERS FOR A TWO-OCEAN NAVY

The story of the World War II carriers began when Germany, Italy, and Japan became Axis allies in the fall of 1938. By this time the Japanese attack on China, and German pressures for territory in Europe made war seem likely. Until this time U.S. national strategy was shaped by the requirements of the most likely war, a war against Japan. Once Germany had created the Axis, it was no longer possible for the United States to contemplate a war fought entirely in the Pacific. Too, Germany and Italy now clearly threatened to penetrate South America; the United States needed the naval strength to prevent any armed assault in the Western Hemisphere. The two problems were linked in that the United States seemed to need access to southeast Asian resources in order to maintain sufficient strength to beat off any Axis attack in the Western Hemisphere. By October 1938 the OpNav War Plans Division was investigating the building program required in a "war of maximum effort," corresponding to the World War II mobilization. In spring 1939 U.S. naval planners began to lay out the requirements of a "Two-Ocean Navy" capable of fighting simultaneous wars in the Atlantic and in the Pacific. The United States began secret staff talks with the British, who would probably also be involved in such a war.

A two-ocean Navy would clearly require more ships, including more carriers. Battleship numbers were set by the need to match all potential enemy navies in both oceans. It did not yet seem that carriers could be dominant—and neither Germany nor Italy had a large carrier fleet the United States would have to match. It is striking in retrospect that this analysis did not take into account the possibility that carrier superiority would change the rules, as when a British carrier strike sank much of the Italian battleship fleet at Taranto in November 1940—or when the Japanese did the same thing to the United States at Pearl Harbor.

The new ships were the *Essex* (CV-9) class designed during the fall of 1939. Because work began after the outbreak of war on 1 September, the previous treaty limit (23,000 tons) did not apply.[27] However, it was possible to work quickly because the new carrier embodied many design features of the earlier 20,000-ton type; thus it was still somewhat limited by the defunct treaties (it displaced 27,200 tons). In drawing up characteristics for the new carrier, the General Board considered and rejected alternative proposals for relatively small carriers with armored flight decks, which would have supported many fewer aircraft. The way in which carrier flight decks had to provide sufficient length for landing-on, parking, and taking off dramatically limited the aircraft capacity of small ships.

As conceived in January 1940, the *Essex* had a long enough flight deck to operate all four squadrons in a single operation. Compared to *Yorktown*, she had a quarter more aviation gasoline. The new carrier had new lightweight efficient high-temperature high-pressure machinery, which dramatically reduced the size of the uptakes in her island structure. Power increased from 120,000 to 150,000 SHP, more than making up for the effect of considerably increased displacement (26,500 rather than 20,000 tons; ultimately 27,200 tons). The machinery was rearranged so that it could not be knocked out by a single hit. Shrinking the island made it possible to place defensive twin 5-inch guns on the flight deck forward and aft of it (the *Yorktown*s had a few flight-deck machine guns). The new design retained four of the eight deck-edge 5-inch guns of the earlier class, those on the island side being eliminated.

Compared to previous carriers, the *Essex* class showed two great innovations. One was reliable powerful hydraulic catapults (H4 type), which by 1945 were often used to launch heavily loaded aircraft. Since rolling takeoffs were no longer necessary, a carrier could place aircraft much closer to her bow: she could operate many more aircraft. Toward the end of the war, because the Japanese used kamikazes against the U.S. fleet, carriers were provided with more fighters, and the ability to use the flight deck more fully became far more important. Catapults also made it possible to launch aircraft under worse sea conditions, because they provided positive control as the airplane ran down the deck. An unusual feature of early *Essex*-class carriers was a cross-deck catapult on the hangar deck. It was intended to launch reconnaissance aircraft even when the carrier's bow was packed with a strike that had recently landed (and had not yet been re-spotted aft). Hangar deck catapults were little used, and they were removed so that more light anti-aircraft guns could be fitted at hangar deck level. The other major change was the deck-edge elevator described above.

Much of the extra tonnage of the new carrier went into more armor. Compared to a *Yorktown*, *Essex* added armor on her hangar deck—which limited the effect of any explosions there (it could resist a 1,000-pound bomb). It was still impossible to provide flight-deck armor. The flight deck was flimsy, but that meant that it could quickly be repaired at sea or in a forward area—and U.S. naval strategy envisaged staging the fleet through the Western Pacific, where it might not have any sort of prepared base. Armor would be fine if it kept bombs out, but any that did penetrate would do damage that could be repaired only in a shipyard. The ships proved remarkably tough, none being sunk. By way of comparison, *Yorktown* (CV-5) and *Hornet* (CV-8) were sunk as well as the huge *Lexington* and the small *Wasp*. Much of the superiority of the new carriers could be traced to much improved damage control measures, such as changed aviation gasoline practices (*Lexington* was fatally damaged by a gasoline vapor explosion). Too, by the time the *Essex* class was in service the United States had sufficient superiority to be able to tow badly damaged ships out of the battle area rather than scuttling them (as with *Yorktown* at Midway) to avoid their seizure by the Japanese. Even so, the survival of ships such as USS *Franklin* and USS *Bunker Hill* was remarkable, a great tribute both to their crews and to their construction. The wartime record of the *Essex* class was later used to show that carriers could survive multiple cruise missile hits, a Japanese kamikaze being quite equivalent to the later anti-ship missiles.

Late in September 1939 OpNav sketched a "two-ocean navy" including thirty-six battleships (of which the U.S. Navy already had twenty-two built and building) and eighteen carriers (of which eight had been either built, laid down, or ordered, including *Essex*). The thinking of the time shows in the proposed initial annual building program: two battleships and one carrier, plus lesser ships (it seemed necessary to expand building capacity before a larger program could be ordered). A March 1938 General Board memorandum written to help lay out a ten-year program argued that "in view of the arising questioned value of aircraft carriers relative to increasing improvement in characteristics of land planes, it is believed that if more carriers are desired they should be built as soon as possible, consequently they are listed for the next two building programs." Congress was more positive: for 1940–1941 it authorized an additional 30,000 tons of carriers, boosting the total to 215,000 tons. The new tonnage was applied to USS *Essex* (CV-9) of the FY41 program. Because carriers were assigned a twenty-year lifetime (by treaty), replacements could not begin until 1945 (the *Lexington*s would become overage in 1947).

In November 1939 Congress passed a 25 percent increase in underage tonnage in each category. That seemed sufficient to build four more 24,000-ton *Essex*-class carriers (CV 10–13). Because designed tonnage had risen to 26,500 tons by May 1940, the number fell to three, leaving a four-ship class (CV 9–12). These ships would bring the total U.S. carrier force to eleven. At this point CV-9 was expected to complete in January 1944, CV-10 in June 1944, CV-11 in July 1944, and CV-12 in February 1945. Once war began, the shipyards did infinitely better, so that CV-9 (*Essex*) was completed in December 1942. The others quickly followed, in April, August, and November 1943.

France collapsed in June 1940. This was far worse than the "two-ocean navy" case considered in 1938–1939, because the United States had relied on Britain and France for a degree of protection against aggression by Germany. In the worst case the Royal Navy might fall into Axis hands. The United States could not possibly, it seemed, quickly build a fleet sufficient for offensive action in both oceans, but the General Board recommended starting at once on a fleet sufficient to maintain a defense in one ocean while mounting an offensive in the other. The recommended fleet gives an idea of the value then being placed on carriers: thirty-two battleships and fifteen carriers. Of these, however, the existing fifteen U.S. battleships were slow and obsolescent, whereas all seven existing carriers were fast, modern ships. To meet the desired force level the General Board asked for another four carriers (CV 13–16), which would more than double the existing carrier force. The "Two-Ocean Navy" Act Congress passed envisaged a 70 percent increase in tonnage, equivalent to seven rather than four more carriers (the Navy did not need 70 percent more battleships, so much of the newly available battleship tonnage went into cruisers and destroyers—but not into carriers). Thus by December 1940 ten new carriers (CV 10–19) were under contract beyond *Essex*.

A July 1941 General Board study showed that in addition it would be possible to complete another seven carriers by December 1946 if the twelve on order were all completed as planned by December 1945, giving a potential total of eighteen carriers in December 1945. The board proposed adding four carriers in FY43, both to replace ships reaching retirement age and to make up for possible war losses. However, in September 1941 an OpNav conference decided tentatively to extend the existing program by, among other ships, six carriers (CV 20–25). A somewhat more optimistic BuShips thought it could lay down the carriers between March 1944 and May 1945 and complete them between August 1946 and November 1947. The first two ships (CV 20–21) were ordered in December 1941. They were part of an initial war program (forty-three ships) approved by the Secretary of the Navy between 15 and 24 December 1941.

CNO Admiral Harold R. Stark had already proposed to President Franklin Roosevelt that new ships be laid down as soon as slips were vacated; that way 900,000 tons of combatant ships could be built. Unlike previous authorizations, this one should allow the tonnage to be used however the Navy decided, to reflect war experience. The president himself urgently wanted new carriers. Against considerable opposition, he pushed through the conversion of nine light cruisers to light carriers (the *Independence*-class CVLs). On 14 March 1942 CNO Admiral King proposed extending the building program to produce *Essex* or better carriers at the rate of at least eight per year beginning in 1943, light carriers to make up deficiencies (in the eight per year), and at least two escort carriers (see below) each month. By March 1942 the projected 1943–1944 program included ten *Essex*es plus four of a new type of heavy carrier (which became the *Midway* class). For several months the program shifted back and forth, but in the end it retained these numbers. The *Independence* class became CVL 22–30, the ten fleet carriers became CV 31–40, and the four big *Midways* were listed as CVB 41–44. Remarkably, nearly all Public Domain of these ships were completed before the end of World War II, although one *Essex* (CV-35 *Reprisal*) and one *Midway* (the unnamed CVB-44) were cancelled. A further program included three more *Essex*-class carriers (CV 45–47, of which one, CV-46 *Iwo Jima,* was cancelled at the end of the war). Two more light carriers (CVL 48–49) were built as such from the keel up, based on a heavy cruiser design. Plans to order

The USS Midway *in a gale off Sicily, February 1949. Photograph taken from the* Essex-*class carrier* Philippine Sea.

six more *Essex* class (CV 50–55) and two more *Midways* (CVB 56–57) were abandoned in March 1945.

The *Essex*es won the great Pacific battles that broke the Imperial Japanese Navy. They became the core of the postwar U.S. carrier force. Of the twenty-four *Essex*-class carriers completed, one (CV-34 *Oriskany*) was suspended at the end of the war and redesigned to operate the new jets.

As a measure of U.S. naval thinking on the eve of war, in September 1941 the Naval War College produced "A Study of the Relative Merits of a Balanced Navy and a Carrier Navy and the Conclusions Reached."[28] The two-ocean fleet then being built (including 60,000-ton *Montana*-class battleships) was compared to a carrier fleet of equivalent cost built around 60,000-ton carriers (rather than battleships) and 27,000-ton carriers instead of cruisers. It was assumed that bases ashore were more efficient than carriers in operating aircraft, and were also more difficult to knock out. There was no question of building an all-surface ship fleet; the study was intended mainly to show that a fleet without any battleships or cruisers (as some air enthusiasts presumably wanted) would be ineffective in important ways. Heavy guns, for example, were all-weather weapons, whereas aircraft were not. The new U.S. program envisaged half as many carriers as battleships, and more carriers (eleven) had recently been ordered than battleships (nine). War experience certainly suggested

Naval History and Heritage Command

that a combination of carriers and heavy gun ships was needed. Only at the end of the war could massed carriers effectively sink battleships, as in the cases of the Japanese superbattleships *Yamato* and *Musashi*.

WORLD WAR II

U.S. carriers underwent three essential wartime modifications. One was multiple radars: surface and air search and height-finding. A related change, begun before the war, was provision of an aircraft homing beacon. That greatly increased effective striking range, and it permitted a carrier to maneuver much more freely while aircraft were in flight beyond the horizon. The navigation beacon also provided a reference point for scouting aircraft and hence for strikes against the targets they found. A second major change was the Combat Information Center (CIC) which correlated the ship's own data with those from other fleet units and from aircraft. Successful fighter control for self-defense was a consequence of the combination of CIC and radar. The CIC operated manually, and could track only a limited number of targets. In 1945 Japanese kamikaze tactics succeeded because attackers split up far more than had conventional attackers, and CICs were flooded with data. CIC also controlled the ship's own defensive guns, and again the kamikazes tended to saturate the ship's ability to handle targets. The combination of radar/CIC success in 1944 and CIC saturation in 1945 led the U.S. Navy to intensive postwar work, ultimately on automating its CICs in the 1960s. The third major change was of course the proliferation of light anti-aircraft weapons, by 1945 often locally controlled to overcome kamikaze saturation.

Carrier operation changed, too. The prewar idea that carriers should be solitary was dropped as large numbers of new fleet carriers entered service beginning in December 1942. It turned out that up to four large carriers (usually three large and one small) could operate together as a carrier task group, such groups working together to form the fast carrier task force (Task Force 38 or 58 depending on whether the fleet commander was Admiral Halsey or Admiral Spruance).

The kamikaze threat again changed the way carriers operated. Fighters multiplied, so that in 1945 an *Essex* might operate as many as seventy-three of them, her bomber complement cut to fifteen dive-bombers (no scouts) and fifteen torpedo bombers. At this time a more conventional combination was thirty-six fighters, thirty-six dive- and scout bombers, and eighteen torpedo bombers.

By this time the U.S. Navy also operated specialized night fighters. From 1943 on, the Japanese exploited the lack of U.S. night fighters to attack with single medium bombers, which sometimes succeeded in torpedoing U.S. carriers. Initially radar was so heavy that aircraft operated in pairs, a torpedo bomber carrying the radar and directing a single-seat fighter. Then a lightweight night fighter radar was developed, and carriers were assigned specifically to operate all night fighter air groups. In 1945, for example, USS *Enterprise* was classed as a night carrier, equipped with thirty-seven night-fighter Hellcats and eighteen radar-equipped Avenger torpedo bombers.

ARMORED FLIGHT DECKS

Prewar the British developed a different kind of fleet carrier, with consequences for the U.S. Navy. Believing that carrier fighters could not possibly provide sufficient protection, the British had two choices: they could follow the U.S. practice of trying to kill the enemy's carriers preemptively, or they could design carriers that could ride out air attacks without losing their capabilities. In 1935 the British found themselves facing Italian air strength in the Mediterranean. The Italians used land bases, and there was little possibility that any pre-emptive strike could eliminate the air threat. In 1936, then, the British designed the revolutionary *Illustrious*-class carrier with an armored hangar (including part of the flight-deck overhead). As U.S. designers had told many U.S. officers, there was a considerable price. In this case it was a smaller flight deck and a small hangar, sufficient for only thirty-six aircraft (the previous British carrier accommodated seventy-two). In U.S. terms, the shorter flight deck dramatically reduced the ship's overall aircraft capacity. Later in the war the Royal Navy adopted the U.S. practice of deck parking aircraft, installing a U.S.-style barrier. The short flight deck seems to have caused problems, the British suffering an undue number of accidents when landing aircraft bounced over the barrier to hit the parked aircraft forward. Ironically, the *Illustrious* design proceeded at just about the same time that the British began to develop their own radar, which made effective fighter control possible and thus made the armored hangar, with its limitations, much less important.

The General Board periodically considered armored-deck carriers. In January 1940 it asked C&R for sketch designs. BuAer's strong preference for open-sided hangars (both to warm up aircraft and for athwartship catapults) greatly complicated any such design, because the flight deck had to be a superstructure. C&R's study envisaged moving an inch of armor from the fourth deck (the protective deck in the *Yorktown*s, and the lower protective deck in an *Essex*) to the flight deck, and adding another inch and a half. The price was at least 2,200 tons, about 7.5 feet more beam, and a knot of speed. The 2.5-inch deck could resist ordinary 1,000-pound bombs (not armor-piercing ones), but they could still enter the hangar if they fell at an angle (as they usually did) and came under the flight deck; after all, the hangar could not be protected at all. To move quickly, moreover, the elevators were made of light alloys; they could not retain both their speed and be protected like the flight deck. Much of the added weight came from the massive supports required by the heavy flight-deck structure to withstand the racking stresses of rolling and beam winds.

Too, the topweight would make the carrier heel more steeply on high-speed turns, with unfortunate effects. The idea died—for the moment.

Initially the British kept the armored flight deck secret, but by the spring of 1940 senior U.S. officers were discussing comments on this type of ship by the British Director of Naval Construction—the same Stanley V. Goodall who had helped C&R in 1917–1918. Initial views were that the Norwegian campaign did not show any need for such protection, although it did show a need for naval aircraft with sufficient performance to challenge land-based ones. Since the U.S. war plan against Japan envisaged seizing Japanese-held islands, the idea that no landing could succeed without sea-based air superiority was a very important lesson of the Norwegian campaign. No particular agitation for a U.S. armored deck carrier followed Goodall's remarks, but Captain John S. McCain (a carrier commander), who had pushed for such a ship since 1939, remained its strong advocate through the fall of 1940. One consequence was that in October 1940 the British were asked for details of the armored carriers. Meanwhile BuShips studied future carriers armored much like *Essex* but with heavier gun batteries (one had 8-inch guns), responding to an August 1940 General Board request. One was armed with the new 5-inch/54 dual-purpose gun, then in the concept stage. By June 1941 it had been developed into a sketch of a 44,500-ton carrier. Its future significance was that it became the basis for a study of a carrier with a protected hangar, which in July 1941 the preliminary designers were about to start. At a June 1941 General Board hearing, the Chief of BuAer suggested building this ship if the decision were taken to replace the planned 65,000-ton *Montana*-class battleships with aircraft carriers. This CV-A would have been 900 feet long, protected against 8-inch cruiser guns. Given her size, she would have accommodated more aircraft: the usual thirty-six fighters, plus thirty-eight dive-bomber/scouts and thirty-eight torpedo bombers. BuAer saw much larger carriers as the only way to retain existing numbers while adopting larger higher-performance aircraft.

Illustrious suffered heavy dive-bombing in 1941 and was sent to Norfolk Navy Yard for repairs under the Lend-Lease program. There she made a considerable impression on U.S. officers—who did not notice that the German armor-piercing bombs actually had made such a mess of her flight deck that she could not keep operating. Those defending U.S. design practices said that the British ship was far better for European waters but that an American-type carrier with many more aircraft made much more sense in a lengthy Pacific campaign. U.S. officers wanted both an American-style air group and British-style protection, accepting that the result would be a larger ship (now unrestrained by treaty, with much relaxed financial limits, too). By July 1941 BuShips had details both of the *Illustrious* design and of the damage she had suffered. The Royal Navy had built a carrier with an armored hangar, not one with a full-length armored flight deck. A heavy German bomb penetrated her hangar roof (part, but not all, of her flight deck) and gutted her hangar.

Because the hangar did not run the full length of the ship, had the bomb hit slightly further forward it would have penetrated deep into the ship, with disastrous consequences. On the other hand, the armor forced the Germans to use a large bomb, and that in turn reduced the scale of the attack, because not all German aircraft could have conducted the attack. Under similar circumstances an *Essex* would also have survived, although the hangar deck might have been penetrated. BuShips developed several designs showing what an *Essex*-like carrier would have to sacrifice to gain some degree of hangar protection. For example, a 28,000-ton carrier (CV-D) with 2.5-inch armor on her flight deck (*Illustrious* had 3 inches) would operate sixty-four aircraft rather than the eighty-three then credited to the *Essex*, and would make 31.5 rather than 33 knots. In November 1941 BuShips offered CV-E, enlarged so that in effect she made no sacrifices to gain a 3.5-inch armored flight deck. She had a 2-inch armored hangar deck. As in the earlier studies, adding armor so high in a ship made for much larger size; in effect the armored flight deck equated to the 8-inch guns of the CV-A study. Given her sheer size, she could operate six squadrons of existing types of aircraft.

In March 1942 the General Board formally proposed building a big carrier based on CV-E with an armored flight deck, arguing that such tough ships were essential. She would be so massive that she could support the larger aircraft then being bought, such as the Grumman F7F Tigercat (which had been conceived, however, to operate from *Essex*-class carriers). This U.S.-style armored flight-deck carrier was soon called the Type B Carrier (CV Type B, then CV-B, and finally CVB, the B often interpreted as "Big" or "Battle"). Six of these *Midway*-class CVB were projected, but three were cancelled at the end of the war.

The British managed to incorporate the heavy armored hangar by making it integral with their hull. U.S. designers could not adopt any such practice, so one great problem in the *Midway* design was how to support the vast weight of a deck treated as a superstructure. One lesson for the designers was never to do that again; in postwar carriers the flight deck was integral with the hull. It was a great triumph of U.S. structural design that large openings could be cut in the ship's side (to provide something like an open hangar) despite the integral-deck structure. The sheer weight of the armored deck made it necessary to reduce freeboard, so the *Midway*-class carriers were far wetter than the *Essexes*. Another problem was how to provide some protection along the sides of the hangar, since surely an enemy would try to get weapons under the armored flight deck. No good solution presented itself, but the partial one was to place the ship's 4-inch guns in protected mounts along the sides of the hangar deck, so that there was a good chance that any weapon fired at the hangar would hit them instead. As a consequence, these ships had clearer flight decks than the *Essex* class.

In 1945 U.S. and British fleet carriers operated together in the face of Japanese kamikazes. U.S. officers noticed that kamikaze hits usually put their ships out of action (although many were repaired in forward areas). They considered the British armored-deck ships far superior, the saying being that after a hit they simply manned sweeps and cleaned up their flight decks. The British saw things very differently. They were painfully aware of how limited their aircraft capacity was and of how their aircraft could not be warmed up in their closed hangars (which were treated like magazines). When the British began to design a new carrier in 1943, they compared open- and closed- (armored) hangar designs. Eventually they selected a U.S.-style open hangar for their final wartime carrier design, HMS *Malta*. The ship was cancelled at the end of World War II, so until records were opened it was not clear just how impressed the British had been with U.S. design practices.

CONVERSION

The British developed another new carrier idea, a converted merchant ship to work with convoys. U-boats had to spend much of their time on the surface, submerging (if at all) only when near their targets. Only when surfaced could they develop sufficient sustained speed to shadow and then to intercept a convoy (very late in World War II the Germans introduced the snorkel, and the situation changed). Aircraft working with a convoy could catch surfaced U-boats. As yet there was no way that aircraft could detect submerged submarines, but the ability to frustrate U-boats trying to intercept a convoy was well worthwhile. British carrier operating practice had produced low-performance aircraft like the Swordfish torpedo bomber, which could operate even from a slow carrier with a small flight deck. By the time the British had their first converted merchant ship carrier (escort carrier), the U.S. Navy was working with the Royal Navy, although the United States was not yet at war. The U.S. Navy had no low-performance bombers, but it became interested in operating auto-gyros (predecessors of helicopters) from a converted merchant ship with a short flight deck. It converted a new freighter into the prototype escort carrier *Long Island*. By this time the U.S. Navy also had the new hydraulic catapult conceived for fleet carriers.[29] These catapults made it possible to operate standard U.S. carrier aircraft from a converted merchant ship. Initially the new low-performance carriers were considered auxiliaries, designated AVG (seaplane tenders were AVs); later they were designated auxiliary carriers (ACV) and finally escort carriers (CVE). Late in 1941 the nominal U.S. requirement was twenty-five, soon cut to sixteen (with fifteen already under contract).[30] The British were allocated another thirty, tentatively designated BAVGs, to be provided under Lend-Lease. Four more conversions were ex-tankers (*Cimarron* class), making a total of fifty such ships.[31]

The *Cimarron* conversion was quite attractive, because it was larger than a C-3 and offered oil fuel for accompanying ships. The maximum effort program planned in 1942 (for 1943–1944) therefore included another twenty-four such ships, to be built as carriers from the keel up. None of these *Commencement Bay*–class ships was ready for combat before the end of the war, but they were used postwar. The earlier ships were reduced postwar to subsidiary roles, the most interesting of which were conversion of *Thetis Bay* into a prototype helicopter assault ship and conversion of *Gilbert Islands* into a communications relay ship (AGMR). In 1942 Henry Kaiser, who was already mass-producing Liberty ships on the West Coast, offered to build escort carriers designed as such from the keel up. The resulting *Casablanca* class was based on a Maritime Commission design for a small passenger ship (had it really been conceived as a carrier from the keel up, the design would have taken far too long). Fifty were built under a program authorized by President Roosevelt (hence not negotiated within the naval staff). Taking into account U.S. ships built for the Royal Navy, well over a hundred escort carriers were completed during World War II.

Conversion did not produce a particularly efficient carrier. The merchant ships were short and slow. Their holds were ill-suited to the shops and other facilities a carrier needed. Carrier facilities were far lighter than the usual cargoes, so the ships had to be ballasted heavily. The island was cut to a bare minimum, smoke pipes being led up alongside the flight deck. This very austere conversion, however, could be carried out rapidly, and in 1942 it was urgent to produce ships to fight the Battle of the Atlantic.

By 1943 the role of U.S. escort carriers had changed dramatically. To fight its war, the U-boat command had to maintain communications with all boats at sea. It directed them to targets, and it needed their reports of, for example, their fuel status and how many torpedoes remained. The Germans thought that their codes were secure and that reports from U-boats, using high-frequency (HF) radio could not be intercepted and certainly could not be subject to radio direction-finding. They were wrong on both counts. Code-breaking and radio direction-finding provided the Allied navies with what amounted to wide-area ocean surveillance of the U-boat force. In May 1943 the U.S. Navy began using this information to hunt down U-boats, rather than merely to screen convoys. Hunter-killer groups built around escort carriers attacked groups of U-boats whose position had been revealed by code breaking. Their aircraft ran down the shorter-range directions provided by the carriers' HF direction finders. The U.S. offensive was unpopular with the British, who feared that the Germans would realize that their codes had been broken, but it proved quite successful (and the Germans never realized why). The U.S. Navy became interested in offensive ASW based on ocean surveillance, an important idea postwar.

In the Pacific, escort carriers were used to ferry replacement aircraft (including Army aircraft for landings) and also to support the Marines directly in the later island battles.

By fall 1941, it seemed obvious that the United States would need many more fleet carriers. An *Essex* would probably take three years to build. Any rapid expansion would have to exploit ships whose hulls had already been laid down. Fortunately the high performance built into new naval aircraft and the new catapults dramatically reduced the requirements any such converted carriers would have to meet. By 1941 the U.S. Navy was building numerous 10,000-ton *Cleveland*-class light cruisers. A study of a full carrier conversion showed that it would be both inefficient and lengthy. The idea was resisted by the General Board.[32] After war broke out, the idea was reconsidered on the basis of the existing escort carriers. This time it seemed well worthwhile, and nine ships were converted into *Independence*-class light carriers (CVL). As measured by the number of aircraft per ton, they were far less efficient than the big *Essex*, but they were still a very useful expedient (the typical air group was twelve fighters, nine bombers, and nine torpedo bombers). Typically one light carrier worked with three fleet carriers in a task group. Once the night carrier concept had been developed, a light carrier offered a full complement of night fighters without complicating the operation of the big strike carriers. The light carrier was considered so attractive that late in the war two ships (*Wright* and *Saipan*) were designed from the outset for this role, using adapted heavy cruiser hulls (which had not been laid down as heavy cruisers).

TRANSITION

The period through 1945 produced a particular type of carrier for both strategic and technological reasons. The strategic reason was that, through this period, the U.S. Navy was designed to seize and then exploit sea control. It was therefore conceived much more to attack an enemy navy—the Imperial Japanese Navy—than to strike at land targets. Aircraft were shaped by that requirement. It was entirely reasonable to expect a dive- or torpedo bomber to take off within the 400-foot length available forward of parked aircraft. U.S. naval aircraft were expected to attack some land targets, particularly when supporting Marines going ashore, but that was very much a secondary role. Perhaps it should be added that even after the Royal Navy regained direct control of its fleet air arm in 1939, it still had to avoid encroaching on the land attack role espoused by the Royal Air Force; there really was a distinct U.S. Navy view of the role of naval aviation. That view would become very important after 1945. In 1945, all existing U.S. naval aircraft could operate from all existing carriers. By 1945 the U.S. Navy was interested in larger carrier aircraft, such as the twin-engine Grumman F7F Tigercat, which would not have been able to operate from small carriers; but it was still true that carrier dimensions and speed shaped naval aircraft, not the other way around. It is not, incidentally, true that some aircraft, such as the Tigercat, were conceived specifically to operate from the big *Midways*—they had not yet been designed when the aircraft specifications were laid out.

The foundation built between the wars made it possible for the U.S. Navy to shift toward a carrier-centered World War II fleet. The huge prewar U.S. naval air establishment was relatively easy to expand to train tens of thousands of new pilots and other personnel. It also trained the senior officers to command a much-expanded carrier fleet. In 1941 the U.S. Navy had seven fleet carriers and one escort carrier. By the end of the war, the U.S. Navy had over a hundred carriers (although most were quick and relatively inefficient conversions of merchant ship and cruiser hulls).

By the time the Imperial Japanese Navy was essentially gone, in 1945, the U.S. Navy had become interested in a new mission, strategic air attack. It was not entirely new: prewar fleet exercises did show valuable potentials for supporting amphibious landings and for attacking enemy shore installations (the U.S. carriers often raided the Panama Canal, Pearl Harbor, and Los Angeles), but they were secondary.

That year the U.S. naval staff studied the contribution that carrier aircraft could make to the bomber attack on Japan by B-29s. It concluded that given the sheer number of carrier aircraft, and the short ranges from which they could be launched, carrier bombers could deliver up to 60 percent of the tonnage available from B-29s. Against this calculation, a January 1945 carrier raid on Tokyo was less than successful, the small carrier bombers finding the high winds over Japan too great a hindrance and probably also finding it difficult to identify targets from the high altitudes then used. They might have performed differently a few months later, when the heavy bombers shifted to incendiary raids mounted from relatively low altitudes. In that case the sheer number of carrier bombers might have made Japanese defense far more difficult. The other advantage of carrier attack was that a carrier could mount attacks from a far wider arc, making it much more difficult for a defender to guess where to place defenses.

Navy interest had probably been spurred by the April 1942 Doolittle Raid, when USS *Hornet* launched sixteen Army B-25 medium bombers to attack Tokyo. They did relatively little damage, but the raid convinced the Japanese that they had to destroy the U.S. carrier force. Their attempt to force a decisive battle, at Midway that June, proved disastrous for them: they lost four carriers, which their limited industrial base could not easily replace. U.S. industrial capacity could more than replace the carriers lost in 1942; newly built U.S. warships dominated the Pacific War from 1943 on. Even before the Doolittle Raid (but probably inspired by planning for it) the U.S. Navy was sponsoring a Grumman design for a carrier-based medium bomber comparable to a B-25 (the TB2F). Although this project died in April 1944 (surprise air attacks were unlikely to succeed now that the Japanese had early warning radar), the idea of heavy land attacks mounted from carriers became very important post-war, largely shaping the new carriers.

NOTES

1. For more details of ships and of carrier designs see the author's *U.S. Aircraft Carriers: An Illustrated Design History* (Annapolis: Naval Institute Press, 1983), and Thomas C. Hone, Norman Friedman, and Mark Mandeles, *American and British Aircraft Carrier Development, 1919–1941.* (Annapolis: Naval Institute Press, 1999). For British development see also this author's *British Carrier Aviation: The Evolution of the Ships and Their Aircraft* (Annapolis: Naval Institute Press and London: Conway Maritime Press, 1988).

2. On 7 October 1915 Captain Mark L. Bristol of the Office of Naval Aeronautics (predecessor of the Bureau of Aeronautics) reported that the British had converted several ships into carriers; he suggested both converting a U.S. merchant ship and considering building a special aircraft ship. Asked for characteristics, the General Board demurred pending the results of the *North Carolina* trials (NARA GB [General Board] 420-7 in RG 80; file 28 October 1915). The General Board was responsible both for war planning (until formation of the OpNav War Plans Division) and (until 1945) for drawing up the characteristics of ships to be built. Given preliminary characteristics, the C&R preliminary design section (and then of its successor the Bureau of Ships) prepared "spring styles" (names after women's clothing styles appearing in the spring) from which the board could choose as a guide to preparing final characteristics. The board also held hearings on characteristics, transcripts of which (almost all from after 1917) have been preserved.

3. GB 420, 17 January 1925, enclosing the report of the special board appointed by the Secretary of the Navy on 23 September 1924 to review the needs of the Navy. The huge number overstated the importance of aircraft. It reflected their rapid development (often a model went from concept to production in a few months), which caused each combatant to buy generation after generation of aircraft. Aircraft were also quickly expended, so vast numbers built reflected much smaller numbers in service at any one time. By way of contrast, World War II was fought by no more than two or three generations of aircraft.

4. The characteristics proposed by the Aviation Division on 23 June 1918 (in GB 420-7, folder 1916–1924) called for a hull at least 700×80 feet (about 15,000 tons) with a clear upper deck divided into a 250-foot forward part, a 150-foot amidships part, and a 300-foot after part, its bridge built over the deck so that airplanes could pass underneath, carrying a mast set amidships so as not to interfere with launching aircraft (as yet there was no thought of an island set to one side of the hull). Speed should be at least thirty knots so that the ship could work with battle cruisers. Uptakes should come up to the ends of the superstructure. Aircraft would be stowed, their wings folded, on the two lower decks and carried up to the main deck. Armament would be limited to four 4-inch anti-aircraft guns at the corners of the superstructure (these guns were suggested because they would be powerful enough to deal with both aircraft and with surfaced submarines; no such dual-purpose weapons then existed, but the idea suggests the extent to which a larger number of single-purpose [AA or surface] guns would have complicated the ship's arrangement). A sketch produced by the Bureau of Ordnance (not the constructors) in July 1918 shows a substantial superstructure about three-quarters of the way forward, bridging the upper deck. This seems to have been much the concept embodied in HMS *Furious*, then being rebuilt as a full carrier with separate landing-on and flying-off decks connected by awkward paths (the U.S. solution, the clear path under the bridge, would have been better). The power plant shown was a big diesel, which would produce less exhaust than a steam plant. A seaplane-handling crane is a prominent feature. Formal characteristics for a FY20

carrier, submitted by the General Board on 10 October 1918, repeated much of what the Aviation Division wanted, but called for funnels and masts to be placed out to the sides of the hull, perhaps hinged outboard. The bridge should be a special design, perhaps a fore and aft bridge outboard (i.e., an island) clear of the flight deck. Full speed was now set at thirty-five knots, the speed planned for the new U.S. battle cruisers and scout cruisers. Reviewing the proposed characteristics, Goodall pointed out that the ship should have good underwater protection and protection against cruiser fire, that her guns were too weak, and that she should have a torpedo battery to deal with heavy enemy ships that she might unexpectedly encounter (as she could not possibly fly off aircraft quickly enough). "Although such a ship should not by any means be regarded as a fighting ship, it should be sufficiently powerfully armed to be able to brush aside light vessels of the enemy, so that its machines can be flown off in comparatively advanced positions." Goodall guessed that she should be about 800 feet long (22,000 tons). By May 1920 characteristics had been rewritten to show sixteen 6-inch/53 (i.e., light cruiser) guns in anti-torpedo (anti-destroyer) batteries, plus one twin torpedo tube on each side. Aviation chief Captain T .T. Craven wanted the ship designed so that "the entire allowance of airplanes can be placed in the air from stowage as quickly as possible."

5. The 1920 program as drafted in September 1918 envisaged carriers (NARA RG 38: GB [General Board] 420-2, 10 September 1918); in its discussion of auxiliaries the General Board wrote that "the need for airplane carriers of high speed to accompany the fleet for the purpose of extending its scouting area has arisen from the experiences of the present war. The General Board recommends that the design and construction of such vessels be not delayed." A list of ships to be completed by 30 June 1925 (i.e., by the end of FY25) included six carriers. This paper included a large aircraft program, but it was limited to large seaplanes, dirigibles, and kite-balloons, plus land-based aircraft then being operated in England, Ireland, and France. No carriers were included in the FY20 program. A 12 October 1919 General Board (GB 420-2) summary of future U.S. naval policy called for one carrier per squadron of capital ships, for a total of seven to work with twelve first-line battleships, and sixteen battle cruisers (seven squadrons, four ships each). That is, at this point carriers were envisaged as supporting arms for capital ships. They were still described as auxiliaries, on a par with destroyer and submarine tenders. The October summary ended with a proposed FY21 building program including two carriers (as well as two battleships, a battle cruiser, ten more scout cruisers, and lesser units). The carriers were expected to be expensive: hull and machinery would cost $20 million, compared to $21 million for a battleship or $23 million for a battle cruiser (but the armor and armament of the gun ships would add considerably; total cost for a carrier was $23 million, compared to $39.5 million for a battleship). Nothing was bought. In November 1920, looking toward the FY22 program, the General Board also vigorously pressed for carriers, arguing that "it is now perfectly evident that the Navy skilled in the use of airplanes and well provided with the most modern types will have a great advantage in war over a Navy not trained in their use or not well supplied [with them]. It is not too much to say that the influence of airplanes upon scouting and information gathering duties may revolutionize former naval practice." On this basis the General Board asked for two to be laid down in FY22 and then one in each of FY23 and FY24 (its recommendations were in the context of a proposed three-year program). In July 1921 the board associated the figure of two with the need for at least one carrier with each fleet, Atlantic and Pacific, urgently recommending that two carriers by authorized in the FY23 program.

6. GB 420-7 File 1916-24, dated 6 May 1920, supporting plans to build fast U.S. carriers. According to the memo, "recent reports" show that the Royal Navy is developing carrier tactics in the Mediterranean with three ships (including the seaplane carrier *Pegasus*), the carrier *Argus* is assigned to the Atlantic Fleet, and a carrier (the seaplane carrier *Ark*

Royal) is assigned to the China Fleet; *Furious* is inactive at Rosyth, and *Hermes* is being completed. Until well into the 1930s the Royal Navy operated the most numerous carrier fleet in the world—but by far not the largest sea-based air arm.

7. The conversion was proposed in May 1920; a converted scout would support a 500 × 60-foot flight deck, and her hangar could accommodate twelve fighters and six torpedo bombers. Increased tonnage would reduce speed from thirty-five to thirty-one knots and the battery would be cut to four 6-inch guns. Conversion plans were submitted on 12 November 1920. The General Board rejected the idea in December 1920.

8. GB (General Board) 420 of 3 February 1921 (in NARA RG 80), calling for a hull 812 × 80 × 30 feet, supporting an 800 × 106-foot flight deck, 46 feet above water. Armament (16 × 6-inch in twin mounts and two triple torpedo tubes) and cruiser-level protection were specified, but not the number of aircraft. However, a 20 November 1920 paper in the same file estimates aircraft capacity for either monoplanes or biplanes, which might be fully or partly assembled (in the hangar). The hangar was to be 290 × 80 feet, i.e., a cavity within the hull rather than a long open space, as in later U.S. carriers, with 45 × 50-foot hatches or elevators at either end. Given assumed airplane dimensions, capacity was estimated. The stowage (hangar) deck could accommodate thirty-five fighters and twenty-three torpedo bombers; half as many again would be carried disassembled in the hold, as replacements for crashed airplanes, for a total of fifty-two fighters and thirty-six torpedo planes. Nothing in these papers suggests any attempt to work out the tactics and hence the ideal numbers of these aircraft. Prior to writing the characteristics, the board issued a memo on carriers, noting that they were a new kind of ship and summarizing British experience. Both the flush-deck *Argus* and the island-equipped HMS *Eagle* had shown excellent results. Their flight decks were 540 × 68 feet and 660 × 100 feet, respectively, and their respective speeds twenty and twenty-four knots. The board noted that HMS *Hermes* had been designed with an island in 1917 before any experience had been gained (it presumably did not know that *Argus* had been tested with a dummy island). In the board's view, none of the British carriers was entirely satisfactory; "it is desired to give the Naval Air Service the highest type of carrier possible with which to experiment in the construction and operation of heavier than air aircraft." General Board files also include a 20,000-tonner sketched in November 1920 as a basis for discussion: 660 × 69 × 23 feet (20,000 tons) with a flight deck 650 × 86 feet (104 feet over sponsons) and two stowage spaces 125 × 64 feet forward and 300 × 55 feet aft, both with 20-foot clear height, each with one elevator, making thirty knots using cruiser machinery (90,000 SHP). She would have a 5-inch belt, considerable by light cruiser standards, and a 2.5-inch protective deck. Stowage on the handling (hangar) deck was given as forty-eight fighters (sixteen ready for flight) and twenty-four torpedo bombers (eight ready for flight), with 40 percent more aircraft stowed in the hold disassembled (figures were developed by filling the spaces involved with airplane silhouettes). Speed was thirty-five knots.

9. GB 420-7 dated 27 June 1921. C&R had submitted alternative sketches with a flush deck (A) and with an island (B) on 12 May. In support of its island design, the bureau commented that so long a ship might not need a flush deck. It now seemed that a carrier should be able to fly aircraft on and off simultaneously, and the deck was so long that she could do so while leaving a neutral area abeam the island. The bureau also pointed out that a flush-deck carrier presented real design problems, not only of disposing of smoke but also of leading air into the boilers from a position forward of the uptakes, which required ducting that would interfere with the forward elevator and also reduce crew spaces. The need to provide telescoping masts, housing radio masts, search lights, and the like (including a pilot house) might well demand unattractive compromises. The same issues arose when the U.S. Navy tried to build huge flush-decked carriers after World War II. The bureau pointed out that permanent masts would give longer radio

range, an important consideration. These designs had clipper bows carried up to the flight deck, to cut through the waves (i.e., keep the flight deck dry). The forward end of the flight deck was squared off so that both of an airplane's wheels would leave the deck at the same time. The open stern was offered to provide cranes to handle seaplanes (a solution the Royal Navy had already adopted in *Eagle* and *Hermes*); it would be closed by a roller curtain 20 × 30 feet. The bureau doubted that a lee could be created aft for seaplane handling, and it pointed out that the open stern would lead directly into the large unobstructed hangar; in a following sea water might easily pour in. The curtain would provide a degree of safety, but the ship would have to be maneuvered carefully if it was open. An island design could provide a big crane abaft the island. A flush-decker could also have cranes, but they would be more difficult to place. Based on hangar area, the B design would accommodate thirty-eight fighters and nineteen torpedo bombers, the former fully assembled and the latter with wings folded (Type A had slightly less hangar area, due to the ducting for uptakes and downtakes).

10. In July 1921 Senator William Borah of Idaho introduced a bill to stop construction of six battleships and three battle cruisers and to convert two of the battle cruisers already under construction to carriers (and also to buy four fleet submarines already authorized). This was advertised as disarmament by example, the emphasis being on the termination of contracts rather than on the new carriers and submarines, and Secretary of the Navy Theodore Roosevelt (a cousin of the late president) urged that the bill be abandoned for fear that it would affect the disarmament conference the United States had just called for the following November. It is significant here because it shows that the idea of converting two battle cruisers was current well before it was inserted into the Washington Treaty.

11. Tonnage was a tricky yardstick, because different navies demanded different amounts of fuel to meet their strategic needs. The solution adopted at Washington was a new standard displacement, defined as the ship's displacement ready for battle less the two main consumables of fuel and reserve feed water. It was difficult to predict standard displacement because ships were designed to operate at a normal displacement including most of their fuel and reserve feed water; one consequence was that many early Treaty designs came out lighter than expected (and many later ones came out heavy, as designers sought to get closer to the limit). The phrase "ready for battle" also caused problems, as navies sought to shave nominal displacement by measures such as including only part of a ship's ammunition or excluding peacetime equipment such as ships' boats. Thus Taylor's 36,000 tons was an estimate based on a design that displaced over 40,000 tons in normal condition.

12. The initial planned aircraft complement was two fighter, two torpedo bomber, and half an observation squadron (the other half of which would be on board Scouting Force battleships). Each fighter squadron consisted of twenty-seven aircraft (eighteen operating, nine reserve), each torpedo squadron of twenty-four aircraft (sixteen operating, eight reserve), and the observation squadron of eighteen aircraft (twelve operating, six reserve). On this basis the ship would operate thirty-six fighters, thirty-two torpedo bombers, and six observation planes, a total of seventy-four aircraft. Undated memo in GB 420-7 files for 1925–1931 from RADM W. A. Moffett, BuAer Chief. This was soon greatly exceeded.

13. Thomas Wildenberg, *All The Factors of Victory: Admiral Joseph Mason Reeves and the Origins of Carrier Airpower* (Washington, DC: Potomac Books, 2003), is Reeves' only biography. It provided the dates used here.

14. This innovation seems to have been made almost immediately, but Wildenberg does not mention it. It may have been associated with the creation of the Landing Signal Officer (LSO) position, as short landings required special assistance. The Royal Navy did not use LSOs. The guess as to the date comes from the way in which carrier design was described in the March 1926 C&R memo. As a motivation for increasing carrier capacity, Wildenberg emphasizes the idea that only a large fighter force could fend off attacks.

15. Memo by BuAer Carrier Section, 1940, in GB 420-7. The equation of high performance and landing deck length helps explain why short Royal Navy carriers using high-performance fighters such as the Corsair and Seafire suffered so many barrier crashes compared to longer U.S. carriers.

16. There was also considerable interest in rigid airships as fleet scouts, in some cases carrying fighters for self-protection. Although these aircraft were retired in the mid-1930s after some spectacular accidents, the idea survived, and the 1940 "Estimate of the Situation" looking toward the FY42 program included a big rigid airship (ZR, 3-million-cubic-feet capacity) in addition to the blimps used for ASW during World War II. It was never built.

17. General Board files include a pair of design studies for maximum-size (27,000-ton) carriers dated 24 May 1924 showing that demanding high speed cost aircraft capacity (seventy-two aircraft in a 27.5-knot carrier, sixty in a 32.5-knot ship). At the other end of the scale, the Washington Treaty did not limit carriers displacing less than 10,000 tons. On 23 March 1925 the Bureau of Aeronautics suggested that such unlimited carriers should be the next considered by the U.S. Navy. It guessed that such a ship could carry sixty-four fighters or twenty-four torpedo bombers. On 31 March 1925 the Secretary of the Navy asked the General Board to consider a ship combining the attributes of a scout cruiser and a light cruiser, a new type of ship. To the General Board, this was much the same as the *Omaha* question raised five years earlier, since Congress would pay either for cruisers or for cruiser-size carriers, but not for both. The BuAer letter actually raised the wider question of carrier size versus aircraft capacity.

18. Contemporary discussions refer to a non-watertight flight deck, well adapted to fittings such as arrester gear. Apparently this was not the superstructure flight deck adopted in the *Ranger* design; it was assumed that a watertight flat would be built a foot or two below the flight deck proper. *Ranger* originally had an open hangar deck mainly to accommodate the planned pair of athwartships catapults, which did not materialize.

19. C&R planned a total of sixteen studies, varying different factors to show their influence on the design, as it had successfully done in the run-up to the first U.S. heavy cruiser design (*Pensacola* class). This systematic approach proved impossible partly because aircraft capability depended more on space and dimensions than on weight, and partly because there was no consensus as to which key factors were involved. The bureau therefore preferred not to submit the studies to the General Board, as they could not be used to draw conclusions accurately enough; however, they did indicate some key limiting conditions. Given the two 33,000-ton ex–battle cruisers, the 135,000-ton treaty total for carriers left 69,000 tons (if the experimental *Langley* were discarded, as the treaty permitted) for two 27,000-tonners, or three 23,000-tonners, or five 13,800-tonners, or six 10,000-tonners. The three tonnages investigated offered, respectively, totals of 192, 220, and 144 aircraft— showing that below a certain point, the ship was too small. C&R also took into account the possibility that the two big carriers would be modified so that their standard displacement could be given as 27,000 tons, leaving 81,000 tons for new carriers (this did not happen), or that the 36,000-ton displacement would be accepted, leaving 62,000 tons. This tonnage could be distributed among up to six carriers displacing between 10,800 tons (for the 62,000-ton total) and 27,000 tons (two ships in each case). No carrier with a mixed air group could be built on about 10,000 tons. Smaller carriers had about 15 percent more flight deck per airplane than larger ones. Although a larger number of smaller carriers would accommodate more aircraft, a smaller number of larger ones would cost much less per airplane; the first cost of five 13,800-tonners would be about 25 percent more than that of three 23,000-tonners, and the cost per airplane would be about 20 percent more. The smaller the carrier, the worse her protection. Although that might not count for above-water weapons that might cause a massive explosion, it certainly did count for torpedo attack.

20. Characteristics were dated 1 November 1927. There had recently been a proposal to convert *Langley*'s sister collier, *Neptune*, into another second-line training carrier, the resulting discussion probably helping to prompt the decision to build a first-line ship instead.

21. Plans called for one to be an athwartships catapult on the hangar deck; cross-wind launches had been tested at the Naval Aircraft Factory (Philadelphia Navy Yard). The hangar deck location was attractive partly because space under the flight deck near the bow (needed for the machinery of a bow catapult) was so limited by the bridge, by the forward anti-aircraft guns, and by hangar equipment. Moreover, a flight-deck catapult would interfere with flight-deck operations. BuAer therefore proposed two double-ended battleship-type powder catapult on the hangar deck, one just abaft the after elevator and one abaft the uptakes, which themselves were abaft the two elevators, BuAer memo dated 10 March 1928 in GB 420-7. The hangar deck catapults were sometimes described as equivalent to the British and Japanese practice of providing a secondary short takeoff deck on the hangar deck level; catapults did not sacrifice as much hangar space. As detail design proceeded, the two elevators were brought together until they were about forty feet apart (General Board 420-7, 16 March 1928). By March 1930 a third elevator had been added, right aft, to make aircraft handling more flexible. This addition was suggested by aviators aboard *Lexington* and *Saratoga*. After aircraft landed, they were immediately re-spotted to the holding area amidships and prepared for another mission; sometimes that required flight-deck crews to work far into the night. The aft elevator could bring some of those aircraft down to the hangar deck, where they could also be prepared, and then back up into the spotting area amidships. Commander Aircraft Squadrons, Admiral Reeves, strongly recommended the third elevator. It became much less useful when operating practice changed to spot aircraft forward rather than amidships.

22. As aircraft became heavier, *Ranger*'s low speed became a real handicap. She could make about 29.4 knots at 16,000 tons, but by April 1939 her displacement was closer to 18,000 and her speed was about 28.7 knots. During a live bombing practice on 29 March 1939, with the surface wind running 4 knots, she was reduced to 24.2 knots and had to resort to long-run (on deck) takeoffs—which dramatically reduced the size of her deck spot, hence the power she could project (GB 420-7, reproduction of 7 April 1939 letter from Commander Aircraft, Battle Force). The point was raised because *Wasp*, 75 percent completed, would also be relatively slow. In 1938–1939 there was some interest in modifying both ships for increased speed, but that proved too expensive, and not worthwhile. *Wasp* actually produced more than her designed power, but nothing like enough to give her the desired carrier speed.

23. In June 1933 the General Board rejected a suggestion that the ships not carry any torpedoes, in line with the earlier feeling that torpedo bombers were far too heavy and too slow to be useful on board carriers. Presumably the board was aware that new engines could substantially improve performance. The new torpedo bomber was the Douglas TBD Devastator, which in the mid-1930s did indeed seem to have spectacular performance. Aviation technology moved so fast that by 1942 (six years after entering service) the TBD was considered a low-performance death-trap at Midway. During the board's discussion, Rear Admiral E. J. King, then Chief of the Bureau of Aeronautics; Commander E. R. McClung of the BuOrd Aviation Ordnance Section; and Lieutenant Smith of the BuOrd Torpedo Section all opposed eliminating carrier torpedoes. The ninety-four-plane loadout is from a 1934 letter from the Supervisor of Shipbuilding at Newport News, mentioning a clause in the detailed specifications for the ship (GB 420-7 file for 1925–1939).

24. BuAer, C&R, and the Bureau of Ordnance jointly suggested installing a small island at the forward corner of No. 2 elevator in a 22 November 1932 memo. Soon a larger island was being proposed; the General Board quickly approved this change. Memo for the record in GB 420-7, dated 23 December 1932, complaining that BuAer had first ruined the ship

by making her a flush-decker and then had demanded that the island be restored. BuAer pointed out that the *Ranger* design was based on experience with the flush-deck *Langley*, which operated only twenty airplanes. The air officer on a deck-edge platform could see far enough aft to see all of them land, controlling them. Once the complement had increased to thirty-two aircraft (i.e., once Reeves' full program had taken effect), it became difficult or almost impossible for the air officer to see aircraft landing after the twelfth or fifteenth. *Ranger* was intended to operate seventy-two aircraft. Once the ex–battle cruisers were in commission it became clear that the island was no problem; as of late 1932 no airplane had ever run into the ship's island, though one did hit an 8-inch turret. BuAer particularly wanted a larger island for *Ranger* to accommodate the air plot through which the carrier's strike aircraft were controlled (the islands of the big ex–battle cruisers accommodated such facilities). In this memo BuAer also admitted that even the low-powered *Langley* had suffered smoke problems.

25. The Second Vinson-Trammell Act (17 May 1938) increased total carrier tonnage by 40,000 tons (29.6 percent, compared to an initial figure of 135,000 tons, left from the 1921 Washington Treaty). By way of comparison, total battleship tonnage increased by 135,000 tons (the whole 1921 carrier allowance) to 660,000 tons (25.7 percent) and cruisers by 20 percent. GB 420-2 contains a two-ocean paper dated 2 May 1939, giving necessary levels of superiority. With 5:3 superiority it would be possible to undertake an offensive in the Western Pacific "under favorable conditions" and the security of U.S. possessions as far west as Guam (but not the Philippines) could be ensured; with 4:3 Wake and the Aleutians would be safe and Guam would probably be safe. This paper strongly advocated fortifying Guam, on the grounds that with 4:3 superiority a fortified Guam would offer the equivalent of 5:3 (and with 5:3, the equivalent of 6:3, which in turn might equate to 380,000 tons of warships). On the other hand, with 4:3 inferiority, the Japanese would be able to attack into the eastern Pacific and perhaps capture the Aleutians. With 4:3 superiority in the Atlantic, U.S. forces should be able to guarantee the Western Hemisphere against German and Italian aggression. Parity would make it dangerous for the Germans and Italians to try to attack South America. The recommendations were based on 4:3 superiority in both oceans. The result was determined mainly by the strengths of the opposing fleets; Germany had ordered two carriers (neither ever completed) and Italy none. Both had, however, considerable battleship forces. Thus analysis based on opposing navies gave a battleship-heavy U.S. fleet (whose desired strength, as calculated in May 1939, was twenty-six battleships and sixteen carriers). A tonnage table included in the paper showed that the United States needed nearly twice the carrier tonnage made available by the 1938 Act (324, 841 versus 175,000 tons); the situation for battleships was only slightly less dire (1,043,169 tons needed versus 660,000 available)—and by no means had all the available 1938 tonnage been built.

26. Thus a 24 November 1939 list of suggested priorities in new ship design (GB 420) produced by C&R (responsible for the designs) shows carriers as priority 5, after light cruisers, submarines, heavy cruisers, and destroyers (but ahead of new battleships, the new *Alaska*-class super-heavy cruisers, destroyer leaders, and a flight-deck cruiser then being discussed). The list was intended as a guide to the General Board for the order in which it should produce characteristics for new designs. They had been developed for light cruisers and submarines (and the flight-deck cruiser was marked "the consensus seems to be against this type").

27. When *Essex* was first inserted into the FY41 program she was envisaged as a repeat *Yorktown* with better machinery (to reach thirty-five-knot speed) and more 5-inch guns (twelve rather than eight), but her maximum displacement was given as the same 20,400 tons as her predecessor *Hornet* (GB 420-2 of 30 June 1939). *Hornet* herself was designated mobilization prototype. By November, CV-9 displacement was being given as 24,000 tons.

28. Copy in GB 420 files, NARA, dated (in pencil) 30 September 1941. The study looked forward to completion of the "two ocean navy" program in 1946. It was intended to help the Navy resist undue political pressure, presumably in favor of aviation at the expense of conventional warships. An interesting feature of the study was the suggestion that, since fighter protection would always be at a premium, an attacker might use robot aircraft to decoy fighters away from the main attack. The report envisaged a global naval war in which the United States would fight in every theater. Thus it took into account conditions in places like the extreme North Atlantic (i.e., the Russian convoy run), in which heavy gun ships could still be quite effective. A point raised by the report was that carriers and their aircraft did not match the naval presence of gun-armed ships; the latter could force maneuver and withdrawal whether or not they actually sank enemy ships, whereas aircraft had little effect at sea *unless* they were lethal. Hence the issue was whether carrier aircraft could actually sink modern battleships maneuvering at sea, something they had not done as of September 1941. The Japanese aircraft that sank the British *Repulse* and *Prince of Wales* in December 1941 were land based (hence numbers were larger than those a carrier could have supported), and Taranto (November 1940) and Pearl Harbor involved static targets. The Italian *Roma* was sunk at sea in September 1943, but by a guided bomb not envisaged in 1943, of which the U.S. Navy had no wartime equivalent. Thus it was not until October 1944 (*Musashi*) that a modern battleship was sunk at sea by the sort of air attack that could have been envisaged in September 1941. Even then it took aircraft from a whole task group to do the job.

29. Most CVEs had the H2 catapult installed on board *Ranger* and *Wasp*. A version of the H4 used by the *Essex* class (H4C) was installed on board the *Commencement Bay* class, and also on some C3 conversions (CVE-25 and CVE 31–54, most of which went to the Royal Navy).

30. Reviewing the building program in June 1941, the General Board observed that there was an urgent need for aircraft to work with convoys, but once *Hornet* was completed about 16 December 1941 no further carriers would be completed until January 1944. The board asked whether it would be advisable to fill the gap with merchant-type carriers, despite their limited aircraft capacity. What should their characteristics be? At a 27 June 1941 hearing, the Chief of BuAer testified that the converted freighters would be useful both to work with convoys (against air attack, surface raiders, and U-boats) and to augment fleet carriers. Six ships were already being converted in the United Kingdom, and C-3 freighters would be useful for this purpose in the United States. The ships could accommodate up to thirty-six fighters, or equivalent numbers of fighters, scouts (cruiser type, with wheels rather than floats), or scout bombers (torpedo bombers were not mentioned). BuAer proposed converting liners to fill the gap between the completion of *Hornet* and *Essex*; preliminary studies of seven liners had been made. Unfortunately all were relatively slow (20.5 to 22 knots) and all had limited capacity (typically eighteen fighters, eighteen dive-bombers, and eighteen torpedo bombers). It might be more useful to convert two fast liners that had been caught in U.S. waters by the war, the French *Normandie* and the Italian *Conte Biancamano*. Four hull numbers were reserved for liner conversions, including one of SS *America*, but none was carried out.

31. Hull numbers 2 through 5 were reserved for planned conversions of liners but never carried out, so the fifty C3 conversions carried numbers through 54 (the ex-tankers were CVE 26–29). CVE 55–104 were the *Casablancas*. The specially built *Commencement Bay* class were CVE 105–127, of which CVE 124–127 were cancelled at the end of the war. The projected CVE 128–139 were never ordered.

32. General Board letter 18 October 1941, following a BuAer letter dated 9 September 1941 and a BuShips letter, describing the proposed conversion, dated 29 August 1941. All of these letters referred to a relatively sophisticated conversion, which would take consider-

able time. The subject was revived in April 1942, but this time a much simpler CVE-like design was envisaged. The General Board still heartily disliked the idea; the U.S. fleet badly needed cruisers, and it did not need mediocre carriers.

CHAPTER 10

Foundation for Victory:
U.S. Navy Aircraft Development, 1922–1945

Hill Goodspeed

The sun shone brightly in the Panama sky as the fighter planes from the aircraft carrier *Saratoga* (CV-3) roared aloft as part of fleet exercises off the coast of the Central American nation. A few days earlier these same planes had launched a surprise "attack" against the Panama Canal that foreshadowed the independent operations of carrier task forces during World War II. On this day, they were part of a mock fleet engagement, with fighter planes escorting bombing and torpedo aircraft. "Climbed so high we near froze to death [and] cruised over to the enemy [battle] line where we discovered all the *Lexington* planes below us," wrote Lieutenant Austin K. Doyle of Fighting Squadron (VF) 2B. With the benefits of altitude and surprise, ideal for fighter pilots ready to do battle, Doyle and his division dove into the "enemy" planes, twisting and turning in dogfights. "When we broke off we rendezvoused . . . [and] strafed every ship in the fleet. . . . No other plane came near us."[1]

The events of a February day in 1929 described above occurred in the midst of a watershed era in naval aviation, the interwar years bringing a host of momentous advancements on multiple levels. From a technological and operational standpoint, none were as important as the aircraft carrier and the tactical and strategic implications of this new weapon of war. Arguably, the key element of the carrier's success was its main battery in the form of the aircraft that launched from its decks, the unparalleled progress made in the design and operation of carrier aircraft providing the foundation for the flattop's success during World War II. Similar progress marked other areas of naval aviation as well. Such was the lasting influence of interwar aircraft development that Lieutenant Doyle, who as a Naval Academy plebe during 1916–1917 served in a Navy with just fifty-eight aircraft of assorted types, could in 1929 write of a carrier strike against the Panama Canal and, later in his career as a carrier skipper, order planes designed on drawing boards of the 1930s to attack Japanese-held beachheads and strike enemy ships over the horizon.[2]

On the day World War I ended, the U.S. Navy's inventory totaled 2,337 aircraft, including heavier-than-air and lighter-than-air types.[3] While this is an impressive total, given the aforementioned aircraft total of fifty-eight when America entered World War I, the number is deceiving. It is true that flying boats built by the Curtiss Aeroplane and Motor Company operated extensively from overseas coastal bases in the antisubmarine role. Yet, when it came to combat types flown at the front, the majority of naval aviators who deployed overseas trained and logged their operational missions in the cockpits of foreign-built airplanes. As the U.S. Navy developed its plan for aircraft production, the realization of the superiority of foreign designs was apparent to, among others, Commander John H. Towers, the Navy's third aviator, who before U.S. entry into the war had observed firsthand operations of British aircraft during a stint in England as assistant naval attaché.[4] Even after the signing of the Armistice, foreign types retained their importance to the U.S. Navy's operations. With overseas observers having witnessed the launching of wheeled aircraft from flight decks built on board British ships, aircraft like Sopwith Camels, Hanriot HD-1s, and Nieuport 29s were procured for use in Navy experiments flying landplanes from temporary wooden platforms erected atop the turrets of fleet battleships. Ironically, the performance of these aircraft, built in the factories of England and France, proved a key factor in the shaping of the interwar aircraft building program.[5]

Indeed, if there was one driving force behind the development of aircraft for the U.S. Navy during the 1920s and 1930s, it was the realization of the importance of shipboard aircraft to naval aviation operations. While this had been on the minds of naval aviation personnel from the beginning—among the earliest experiments conducted were the testing of catapults for launching aircraft from ships—most naval aviators were initially wedded to seaplanes. Upon arriving in Pensacola, Florida, to establish the Navy's first aeronautical station there in January 1914, Lieutenant Commander Henry Mustin wrote to his wife of the difficulties of finding a suitable site for an airfield from which to operated landplanes and dirigibles: "Personally, I don't approve of the Naval flying corps going in for those two branches because I think they both belong to the Army."[6] This philosophy would guide aircraft operations during naval aviation's first decade and beyond, with naval aviator training and operations centered on seaplane operations.[7]

British experience in World War I, namely the operation of wheeled-aircraft from ships, coupled with the aforementioned experiments on U.S. Navy battleships carried out during winter maneuvers at Guantanamo Bay, Cuba, in 1919, prompted a shift in thinking. Weighed down by pontoons, floatplanes simply could not compare with landplanes when it came to speed and maneuverability. Also, ships operating floatplanes, while they could launch them relatively quickly, had to disrupt operations to come alongside a returning aircraft and crane it back aboard. The aircraft carrier, with a deck devoted to the launching and recovery of aircraft, offered the most promise of maximizing the potential of aircraft in fleet operations.[8]

By 1927, three aircraft carriers—*Langley* (CV-1), *Lexington* (CV-2), and *Saratoga* (CV-3)—had been placed in commission, their presence giving naval aviation heretofore unrealized capabilities in fleet operations and a potential as offensive weapons at sea or against land targets. "The value of aircraft acting on the defensive as a protective group against enemy aircraft is doubtful unless it is in connection with an offensive move," wrote naval aviator Commander Patrick N. L. Bellinger in his Naval War College thesis in 1925.

> The most effective defensive against air attack is offensive action against the source, that is enemy vessels carrying aircraft and therefore, enemy aircraft carriers, or their bases and hangars on shore as well as the factories in which they are built. The air force that first strikes its enemy a serious blow will reap a tremendous initial advantage. The opposing force cannot hope to surely prevent such a blow by the mere placing of aircraft in certain protective screens or by patrolling certain areas. There is no certainty, even with preponderance in numbers, of making contact with enemy aircraft, before they have reached the proper area and delivered their attack, and there is no certainty even if contact is made, of being able to stop them.[9]

Nine years later, the Navy's war instructions for 1934 emphasized the importance of seizing the offensive during a fleet engagement. "*If the enemy aircraft carriers have not been located*, our fleet is in danger of an air attack. In this situation, enemy carriers should be located and destroyed," the document read. It further stated that if enemy carriers had been located, either with their aircraft on board or their strike groups having been launched, U.S. carrier planes would "vigorously" attack them, "destroy[ing] their flying decks."[10]

This realization of the threat of enemy air power in a fleet action stimulated tactical thought, which in turn influenced the design of the planes tasked with delivering the blows against enemy carriers. Initially, it was conventional wisdom that torpedoes would be the most effective method of attack against enemy ships, but whether an aerial torpedo or a bomb, the struggle facing aircraft designers was developing aircraft that could carry the weight of the ordnance without compromising too much in the way of speed, maneuverability, and range.[11] The first successful torpedo plane design introduced into fleet service was Douglas Aircraft Company's DT, which was important in more than one respect. First, it was the maiden military plane produced by the company, symbolizing the emergence of a postwar aircraft manufacturing

Naval History and Heritage Command, *Naval Aviation News*, June 1975

The first successful torpedo plane design was Douglas Aircraft Company's DT.

base marked by the opening of such companies as Douglas and Grumman Aircraft Engineering Corporation. These firms, founded after World War I, joined such wartime entities as the Curtiss Aeroplane and Motor Company, Boeing Company, Glenn L. Martin Company, and the Naval Aircraft Factory—the latter a Navy-owned center for manufacturing and testing of airplanes—in meeting the demands of the Navy's aircraft programs. Second, due to the weight of aerial torpedoes, while earlier torpedo plane designs were twin-engine ones that were unsuitable for carrier use, the single-engine DT was capable of shipboard operations and of carrying a payload of 1,835 pounds. In fact, on 2 May 1924, a DT-2 version of the design carrying a dummy torpedo successfully catapult launched from *Langley* anchored at Naval Air Station (NAS) Pensacola, Florida. Finally, the DT pointed to the future in its composition, the traditional wood and fabric used in aircraft, while still present, accompanied by sections of welded steel.[12]

Following the DT into production was Martin's T3M/T4M torpedo planes (versions were also built by Great Lakes with the designation TG), which boasted a higher speed than the DT and could carry versions of the Mk-VII torpedo that was in the Navy's weapons arsenal during the late 1920s. Its introduction coincided with the first significant involvement of aircraft carriers in fleet exercises, which revealed much about the employment of torpedo planes. Fleet pilots all too quickly found that the operational parameters of their torpedoes left much to be desired, any hope of a successful attack necessitating that the weapon be dropped at an altitude of no more than twenty-five feet with the aircraft flying at a maximum speed of eighty-six miles per hour. Malfunctioning torpedoes were the norm rather than the exception, and the survivability of torpedo planes flying "low and slow" was questionable. Noted a section of the Aircraft Squadrons, Battle Fleet document "Aircraft Tactics—Development of" dated 3 February 1927: "Even with anti-aircraft gunfire in its present underdeveloped stage, torpedo planes cannot hope to successfully launch [an] attack from 2,000 yards and less." By 1930, there were serious questions as to the wisdom of operating torpedo planes at all.[13]

The introduction of the Mark XIII torpedo held enough promise for the continuation of the torpedo mission, the weapon capable of being launched at a range of 6,300 yards from altitudes of between 40 and 90 feet and at a speed of 115 mph. The weapon's weight of 1,927 pounds mandated the introduction of a more capable torpedo plane, the Navy selecting another Douglas design, the TBD Devastator. First flown in 1935, the TBD was cutting edge for its era given the fact that it was a monoplane of all-metal construction with a top speed of over 200 mph. It would be upon the wings of the TBD that torpedo squadrons went to war in 1941 and 1942.[14]

Developing alongside airborne torpedo attack as an element of naval aviation's offensive arsenal was aerial bombing. Before World War I and in the years immediately following, battleship officers remained skeptical of the ability of an aircraft to sink a capital ship with bombs. Though bombing tests conducted by Army and Navy airplanes against antiquated U.S. ships and captured German vessels during 1921 proved a success in the damage they inflicted, the fact that the target ships were at anchor with no anti-aircraft defenses left many Navy officers skeptical. Yet, as the first decade of the 1920s progressed, bombing offered increasing promise. "The relative merits of the torpedo plane and the bombing plane has [sic] been a much mooted question recently," Chief of the Bureau of Aeronautics Rear Admiral William A. Moffett told an audience at the Army War College in 1925. "Potentially, the aircraft bomb is, I believe, the most serious menace which the surface craft has to face at the present time."[15] The following year, operations in the fleet focused on a particular type of bombing attack that offered the best chance to make Moffett's potential menace a real one. On an October day off the coast of San Pedro, California, sailors on the decks of the battleships of the Pacific Fleet heard the whine of aircraft engines and spotted dark specks diving toward them. What they saw and heard were F6C Hawks of Fighting VF Squadron 2 making a simulated attack, the pilots positioning their planes in steep dives as they roared down on their targets. The event marked the first fleet demonstration of the tactic of dive-bombing, and less than two months later squadrons of Aircraft Squadrons, Battle Fleet completed their first dive-bombing exercise.[16]

As was the case with the development of torpedo aircraft, the evolution of bomber designs during the interwar years was in part driven by the increasing weight of the ordnance, their reason for being. Yet, most of the aircraft initially filling the "light bombing" role were not employed solely in that mission, the Bureau of Aeronautics as late as 1927 issuing the opinion that there was no need for a specialized aircraft for that task alone. Four years later the air groups in *Lexington* and *Saratoga* did not even include a bombing squadron, each carrier instead embarking two fighting squadrons with one devoted to the fighting mission and one to light bombing. Even the aircraft considered the first Navy design built specifically for dive-bombing, the Curtiss F8C, was a dual mission aircraft that operated in the fleet as a fighter bomber.[17]

During the prewar years the fleet would never divest itself of using a multi-mission aircraft as a dive-bomber, but during the early 1930s the Bureau of Aeronautics issued requests for proposal for a new classification of aircraft called the scout-bomber to equip carrier-based scouting and bombing squadrons. This aircraft would fulfill the missions outlined in the war instructions of attacking enemy surface ships and scouting tactically.[18] Among naval aircraft, the scout-bombers designed in the decade preceding World War II were among the most technologically advanced. The SBU was the first capable of exceeding 200 mph, its wings reinforced to handle the stress of steep dives carrying a 500-pound bomb, while the BF2C-1 Goshawk possessed an all-metal wing structure that made it even more durable in a dive. The SB2U Vindicator, ordered in 1934, was the sea service's first monoplane scout-bomber. However, the greatest developments came with the Northrop BT-1 and the SBD Dauntless. The former, delivered in 1937, incorporated unique split flaps, the upper and lower flaps opening when the airplane was in a dive. When flight tests revealed extreme buffeting in the horizontal stabilizer, engineers added holes to the flaps, which remedied the problem and in dive-bombing runs slowed the aircraft and made it a stable bombing platform. This technology carried over to Douglas Aircraft Company's SBD Dauntless, which boasted a top speed of 256 mph, could carry a 1,000-pound bomb, and had a maximum range of 1,370 miles in the scouting configuration. Enhancing the capabilities of these aircraft as dive-bombers was equipment such as telescopic sights and a bomb crutch, the ladder swinging ordnance away from the fuselage during a dive so that falling bombs did not strike the aircraft's propeller.[19]

In comparison to dive-bombers and torpedo planes, fighter aircraft had a sound foundation upon which to build during the interwar years, air-to-air combat having advanced more during World War I than other arenas of air warfare. Fighters provided cover for bases and ships against enemy air attack and protected bombing and torpedo planes en route to bomb enemy targets, their missions also including clearing the skies of enemy fighters and shooting down enemy scouting planes to deny information to enemy commanders.[20] In short, on the wings of fighter planes rested the responsibility of gaining control of the air and maintaining air superiority, the ideal characteristics for aircraft tasked with this mission being speed, rate of climb, and maneuverability. These characteristics were greatly enhanced in naval aircraft by the introduction of air-cooled engines, embodied by the Pratt & Whitney Wasp. Unencumbered by a radiator that was standard on water-cooled engines, the Wasp was lighter, the savings in weight translating into improved performance. Endurance tests also revealed that air-cooled engines were more reliable, which was appealing for naval aircraft that operated over open ocean far removed from land bases.[21]

As mentioned above, Navy fighters of the interwar era were viewed as multi-mission platforms, as evidenced by the fact that it was fighters that delivered the first successful fleet demonstration of a dive-bombing attack. The Bureau of Aeronautics, in issuing specifications to aircraft companies for the design of new fighter planes, routinely included parameters for the aircraft in the bombing role. As tactics developed during the 1920s and 1930s, however, air-minded officers came to the realization that saddling fighters with a bomb diminished their ability to provide air superiority. As Rear Admiral Harry E. Yarnell commented in 1932 during his tour as Commander, Aircraft Squadrons, Battle Force, "It is becoming increasingly evident that if the performance of fighters is to be improved . . . bombing characteristics of fighters must be made secondary to fighting characteristics."[22]

Yarnell's letter coincided with the emergence of the first fighter designed by the relatively new Grumman Aircraft Engineering Corporation, the FF-1. Delivered in 1933, the airplane boasted features new to Navy fighters, including an enclosed cockpit canopy, an all-metal fuselage, and retractable landing gear. Though its forward fuselage was bulbous in order to house the latter, the FF-1 had a top speed of 207 mph, this attribute becoming readily apparent to a U.S. Army Air Service squadron commander, who upon seeing one of the "Fifis" during a tactical exercise over Hawaii in 1933 decided to make a run on it. "Great was his amazement when his dive upon the innocent looking target failed to close the range."[23] One other aspect of the FF-1's design was that it was a two-seater, with room for a pilot and observer, an arrangement more in line with torpedo and bombing planes. This fact sparked a debate among fighter pilots over the direction of design of future aircraft. In a 1935 memorandum to the Chief of the Bureau of Aeronautics, the commanding officer of VF-5B noted the two-seat fighter's superiority in escorting strike groups was possible because of the observer's ability to scan the skies for enemy aircraft and proclaimed it less vulnerable to diving attack by enemy fighters for the same reason. The VF-5B skipper argued that the two-seater was equal to or superior to the single-seater in all tactical missions required of fighter aircraft. Conceding the general advantage of smaller, single-seat fighters in speed and maneuverability, he concluded that in naval warfare control of the air was obtained not by air-to-air superiority over enemy aircraft formations, but by knocking out the carriers from which the enemy planes operated. "In this the superior characteristic of the single-seater [sic] fighter can play little or no part."[24]

A tactical board convened by Commander, Aircraft Squadrons, Battle Force issued a report on the issue the following January, defining a fighter plane as a "high speed weapon of destruction against other aircraft." The board criticized the dismissal of this fundamental mission of Navy carrier fighters, writing that the VF-5B commander's report "gives undue importance to secondary fields of employment . . . emphasizing the suitability of the airplane for a function which is not one for which a VF [fighter plane] is properly suited." The board concluded that "present VF aircraft in service are of practically no value as VF. They lack either necessary speed superiority over other types or necessary offensive armament, or both."[25]

This quest for speed would endure, with Grumman following up the FF-1 with first the F2F and then the F3F biplanes, each faster but limited in capability when compared with the Japanese A6M Zero also under development in the late 1930s (the A6M-2, which was operational in 1940, had a top speed of 331 mph compared to 264 mph for the F3F-3).[26] Throughout the late 1930s the Bureau of Aeronautics initiated requests for proposals to the nation's aircraft industry for fighter designs that emphasized speed and improved armament. In this approach of casting a wide net, the Navy received a variety of designs. Some, including the unorthodox twin-engine F5F Skyrocket, did not enter production, while others, namely Brewster's F2A Buffalo monoplane, were put into production, but proved disappointing. The aircraft that emerged as the best that could be placed in production most quickly was Grumman's F4F Wildcat, a monoplane successor to the company's earlier biplane fighter designs, which with its super-charged engine achieved a maximum speed of 333.5 mph at an altitude of 21,300 feet and boasted four .50-caliber machine guns for armament. On it would rest the fortunes of Navy and Marine fighter squadrons until 1943.

The aircraft carrier and the airplanes that flew from her deck represented the cutting edge of naval aviation operations of the interwar years, with *New York Times* reporter Lewis R. Freeman capturing the public's excitement over the ship's unique operations in an article written in the aftermath of Fleet Problem IX. "Just about the most spectacular show in the world today . . . is the handling and manoevering [*sic*] of the great carriers *Lexington* and *Saratoga*," he wrote. "The spectacle of launching and landing planes is fully up to the superlative scale of the ship itself. . . . In the darkness of early morning the effect is heightened by circles of spitting fire from the exhausts and the colored lights of the wings and tail."[27] However, the foundation upon which the airplane entered naval service was seaplanes and flying boats, and in the immediate postwar years they provided naval aviation's first real integration with fleet operations.

Established in early 1919, Fleet Air Detachment, Atlantic Fleet, put to sea in exercises with surface forces, part of its operations being flights of wheeled aircraft from improvised decks on board battleships. However, significant attention was also devoted to flying boat operations and their support of surface ships, particularly in the spotting of naval gunfire. "For the first time in the history of the Navy, the actual setting of the sights was, to a large extent, controlled by the officers of the Airboat squadron," read an air detachment report of 1920. "This marks the beginning of a new era in our naval gunnery."[28] Success in this role, the spotting of naval gunfire, led to the eventual assignment of detachments of seaplanes to cruisers and battleships as part of cruiser scouting (VCS) and observation (VO) squadrons, respectively. To fill this requirement, a number of aircraft procured by the Navy during the interwar years, including the VE-7, UO/FU, and O2U, could be operated in both the landplane and floatplane configuration. By the time the United States entered World War II, the principal aircraft flying in the scouting and observation roles were the Curtiss SOC Seagull and Vought OS2U Kingfisher, the latter a monoplane of which over a thousand were eventually produced.[29]

Long-range scouting would become the domain of flying boats, the detachment demonstrating their endurance in a lengthy seven-month cruise with the fleet, logging 12,731 nautical miles, some 4,000 of which were in direct maneuvers with the fleet. Meanwhile, in the Pacific, flying boats and seaplane tenders formed Air Force, Pacific Fleet in July 1920, putting to sea for joint fleet exercises that demonstrated the scouting capabilities of Navy flying boats. During the cruise, wartime F-5L flying boats covered a distance of 6,076 miles in operations between California and Central America. Wrote Admiral Hugh Rodman, Commander in Chief, Pacific Fleet, at the conclusion of the exercises, "The scouting work performed by the seaplanes was carried out to a distance of about one hundred and sixty-five miles from the bases and in weather which, except under war conditions, might have caused the commander of the force to hesitate about sending the planes into the air."[30]

During the late 1920s flying boat operations in the Navy began to stagnate as increasing emphasis and funding was devoted to aircraft carrier development. Though over the course of the ensuing years new designs appeared, they were, in the words of Rear Admiral A. W. Johnson in a paper on the development and use of patrol planes, "of no useful purpose except for training and utility services."[31] In contrast to the seagoing force that had demonstrated so much the potential of the flying boat in fleet operations in the immediate postwar years, Johnson, who commanded Aircraft, Base Force, noted that "patrol plane squadrons became in reality a shore based force," with cruising reports of seaplane tenders during the late 1920s and early 1930s proof of the diminished employment of flying boats in fleet operations.[32] Even the Consolidated Aircraft Company's P2Y, which achieved fame when it equipped Patrol VP Squadron 10F in a record-setting non-stop flight between California and Pearl Harbor, Hawaii, in January 1934, had limitations: "[It] must operate from sheltered harbors, and can do nothing in the way of scouting and bombing that cannot be as equally well done by large land planes operating from established shore bases equipped with good flying fields."[33] Yet, landplanes for distant overwater flights were the exclusive domain of the Army Air Corps, a 1931 agreement between Army Chief of Staff General Douglas MacArthur and Chief of Naval Operations Admiral William V. Pratt preventing the Navy from operating long-range land-based aircraft.[34]

Johnson's comments came at a critical juncture for both the development of flying boats and the strategic requirements for their employment in the event of war. By the early 1930s, those officers working on War Plan Orange, the constantly evolving American strategy in the event of war with Japan, had begun to more appreciate the role of air power in a fleet engagement. With ships able to engage at greater distances, advance scouting, particularly in the open expanses of the Central Pacific, could prove a deciding factor between victory and defeat.[35] For proponents of patrol aviation, this tactical and strategic requirement for flying boats coincided with the introduction of a plane that represented a tremendous advance in flying boat technology—the PBY Catalina.

With a maze of struts and wires between wings limiting the performance of earlier biplane designs, Consolidated Aircraft Company engineers drew up a flying boat built around a high-mounted parasol wing with minimal struts necessary because of internal bracing; this reduced drag, as did wing floats that retracted once airborne to form wingtips. Despite a gross weight that exceeded that of the P2Y it replaced, the PBY boasted a top speed nearly 40 miles per hour faster than that of the P2Y. Deliveries of the PBY began in 1936, and two years later fourteen Navy patrol squadrons operated the type.[36] "I feel very strongly that when the PBY's [sic] come into service, the Fleet will begin to realize the potentialities of VP's [sic] [patrol planes]," wrote Rear Admiral Ernest J. King on the eve of the aircraft's delivery, "and will begin to *demand* their services."[37]

Performance in fleet exercises validated the PBY's capabilities as a long-range scout. Comments on patrol plane activities in Fleet Problem XVIII held in early 1937 concluded that they were capable of locating an enemy force within a five hundred- to one thousand-mile radius of their bases, night tracking, and high-altitude bombing.[38] "Your patrol planes have certainly changed the whole picture in regard to tactics and even strategy," Captain W. R. Furlong of the Bureau of Ordnance wrote King. Such was the range that the newly arrived Catalinas could reach; planners of future war games would have to "put the brakes on the patrol planes to keep them from finding out everything long before we could get the information from the cruisers and other scouts."[39]

The capabilities of the PBY, coupled with fatal crashes, spelled the end of the use of rigid airships as long-range scouts, an idea long championed by Rear Admiral William A. Moffett, the first chief of the Bureau of Aeronautics. However, non-rigid airships, notably of the K-class would prove effective in long-range antisubmarine patrols during World War II.[40]

Not as clear in discussions about patrol aviation was the advisability of using flying boats in a bombing role. There was indeed a precedent in the practice, F-5Ls having participated in the famous 1921 bombing tests against captured German warships and stricken U.S. Navy vessels.[41] In 1934, while serving as Chief of the Bureau of Aeronautics, Rear Admiral Ernest J. King had suggested that flying boats could serve as a first strike weapon in an engagement at sea, their attacks preceding those of carrier planes and surface forces.[42] Correspondence between Captain John Hoover and Admiral Joseph Mason Reeves, the latter Commander in Chief, United States Fleet, the following year illuminated the problems with flying boats operating in this capacity. Umpires in fleet exercises determined that patrol planes would incur heavy losses and inflict insignificant damage to capital ships when used in the strike role, with Hoover pointing to the fact that the slow speeds and low service ceilings of patrol planes then in operation (the Consolidated P2Y and Martin PM) made attacks by them "suicidal." "The way to utilize patrol planes for attacking must by re-studied from a *practical viewpoint*."[43] The introduction of the PBY Catalina ("PB" being the Navy designation for patrol bomber), which incorporated a nose compartment for a bombardier and provision to carry the Norden bombsight, offered more promise when it came to patrol bombing operations. However, as the author of the foremost study of planning for the war against Japan has noted, by 1940 the notion of operating flying boats as patrol bombers had been discounted.[44] Yet, wartime necessity would awaken interest in flying boat offensive operations for the PBY and other flying boat designs of the 1930s, including the PBM Mariner and PB2Y Coronado.

By mid-1941, the year in which naval aviation entered the world's second global war, the Secretary of the Navy could report a net increase of 82 percent over the previous fiscal year in the number of service aircraft on hand in the Navy's inventory. His annual report noted emphasis being placed on development of dive-bombing and fighting aircraft of greater power, which was "vindicated in the service reports received from belligerents abroad."[45] Other technical adaptations based on wartime observations included such equipment as self-sealing fuel tanks and improved armor and firepower. "With the present international situation," the secretary concluded, "it is imperative that all construction work on ships, aircraft and bases be kept at the highest possible tempo in order that the prospective two-ocean Navy become a reality at the earliest possible date."[46] The sudden events of the morning of 7 December 1941 shifted this tempo into previously unimagined levels, the events that occurred between that day and September 1945 representing the ultimate test for the technology and tactics that evolved during the previous two decades.

"When war comes," Captain John Hoover wrote in 1935, "we will have just what is on hand at the time, not planes on the drafting board or projected."[47] For naval aviation, the combat aircraft flying from carrier decks, fleet anchorages, and airfields when war came had entered service between 1936 and 1940. Fortunately, however, the planes that eventually would replace or complement them were far removed from the drafting board. The prototype of the F6F Hellcat made its first flight just months after the Pearl Harbor attack, while the XF4U-1 Corsair had already demonstrated speeds of over four hundred mph during test flights in 1940. Similarly, prototypes of the SB2C Helldiver and TBF Avenger had already taken to the air by the time the United States entered World War II. And with the coming of war, the mobilization of industry translated into rapid transformation of prototypes into production versions of airplanes ready for combat, with American factories turning out an average of 170 airplanes per day from 1942 to 1945.[48]

How did these airplanes fare in the crucible of combat? A telling statistic is found in an examination of air-to-air combat: During the period 1 September 1944–15 August 1945, the zenith of naval aviation power in the Pacific, in engagements with enemy aircraft, a total of 218 naval carrier–based and land-based fighters were lost in aerial combat, while Navy and Marine Corps FM Wildcat, F6F Hellcat, and F4U Corsair fighters destroyed 4,937 enemy fighters and bombers.[49] Even during the period 1942–1943, when naval aviators flew the F4F Wildcat, which in comparison to the heralded Japanese Zero had an advantage only in its defensive armor and self-sealing fuel tanks, carrier-based and land-based Wildcat pilots splashed 905 enemy fighters and bombers. This came at a cost of 178 Wildcats destroyed and 83 damaged.[50] Comparing the two eras, in all the action sorties flown by naval aircraft during 1942, 5 percent ended in the loss of the aircraft. In 1945, less than one-eighth of 1 percent of all action sorties resulted in a combat loss.[51] While direct comparisons are not possible with other classes of aircraft, a look at the total number of sorties flown against land and ship targets by year is revealing. In the first two years of the war, 19,701 sorties were directed against ship and shore, a figure that for the years 1944–1945 jumped to 239,386![52]

A key reason for this increase was aircraft development. The carrier *Enterprise* (CV-6), at sea when the Japanese attacked Pearl Harbor, had none of the same aircraft types on board when she operated off Japan in 1945. The F4U Corsair and F6F Hellcat by that time in the war boasted better top speeds, rate of climb, and performance at altitude than the most advanced versions of the Japanese navy's Zero fighter. Similarly, the SB2C Helldiver and TBF/TBM Avenger, particularly once technical maladies were corrected in the former, proved to be more than comparable to the aircraft operated by the Japanese in the torpedo and bombing roles. In addition, Japanese aircraft to a great extent suffered from deficiencies in their armor protection, making them more susceptible to being shot down by Allied aircraft and anti-aircraft gunners. Even though the Japanese did produce some very capable aircraft as the war progressed—among them the all-metal Yokosuka D4Y Suisei bomber that had a top speed comparable to many fighters and the Kawanishi N1K1-J/N1K5-J Shiden and Shiden Kai fighter, which in the hands of an experienced pilot could be more than a match for an Allied fighter—they appeared in too few numbers to have much effect on the outcome of the war. In addition, due to increasing Allied superiority in material, the successful campaign against Japanese merchant and combat ships, and the increasing conquest of territory, Japanese planes were at a strategic and tactical disadvantage before they even left the ground.[53]

There is more to the story behind the statistics. First, sortie rates and the number of enemy aircraft destroyed rose in direct proportion to the growth of U.S. naval aviation. In 1941 there were 1,774 combat aircraft on hand in the U.S. Navy. By 1945 that figure had grown to 29,125.[54] When the Japanese attacked Pearl Harbor, the Navy had a total of seven fleet carriers and one escort carrier in commission. Between that time and the end of the war, the Navy commissioned 102 flattops of all classes.[55] Then there was the human factor. Imperial Japanese Navy and Army pilots generally remained in combat squadrons until they were killed or suffered wounds that rendered them unable to fly, this policy of attrition steadily reducing the quality of enemy pilots faced as the war progressed. This was apparent as early as late 1942, a Report of Action of Fighting Squadron (VF) 10 in November 1942 noting that the "ability of the enemy VF [fighter] pilots encountered in the vicinity of Guadalcanal is considered to be much inferior to the pilots encountered earlier in the war."[56] In contrast, experienced U.S. naval aviators rotated in and out of combat squadrons. For example, Lieutenant Tom Provost, designated a naval aviator during the late 1930s, flew fighting planes from the carrier *Enterprise* (CV-6) during the early months of World War II, including service at the Battle of Midway. His next tour was as a flight instructor, imparting knowledge to fledgling pilots before returning to the fleet in 1944 and 1945 to fly F6F Hellcat fighters off an *Essex*-class carrier.[57] These naval aviators were well led and well trained. Fighter squadron commanders during the early months of the war, notably Lieutenant Commanders John S. Thach and James Flatley, proved adept at developing tactics to maximize the advantages of their aircraft over those of the enemy while the U.S. Navy's longtime emphasis on teaching deflection shooting paid dividends in actual combat.[58] The same imparting of lessons learned was standard in other types of squadrons as tactics developed throughout the war.

During World War II, were U.S. Navy aircraft employed in a manner envisioned during the interwar years and how did the ever-changing tactical environment affect the operations of naval aircraft? The answers to these questions provide an important framework in which to assess the history of aircraft development between 1922 and 1945.

Much prewar discussion centered on how naval aircraft could be most effective in a fleet engagement, and concerns expressed at that time about the vulnerability of torpedo planes proved well founded, with carrier-based torpedo squadrons at Midway suffering grievous losses. Despite the fact that even as late as May 1945, experienced carrier task force commander Vice Admiral Marc A. Mitscher still considered the torpedo "the major weapon for use against surface ships," the number of torpedoes dropped at sea decreased as the war progressed.[59] For carrier-based aircraft and land-based aircraft, during the first year of the war torpedoes accounted for 73 percent and 94 percent, respectively, of the total ordnance expended on shipping by weight. By 1945, those figures had dropped to 16 percent and 0 percent, respectively, and throughout the war only 1,460 torpedoes were dropped by naval aircraft.[60] Factors contributing to these low numbers included the problematic aerial torpedoes in the U.S. inventory early in the war and the focus of carrier strikes in the war's latter months being increasingly centered on hitting land targets. During 1945 the total tonnage of bombs dropped on land targets by Navy and Marine Corps aircraft was 41,555 as compared to just 4,261 tons of ordnance dropped on ships of all types during the same period.[61]

Dive-bombing lived up to expectations as a tactic that could influence the outcome of a sea battle, a fact demonstrated in dramatic fashion in the sinking of four Japanese carriers at the Battle of Midway. However, as evidenced by the statistic above, as the war moved ever closer to the Japanese home islands, targets for carrier-based dive-bombers were increasingly located ashore rather than afloat, with planes attacking harbor areas, transportation networks, and enemy airfields. It was in the bombing mission that wartime experience shuffled the prewar and early war composition of carrier air groups. Scouting squadrons, which in 1942 were equipped with the same airplane—the SBD Dauntless—as bombing squadrons on board carriers, were eliminated from carrier air groups by 1943. In addition, torpedo planes and fighters increasingly assumed some of the ground attack mission, the latter reawakening the fighter versus fighter bomber debate of the 1930s. Commanders had no choice but to use fighters in the bombing role during 1944 and 1945 when the advent of the kamikazes necessitated that the number of fighter planes in a carrier air group be increased dramatically. By war's end, their numbers were double that of the combined number of torpedo and scout-bombers.[62] In the fighter-bomber role, naval single-engine fighters from land and ship logged a comparable number of ground attack missions as that of airplanes designed as bombers. However, on these missions they expended primarily rockets and machine gun ammunition.[63] The SBD Dauntless, SB2C Helldiver, and TBF/TBM Avenger proved the mainstay of the bombing mission, the latter aircraft proving to be one of the most versatile naval aircraft of the entire war. The dive-bombers carried 34 percent of all naval aviation's bomb tonnage, while Avengers delivered 32 percent of the bomb tonnage and launched 29 percent of all rockets.[64]

U.S. Navy Curtiss SB2C Helldiver returns from a strike on Japanese shipping.

The employment of fighters in the bombing role was central to the debate about the composition of carrier air groups, the subject of much discussion as the war drew to a close. A 1944 survey of carrier division commanders on the subject revealed a consensus that the majority of airplanes on deck should be fighters, the problematic SB2C Helldiver perhaps influencing calls for fighters to assume a ground attack role in addition to the air-to-air mission. Vice Admiral Mitscher preferred dive-bombers over fighter bombers, telling Captain Seldon Spangler, who was on an inspection tour of the Pacific in 1945, that dive-bombers, even given the inadequacies of the SB2C, were better than the F4U Corsair in the bombing role. Wrote Spangler, "He thought it would be most desirable to get down to two airplane types aboard carriers, one to be the best fighter we can build, the other to be a high performance torpedo dive bomber." Rear Admiral Gerald F. Bogan concurred to some degree. Although favoring the intensification of dive-bombing for fighting planes, he wrote "Do not emasculate the VF plane."[65] Interestingly, in production were two airframes that met Mitscher's requirements, the BT2D (later AD) Skyraider, which combined the torpedo and bombing missions into one attack mission, and a pure fighter in the form of the F8F Bearcat. Interestingly, the F4U Corsair, which, after some technical problems were solved, became an excellent carrier plane and served for years after World War II on the basis of its capabilities as a fighter bomber.

"The Fleet is well satisfied with PBY-5A airplanes for use at Guadalcanal for night reconnaissance, bombing, torpedo attack, mining, etc.," read an 28 April 1943, report to the Director of Material in the Bureau of Aeronautics. "They are not using these airplanes in the daytime except in bad visibility."[66] This concise summary of operations in the first part of the Pacific War reveals that in their decision to remove the flying boat from consideration as a long-range daylight bomber, prewar officers were correct about the platform's capabilities. Action in the war's early weeks proved the vulnerability of the lumbering PBYs to enemy fighters, with four of six PBYs of VP Patrol Squadron 101 shot down on a 27 December 1941, raid on Jolo in the central Philippines.[67] However, under the cover of darkness, the aircraft proved highly effective in the ground attack mission. As prewar exercises demonstrated, PBYs performed well as long-range scouts, most notably in their locating elements of the Japanese fleet at Midway. Their ability to patrol wide expanses of ocean also made them effective as antisubmarine platforms against German U-boats as well as very capable search and rescue aircraft.[68]

What could not have been foreseen during the 1930s in light of the division of roles and missions between the armed services was the successful operation of long-range multi-engine landplanes in naval aviation. As noted above, the Pratt-MacArthur agreement had given the Army Air Corps exclusive use of long-range land-based bombers to fill their role in coast defense, but with flying boats limited in daylight bombing, the Navy began pressing for the ability to operate multi-engine bombers from land bases. In July 1942 the Sea Service reached an agreement with the Army Air Forces (re-designation of Army Air Corps in 1941) to divert some production B-24 Liberators to the Navy for use as patrol bombers. The first of these airplanes, designated PB4Y-1s, were delivered to the Navy in August, and the following year, with its focus on the strategic bombing campaigns in Europe and the Pacific, the Army Air Forces relinquished its role in antisubmarine warfare. Other aircraft eventually joined the PB4Y-1 in the patrol bombing role in both the European and Pacific theaters, including a modified Liberator designated the PB4Y-2 Privateer, the PBJ (Army Air Forces B-25) Mitchell, and the PV Ventura/Harpoon.[69]

While the Army Air Forces employed their bombers in primarily in horizontal attacks, which were also carried out by Navy and Marine Corps medium bombers, many Navy crews specialized in low-level bombing, oftentimes dropping on enemy shipping at masthead level. A review of 870 PB4Y attacks against shipping revealed that over 40 percent of them resulted in hits. In addition, they were credited with downing over three hundred enemy planes, the PB4Ys being heavily armed with machine guns. Marine PBJs proved the workhorse of land-based patrol bombers, flying more than half of all action sorties flown. All told, patrol bombers, while flying just 6 percent of naval aviation's action sorties, dropped 12 percent of all bomb tonnage delivered on targets during World War II.[70]

A number of other operations involving naval aircraft are worthy of discussion in drawing conclusions about the development of naval aircraft through World War II. Radar-equipped aircraft made tremendous strides in operations after dark during World War II, completing some 5,800 action sorties from carriers and land bases. From a total of only 76 attacks (air-to-ground and air-to-air) against enemy targets in 1942, naval aviation night operations grew to include 2,654 nocturnal attacks in 1944. The PBYs would not have been able to have as much of an offensive impact as they did without their night attack capability.[71] Carrier aircraft, despite fears about tying carriers to beachheads in support of amphibious operations, achieved a great deal of success in providing close air support to assault forces, primarily flying from escort carriers. Naval aircraft, including carrier-based ones, proved that they could neutralize land-based air power, with fighter sweeps focusing on enemy airfields on island chains and the Japanese homeland serving the purpose of striking potential attackers at their source. "Pilots must be impressed with the double profit feature of destruction of enemy aircraft," read a June 1945 memorandum on target selection for Task Force 38 carriers operating off Japan. "Pilots must understand the principles involved in executing a blanket attack. The Blanket Operation is NOT a defensive assignment. It is a strike against air strength."[72] Finally, in the field of weapons development, the advances like electronic countermeasures equipment to thwart enemy radar and the introduction of high-velocity aircraft rockets (HVAR) made carrier aircraft more capable platforms, the latter yielding positive results particularly in close air support against enemy defensive positions.[73]

In a speech delivered during the 1920s, Admiral William S. Sims remarked, "One of the outstanding lessons of the overseas problems played each year is that to advance in a hostile zone, the fleet must carry with it an air force that will assure, beyond a doubt, command of the air. This means not only superiority to enemy fleet aircraft, but also to his fleet and shore-based aircraft combined."[74] This statement reflected the essence of naval air power, and it can be argued that during the interwar years all aspects of aircraft development, from design to tactics, supported the drive of naval aviation advocates toward a fleet that reflected this vision. By 1945, at the end of the greatest war the world has ever known, a triumphant flight of hundreds of carrier planes over the battleship *Missouri* (BB 63) as the instrument of surrender was being signed on her deck was proof that the vision had been realized.

NOTES

1. Lieutenant Austin K. Doyle to Mrs. Jamie R. Doyle, 13 February 1929 (Admiral Austin K. Doyle Papers, Emil Buehler Naval Aviation Library, National Naval Aviation Museum (hereafter cited as Doyle Papers).

2. Doyle graduated from the U.S. Naval Academy in 1919 as a member of the class of 1920, his graduation date moved up because of World War I. He commanded two carriers, *Nassau* (ACV-16) and *Hornet* (CV-12), during World War II.

3. Roy Grossnick, ed., *U.S. Naval Aviation, 1910–1995* (Washington, DC: GPO, 1995), p. 37.

4. Peter M. Bowers, *Curtiss Aircraft, 1907–1947* (Annapolis: Naval Institute Press, 1987), pp. 74–75; Clark G. Reynolds, *Admiral John H. Towers: The Struggle for Naval Air Supremacy* (Annapolis: Naval Institute Press, 1991), pp. 99, 117.

5. Charles M. Melhorn, *Two-Block Fox: The Rise of the Aircraft Carrier, 1911–1929* (Annapolis: Naval Institute Press, 1974), pp. 27–30, 37; Grossnick, *U.S. Naval Aviation,* p. 38.

6. Lieutenant Commander Henry C. Mustin to his wife, 23 January 1914 (Captain Henry C. Mustin Papers, Emil Buehler Naval Aviation Library, National Naval Aviation Museum).

7. Grossnick, *U.S. Naval Aviation,* pp. 505–6.

8. Melhorn, *Two-Block Fox,* pp. 37–38.

9. "Tactics," Thesis submitted by Commander Patrick N. L. Bellinger as a member of the class of 1926 at the U.S. Naval War College (copy in Emil Buehler Naval Aviation Library, National Naval Aviation Museum).

10. *War Instructions, United States Navy, 1934* (copy in Emil Buehler Naval Aviation Library, National Naval Aviation Museum).

11. Norman Friedman, *U.S. Naval Weapons* (Annapolis: Naval Institute Press, 1982), p. 186; Grossnick, *U.S. Naval Aviation,* p. 31.

12. René J. Francillon, *McDonnell Douglas Aircraft since 1920,* vol. 1 (Annapolis: Naval Institute Press, 1988), pp. 46–52.

13. Thomas Wildenberg, *Destined for Glory: Dive Bombing, Midway, and the Evolution of Carrier Airpower* (Annapolis: Naval Institute Press, 1998), pp. 104–7; "Aircraft Tactics—Development of," Aircraft Squadrons, Battle Fleet, 3 February 1927 (copy in Emil Buehler Naval Aviation Library, National Naval Aviation Museum); Friedman, *U.S. Naval Weapons,* p. 116.

14. Wildenberg, *Destined for Glory,* p. 167; Barrett Tillman, "Douglas TBD: The Maligned Warrior," *The Hook* (August 1990), pp. 18–22.

15. Grossnick, *U.S. Naval Aviation,* p. 49; "The Naval Air Service," A lecture delivered at the Army War College by Rear Admiral William A. Moffett, Chief , Bureau of Aeronautics, 10 November 1925 (copy in Emil Buehler Naval Aviation Library, National Naval Aviation Museum).

16. Grossnick, *U.S. Naval Aviation,* pp. 65–66.

17. Friedman, *U.S. Naval Weapons,* p. 190; "Organization of Naval Aviation Battle Fleet, Aircraft Squadrons, Battle Fleet, 1931" (copy in Emil Buehler Naval Aviation Library, National Naval Aviation Museum); Bowers, *Curtiss Aircraft,* pp. 205.

18. *War Instructions, United States Navy, 1934.*

19. Gordon Swanborough and Peter M. Bowers, *United States Navy Aircraft since 1911* (Annapolis: Naval Institute Press, 1990), pp. 443–46; Wildenberg, *Destined for Glory,* pp. 136–37; Bowers, *Curtiss Aircraft,* p. 264; Friedman, *U.S. Naval Weapons,* p. 190.

20. Moffett, "The Naval Air Service."

21. *The Pratt & Whitney Aircraft Story* (Hartford: Pratt & Whitney Aircraft Division of United Aircraft Corporation, 1950), pp. 49–51.

22. Quoted in Wildenberg, *Destined for Glory*, p. 114.

23. Swanborough and Bowers, *United States Navy Aircraft*, pp. 212–13, quoted in *Bureau of Aeronautics Newsletter* (1 March 1933).

24. Commanding Officer, VF-5B, to Chief of the Bureau of Aeronautics, 22 May 1935 (copy in Doyle Papers).

25. Aircraft Tactical Board, Aircraft, Battle Force to Commander, Aircraft Battle Force, 21 January 1936 (Doyle Papers).

26. Swanborough and Bowers, *United States Navy Aircraft*, pp. 217–18; René Francillon, *Japanese Aircraft of the Pacific War* (Annapolis: Naval Institute Press, 1990), p. 377.

27. *New York Times*, 10 February 1929.

28. Grossnick, *U.S. Naval Aviation*, p. 38; Commander Air Detachment to Air Detachment, 28 June 1920 (William W. Townsley Papers, Emil Buehler Naval Aviation Library, National Naval Aviation Museum).

29. Swanborough and Bowers, *United States Navy Aircraft*, pp. 428–48.

30. Grossnick, *U.S. Naval Aviation*, p. 48; Reynolds, *Admiral John H. Towers*, 174–76; Admiral Hugh Rodman to Captain Henry C. Mustin, 9 October 1920 (Correspondence File, 1917–1920, Box 2, Henry C. Mustin Paper, Library of Congress).

31. Rear Admiral A. W. Johnson, *The Naval Patrol Plane: Its Development and Use of the Navy*, 1935 (copy in Kenneth Whiting Papers, Nimitz Library, United States Naval Academy).

32. Ibid.

33. Grossnick, *U.S. Naval Aviation*, p. 86.

34. Edward S. Miller, *War Plan Orange: The U.S. Strategy to Defeat Japan, 1897–1945* (Annapolis: Naval Institute Press, 1991), pp. 175–76.

35. Ibid.

36. Swanborough and Bowers, *United States Navy Aircraft*, pp. 95–96.

37. Rear Admiral Ernest J. King to Rear Admiral Arthur B. Cook, 21 July 1936 (Correspondence File-Arthur B. Cook, Box 5, Ernest J. King Papers, Library of Congress).

38. Commander Aircraft, Base Force to Commander in Chief, U.S. Fleet, 1 June 1937 (Memoranda File, 1936–1937, Box 4, Ernest J. King Papers, Library of Congress).

39. Captain William R. Furlong to Rear Admiral Ernest J. King, 4 September 1937 (Correspondence Files E–F, 1936–1938, Box 5, Ernest J. King Papers, Library of Congress).

40. Miller, *War Plan Orange*, p. 176.

41. Grossnick, *U.S. Naval Aviation*, p. 49. These tests were more famous for the publicity garnered by Army bombers that supported General William Mitchell's efforts to form an independent air service.

42. Bureau of Aeronautics Memorandum, 13 December 1934 (Correspondence H-R, 1933–1936, Box 4, Ernest J. King Papers, Library of Congress).

43. Admiral Joseph M. Reeves to Captain John H. Hoover, 9 April 1935 (Correspondence Files H, 1936–1938, Box 5, Ernest J. King Papers, Library of Congress); and Captain John H. Hoover to Admiral Joseph M. Reeves, 10 January 1935 (Correspondence Files R, 1936–1938, Box 6, Ernest J. King Papers, Library of Congress).

44. Miller, *War Plan Orange*, p. 179.

45. *Annual Report of the Secretary of the Navy for the Fiscal Year 1941* (Washington, DC: GPO, 1941).

46. Ibid.

47. Captain John Hoover to Admiral Joseph M. Reeves, 10 January 1935 (Correspondence Files R, 1936–1938, Box 6, Ernest J. King Papers, Library of Congress).

48. See entries in Swanborough and Bowers, *United States Navy Aircraft*, for respective aircraft; Barrett Tillman, "Cost of Doing Business," *Flight Journal*, Vol. 14, No. 6 (December 2009), p. 31.

49. *Statistical Information on World War II Carrier Experience: Special Study-Aircraft Performance Characteristics* (copy in Emil Buehler Naval Aviation Library, National Naval Aviation Museum).

50. *Naval Aviation Combat Statistics—World War II* (Washington, DC: Air Branch, Officer of Naval Intelligence, Office of the Chief of Naval Operations, 1946), p. 60.

51. Ibid.

52. Ibid., p. 84.

53. Mark R. Peattie, *Sunburst: The Rise of Japanese Naval Air Power, 1909–1941* (Annapolis: Naval Institute Press, 2001), pp. 183, 187; René Francillon, *Japanese Aircraft of the Pacific War* (Annapolis: Naval Institute Press, 1990), pp. 454–61, 320–29; *Statistical Information on World War II Carrier Experience: Special Study-Aircraft Performance Characteristics* (copy in Emil Buehler Naval Aviation Library, National Naval Aviation Museum).

54. Grossnick, *U.S. Naval Aviation*, p. 448.

55. Ibid., pp. 423–31.

56. Commander, Fighting Squadron Ten to Commanding Officer, USS *Enterprise*, Report of Action—10–17 November 1942 (copy in files of Emil Buehler Naval Aviation Library, National Naval Aviation Museum).

57. Clark G. Reynolds, *The Fast Carriers*, 2nd edition (Annapolis: Naval Institute Press, 1992), p. 62; Papers of Thomas Provost (Emil Buehler Naval Aviation Library, National Naval Aviation Museum).

58. John B. Lundstrom, *The First Team: Pacific Naval Air Combat from Pearl Harbor to Midway* (Annapolis: Naval Institute Press, 1984), pp. 458–68.

59. Captain Seldon B. Spangler to Chief, Bureau of Aeronautics, Report on Trip to Pacific Area, 5 May 1945 (Vice Admiral Seldon B. Spangler Papers, Emil Buehler Naval Aviation Library, National Naval Aviation Museum).

60. *Naval Aviation Combat Statistics—World War II*, pp. 112–13.

61. Ibid., p. 109.

62. Reynolds, *The Fast Carriers*, p. 357.

63. *Naval Aviation Combat Statistic—World War II*, p. 102.

64. Ibid.

65. Captain Seldon B. Spangler to Chief, Bureau of Aeronautics, Report on Trip to Pacific Area, 5 May 1945 (Vice Admiral Seldon B. Spangler Papers, Emil Buehler Naval Aviation Library, National Naval Aviation Museum); Commander William N. Leonard to Vice Admiral John S. McCain, circa 1944 (copy in John S. Thach Papers, Emil Buehler Naval Aviation Library, National Naval Aviation Museum).

66. Commander Seldon B. Spangler to Director of Material, Bureau of Aeronautics, Comments on Various Airplanes (Vice Admiral Seldon B. Spangler Papers, Emil Buehler Naval Aviation Library, National Naval Aviation Museum).

67. Michael D. Roberts, *Dictionary of American Naval Aviation Squadrons*, vol. 2 (Washington, DC: Naval Historical Center, 2000), p. 443.

68. See Captain Richard C. Knott, *The American Flying Boat: An Illustrated History* (Annapolis: Naval Institute Press, 1979).

69. Swanborough and Bowers, *United States Navy Aircraft*, p. 103.

70. *Naval Aviation Combat Statistics—World War II*, pp. 15, 124.

71. Ibid., pp. 119–20.

72. Miller, *War Plan Orange*, p. 350; Commander, Task Force 38 to Task Force 38, 26 June 1945, Selection of Japanese Targets for Carrier Based Attack (copy in John S. Thach Papers, Emil Buehler Naval Aviation Library, National Naval Aviation Museum).

73. For HVAR use, see *Naval Aviation Combat Statistics—World War II*, pp. 33–35.

74. In Chronological Section, 1904–1921, Rear Admiral William A. Moffett Papers (Microfilm copy in Nimitz Library, U.S. Naval Academy).

CHAPTER 11

Straight Up:
Vertical Flight in the U.S. Navy

Kevin J. Delamer

THE EARLY DEVELOPMENT OF NAVAL HELICOPTERS:
SOMEONE ELSE'S PROBLEM

The story of naval aviation is the tale of a century spent surpassing artificial boundaries and constraints, often imposed by individuals who were not themselves naval aviators. The history of rotary-wing aviation in the naval Services is a parallel story. The first demonstration of the capability of a helicopter to operate from a ship was sponsored by the Maritime Commission and was conducted by an Army Air Force pilot on 7 May 1943. Colonel R. F. Gregory completed his preflight checks at Stratford, Connecticut, started the aircraft and "pulled pitch"—that is to say, raised the control lever in his left hand, the collective, increasing the pitch on all of the main rotor blades simultaneously. This increased pitch generated increased lift and the XR-4 helicopter rose into the air, stabilized for a moment, and headed for the Long Island Sound, where the SS *Bunker Hill* lay at anchor with U.S. Navy representatives embarked to witness the demonstration. The ship was a tanker modified with a plywood landing platform amidships. The arrangement of the landing platform, athwartships and surrounded by cargo-handling posts and booms, was less then optimal. Like many of the conditions in which naval rotary-wing aviation developed, this arrangement was a precedent that would require time to overcome. Colonel Gregory completed twenty-four[1] flights from the deck of *Bunker Hill* that day, with intervening landings of the pontoon-equipped XR-4 on the water of Long Island Sound.[2] In a sense, naval rotary-wing aviation was born that spring day, with an Army pilot at the controls. But the decisions that gave birth to naval rotary-wing aviation predate this demonstration. They were largely decisions made by officers of the United States Coast Guard.

There were a number of promoters of military helicopters. Colonel Gregory was a supporter, having been involved in efforts to adapt the Sikorsky VS-300 into a militarily useful aircraft. The senior leadership of the U.S. Navy did not include any advocates for this new technology. Far from embracing the helicopter, a series of attempts were made to assign the tasks associated with developing this new technology to someone else—anyone else! Initially, the Office of the Chief of Naval Operations declined to participate in the development of military helicopters, requesting instead that the U.S. Army Air Force proceed with the development and advise the Navy once a suitable model was available.[3] Even after the Army had determined that the VS-300 met the established criteria, the Navy remained skeptical. The Bureau of Aeronautics did issue a planning document in July 1942 calling for the procurement of four helicopters to be used in experiments, but in February 1943, Commander in Chief, U.S. Fleet assigned the task of exploring the use of ship-based helicopters for anti-submarine warfare to the Coast Guard.[4] The U.S. Coast Guard operated as part of the U.S. Navy during time of war, but the assignment of the development task to that Service did not represent a ringing endorsement of the new technology.

The pontoon-equipped XR-4 flights from the USS Bunker Hill *in May 1943 marked the birth of naval rotary-wing aviation.*

The simple fact is that Navy helicopters, now so ubiquitous a part of every naval operation, owe their existence to the U.S. Coast Guard. The development of naval rotary-wing aviation begins before the U.S. Navy expressed any interest. In May 1940, when Igor Sikorsky conducted his first public demonstration, officers of the U.S. Coast Guard were present. Commander Watson Burton, the Commander of Air Station, Floyd Bennett Field, and Commander William Kossler, Chief of the Aviation Engineering Division at Coast Guard Headquarters immediately recognized the capabilities that the new technology represented. Additional demonstrations for the U.S. military followed, witnessed by an expanding circle of Coast Guardsmen including Lieutenant Commander Frank Erickson.

Erickson was destined to have a profound impact on the development of Navy helicopters. An early helicopter enthusiast, having read about Sikorsky's prewar experiments, he "saw great possibilities for an aircraft that could be operated from the deck of a small ship."[5] In June 1942 Erickson had reported to Air Station Floyd Bennett Field in Brooklyn, New York, as the executive officer. Shortly after his arrival, Commander Kossler, who had taught at the Coast Guard Academy when Erickson was a cadet, made a routine visit to Floyd Bennett Field. The substance of their discussions revolved around Sikorsky's helicopters. Before the end of the month Kossler's assistant, Lieutenant Bill Kenly, was sent to an appointment with Igor Sikorsky—by way of Brooklyn. Kenly asked if he could get someone to fly him to Stratford, Connecticut, for his meeting. Erickson later learned that the stop at Brooklyn was a subterfuge aimed at judging the true level of his interest in the project.[6] If Kossler had any doubts, they were alleviated by the enthusiastic response of the executive officer. The date was 26 June and Erickson was en route to becoming Coast Guard Helicopter Pilot Number One.

The fervor demonstrated by these Coast Guard pioneers was arrayed against determined skeptics at the Navy's Bureau of Aeronautics. In November 1941 President Franklin Delano Roosevelt issued an executive order placing the Coast Guard under the operational control of the Navy.[7] This fact constrained the efforts of the Coast Guard to purchase helicopters. By law, Coast Guard aircraft procurement was controlled by the Bureau of Aeronautics (BuAer), an organization hostile to the idea of developing rotary-wing aircraft. In 1942 it was a large bureaucratic organization with a wide scope of responsibility including fleet operations, procurement, research, development of shipboard systems supporting aircraft, and numerous other functions. The divisions, committees, and boards that performed these functions had evolved into a variety of fiefdoms, none of which experimental helicopters fell into comfortably. The attitude of the Navy as perceived by the Coast Guard leadership was simple. The helicopter had originally been proposed as a "flying lifeboat." When Commander Kossler initially discussed the procurement of helicopters with Coast Guard flag officers the response was emphatic: "Hell, Bill, the

Navy is not interested in lifesaving, [sic] they just want to get on with the business of killing the enemy."[8] While the later assignment of submarines and patrol aircraft to the recovery of downed airmen belies this attitude, the realities in early 1942 of an avalanche of immediate, critical tasks assigned to the bureau at the very least drove experimentation on helicopters to a very low priority.

Against this backdrop, Erickson accompanied Kenly to Stratford, Connecticut. After conducting what the official history termed an "inspection,"[9] he spent two nights composing his report.[10] The proposal was also shaped by the state of the war in the Atlantic. May and June 1942 were the months in which the Allies lost the greatest tonnage to date to submarines. Of over 1.2 million tons of merchant shipping lost in two months, over 90 percent was lost on the fringes of North America.[11] Erickson recognized the potential utility of the helicopter for anti-submarine warfare. Initially envisioning these aircraft as scouting platforms that could extend the search horizon of convoy escorts, the proposals redefined the proposed use of rotary-wing aircraft from the Coast Guard–specific task of rescue operations to a task with which the Navy was struggling: anti-submarine warfare. Erickson's concept involved the operation of helicopters from platforms mounted on merchant vessels, providing additional search assets and allowing a smaller number of escorts to protect effectively a larger convoy. Unescorted merchantmen could also be provided with a means of detecting and thus avoiding submarines.[12] Erickson also posited the use of helicopters to deliver depth charges more accurately than did fixed-wing aircraft. He proposed a procedure that would later become helicopter in-flight refueling (HIFR) and suggested that helicopters could rescue the crews of vessels that did fall victim to submarines. These rescue operations, while a core Coast Guard capability, were couched in terms of relieving other ships in convoys of this dangerous task that made them more vulnerable to submarines. While the broad array of potential benefits did convince his immediate superiors within the Coast Guard, the Navy remained skeptical. The Bureau of Aeronautics did issue a planning directive that called for the procurement of four Sikorsky helicopters for further research and development.[13] A planning directive proved to be a far different thing than an aircraft on hand.

Erickson's proposals did receive strong support from his chain of command. The Commanding Officer of Air Station Floyd Bennett Field and the District Commander, Rear Admiral Stanley Parker, who was a qualified aviator himself, both strongly endorsed Erickson's letter.[14] In November 1942, Parker also made the pilgrimage to Stratford to see Sikorsky and his machine. More importantly, Parker wrote a personal letter to Vice Admiral Russell Waesche, Commandant of the Coast Guard, suggesting that the commandant view a demonstration of the Sikorsky helicopter. On the advice of Parker, Coast Guard pilot number seven and the senior aviator in the Coast Guard, Vice Admiral Waesche, did just that on 13 February 1942, witnessing what Erickson called "a very impressive demonstration."[15] So impressed was the commandant that upon his return to Washington he requested a meeting with Admiral Ernest J. King, Chief of Naval Operations (CNO).

Outside the Coast Guard, events were in motion that would further the cause of developing Navy helicopters. Grover Loening, a German immigrant who received the first postgraduate degree in aeronautical engineering granted by Columbia University, was an aviation pioneer. He was also a consultant to the War Production Board, an organization chartered to regulate the production of war material and the allocation of resources. Loening supported development of helicopters for anti-submarine warfare. He also advocated that the project not be carried forward by the Navy Bureau of Aeronautics, but rather that it be assigned to the Maritime Commission, War Shipping Administration, or the Coast Guard. Concurrent with Loening's intercession on behalf of rotary-wing, anti-submarine aircraft, Britain weighed in with an order for two hundred Sikorsky helicopters for anti-submarine work.[16] If the U.S. Navy was not sold on the concept, the Royal Navy certainly was.

All these events converged to provide the background for the meeting between Admirals King and Waesche. King remained under significant pressure to stem the losses among merchant shipping caused by submarines.[17] The British support for helicopters was a double-edged sword, as King and his British counterparts were famously adversarial.[18] In the end, the needs of the Battle of the Atlantic prevailed. Waesche offered another tool with which to combat the German U-boats. Two days after Waesche returned from Connecticut, King, either in his capacity as CNO or as Commander in Chief, U.S. Fleet, began issuing a series of directives. The Coast Guard was given responsibility for developing helicopters to combat the submarine threat. The Bureau of Aeronautics was directed to carry out tests to determine the suitability of the Sikorsky helicopter for ship-based anti-submarine warfare. The Commandant of the Coast Guard, in turn, appointed Kossler to lead the Coast Guard effort, which, in effect, made him responsible for the development of all naval helicopters. Kossler, in turn, arranged for orders for his friend Frank Erickson to report to Stratford, Connecticut, to begin training as a helicopter pilot. His instructors were Igor Sikorsky and C. L. "Les" Morris, Sikorsky's chief test pilot.

In May, a Combined Board for the Evaluation of Ship-Based Helicopter in Antisubmarine Warfare was appointed, with representatives drawn from the staffs of Commander in Chief, U.S. Fleet; the Admiralty (Royal Navy); the British Air Commission; the U.S. Coast Guard; and the Bureau of Aeronautics. Representatives of the Army Air Forces, the War Shipping Board, and the National Advisory Commission on Aeronautics—the predecessor of NASA—later joined the board. This board was, in today's lexicon, an interagency effort. Some question exists whether this helped or hindered the effort.

Colonel Gregory's demonstration on board SS *Bunker Hill* occurred three days after the creation of the board, long before the board would reach any decisions.

The U.S. Maritime Commission did not provide a representative to the Combined Board but did work closely with the War Shipping Administration, which had split off from the commission. The commission did provide the ship for the demonstration. Grover Loening, observing as a consultant to the War Production Board, pronounced the tests successful and described the takeoffs as "remarkable."[19] The Bureau of Aeronautics was less sanguine, citing the calm conditions under which the tests were conducted. The board met ten days after the test and raised a series of additional questions. The most important questions revolved around the manner in which the helicopters would be employed operationally.[20] Specifically, questions of basing the aircraft on merchant vessels versus escorts, the number of aircraft needed for an effective screen, and the number of flight hours between overhauls for the helicopters as compared to the hours required to cover convoys at all points to the acceptance of their value.

The tenor of the board's deliberations demonstrated a shift in the direction the Navy was pursuing. As the board was chartered by Admiral King as Commander in Chief, U.S. Fleet, and included a substantial number of Navy members, the former policy could have been preserved or at least the requirements set forth could have impeded development rather than focus the effort on creating an effective weapons system. While the initial test had been arranged by Igor Sikorsky before the board began functioning, the initial meetings, conducted to consider the implications of the test on *Bunker Hill*, demonstrated the synergistic effects of an interagency team. The obstructionism of the Bureau of Aeronautics was transformed into a more constructive conservatism, grounding the project's sound logistic and operational principles. The enthusiasm of the Coast Guard and the Maritime Commission was tempered, avoiding attempts to overstate the effectiveness of the new technology, an all too common fault of advocates of any new weapon system or doctrine. In the end, the board sought to define the doctrinal parameters within which the helicopters would be utilized and to ensure the decisions were made on the ability to operate effectively over the longer term.

The immediate result of these deliberations was to schedule three additional tests. Modern flight tests are still conducted in a "build up" fashion, beginning with familiarization and relatively simple tasks and expanding the operating envelope by stages. This process minimizes the additional risk incurred with each progressively more difficult phase of testing. The design of this series of tests employed this same philosophy. The first test was to be conducted in calm water, replicating Gregory's success on the *Bunker Hill* and familiarizing the new helicopter pilots with the necessary procedures. These airmen would, in turn, conduct further tests. The second phase was designed to explore the effects of ship motion in a seaway on the operability of helicopters. The third phase, what today would be termed operational test and evaluation, involved conducting operations from a vessel in convoy to and from Europe.[21]

The merchant vessel SS *James Parker*, the former SS *Panama*, was a troop transport. Fitted with a trapezoidal platform on the stern, she foreshadowed the flight deck configuration of most future vessels operating helicopters.[22] On a short run from New York to the Virginia Capes, she was the platform for three days of testing in the Chesapeake Bay. The tests were successful in their stated aim with ninety-eight flights completed by the embarked helicopters, the XR-4 used in the original test on *Bunker Hill* and the improved YR-4A version.

The second phase of the tests was conducted aboard MV *Daghestan*, a bulk freighter acquired by the British under Lend-Lease. The "seaway" in question was the Long Island Sound. While the sound has a fearsome reputation as a dangerous body of water in a storm, the sea was smooth for the majority of the test. A team of twenty-six pilots and observers, led by Coast Guard Lieutenant Commander Frank Erickson, conducted over three hundred launches and recoveries in November 1943. The only deficiency noted was one familiar to a later generation of helicopter pilots—starting and stopping the rotor blades in high winds proved difficult or impossible unless the ship maneuvered to reduce the apparent wind over the deck.[23] The "success" triggered the third and most challenging phase of the test series. The unfortunate choice of the Long Island Sound as the test location would have serious implications for Lieutenant (jg.) Stewart "Stu" Graham, Coast Guard Helicopter Pilot Number Two, who would lead the next effort.

The third phase, an operational test under combat conditions as part of a convoy, followed in January 1944. Stu Graham would embark with the British Helicopter Service Trial Unit and two YR-4B helicopters aboard *Daghestan*. The test proved to be a grueling trial. High sea states, high winds, and convoy doctrine that precluded the *Daghestan* from varying from her assigned course and position in the convoy effectively grounded Graham for all but two days of the voyage. The ship rolled, pitched, and yawed. Her bulk cargo of grain shifted in the hold, giving it a permanent list of 5 degrees. In the end, the helicopters did very little patrolling. The brief windows of opportunity for flying were spent demonstrating that the helicopters could launch and recover under open-sea conditions. The fragile nature of the aircraft and the limited utility due to operational restrictions led the board to recommend that no further ship-based helicopter operations be conducted until a more robust aircraft became available. Admiral Waesche reluctantly agreed, downgrading the R-4, re-designated the HNS-1, to service as a training aircraft. This setback did not dampen Frank Erickson's determination to demonstrate the potential of the helicopter.

Newly promoted and assigned as the Commanding Officer of Air Station Floyd Bennett Field, Commander Frank Erickson continued to apply his drive and imagination to the development of the helicopter. In December, before the *Daghestan* debacle, the Chief of Naval Operations had directed the establishment of a separate helicopter training program, to be established at Floyd Bennett Field. Erickson found himself in charge of establishing a naval helicopter training program. Having trained Graham and others, he had the credentials. His fertile imagination put in place various innovations. A 40-foot by 69-foot movable platform was developed to simulate ship motion ashore. Pilots could experience worst-case conditions in an environment where a stable landing surface was readily available in the event of mechanical problems or student difficulties. The Royal Navy still maintains a similar device today, used primarily for flight test; while mechanically more sophisticated, it is essentially the same device invented by Erickson and his command.

Erickson had been instrumental in equipping the test aircraft with float-type landing gear. He continued to pursue a variety of other innovations. Under Erickson's direction, and frequently with him at the controls, various new devices were introduced. Development of an autopilot for the HNS-1 was begun in 1944. In a parallel effort, the Hayes dunking sonar, originally developed for blimps, was successfully mated to the XHOS-1 helicopter, the newest Sikorsky variant. In March 1945 the tests were reported complete and successful. Unfortunately by the time an effective antisubmarine helicopter had been developed, the submarine threat in the Atlantic had been extinguished, as would be the Nazi regime that spawned that threat. A sling for carrying a stretcher was demonstrated and a hydraulic rescue hoist was also developed, but the Navy was still not interested in the helicopter as a rescue vehicle. Budget cuts, programmatic cuts, and further delays were on the horizon, but the concept had been proven. It would require further crises to spur further development.

EARLY HELICOPTER OPERATIONS: SOMEONE ELSE'S SOLUTION

Erickson's innovations charted the course for Navy helicopters for over half a century. In possession of these fragile, awkward aircraft, the Bureau of Aeronautics included them in a series of postwar tests. In the changing strategic environment, these tests were part of an effort to demonstrate the capability of the carrier to operate in the arctic regions, where potential crises involving the United States and the Soviet Union were expected to play out. The embarked HNS-1 helicopters, wearing Coast Guard colors and flown by Coast Guard pilots, demonstrated an ability to cope with the extreme conditions. The confluence of events again furthered development of Navy helicopters.

Following the conclusion of World War II, the Coast Guard successfully navigated the delicate passage between operational control of the Navy and its administrative home waters within the Department of the Treasury. In doing so, Coast Guard helicopters also departed the Navy inventory. In response, the Navy acknowledged the potential of these assets, establishing Helicopter Development Squadron THREE (VX-3) to "study and evaluate the adaptability of helicopters to naval purposes."[24] The critical fact remained the need to adapt equipment that had not been designed for shipboard operations to that most demanding environment. During the war, the Coast Guard leadership had been skeptical of the Navy's commitment to rescue operations. It proved to be an inaccurate assessment in the long term. Plane guard, providing an airborne alert for conducting the rescue of downed aviators, was the principal mission delegated to the helicopters. "Study" by VX-3 led to evaluation, including assigning a detachment of HOS-3 helicopters to the spring Atlantic Fleet exercise of 1947. During this period, the helicopters conducted twenty-two plane guard missions, leading to six rescues. A contemporaneous article in the *Proceedings* of the Naval Institute extolled the superiority of the helicopter as a rescue platform, as well as its versatility in performing numerous other missions.[25]

The deployment proved a fateful one, leading to the establishment of two helicopter utility squadrons. These squadrons would form the nucleus around which the rotary-wing community would grow over the ensuing seven decades. The Helicopter Utility Squadron TWO (HU-2) would be assigned the responsibility of training future rotary-wing naval aviators, assuming this responsibility from VX-3, which was disestablished at the same time HU-2 began operations. This would raise questions regarding the standardization of helicopter training. Some aviators, like Lieutenant William Knapp, the first Navy helicopter pilot to be so designated, were trained by the Coast Guard. Others obtained their qualifications through VX-3, while still others were designated after receiving training at Helicopter Utility Squadron ONE, or at the Naval Air Technical Center at Patuxent River, Maryland, or from the Sikorsky Aircraft Company directly. Standards for the qualification of aviators as helicopter pilots were issued by the Chief of Naval Operations in June 1948. These standards provided for the recognition of these variously obtained qualifications but placed the responsibility for future qualifications on HU-2.[26] Providing this training while simultaneously supporting detachments for utility and search and rescue missions would prove a daunting task, so daunting, in fact, that it would rapidly become apparent that a dedicated training establishment would be required.

A new command, in a new location, would assume the responsibilities of training Navy helicopter pilots. As Pensacola, Florida, assumed a larger role in the peacetime naval aviation training establishment, it was only logical that dedicated helicopter training would be transferred south as well. In December 1950, Helicopter Training Unit ONE (HTU-1) was established at Ellyson Field. In January of the following year, the training and qualification responsibilities of HU-2 were reassigned to HTU-1.[27] The subsequent evolution of the training mission would see various re-designations of this command, but Helicopter Training Squadron EIGHT

(HT-8) still provides "advanced helicopter flight instruction to all U.S. Navy, U.S. Marine Corps and U.S. Coast Guard helicopter flight students."[28]

Strategic considerations would shape the future development of rotary-wing aviation. In 1946, Deputy Chief of Naval Operations Vice Admiral Forrest Sherman focused on a new maritime strategy. Forward, offensive operations dominated the new strategy and anti-submarine warfare was central to the operational concept. The introduction of the German Type XXI submarines at the end of World War II had sparked a revolution in submarine warfare.[29] The acquisition of numerous Type XXI boats by the Soviet Union at the end of the war, combined with tensions between the emerging superpowers, would have a dramatic impact. Sherman focused on offensive operations against the bases for hostile submarines, but the lessons of the recently concluded conflict were not lost. The difficulty inherent in degrading the submarine threat at the source was recognized, but so too was the reduced effectiveness of aircraft as ASW assets as a result of the Type XXI–induced revolution. During the war, the mere presence of an aircraft was enough to disrupt submarine attacks. The new generation of submarine was far less vulnerable.[30] New technologies would be required to augment the defensive measures that would facilitate Sherman's offensive posture. Frank Erickson's foresight in mating the dunking sonar to the helicopter would provide part of the answer.

The Hayes dunking sonar used in World War II experiments would evolve, as would the underpowered helicopters. In the immediate postwar years, twin rotor–configured aircraft like the McDonnell XHJD-1 and the Piasecki H-21 would garner increasing attention. Sikorsky Aircraft would develop a competing model based on the earlier successful configuration of a single main rotor. Originally developed to compete for the Air Force rescue helicopter contract, the S-55 was adapted for a Navy operational investigation of helicopter ASW using dipping sonar. Designated the HO4S-series in naval service, it was underpowered and could carry either the dipping sonar or antisubmarine torpedoes, but not both simultaneously. Naval rotary-wing aviation continued to be an exercise in adapting equipment originally intended for other purposes. In spite of this handicap, the project would succeed and would set the stage for the next generation of ASW helicopters.

Concurrent with the demonstration of the ASW capabilities of the Sikorsky variant, Piasecki would also enter the competition with a tandem-rotor variant, the HUP series aircraft. When Helicopter Antisubmarine Squadron ONE (HS-1), the first squadron of its type, was established in October 1951, it was equipped with HUP-1/2 aircraft. As with the rapid development that occurred in all naval aviation communities during the decade following the end of World War II, the early HS squadrons would experience a rapid transition through a series of airframes including the HUP and the Sikorsky HRS, HO4S, and HSS-1 helicopters. This rapid evolution would slow with the introduction of this last model beginning in 1955.[31]

Representing the highest evolution of the piston-engine helicopter, the night-capable HSS-1N Sea Bat (Sikorsky S-58) would remain the standard antisubmarine helicopter until the advent of the turbine-engine helicopters in the following decade. Following the transition to turbines, the Sea Bat, by then re-designated the H-34-series, would continue to serve as a search and rescue platform as well as in the Marine Corps. Various foreign navies would continue to fly it for decades.

Wartime has historically spurred innovation. One enduring concern in conducting combat flight operations is the retrieval of downed aircrewmen in hostile territory. During the conflict in Korea, the logical evolution from utilizing helicopters for rescue operations at sea to recovery of pilots ashore came to fruition. Primarily relying on the older HO3S helicopters, rescue units were staged forward in order to speed these recoveries. Even after the Chinese offensive had pushed United Nations forces well south of Wonsan, the waters of the harbor served as a haven for naval operations. Yo Do, an island in the harbor, remained under the control of U.S. forces and was the site of an emergency landing strip. In early 1951 LST-799 was modified to include a mid-ship flight deck for the launch and recovery of helicopters and was assigned to the Wonsan Harbor Control System.[32] From this location, it and other modified LSTs provided a secure base from which rescue operations could be mounted swiftly. A new, dramatic, and dangerous chapter in the employment of Navy helicopters had opened.

Between the establishment of the force at Wonsan and the end of active hostilities, twenty-two successful helicopter rescues were conducted. Such high-risk missions were not, however, without a cost. In July 1951, Lieutenant (jg) John Koelsch and his observer, Aviation Radioman George Neal, launched in an effort to recover a Marine aviator down near Wonsan. Successfully locating Captain James Wilkins, their helicopter was hit by ground fire and crashed while attempting to hoist him aboard. Successfully evading the enemy for nine days, Neal and Koelsch carried the injured Marine to the coast before being captured. Koelsch did not survive captivity, but in 1955 was posthumously awarded the Medal of Honor, becoming the first helicopter pilot so honored.[33] He would not be the last. CPO Duane Thorin, the model for the helicopter pilot in James Michener's novel *The Bridges at Toko-ri*, Lieutenant (jg) John Thornton, Lieutenant Edward Moore, and their crews all faced capture or death rescuing fellow aviators during the conflict.[34] The tales of heroism by helicopter crews would fill an entire volume.

DESIGN WITH A PURPOSE

The year 1960 saw the transformation of rotary-wing aviation. The Sikorsky S-58 had been designed to meet U.S. Navy requirements, but with an eye toward meeting the requirements of other Services and commercial markets. In 1957 Sikorsky

SH-3A (HSS-2) flown publicly for first time, 24 March 1959.

Aircraft began design efforts to meet a U.S. Navy circular of requirements for the next generation anti-submarine helicopter. The resulting aircraft, tested and accepted by the Navy in 1959, would become the H-3 series helicopters. The Sea King would remain the backbone of aircraft carrier–based, rotary-wing aviation for over thirty years. In a search and rescue capacity, they would serve into the twenty-first century and in Marine colors as of 2010 they still fly the president of the United States. While Sikorsky developed this large, turbine-engine helicopter, Vertol and Kaman married the increased power of the "jet" engines to design concepts for other Navy requirements. The engine in question, powering all three designs, would be the General Electric T-58. The H-2 Sea Sprite and the H-46 Sea Knight, in conjunction with the Sea King, would lay the foundation for successful naval operations into the next century. They were also the first helicopters point-designed to meet the Navy's requirements. It is not surprising that these platforms proved so enduring.

The turbine era would see the rise of a submarine-centric Soviet navy, war in Southeast Asia, and support to a range of humanitarian, scientific, and space missions. These three models would bear the brunt of these efforts.

Countering the expanding Soviet submarine threat proved to be the principal challenge. The development of nuclear-powered submarines added complexity to an already difficult problem. The need to track these adversaries using passive acoustics, prosecute them with active sonar, and, if necessary, attack them with rapidity would dictate the need for larger, more capable helicopters. The Sea King was the first to meet the requirement. Operationally capable of carrying two torpedoes, a dozen expendable sonobuoys, and equipped with a dipping sonar, this was the platform of choice for holding contact with the submarines deployed by an adversary.

The small number of sonobuoys carried rendered it less effective as an open-ocean search platform, but once integrated into an anti-submarine team, the precision with which the sonar could locate a submarine and rapid rate at which that sensor could be repositioned made it difficult for a submarine to break contact.[35]

Another approach to improving this capability resulted in a program that was innovative, if perhaps ahead of its time. There were persistent efforts, culminating in 1960, to develop an unmanned platform for weapons delivery combined with improved, longer-range ship-mounted sonars. The Drone Antisubmarine Helicopter (DASH) program continued throughout the decade with mixed results. Simulated attacks using exercise torpedoes were demonstrated over 19,000 yards from the controlling ship, but anti-submarine rocket (ASROC) launchers could obtain greater ranges; the greatest difficulty continued to be the initial acquisition of contact and the difficulty of recovery aboard a DD. The requirement for a sensor deployment platform would be met with a rotary-wing aircraft, one that was originally designed as a utility aircraft.[36]

The Kaman H-2 Sea Sprite was not built as an ASW platform. As requirements evolved, so did the weapon system. The initial configuration involved a single engine, but by 1970 virtually all models had been converted to a twin-engine configuration. Many of these aircraft were also converted to the interim Light Airborne Multi-Purpose System (LAMPS) configuration. These SH-2D aircraft were the forerunner of the SH-2F, a fully integrated anti-submarine warfare platform. The problem of initial submarine detection would be answered by delivering sensors across a broader area and linking them back to the ship. The Sea Sprite would also possess some capability to monitor these sensors internally and was equipped with a magnetic anomaly detector (MAD). By 1973 most H-2 Sea Sprites had been converted to the LAMPS configuration.[37] A small number of utility versions were retained for specialized missions. Sea Sprite detachments supported oceanographic research vessels and some search and rescue missions, but the end of the Vietnam War had relieved them of the missions that perhaps garnered the most fame. H-2 and H-3 aircraft had figured prominently in the air war over Vietnam; these would be the recovery vehicles for combat search and rescue, retrieving downed aviators under fire.

As with the air war in Korea, some consideration had been given before the war to the use of helicopters for the recovery of downed airmen. In the Navy, this consideration stopped well short of an integrated concept of operations. Upon the commencement of punitive strikes after the Tonkin Gulf incident, utility helicopters already on station on the aircraft carriers were pressed into service. In addition, the helicopter anti-submarine squadrons also answered the call. Three squadrons were pressed into service in succession: HS-2, HS-6, and HS-4. During 1966, the Black Knights of HS-4 would establish a record that still stands. The squadron would conduct twenty-four combat rescues, earning special recognition. The color guard of

HS-4 is attired in black berets in recognition of this remarkable deployment.[38] The other squadrons that participated in this rotation also conducted dramatic rescues under duress, but this was not without a heavy cost. The toll taken would lead the Navy to re-evaluate procedures for combat rescues and would give birth to a new squadron and new procedures to increase the survivability of the rescuers going in harm's way.

Author James Michener, serving as a war correspondent on board an aircraft carrier in Korea, was a second-hand witness to several dramatic rescue attempts. On one occasion the price of a failed attempt to rescue one pilot included the loss of five additional escort airplanes and the loss of the rescue helicopter and crew. Operations in Vietnam would lead to similar heroics and to similar losses. Serious efforts were made to learn lessons from both the successes and from the failures. New syllabi were developed to give pilots bound for duty in the combat zone the skills necessary for survival. This effort was strengthened by the establishment of a new squadron to conduct search and rescue efforts in the Vietnam Theater.

In 1965, HU-1 was re-designated Helicopter Combat Support Squadron ONE (HC-1). With detachments supporting aircraft carriers and logistic support ships, conducting combat search and rescue, minesweeping, and helicopter gunship operations, it rapidly became obvious that the diverse platforms and missions could best be served by splitting off unique missions as separate squadrons. The parent squadron retained the search and rescue detachments on board the aircraft carriers, but the specialized detachments supporting overland search and rescue and mine-sweeping elements that were stationed at Cubi Point in the Philippines and Atsugi, Japan, became Helicopter Combat Support Squadron SEVEN (HC-7), a unit that would be awarded medals for valor out of proportion to its size and brief history. In an article in the aviation journal *Foundation*, former HC-7 detachment Officer in Charge Robert Jones made a persuasive argument that it was the most decorated Navy squadron in the Vietnam War.[39]

The detachments that consolidated to form HC-7 drew on the experiences of the anti-submarine squadrons and HC-1 detachments that had been pressed into service earlier. Between the establishment of the squadron in September 1967 and its final mission in 1975, 156 individuals were rescued. These missions included routine missions and medical evacuations, but at least 58 of those rescued were recovered during combat missions.[40] During the war, the squadron transitioned from single-engine UH-2A helicopters to a mix of HH-2C and HH-3A aircraft, the latter two better armed and armored to withstand the rigors of the combat mission. The combination of more capable aircraft, dedicated crews, and an inherently heroic mission produced a Medal of Honor and four Navy Crosses as well as a host of other awards for valor.

Lieutenant (jg) Clyde Lassen became the second Navy helicopter pilot to be awarded the nation's highest medal following a pre-dawn mission to recover the crew of an F-4 Phantom, making multiple approaches under fire in the UH-2A.[41] The level of bravery would not slacken, even in the face of more determined opposition as the war progressed. During the bombing halt ordered by President Lyndon Johnson, the squadron's exploits were limited to "routine" rescues, but following the resumption of strikes against North Vietnam combat rescues also resumed. In the squadron's brief history, 1972 would prove the busiest year, with fifty-nine personnel rescued. Perhaps the most dramatic recovery belonged to Lieutenant Harry Zinser's crew, with both pilots awarded the Navy Cross after a harrowing series of flights during which they plucked a downed pilot from under the field of fire of a 37-mm anti-aircraft gun.[42] All this came from a squadron once described as the "Orphans of the 7th Fleet."[43] The search and rescue detachments would be deployed on over 2,100 consecutive days in support of combat operations in Southeast Asia.

Four other detachments from HC-1 formed yet another squadron that engaged in dramatic operations in Vietnam. These units were re-designated as Helicopter Attack (Light) Squadron THREE (HAL-3). Equipped with former Army UH-1B gunships, these crews performed critical missions in support of the riverine patrols of Operation Game Warden, the interdiction of Viet Cong supplies along Vietnam's inland waterways. This mission was essential to pacification efforts in the Mekong Delta and in attempts to preserve the Saigon government. Armed with pilot-operated mini-guns, rockets, and crew-served .50-caliber machine guns, these were formidable weapons against enemy concentrations that sought to interfere with the operations of the patrol boats of the "brown water navy" that they supported.

At the same time that HC-7 was engaged in dramatic, high-risk missions, the squadron also participated in groundbreaking work in other mission areas. These tasks, while more mundane, are perhaps even more critical to the success of naval operations. Specially modified H-3 Sea Kings would be configured for airborne minesweeping and would see service off the Vietnamese coast. The squadron would also begin experiments with the UH-46A Sea Knights originally inherited from HC-1. Similar experiments were conducted in the Atlantic by Helicopter Combat Support Squadron FOUR (HC-4), and eventually the Pacific Fleet mission would be transferred to Helicopter Combat Support Squadron THREE (HC-3) in San Diego. The speed and efficiency with which pairs of "phrogs" (as the H-46 was nicknamed due to resemblance to a frog when viewed from the front) could transfer cargo between ships was truly remarkable. Over time this vertical replenishment mission would become so critical to Battle Group operations that five squadrons would eventually be established supporting this mission. The ubiquitous "phrog" would symbolize the Navy's ability to sustain extended operations at sea, yielding only when these aging aircraft gave way to a successor after over a quarter of a century.

BACK TO THE FUTURE?

The decade following the end of the conflict in Vietnam would see a continued high operational tempo for the Navy. This tempo was necessary to meet an increasingly aggressive Soviet presence throughout the world. A significant element of this threat was composed of an ever-quieter, ever-more sophisticated submarine force. Among the weapons employed by these vessels, mines proved particularly problematic. An integrated approach was required to counter the many capabilities of this potentially hostile force.

First and foremost, individual ships and Battle Groups would be required to spend longer periods at sea. To maintain the level of operations necessary to monitor Soviet activity, rapid re-supply of ships at sea was essential. Vertical replenishment was the only effective answer.

Beyond critical logistic support, better detection and tracking of submarines was required. The original helicopter-based solution to this problem, DASH, had proved unsatisfactory due to the inability to deploy sensors, among other technical problems. The first solution was the LAMPS-configured SH-2D aircraft. While providing a dramatic improvement over ship-based sensors, this aircraft and the successor SH-2F proved to have limitations. All acoustic data were data-linked back to the ship and evaluated there with an inherent time delay in transmitting critical tactical data to the helicopter crew. On board the helicopter, the aircrew could listen to the sonar signals aurally and had real-time data from the MAD and radar, but relied heavily on communications with the destroyer or cruiser on which they were embarked. In addition to the time lag, the communications between the ship and the helicopter also served to make the ship more vulnerable by pinpointing its location.

The foundations of the Navy helicopter community rest on adaptation of aircraft developed for other purposes and other Services. The Navy would seem to have returned to this method in developing the next generation of shipboard helicopter. When the decision was made to replace the H-2 with a larger airframe, capable of supporting on-board acoustic processing, it did not simply adapt the Army UH-60 Blackhawk to Navy purposes. The entire airframe was completely redesigned, shifting the main structural supports to accommodate the stresses of shipboard landings and the low-mounted hard points necessary for torpedoes and external fuel tanks. The SH-60B Seahawk, also called LAMPS-III, proved a remarkably reliable and robust platform. More than an airborne adjunct to the ship, the Seahawk was capable of independent prosecution of submarines while maintaining contact with the ship through a discreet, directional data link that did not give away the ship's position. It proved so reliable that when the time came for a replacement for the venerable H-3 on the carriers, another version of the H-60 would be chosen.

Following the end of the Vietnam War, Navy helicopters returned to their traditional missions. Frank Erickson had proposed, and Commander Malcolm Cagle had extolled, the value of helicopters for ASW, logistics, and search and rescue. The valuable contributions of helicopters in other mission areas were willfully ignored. The Vietnam missions—gunship and combat search and rescue—were delegated to the reserves. The future would require a re-examination. Operations in Grenada would develop too quickly to admit the mobilization of the reserve CSAR squadron. The HS community would once again be pressed into service. The gunship squadrons, one on each coast, would transform into special operations support squadrons with CSAR as a secondary mission, equipped with yet another variant of the H-60. These squadrons would also experience obstacles in deploying for Operation Desert Storm. While they would be sent to the desert, their assignment to the Special Operations organization would preclude taking part in the Navy CSAR Task Force that operated in the Arabian Gulf. Instead, the HS squadrons, flying SH-3H airframes, armed with only M-60 machine guns and without self-sealing fuel tanks, would again be called on. Ironically, it was not the HS-12 Wyverns who established the CSAR helicopter detachment in the northern gulf, nor the other HS squadrons with whom they shared that duty, but a LAMPS detachment that would record the only opposed Navy rescue of Desert Storm.

Most of the drama for Navy helicopters in Desert Storm proved to be reserved for the LAMPS detachments. While the destroyer on which the CSAR helicopters were based was repositioned southward for replenishment, Lieutenant Kenneth Szmed and his crew were called on to rescue an Air Force pilot down in the water off Kuwait City. LAMPS crews also provided radar guidance to British Lynx helicopters, enabling them to approach enemy patrol boats at wave-top heights to avoid detection before firing their ship-killing missiles. The CSAR detachments did participate in the liberation of the first Kuwaiti territory set free, Qaruh Island, which was liberated by embarked SEALs, transported in Wyvern H-3s, covered by Army OH-58 helicopters.[44]

The successors to the RH-3 minesweepers of Vietnam were also busy. In the intervening years, a new helicopter community was born. The increasing sophistication of Soviet mines required larger and more sophisticated detection and sweeping gear. To handle these larger payloads, the massive H-53 heavy-lift helicopters were adapted to the mine countermeasure mission. These MH-53E aircraft swept channels to allow ships to approach the Kuwait coast, a key enabler for devastating naval gunfire support missions.

The collapse of the Soviet threat, combined with the lessons of Desert Storm, demonstrated a need for a re-evaluation of the structure, missions, and equipment of Navy helicopters. New missions, or rather old ones re-acknowledged, have come to dominate training and planning. Combat search and rescue, support to naval

Special Warfare, armed helicopters for striking small craft, surveillance using infrared sensors—all these missions reflect the legacy of Vietnam. They also represent necessary changes as other platforms have left the naval inventory. With the departure of the S-3 Viking from the scene, a new set of missions falls to Navy helicopters.

As naval aviation shapes a course for the future, rotary-wing aviation continues to play in increasingly important role. Ironically, as Navy helicopters assume more roles and a larger place in plans, fewer models will be available. In the end, after fifty years, only three H-3s remained in Navy service, performing SAR duty at NAS Patuxent River. These too were retired in 2009. Both the H-2 and H-46 airframes have been retired. The Navy is moving toward two H-60 models for all missions— the MH-60R and MH-60S. However, in recognition of the growing requirement for more helicopters and more pilots to fly them, a third helicopter training squadron was established at Naval Air Station Whiting Field on 25 May 2007. The Helicopter Training Squadron TWENTY-EIGHT Hellions will help train the increasing percentage of naval aviators who fly these rotary-wing aircraft. "The helicopter community remains at the core of Naval Aviation, and a robust and highly capable helicopter fighting force is a fundamental requirement for any Navy operation,"[45] so opined the Navy's director, Air Warfare, in a 2004 article in *The Hook, the Journal of Carrier Aviation*. These sentiments, by a career fixed-wing pilot, represent a sea change. Naval helicopters have come of age.

NOTES

1. Sikorsky Aircraft, press release, n.d., "High Lights in the Development of the Sikorsky Helicopter," Igor I. Sikorsky Historical Archives. While some sources indicate that fewer flights were completed, twenty-four is a consensus number and is supported by this and other documentation from the Sikorsky Archives.

2. U.S. Navy, Chief of Naval Operations, *United States Naval Aviation, 1910–1970*, NAVAIR 00-80-P-1 (Washington, DC: GPO, 1970), p. 120.

3. Robert M. Browning Jr., *The Eyes and Ears of the Convoy: Development of the Helicopter as an Anti-submarine Weapon* (Washington, DC: United States Coast Guard Historian's Office, 1993), p. 9.

4. U.S. Navy, *United States Naval Aviation*, p. 119; Browning, *The Eyes and Ears of the Convoy*, pp. 5–6.

5. Frank Erickson, "A Brief History of Coast Guard Aviation," *The Bulletin*, (November–December 1966), p. 422.

6. Ibid.

7. Franklin Delano Roosevelt, Executive Order 8929, 6 FR 5581, 1941 WL 4041, http://www.presidency.ucsb.edu/ws/index.php?pid=60917 (accessed 19 August 2009).

8. Browning, *The Eyes and Ears of the Convoy*, p. 4.

9. U.S. Navy, *United States Naval Aviation*, p. 114.

10. Erickson, "A Brief History," p. 423.

11. Samuel Eliot Morison, *History of United States Naval Operations in World War II,* vol. 1, *The Battle of the Atlantic, 1939–1943* (Boston: Little, Brown, 1947; Edison, NJ: Castle Books, 2001), pp. 412–13.

12. Frank Erickson, letter to Headquarters, U.S. Coast Guard of 29 June 1942; cited in Robert M. Browning, "The Development of the Helicopter," Igor I. Sikorsky Archives, http://www.sikorskyarchives.com/tdoth.html (accessed 10 July 2009).

13. U.S. Navy, *United States Naval Aviation,* p. 115.

14. Erickson, "A Brief History," p. 423.

15. Ibid.

16. Browning, *The Eyes and Ears of the Convoy.*

17. Papers of Ernest J. King, Operational Archives Branch, Naval Historical Center, Washington, DC.

18. Thomas B. Buell, *Master of Sea Power: A Biography of Fleet Admiral Ernest J. King* (Boston: Little, Brown, 1980), p. ix; Williamson Murray and Allan Millett, *A War to Be Won: Fighting the Second World War* (Cambridge, MA, and London, England: The Belknap Press of Harvard University Press, 2000), p. 189.

19. Grover Loening, memorandum to War Production Board, dated 14 May 1943, cited in Browning, *The Eyes and Ears of the Convoy.*

20. Browning, *The Eyes and Ears of the Convoy,* pp. 9–10.

21. Discussion of the similarity of the design of these tests and modern flight test procedures is based on the author's experience as a rotary-wing test pilot, including participation in seven dynamic interface tests conducted to determine the compatibility of the H-60 and H-3 series aircraft with a variety of naval and naval service vessels.

22. Most ships that routinely operate helicopters have a flight deck located at the stern or have no superstructure aft of and above the flight deck. The few exceptions tend to be vessels like the hospital ships USNS *Mercy* and USNS *Comfort,* which were not originally designed to operate helicopters.

23. Arthur Pearcy, *A History of U.S. Coast Guard Aviation* (Annapolis: Naval Institute Press, 1989), p. 59. All naval helicopters experience these problems to some degree, with the extreme case being the H-46 series. The problems of "tunnel strikes" while starting and stopping the rotors led to an extensive flight test program in the mid-1990s, in which the author was involved, to determine the cause and remediation.

24. U.S. Navy, *United States Naval Aviation,* p. 163.

25. Malcolm W. Cagle, "The Versatile Windmills," *United States Naval Institute Proceedings* (July 1948): 833–35.

26. Roy A. Grossnick, *United States Naval Aviation, 1910–1995* (Washington, DC: GPO, 1997), p. 171.

27. Ibid., p. 756.

28. U.S. Navy, "HT-8 Eight Ballers: Squadron History," https://www.cnatra.navy.mil/tw5/ht8/history.asp (accessed 15 December 2009).

29. Marcus O. Jones, "The Type XXI and Innovation in the German Navy during the Second World War," paper presented at the Naval History Symposium, U.S. Naval Academy, Annapolis, 10–11 September 2009.

30. Michael A. Palmer, *Origins of the Maritime Strategy: The Development of American Naval Strategy, 1945–1955* (Annapolis: Naval Institute Press, 1990), pp. 32–34.

31. Rick Burgess, "HS-1 Seahorses," *Naval Aviation News* 81, no. 1 (November/December 1998), p. 12.

32. U.S. Navy, *Dictionary of American Naval Fighting Ships,* vol. 3 (Washington, DC: GPO, 1977), pp. 153–54.

33. Malcolm W. Cagle and Frank A. Manson, *The Sea War in Korea* (Annapolis: Naval Institute Press, 1957), p. 416; Hill Goodspeed, "Whirlybirds over Korea," *Naval Aviation News* 85, no. 1 (November/December 2002), p. 33.

34. Richard F. Kaufman, "Behind the Bridges at Toko-ri," *Naval Aviation News* 84, no. 3 (March/April 2002), pp. 18–23; Goodspeed, "Whirlybirds over Korea," p. 33.

35. Personal experience of author over eleven years in HS squadrons and in flight test; also author conversations with Lieutenant Commander David Moran, USN; Captain Douglas Roulstone, USN; and Captain Paul A. "Tony" Laird, USN, during the course of these tours.

36. Andreas Parsch, *Directory of U.S. Military Rockets and Missiles,* Appendix 4, QH-50 DASH (28 April 2004), http://www.designation-systems.net/dusrm/app4/qh-50.html (accessed 25 November 2009); "DASH History," http://www.gyrodynehelicopters.com/ dash_weapon_system.htm (accessed 5 December 2009).

37. Bill Gunston, *An Illustrated Guide to Military Helicopters* (Upper Saddle River, NJ: Prentice Hall, 1986).

38. The black berets and the reading of the CNO order authorizing their wear was an integral part of the HS-4 change of command ceremonies during the period the author served on the CVW-14 staff and as a department head in the squadron.

39. Robert E. Jones, "The Most Highly Decorated Navy Squadron in Vietnam?" *Foundation* 2, no. 1 (1981), pp. 91–97.

40. HC-7 Rescue Log, 3 October 1967 to 8 April 1975, unofficial document, http://www .hc7seadevils.org/draftrescuelog.pdf (accessed 10 December 2009).

41. Hill Goodspeed, "Into the Night," *Naval Aviation News* 84, no. 6 (September/October 1998), pp. 27–29.

42. James R. Lloyd, "To Those Who Returned for Me," *The Hook* 25, no. 4 (Winter 1997), pp. 33–36.

43. Mark Morgan, "Orphans of 7th Fleet," *The Hook* 26, no. 2 (Summer 1998), pp. 26–37.

44. Edward J. Marolda and Robert J. Schneller Jr., *Shield and Sword: The United States Navy and the Persian Gulf War* (Washington, DC: Naval Historical Center, 1998; Annapolis: Naval Institute Press, 2001), pp. 221–25.

45. Rear Admiral Thomas J. Kilcline, "Navy Helicopters at the Core of Strike Group Capability," *The Hook* 32, no. 4 (Winter 2004), pp. 8–10.

CHAPTER 12

The Transition to Swept-Wing Jets

Robert C. Rubel

Definition of an optimist: a naval aviator with a savings account.

—Naval aviation quip

In this centennial year of naval aviation's history, the jet engine and jet-powered aircraft are ubiquitous. Millions travel safely in jet airliners, and the military jet fighter is almost a cultural icon. However in the late 1930s the prospect for powering aircraft with anything but piston engines seemed remote to all except for a few visionary engineers in Great Britain and Germany. Their work resulted in the first flights of jet-powered aircraft in the early 1940s, but due to the low thrust of their engines these aircraft were outclassed by existing piston-engine fighters. Additional advances in engine design in Germany resulted in the fielding of the ME-262 "Swallow" fighter, which, although not as maneuverable as the American P-51 Mustang and other Allied fighters, had a top speed 100 mph greater due to its jet engines and swept wings, giving it significant operational advantages. After the war, aeronautical engineers from all the Allies studied German technical advances and strove to incorporate them into their new generation of fighters.

The U.S. Navy, accustomed to working with Westinghouse on turbochargers for its piston-engine fighters, let a contract with them during World War II to develop a jet engine, and most of the early Navy jets were powered by Westinghouse engines. Westinghouse experienced significant difficulties in producing jet engines, which proved to be a serious impediment to the success of Navy jet designs in the late 1940s and early 1950s. Whether developed by Westinghouse, General Electric, or other manufacturers in the United States and elsewhere, all early jet engines suffered from low thrust and high fuel consumption and were slow to power up and power down, as well as having poor reliability. Thus the first generation of jet fighters such as the Air Force's P-80 Shooting Star and the Navy's FH-1 Phantom were of limited operational utility despite having the high-speed and high-altitude capabilities characteristic of jet-powered planes. It was not until the second generation of jet engines was produced that viable operational jets could be fielded.

When the Navy introduced its first operational jet, the McDonnell FH-1 Phantom, in 1947, it began a transition phase that turned out to be extended and very costly in terms of aircrew lives and airplanes lost. The higher speeds and altitudes of jets presented a new set of problems to the aircraft designers and manufacturers as well as to the Navy squadrons that operated them. In 1946 nobody knew that a high-performance jet fighter needed such appurtenances as a stabilator (instead of an elevator); irreversible, hydraulic flight controls with artificial feel; redundant hydraulic systems; pitch and yaw stability augmentation; ejection seats; air conditioning; and others.[1] Learning these lessons required a trial-and-error process that resulted in the fielding and rapid obsolescence of a series of different jets, each reflecting solutions to the defects discovered in earlier models.

It is central to the story presented in this chapter to consider how long the "transition" to jets lasted. Some histories of naval aviation regard the transition to jets to be substantially complete with the phaseout of the last propeller-driven fighters, while others maintain that the transition lasted until the introduction of the F-8 Crusader and F-4 Phantom II—the first Navy carrier-based fighters that were the equals in performance of their land-based counterparts. Yet another way of looking at it is via the lens of safety; one might declare the transition to have been complete when the Navy aviation accident rate became comparable to that of the U.S. Air Force. The logic behind this reasoning is that there are a multitude of factors—technical, organizational, and cultural—that constitute the capability to operate swept-wing jets, and mishap rate is an indicator of how successful overall an organization is in adopting a new technology. Using this criterion, the Navy's transition process lasted until the late 1980s, which is not coincidentally the era in which the F/A-18 was arriving in the fleet in numbers. The basis for this argument is that tactical jet aircraft design and technology presented Navy aircrews, maintenance personnel, and leadership with several major challenges that were not substantially overcome until the introduction of the F/A-18 Hornet in 1983. These challenges included technical problems such as engine reliability and response times, swept-wing flight characteristics, and man-machine interface problems. The Air Force also encountered these challenges, but the Navy's operating environment and indeed its organizational culture presented significant impediments to achieving a fully successful transition until well after the Air Force had.

Between 1949, the year jets started showing up in the fleet in numbers, and 1988, the year the Navy/Marine mishap rate finally got down to Air Force levels, the Navy and Marine Corps lost almost 12,000 airplanes and over 8,500 aircrew of all types (helos, trainers, and patrol planes in addition to jets), in no small part as a result of these issues. Perhaps the statistics about the F-8 Crusader, a supersonic fighter designed by Vought in the late 1950s, provide a good illustration of the problem. Always known as a difficult airplane to master, 1,261 Crusaders were built. By the time it was withdrawn from the fleet, 1,106 had been lost to mishaps. Only a handful of them were lost to enemy fire in Vietnam.[2] While the F-8 statistics might be worse than most models, the magnitude of the problem is clear. Whether from engine failure, pilot error, weather, or bad luck, the vast majority (88 percent!) of Crusaders ever built ended up as smoking holes in the ground, splashes in the water, or fireballs hurtling across the flight deck. This was naval aviation from the start of the jet era through about 1988. Today the accident rate is normally one or fewer per 100,000 hours of flight time, making a mishap an unusual occurrence. This is in stark contrast to the landmark year of 1954, when naval aviation (USN and USMC) lost 776 aircraft and 535 aircrew, for an accident rate well above 50 per 100,000 flight hours—and the rate for carrier-based tactical aviation was much higher than that.

During this extended transition period naval aviation participated in three major wars and numerous crises, and of course many planes and crews were lost to enemy fire. However, the vast majority of aircraft losses over this period were due to mishaps, many of which were associated with the technical and organizational problems just discussed. In other words, the airplanes that populated the flight decks of aircraft carriers from the introduction of the FH-1 Phantom through the retirement of the F-14 Tomcat were, with several exceptions, hard to fly and maintain, and would kill the unwary crew. Many men and a few women gave their lives trying to operate these machines in the challenging environment of the sea. This chapter is meant to recognize their sacrifice and honor their service.

THE OPERATIONAL IMPERATIVE

U.S. naval aviation ended World War II at the top of its game; its collection of aircraft was the best in the world and the requirements of carrier suitability did not compromise their performance versus land-based fighters. By the early 1940s the Navy's Bureau of Aeronautics had received word of jet engine developments in Germany and Great Britain, and had commissioned Westinghouse and Allis Chalmers to build American versions. However, high fuel consumption, low power at takeoff, and poor reliability of early engines did not make the engines attractive for use in carrier-based planes. Moreover, when details of German aerodynamic advances, specifically the swept wing, became known, Navy planners felt that their high landing speeds and adverse handling characteristics would make aircraft equipped with them unsuitable for carrier use.

On the other hand, the Navy was faced with a new opponent, the USSR, which had also capitalized on captured German knowledge. If they were to build a jet bomber, then carriers might be defenseless unless they could launch high-speed interceptors from their decks. As the Cold War came into being, this knowledge pressurized the development of jet aircraft, adding to the rapidity with which it took place but also imposing brutal material and human costs.

An additional source of pressure was the new U.S. Air Force, whose leadership in the postwar environment believed that the combination of the atom bomb and the ultra-long-range bomber rendered naval aviation irrelevant. The Navy had long regarded strikes against land targets to be a fundamental mission of its air arm, and the prospect of being sidelined in the business of nuclear attack seemed to threaten the very existence of naval aviation. In April 1949 the Secretary of Defense, Louis Johnson, cancelled the construction of USS *United States*, a very large straight-deck aircraft carrier with no superstructure above the flight deck (flush deck being the technical term) that was designed to support a new generation of big Navy jet bombers capable of carrying the large and heavy nuclear weapons of the day. This cancellation, along with USAF efforts to push the huge B-36 bomber program at the expense of the other Services, produced in October 1949 an incident that has been termed the "Revolt of the Admirals" in which Admiral Arthur Radford (CINCPAC) and other aviation flags as well as the CNO, Admiral Louis Denfeld, testified before Congress on the need for an atomic delivery capability for naval aviation and on the deficiencies of the B-36—in direct contravention of the Secretary of Defense's wishes. Although Admiral Denfeld was subsequently fired by the secretary, Congress was sufficiently convinced of the Navy's utility in strike warfare to authorize in 1951 the construction of USS *Forrestal*, the first of the "super carriers" that could adequately handle the operations of heavy, fast jets.[3] However, the Navy still needed a jet to perform the mission of nuclear strike, and development pressures continued.

The early Cold War operational environment was challenging for naval aviation, to say the least. Knowing that the Soviet Union was working on jet fighters and jet bombers that could carry nuclear weapons and drop them on naval formations, the Navy needed to develop fighter/interceptor aircraft that could defend the carrier and its escorts from attack while sailing into position for a strike and could also strike aircraft that had enough range to hit meaningful targets and enough speed to survive enemy defenses. These general requirements propelled naval aviation development efforts throughout the period from the late 1940s through the 1970s. During this period, the actual employment of naval aviation in three wars, Korea, Vietnam, and Desert Storm, demanded of Navy jets the flexibility to conduct conventional bomb delivery, close air support, and dogfighting. Thus the development of carrier jets morphed over time to designs that were more general-purpose, resulting ultimately in the introduction of the F/A-18 Hornet, an aircraft that is a true strike-fighter.

Thus there was no opportunity for naval aviation to rest on its laurels after World War II. In combination with a massive postwar demobilization, it had to forge ahead with a program to adopt the new engine and aerodynamic technology. It approached this task by attempting to reduce strategic risk through the letting of multiple contracts to different aircraft companies in hopes that at least one of the designs would be viable. On the other hand, it accepted a high degree of operational risk by ordering series production of various models before flight testing was complete. The net effect of this strategy was that between 1945 and 1959, twenty-two Navy fighters made their first flights, whereas over the following forty-six years there were only five.[4] Some of the designs spawned during the early period such as the F2H Banshee were useful machines that had lengthy service lives while others such as the F7U Cutlass and F-11 Tiger were disappointments and had only brief service.

As mentioned previously, the first years of the jet era in the Navy were a disaster in terms of aircraft and crews lost, but the Navy had little choice but to continue sending jets to sea. The gas-guzzling nature of jets made getting them back aboard the carrier in a timely manner a matter of utmost urgency and increased the pressure on carrier captains, admirals, and their staffs to adapt to a very different operational tempo. Future Vice Admiral Gerald Miller was a on a Carrier Group staff in 1950 as they operated F9F-2 Panthers in the Korean theater of operations. They were going to swap sixty-four Panthers from an out-going carrier to one just coming into theater. The weather was bad ashore and the heavy seas were causing the decks to pitch. The staff work and planning to set up the operation did not adequately take into account the limited endurance of the new aircraft. Miller's description of what happened illustrates the consequences of learning to operate jets in a wartime environment:

> We had a lot of these fighters in the air. Then we tried to bring them down and it was a tough job of getting them on board. They were running out of fuel and there was no base on the beach to send them to. We had to get them back on board those two carriers, and we broke up those planes in some numbers.
>
> It was awful. It was so bad, I can still remember the Admiral walking over to the opposite side of the bridge, putting his head down on his hands and shaking. It was so bad he couldn't even get mad. It was a horrible mess. Well, that was all because of the size of the ship, the nature of the airplanes and straight deck operations. We started from debacles of that kind to get something better.
>
> Considering the upheaval in the navy caused by demobilization and the introduction of new technologies, it's amazing that we kept together as much as we did. . . . We worried, but we did proceed with the jet program.[5]

At the same time as naval aviators were attempting to master the new jet aircraft, they were grappling with two new missions that increased the degree of difficulty even more: night and all-weather operations and nuclear weapons delivery. In a sense, these two missions were connected, in that it was felt that when the call came, weather or darkness could not stand in the way of getting the nuclear weapon to its target. These two missions exerted considerable pressure on aircraft design and on the risks naval aviation was willing to endure to put these capabilities to sea. Coupled with the risks inherent in jet-powered aviation in those years, these mission areas significantly contributed to the loss of aircraft. To get a feel for the nature of the environment in which naval aviators operated, listen to Captain Gerald O'Roarke, USN (Ret.) describe the environment in VC-4, the Navy's East Coast night/all-weather fighter squadron in the early 1950s:

> All naval aviators are routinely exposed to, or involved in, aircraft accidents. That's accepted as almost a hazard of the trade. In carrier work, where dangers abound, accidents tend to be more frequent. In the night carrier operations of those days, accidents were so frequent that they were considered commonplace and unexceptional. Whenever a det [detachment of four to six aircraft sent out on a carrier] departed, the aircraft they flew off were more or less written off. No one expected that all of them would ever come back to Atlantic City. . . . Unfortunately, the same negativism tended to extend to the pilots as well, whose safe return wasn't much better than the aircraft. Between pilots lost, the pilots maimed, and the pilots who decided to throw in their wings, precious few dets ever returned with the same resources they took with them.[6]

ECHELONS

Although the development process of naval jet aircraft has been virtually continuous since 1945, and the service lives of various models of jets have significantly overlapped those that have followed, it is still possible and useful to think of the transition process as a series of waves or echelons.[7] From the first flight of the FH-1 Phantom to the introduction of the F/A-18 Hornet there have been six identifiable waves or echelons of Navy jets.

Echelon I: The First Jets

The first jets that entered into Navy service were procured in relatively low numbers and were used primarily to develop operating procedures. These included the McDonnell FH-1 Phantom and F2H Banshee, the North American FJ-1 Fury, Vought F6U Pirate, Grumman F9F-2 Panther, Douglas F3D Skyknight, and the Vought F7U-1 Cutlass. All but the Cutlass were straight-winged jets. The first operational squadrons received the Phantom and Fury in 1949. These jets proved to be reasonably compatible with the straight-deck carriers of the day as their approach speeds were not much higher than propeller aircraft and their handling characteristics were not too different. However they lacked thrust, they had little in the way of weapons systems beyond guns, and their gunsights were little improved over their World War II kin. After about a year of operations (none were deployed) they were replaced by the more capable second-echelon jets.

Vought's Cutlass was one of this first echelon of jets, at least from the standpoint of when development started. It was one of only a few Navy jets over the years that could be said to be ahead of its time. First flown in 1948, it was a futuristic-looking tailless fighter whose potential was never fully realized due to the deficiencies of the engine (Westinghouse) technology of the day. Originally conceived of as a high-speed interceptor, it took nine years to get it from the drawing board in 1946 to its first deployment in 1955, and by the time it became operational, other swept-wing jets such as the F9F-6 Cougar and the F3H Demon had cornered the market on fighter operations. Due to its lack of thrust (for its weight and the nature of the airframe) and difficult handling characteristics, especially in landing on straight deck carriers, it only made a few deployments.

Echelon II: Korean War Era Jets

It was the Banshees, Panthers, and Skyknights that provided the Navy's inventory of jet fighters during the Korean War. The McDonnell Banshee was essentially an up-sized and upgraded Phantom. Initially deployed on the East Coast, as the Korean War developed Banshee squadrons eventually made an appearance. Its key strengths were its high-altitude capability and decent range. The Panther is perhaps the most famous of the early Navy jets, figuring prominently in the movie *The Bridges at Toko-Ri*. Neither the Banshees nor the Panthers had many MIG confrontations because of where they operated, which was probably a good thing due to their performance deficits vis-à-vis the Soviet-built fighters. However they did manage to come out of the war with a positive kill ratio, and they performed highly useful service in the attack of ground targets. The F3D Skyknight, a rather slow and ungainly looking aircraft, actually had the best record against the swept-wing MIGs because it was designed and equipped to be operated at night. The Banshees eventually became the Navy's key night fighter in the early to mid-1950s and both the Banshee and Panther served long and usefully in the reserves and for other functions after they were superseded in the fleet.

Echelon III: The First Swept-Wing Jets

Concerned about the low-speed handling characteristics of swept-wing jets, in 1946 the Navy had Bell Aircraft Corporation modify a P-63 King Cobra propeller fighter with a swept wing that was designated an L-39. Low-speed approach tests with this machine, especially when equipped with leading edge slats, indicated that swept-wing aircraft handling characteristics would be acceptable for a carrier approach and landing. The Navy also contracted with Douglas Aircraft Corporation in 1945 to develop a high-speed test aircraft dubbed the D-558. Actually, this became two aircraft, the straight-winged D-558-1 Skystreak, a jet-powered aircraft used to explore the transonic region, and the swept-winged D-558-2 Skyrocket, powered by both jet engines and rockets, that eventually got up to Mach 2. Interestingly, these sleek test beds hardly stayed ahead of operational jet aircraft performance, but they did highlight the phenomena that would be encountered in high-speed flight and pointed the way to the design elements that would be needed there.

Due primarily to engine problems, three of the Navy's first five swept-wing fighters had extended development periods. The Cutlass' first flight was in 1948; the initial models of the F3H Demon and the F4D Skyray took place in 1953 and 1954. However, due to not only the presence of swept-wing MIGs in Korea, but also continued pressure from the Air Force, the Navy was desperate to put a swept-wing fighter to sea. Thus it turned to modified versions of existing fighters. With the substitution of swept wings for straight wings, the F9F-4 Panther became the F9F-6 Cougar, and FJ-3 Fury was derived from the Air Force's successful F-86 Sabre. The Cougars deployed first in 1953, with the Fury going to sea in 1955. By 1957 both the missile-toting Demon and the delta-winged Skyray were found on fleet carriers. The ultimate model of fighter in this echelon was the F-11 Tiger, a barely supersonic aircraft that was only produced in small numbers and saw only a few deployments because of its deficient range and endurance and because more capable fighters were about to be fielded.

This echelon of jets also included the A-3 Skywarrior, a large twin-engine jet designed to deliver the large atomic bombs of the day. The "Whale" as it was known, had the speed of a fighter but had an operational radius in excess of 1,600 nautical miles. First deployed in 1956, the Whale could be operated from converted *Essex*-class carriers, although at almost 70,000 pounds gross weight and a wingspan of 72 feet, it was a challenge. The A-3 represented the jet-powered nuclear bomber the Navy felt was necessary for the survival of naval aviation, but within several years of its introduction, the size and weight of tactical nuclear weapons had decreased to the point where fighter-sized jets could carry them. Eventually the A-3 lost its nuclear delivery mission, but it was found to be a very useful airframe for aerial tanking and an array of electronic warfare missions. It remained in service until 1987. Reflecting the challenges of flying the early jets, of the 281 A-3s built, 108 (38 percent) were lost to mishaps and only three in combat.[8]

At the other extreme in terms of size and weight was the Douglas A-4 Skyhawk, often referred to as the Tinker Toy Bomber or the Scooter. Due to the decreasing size and weight of tactical nuclear weapons, it became feasible to design a fighter-sized aircraft as a nuclear bomber. This approach had several advantages, including less expense, less room taken up on a carrier's flight deck, and exposure of only one crewmember to risk on a nuclear mission. The A-4 had long, spindly landing gear so that a nuclear weapon could be slung beneath it. The Skyhawk was so small, including a very cozy cockpit, that pilots joked that you wore it instead of getting in it. First deployed in 1957, the A-4 represented a significant improvement in speed, reliability, and handling over its contemporaries. By the time Vietnam began, the A-4 proved to be a versatile and effective general-purpose light attack aircraft. After its fleet service was over, it found further use as an adversary aircraft and as a two-seat trainer well into the 1990s.

Echelon IV: Faster Fighters, Better Bombers

By the late 1950s, jet engine and aerodynamics technology had advanced to the point that designers could produce aircraft that could generate high top-end speeds in the Mach 2 range and also attain respectable turn performance for dogfighting. The Vought F-8 Crusader was the first of these improved fighters, replacing the earlier jets starting in 1957. The Crusader could better Mach 1.5, but was a difficult aircraft to bring aboard a carrier and was designed and operated as a day fighter, having only a marginally capable radar. Perhaps the quintessential jet fighter coming out in this period was the F-4 Phantom II. Excelling as both a fighter and a bomber, it enjoyed a particularly long service life and was well loved by its crews. Able to approach Mach 2, the Phantom II was a crewed fighter, with a radar intercept officer in the backseat.

Also introduced in this era was the A-5 Vigilante; although originally designed as a Mach 2 nuclear bomber, it morphed into a very good reconnaissance aircraft.

The other attack jets introduced in this period were the A-6 Intruder, a two-place, all-weather medium bomber, and the A-7 Corsair II, a single-seat light attack and close air support machine. Neither of these latter two subsonic aircraft could be considered fighters, but their electronic weapons systems shared the generational technology that inhabited the F-4: analog and early digital mission computer systems and multi-mode radars.

McDonnell FH-1 Phantom.

Echelon V: High-Tech Jets

This echelon contains only two jets, the F-14 Tomcat and the F-18 Hornet. The naval version of the McNamara-mandated TFX, which later became the Air Force F-111, is not counted as it was never produced. As previously mentioned, in the first fifteen years of the jet era, there were five times as many models introduced as in the next forty. This reflects not only the spiraling costs of producing a modern jet fighter, but also the longevity of service of echelon IV aircraft in the fleet. As well, the evolution of carrier aircraft has narrowed to the point that one airframe serves both the fighter and attack roles, and in the case of the Hornet, the electronic warfare and refueling roles too.

The F-14 Tomcat, immortalized in the movie *Top Gun*, was developed to provide the Carrier Battle Group with protection from raids by Soviet missile air assault regiments of Badger and Backfire bombers. Possessing a variable geometry wing and a powerful air-to-air radar, the Tomcat could carry six long-range Phoenix missiles as well as a variety of other missiles and inhabit combat air patrol stations three hundred miles or more from the carrier. Late in its career, it became a true strike-fighter with the addition of a bomb-dropping capability.

By the mid-1970s, another leap in engine, aerodynamics, and systems technology was in the works. The Air Force Light Weight Fighter Program spawned two competitive designs, the YF-16 and YF-17, which were revolutionary. The Air Force selected the F-16, and eventually Congress directed the Navy to use one of these aircraft as the replacement for its aging A-7 Corsair. It chose the Northrup YF-17 and developed it into the F-18 Hornet. The Hornet is characterized by the extensive application of digital computer technology that results in fly-by-wire control systems in which the pilot's control inputs are fed to a computer that calculates actual control surface movements, highly capable radars, and refined digital cockpit displays. The F-18 is also highly maneuverable as well as capable of supersonic speeds.

Echelon VI: The Last Manned Fighters?

We now enter the future. New aircraft such as the Air Force's F-22 Raptor and the F-35 Joint Strike Fighter (now called the Lightning II) bring even more advanced capabilities and characteristics to the air combat arena. These include a high degree of stealthiness, major increases in on-board data processing, as well as huge increases in sensing and communications capacity. These aircraft will be flying network nodes as well as highly lethal fighters. They will be supersonic, but their top-end speeds will be no higher and in some cases less than earlier generation machines because such high speeds are not considered a worthwhile tradeoff for maneuverability, stealth, and systems capacity.

Although this chapter is a history of naval aviation's transition to jet aircraft, it is worthwhile to look even further ahead. Although to some degree speculative, the outlines of a future echelon of Navy carrier aircraft is becoming increasingly clear: they will be unmanned. Emerging control technology based on artificial intelligence is already producing an array of unmanned drones that have proven useful and effective in current wars in Iraq and Afghanistan as well as in other operations around the world. There are a number of reasons for the Navy to develop a new generation of what are termed "Unmanned Combat Aerial Systems" or UCAS. Freed of the requirement to house humans aboard, these aircraft will have even greater stealth and huge increases in range and endurance. If, as seems probable at this point, missiles will dominate all arenas of naval warfare, UCAS will not need to dogfight like traditional manned fighters.

DEAD ENDS: SEAPLANES AND VERTICAL TAKEOFF AND LANDING

From the Sea

For much of its early history the Navy made extensive use of seaplanes, either utilizing floats fitted to aircraft that were otherwise designed for land use, and true flying boats. By the late 1930s, the Navy had abandoned the idea of floatplane fighters and instead used the type as scouts operating from battleships and cruisers. After World War II, the Navy again revived its interest in sea-based fighters, this time swept-wing jets, thinking that swept-winged fighters might not be suitable for carrier operations. It let a contract in 1951 with Convair to produce a delta-winged, supersonic fighter called the Sea Dart. A small flying boat that floated on its fuselage, it used an extendable "hydro ski" to handle the forces of takeoff and landing. Several Sea Darts flew, but their performance was disappointing due to deficient engine thrust. However one did exceed Mach 1 in a shallow dive on a test flight, becoming the only seaplane to break the sound barrier. After several catastrophic accidents, and with the development of carrier-capable swept-wing jets, the Sea Dart project was abandoned.

The Navy had far more success with larger flying boats. Its PBY Catalina series was used extensively in World War II as a scout and for transport to areas with no airfields. Larger flying boats were put into operation after the war as anti-submarine patrol planes and transports. The idea for a large, jet-powered seaplane emerged from the inter-Service rivalry of the late 1940s and early 1950s with the Air Force, in which the large aircraft carrier *United States* was cancelled. Seeking to establish its own nuclear strike capability using jet seaplanes, the Navy issued a requirement in 1951, which Martin Aircraft Company eventually won. The result was the P6M SeaMaster, a four-engined, swept-winged aircraft that was to be capable of carrying 30,000 pounds of ordnance on a combat radius of 1,500 miles. It was to be capable of a 0.9-Mach attack speed at sea level. As with the Sea Dart, the SeaMaster showed early promise, with its first flight in 1955, but two catastrophic accidents precipitated a significant redesign. By the time the second model was ready for testing in 1959, the incipient introduction of the Polaris ballistic missile submarine and defense budget cuts resulted in the demise of the program.

Going Vertical

The Navy has always had an interest in aircraft that could take off and/or land vertically. Helicopters are ubiquitous and serve the Navy in many ways, but they are not capable of replacing conventional fighter and attack aircraft. Early in the jet era, the Navy experimented with several types of turboprop vertical takeoff and landing (VTOL) aircraft including the XFY-1 Pogo. None of the early turbojet engines had enough thrust to lift an aircraft vertically, nor was there sufficient technology to design a machine that would be controllable in the shipboard environment. The attractions of vertical takeoff and landing are many for the Navy. Without having to worry about catapults and arresting gear, an aircraft carrier could operate significantly more aircraft for a given size, and construction expenses would be less. Moreover, freed from the many safety restrictions and the intricate ballet of on-deck aircraft movements that confine the operations of an aircraft carrier to cycles of an hour and thirty minutes—more or less—a VTOL-equipped carrier would have far greater operational flexibility and rapid response to changing tactical situations.

However, the price for vertical flight has been too high. The British-designed AV-8 Harrier was the first and most successful "jump jet," and was the difference between victory and defeat in their Falklands War with Argentina. It also became a workhorse for the U.S. Marine Corps, operating from the decks of catapult-less amphibious ships and austere expeditionary airfields. However, the Harrier has relatively little payload and range. The Navy has passed up this jet because it could not be used as a fleet defense fighter or as a practical attack aircraft, given the mostly long-range missions the Navy has envisioned for its bombers. Even today, with a short takeoff/vertical landing version of the new, fifth-generation Joint Strike Fighter due to be introduced, the Navy is sticking with a conventional catapulted takeoff and arrested landing version. It seems that the Navy may never realize the dream of vertical flight for its tactical aircraft.

LIVING THE TRANSITION

As the Navy proceeded into the jet age, it fielded in rapid succession a number of different designs, each representing a significant advance in speed and capability. Some of the early models only had an operational career of two or three years before being superseded by a more advanced design. Many things were changing rapidly in the early 1950s, including ship design and airwing composition. The catastrophic accident rates were due in part to this turbulence—pilots would transition from type to type without adequate training. Some of these jets, like the F9F-2 Panther and F4D Skyray, were relatively easy to handle and bring aboard the carrier, while others such as the F7U Cutlass and the F-8 Crusader were notorious for their difficult handling characteristics. All suffered from engine and system reliability problems, and the advent of more challenging missions, such as night and all-weather operations, exacerbated vulnerabilities inherent in the aircraft and the naval aviation culture.

Each succeeding echelon of Navy jets represented an improvement over the last. However, echelons II through IV shared a set of design problems that were not substantially overcome until the advent of the F-18. Low thrust and unreliable engines, adverse handling characteristics, especially in the carrier landing approach, and complex man-machine interfaces made flying Navy jets a dangerous business. Military jet flying is loaded with challenges including dogfighting, dive-bombing and formation flying; design defects and difficulties added to the challenges and exacted a frequently fatal price for any deficiencies in aircrew technique. The following sections provide some insight into the challenges of dealing with the characteristics of Navy jets.

Handling

We will start with the handling characteristics of a swept-wing jet. Anyone who has ever piloted an airplane knows that as airspeed decreases, there comes a point at which the wings can no longer sustain flight. In primary training, at a safe altitude the instructor has the student reduce power and hold altitude by easing back on the control stick until the airplane is pitched up at such an angle relative to the oncoming air that the airflow over the wings cannot flow smoothly over the top, and lift is lost. This is termed a stall. In straight-wing airplanes, this stall happens abruptly because the whole wing loses lift at the same time (although most designs have a bit of "twist" put in the wing shape to ensure the stall starts at the wing root near the fuselage and propagates outward, contributing to keeping the wings level in a stall). A swept wing does no such thing. It loses lift more gradually. Moreover, as the jet's angle of attack increases to compensate for the loss of lift, the wings generate large amounts of induced drag, the air resistance incurred by generating lift. As airspeed slows, lift decreases and induced drag increases, and the swept-wing jet, regardless of how powerful the engines are, can get into a predicament in which it has a high rate of sink but is not fully stalled, and full power cannot get it out of it. The only way out is to drop the nose of the aircraft, at which point the jet drops like a rock until flying speed is regained. If the jet is near the ground, like in a landing pattern, it is doomed.

As the Navy started introducing swept-wing jets, pilots who were used to the characteristics of straight-wing machines could get themselves into a terminal situation because their habit pattern would cause them to pull up on the nose to control rate of descent rather than add power. If they were slow in recognizing the developing problem, they would find themselves in a high rate of descent near the ground that they could not get out of. Early ejection seats could not handle high rates of descent near the ground. The end result was a lost jet and dead pilot. This was an all-too-common occurrence throughout the early jet era. Of course, this characteristic was exacerbated in the aircraft carrier operating environment. Swept-wing aircraft have higher approach and landing speeds than straight-wing aircraft, and they must be operated much nearer to stall speed to keep arrested landing speeds down and reduce the risk of damage on landing. Stalling and crashing in the landing pattern was a definite occupational hazard for Navy jet pilots. Even as late as the early 1990s, crashes of this sort were occurring in the A-7 and F-14 communities.

However, gradual stall was not the only adverse handling characteristic of swept-wing jets. Each particular model had its own idiosyncrasies that could lead to loss of control. The F-14 had a flat spin mode that could be entered if the pilot pulled too hard in a slow speed dogfight, which was frequently unrecoverable. The A-7 had a rather violent way of departing from controlled flight at high speeds that would result in an "auger," a high-speed roll heading straight down. Early A-7 pilots interpreted the auger as a spin (a slow speed stalled and twirling condition) and put in anti-spin controls that only made the situation worse. A number of Corsair drivers flew into the ground at six hundred knots trying to get out of what they thought was a spin. It took several fatalities until the accident boards finally figured out what had happened, and ordered additional training instituted for pilots to recognize and recover from the condition. This is typical of what happened in some form for almost every new jet design the Navy introduced during the transition period. All tactical jet crews engaged in dogfight training, a demanding environment in which it is necessary to fly the airplane to the limits of its capability, especially in the slow speed realm. A steady stream of lost aircraft progressively taught the Navy and the aircraft designers about the deficiencies of each design, some of which did not come to light until years after the aircraft's introduction. Aircrews were only too aware of the dangers, but there was a special pride in being able to master a hard-to-fly jet. There was a picture of a Marine Corps F-4 Phantom that hung for many years behind the bar at the Naval Air Station in Fallon, Nevada. On the matting was an inscription that said: "If it don't buck, there ain't no rodeo."

Engines

Stepping on the gas of a car yields instant response—the same as when a pilot moves the throttle forward on a propeller-driven airplane. This is because the increased gas flow to the cylinders causes bigger explosions and moves the pistons faster right away. Not so in a jet engine. Increasing the fuel flow causes a hotter fire and higher pressures to be generated in the combustion chambers, but this high-pressure gas must now travel aft to the turbine section and cause it, and the attached compressor section up front, to spin a bit faster. This faster spin compresses the incoming air more, which in turn generates higher pressures in the combustors, which then cause the turbine to spin faster, and so on. Obviously, this takes a finite amount of time. The heavier the compressor and turbine assembly, the more inertia it has, and the more time required to spin up and get to full power. Early jet engines had heavy rotating cores and lower operating temperatures due to less advanced metallurgy, so the lag time between the pilot putting the power lever forward and full thrust being produced was significant. Slow engine response, coupled with the difficult slow-speed approach and landing characteristics of swept wings, produced a lethal combination for Navy pilots. Some early jets such as the Panther and Cougar had centrifugal flow jet engines in which the compressor sent air outward instead of straight back. A centrifugal flow compressor was heavier and less efficient than an axial flow one, and thus increased engine lag even more.

However, jet engine spool-up lag was only half of the problem; engines also lagged in spooling down when the pilot pulled back on the throttle. In piston-engined propeller aircraft, not only did the engine immediately stop putting out power, the propeller acted as a kind of speed brake. Thus, on the straight deck carriers, the Landing Signal Officer (LSO) would give a "cut" signal when the aircraft had the deck made, and the prop plane would settle into the wires. If, for some reason, the hook did not engage the wires, there was a barrier set up to snag the landing gear and stop the plane before it ran into the aircraft parked on the forward part of the flight deck. This system did not work well for jets. Engine lag tends to bedevil student pilots when they first attempt to fly a jet straight and level, causing over-controlling and a rather sinusoidal flight path until they get the hang of leading the power, both in adding it and reducing it. Combined with the lack of a robust and disciplined transition program from propeller aircraft, which was precisely the case in the late 1940s and early 1950s, jet engine lag set the stage for disaster aboard straight deck aircraft carriers. The straight-winged jets such as the Banshee and Panther tended to "float" anyway, the wings continuing to generate lift even when the aircraft speed was just above stall. As a result, if a pilot added too much power in close to the carrier on the final few seconds of an approach, say, to compensate for going below glidepath (remember, the pilot probably added a little power and got no instant response like in a prop, and so added more), then realized he had over-corrected and pulled the power to idle on the LSO's cut signal, the engine would continue to pump out some residual thrust as it spooled down and the jet would level off (float, especially as it got instantly into the "ground effect" of the carrier's flight deck) and not only miss the wires, but also the mid-ship barriers. Most of the time there were many aircraft parked up on the bow, protected, in theory, by the barriers. The result was a catastrophe in which the floating jet ploughed into the parked machines. This happened more than once. Even with improved jet engines, problems with residual thrust did not entirely disappear, but the arrival of the angled flight deck turned potential catastrophes into harmless "bolters" in which the jet simply continued off the angle and into the air to try again.

As metallurgy and jet engine design improved, response lag was reduced. The J-79 turbojet that powered the F-4 Phantom had very quick response and pilots loved it. Moreover, it proved to be highly reliable. However, a trend developed in the 1960s to place fan jet engines in tactical jets. A fan jet engine has a greater diameter compressor section so that some of the compressed air bypasses the "hot section" of the engine and flows directly out the tailpipe. This adds efficiency to the engine, giving the airplane better "mileage." For tactical jets, which always lack space for fuel, increased mileage means greater radius of action; a good thing generally. However, there was a price to be paid. Fan jets originated in the airline industry, where the engines are treated tenderly, being brought to full power gradually and left unmolested at cruising power for most of the flight. Not so with fighters. The requirements of combat and carrier landing demand constant and rapid throttle movements. Obviously, the addition of a fan section adds weight to the rotating core, so it is easy to imagine the impact on throttle response times. Moreover, the constant stress of having to accelerate that heavy fan imposes much greater stress on the turbine section. Sure enough, Navy fighters and attack aircraft equipped with fan jets started suffering high rates of engine failure. This was bad enough in a two-engine F-14, but catastrophic in the single-engine A-7 Corsair. At one point, the Navy made Corsair pilots limit their throttle movements so the temperatures on the turbine blades could be controlled. In addition, the engines were being preemptively replaced every two hundred hours of operation. Even with these restrictions Corsairs were falling out of the sky. The TF-30 engine, which powered both the early A-7 models and the F-14, also had a tendency to develop compressor stalls, where the airflow through the compressor burbles, like in a wing stall. The engine bangs like crazy and loses power. Many jets were lost to such stalls.

Man-Machine Interface

Cockpit design—the arrangement of gauges and controls—has always been an issue of intense interest to designers and aircrew. Prior to the introduction of jet fighters, the cockpits of Navy aircraft were relatively simple, consisting of sufficient gauges to exert basic control, and in some cases to "fly blind" in clouds and bad weather. Navigation was generally via a compass and a map. As jets were introduced, so were more advanced electronics systems such as radar, weapons control, and eventually electronic navigation. The operation of these systems required quite a bit of attention and effort by the pilot; so much so that pilot distraction caused more than a few accidents. This was exacerbated by the introduction of surface-to-air missiles, which forced attack aircraft to adopt the tactic of low-level approach to their target. Flying a jet at high speed, close to the ground required intense concentration and a highly disciplined approach to using the various electronic systems. If the pilot spent just a little too much time focused inside the cockpit trying to update his navigation system or change channels on his radio, he could be annihilated in a cloud of fire and dirt as his airplane hit the ground at high speed. This was the fate of perhaps dozens or scores of aircrew over the years as they struggled to carry out their missions using cockpit systems that required lots of attention. One fix for this problem was to insert another crewmember (Radar Intercept Officer, Bombardier-Navigator, etc.) whose whole job was to manage aircraft systems. While the "crew concept" did indeed improve the operational effectiveness of aircraft with complex systems, it did not eliminate the problem of aircrew distraction altogether.

Perhaps the most demanding environment was the low level nuclear mission, which had to be carried out day or night and in almost any kind of weather. While early jets simply could not operate at low level at night or in bad weather, the introduction of both the A-6 Intruder and the A-7 Corsair was supposed to open up this regime to naval aviation. Crews were forced to train in these conditions, and defects in man-machine interfaces soon produced a number of crashes and fatalities, especially in mountainous terrain, where the planes' radars were supposed to alert the pilot of impending obstacles. The A-6 system proved reasonably effective at keeping the plane from hitting mountains, but less so at avoiding power lines. The A-7 system was judged unsuitable after several fatal crashes in which the pilot under instruction was head down under a view-blocking canopy and chased—for safety— by an instructor in another aircraft. Apparently the terrain following radar did not generate a climb signal in time and the instructor pilot's warning came just a little too late.

Nor was low altitude, high-speed navigation the only regime in which systems design flaws proved fatal. In the age before computers, many basic "housekeeping" tasks had to be handled by the aircrew. Fuel management was a constant source of problems and indeed contributed to the deaths of some early jet test pilots. In most Navy jets from FH-1 Phantom to the A-7 Corsair II, the crew either had to take some action to get fuel to transfer in the right sequence from each of the plane's tanks, or had to go through some sequence of switch flipping if the automatic fuel transfer sequence did not occur correctly. Complicated relay logic and cockpit switch sequences caused any number of jets to quit running with plenty of fuel still aboard. Fuel management headaches were multiplied by the introduction of mid-air refueling. In the A-7 for instance, if the refueling probe was bent, and this was not an uncommon result of trying to get fuel from an Air Force KC-135, fuel transfer from the drop tanks was inhibited, so the Corsair driver could have four-thousand pounds or more of unusable fuel hanging from his jet. Because most jets required hydraulically boosted flight controls to compensate for transonic shockwaves, unreliable hydraulic systems posed similar problems. Thus most jets were equipped with multiple hydraulic systems that commonly required somewhat complicated "switchology" drills if one or more failed. Again, many airplanes were lost when pilots flipped the switches in the wrong order.

Armed with this mini-education about the hazards of flying swept-wing jets, we can go on to review with greater insight and appreciation the transition from straight-wing piston-engine propeller planes to swept-wing jets on board the Navy's aircraft carriers.

GETTING ON AND OFF THE AIRCRAFT CARRIER WITH JETS

By the end of World War II, the U.S. Navy had become very adept at operating aircraft carriers. It had an extensive cadre of highly experienced pilots that provided leadership in the air wings and squadrons and excellent instruction in the training command, and it knew how to get the air wings on and off the carriers. In the 1920s and 1930s naval aviation had developed technologies that allowed the carriers to operate sixty or more aircraft. Of course, a key technology was the arresting wires stretched across the flight deck of the carrier and the arresting hook attached to the tail of the airplane. However, the real key to operating large numbers of aircraft was the midship barrier, a series of elevated wires that would catch the landing gear of any aircraft that happened to miss the arresting wires or whose hook bounced over them or perhaps just broke. This allowed the ship to park aircraft up on the bow for refueling and rearming without having to send them down to the hangar deck. In addition, naval aviators had devised a circling landing approach that allowed the pilot to observe the LSO who was standing on a small platform well aft on the flight deck on the port side of the ship. Armed with two paddles, the LSO would let the pilot know if he was too high or too low, and gave him a "cut" signal to reduce power to idle when he had the deck made. This whole system worked well for propeller aircraft, with their relatively low approach speeds, light weight, and instant power response.

The first jets had straight wings and were relatively light, so their approach speeds weren't that much different from props. However, given jet engine lag, pilots had to be careful not to pull off too much power when they got a little high on the glide slope. A number of ramp strikes occurred when they did. Conversely, if the pilot jammed on too much power to correct for a low, the jet engine also took its time spooling down, and there were cases, as previously mentioned, of the jet floating over the barrier and crashing into the "pack" of parked aircraft with catastrophic results. The Navy understood that bringing swept-wing jets into the picture would only exacerbate the problems and so delayed the fleet introduction of these machines until several years after they became operational in the Air Force. When the F9F-6 Cougar, a modification of the straight-winged Panther, showed up in squadrons in November 1952, the difficulties of getting it aboard safely were magnified. If a swept wing is dicey to handle at slow speed and wings level, it's doubly so in an approach turn. In order to make the approach a bit easier for the pilot, the pattern was extended a bit to give him more wings level time in the "groove." However, this made it harder for the pilot to see the LSO.

Two pieces of British technology came to the rescue for the Navy. The first was the angled flight deck. The flight deck was widened amidships, allowing the landing area to be canted about 10 degrees to port. This permitted aircraft that missed the wires or bounced to add power and go around for another try without crashing into the barrier or the pack of parked airplanes; equally important, it allowed jet pilots to fly a power-on, constant angle of attack approach all the way to touchdown. That way, with the engine already at a relatively high power setting, the lag to attain full power if the wires were missed was minimal. In fact, standard procedure quickly became adding full power immediately on touchdown, arrested stop or not. If the plane caught the wire, the jet would just sit there momentarily at full power, held stationary by the hook. Once stopped, the pilot would reduce power and taxi out of the landing area. USS *Antietam*, an *Essex*-class carrier, was the first to receive this modification and returned to the fleet in 1953. In 1955, USS *Forrestal*, the Navy's first super carrier, expressly designed to accommodate the heavier swept-wing jets, was commissioned with an angled deck. In 1955 another British invention, the optical mirror landing system, was introduced aboard U.S. carriers. This apparatus allowed the pilot to see clearly whether he was on glideslope or not from over a mile behind the ship. Later, the mirror was replaced with a series of Fresnel lenses that performed the same function of providing a visual indication of glideslope, but using much less space. The influence these innovations had on the safety and operational efficiency of aircraft carriers was dramatic: the carrier embarked accident rate per ten thousand landings dropped from thirty-five in 1954 to seven in 1957.[9]

Jets also had to get off the carrier, and this required a third British invention, the steam catapult. The Navy had been using catapults since the early days of naval aviation. Initially run by compressed air, ungainly looking catapults were installed on cruisers and battleships to launch their scout floatplanes. The Navy subsequently developed hydraulic catapults prior to World War II, but the fast carriers operated almost exclusively using free deck rolls because the Hellcats, Dauntlesses, and Avengers didn't need them. However, the hydraulic catapults were a necessity on the smaller light and escort carriers. It soon became clear that jets could not use free roll takeoffs due to their higher minimum flying speeds, and so the hydraulic catapults were used initially. However, as the jets got heavier and required yet greater launch speeds, the need for better catapults became manifest. The Royal Navy came to the rescue again with the steam-powered catapult. The steam catapult used steam from the ship's propulsion plant, could be built with a much longer power stroke, and was considerably lighter than a comparable hydraulic unit. These three innovations, the angled deck, the optical landing system, and the steam catapult set the stage for the effective operation of supersonic swept-wing jets at sea.

GETTING OUT

In propeller aircraft, if the engine quit or the plane caught fire, the pilot and any crew could "bail out," that is, open the canopy, door, or hatch and just jump, pulling the rip cord on the parachute once clear of the plane. Moreover, one could reasonably think about ditching a prop; pancaking down on the water at 80 knots or so was eminently survivable. All of this changed with jets. At 300 or 400 knots, trying to bail out in a traditional manner was impossible. At jet landing speeds, ditching a swept-wing fighter was almost certain suicide. The answer was the ejection seat. Initially powered by a small explosive charge, seats were later equipped with a rocket engine under the seat pan and had provisions for restraining the pilot's arms and legs in the brutal blast of air that was encountered when ejecting from airplane at high speed. The ejection seat was supposed to be the pilot's savior, and indeed it was—sort of. The first successful ejection from a Navy aircraft was in 1949 when the pilot of a Banshee was forced to eject over South Carolina at 597 knots.

As with the jets themselves, ejection seats went through a development process, with early seats being less sophisticated and capable than later ones. An ejection seat can be characterized by its capability in two modes: low speed and close to the ground and high speed and high altitude. Once introduced, the ejection seat generated an interesting dilemma for the pilot and crew—when do they pull the handle? The author of this chapter had an introduction to swept-wing jets that was marred by two accidents illustrating the problem. In advanced flight training using the TA-4J Skyhawk, an instructor and fellow student were killed when they ejected too late after their engine failed on takeoff. The instructor was apparently trying to get the aircraft turned around to execute an emergency landing. It was later learned in the accident investigation that he had been fudging his logbook with instrument time so that he would not lose his instrument rating. We surmised that fear of this coming to light if he ejected caused him to delay pulling the handle. The second incident was an A-7 pilot (another fellow student on his first A-7 flight—solo) that ejected late after his engine quit after a touch-and-go landing. He survived, but was so injured he never flew again. Although a qualified aviator, he had not yet developed the reactions and instincts to handle an engine failure at such a critical juncture on his first Corsair flight.

These gruesome anecdotes illustrate a phenomenon with ejection seats. Despite the progressively increased capability of the ejection seats in each new type of aircraft, the survival rate of ejections did not rise the way you would expect. Many aviators believed this was because (a) there were sometimes external mental or emotional factors that caused pilots to delay their ejection, (b) pilots would ascribe too much capability to the seat and thereby delay pulling the handle, and (c) things happened too damned fast.

Interestingly, in the first decade of the jet era, the number of crew fatalities was significantly less than the number of lost aircraft. After that the two statistics gradually match up, with the number of fatalities becoming equal to or exceeding the number of aircraft lost. Part of this is undoubtedly due to the residual propeller aircraft in the fleet, including the F4U Corsair and the A-1 Skyraider. But it may also be due to the number of straight-wing jets that could be ditched with reasonable hope of crew survival. The arrival of crewed aircraft also meant that a fatal accident produced multiple deaths for the loss of a single aircraft.

KEEPING THEM FLYING

Just as flying was considered an art born of individual experience in the piston-engine years of naval aviation, so was maintenance. The aircraft, except for the engines, were relatively simple and maintenance was mostly a matter of senior petty officers handing down their knowledge and wisdom to the new "airdales" (sailors in naval aviation ratings). Piston engines were complex machines, but by the 1940s were pretty reliable. The introduction of jets changed things. To start with, the early jet engines had a very limited service life. Whereas an air-cooled radial piston engine might run for several thousand hours before needing to be replaced, a jet engine would require replacement after only several hundred. As jets got faster, they required more complex hydraulic and electrical systems, including such exotic (for the time) accessories as yaw dampers, cockpit pressurization, and ejection seats. The old ways of maintenance came under extreme pressure. To quote a *Naval Aviation News* article from 1961: "Compared to the fighters of 1940, the fighters of today are five times as heavy, have six times as many inspection items, ten times as many switches, twenty times as many valves, sixty times as many electron tubes, require ten times as many items of support equipment, and cost about eighty times as much."[10]

The Naval Aviation Maintenance Program (NAMP) was established in 1960 to standardize maintenance practices and improve aviation logistics. The idea was to standardize both terminology and procedures so that a maintenanceman would be instantly familiar with maintenance and repair procedures regardless of what ship, air station, or squadron he was assigned. Moreover such a system required extensive documentation, and naval aviation produced progressively more sophisticated methods over the years.

However, change has always come hard to the Navy and the imposition of standardized maintenance methods was no exception. To quote from the same *Naval Aviation News* article: "While it is hard to find anyone in our time who does not appreciate the value of interchangeable parts in machines, it is not so generally recognized that the same principles apply in human organizations."[11] The effective transition from aviation maintenance as an individual art to a formalized human-machine system took years, and many jets were lost, even through the 1980s, to maintenance errors resulting from squadron maintenance chiefs "doing their own thing" and subverting the system in various ways. The informality of naval aviation maintenance was nowhere more evident than in the cases where naval aviators undertook to fix their own aircraft on a cross-country flight. If a starter, hydraulic pump, or similar part failed, it was not uncommon for the pilot to call back to the squadron and have a new part sent out in another jet toting a "blivet," an external fuel tank modified with a door and shelves to carry cargo. The sight of a Navy pilot taking a wrench to his own airplane always shocked and dismayed Air Force personnel (if it took place at an Air Force base) who witnessed it, as the Air Force had a much more disciplined and structured system. This practice continued at least into the 1980s.

Naval aviation maintenance is a highly challenging business even under the best of circumstances. Squadrons must regularly move their operations from a shore base to an aircraft carrier and back again, sometimes splitting up into small detachments. Moreover, airdales must perform maintenance on the flight deck of an aircraft carrier, at night and in some miserable weather conditions. As if that were not enough, they have to be ready to scurry out to the middle of a flight deck during launch operations to try and fix a jet that developed a problem after start-up. Although the dangers of whirling propellers and jet engines that could blow a man over the side or suck him into the intake were well appreciated, over the years a steady stream of aviation sailors were lost or injured to these hazards. As with aircrew, airdales who could not maintain their composure in the rapid-fire and dangerous environment they faced were weeded out by death or injury, or if they could not deal with the fear and strain, left the business. Those who remained were tough and savvy and they made naval aviation a success.

NAVAL AVIATION CULTURE AND THE TRANSITION TO JETS

In order to understand the catastrophic price the Navy paid in its march to operate swept-wing jets from aircraft carriers, we must look at the organizational culture onto which this new technology was grafted. After all, the majority of the mishaps that occurred were due to aircrew error of some sort, whether it was precipitated or exacerbated by the design problems previously identified—or gross error, negligence, or irresponsibility not connected with them.

Naval aviators always viewed themselves as daredevils. The difficulties of taking off from and landing on a ship were unequalled in the land aviation domain, and naval aviators therefore considered themselves both exceptionally skilled—and expendable. The naval aviation accident rate (if not the sheer numbers) from its inception through World War II was hardly less than the awful rates experienced in the early jet era. Naval aviators have always regarded themselves as a different breed than their surface Navy brethren, but for all that, have shared in the Navy's culture of independence and self-reliance. The simplicity and relative inexpensiveness of early naval aircraft allowed this culture to thrive, in that flight instruction was personal and aviators had few detailed procedures or rules to follow in mastering their aircraft. Seat-of-the-pants flying and individuality in technique were the order of the day. But since the piston-engine aircraft all operated essentially in the same way and roughly at the same speeds, especially when landing, and since they rarely operated at night or in bad weather, pilots could transition between aircraft easily and informally. Mr. Richard "Chick" Eldridge, a member of the Naval Safety Center for several decades remembers his Navy flight training in 1943: "To my recollection, there was little emphasis on aviation safety. What safety information was imparted to the fledgling aviator came from the primary instructors. Lessons learned usually came in the form of 'gems of instructor wisdom.' You were simply told to fly certain maneuvers in a specific way or wind up as a statistic."[12]

The first thing to change was the technology. Culture change lagged by more than a decade, causing a virtual bloodbath. In addition to the specific challenges of flying jets mentioned previously must be added the greatly increased speeds. Things happen much faster in jets and a different mindset and discipline are called for to avoid disaster. Pilots who spent significant time flying at propeller aircraft speeds tended to have more difficulty adjusting to jet speeds than those who were introduced to them early. The author observed this during the Navy's transition from the piston-engine S-2 Tracker carrier anti-submarine aircraft to the jet-powered S-3 Viking. The more senior pilots seemed to have the most difficulty, and indeed a number of them either quit, had accidents, or failed to pass flight checks. This was a serious issue that attended the fleet introduction of the A-3 Skywarrior. Initially, the Navy brought in senior aviators from the land-based patrol community as well as some carrier pilots. A series of accidents and difficulties involving former patrol pilots prompted the Commander of the Sixth Fleet to write a letter to the CNO recommending only carrier-trained pilots be assigned to A-3 squadrons.[13]

In the early years of the jet transition, naval aviation remained wedded to its individualistic culture. Structured programs of training, detailed reference manuals, and disciplined evaluation of pilot performance did not exist in any coherent way across naval aviation. But jets, with their higher speeds, challenging handling characteristics, and ever-more complex systems required just that. The horrible accident rates eventually drove the Navy to do something. The Air Force had been suffering an increase in mishaps also and formed a Flight Safety Directorate with 525 personnel and undertook to impose discipline on the aviation corps by disciplining crew when fault and culpability could be assigned. In contrast, the Navy's first effort was puny by comparison with only twenty-five personnel. However, war hero Captain James F. "Jimmy" Flatley wrote up a highly critical and influential report on naval aviation safety in 1953 that generated organizational and procedural changes that went far to change the culture.[14] Along with these changes, a more structured program of flight training was introduced, eventually culminating with the establishment of replacement training squadrons that provided intensive and detailed instruction for newly winged aviators in the aircraft they would fly in the fleet. These squadrons would also become the centers of flight and maintenance evaluation of the fleet squadrons based with them. A variety of other measures also served to further professionalize and discipline the naval aviation culture, including formal training for squadron safety officers, improved accident investigation techniques, specially trained medical personnel called flight surgeons, the publication of a safety magazine to share stories of accidents and near misses, and top-down leadership that countered the laissez-faire cultural heritage.

However, as with naval aviation maintenance, the "ready room" culture was resistant to change. Thus the authors of another 1961 *Naval Aviation News* article felt compelled to say "Some people view the idea of everyone in naval aviation doing everything 'the one best way' with some misgivings. They fear that general use of standardized procedures, while it may reduce the accident rate, will result in a reduction of a pilot's ability to 'think on his feet' and deal flexibly with emergencies and combat situations. Experience in other fields has proved that fear unfounded."[15] A major element of the resistance to change was the fact that adaptation to the new technology had a value content; that is, it made irrelevant certain skill sets that were associated with being a respected, professional aviator in the propeller-driven era. It wasn't so much the difficulty in learning new skill sets as it was abandoning old ones that were associated with professional virtue. The naval aviation culture that grew up from 1911 to 1947 was intense, insular, and value-centric. Moreover, likely because of the acrimonious relationship that developed between the Navy and Air Force in the late 1940s, there was a reluctance to view anything the USAF did as appropriate for naval aviation, and it took a long time for the Navy to adopt or adapt Air Force best practices.

Despite the organizational and procedural progress that was made in the 1950s and 1960s, the social culture of naval aviation lagged. Apart from the drinking and partying that contributed to any number of one-car fatal accidents after happy hour at the officers club, there existed a testosterone-heavy atmosphere of pressure in the ready rooms that put pilots in a difficult position when they manned up their aircraft. It was almost normal to find on start-up that some piece of equipment on a multi-system jet was malfunctioning. The pilot or crew now had to decide whether the problem was of sufficient severity to warrant "downing" the airplane and canceling the flight. However, such a decision was not straightforward. Many a CO, Air Wing Commander, or carrier skipper was hell-bent on making all scheduled sorties or setting new operational records. The pilot that downed too many aircraft, especially in night or bad weather conditions, would quickly get a reputation as a coward. Thus pilots were under considerable pressure to get their aircraft in the air. How many mishaps were caused by pilots launching with defective aircraft is not clear, but the number was significant. The arrival of the F-18 changed this aspect of the culture significantly. The airplane was extremely reliable, and its design meant that any defects encountered on start-up were more clearly either insignificant or were cause for not launching.

The Navy has always placed considerable responsibility and authority into the hands of the individual officer. An imperative of war at sea, this delegated style of command and control has both enhanced and afflicted naval aviation. Throughout the history of naval aviation, outstanding decision making by relatively junior officers has made the difference in battle, such as Lieutenant Commander Wade McClusky's decision to take his strike group in the direction a Japanese destroyer was headed and thus find the Japanese aircraft carriers at the Battle of Midway. However, faced with the imposition of new technology that demanded new types of procedural discipline and centralized management, the culture was slow to adapt, and literally thousands of naval aviators lost their lives as a result.

FINDING THE RIGHT COMBINATION OF INGREDIENTS

The development of aviation technology between the time of the Wright brothers' first flight and 1947 was amazingly fast. In just forty-five years aviation had progressed from machines that were hardly more than powered kites to jets that pushed the speed of sound. This rapid development meant that individual models of combat aircraft became obsolete fairly quickly. This had been the case prior to and during World War II, and was to be the case over the early years of jet transition in the Navy. The initial echelon of straight-wing jets had an operational lifespan in the fleet of only a few years, although some of them had a longer second life in the reserves or through other specialized shore-based uses such as the training command. In the late 1940s and the early 1950s, as whole squadrons transitioned from propeller airplanes to jets, pilots—who had developed a set of habit patterns molded to straight-wing propeller planes that flew slower and used gas slower and were lighter and simpler—were put into fast, gas-guzzling jets with the challenging operating characteristics we have previously described. It was a lethal combination. Rear Admiral Thomas Brown III, who was a mid-grade officer in those days, summed things up pretty well in his oral history to the Naval Historical Foundation:

Something that is important to understand about that era is that the Navy introduced a number of different jet aircraft into the fleet in the middle '50s. Among them were the FJ3, FJ4, the A-4 Skyhawk, the F4D Skyray, the F8U Crusader, and the F-11 Tiger. Also, we had a whole bunch of pilots that had transitioned from props to jets, from slower to faster airplanes, from straight wing to swept wing, and the accident rate was horrendously high. It was almost off the graph how many accidents we were having in large part because of poor training. In our squadron alone [flying A-4s] we killed three people in our first year in the Skyhawk.[16]

Admiral Brown was talking about the state of affairs in 1956 and 1957, a period when the mishap rate was falling sharply due to the introduction of the angled deck and the optical landing aid. A number of institutional fixes were generated, such as the founding of the Naval Aviation Safety Center in 1953, the Naval Aviation Maintenance Program in 1959, and the Naval Aviation Training and Operational Procedures Standardization (NATOPS) program in 1961. These measures had a dramatic effect; the accident rate per 100,000 flying hours plummeted from about fifty-five in 1954 to less than ten in 1971. None of this includes combat losses in Vietnam; the numbers reflect the total naval aviation rate, which includes shore-based patrol planes that had a much better safety record; even through the 1990s carrier-embarked mishap rates were always higher. Given that a single carrier air wing can fly 10,000 hours in less than three months of deployed operations, even a rate of ten is ruinous. By comparison, today's rate hovers between one and two per 100,000 hours, commensurate with that of the Air Force—an indication of the maturity of the naval aviation professional culture.

Another factor that may have contributed to the brutal accident rates of the 1950s and early 1960s was the number of different models of jets operated by the fleet. Up through 1957 new types of jets were being introduced almost every year. Combined with the lack of an effective training and standardization program, pilots would switch back and forth between models, the newer of which possessed ever-more-complex systems and more challenging flight characteristics. Mishaps were a virtual inevitability. Again, Captain O'Roarke:

But for the kids newly arrived at VC-4 [the Navy's night specialty squadron on the East Coast] from the all-prop training command and a short, night/radar course in props at Key West, sporting only about four hundred hours of total flight time, the simultaneous introduction to night, weather and jets, all done in an informal, casual manner, presented a real exercise in personal survival. This demanding environment, as might well have been expected, exacted a very heavy toll in fatal accidents.[17]

A-6 Intruder on the USS Independence's *catapult, March 1965.*

By the mid-1960s, Air Wing composition was starting to stabilize, with the introduction of the A-6, F-4, and A-7. Pilots could build up considerable experience in one type of airplane and by 1973 naval aviation had more than halved its accident rate.

Of course, some of the Navy's jets were easier to fly and more reliable than others. The F9F Panther, and its swept-wing cousin, the Cougar, were well regarded by pilots, even if they were a bit underpowered. Perhaps the most infamous of the early jets was the F7U Cutlass, a tailless fighter unaffectionately known as the "Ensign Eater." Part of the combination was also due to the operational mission of the aircraft. Some of the jets were almost exclusively used as "day fighters," which tended to limit their exposure to the more threatening flight regimes such as low-level bombing and night or bad weather carrier operations. Newer models brought both improvements—designers learned from the defects of current aircraft that were brought to light via fleet operations—but also new problems as the limits of technology were pushed. Aircraft like the F-8 Crusader and F-4 Phantom achieved much higher airspeeds than their predecessors, but at the cost of higher approach and landing speeds that reduced the margin for error in landing them aboard the carrier. Perhaps the ultimate aircraft in terms of speed and difficulty of bringing aboard was the RA-5C Vigilante. A large aircraft at around 70,000 pounds takeoff weight, it was beautiful, fast—and fragile. The combination of high approach speed, heavy weight, and no-margin structural design (to save weight) made every landing a potential accident—and many were.

However, chasing higher airspeeds was not the only technological limit that was being pushed. The introduction of the A-6 Intruder brought an all-weather, day and night attack capability to the fleet. Although the A-6 had a robust airframe and two reasonably reliable engines, it also had a complex radar navigation and attack system. Crewed by both a pilot and a Bombardier-Navigator (BN), the airplane had an incredible ability to sneak around at low level, in the mountains, at night to deliver weapons. However, there were limits to the system's reliability, and in the low level, night regime, margins for error disappeared. Many Intruders and their crews were lost in those conditions. In theory, the A-7 Corsair was supposed to operate in a similar way with a single pilot and a single engine. A rash of training accidents quickly demonstrated that this was not feasible. By comparison the night strike version of the single-seat F/A-18 proved to be perfectly capable of flying low-level night missions in the mountains, albeit in a clear air mass. The difference was massive improvement in cockpit automation and display, and the introduction of imaging infrared and light amplification technologies.

In this centennial year of naval aviation, the Navy's air arm has been jet powered for over half of its history. The transition was long and brutally expensive in terms of loss of life and aircraft. However it was, by any measure, a success. Throughout the Cold War and a series of hot wars including Korea, Vietnam, Desert Storm, and others, naval aviation has been able to provide effective tactical air power from the sea. Its ability to do this despite a long and difficult process of learning how to operate jet aircraft at sea is a tribute to the brilliance of various aircraft designers, the ingenuity of countless airdales, the sailors who struggled to keep those complex and touchy machines flying, and the bravery and perhaps foolhardiness of the crews that would climb into jets, which were hard to fly and lacked reliability, and perform missions that took them to the edge of what man and machine could do.

NOTES

1. Tommy H. Thomason, *U.S. Naval Air Superiority: Development of Shipborne Jet Fighters 1943–1962* (North Branch, MN: Specialty Press, 2007), p. 123.
2. Naval Safety Center aviation safety database. Unless otherwise cited, all mishap statistics were obtained from this source.
3. Jeffery G. Barlow, *Revolt of the Admirals* (Washington, DC: Naval Historical Center, 1994), pp. 233–89.
4. Thomason, *U.S. Naval Air Superiority*, p. 265.
5. Vice Admiral Gerald E. Miller, "Transition to the Jet Age," *Into the Jet Age*, pp. 12–13.
6. Captain Gerald O'Roarke, USN (Ret.), "We Get Ours at Night," *Into the Jet Age*, ed. Captain E. T. Wooldridge, USN (Ret.) (Annapolis: Naval Institute Press, 1995), pp. 31–32.
7. Although it might seem more appropriate to use the term "generations," it is avoided here to prevent confusion with the technical term "generations of fighters"—coined by the Navy Fighter Weapons School (Top Gun)—to describe various classes of fighters based on their performance characteristics.

8. A-3 Skywarrior Association, http://www.a3skywarrior.com/memorial/full_accident_date .htm (accessed 12 April 2009).

9. U.S. Navy LSO School, http://www.robertheffley.com/docs/CV_environ/Basic%20IFLOLS%20 Lecture%5b2%5d.ppt#259,3,From Paddles to IFLOLS (accessed 15 August 2009).

10. Major Richard A. Bauer, USMC, and Lieutenant Leo L. Hamilton, USN, "Naval Aircraft Maintenance Program," *Naval Aviation News*, February 1961, p. 25.

11. Ibid., p. 28.

12. Richard A. Eldridge, "A Look Back: Forty Years of Reminiscing," http://safetycenter.navy .mil/media/approach/theydidwhat/eldridge.htm (accessed 24 March 2009).

13. Jerry Miller, *Nuclear Weapons and Aircraft Carriers* (Washington, DC: The Smithsonian Institution Press, 2001), p. 104.

14. Steve Ewing, *Reaper Leader* (Annapolis: Naval Institute Press, 2002), pp. 198–99.

15. "The One Best Way, New Standards for Naval Air," *Naval Aviation News*, August 1961, p. 6, http://www.history.navy.mil/nan/backissues/1960s/1961/aug61.pdf (accessed 28 May 2009).

16. Oral history of Rear Admiral Thomas F. Brown III, conducted by Joseph Smith, 5 March 2002 to 24 March 2002. Naval Historical Foundation Oral History Program, 2004.

17. O'Roarke, "We Get Ours at Night," p. 26.

CHAPTER 13

Naval Aviation in the Korean and Vietnam Wars

Gary J. Ohls

THE KOREAN CONFLICT

On Sunday, 25 June 1950, the North Korean People's Army—the *In Min Gun*—attacked across the 38th parallel into the Republic of Korea (ROK) thereby initiating the Korean War.[1] Numerous provocations over the preceding two years such as raids, sabotage, guerrilla activity, infiltration, propaganda, and economic pressure had failed to bring down the Syngman Rhee government or persuade a majority of South Koreans to support a Communist takeover.[2] Meanwhile, the United States had sent ambiguous diplomatic signals regarding its commitment to Korea, and all of Asia for that matter, beyond its vital interests in Japan and the Philippines.[3] The general weakness of American military forces in the Far East coupled with their withdrawal from Korea after the establishment of the Rhee government in 1948 created an impression among Communist leaders that a conventional assault from the North could succeed where numerous subversive efforts had failed.[4] Additionally, the 1949 Communist takeover of mainland China had reinforced the notion that America would not commit ground forces on the mainland of Asia.[5] The United States had stood by as Mao Zedong's Communists forces defeated the Nationalist Chinese—an America ally throughout and after World War II—and drove them to the island of Formosa (Taiwan), at some cost to America's international stature.[6] In light of all these considerations, Communist leaders in Pyongyang, Beijing (Peking, as it was then called), and Moscow believed attacking South Korea would be a relatively low-risk operation, which could produce great strategic advantages throughout Asia.[7]

During the months leading up to the North Korean attack, U.S. intelligence services observed increasing signs of its possibility, yet the actual event achieved strategic and tactical surprise.[8] Despite the fact that many ROK units and individuals fought courageously and in some cases effectively, their weapons, equipment, training, and leadership could not match that of the North Korean People's Army (NKPA). The ROK Army had no armor to oppose the T-34 tanks—provided to North Korea by the Soviet Union—nor did they possess antitank weapons capable of stopping them.[9] They had no heavy artillery comparable to the Soviet-supplied systems, and did not have fighter planes or antiaircraft weapons with which to oppose North Korea's Soviet-supplied aircraft.[10] When coupled with the element of surprise, these deficiencies proved far too great to overcome.[11] The blatant nature of the North Korean attack supported by weapons, material, and training from the Soviet Union caused many American leaders to see a similar pattern in which "Hitler, Mussolini and the Japanese had acted ten, fifteen, and twenty years earlier."[12]

In the days immediately following Kim Il-sung's invasion of the Republic of Korea, important events took place in New York and Washington D.C. The United Nations passed a resolution that condemned the attack as an act of aggression, ordered North Korea to cease operations and withdraw its forces, and called on member nations to assist the United Nations in resisting the action.[13] The Soviet delegation would surely have blocked this resolution had they not been boycotting Security Council meetings at the time, in protest against its refusal to seat the People's Republic of China.[14] Ostensively the war in Korea would be fought under the auspices of the UN; but in essence, it would be an American conflict despite the small contribution of a few allies.[15] The UN action provided the Truman administration a certain amount of international and domestic cover, allowing the United States to take action that might otherwise be problematic.

Among other things, the president of the United States ordered General Douglas MacArthur to take command of all U.S. forces in Korea, conduct evacuation of American citizens, provide ammunition and equipment to South Korean forces, and move the U.S. Seventh Fleet—under command of Vice Admiral Arthur D. Struble—north from the Philippines. He also authorized the use of air and naval forces to protect all such activity and for a survey team to evaluate the situation on the peninsula and determine what the United States could do to assist the Republic of Korea.[16] The president expanded MacArthur's area of responsibility to include Formosa and ordered the Seventh Fleet to protect that island nation against attack from Communist China.[17] In addition to defending Formosa, Seventh Fleet would also inhibit Chiang Kai-shek from using the crisis as a pretext to attack mainland China, thereby expanding the war.[18] The earliest American combat action of this conflict involved an effort to keep open the air and sea points of embarkation for emergency evacuation. When North Korean YAK fighters attacked U.S. Air Force

F-80 Shooting Star and F-82 Twin Mustang aircraft covering the evacuation of civilians over Inchon, American pilots splashed three of the Communist aircraft and later shot down four more over Seoul.[19]

Despite the unpreparedness of U.S. forces, President Harry S. Truman believed he must prevent a Communist takeover of South Korea even if it meant going to war.[20] In Truman's view, this crisis constituted a critical test of will between the two international blocks—free democracies and totalitarian Communism—that had evolved since the end of World War II.[21] It was a decision widely supported at the time by the American people and the U.S. Congress.[22] Within days of the North Korean attack, the Truman administration authorized MacArthur to use American ground forces to halt the North Korean advance.[23] Of course, this would be problematic since the United States had chosen to scuttle its military might in the aftermath of World War II.[24] Ultimately, it would take full application of American air, naval, and amphibious capability as well as the activation of four National Guard divisions and numerous reserves to reverse the fortunes of war in Korea.[25] Carrier-based naval air power along with land- and carrier-based Marine Corps close air support would prove crucial in the hard fighting American forces faced during three years of the Korean War.[26]

American planes of the Far Eastern Air Force—under command of Lieutenant General George E. Stratemeyer—not only engaged North Korean YAKs during evacuation operations at Inchon and Seoul, but also conducted some to the earliest offensive actions of the Korean War. B-29 Superfortresses and B-26 Invaders flew missions against targets in North Korea, and—in conjunction with F-80 Shooting Stars—attempted to provide support to allied ground troops in the South.[27] The U.S. Navy also conducted early offensive action with the first major strike coming from aircraft of Seventh Fleet's Task Force 77 off USS *Valley Forge* on 3 July 1950. These carrier planes, consisting of F9F Panthers, F4U corsairs, and AD Skyraiders, attacked the North Korea capital at Pyongyang and other targets, destroying much of the North Korean air force in the process.[28] Throughout the month of July, Task Force 77—including the Royal Navy's HMS *Triumph* and several British escorts—attacked enemy targets in both North and South Korea, while Task Force 96 (a surface action group consisting of one cruiser and four destroyers) provided naval gunfire in support of South Korean forces retreating down the peninsula toward Pusan.[29] The F-80 Shooting Star served as the preeminent U.S. Air Force plane in the theater at that time, but it was primarily a fighter-interceptor. Although superior to anything the North Koreans had, these planes were not ideal in the ground support role. Additionally, they primarily flew out of bases in Japan carrying limited ordnance loads due to their fuel requirements. Therefore, they had minimal time on station once they arrived over Korea. As a result, the only substantial air support available to U.S. and ROK ground forces during much of the early fighting came from carrier-based tactical air.[30]

U.S. Navy Fighters F4U Corsairs return to carrier USS Boxer *(CV-21) after a strike over Korea, September 1951.*

The outbreak of the Korean War found the United States near the nadir of its post–World War II disarmament. Although the National Security Act of 1947 and its addendum of 1949 purported to strengthen the U.S. military, they fell far short of that goal. Besides, even the most effective legislation could not have overcome the severe budget reductions imposed on the military by Congress and enthusiastically carried out by the Truman administration.[31] Of course, this created enormous inter-Service rivalry for resources, roles, and missions.[32] Additionally, the newly formed U.S. Air Force had made a disruptive play for control of all air missions during the postwar unification battles, including those developed and performed by naval aviation.[33] Many leaders within the defense establishment questioned the need for carrier-based air power anyway, believing that land-based bombers could assume all Navy missions. Secretary of Defense Louis A. Johnson had ungraciously stated to Admiral Richard L. Conolly just six months before the Communist invasion of South Korea, "Admiral, the Navy is on its way out. . . . There's no reason for having a Navy and Marine Corps. General [Omar] Bradley tells me that amphibious operations are a thing of the past. We'll never have any more amphibious operations. That does away with the Marine Corps. And the Air Force can do anything the Navy can nowadays, so that does away with the Navy."[34] Johnson underscored his myopic view of defense planning by canceling the Navy's modern super carrier project, USS *United States,* and promoting a strategic bomber of questionable design and excessive cost named the B-36 Peacemaker.[35] The subsequent B-36 debate and controversy had the unfortunate effect of focusing the Air Force's thinking primarily on strategic air power at the expense of tactical capability.[36] To the extent that naval aviation continued to develop in the constrained and conflicted environment of the late 1940s, it did so in an era of technological change, including the transition from propeller to jet propulsion and the consequent need to move toward more capable carriers.[37]

By 1950, cost-cutting measures had programmed the Navy to retain only five fleet carriers despite the clear beginnings of a Cold War with the Soviet Union. Of course, the U.S. government had mothballed large quantities of ships and other combat systems at the end of World War II with the intention of refurbishing them for future wars, if and when necessary.[38] In the event, nineteen enhanced *Essex*-class carriers eventually returned to service by the end of the Korean War, fully equipped with operational air groups. This revitalization of naval aviation permitted four carriers to operate continuously in Korean waters while maintaining two in the Mediterranean in support of NATO strategy through the end of the war. Despite Secretary Johnson's arrogant claims of the demise of the Navy and Marine Corps, carrier aircraft—under Navy and Marine Corps leadership—flew more than 30 percent of all combat sorties of the Korean War.[39] This naval air power, coupled with land-based Air Force capability, proved essential to American operations against the vastly superior manpower that the Chinese Army brought to the fighting when it entered the war in the final months of 1950.

Despite air attacks against the invading *In Min Gun* and introduction of U.S. ground units, American and South Korean forces could not halt the Communist onslaught until sufficient reinforcements arrived in country. The cumulative effect of the fighting by sea, land, and air forces, coupled with an effective reinforcement effort, eventually halted the North Korean offensive just short of the city of Pusan, thereby permitting American and South Korean forces to retain a toehold on the southeast corner of the peninsula. The American ground troops initially introduced into Korea consisted of ill-trained and inadequately equipped elements of Major General William F. Dean's 24th Infantry Division based in Japan.[40] Subsequent reinforcements included the 1st Cavalry Division—which landed unopposed at the port of Pohang just north of Pusan—and the 25th Infantry Division. None of these units was combat ready in terms of their authorized strength, the adequacy of their weapons, or the state of their training. Largely, this resulted from a general view among Americans and their leaders that the United States would fight any future war principally with air power and nuclear weapons. Few believed that hard fighting by ground forces such as occurred in World War II would ever again be required.[41]

During the latter part of July, the defenses of the Pusan Perimeter began to stabilize under command of Lieutenant General Walton H. Walker's Eighth Army headquarters. By early August, Walker's forces included five ROK divisions, three U.S. divisions—the 24th, the 25th, and the 1st Cavalry—along with the 5th Regimental Combat Team from Hawaii. Additionally, U.S. replacements, reinforcements, and supplies continued pouring in at the port of Pusan from around the world.[42] Shipments included weapons more able to deal with the Communist T-34 tanks, which had previously been difficult to stop by ground forces.[43] In these early weeks of fighting in Korea, several things became obvious to American commanders. Most significantly, the Communists had found a way to negate America's nuclear advantage by waging war at a level below the nuclear threshold. It was equally apparent that although air power could not win the conventional war that Communist forces had imposed, "it could and did prevent the North from overrunning the South."[44]

By early September, it became clear that "the United States would not be driven off the Korean Peninsula."[45] Also by this time, the United States had three aircraft carriers on station, which provided air support to American and South Korean forces while attacking the *In Min Gun*'s lengthening lines of communications.[46] These, and subsequent carriers assigned to Task Force 77, consisted of *Essex*-class fleet carriers capable of conducting jet aircraft operations. In addition to *Valley Forge,* the carriers on station early in the war included *Philippine Sea, Leyte,* and *Boxer.* In August, elements of the 1st Marine Aircraft Wing arrived from the United States with F4U Corsair squadrons embarked on the escort carriers *Badoeng Strait* and *Sicily* thereby constituting Task Element 96.23.[47] This Marine Air Group, MAG-33, was actually a task organized element of the 1st Provisional Marine Brigade that included the 5th Marine Regiment as its ground combat element.[48] Although the Marine Corsairs flew close air support missions for all ground forces fighting in Korea, they primarily supported units of the 1st Marine Division through a highly synergistic relationship that presaged the modern Marine Air Ground Task Force (MAGTF). In the course of the war, six escort carriers with Marine Corps squadrons embarked served in Korean waters.[49]

The typical air group on *Essex*-class fleet carriers consisted of two F9F Panther jet squadrons, one F4U Corsair squadron, and one AD Skyraider squadron.[50] Ideal in the fighter-intercept role, the Panther also saw service in support of ground operations, and its bomb- and rocket-carrying capacity increased during the war to where it could routinely carry 1,200 pounds of ordnance. The propeller-driven Corsairs could carry 3,000 pounds and the Skyraiders 8,000.[51] The U.S. Far East Air Force quickly recognized the superiority of the Navy's aircraft mix for the ground attack mission, and sought to improve its ability to support directly the fighting troops. Since Navy squadrons received all available Corsairs and Skyraiders, the Air Force drew on an outstanding World War II fighter that also performed relatively well in the ground attack role, the F-51 (P-51) Mustang.[52] They also upgraded their fighter-intercept capability to the F-84 Thunderjet and then to the F-86 Sabre, the only American or allied airplane that could consistently defeat the Communists' MiG-15, which entered the fray in November 1950.[53] Once the U.S. Air Force established its squadrons on the Korean peninsula—after a reversal in the fortunes of war—it proved to be a formidable force in the fighting.[54] As the war played out, tactical air support came from 7th Fleet's Task Force 77, Marine Corsairs off escort carriers and land bases, and ground-based squadrons within South Korea under Fifth Air Force. Once the Air Force established F-86 Sabres on the peninsula to provide fighter cover against the MiG-15, American air superiority in Korea was never in question, although the duel between MiG-15s and F-86 Sabres continued throughout the war.[55]

In the early weeks of the Korean War, as the *In Min Gun* drove down the peninsula, circumstances constrained the Air Force's ability to provide close air support to American and South Korean ground forces. The F-80 Shooting Star was not ideally suited for this mission, and it had to restrict the ordnance carried due to the fuel requirements of flying from bases in Japan. This limited firepower, coupled with the short time the jets could remain on station, made for inefficient use of the aircraft. But the Navy and Marine Corps could fly support missions from carriers, which moved close to the battle areas and delivered Corsairs and Skyraiders with generous ordnance loads.[56] Of course, many problems remained, including communications between air and ground forces as well as coordination between Task Force 77 and Fifth Air Force's Joint Operation Center.[57] Yet these problems improved as the war progressed. Once Air Force squadrons relocated their operating bases from Japan to South Korea, after the Army pushed back the *In Min Gun*, their contribution became much greater. Throughout the Korean War, the close air support provided by Navy, Marine Corps, and Air Force aircraft remained the key to success for units fighting on the ground.[58]

Even though close air support constituted the most crucial mission for naval air power in the early weeks of the Korean War, pilots also performed other important tasks. On 18 July, *Valley Forge* launched seven F9F Panther jets to conduct an armed reconnaissance along the eastern coast of North Korea. At the port of Wonsan, they identified the vital Wonsan Oil Refining Factory entirely untouched by the war. Later that afternoon, *Valley Forge* launched a flight of ten Corsairs loaded with rockets and 20-mm ammunition along with eleven Skyraiders carrying rockets, 500-pound bombs, and 1,000-pound bombs. Arriving over Wonsan, the Navy planes swarmed above the refinery attacking first with rockets, then with bombs, leaving it in a state of twisted steel and piled rubble. The naval aviators could observe the towering column of smoke from sixty miles away and it took four days for the fire to burn out. The attack damaged the facility beyond repair and destroyed some 12,000 tons of refined petroleum, at no loss of American planes or pilots.[59] Like the earlier attacks against Pyongyang and other North Korean targets, this assault obliterated its target area, demonstrating the flexibility and destructive capability of U.S. naval air power.

In the early weeks of the Korean War, American naval aviation units implemented a number of innovations. The first combat use of an ejection seat occurred during August when Lieutenant Carl Dace's F9F Panther received ground fire while strafing a North Korean target. After some considerable maneuvering, Dace made it out to sea where he jettisoned his canopy, shot into the air, separated from his seat, opened his parachute, and descended into the water below. Several hours later, a destroyer rescued the damp aviator from his raft.[60] Another innovation involved the military application of rotary-wing aircraft. Helicopters were just beginning to come of age in 1950, and the Navy and Marine Corps found numerous opportunities for their use. Relying primarily on the Sikorsky HO3S, the Sea Service's aviators initially used these new machines for air rescue and as plane guard during carrier operations.[61] As we shall see, the role of helicopters continued to grow throughout the course of the Korean War.

During the first weeks of August, General Walker and his Eighth Army fought a continuous series of hard battles to prevent the *In Min Gun* from breaking through the Pusan Perimeter.[62] Much of this fighting benefited from the close air support provided by Marine Corsairs flying off *Badoeng Strait* and *Sicily*.[63] On 17 August, Walker attacked a particularly dangerous North Korean position known as Obong-ni (also known as No Name Ridge because reporters did not initially know its real name) that formed a bulge into the American lines. Previous efforts to dislodge the *In Min Gun* had been unsuccessful, but this time Walker's attack included a relatively fresh unit, the 1st Provisional Marine Brigade commanded by Brigadier General Edward A. Craig. The ground combat element of the brigade amounted to nothing more than a reinforced Marine regiment. A week earlier, ground combat Marines of the 1st Provisional Brigade, teaming with their aviation brethren, had demonstrated the effectiveness of the Marine Air-Ground concept by devastating an NKPA motorized regiment during an attack near the town of Kosong in the southern part of the Pusan Perimeter.[64]

Consisting of the 5th Marine Regiment, Marine Air Group 33, and a combat logistics element, the 1st Provisional Marine Brigade was the lead component of the 1st Marine Division and the 1st Marine Aircraft Wing. General MacArthur had specifically requested this force for the amphibious counterstroke he planned to launch against the North Korean Army.[65] But the situation in the Pusan Perimeter proved too critical to reserve the Marines for some future action. From the time of their arrival off Korea, the Marine Corsair squadrons launched ground-attack sorties, often in conjunction with naval carrier aircraft and Air Force F-51 Mustangs flying out of tightly packed bases within the Perimeter.[66] The 5th Marines, under command of Lieutenant Colonel Raymond L. Murray, working in conjunction with U.S. Army units, would now assault the most critical threat to the Pusan Perimeter, and they would do so under the cover of Marine Corsairs flying off *Badoeng Strait* and *Sicily*.[67]

In two days of very hard fighting, Marines on the ground teamed with Marines in the air to drive the North Korean forces from Obong-ni ridge and across the Nakton River thereby eliminating the dangerous salient.[68] This did not end the fighting along the Pusan Perimeter as the *In Min Gun* desperately tried to drive American and South Korean forces off the peninsula before reaching their culminating point. But U.S. Army and ROK forces on the ground and Navy, Air Force, and Australian planes in the air would undertake the subsequent fighting at Pusan without their Marine component.[69] In the first week of September, Marines of the 1st Provisional Brigade loaded on amphibious shipping and joined their fellow units of the 1st Marine Division then arriving from the United States. Their destination would be the port city of Inchon where they would conduct a remarkable amphibious landing, resulting in a dramatic reversal in the fortunes of war.

Operation Chromite, the amphibious landing at Inchon and subsequent capture of Kimpo airfield and the capital city of Seoul, began on 15 September 1950 with the Marine landing force securing Wolmi-do Island under fire.[70] Of course, the planning and preparation had begun well before that date including an extensive effort by General MacArthur to persuade civilian and military leaders in Washington of the efficacy of his plan.[71] In the minds of many high-ranking leaders, MacArthur's concept was not only bold, but also highly risky. The geography and hydrography of that area made the approaches treacherous, with tides averaging twenty-three feet and a strong tidal current that further complicated navigation.[72] In the Supreme Commander's view, all these difficulties would cause his enemy to discount the possibility of a landing at Inchon and thereby ensure the element of surprise. In MacArthur's mind, catching the NKPA unaware and unprepared would more than make up for the physical and tactical problems of landing at Inchon. Ultimately, MacArthur got his way as well as the forces he believed he needed to conduct the operation.[73] These included the 1st Marine Division, the 7th Infantry Division, and the largest assemblage of naval air power since the end of World War II. The Fifth Air Force provided a supporting role by neutralizing North Korean airfields, cutting railroads and bridges, conducting reconnaissance, and providing tactical air support to Eighth Army at the Pusan Perimeter.[74]

During the transit from Japan and the Pusan Perimeter to Inchon, naval aircraft operating from *Sicily, Badoeng Strait, Valley Forge, Philippine Sea,* and HMS *Triumph* lashed out at targets in the objective area as well as other locations along the coast to diminish enemy capability and keep them guessing as to the actual landing site.[75] Additionally, aircraft flying off *Valley Forge* flew regular photoreconnaissance missions, providing current intelligence and updated targeting information. As the Amphibious Task Force moved toward the objective area on 14 September (D-1), carrier aircraft attacked the landing sites, followed by surface fires from supporting cruisers and destroyers.[76] The carrier planes alternated with surface guns throughout the day, focusing much of their fires on Wolmi-do Island where the Marines would make their initial landing. As the assault force made its way to Green Beach on Wolmi-do in the early hours of 15 September, twenty-eight Marine Corsairs covered the final run-in as four destroyers continued to provide surface gunfire support.[77]

The Marines of 3rd Battalion, 5th Marines, captured Wolmi-do Island by 0800 in the morning on D-day, and turned toward So Wolmi-do (a small island attached by causeway to Wolmi-do) which they captured by late morning. On receiving a message that the beachhead had been secured, MacArthur turned to Rear Admiral James H. Doyle, Commander of the Amphibious Task Force, and said: "Please send this message to the fleet: 'The Navy and Marines have never shone more brightly than this morning.'"[78] In accomplishing this first phase of the operation, the Marines suffered only seventeen casualties, none of which proved fatal. They now prepared for a potential counterattack across the causeway from Inchon and waited for the tide to rise for the next phase of the complex operation. During this time, Skyraiders from Task Force 77 continued to isolate the battlefield by interdicting enemy movement and attacking various targets.[79] Carrier-based aircraft also concentrated fire on the next landing sites including Beach Red, north of Wolmi-do Island in Inchon proper, and Beach Blue, south of Wolmi-do in slightly more open country. The task force commander set H-hour for 1750 at which time the First and Second battalions of the Fifth Marines under Lieutenant Colonel Raymond Murray assaulted Red Beach and the First Marines under legendary Colonel Lewis B. "Chesty" Puller assaulted Blue Beach.[80] By the end of the day, the Navy had landed 13,000 troops along with their weapons and equipment, and the landing force had secured all objectives. The cost in blood for the first day of fighting amounted to 21 killed and 174 wounded.[81] The uniform success of this D-day operation owed much to the professionalism and courage of the Marines of the landing force, of course. Yet the importance of overwhelming close air support provided by Navy and Marine carrier aircraft on this day and in subsequent fighting ashore cannot be overstated. On D-day alone, these pilots flew 344 sorties at the loss of two aircraft. The carriers would maintain that high-intensity level throughout the two weeks of the Inchon-Seoul operation.[82]

On 16 September, the Marines continued the attack to capture Kimpo airfield while the 7th Infantry Division landed in trace (i.e., behind the 1st Marine Division, the initial assault force) and moved south toward Suwon to recapture its airfield and prepare for a linkup with the Eighth Army upon its breakout from the Pusan Perimeter.[83] Much of this fighting by Eighth Army and X Corps (the parent command of the Marines and Army units conducting the Inchon-Seoul operation) proved to be very fierce. By 20 September, the Marines began their assault on Seoul and one week later secured the city. On 29 September 1950, MacArthur returned Seoul to Syngman Rhee and restored civil government to the Republic of Korea.[84] As Walker's Eighth Army attacked out of the Pusan Perimeter, it met desperate resistance initially, "but with supplies gone, caught between pincers, and without retreat routes available, he [the enemy] gave way at an accelerated rate."[85] The collapse of the *In Min Gun* went from a precipitate withdrawal to complete disintegration in which Kim Il-sung's experienced and hardened troops abandoned their arms and equipment while surrendering in droves. "Within a month, the total of Red captives rose to 130,000."[86]

In late September, MacArthur received amplifying instructions directing the destruction of remaining North Korean units, including operations north of the 38th parallel.[87] By 20 October, Eighth Army initiated an attack on the North Korean capital city of Pyongyang, which quickly fell, while X Corps landed at Wonsan on the east coast of Korea.[88] Over 3,000 expertly laid magnetic and contact mines delayed the landing, and it ultimately required a concerted effort by naval aircraft, helicopters, and surface minesweepers to clear Wonsan Harbor and land the Marines. The NKPA commanders had clearly learned a hard lesson from the Inchon operation, and thereafter mined all the major harbors they could access. By the time the Wonsan landing occurred, ROK Army units had cleared the area of light *In Min Gun* resistance, and the Marines went ashore unopposed.[89] Subsequently, X Corps landed U.S. 7th Infantry further north at Iwon and an ROK force at Tanchon. Despite the delay at Wonsan, the drive to the Yalu had begun.

For the march into North Korea, MacArthur's Far East Command divided air support between Fifth Air Force, which supported Eighth Army moving north from Pyongyang on the west side of the peninsula, and Task Force 77 supporting X Corps to the east. Initially, Task Force 77 controlled all air activity in the Wonsan area, but that changed when Air Force leaders argued that the arrangement would lessen coordination of Allied tactical air in Korea. As a result, MacArthur placed 1st Marine Air Wing under control of Fifth Air Force although it remained primarily in support of X Corps.[90] Doctrinal differences between Air Force procedures and those of the Navy and Marine Corps created problems that became apparent early in the war and were never fully reconciled.[91] Yet this command arrangement for aviation units remained in place through the end of the war. Despite ongoing problems and general dissatisfaction among Navy and Marine Corps commanders, the relationship worked, as evidenced by subsequent combat actions in both North and South Korea.[92] For example, during the fighting around the Chosin reservoir and subsequent march to the sea in December 1950, after the Chinese Communists entered the war, ground units of the 1st Marine Division were covered by one of the heaviest concentrations of aircraft of the whole war, consisting exclusively of carrier-based planes of the Marine Corps and Navy.[93]

Clearly, close air support proved to be among the most important missions for both carrier air power and the fighting units on the ground; and this remained true throughout the Korean War. Yet naval aviation provided numerous other functions that contributed substantially to American's military effort during the conflict. Among the more important of these were interdiction missions, armed reconnaissance, and Air Group strikes. The latter involved scheduled attacks consisting of thirty to fifty aircraft against fixed objectives such as bridges, dams, or industrial areas. In these strike packages, the Corsairs and Skyraiders typically carried heavy ordnance loads while Panther jets provided air cover and suppressed ground fire with rockets and 20-mm gunfire. Air Group strikes proved particularly significant early in the war before American air power had destroyed most high-value targets.[94]

The interdiction missions involved strikes to disrupt the flow of war material from enemy supply bases to their front lines. Once the Chinese entered the war in late 1950, this became a particularly lucrative, though difficult, area for exploitation. Since the U.S. Navy controlled the seas and dominated major ports such as Wonsan, Hungnam, and Chongjin, Communist leaders had to rely on railroads and the primitive road system for re-supply. This resulted in a cat-and-mouse game between the planes of Task Force 77 and their enemy on the ground who frustrated the aviators by hiding trains within tunnels, moving primarily at night, and emplacing automatic weapons at key positions to protect locomotives and major staging areas. As the war progressed, these missions became increasingly dangerous for the planes and pilots of Task Force 77.[95] Yet the interdiction sorties had a major impact on deliveries at the front, particularly ammunition of all types, which Mao Zedong's army used in great quantities. The deep interdiction mission also focused against troop concentrations and key transportation centers twenty to forty miles behind the front, especially after the Chinese entered the war.[96] The most famous interdiction operation of the war occurred during March and April 1951 against two bridges in the Kilchu-Songjin area. This action became known as the Battle of Carlson's Canyon due to the damage inflicted by a squadron of Skyraiders commanded by Lieutenant Commander Harold G. "Swede" Carlson flying off USS *Princeton*.

The Battle of Carlson's Canyon involved a thirty-day sequence of bridge bombing, bombing the efforts to repair the bridge, and confronting clever efforts to bypass the bridge.[97] Not only did this prove frustrating, but also these and other targeted bridges became great anti-aircraft traps for the pilots of Task Force 77.[98] The Battle for Carlson's Canyon became the real-life model for James A. Michener's novel *The Bridges at Toko-ri* and subsequent movie of the same name. In his role as correspondent, Michener spent several weeks on board *Essex* and *Valley Forge,* becoming familiar with the people and missions of their Air Groups, whom he also used as models for his fictionalized version of the naval air war in Korea.[99] Carlson's squadron of Skyraiders later succeeded in destroying the sluice gates of the Hwachon Dam after previous efforts by air and land had failed, earning his unit the nickname "Dambusters." The complexity of this mission required an unconventional approach and the *Princeton*'s aviators responded by using aerial torpedoes left over from World War II. If other missions had established the destructive power of naval aviation, the attack on Hwachon Dam demonstrated its flexibility and capacity for innovation.[100]

The armed reconnaissance mission proved particularly valuable in areas that artillery or naval gunfire could not cover, such as mountainous areas of North Korea. Conducted primarily by F9F Panther jets of Task Force 77, these actions focused on the primitive road network. A typical mission consisted of four Panthers (two sections of two planes each) loaded with rockets, bombs, and 20-mm ammunition. After clearing the beach at ten thousand feet, the aircraft would descend and move to their patrol area looking for targets to attack. The lead plane would fly at three hundred feet followed by a second plane at one thousand. The second section consisting of the third and fourth plane would follow at about three thousand feet to provide air cover and assist in navigation. The lead pilot served as a spotter in identifying targets and threats for the second, which conducted the actual attack. This action would occur at a speed of about 250–300 knots, and typically in very rugged terrain. After the attacking plane expended its ordnance, it would rotate with the lead plane, and then the sections would rotate until all aircraft had exhausted their loads.[101]

The military use of helicopters evolved significantly during the course of the Korean War. Initially used for observation and evacuation, innovative leaders quickly devised other important applications such as laying communications wire and telephone cables, night casualty evacuation, search and rescue, covert operations, gunfire spotting, minesweeping, and transporting troops and supplies through vertical envelopment, including ship-to-shore movement.[102] Arrival of Marine Helicopter Transport Squadron (HMR)-161, operating the larger Sikorsky HRS-1 transport helicopter in the spring of 1951, made possible the first mass helicopter re-supply in history, named Operation Windmill 1, in which 18,848 pounds of gear and seventy-four Marines were moved a distance of some seven miles in twenty-eight flights. Similar evolutions including operations Summit and Bumblebee occurred in the following weeks, helping to establish the helicopter as an important tactical system. Helicopters evacuated nearly ten thousand Marines in the course of the Korean War during which over one thousand flights occurred at night. Although the Navy made use of helicopters in Korea as well, Marines accomplished most of the battlefield innovation with the Army and Air Force essentially uninvolved until the latter part of the war.[103]

After the large-scale Chinese entry into the war in November and December 1950, the battles moved several times into South Korea and then back to the north as each side launched major offensive operations.[104] During this fighting from 1951 through 1953, naval aviation executed numerous and various roles. Planes of Task Force 77 undertook considerable air action in conjunction with the Air Force's massive interdiction effort known as Operation Strangle and its successor, Operation Saturate.[105] Other functions included, on 25 August 1951, the first ever use of carrier fighters to escort Air Force bombers over hostile territory. This period of the war also marked a time of greater cooperation between the Air Force and naval aviation units in joint targeting and operational planning.[106] Of course, as the war progressed, numerous changes occurred in the nature of the naval air war. Among other things, the ratio of jet aircraft sorties to propeller planes increased significantly. This resulted from adjustments made in aircraft employment as well as introduction of the F2H Banshee jet in the fighter-bomber role.[107] The Banshee could outperform the Panther in both the intercept and ground attack mode, and proved particularly effective against bridges and railroads. It also served as a superb photoreconnaissance aircraft in its F2H-2P variant. Additionally, introduction of the F3D Skyknight night fighter during the war augmented the Panther and Banshee in their fighter-intercept role. Among other advantages, the Skyknight had a sophisticated radar system that could identify enemy aircraft approaching from both front and rear. It proved particularly valuable in escorting Air Force B-29s on nighttime bombing runs. Although not as effective against the MiG-15 as the F-86 Sabre, all three of these Navy fighters could often defeat MiG challengers due to the superior training of the Navy and Marine Corps pilots.[108]

Changes in the concept of carrier employment also occurred in the course of the war from a blue-water replacement for the battleship to that of a more littoral and land-focused platform. This led to the idea of aircraft carriers operating throughout the world in environments where land-based air power may not be available. Secretary of State Henry Kissinger personified his evolving view of the utility of the carrier many years later with his famous question during times of crisis, "Where are the carriers?"[109] Of course, carriers themselves underwent significant enhancements beginning with upgrades to *Essex*-class ships. This led to development of the big deck super carriers including the *Forrestal* class in 1955 followed by the nuclear-powered *Enterprise* and *Nimitz* classes.[110]

A need for carrier-based fighters that could compete with the Communist MiG-15 in air-to-air combat as effectively as the Air Force F-86 Sabre influenced the development of the F-8 Crusader and F-4 Phantom II, both of which performed well against the MiG-17, MiG-19, and MiG-21 in Vietnam. Modernization of naval ground attack capability resulted in production of the superb A-4 Skyhawk light attack jet.[111] Further, the need for an all-weather, night strike plane led to production of the A-6 Intruder (along with its electronic warfare variant, the EA-6B Prowler), another weapon system that performed very well in Southeast Asia and subsequently. The tactical maturing of the helicopter during the war had an impact on land combat like few innovations in military history. This constitutes another important area where the experiences and lessons of the Korean War profoundly affected events a few years later in Vietnam.[112] Regrettably, this good use of lessons learned and improvement in warfighting did not extend itself to an understanding of the role of strategy in warfare—and the importance of adequacy in strategy—once the United States committed itself to the conflict in Southeast Asia.[113] Having accepted war without victory in Korea, American leaders twenty years later found it possible to accept defeat for the first time ever in Vietnam.[114] The most important lesson of Korea and of the history of warfare in general is that wars are won by adequate strategy and not tactical or operational excellence alone. This seems to have been completely lost on America's leaders of the 1960s.[115]

THE VIETNAM CONFLICT

The United States went to war in Vietnam to stop aggressive Communism, just as it had in Korea, but numerous differences existed in both the road to war and in its execution. Among the most notable was the gradual nature in which American leaders moved the nation toward engagement. Unlike the Communist invasion of South Korea in 1950, there was no main force attack across a recognized border that could rally international outrage. Apparently the Vietnamese Communists had learned from the mistake of Kim Il-sung in this regard.[116] The leaders of North Vietnam cloaked their aggression under a banner of ideology and nationalism with a heavy coating of ambiguity. Unlike North Korean leaders, they cleverly avoided creating an image in their persons or actions that would stand comparison to the aggressive acts of Nazi Germany and Imperial Japan (or for that matter, Communist North Korea).

Another significant difference between Vietnam and Korea involves the state of American military preparedness. Unlike the almost criminal neglect of the U.S. armed forces in the late 1940s, American's military Services entered Vietnam well prepared, probably better prepared than in any of its previous wars. Of course, the U.S. Army was primarily prepared to fight a conventional war and not an insurgency, which constituted a major part of the Vietnam War in its earlier phases.[117] This situation resulted from the Cold War orientation of military leaders of that period, and should not detract from the general quality of the Services. As noted before, all Services had learned many lessons from the Korean War and integrated subsequent improvements into their planning, procurement, training, and Service cultures. It seems the only lesson unlearned was the need for an adequate strategy that would match U.S. policy objectives, adapt America's superb military capability to the needs of the Vietnam War, and turn tactical and operational supremacy into strategic success.[118] That lesson was the responsibility of America's civilian and military leaders at the highest level, and one in which they failed utterly.

North Vietnam's Communist leader, Ho Chi Minh, initially thought that he could bring down the South Vietnamese government through political action and internal agitation. Yet the government of Ngo Dinh Diem not only survived those efforts, but also began taking effective action against Communist leaders and organizations throughout the South. By 1959 Ho and his colleagues believed it necessary to launch an armed insurgency to achieve their objective. This began on a large scale in July of that year with the infiltration of some four thousand well-trained cadre men into South Vietnam. From that point on, events began to favor the Communists, and by 1961, the Viet Cong appeared on the verge of victory.[119] By this time, the United States was deeply involved in the affairs of South Vietnam and the prospect of its collapse revived memories of the Communist victory in the Chinese civil war, and the political recriminations it created within the United States.[120] This presented a problem requiring delicate attention at the highest level of government.

As early as 1950, the United States had established a Military Assistance Advisory Group (MAAG) in Saigon to oversee disbursement of financial aid and delivery of armaments to the French during their Indochina War.[121] This grew into a mechanism for supporting the government of South Vietnam and eventually included U.S. military advisers to the South Vietnamese armed forces.[122] In the early 1960s, President John F. Kennedy and his administration began to consider, for the first time, the prospect of sending U.S. ground combat forces into the conflict. It was an unappealing prospect, and one that Kennedy avoided, deciding instead for increased financial and material support along with sending additional military advisers.[123] This surge of American support, coupled with more aggressive action by South Vietnamese forces, stabilized the situation for a time. The increased American commitment included contingents of U.S. Army and Marine Corps helicopters designed to enhance the mobility of the Army of Vietnam (ARVN). The Marine element—named Operation Shufly—continued to perform that mission until March 1964 at which time it was absorbed into the larger effort under way in Vietnam.[124] In addition to advisers, aviation units, and support elements in South Vietnam, U.S. carriers patrolled the Vietnam coastline throughout the early 1960s, launching unarmed reconnaissance aircraft as well as search and rescue helicopters when any of the aircraft were lost.[125] The role of naval aviation in the Vietnam War began with America's earliest involvement and remained an essential element across a wide spectrum of missions throughout.

The aircraft carriers of the Vietnam era included *Essex-* (upgraded), *Midway-*, and *Forrestal*-class ships and USS *Enterprise*. They typically carried Air Wings of two fighter squadrons, two or three attack squadrons, early warning and photoreconnaissance planes, and varying detachments of helicopters. The *Essex* carriers could

U.S. Navy F-4B Phantom II from the USS Ranger, *February 1968.*

support F-8 Crusader fighters, A-1 (formerly AD) Skyraiders, and A-4 Skyhawk attack planes. When the Skyraiders were withdrawn from the fleet in early 1968, they were replaced with additional squadrons of Skyhawks. On the big-deck *Forrestal* carriers, at least one of the fighter squadrons would consist of F-4 Phantom II jets. When the A-6 Intruder bombers reached the fleet in 1965, they also resided on *Forrestal* carriers as did the next generation of light attack planes, the A-7 Corsair II.[126] These carriers and their escorts were less mobile in Vietnam than during Korea due primarily to geography. Whereas the peninsular character of Korea provided ample opportunity for carriers to reposition themselves to best support their missions, the linear coastline of Vietnam along the South China Sea did not lend itself to such action. The carriers in Southeast Asia operated about 150 miles offshore from a reference point east of the Demilitarized Zone (DMZ) named Yankee Station. As in the Korean War, carriers and Air Groups from Seventh Fleet's Task Force 77 performed a variety of missions in support of the war effort.

Although carrier air tended to focus on North Vietnam early in the war, it so impressed General William Westmoreland that he requested a second station farther south from which to conduct naval air operations in South Vietnam. In response, the Navy created a point off the South Vietnamese coast southeast of Cam Ranh Bay, which it named Dixie Station. This southern position normally had a lower priority for carriers than Yankee Station because Air Force and Marine Corps tactical aircraft were also available from land bases in South Vietnam and Thailand with which to support ground operations.[127] Since Yankee Station primarily supported operations in North Vietnam, it was usually more active and typically had at least three carriers on station permitting twenty-four-hour operations. It was not unusual for there to be four or five carriers on Yankee Station and the count even went as high as six at one point late in the war.[128]

By the end of 1962, the United States had over 11,000 military personnel in South Vietnam consisting primarily of advisers, pilots, and support personnel. Throughout this early period, officials denied that Americans engaged in combat in South Vietnam. Yet advisers went into battle with their assigned units, and pilots flew combat missions in support of operations from the earliest days, often under the guise of training or advising. Predictably, Americans began taking casualties during this time, including thirty-two killed in action during 1961–1962.[129] In February 1962, Washington transformed the MAAG into an overarching organization to coordinate assistance and operations, renaming it the Military Assistance Command, Vietnam (MACV), with General Paul D. Harkins assigned as commander.[130] General William Westmoreland would replace Harkins in this role during July 1964. In November 1963, before Washington had made any key decisions regarding the introduction of American ground combat forces, assassins had taken the lives of Presidents Diem and Kennedy, leaving the new American president, Lyndon B. Johnson, in the position of deciding Vietnam's future.[131] Regrettably, Johnson would prove to be America's least resolute wartime president.

When Johnson acceded to the presidency, he faced an increasingly aggressive Communist campaign in South Vietnam, yet his initial reaction was to continue the policy of equivocation, even in face of direct attacks on American personnel and facilities.[132] That would change somewhat in August 1964 with the Gulf of Tonkin incident in which three North Vietnamese patrol boats attacked the American destroyer USS *Maddox* in international waters. *Maddox* was part of the Navy's DeSoto intelligence-gathering program that supported South Vietnam's covert operations in the North. When the enemy boats fired torpedoes at *Maddox*, its captain returned fire and vectored in a flight of F-8 Crusaders from USS *Ticonderoga*, which attacked with rockets and cannon fire, adding to the damage inflicted by *Maddox* and sinking at least one of the boats. Two days later, during hours of darkness, a second attacked occurred, which the sailors of *Maddox* and *Turner Joy* (which had joined *Maddox* after the first attack) believed to be real, but many historians consider illusionary.[133] Regardless of the veracity of the second attack, the Gulf of Tonkin incident(s) marked the beginning of a greater level of American involvement in the Vietnam War. Within hours, President Johnson ordered retaliatory air raids, known as Operation Pierce Arrow, against five patrol boat bases along the North Vietnam coast, on any enemy boats observed, and at the fuel installation at Vinh. Crusader, Skyhawk, and Skyraider aircraft from *Ticonderoga* and *Constellation* launched their attacks on 5 August, sinking eight boats, damaging twenty-one, and destroy-ing the fuel installation at Vinh. The Navy lost two planes in the attack including an A-4 Skyhawk flown by Lieutenant (jg) Everett Alvarez from *Constellation.* Alverez became the first Navy prisoner of war in Vietnam, remaining so for the next eight and a half years.[134] Regrettably, the pilot of the second plane, Lieutenant (jg) Richard Sather did not survive. Both losses resulted from ground-based anti-aircraft artillery (AAA) fire.[135]

The most important result of the Gulf of Tonkin incident(s), of course, was the Southeast Asia Resolution (commonly called the Gulf of Tonkin Resolution) of 10 August 1964 in which the U.S. Congress granted President Johnson broad authority to assist South Vietnam and other U.S. allies in Southeast Asia.[136] After the 5 August attack on the North Vietnam naval facilities, President Johnson fell back into the pattern of inaction, declining to react even to direct and intentional attacks against American personnel and aircraft in South Vietnam. To some extent, the upcom-ing November 1964 election, in which Johnson was running for president of the United States as a peace candidate, may have influenced his decisions.[137] His oppo-nent, Senator Barry Goldwater, was widely viewed as a dangerous hawk who would embroil the United States in a war in Southeast Asia if elected. Regardless of the rea-son, this lack of American action gave heart to Communist leaders, and the situation in South Vietnam continued to deteriorate.[138]

In late 1964 and early 1965, the North Vietnamese government began moving main force North Vietnamese Army (NVA) units into the South for a war-winning push.[139] Communist guerrilla activity increased, including attacks against American personnel and facilities. The administration finally reacted to Viet Cong provo-cations in February 1965 (after Johnson's re-election and inauguration) when Communists attacked the U.S. base complex at Pleiku, South Vietnam, killing nine Americans, wounding one hundred, and inflicting heavy damage on U.S. aircraft and structures.[140] In response, some eighty-three planes from *Coral Sea, Hancock,* and *Ranger,* along with an element of the South Vietnamese Air Force struck back in an operation named Flaming Dart I. This action included strikes on the North Vietnamese barracks at Dong Hoi and Vit Thu Lu as well as targets in Vinh, all at the cost of one A-4 Skyhawk. Critics consider these objectives relatively insignificant, selected by civilian leaders back in Washington and not military commanders who sought a stronger response against more legitimate and vital targets.[141]

Shortly after Flaming Dart I, the Viet Cong struck the U.S. barracks at Qui Nhon, killing twenty-three Americas and wounding many more. Ninety-nine planes from *Coral Sea, Hancock*, and *Ranger* immediately responded with Flaming Dart II, which attacked the Chanh Hoa barracks just north of the DMZ. Weather problems unique to this area, particularly during the winter months, minimized the effective-ness of this strike. Additionally, ground fire brought down three Navy planes while damaging several others. These were the first of the Alpha Strikes, which utilized all available elements of a carrier wing.[142] Alpha strikes could put a very heavy weight of ordnance on targets in a very short period of time, "either for shock effect or to penetrate very heavy defenses."[143] Despite the quantity of firepower used, the Flaming Dart operations proved ineffective in reducing attacks on American personnel and installations. Therefore, President Johnson initiated an air campaign against North Vietnam on 13 February 1965 named Operation Rolling Thunder, which purported to increase gradually the pain of war to the point that North Vietnamese leaders would give up their effort.[144]

The execution of Operation Rolling Thunder involved carrier aircraft from Task Force 77 along with land-based Marine Corps and Air Force planes flying from South Vietnam and Thailand.[145] There were many problems with Rolling Thunder, including the fact that the first attacks did not launch until 5 March and then mostly against insignificant targets. Additionally, the missions were initially limited in frequency, placing little or no pressure on North Vietnamese leaders and certainly having no effect on their behavior.[146] Unlike the aggressive, hard-hitting interdiction and strike packages against North Korea during 1950–1953, Rolling Thunder amounted to an ineffective, highly restricted, low-impact effort entirely wanting in its effect.[147] This did not result from the lack of effort by American aviators, but from restrictive targeting. In other words, Rolling Thunder was an intense effort against second- and third-level targets and not a thrust for the enemy's jugular. Of course, none of this kept the operation from being highly dangerous to the pilots flying the missions. Despite the effort expended, Rolling Thunder failed to communicate American determination to the Communist enemy as President Johnson had intended. Hanoi took the gradual and minimalist approach of Rolling Thunder as an indication of lack of will rather than a demonstration of American resolve.[148] Additionally, the strategy, tactics, and target selection that underlay Rolling Thunder were inconsistent with the advice of most military commanders, the director of the Central Intelligence Agency, and eventually even the American ambassador to South Vietnam.[149]

Ironically, the decision to place inordinate restrictions on the air campaign in North Vietnam occurred simultaneously with the commitment of American ground combat forces into the South. Many commanders considered this disconnect to be a serious mistake. In the words of Admiral U. S. Grant Sharp, Commander in Chief of Pacific Command at the time: "Despite John McCone's (the Director of the Central Intelligence Agency) perceptive warning vis-á-vis the implications of deploying those ground forces without making full use of our air power against the north, Secretary McNamara chose to do just that; i.e., to downgrade the U.S. air effort in North Vietnam and to concentrate on air and ground action in the south. This fateful decision contributed to our ultimate loss of South Vietnam as much as any other single action we took during our involvement."[150] Of course, not everyone agrees with Admiral Sharp's point of view on the potential of air power to win the Vietnam War; yet when Rolling Thunder ended in October 1968, few would argue that it had been an effective campaign.[151]

The Rolling Thunder campaign that began so inauspiciously in February 1965 was designed to progress from near the DMZ northward, under the assumption that the Communists would give up the war rather than risk destruction. But the effort never had the conviction necessary to impress North Vietnamese leaders.[152] The restrictions placed on the operation ensured it would not be effective, and the policy of gradualism permitted the Communists to adjust to every measure.[153] Such requirements as administration approval before every strike, no pre-strike reconnaissance, no follow-up secondary strikes, and positive identification of enemy aircraft before engagement (at closing speeds of up to one thousand miles per hour) incensed commanders and pilots alike. Additionally, prohibiting pilots from attacking surface-to-air missile (SAM) sites before they were fully functional (and not always then) and not allowing pilots to use unexpended ordnance on targets of opportunity were initially frustrating and ultimately deadly. Should it be necessary to cancel a mission for any reason whatsoever, including weather, the flyers could not simply re-schedule it, but had to go through an entirely new planning and approval cycle.[154] Additionally, President Johnson ordered periodic bombing halts intended to cause the North Vietnamese to reconsider the situation, all of which had no more impact than the ineffectual bombing itself.[155]

Eventually, the administration lifted some of the bombing restrictions, at least during certain periods. On 30 June 1966, a forty-six plane strike off *Ranger* hit an oil storage facility in the outskirts of Haiphong. Four days later, planes from *Kitty Hawk* struck an electrical power plant near downtown Haiphong, and in May 1967, *Bon Homme Richard*'s planes hit targets near downtown Hanoi. Several months later, Task Force 77 aircraft began bombing bridges between Haiphong and Hanoi. Of course, these and other missions flown constantly by Task Force 77 had their price. Numerous aircraft were lost and serious accidents occurred on board *Oriskany* and *Forrestal* due in part to the high operational tempo. Needless to say, the greatest misfortune in all this involved the loss and injury to pilots, crews, and sailors in support of a strategy that American leaders had not adequately crafted.[156] Communist losses were undoubtedly far greater, but to the amazement of American leaders, the North Vietnamese could sustain these losses within their strategic model. It appears that officials in Washington erroneously assumed their counterparts in Hanoi would be the mirror image of their thought processes and cultural values.

Ostensibly, the decision to insert U.S. ground forces into the war resulted from the need to secure America's air base at Da Nang. American leaders doubted the ability of ARVN forces to protect the huge base where the United States had located substantial assets. On 26 February 1965, at the request of General Westmoreland,

President Johnson approved the landing of U.S. Marines to provide security for America personnel, aircraft, and material at Da Nang.[157] On 8 March, the lead element of the Ninth Marine Expeditionary Brigade, under command of Brigadier General Frederick J. Karch, landed at Da Nang with the mission to protect its air base from enemy attack.[158] During the following weeks, Marine fixed-wing squadrons began landing in quick order and by midyear, much of the 1st Marine Air Wing had arrived in Vietnam. By the end of 1965, all the Wing's squadrons were operating in country as well as a Marine fighter squadron deployed on board USS *Oriskany*, which arrived in Vietnamese waters in May 1965.[159] Additionally, Marine ground forces quickly grew to brigade and then division size followed by authorization to conduct offensive operations.[160] The first major American ground action of the war, Operation Starlite, occurred in August 1965 with Marines attacking a Viet Cong regiment of some three thousand troops south of Da Nang near Chu Lai.[161] Starlite consisted of three Marine infantry battalions, five helicopter squadrons, and two fixed-wing squadrons flying F-4 Phantom and A-4 Skyhawk jets. The operation shattered the Viet Cong regiment, killing over six hundred Communist troops at the cost of fifty Marine dead.[162]

About the same time the United States initiated Rolling Thunder, the Navy began an important maritime surveillance program entitled Operation Market Time. Consisting of surface and air units of the American and South Vietnamese navies, Market Time attempted to detect Communist waterborne supply and infiltration efforts along the South Vietnamese coastline.[163] In addition to some 220 American and South Vietnamese naval surface craft, Market Time utilized P-2 Neptune, P-3 Orion, and P-5 Marlin patrol aircraft.[164] These actions could occasionally become very exciting with patrol aircraft exposed and at risk, but mostly they involved long flights of ten to thirteen monotonous hours receiving very little attention outside the units conducting the missions.[165] Market Time operations proved to be quite successful in reducing infiltration from coastal waters into South Vietnam, thereby forcing greater reliance on the Ho Chi Minh trail by Communist leaders.[166] American air efforts to interdict the Ho Chi Minh trail never enjoyed the success of Market Time, even after October 1968 when the end of Rolling Thunder allowed assets to be shifted to that mission.[167]

Another naval operation named Game Warden conducted riverine actions in the brown water areas of southern South Vietnam. Consisting of river patrol boats, mine sweepers, and helicopters, the Game Warden operation began in the Mekong River delta and expanded into virtually every river and slough network from Cambodia to the South China Sea.[168] Intended to deny these marshy alluvial plains and their associated river networks to the Viet Cong, Operation Game Warden proved relatively successful and occasionally very violent when American or South Vietnamese patrol boats encountered Communist formations.[169] Like Operation Market Time, Game

Warden did not receive the same level of attention from correspondents and historians, as did the larger and more dramatic events of the Vietnam War. Yet both operations contributed to the war effort and underscored the value of naval aviation in what were essentially surface operations.

As the air war over North Vietnam wore on, Soviet-supplied air defense system became an ever-increasing problem for American aviators. This threat included both surface anti-aircraft defense systems and airborne fighters, especially the MiG-21. Initially, the greatest surface-based threat came from conventional anti-aircraft artillery, which proved effective even against modern high-speed aircraft. Simply by projecting the route of flight from an attack plane's roll-in point to its target, AAA gunners could fill that kill box with as much flak as possible. This tactic proved particularly lethal when multiple systems fired in barrages accompanied by the small-arms fire available from other defenders. Antiaircraft artillery had proven quite effective in Korea as well as in the early phases of the Vietnam air war. It was one of the lessons we either failed to learn properly, or dropped from our institutional memory. Of course, emergence of the surface-to-air missile (SAM) threat somewhat distracted air power leaders from addressing the dangers of AAA. During Vietnam, 58 percent of naval combat losses, 73 percent of Air Force casualties, and 64 percent of Marine Corps losses are attributable to AAA gunfire. The fact that the Air Force and Marine Corps flew more missions over South Vietnam and Laos where AAA was the only threat helps explain why they had greater losses from these systems.[170] Of course, naval aviators developed countermeasures against the AAA fire, which included escort planes that attacked suspected and identified sites with Zuni air-to-ground missiles and 20-mm gunfire just seconds before attack planes made their bombing runs. Although evidence suggests that these suppression efforts took a high toll in enemy gunners and weapons, the North Vietnamese could constantly replace both, and AAA fire remained a threat throughout the war.[171]

In the spring of 1965, Soviet SAMs made their appearance in North Vietnam. Despite photoreconnaissance confirmation of the sites, administration policy did not permit American aviators to attack them before they began taking losses.[172] Apparently the administration feared offending the Soviet Union should attacks against the SAM constructions sites kill some of its citizens. Additionally, as naive as it may seem now, several high-level officials in Washington refused to believe the North Vietnamese would actually use SAMs against Americans. In July 1965 the United States lost its first plane to a Communist SAM, an Air Force F-4 Phantom II aircraft.[173] By the end of 1967 there were some two hundred SAM sites in North Vietnam with about five hundred missiles available at any one time. By 1972 there were three hundred sites throughout the country, some as far south as the DMZ. Even more astonishing, the North Vietnamese were allowed seven years of uninterrupted re-supply of launchers and missiles from the Soviet Union. Yet despite all the disadvantages the administration placed on its warfighters, American aviators learned to adjust to the SAM threat by developing tactics that could destroy launch sites on the ground and avoid their missiles in the air. The introduction of Shrike anti-radiation missiles in March 1966 helped in this regard, providing a means of defeating SAM sites once they activated their radars. SAMs shot down approximately two hundred planes, from their introduction through 1972. Carrier aviation lost twice as many planes to SAMs than did the U.S. Air Force, primarily because they flew more frequently in North Vietnam where the SAM defenses were the strongest.[174]

The airborne fighter defense system in North Vietnam consisted of MiG-17, MiG-19, and MiG-21 aircraft.[175] Although American pilots occasionally lost engagements with the Communist MiGs, they never really threatened U.S. air superiority in the skies over North Vietnam. Ground-based AAA and SAM capability remained the major threat to American air power throughout the war. Only 16 of the 473 naval aircraft and 60 of the 618 Air Force planes lost over North Vietnam resulted from MiG interceptors.[176] American pilots first drew blood in the air-to-air battle on 17 June 1965 when two F-4 Phantom II jets from *Midway* shot down two MiGs in an engagement involving closing speeds in excess of one thousand miles per hour. Three days later, two MiG-17s attacked four A-1 Skyraiders that were covering a rescue mission. The Skyraiders tightly maneuvered until one closed behind a MiG and splashed it with 20-mm cannon fire. The second MiG departed the fray following one of the truly unique aerial fights of the war.[177] Not all engagements proved this successful, of course, but North Vietnamese fighter-intercept aircraft could never control their airspace. No Navy strike was ever turned back, and no Air Force mission was ever deterred by enemy air actions. Yet even this minimal air threat need not have existed except for misguided policies out of Washington, which kept most of the major MiG bases off-limits until well into 1967. Even then, the authority to crater runways and destroy enemy planes on the ground was intermittent, reflecting the wavering policies of the Johnson administration.[178]

Although Marine air flew in support of Rolling Thunder and other missions during the Vietnam War, its primary role involved support of ground combat units, especially Marine forces. This included close air support of troops in contact with enemy forces, and tactical movement of troops by helicopter. The primary aircraft used for Marine close air support during Vietnam included the F-8 Crusader, F-4 Phantom II, A-4 Skyhawk, and A-6 Intruder. At the beginning of the war, the Marine Corps helicopter mix consisted of the UH-34 Seahorse and CH-37 Mojave aircraft and, during the course of the war, transitioned to the CH-46 Sea Knight, CH-53 Sea Stallion, UH-1 Huey, and AH-1 Cobras.[179] If support of ground operations was the mainstay of Marine aviation, it was also an important mission for carrier-based naval aviation in Vietnam just as it had been in Korea. For example, during the siege of Khe Sanh in the aftermath of the 1968 Tet offensive, Navy pilots flew some 3,100 sorties in support of the Marine defenders. This was in addition, of course, to the 2,548 sorties conducted by Air Force B-52 Stratofortress bombers that pounded enemy positions surrounding the firebase during the same period.[180] The Battle of Khe Sanh would not be the last time naval aviation would team with B-52 bombers in conducting operations during the Vietnam War.

Upon assumption of the American presidency in January 1969, Richard M. Nixon initiated a new war strategy entitled Vietnamization. It actually constituted one element of the larger approach to security within Asia called the Nixon Doctrine. Vietnamization reflected the reality that support for the controversial war was waning beyond repair within the United States. President Nixon's concept involved turning over ground combat operations to South Vietnamese forces while providing American air, naval, and logistical support.[181] Concurrent with this undertaking, the United States attempted to engage North Vietnamese leaders in negotiating a peace that would leave South Vietnam intact. This effort enjoyed no success until 1972 at which time Nixon ordered renewed bombing of North Vietnam on a massive scale along with the mining of its harbors. This culminated in Operation Linebacker II (also known as the Christmas bombings), in which B-52 bombers, other Air Force planes, and carrier aircraft from Task Force 77 conducted devastating assaults on the Hanoi-Haiphong area.[182] Unlike Rolling Thunder, these attacks focused on significant military targets such as transportation and logistics nodes, air bases, electrical power plants, and communications centers. Additionally, they lacked the presidential micromanagement of Rolling Thunder and the restrictive rules of engagement that inhibited militarily sound air tactics.[183] The severity of these attacks caused Communist leaders to negotiate in earnest, coming to a cease-fire agreement in January 1973.[184]

Ostensively, this accord permitted the United States to end its involvement in Southeast Asia while ensuring the release of American and South Vietnamese prisoners of war.[185] The settlement was a sham, of course, merely setting the stage for a North Vietnamese conventional attack against the South in March 1975, leading to a Communist victory.[186] By that time, the U.S. Congress and American people opposed the war so completely they would not even support the use of air and naval forces to assist South Vietnamese forces. That formula had proven successful in halting the 1972 Easter Offensive by North Vietnam, and many believed it could work again. But in 1975, the Watergate scandal had weakened the American presidency and forced President Nixon from office. His successor, Gerald R. Ford, could not overcome congressional resistance, and the United States allowed South Vietnam to face the North Vietnamese onslaught alone.[187] By 30 April, Saigon fell to Communist forces, and the United States had lost its first war.[188]

The Korean and Vietnam wars were actually wars within a war; they were hot wars within a Cold War. Korea had been a conventional war whereas Vietnam was primarily a guerrilla war in the early years and predominately a conventional war in its later phases.[189] These wars exhibited the more violent aspects of America's policy of containment. Had it not been for the superpower competition of that era, the United States would never have engaged in these conflicts. The risk of a superpower clash during Korea and Vietnam somewhat constrained the actions of both sides, of course.[190] Although this backdrop of nuclear superpower confrontation does not excuse deficiency in strategic thinking and policy formulation, it does help explain it. American leaders, particularly presidents Truman and Johnson, found themselves beyond their depth in the constrained warfare of the post–World War II era. Although able men in many ways, they proved unable to devise winning solutions for the conflicts that destiny presented to their generation of leadership. These are the first American presidents for whom this is true.

A general lack of understanding by American leaders regarding the strategic reality of the late 1940s almost resulted in the demise of naval aviation, and perhaps elimination of the Marine Corps. But the harsh reality of the Korean War and the concomitant realization that war could be fought on many levels resulted in the revitalization of these important components of national security. Naval aviation proved crucial to saving allied ground forces in the early weeks of the Korean War and for sustaining the subsequent war effort, thereby denying the Communist aggressors their intended goal. By the time of Vietnam, the capability and flexibility of naval aviation had been reestablished and well accepted. Carrier aviation, like other elements of American military power, performed effectively and efficiently to the extent permitted by U.S. policy and strategy. The credibility established by naval aviation during these two hot wars proved important in the deterrence strategy of the subsequent Cold War years. Additionally, naval aviation served America well during the strategically confusing years after the fall of the Soviet Union, and proved an essential and effective element in the expeditionary era that followed.

NOTES

1. T. R. Fehrenbach, *This Kind of War* (Washington, DC: Brassey's, 1963, 1994), pp. 1–9.

2. Ibid., p. 32; David Rees, ed., *The Korean War: History and Tactics* (New York: Crescent Books, 1984), p. 11; Harry S. Truman, *Memoirs by Harry S. Truman*, vol. 2 (Garden City, NY: Doubleday, 1956), pp. 328, 331.

3. Richard P. Hallion, *The Naval Air War in Korea* (Baltimore, MD: Nautical & Aviation Publishing Company of America, 1986), pp. 27–29; Rees, ed., *The Korean War: History and Tactics*, p. 13; Craig L. Symonds, *Historical Atlas of the U.S. Navy* (Annapolis: Naval Institute Press, 1995), pp. 194–95; Truman, *Memoirs*, pp. 325–26.

4. John Lewis Gaddis, *We Now Know: Rethinking Cold War History* (Oxford: Clarendon Press, 1997), p. 73.

5. Ibid., p. 74.

6. Fehrenbach, *This Kind of War,* p. 33; John Lewis Gaddis, *The Cold War* (New York: Penguin Press, 2005), p. 42; Douglas MacArthur, *Reminiscences* (New York: McGraw-Hill, 1964), pp. 320–22; Max Hastings, *The Korean War* (New York: Simon and Schuster, 1987), pp. 48–49.

7. Fehrenbach, *This Kind of War,* pp. 32–33; Hastings, *The Korean War,* p. 51.

8. Gaddis, *We Now Know,* p. 75; Hastings, *The Korean War,* p. 52; James L. Holloway III, *Aircraft Carriers at War: A Personal Retrospective of Korea, Vietnam, and the Soviet Confrontation* (Annapolis: Naval Institute Press, 2007), p. 49; Truman, *Memoirs,* p. 331.

9. F. A. Godfrey, "The Attack from the North," in Rees, ed., *The Korean War: History and Tactics,* p. 16.

10. Hastings, *The Korean War,* p. 45; Rees, ed., *The Korean War: History and Tactics,* p. 12.

11. Fehrenbach, *This Kind of War,* pp. 42–49.

12. Truman, *Memoirs,* pp. 333, 336–37.

13. Gaddis, *The Cold War,* p. 43; Truman, *Memoirs,* pp. 334.

14. Gaddis, *We Now Know,* p. 767; Hastings, *The Korean War,* pp. 55–56; Hallion, *The Naval Air War in Korea,* p. 30.

15. Symonds, *Historical Atlas of the U.S. Navy,* p. 196.

16. Fehrenbach, *This Kind of War,* pp. 50–52; Truman, *Memoirs,* p. 336.

17. Hastings, *The Korean War,* p. 60.

18. Gaddis, *We Now Know,* p. 77; Truman, *Memoirs,* p. 334.

19. Bevan R. Alexander, *Korea: The First War We Lost* (New York: Hippocrene Books, 1986), pp. 29–30; Fehrenbach, *This Kind of War,* pp. 52–53; Hallion, *The Naval Air War in Korea,* pp. 14, 30; Anthony Robinson and David Rees, "The Air and Sea War," in Rees, *The Korean War: History and Tactics,* p. 105.

20. Hastings, *The Korean War,* p. 60; Harry G. Summers Jr., *On Strategy: A Critical Analysis of the Vietnam War* (Novato, CA: Presidio Press, 1982), p. 192.

21. Holloway, *Aircraft Carriers at War,* pp. 45–46; Truman, *Memoirs,* pp. 337, 358, 463–64.

22. Hastings, *The Korean War,* pp. 61–62.

23. Truman, *Memoirs,* pp. 342–43.

24. Hastings, *The Korean War,* p. 58; Holloway, *Aircraft Carriers at War,* pp. 44–45; Truman, *Memoirs,* p. 345.

25. Fehrenbach, *This Kind of War,* pp. 111–12; Truman, *Memoirs,* pp. 345, 347–48.

26. Paolo E. Coletta, *The United States Navy and Defense Unification: 1947–1953* (Newark: University of Delaware Press, 1981), p. 247; Holloway, *Aircraft Carriers at War,* pp. xii–xiii, 33.

27. Hallion, *The Naval Air War in Korea,* p. 40.

28. Ibid., pp. 34–35; Holloway, *Aircraft Carriers at War,* pp. 46, 62.

29. Hallion, *The Naval Air War in Korea,* p. 30; Symonds, *Historical Atlas of the U.S. Navy,* pp. 194–95; Korean Institute of Military History, *The Korean War,* vol. 1 (Lincoln: University of Nebraska Press, 1997), p. 340.

30. Hallion, *The Naval Air War in Korea,* pp. 40–41; Holloway, *Aircraft Carriers at War,* p. 62; Richard C. Knott, *Attack from the Sky: Naval Air Operations in the Korean War* (Washington, DC: Naval Historical Center, 2004), p. 12.

31. Fehrenbach, *This Kind of War,* pp. 56, 59–61; Victor H. Krulak, *First to Fight: An Inside View of the U.S. Marine Corps* (Annapolis: Naval Institute Press, 1984), pp. 120–23; James R. Locher III, *Victory on the Potomac: The Goldwater-Nichols Act Unifies the Pentagon* (College Station: Texas A&M University Press, 2002), pp. 26–27.

32. Coletta, *The United States Navy and Defense Unification*, p. 230.

33. Ibid., pp. 64, 142–43.

34. Thomas B. Buell, *Naval Leadership in Korea: The First Six Months* (Washington, DC: Naval Historical Center, 2002), p. 7; Coletta, *The United States Navy and Defense Unification*, p. 213; Krulak, *First to Fight*, p. 120.

35. Coletta, *The United States Navy and Defense Unification*, pp. 187, 156–57, 160–61; Hallion, *The Naval Air War in Korea*, pp. 13–18; Alwyn T. Lloyd, *A Cold War Legacy: A Tribute to Strategic Air Command—1946–1992* (Missoula, MT: Pictorial Histories Publishing Company, 1999), pp. 126–28; Russell F. Weigley, *The American Way of War: A History of United States Military Strategy and Policy* (New York: Macmillan, 1973), pp. 372–73, 376–79.

36. Hallion, *The Naval Air War in Korea*, p. 20.

37. Ibid., pp. 9, 24.

38. Symonds, *Historical Atlas of the U.S. Navy*, pp. 191–92.

39. Holloway, *Aircraft Carriers at War*, p. xii.

40. Coletta, *The United States Navy and Defense Unification*, p. 247; Fehrenbach, *This Kind of War*, pp. 65–71.

41. Alexander, *Korea: The First War We Lost*, pp. 46–52.

42. Fehrenbach, *This Kind of War*, pp. 108–9.

43. Alexander, *Korea: The First War We Lost*, p. 2.

44. Hallion, *The Naval Air War in Korea*, p. 56; Weigley, *The American Way of War*, pp. 384–85.

45. Holloway, *Aircraft Carriers at War*, pp. 47, 62.

46. Ibid., p. 62.

47. Ibid., p. 64; Krulak, *First to Fight*, p. 124.

48. Peter B. Mersky, *U.S. Marine Corps Aviation: 1912 to Present* (Baltimore, MD: Nautical & Aviation Publishing Company, 1983, 1987, 1997), p. 130.

49. Holloway, *Aircraft Carriers at War*, p. 65.

50. Ibid., pp. 63–64.

51. Ibid., p. 63; Knott, *Attack from the Sky*, p. 51.

52. Hallion, *The Naval Air War in Korea*, pp. 40–41.

53. Ibid., pp. 70–71.

54. Holloway, *Aircraft Carriers at War*, pp. 69–72.

55. Ibid., p. 72.

56. Hallion, *The Naval Air War in Korea*, pp. 41, 46–47.

57. Knott, *Attack from the Sky*, p. 14.

58. Hallion, *The Naval Air War in Korea*, p. 39.

59. Ibid., pp. 38–39.

60. Ibid., p. 54.

61. Ibid., pp. 55–56; Knott, *Attack from the Sky*, p. 45.

62. Fehrenbach, *This Kind of War*, pp. 119–27.

63. Alexander, *Korea: The First War We Lost*, p. 126; Knott, *Attack from the Sky*, pp. 16–17.

64. Alexander, *Korea: The First War We Lost*, pp. 129–31.

65. Coletta, *The United States Navy and Defense Unification*, p. 238; Robert Debs Heinl Jr., *Victory at High Tide: The Inchon-Seoul Campaign* (Philadelphia: Lippincott, 1968), pp. 19–21; Krulak, *First to Fight*, pp. 124–26.

66. Warren Thompson, *F4U Corsair Units of the Korean War* (Oxford: Osprey Publishing, 2009), p. 51.

67. Hallion, *The Naval Air War in Korea*, pp. 50–54.

68. Alexander, *Korea: The First War We Lost*, pp. 138–40; Fehrenbach, *This Kind of War*, pp. 127–34.

69. Alexander, *Korea: The First War We Lost*, pp. 147–48.

70. Hallion, *The Naval Air War in Korea*, p. 57.

71. MacArthur, *Reminiscences*, pp. 348–52.

72. Symonds, *Historical Atlas of the U.S. Navy*, p. 196.

73. Joseph H. Alexander and Merrill L. Bartlett, *Sea Soldiers of the Cold War: Amphibious Warfare 1945–1991* (Annapolis: Naval Institute Press, 1995), pp. 16, 20, 25; Hallion, *The Naval Air War in Korea*, p. 57; Heinl, *Victory at High Tide*, pp. 32–60, 63–64.

74. Hallion, *The Naval Air War in Korea*, pp. 59–60.

75. Heinl, *Victory at High Tide*, pp. 77–80; Knott, *Attack from the Sky*, pp. 18–19.

76. MacArthur, *Reminiscences*, p. 353.

77. Hallion, *The Naval Air War in Korea*, p. 63; Heinl, *Victory at High Tide*, pp. 87–90.

78. MacArthur, *Reminiscences*, p. 353.

79. Knott, *Attack from the Sky*, p. 20.

80. Heinl, *Victory at High Tide*, pp. 92–96, 98–117.

81. Ibid., pp. 119–20; Knott, *Attack from the Sky*, pp. 20–21.

82. Hallion, *The Naval Air War in Korea*, pp. 63–64; Heinl, *Victory at High Tide*, pp. 221–24.

83. Heinl, *Victory at High Tide*, p. 183; MacArthur, *Reminiscences*, p. 354.

84. Alexander and Bartlett, *Sea Soldiers of the Cold War: Amphibious Warfare, 1945–1991*, p. 23; Heinl, *Victory at High Tide*, pp. 254–55; MacArthur, *Reminiscences*, pp. 355–56.

85. MacArthur, *Reminiscences*, p. 354; Weigley, *The American Way of War*, pp. 386–87.

86. MacArthur, *Reminiscences*, p. 354.

87. Heinl, *Victory at High Tide*, p. 358.

88. MacArthur, *Reminiscences*, pp. 358–59.

89. Hallion, *The Naval Air War in Korea*, pp. 68–70; Knott, *Attack from the Sky*, p. 23.

90. Pat Meid and James M. Yingling, *U.S. Marine Operations in Korea 1950–1953*. Vol. 5, *Operations in West Korea* (Washington, DC: Historical Division, Headquarters, U.S. Marine Corps, 1972), pp. 487–88.

91. Knott, *Attack from the Sky*, p. 23.

92. Hallion, *The Naval Air War in Korea*, p. 67.

93. Ibid., pp. 80–85; Knott, *Attack from the Sky*, pp. 28–29; Meid and Yingling, *U.S. Marine Operations in Korea 1950–1953*, pp. 488–89.

94. Holloway, *Aircraft Carriers at War*, pp. 94–95; Weigley, *The American Way of War*, pp. 391–93.

95. Knott, *Attack from the Sky*, pp. 36–37, 39.

96. Holloway, *Aircraft Carriers at War*, pp. 95–96, 100–102.

97. Knott, *Attack from the Sky*, pp. 42–43.

98. Hallion, *The Naval Air War in Korea*, pp. 94–95.

99. Ibid., p. 95; Holloway, *Aircraft Carriers at War*, pp. 129–30; Knott, *Attack from the Sky*, p. 38.

100. Hallion, *The Naval Air War in Korea*, pp. 120–22; Knott, *Attack from the Sky*, p. 43.

101. Holloway, *Aircraft Carriers at War,* pp. 102–9.
102. Hallion, *The Naval Air War in Korea,* p. 198; Knott, *Attack from the Sky,* pp. 33, 47–48.
103. Meid and Yingling, *U.S. Marine Operations in Korea 1950–1953,* pp. 493–98; Mersky, *U.S. Marine Corps Aviation,* pp. 142–43.
104. Knott, *Attack from the Sky,* p. 35.
105. Hallion, *The Naval Air War in Korea,* pp. 102–3, 131; Symonds, *Historical Atlas of the U.S. Navy,* p. 198.
106. Hallion, *The Naval Air War in Korea,* pp. 125–26.
107. Ibid., pp. 127–29.
108. Knott, *Attack from the Sky,* p. 51.
109. Holloway, *Aircraft Carriers at War,* p. xi.
110. Knott, *Attack from the Sky,* p. 65.
111. Hallion, *The Naval Air War in Korea,* p. 191–93.
112. Ibid., pp. 196–98.
113. Summers, *On Strategy,* p. 4.
114. U. S. Grant Sharp, *Strategy for Defeat: Vietnam in Retrospect* (San Rafael, CA: Presidio Press, 1979), p. 269.
115. Ibid., pp. 259–71; Summers, *On Strategy,* pp. 104–5.
116. Summers, *On Strategy,* pp. 85–86.
117. Andrew F. Krepinevich Jr., *The Army and Vietnam* (Baltimore, MD: Johns Hopkins University Press, 1986), pp. 6–7.
118. Summers, *On Strategy,* pp. 88–90.
119. Philip B. Davidson, *Vietnam at War: The History: 1946–1975* (Novato, CA: Presidio Press, 1988), pp. 289–92; Dave Richard Palmer, *Summons of the Trumpet: U.S.-Vietnam in Perspective* (Novato, CA: Presidio Press, 1978), pp. 75–78.
120. H. R. McMaster, *Dereliction of Duty: Lyndon Johnson, Robert McNamara, the Joint Chiefs of Staff, and the Lies that Led to Vietnam* (New York: HarperCollins, 1997), p. 48.
121. Holloway, *Aircraft Carriers at War,* p. 191.
122. Eventually, the MAAG was re-designated as Military Assistance Command, Vietnam (MACV) with expanded operational tasks. Davidson, *Vietnam at War: The History: 1946–1975,* pp. 293, 297, 301.
123. Palmer, *Summons of the Trumpet,* pp. 22–26; Weigley, *The American Way of War,* p. 460.
124. Mersky, *U.S. Marine Corps Aviation,* pp. 203–9.
125. Davidson, *Vietnam at War,* pp. 292–300; Peter B. Mersky and Norman Polmar, *The Naval Air War in Vietnam* (Annapolis: Nautical and Aviation Publishing Company of America, 1981), pp. 11–12.
126. John B. Nichols and Barrett Tillman, *On Yankee Station: The Naval Air War over Vietnam* (Annapolis: Naval Institute Press, 1987), pp. 2–3,113–14; Tommy H. Thomason, *Strike from the Sea: U.S. Navy Attack Aircraft from Skyraider to Super Hornet 1948–Present* (North Branch, NM: Specialty Press, 2009), p. 132.
127. Mersky and Polmar, *The Naval Air War in Vietnam,* pp. 28–29.
128. Holloway, *Aircraft Carriers at War,* pp. 194, 234–38.
129. Davidson, *Vietnam at War,* p. 301.
130. Palmer, *Summons of the Trumpet,* p. 21.
131. William M. Hammond, "U.S. Intervention and the Fall of Diem," in Ray Bonds, *The Vietnam War: An Illustrated History of the Conflict in Southeast Asia* (New York: Crown

Publishing, 1979), pp. 12, 64–70; Davidson, *Vietnam at War,* pp. 303–4; McMaster, *Dereliction of Duty,* p. 248.

132. Davidson, *Vietnam at War,* pp. 323–24, 327.

133. William M. Hammond, "Communist Aggression Provokes US Retaliation," in Bonds, *The Vietnam War* (see note 131), pp. 74–76; Holloway, *Aircraft Carriers at War,* pp. 191–92; McMaster, *Dereliction of Duty,* p. 107.

134. Sharp, *Strategy for Defeat,* pp. 35–49; Mersky and Polmar, *The Naval Air War in Vietnam,* pp. 13–26; Thomason, *Strike from the Sea,* p. 102.

135. Nichols and Tillman, *On Yankee Station,* p. 50.

136. Sharp, *Strategy for Defeat,* pp. 45–46.

137. Davidson, *Vietnam at War,* pp. 334–35.

138. Sharp, *Strategy for Defeat,* pp. 53–54.

139. Davidson, *Vietnam at War,* pp. 325–29; Sharp, *Strategy for Defeat,* pp. 46–49.

140. Davidson, *Vietnam at War,* pp. 333, 335–36; Sharp, *Strategy for Defeat,* p. 56.

141. Mark Clodfelter, *The Limits of Air Power: The American Bombing of North Vietnam* (New York: The Free Press, 1989), pp. 82–84; Mersky and Polmar, *The Naval Air War in Vietnam,* pp. 18–21; Sharp, *Strategy for Defeat,* pp. 56–62.

142. Mersky and Polmar, *The Naval Air War in Vietnam,* pp. 21–26; Sharp, *Strategy for Defeat,* pp. 59, 66–67.

143. Holloway, *Aircraft Carriers at War,* pp. 238–39.

144. Weigley, *The American Way of War,* p. 463.

145. Holloway, *Aircraft Carriers at War,* pp. 193, 234–36.

146. Clodfelter, *The Limits of Air Power,* p. 65.

147. Nichols and Tillman, *On Yankee Station,* p. 16.

148. Davidson, *Vietnam at War,* p. 339; Symonds, *Historical Atlas of the U.S. Navy,* p. 208.

149. Holloway, *Aircraft Carriers at War,* p. 235; Mersky and Polmar, *The Naval Air War in Vietnam,* p. 27; Sharp, *Strategy for Defeat,* pp. 63–80.

150. Sharp, *Strategy for Defeat,* p. 80.

151. Clodfelter, *The Limits of Air Power,* pp. 143–45; Bernard C. Nalty, "The Air War against North Vietnam," in Bonds, *The Vietnam War* (see note 131), p. 94.

152. Palmer, *Summons of the Trumpet,* pp. 75–78.

153. Clodfelter, *The Limits of Air Power,* pp. 144–45.

154. Mersky and Polmar, *The Naval Air War in Vietnam,* pp. 27–29; Land Rogers, "US Navy and Marine Corps Operations in Vietnam," in Bonds, *The Vietnam War* (see note 131), p. 130.

155. Krepinevich, *The Army and Vietnam,* p. 184; Palmer, *Summons of the Trumpet,* pp. 72–79.

156. Symonds, *Historical Atlas of the U.S. Navy,* p. 208.

157. Davidson, *Vietnam at War,* pp. 343–44.

158. Krulak, *First to Fight,* p. 181; McMaster, *Dereliction of Duty,* p. 248.

159. Mersky, *U.S. Marine Corps Aviation,* pp. 213–15.

160. Weigley, *The American Way of War,* pp. 463–64.

161. Nichols and Tillman, *On Yankee Station,* p. 18; Symonds, *Historical Atlas of the U.S. Navy,* p. 214.

162. Mersky and Polmar, *The Naval Air War in Vietnam,* pp. 47–48.

163. Sharp, *Strategy for Defeat*, p. 140.

164. Anonymous, "From the Vietnam Front: On Coastal, Air and River Patrol, All Hands: The Bureau of Naval Personnel Career Publication" (December 1966), p. 17.

165. Mersky and Polmar, *The Naval Air War in Vietnam*, pp. 30–34.

166. Sharp, *Strategy for Defeat*, p. 140.

167. Clodfelter, *The Limits of Air Power*, p. 147.

168. R. Blake Dunnavent, *Brown Water Warfare: The U.S. Navy and the Emergence of a Tactical Doctrine, 1775–1970* (Gainesville, FL: University of Florida Press, 2003).

169. Sharp, *Strategy for Defeat*, p. 140; Symonds, *Historical Atlas of the U.S. Navy*, p. 212.

170. Nichols and Tillman, *On Yankee Station*, pp. 49–52.

171. Ibid., pp. 53–54.

172. Nalty, "The Air War against North Vietnam," p. 88.

173. Nichols and Tillman, *On Yankee Station*, pp. 54–55.

174. Ibid., pp. 56–62.

175. Nalty, "The Air War against North Vietnam," p. 88.

176. Nichols and Tillman, *On Yankee Station*, pp. 67–68.

177. Nalty, "The Air War against North Vietnam," p. 90; Rogers, "US Navy and Marine Corps Operations in Vietnam," p. 132.

178. Nichols and Tillman, *On Yankee Station*, pp. 67–68, 70.

179. Mersky and Polmar, *The Naval Air War in Vietnam*, pp. 86–87.

180. Rogers, "US Navy and Marine Corps Operations in Vietnam," pp. 136–38; John T. Greenwood, "B-52: Strategic Bombers in a Tactical Role," in Bonds, *The Vietnam War* (see note 131), p. 202.

181. Jeffrey J. Clarke, "Vietnamization: The South Must Save Itself," in Bonds, *The Vietnam War* (see note 131), pp. 172, 180; Summers, *On Strategy*, pp. 176–77.

182. Holloway, *Aircraft Carriers at War*, pp. 326–27; Sharp, *Strategy for Defeat*, p. 252.

183. Holloway, *Aircraft Carriers at War*, pp. 335–34; Sharp, *Strategy for Defeat*, pp. 252–54.

184. John T. Greenwood, "B-52: Strategic Bombers in a Tactical Role," in Bonds, *The Vietnam War* (see note 131), p. 204.

185. William L. Allen, "Spring 1972: Northern Invasion Repulsed," in Bonds, *The Vietnam War* (see note 131), p. 226.

186. Mersky and Polmar, *The Naval Air War in Vietnam*, p. 211; Palmer, *Summons of the Trumpet*, pp. 262–63.

187. Holloway, *Aircraft Carriers at War*, p. 334; Sharp, *Strategy for Defeat*, pp. 259–65; Summers, *On Strategy*, pp. 113–15.

188. Palmer, *Summons of the Trumpet*, pp. 261–62.

189. Summers, *On Strategy*, pp. 90–91.

190. Clodfelter, *The Limits of Air Power*, p. 209.

CHAPTER 14

By Land and Sea:
Non-Carrier Naval Aviation

Sterling Michael Pavelec

ircraft presented an interesting new technology to the U.S. military. At the
turn of the twentieth century, both the land and sea Services—the Army
and the Navy—considered how to incorporate aviation into their branches.
The Navy saw great potential in aviation technology and quickly integrated it into
Navy doctrine, strategy, and thinking, as well as dedicating funds for procurement of
aircraft and peripheral technologies. Over time, with frequent fits and starts along the
way, the Navy developed coherent doctrine and aviation assets to perform uniquely
naval roles. In this chapter, I will outline some of the ideas that the Navy tried and
eventually adopted, and introduce the various airframes beyond carrier aviation that
the Navy has employed over the past one hundred years. At the start of the twentieth century, a new technology emerged that changed the grammar of warfare.[1] The
introduction of aircraft and submarines transformed naval warfare to include the
third dimensions: undersea and aerial operations. New technologies translated into
new strategies as planners attempted to gain strategic advantages.

The great naval theorists, Corbett and Mahan,[2] were the founding fathers of naval
and maritime strategy up to and including World War I (1914–1918).[3] However,
by the end of the Great War, technology forever altered naval warfare. Fortunately,
American military planners and strategists were at the leading edge of technological
adaptation and envisioned the incorporation of the third dimension into strategy.
Unfortunately, they were not the only ones.

As seen elsewhere in this book, others are recounting lighter-than-air naval aviation[4] and the development of carrier aviation.[5] This chapter will focus specifically on

land- and sea-based naval aviation, and the doctrine and development of the naval air arms that were not based on ships at sea.

As aviation technology evolved, presenting a new idea for warfighting, both the Army and Navy became interested in the possibilities.[6] The Army, into and after World War I, adopted aviation as an Army branch (Signal Corps, Air Services, and by 1941 U.S. Army Air Forces) for two types of operations: support for land forces and as strategic bombers. The Navy, on the other hand, incorporated air assets to perform uniquely naval missions and to fill roles that the Army was unwilling to perform. The early Navy missions were twofold: support the fleet and a secondary mission of aerial support of naval missions aground (observation and attack). In 1913, Secretary of the Navy Josephus Daniels commissioned a board under Captain (Navy) Washington Irving Chambers to "consider all views and prepare a comprehensive plan for the organization of a Naval Aeronautic Service."[7] The Chambers Board studied the chaotic program to that point and subsequently recommended a separate bureau—which was denied—as well as procurement. Naval aviation was relegated an office status, the Office of Naval Aeronautics, with representatives from Navigation, Construction and Repair, Steam Engineering, Ordnance, and the Marine Corps.[8] Finally, the board requested fifty planes and estimated the costs at just under $1.3 million for the aircraft and support equipment and men.[9] The Navy was taking a vested interest in naval aviation.

Early aviation experiments in the Navy were multifaceted. The Navy considered a number of ways to adapt air power for naval applications. Everything was tried; most were adopted. With the technology of the 1910s, the Navy looked into lighter-than-air (LTA) as a viable possibility for fleet support. Given that LTA was at the time comparable technology to heavier-than-air, the Navy began an expanded program of LTA development.[10] In addition to LTA, the Navy embraced land-based aircraft in experiments both onboard ships as well as from land bases. Further, the Navy was interested in sea-based floatplanes and flying boats for the flexibility they promised. Beginning with the 1911 USS *Pennsylvania* experiments, the Navy sought ways to incorporate air power into existing doctrine. In January, test pilot Eugene Ely made aviation history when he landed his Curtiss pusher on a modified deck, proving the feasibility of aviation for naval applications. Further Navy tests proved the viability of aircraft wedded to ships, aircraft carrier technology received due attention, and floatplanes were assigned to seaplane tenders, battleships, and cruisers. As Navy experiments progressed, Navy doctrine began to form. In the end, developing doctrine focused on the core naval roles that aircraft provided in support of the fleet.

The Great War brought rapid expansion to the naval air arm; during the war Congress appropriated the necessary funds.[11] At one point, an idea was floated to define U.S. naval aviation as a separate component of the Navy, like the semiautonomy of the Marine Corps, which was unsuccessful.[12] During the war, naval aviation came into its own. Planes and balloons were employed to support the fleet in the Atlantic. Early roles included using air assets in the observation role to protect the fleet against German surface and sub-surface threats. The U-boat (*Unterseeboote*— submarines) was emerging as a threat to the U.S. Navy and merchant marine when transporting goods to the war zone. Naval aviation found its niche: protecting fleets and convoys from the German *Hochseeflotte*. However, the first "Battle of the Atlantic" was fought with very primitive technology; the United States did not yet have aircraft carriers. The Navy employed balloon ships and seaplane tenders (which used cranes to lower and recover seaplanes for use) in the role of fleet protection. Interestingly, the Navy did set up static bases on land in the United States, using land-based aircraft for fleet support and for anti-submarine warfare close to the East Coast. Along the Atlantic coast of the United States, the Naval Reserve Flying Corps was tasked with practicing flying and providing observation for the Navy. Among the corps were a group known as the "Yale Unit," formed into the Aerial Coast Patrol, flying out of Gravesend Bay (New York) spotting for mines.[13] However, when the war started for the Americans,[14] the Navy still only had fifty-four planes, three balloons, and forty-eight Navy and Marine Corps officers. With the commitment to the war, the Navy expanded rapidly.

The first component was money. Immediately after the declaration of war, the Navy was given $3 million for aviation procurement, followed by $11 million in June and another $45 million in October. Money was not the issue. Unfortunately, planes were not easily built, and pilots took time to train. The Aircraft Production Board, headed by Howard Coffin, streamlined aircraft production for both the Army and Navy, providing the much needed airframes for war. As part of the later-termed military-industrial complex, a dedicated Naval Aircraft Factory was established in Philadelphia to produce flying boats and seaplanes for the Navy. Although production promises were extravagant, the first H-16 flying boats did not start to roll off the production line until March 1918. Training was even more erratic. Most of the training was farmed out to established training facilities, including one in Toronto, Canada; most Navy pilots were trained at NAS Pensacola (Florida).

In addition, in order to show good faith to the French, U.S. Navy aviators were sent to France in June 1917. A liaison was sent to Paris; the Navy was determined to support France's war effort in any way possible. The French demanded that American pilots be retrained by French aviators who already had combat experience, while American mechanics received remedial instruction in country as well. The Americans then set up coastal bases in order to free up French pilots for other duties. By taking over some French bases and building others, the Navy began providing air cover with coastal patrols. Extending their influence across the channel and into the North Atlantic, the Navy also set up bases for operations, training, and repair in England including Eastleigh and Killingholme and in Italy.

The Navy's role in World War I air power was mixed and controversial. The Navy was dedicated to providing fleet support, spotting for mines, and conducting anti-submarine warfare in the Atlantic and English Channel. But when the Navy requested land-based bombers for offensives against German submarine pens and various land targets, in an early form of strategic bombing, the Army balked. U.S. Army Major General Benjamin Foulois, Commander of the U.S. Army Air Services in theater, blocked Navy procurement of land-based bombers, arguing that strategic bombing was an Army role. The tensions created during the war were continued into the postwar, interwar, era.[15] The Army was not only obstreperous about the Navy mounting bombing attacks, it was also vehemently against separating the air services altogether, an argument that would continue to rear its ugly head. In the end, General John Pershing, Commander of the American Allied Expeditionary Forces, was given the final vote; he allowed the Navy to have bombers after the Army's requirements had been met. The Navy finally had the equipment and manpower to launch bombing raids in September 1918, but only in piecemeal attacks against German targets. By the end of the war, the Navy had discovered two important lessons: first, the need and viability of aircraft for fleet protection, and second, the uphill battle they would face in competing with the Army for aviation resources.

As well, the Navy realized the effort and costs of the new modern arm. By the end of the war, the Naval Air Arm had grown to include 1,147 officers and more than 18,000 men assigned overseas.[16] Naval aviators had flown 22,000 sorties during the war, in a variety of airframes, mostly French and British. By the armistice, the Navy owned 570 aircraft in theater as well as 15 dirigibles and another 215 balloons of all types. Naval expansion illustrates the importance of the new technology to naval strategy.

The immediate postwar period brought downsizing and doctrinal changes to the Navy. Most of the changes were imposed; but significant changes also came from within. The U.S. Navy made a concerted effort to retain the important new air arm into the post–World War I era in the face of external limitations and internal reassessment.

Immediately after the war, in historical fashion, the U.S. military—guided by the government—began to radically downsize. Contracts for uncompleted material were cancelled, soldiers and sailors were discharged from duty, and the military demobilized. Navy aviation, while considered important, returned to prewar numbers of men and equipment. However, this was not all bad; the pilots and aircrew were more experienced after the war, and the equipment was substantially better. Naval airframes went on sale as surplus; wartime naval aviators began civilian careers as commercial pilots and instructors, often in the same surplus military aircraft they had flown during the war.

The early 1920s brought a number of significant changes to naval aviation. The first was good news, in the form of spending. The Naval Appropriations Act (1920) gave money to the Navy, some of which was put toward naval aviation. From the 1920 Act, the Navy commissioned the USS *Jupiter* (later *Langley*), the first U.S. Navy aircraft carrier. Two other ships were commissioned as seaplane tenders,[17] and money was set aside for two dirigibles—one built, and one bought from England. Six coastal bases were also funded.[18]

At the highest levels of Navy command—as well as the Navy's most prestigious schools—naval aviation was a hot topic. In a series of memos between the Chief of Naval Operations (CNO) and the President of the U.S. Naval War College (NWC) in Newport, Rhode Island, naval aviation emerged as a front-burner subject.[19] The CNO asked the president of the NWC about current thought on the theme, and the president responded with a memo to the CNO.[20] The two-page memo discussed the importance of naval aviation and how it could best serve the Navy. The NWC president was adamant that the Navy retained its aviation capabilities—under no circumstances should it give control of the sphere to the Army.[21] At the behest of the president, the NWC began instruction and lectures on the importance and employment of naval aviation as a key component to an integrated Navy doctrine.[22] The Navy began a lasting tradition of exploring and explicating the role of aviation in naval doctrine.

But perhaps most importantly, events in September 1921 solidified Navy concerns about the significance of aviation in the maritime sphere. Ironically it was an Army officer who illustrated the value of aviation to the Navy: William "Billy" Mitchell. Mitchell, who set out to prove the importance of air power to the Army—in order to argue the point of an independent air force[23]—embarked on aviation trials at the expense of the Navy. In order to show the impotence of the Navy and how air power could be successful, he fabricated an aerial exposition to demonstrate the eclipse of U.S. naval power. With a few planes loaded with bombs, his pilots successfully bombed and sank captured German warships anchored for the demonstration.[24] Mitchell did not get an independent air force, angered numerous Army generals and Navy admirals in his path, and was eventually court-martialed for insubordination. What he did achieve, unwittingly, was a determination in the U.S. Navy to pursue naval aviation as part of the Navy, for specifically naval roles. His actions widened further the existing schism between Army and Navy air early in the interwar period.

Thus, into the 1920s the Navy combined institutional awareness with outside pressure to focus on the importance of aviation. Further, technology was catching up to the promises of effectiveness, and land- and sea-based aircraft were coming into their own. The Navy was still a few years away from carrier-based aviation in a definitive role at the same time that LTA technology was being eclipsed.[25] The Navy

continued development of aircraft technology as well as serious study on the importance of aviation to the Navy.

Organizationally, the Navy attempted to conceptualize the role of naval aviation.
By 1921, in an effort to retain its aviation arm, the Navy instituted the Bureau of
Aeronautics. Citing the importance of the air arm to the Navy, and with the support of the secretary as well as the president, the proposal was signed into effect on
12 July 1921.[26] Rear Admiral William Moffett became the first Chief of the Bureau
of Aeronautics (BuAer), who was tasked with advising the CNO on "all aeronautic
planning, operation[s], and administration."[27] Friction emerged over procurement,
with competition between BuAer, Plans, and Material divisions; however, coordination within the Navy—even with overlap—allowed Navy aviation to proceed with
renewed importance.

But, what to do with airplanes in a purely naval role remained the dominant
question. The Navy was willing to let the Army continue its pursuit of "strategic"
bombing as an Army role; the focus was instead on what airplanes could do for the
Navy. By 1931 the Navy thought it had a compromise that everyone could work
with. In a meeting between the CNO, Admiral William Pratt, and Chief of Staff
of the Army General Douglas MacArthur—later known as the Pratt-MacArthur
Agreement—it was decided that naval aviation would be "based on the fleet and
move with it as an important element in solving the primary missions confronting
the fleet . . . thus assuring the fleet absolute freedom of action without any responsibility for coast defense."[28] The presupposition was that the Navy would control all
of the air over the water, the Army over the land; each service would stay on its own
side of the coast. An immediate issue was that the Navy was still in the experimental phases with their first few aircraft carriers,[29] and it was unclear that the Army
would attend to coastal defense when called upon.[30] With these limitations in mind,
the Navy continued development of sea-based aircraft and retained a considerable
number of land-based planes for use.[31]

In subsequent meetings, there was a lack of consensus about the jurisdiction
over coastal defense.[32] Throughout the 1930s the Army and Navy bickered over
who would watch the coasts in case of enemy action close to the continental United
States. The Army, as supported by the Joint Staff in the Drum Board report (1933),
indicated that the coasts were the Army's responsibility, even if under Navy command.[33] Likewise, Navy aircraft operating within a two hundred- to three hun-
dred-mile distance from the coast may fall under an Army commander, again, as
proposed by the Joint Board in 1935.[34] However, it is important to note that while
the Joint Board considered it an important issue (with meetings and publications
up to and including 1939), and the Navy wanted the Army to commit, the Army
did not consider it an important task in their doctrinal writings.[35] The Army was
more concerned with the doctrines of strategic bombing and slightly less concerned

with support of the land forces; there was little writing or intellectual time given to coastal patrol. Interestingly, the Army was so concerned with its monopoly on land-based aircraft that the Secretary of War brought the issue to the president when he found out that the Navy was deploying (land-based) torpedo bombers to Coco Solo and Pearl Harbor. The secretary asked the president to deny future purchases of land-based aircraft for the Navy, citing conflict of interest and duplication of effort.[36] Even though the Navy was allowed to continue procurement of land-based aircraft, the dilemma continued, with frequent heated conversations between the Army and Navy over jurisdiction and procurement.

However, even with inter-Service rivalries with the Army, the naval air arm prospered in the 1930s. Government spending, while curtailed due to the Depression, was forthcoming: bases were built and expanded and aircraft technology evolved. The Hepburn Board (1938) asked for funds for planes and bases; the Navy realized that their duties to protect the fleet and provide necessary aviation assets were important.[37] However, the funds were not up to the tasks as proposed, and the Navy lacked another important component: pilots and aircrew. When the government did finally relent and provide the necessary funds, there was little time to prepare, so that the old maxim held true: "When there is time, there is no money; when there is money, there is little time." Navy aviation faced a crisis in 1939 when wars on two continents boiled over. When the Germans invaded Poland in September 1939, the Navy began "neutrality patrols" in the Atlantic and Caribbean with a mere 90 planes,[38] some 700 frontline aircraft in total in the Pacific, flying from land bases and aircraft carriers.[39] It was simply not enough, and war was at hand. Germany boasted an overoptimistic force of 5,000 aircraft,[40] the Japanese were thought to have as many as 900 naval aircraft and 1,800 Army aircraft.[41] The United States in general, and the Navy in particular, found themselves behind in aircraft production and pilot training as war exploded across the globe.

In spring 1940 the president stepped in to address the situation. In May, Franklin Roosevelt ordered funds for 50,000 aircraft for the Army and Navy. In order to facilitate production at undreamed of levels, the National Defense Advisory Committee was formed to rethink American production. Industry was encouraged with contracts and funding, and the massive buildup for war began. The Navy, with only 1,741 aircraft in June 1940, prepared to accept thousands of planes rather than dozens, Congress authorized 4,500 new aircraft on the 14th, raised it to 10,000 on the 15th, and when France fell at the end of the month, funded 15,000. The immediate problem was the ability to produce the numbers necessary, but at least the Navy did not have to worry about money. The diverse inventory included multiple types for carrier aviation, but also included flying boats like the Consolidated PBY Catalina and PB2Y Coronado as well as the Martin PBM Mariner. The Navy asked for and eventually received (after bitter haggling with the Army) their version

P-3 Orion conducting ship surveillance in mid-Pacific, September 1974.

of the Consolidated B-24 Liberator (Navy designation PB4Y-1) as well as other land planes from the Army such as the Lockheed Hudson and Vega Ventura. The race against time was on; the Navy prepared as best it could for imminent hostilities against Germany—for the control of the Atlantic and protection of shipping headed to Britain as well as a potential conflict in the Pacific against Japan. When war came in December 1941, in addition to the reinvention of American industry, the Navy had 5,260 aircraft of all types as well as 6,750 pilots available.[42]

After the attack on Pearl Harbor, the Navy was forced to fundamentally reconceptualize doctrine. With the great battleship fleet either sunk or damaged, the only tool left to fight the war was naval aviation. Emphasis was placed on air power assets in both the Atlantic and Pacific theaters of war.

EUROPE, THE NORTH ATLANTIC, AND THE FIGHT AGAINST GERMANY

In the Battle of the Atlantic, the Navy took immediate action to secure sea lines of communication (SLOCs) to supply Britain and keep it in the war. After the fall of France, the British relied heavily on the United States for materials (both civilian and military) for their struggle against Nazi Germany. The enemy retaliated with the naval Battle of the Atlantic, sending German U-boats to sink Allied merchant ships to starve out Britain. The combined U.S. and British response was threefold:

the convoy system for merchant shipping, surface escorts for the fleets, and air cover from long-range aircraft. As early as summer 1942 Patrol Squadron (VP) 73, flying PBY Catalinas, was sent from Quonset Point, Rhode Island, to Iceland to fly anti-submarine patrols across the North Atlantic.[43] However, there were immediate problems: the "Cats" were ineffective at night, they could not shadow the fleets throughout their journey, and there were too few aircraft necessary for the task. Further squadrons were dispatched to Atlantic bases to provide protection for the convoys; Fleet Air Wing (FAW) 7 was established at Dunkeswell, England, made up of VP-103, 105, and 110. Another three squadrons were eventually sent to provide this invaluable service.

A point of friction emerged between the Army and Navy. The Navy wanted a more robust airframe for attacking U-boats, the Army was reluctant to give up strategic resources to the Navy. The Navy had requested B-24s; the Army became concerned that the Navy wanted to infringe on their mission of strategic bombing. Eventually, with the Navy's promise to confine themselves to anti-submarine patrol, the Army relented and began to supply B-24s to the Navy—which were re-designated PB4Y-1.[44] The Navy complained that the airframes were either too old or unfit for Army use, a rumor that was uncontested by the Army, but nonetheless false.

In the ensuing Battle of the Atlantic, the land- and sea-based naval aircraft were invaluable in the final outcomes: both the defeat of the German U-boat threat and the successful supply of Britain and later the Soviets. Combining endurance and effect with new technologies, the Navy planes turned the tide against the German submarine forces and allowed the United States to build up in Britain for the invasion of Normandy and liberation of Europe. During the Battle of the Atlantic, the new technologies of centemetric radar, sonar (on ships), improved ordnance, Leigh Lights, and aircraft improvements overcame traditional problems of night and bad weather to defeat the U-boat threat. In the end, American production, anti-submarine warfare (ASW) doctrine, and technology all combined to destroy the German submarines and win the battle. These successes were built on as the Navy developed an operable ASW doctrine that outlasted the war.

U.S. NAVY LAND- AND SEA-BASED AIRCRAFT IN THE PACIFIC

The history of Navy air power in the Pacific War is usually footnoted by the role of land- and sea-based platforms; the bulk of the research and writing is devoted to the successes of carrier aviation against the Japanese. While carrier-borne aviation was a key component to American victory, no small part was played by the men and machines that were based on the land and sea. The same structure was followed in the Pacific as in the Atlantic, with VP squadrons—and later VB and VPB (for Bombing and Patrol/Bomber)—ringed around the Pacific and advanced as the

Navy and Marine Corps conquered islands. The role of Navy aircraft in the Pacific was even more strategic than in the Atlantic. Heavy bombers (land based) and seaplanes were used in the role of observation, mapping, photography, and patrol, and also took part in operational and strategic bombing missions as U.S. troops advanced across the Pacific toward Japan. The vast expanses of the Pacific were overcome by the Navy's long-range bombers and seaplanes. The Catalinas, Coronados, and Mariners were used in a number of roles, employing their long-range capabilities, playing a key role in rescuing downed airmen, and spotting for Japanese fleet movements. One especially interesting example are the Catalinas of VP-12, one of the famed "Black Cat" squadrons who painted their planes flat black and conducted nighttime commerce raiding and bombing missions.[45] Their counterparts, the land-based Navy squadrons, flew B-24s (Navy designation PB4Y-1), B-25s (PBJ-1), and B-17s (PB-1).[46] The Navy bombers were used in similar ASW and anti-shipping roles, as well as on missions to prepare battlefields for invasion throughout the Pacific campaign. One example among many is the pre-invasion bombing of Guadalcanal by Navy bombers, then the subsequent re-supply of the island with similar aircraft. The "heavies" were some of the first aircraft to use Henderson field after it was captured, helping secure the hard-fought island for American forces.[47]

Organizationally, the Navy's Bureau of Aeronautics went through additional transformation during the war in order to bring naval aviation under a more coherent leadership. In August 1943, in response to the argument that aviation was not receiving proper treatment within the Navy, a deputy chief was added to the staff of the CNO: the Deputy Chief of Naval Operations (Air).[48] The Chief of BuAer Rear Admiral John "Slew" McCain, became the DCNO (Air) and was "charged with the preparation, readiness, and logistics support of the naval aeronautic operating forces included within several fleets, seagoing forces and sea frontier forces of the United States Navy, and with the coordination and direction of the effort to this end of the bureaus and offices of the Navy Department."[49] BuAer became a technical bureau; operations fell under the guidance of the new DCNO (Air). The chain of command was altered slightly so that the CNO (and his offices) had increasingly more jurisdiction over aviation assets.

Nonetheless, it was ultimately the Army bombers that were the bookends for the Pacific War, even if it was with the extensive help from the Navy. The first raids on the Japanese home islands were carried out by Army B-25s flown off the aircraft carrier USS *Hornet*; the final raids of the war were only possible after the Navy and Marines captured airfields at Iwo Jima and Okinawa for Army (Air Forces) use. For all the infighting between the two Services, when it came time to cooperate to defeat an enemy, they did.

V-J Day came on 15 August 1945 (in Japan and the UK but on 14 August in the United States) when the Japanese surrendered to the United States aboard the

USS *Missouri*. General MacArthur and Admiral Nimitz, the heroes of the Army and Navy, respectively, accepted the Japanese surrender aboard the newest and finest battleship in the fleet, even as the era of the battleship was being eclipsed by aircraft carriers.

THE START OF THE COLD WAR

The end of World War II marked a turning point for U.S. naval aviation. The rise of carrier aviation as well as the changing nature of technology ushered in a new era of doctrine, procurement, and missions for naval aviation. Like the eclipse of LTA equipment, the advent of atomic weapons and jet power introduced a sea change. The Navy's focus remained on the missions of World War II: observation, ASW, fleet protection, and a modicum of bombing missions. However, events and technology conspired against the Navy's use of land- and sea-based platforms into the jet era.

The first event the Navy faced in the postwar era was the National Security Act (1947). President Harry Truman consolidated the Department of the Navy and War Department into the Department of Defense, with each of the service chiefs as representatives on the new Joint Chiefs of Staff (JCS). One dispute developed over the role of aircraft when the U.S. Air Force was established. Some argued that the new Air Force should shepherd all air assets; each of the Services argued for their own organic air component. The Air Force insisted that they had won World War II with air power and strategic bombing, and had a strong case when considering the atomic bombs and heavy bombers that helped defeat Japan in 1945. The Army was worried that the divorce of the Air Force would remove the ground support mission of Army aviation, in response the Air Force assured the Army they would continue these operations. To make a long story short, the Air Force did not; the Army had to resurrect this mission with the new technology of helicopters. The Marines did not want to be folded into the Navy, and maintained their independence. The Navy did not want to lose their air component, so allowed the Air Force jurisdiction over strategic bombing missions. In the end, the Navy was willing to forgo development and procurement of heavy bombers in order to maintain a naval air arm.

While still arguing that the Navy had a strategic role to play, the technology posed a paradox. Atomic weapons were seen as the focus of future warfare, and the Navy had to rationalize how to incorporate them into Navy doctrine. While they could provide unprecedented capabilities, they also presented an interesting dilemma. The Navy wanted to be able to use them and began planning for a supercarrier, the USS *United States*, to carry nuclear-armed bombers. But at the same time, it was demonstrated that the carrier was vulnerable in Navy nuclear experiments such as the Bikini Atoll demonstration. Further, the proposal for supercarriers (the Navy wanted five) offended the Air Force as it was building its new generation of strategic bombers, specifically the Convair B-36 *Peacemaker*. The debate raged on. The Navy argued that supercarriers were invaluable to maintaining open sea-lanes, the Marines offered that they were required for any overseas expedition. The Air Force wanted a monopoly on strategic bombing, and in Douhetian fashion maintained that they were the only force necessary for future nuclear war. The Army felt secure in their role, but understood that they had to stay in the fight for numbers and funding. Each of the Services fought for attention, funding, and independence. By 1949 the argument reached a crisis point. New Secretary of Defense Louis Johnson cancelled the USS *United States* five days after the building program began, leading to what became known as the "Revolt of the Admirals."[50] The Secretary of the Navy and the CNO both spoke out in public against the decision to cut the program, and each lost his job. The Navy spoke out against Johnson's decision, citing his personal interest in the B-36 and his open preference for the Air Force. The acrimony was obvious enough that the House Armed Services Committee investigated the matter, dismissing a number of additional Navy officers for their opinions, but did not force the Navy to give up its aviation assets. The widening gulf between the Air Force and the other Services was not repaired when the findings allowed for the continuation of B-36 contracts. The Navy, barely placated by the decisions, returned to the design tables to reinvent their postwar carriers. Navy animosity remained high when the North Koreans invaded South Korea in June 1950.

The Korean War began just as the Navy was locked in a struggle with the new Air Force for the control of the air. Further, the Navy, just like the other Services, was drawing down from World War II, and trying to do as much with fewer men and less material. Demobilization was a high priority after World War II; no one thought that there would be another war for the foreseeable future. But the bipolar world of Capitalism and Communism brought new challenges for the U.S. military. The new Department of Defense struggled to find solutions for the potential problem of fighting the Communists; each of the branches tried to define their future military needs. The Air Force stepped up with strategic nuclear bombing, and was rewarded with new technology for the role. The Navy mission was similar to the World War II era, but began the 1950s with new technology for similar roles. By the outbreak of the Korean War, the Navy had access to both new and old as it defined its role in the new conflict. Carrier aircraft were being replaced with new jets, but the traditional missions of observation and ASW continued with World War II era airframes.

When the Korean War broke out, the Navy deployed to the theater with a handful of carriers as well as their patrol squadrons. The land- and sea-based planes shouldered the work of observation and spotting, as well as ASW patrol and at times search and rescue. At the outbreak of war, the Navy committed two task groups (70.6 and 96.2) to the fight. Under Task Group 70.6 fell Fleet Air Wing 1 (FAW-1) and Marine Air Wing 1 (MAW-1). Four squadrons made up FAW-1: VP-1, VP-28,

VP-46, and VU-5. Task Group 96.2 included FAW-6, which had three squadrons (VP-6, 42, and 47).[51] While this may sound like a massive commitment of land- and sea-based aircraft, it in fact represents only a total of fifty-three aircraft.[52] These planes began immediate ASW and observation patrols, to great success. The Korean War was fairly uneventful for the Navy's VP squadrons. Flying their old Privateers (late World War II–vintage, highly modified B-24s) as well as some new Neptunes and the flying boat Mariners, the VP squadrons performed admirably during the conflict, flying long hours on patrol and suffering few casualties. In three years of combat the VP squadrons flew over 21,000 sorties for 145,000 hours and suffered only forty-one losses from all causes, only four losses due to enemy action.[53] By the end of the "active" portion of the war, there were still only fifty-four aircraft in the VP squadrons in Korea, suggesting that they were superfluous or that these few aircraft were doing all that was necessary of them. While the numbers for Army, Air Force, and Navy carrier aircraft increased throughout the conflict, the patrol squadrons stayed steady at fifty to seventy airframes. Considering the nature of the war, it can be argued that the patrol planes were used in a successful way to isolate the battlefield (the Korean Peninsula) and did their job of keeping sea-borne outside influences from affecting the battlefield. The Army and Air Force had to deal with the Chinese (land) border; the Navy's patrol squadrons were successful at keeping the seas clear of enemies and open for allies.

At the end of the Korean War, the Navy revisited the mission statement for sea- and land-based aviation assets. The Navy was still concerned about fleet support, observation, and ASW warfare, but once again, technology was increasingly successful at marginalizing previous airframes. Sea-based aircraft were slowly overshadowed by land- and carrier-based platforms; increasing performance from jet aircraft, as well as the introduction of Navy and Marine Corps helicopters that took care of short-range missions for the fleet.[54] Fleet support could be handled by the jets; search and rescue was increasingly taken over by rotary-wing aircraft. As other airframes took over these tasks, the Navy produced fewer seaplanes for service. Other missions were also adopted by carrier aircraft. Observation and photography, as well as short-range ASW were assumed by new carrier aircraft like the Guardian,[55] the Tracker,[56] and by 1964 the Hawkeye.[57] In-flight refueling increased the ranges of aircraft, providing longer-duration flights previously possible only in multi-engine land- and sea-based aircraft. The Navy began to transition away from land-based aircraft as their ideas about deep attack and long-range changed and at the same time were taken over by other Navy aircraft and the U.S. Air Force.

One mission that remained specifically naval was ASW. In 1962 the Navy took delivery of its most advanced long-range, land-based ASW and patrol platform, the Lockheed P-3 Orion.[58] The large, four-engine ASW specialist filled the Navy's need for an extended-range platform that could simply not be covered by carrier aircraft.

Navy VP squadrons were in the process of refitting with P-3s (from P-2 Neptunes) when the Navy was called to action in Southeast Asia.

The conflict in Vietnam exploded in August 1964 with the Gulf of Tonkin incident and subsequent escalation by President Lyndon Johnson. The Navy entered the fray with carrier-based aircraft along with seven VP squadrons.[59] As early as February 1965, SP-5B Marlins were moved to Danang as VP-47, part of 7th Fleet, to patrol for submarines. Vice Admiral William Martin, Deputy CNO (Air) wanted to show the viability of the Navy's last seaplane, but was quickly thwarted, not because of the aircraft's impending obsolescence, but because his superiors were worried about VC sabotage of the seaplane base. Only a week after deploying to Vietnam they were moved back to the Philippines for their protection; the Marlins flew patrols from there.[60]

Other Navy efforts in Vietnam met with more successes. In Operation Market Time, a number of VP squadrons, including VP-4, 17, and 40, flew observation and anti-shipping patrols along the coast of South Vietnam which, in conjunction with naval forces on the surface, aimed to deny the sea routes for VC infiltrators. The patrols came in three flavors: Yankee Station, missions in the Gulf of Tonkin, usually flown at night; the Market Time operations observing the coast of South Vietnam for infiltrators; and Ocean Surveillance Patrols (OSAP).[61] One squadron (VP-2, based out of Tan Son Nhut) added five Navy-designated Douglas A-1H Skyraiders to their inventory to bolster their attacking abilities. Patrol aviation's Neptunes would locate bad guys and the Skyraiders could intercept them. While the Skyraiders could, and did, fly from carriers, they were primarily a land-based, single-engine attack aircraft, designed for slow and low flight to attack ground targets. Blessed with excellent range and durability, the A-1s were successful in interdicting Viet Cong (VC) supplies spotted by their observation counterparts.[62] In another interesting use of Navy land-based aircraft, this time OP-2E Neptunes from VO-67 based at Nakhon Phanom, aircraft dropped acoustic sensors to listen for seismic anomalies on the Ho Chi Minh Trail. The "Spikebuoy" and "Adsid" monitors indicated when heavy boot and truck traffic moved along the re-supply route, alerting attack planes, through communications channels, when and where to strike. In some opinions the sensors allowed for more frequent and successful attacks against the VC supply lines, cutting down the resources headed to the insurgency in the South.[63]

Perhaps the best example of Navy land-based aircraft were the Flying Black Ponies of VAL-4.[64] This group flew OV-10s to assist Navy riverine forces and SEAL special operations teams in South Vietnam. The erstwhile Air Force frame was a twin-engine ground attack and observation plane—one squadron given to the Navy—and filled an important if often forgotten role in the counterinsurgency in South Vietnam. Operating from January 1969 to April 1972, this squadron was an odd, uncommon but essential component of the Navy's efforts in the war, and a singular example of Navy land-based aircraft used experimentally to great effect.

Although it was disbanded at the end of the war and never replicated, it remains a shining example of ingenuity and adaptation in unconventional warfare.

In the aftermath of the Vietnam War, the Navy once again ran headlong into postwar constraints. The United States ended the draft and became an all-volunteer military. The defense budget was cut and continued a downward trend (as compared to the gross domestic product [GDP]). The Cold War continued, but the Navy faced continuing operations with fewer sailors and less equipment. And again, Navy missions were influenced by technological change. In the years between World War II and the end of Vietnam, the Navy increasingly relied on carrier aircraft for bombing; with the advent of precision munitions (in and after Vietnam), the standard fighter and fighter/bomber on board aircraft carriers could fill the role of strategic bomber, circumventing the need for a land-based bomber. The Navy found that its F-14s and later F/A-18s, coupled with aerial refueling, could manage the tasks of bombing once relegated to heavy (land-based) bombers. Short-range ASW and fleet protection was assumed by S-3A Vikings after 1974.[65] Maritime patrol by flying boats ended because of financial constraints as well as other, better technology that replaced them; the last P5M-2 Marlin squadron (VP-40) was converted to P-3s in 1968. The Navy experimented with three more seaplanes, but did not use them in service. The final Navy propeller seaplane was the Convair XP5Y-1 Tradewind (later designated R3Y-1),[66] intended as a flying boat for long-range patrol and transport. It was the only turboprop seaplane delivered to the Navy. The final two experimental seaplanes were jets: attempts to combine jet technology of the 1950s with the Navy's perceived need for seaplanes. The first was the Martin XP6M-1 SeaMaster,[67] a four-jet engine seaplane envisioned as a seaborne heavy bomber and patrol plane. Although the SeaMaster was a spectacular aircraft, the program was cancelled in 1960 as the Navy turned away from long-range strategic bombing. After the cancellation of the SeaMaster, the Martin Company got out of the seaplane business to refocus on avionics and missile development. The final Navy seaplane experiment was an attempt at a sea-based air superiority jet fighter, the Convair XF2Y-1 Sea Dart.[68] This aircraft was an offshoot of the Convair F-102 Delta Dagger, an air superiority jet fighter built for the Air Force. The Sea Dart was envisioned to be a Navy platform similar to its Air Force cousin, a supersonic interceptor. But despite its high-technology and coolness factors, there were problems with a sea-based jet fighter; it was obsolete before experimental trials began.[69] The program was cancelled after the first two experimental aircraft suffered catastrophic failure; the Navy gave up on sea-based flying boats. Today flying boats are still used by the U.S. Coast Guard for search-and-rescue (SAR) operations, as well as continued Soviet/Russian experiments with the technology. The Japanese and Chinese have a few flying boats in their inventories and Canada uses them for military purposes. The remaining flying boats fill niche markets for sport flyers and water-bombers for forest firefighters.

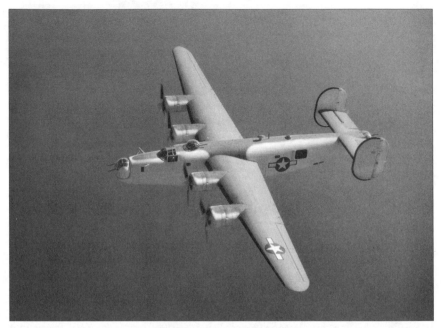

Consolidated B-24 Liberator designated by the U.S. Navy as the PB4Y-1.

The only combat-related mission left to the Navy that could not be filled by carrier aircraft was long-range ASW patrol. For this mission, the Navy relied on the
venerable Lockheed P-3 Orion.[70] Throughout the Cold War, the P-3 remained the
workhorse of the Navy, flying patrols around the globe searching for Soviet submarines. Designed as a long-range patrol plane, the four-turboprop engine aircraft was
packed with electronics and anti-submarine weapons to find and potentially destroy
enemy subs. Distinguishable by its long "tail," the magnetic anomaly detection
(MAD) boom extends to the rear, making the aircraft easily distinguishable. The
eleven-man crew typically flew extended long-range patrols—up to eighteen hours
at a time—searching the seas for Soviet subs and enemy warships. The P-3 could
maintain altitude and speed—cruising speed of 378 mph—by flying on only three
or even two engines, thus extending range and conserving fuel. The plane was
designed to fly low and slow, searching the seas for the enemy.

The last land-based Navy aircraft in the inventory (excepting a few transports and
VIP "limousines"), the P-3 Orion continues to provide essential long-range capabilities to the Navy into the twenty-first century. Even after the fall of Communism, the
Orion continues service for the Navy, extending the Navy's reach across the oceans
of the world. The P-3 saw service in the 1991 Gulf War, as one of the first combat
components on site after Iraq invaded Kuwait. Upgraded P-3s were instrumental in

identifying and targeting Iraqi surface ships in the Persian Gulf during Operation Outlaw Hunter. The Navy's P-3s provided electronic and targeting information in the protection of U.S. and Saudi equipment in the combat area.[71]

The need for the Navy's land-based long-range patrol capability was assured and continued into the twenty-first century. As the Navy began to shop around for a new airframe, an unfortunate incident occurred on patrol off the coast of China. In April 2001 a P-3C had an unfortunate midair collision with a Chinese PLA Naval Air Force J-811 (some reports say J-8D) fighter/interceptor, killing the Chinese pilot. The American crew made an emergency landing at an airfield on Hainan and were immediately detained. The international incident was compounded by the death of the Chinese pilot and the fact that the P-3 was an electronics warfare aircraft. The American crew of twenty-four was returned to the United States a week after the crash; the P-3 was held (and undoubtedly studied) for three months.[72] The Hainan Island incident—as it became known—was reminiscent of the Gary Powers incident in 1960, when his U-2 spy plane was shot down over the Soviet Union.

After the events of 9/11, Navy P-3s were employed in the War on Terror as long-range mobile electronics platforms to combat conventional and terrorist threats. With the invasion of Afghanistan and Iraq, Navy P-3s once again provided invaluable effects for the Navy and the U.S. military as a whole. In Afghanistan, Navy P-3s, equipped with new electronics packages, were equipped for anti-surface warfare improvement platforms (AIP) to combat threats in there. Flying out of Kandahar, they provide electronics intelligence and targeting information for ground troops and air support platforms.[73] In Iraq, after 2003, the Navy provides P-3s for both the land battles and maritime patrol operations in the Persian Gulf on a regular basis. In the troubled waters off Somalia, Navy P-3s patrol for Somali pirates, protecting merchant ships and helping with the anti-piracy efforts off the Horn of Africa. As part of Combined Joint Task Force–Horn of Africa (CJTF-HOA) Combined Task Force 150 (part of the U.S. Sixth Fleet), the P-3s continue to combat Somali pirates as part of the efforts in Operation Enduring Freedom–Horn of Africa.

Into the twenty-first century, the Navy preserves the mission of long-range land-based maritime patrol with the aging P-3 fleet.[74] Now operating twelve squadrons of P-3s, the Navy is searching for a new aerial platform to replace the forty-seven-year-old design. Currently the Navy is considering the MMA (multi mission aircraft) from Boeing (Navy designation P-8 Poseidon) as a replacement for the P-3. Based on the Boeing 737, the aircraft will provide the same mission capabilities as the P-3 with a new all-jet design.[75] Although there are some detractors for the new airframe, the program is needed to replace the aging aircraft. The most commonly cited deficiency in the MMA is that the jet will not be able to fly low and slow for anti-submarine and anti-shipping duties. Nonetheless, the Navy is determined to continue the role in a new airframe with improved qualities.

Today the Navy continues to preserve the patrol mission with land-based naval aircraft. All other missions from World War II have been given over to the Air Force and carrier aircraft, but the long-range ASW and anti-shipping roles have been maintained. The Navy will continue these roles well into the twenty-first century with a mix of old and new aircraft, some land based, some from carriers as needed. The legacy of land- and sea-based Navy aircraft has been missions born of necessity and marked with adaptation and innovation. Into the future, the Navy will continue to employ land-based aircraft to protect the fleet and provide comprehensive mission support in the spirit of jointness for the U.S. military as a whole. The future of U.S. Navy aviation still has a place for land-based aircraft to maintain the Navy's missions around the globe.

NOTES

1. Carl von Clausewitz discusses the grammar and logic of warfare in his epic tome, *On War*, trans. Michael Howard and Peter Paret (Princeton, NJ: Princeton University Press, 1976).

2. Sir Julian Corbett, *Principles of Maritime Strategy* (New York: AMS Press, 1972), and Alfred Thayer Mahan, *Influence of Sea Power Upon History, 1660–1783* (Boston: Little Brown, 1918).

3. It is this author's contention that naval warfare traced a distinctly evolutionary track of the superiority of capital ships from the ancient triremes to the *Dreadnought*-class battleships of World War I. Aviation and submarine technology showed the potential to radically (disruptively) alter the naval strategy paradigm.

4. See chapter 4, this volume, on lighter-than-air naval aviation.

5. See chapters 9 and 15, this volume, on U.S. Navy carrier aviation.

6. Note that up to 1947 when the War Department was reorganized, there were only two Services, the Army and the Navy. Each procured air assets for specific roles related to the land and sea, respectively.

7. Archibald Turnbull, *History of United States Naval Aviation* (Manchester, NH: Ayer Company Publishing, 1971), p. 33.

8. Ibid., pp. 33–34. See also chapter 2, this volume, by Dr. Stephen Stein on the early days of the Navy's Bureau of Aeronautics.

9. Ibid., p. 34.

10. See specifically chapter 4, this volume, Dr. John Jackson's excellent overview of U.S. Navy LTA.

11. Naval Appropriations Act, March 1915, $1 million, and further monies throughout the war for all types of naval aviation and R&D.

12. In Turnbull, *History,* p. 63, Commander Mustin, to the Navy General Board in 1916, argued that the "Navy be given a separate flying corps similar to the Marine Corps."

13. Ibid., pp. 91–92.

14. Officially in April 1917.

15. Turnbull, *History,* pp. 137–38.

16. Of the total number of naval officers (6,716) and men (30,693) by the end of the war. Added to these figures were another 282 officers and 2,180 Marines in aviation roles.

17. Only one was completed: the USS *Wright* (AZ-1, later AV-1).

18. Wilbur Morrison, *Pilots, Man Your Planes* (Ashland, OR: Hellgate Publishing, 1999), pp. 40–41.

19. See specifically letters from the CNO to the President of the NWC in the U.S. Naval War College Archives (hereafter NWC Archives), Record Group 8, Box 30, multiple files.

20. Specifically NWC Archives RG8, Box 30, File 9.

21. Ibid.

22. See specifically documents in the NWC Archives in RG8, RG15 (lectures), and RG64.

23. See specifically his ideas on air power in William Mitchell, *Winged Defense*, (Mineola, NY: Dover Publications, 2006).

24. Among the many books on Mitchell, the (anti-) Navy demonstrations, and Mitchell's subsequent falling-out with both the U.S. Navy and Army, see specifically Alfred Hurley, *Billy Mitchell: Crusader for Airpower* (Bloomington: Indiana University Press, 2006).

25. See specifically the devastating losses of Navy dirigibles during this time, and subsequent abandonment of this technology. Mitchell enters the picture again, when he publicly excoriated the U.S. Navy as incompetent in aerial technology and employment.

26. "The Bureau of Aeronautics," in Turnbull, *History,* pp. 186–92.

27. Ibid., p. 190.

28. Pratt-MacArthur Agreement, Air Force Historical Research Agency (AFHRA), USAF Collection, IRIS No. 123080 (AFHRA, Maxwell AFB, AL).

29. CV-1 USS *Langley,* CV-2 USS *Lexington,* and CV-3 USS *Saratoga* were on the Navy register, but the Navy still relied heavily on battleships (BB) for power projection. To say that carrier aircraft development was still in its embryonic phases would not be an understatement. See specifically Thomas Hone et al., *American and British Aircraft Carrier Development, 1919–1941* (Annapolis: Naval Institute Press, 1999).

30. Turnbull, *History,* pp. 277–79, gives an excellent account.

31. NWC Archives, RG8, Box 31, File 11: multiple listings for Navy procurement of aircraft, first citation 1922.

32. AFHRA, USAF Collection, IRIS No. 467748, "Alleged 100 Mile Limitation on Army Aviation in Coast Defense, 1931," compiled and published (as a classified document) 1 November 1946 (Maxwell AFB, AL).

33. Ibid., pp. 1–2.

34. Cited in ibid., p. 2.

35. See multiple Army Air doctrinal documents from the interwar periods, including "Employment of the Air Forces for the Army" (1935) as well as AWPD-1, where the issue did not even warrant mention.

36. As recounted in Turnbull, *History,* p. 279, from the winter 1929/30.

37. Ibid., pp. 300–301. Admiral Arthur Hepburn recommended the expansion of naval aviation including planes and bases. See specifically his report for expansion of the eleven existing bases and construction of sixteen new ones, including bases in the Pacific.

38. According to Turnbull (ibid., p. 311), Patrol Wings 3 and 5 had fifty-four aircraft between the two of them, the battleship fleets had twenty-five.

39. According to *The United States Strategic Bombing Survey (Japan)* (Maxwell AFB, AL: Air University Press, multiple volumes). See specifically USSBS, *The Campaigns of the Pacific War* (published in 1946), which states more precisely that there were 1,426 Allied planes in the Pacific, 688 frontline aircraft (the rest obsolete and obsolescent), and of these 332 were British and Australian.

40. It was actually closer to 2,000 combat aircraft with an additional 1,250 trainers and transport.

41. Again, overestimations; the Japanese did not have nearly that many, but American intelligence was remiss. However, it must be mentioned that the Japanese, while lacking in numbers, by 1939 (and into 1941) had the world's finest collection of naval aircraft and pilots. See specifically *The United States Strategic Bombing Survey (Japan),* p. 4.

42. Turnbull, *History,* p. 317. The number of pilots included Navy, Marine Corps, and Coast Guard pilots ready for duty.

43. Robert Carlisle, *Cats over the Atlantic, VPB-73 in WW II* (Santa Barbara, CA: Fithian Press, 1995), p. 28.

44. See Allan Carey, *U.S. Navy PB4Y-1 (B24) Liberator Squadrons in Great Britain during World War II* (Atglen, PA: Schiffer Military History, 2003), pp. 21–22.

45. Richard Knott, *Black Cat Raiders of World War II* (Annapolis: Naval Institute Press, 2000).

46. Special thanks to Curt Lawson of the U.S. Naval Aviation Museum (Pensacola NAS, FL) for his well-researched and detailed listing of Navy aircraft, their acceptance dates, numbers built, and roles in the Navy. In addition to his research, this author benefited from his extensive knowledge in numerous conversations.

47. Samuel Griffith, *The Battle for Guadalcanal* (Champaign: University of Illinois Press, 2000).

48. Julius Furer, *Administration of the Navy Department in World War II* (Washington, DC: GPO, 1959), pp. 391–92.

49. Ibid., p. 392.

50. Jeffrey Barlow, *Revolt of the Admirals: The Fight for Naval Aviation, 1945–1950* (Washington, DC: Naval Historical Center, 1994).

51. Korean War Documents, Aviation Statistics Specific Report 2-50, "Combat Activity of Navy Aircraft in Korean Theater June 1950–July 1953," June 1950 entry, pp. 3–5 (Aviation Statistics Section, Aviation Plans Division, U.S. Naval Aviation Museum, Pensacola NAS, FL). The massive binder is divided by month of the conflict.

52. Ibid., pp. 7, 9–11. The breakdown is: VP-1 (8 aircraft), VP-6 (7), VP-28 (9), VP-42 (9), VP-46 (7), VP-47 (8), VU-5 (5).

53. Ibid., July 1953 overview, pp. 71–81 (tables 15, 16, 20, and 21). Two patrol planes were shot down by enemy AA; 32 lost to "operational" losses (accidents, crashes, etc.), and 7 were lost to "All other causes." Of the 41 lost, 26 were seaplanes and 15 were landplanes.

54. For more details see the corresponding chapters in this Korean War Documents collection on the development of aircraft carriers and aircraft.

55. Grumman AF-2W, first in service in 1950.

56. Grumman S2F-1, first in service in 1954.

57. Grumman W2F-1 (E-2A), first in service in 1964.

58. See specifically the P-3 entry in Rene Francillion, *Lockheed Aircraft since 1913* (Annapolis: Naval Institute Press, 1987), pp. 408–19.

59. Specifically, VP-2, 4, 16, 17, 31, 40, and 50.

60. Edward Marolda and Oscar Fitzgerald, *The United States Navy and the Vietnam Conflict,* vol. 2, *From Military Assistance to Combat 1959–1965* (Washington, DC: Naval Historical Center, 1986), pp. 494–95.

61. Peter Mersky and Norman Polmar, *The Naval Air War in Vietnam* (Baltimore, MD: Nautical and Aviation Publishing Company of America, 1986), pp. 31–34.

62. Marolda and Fitzgerald, *The United States Navy*, pp. 518–21.

63. Mersky and Polmar, *The Naval Air War*, pp. 171–72.

64. Kit Lavell, *Flying Black Ponies* (Annapolis: Naval Institute Press, 2000).

65. Lockheed S-3A and later B *Viking*, first delivered in 1974.

66. Convair R3Y-1, 2 Tradewind, first flown in 1954, twelve delivered.

67. Martin XP6M-1 SeaMaster, first flown in July 1955, five built (two experimental, three pre-production).

68. Convair XF2Y-1 Sea Dart, first flown in April 1953, five built.

69. B. J. Long, "Sea Dart," *Journal of American Aviation Historical Society* 24, no. 1 (Spring 1979), pp. 2–12.

70. Lockheed P-3A/B/C/D/E/F Orion, first delivered in 1962, 516 built to date. See specifically Francillion, *Lockheed Aircraft*, pp. 408–19.

71. David Reade, *The Age of Orion, the Lockheed P-3 Orion Story* (Atglen, PA: Schiffer Military History, 1998), pp. 42–49. Reade suggests that the P-3s actively targeted 55 of the 110 Iraqi ships destroyed in the Gulf War (1991).

72. Although there is little in the secondary research on this as of yet, and the official documents are still classified, the open source news media (CNN, BBC, etc.) covered this story extensively from 1 to 11 April 2001, and in subsequent news stories. Today (in 2009) it seems as if the incident has been forgotten in diplomatic circles, with increasingly friendly relationships with China.

73. See specifically http://www.military.com/NewContent/0,13190,SS_070505_Navy,00.html (accessed 18 November 2009), for a discussion of Navy P-3s in Afghanistan.

74. See "A Cooperative Strategy for 21st Century Seapower," as proposed by the U.S. Navy in 2007, http://www.navy.mil/maritime/MaritimeStrategy.pdf (accessed 18 November 2009).

75. See Boeing's Web site on the P-8 (MMA), http://www.boeing.com/defense-space/military/p8a/index.html (accessed 18 November 2009).

CHAPTER 15

U.S. Aircraft Carrier Evolution: 1945–2011

Norman Friedman

In dramatic contrast to the carriers that won World War II, the carrier fleet built since World War II was conceived primarily to strike land targets.[1] The strike missions conceived in 1945–1950 defined a new generation of carrier-based bombers. These aircraft in turn shaped the new carriers, beginning with USS *Forrestal*. The *Forrestal* design in turn defined succeeding aircraft, all of which were designed to fit essentially the same flight deck, hangar deck, and catapults and arresting gear. It turned out, unexpectedly, that many of the same aircraft could operate from existing carriers, once they had been modernized. Although U.S. carriers have changed considerably since the 1950s, their modern form is recognizably that of the *Forrestal*, so this account will concentrate on the first postwar decade, which shaped her.

The postwar carrier force was shaped by a combination of new (and changing) strategic conditions and rapidly changing technology, the latter occurring particularly in the years immediately after World War II. Another factor, until about 1970, was the large inventory of carriers remaining after World War II, comprising two classes of fleet carriers (*Midway* and *Essex*) and numerous smaller ones (particularly the wartime light carriers and the *Commencement Bay*–class escort carriers).

The major new technologies were the atomic (and then hydrogen) bomb, jet aircraft, guided missiles, nuclear power for ships, and new kinds of submarines (first fast diesel-electric types and then nuclear submarines), electronics, navigation, and communications. All changed during the fifty postwar years to interact in various ways.

NEW STRATEGIC CONDITIONS

By the end of World War II, carriers were operating in two rather different roles. One was land attack, either strategic (the strikes on Tokyo) or tactical (direct support of troops, particularly as they landed) the other was anti-submarine warfare either in the hunter-killer role or in direct support of convoys.[2] Which would be the dominant postwar role? It seemed unlikely that the struggle with the powerful Japanese surface fleet would be repeated. The Soviet Union, a dominant land power, would probably be the next enemy. The main naval component of Soviet power was a large submarine fleet. The Soviets also operated a large land-based naval air arm, but it seemed far less significant (at least to the U.S. Navy) than the submarines in the immediate postwar period.[3]

From a strategic point of view, the United States was an island that would be supporting a war on the periphery of Eurasia. Throughout the Cold War, there were three opposing views of what that might mean. One view, the Navy's, was that the sea gave U.S. forces enormous mobility. They might not match sheer Soviet numbers, but the threat of powerful attacks around the periphery could force the Soviets to split up their forces, denying them the superiority in any one place that might be fatal to the West. This was much the Western strategy of World War II. The opposing view was that peripheral attacks were pointless because only one land theater mattered: the Central Front along the inter-German border. In this view, the point of sea power was to guarantee re-supply of the Western force fighting in central Europe.

A third view emerged from the successful bombing of Japan. Until 1949 the United States had a monopoly on nuclear weapons. The Truman administration hoped that the threat of such weapons, which at the time could be delivered only by heavy land-based bombers, might deter the Soviets even though the United States and other Western countries could not maintain sufficient land forces in Western Europe. The situation became particularly difficult in 1948–1950. U.S. rearmament (after the Soviets seized power in Czechoslovakia by a coup, and thus convinced doubters that there was indeed a Cold War in progress) stalled because funds were split between Marshall Plan aid to Europe and defense. The argument was that the Marshall Plan was in effect defense against the real possibility that Soviet-controlled Communist parties would simply seize power in weakened countries like France, Germany, and Italy. The outbreak of war in Korea in June 1950 effectively demonstrated the limits of nuclear deterrence.

These alternatives had radically different consequences for the shape of the Navy and its carrier force. The Navy view was that the strike carrier capability developed during World War II and demonstrated so dramatically in the Pacific should be adapted to the new conditions. For example, if the Soviets decided to advance into Western Europe, a powerful naval force in the Mediterranean and the North

Sea could land U.S. ground forces on their flanks, slowing or stopping them. Such a force, so employed, would be far more effective than it would be if simply placed in the path of an overwhelming Soviet Army in Germany.

Strike carriers might also be the best way to deal with Soviet submarines. Although the Soviet submarines available in 1945 were obsolescent at best, the Soviets (like the Western Allies) had captured new German technology. Within a few years they would be building submarines that could probably defeat the anti-submarine measures that had won the Battle of the Atlantic. There was little chance that the Western navies would be able to build enough escorts to conduct a World War II–style convoy defense of their vital shipping. In that case the choices would be either to hunt down the submarines or to destroy them at their bases ("at source").

These issues were not particularly contentious during the run-down of U.S. military strength after 1945. The Navy lived mainly off the massive wartime investment in ships and aircraft. By 1948, when rearmament began, new weapons, particularly aircraft, were coming into service, and new production was needed. For the Navy, among the first fruits of rearmament was approval to build the first of a new generation of very large carriers, USS *United States.* Meanwhile the political choice had been made to create a new U.S. Air Force and to achieve efficiency by unifying the (newly) three Services and parceling out their roles. The new Air Force wanted much what the Royal Air Force had achieved in 1918, a monopoly over aircraft. Because the Air Force emerged from the Army, it certainly achieved that in terms of Army aviation. The U.S. Navy, however, was well aware that carriers—and their aircraft—would be its core. It successfully resisted attempts to eliminate naval aviation, although there were extremely acute questions as to which Service would be responsible for which kinds of air operation. During the debate over Service unification, the U.S. Army tried to eliminate the Marine Corps as unnecessary duplication of effort (President Harry Truman, a former Army artillery officer, favored this move), but the Marines successfully resisted. That resistance preserved Marine aviation, with important consequences for Navy aviation (which included the Marines) as a whole.

Inter-Service arguments became crucial because the defense budget suffered in 1949. The necessary cut was so deep that no Service could avoid cutting core capabilities. The new U.S. Air Force decided to emphasize its nuclear role, which promised an affordable kind of defense. The new supercarrier USS *United States* had been conceived for nuclear attack. Many in the Air Force clearly saw it as a direct threat; if the only viable Air Force role was nuclear attack, only a monopoly would guarantee the Service's survival. Indeed, a monopoly would make the Air Force the dominant Service. In 1949 the two largest programs were the supercarrier (which would have been the first of four) and the Air Force's B-36 intercontinental bomber. Secretary of Defense Louis Johnson cancelled the carrier. To many in the Navy, he was reducing the Service to a subsidiary role, supplying forward bases (which might not even be needed if the B-36 succeeded). The Secretary of the Navy resigned. The Navy forced a congressional debate—and lost. The Navy's fight was known as the "Revolt of the Admirals." In effect the outbreak of war in Korea about a year later showed that the Navy had been right: nuclear deterrence was a limited weapon. Events after the out-break showed that the problem had been budgetary: the Truman administration roughly tripled the defense budget, and it became possible to build balanced U.S. forces, including a new generation of aircraft carriers.

The Navy had always argued that the value of the carrier lay in its flexibility. That was dramatically demonstrated in June 1950, when U.S. and British carriers provided much of the critical air support when the North Koreans invaded South Korea, overrunning airfields. Later, jets operating from the U.S. carriers challenged the Russian-supplied (and often Russian-operated) MiG-15s supporting the Chinese and the North Koreans. It was crucial for U.S. carrier aviation that existing carriers were able to operate aircraft with performance entirely comparable to that of land-based fighters (and bombers).

Dwight D. Eisenhower became president in 1953. As the first Commander of NATO forces in Europe, he was acutely aware of the weakness of Western armies compared with those of the Soviet Union. As former Commander of Allied Armies beginning with D-day, he was also well aware of the value of sea-based forces. He remarked that Western Europe should be seen as a peninsula, with sea flanks on both sides that the defenders could and should exploit. He was also well aware that

Official 1948 sketch of the supercarrier United States, *which was designed to carry heavy bombers.*

U.S. Navy

nuclear deterrence made the big war in Europe unlikely—but did not affect peripheral wars such as Korea. President Eisenhower saw American sea power as a way of
forcing the Soviets and their clients to defend their entire periphery. For him, therefore, strike carriers armed with nuclear weapons were the only affordable way to deal
with the sheer mass of Soviet and client land forces. This mass had recently been
demonstrated by Chinese intervention in Korea.

At the same time, nuclear-armed carrier aircraft were considered an important addition to the U.S. strategic deterrent. Because they operated around the
edges of Eurasia, carriers could attack the Soviet Union from unexpected directions.
The Soviets maintained a massive national air defense system. Just as in the case of
ground forces, the U.S. ability to strike from the sea forced the Soviets to stretch out
that system; that investment imposed other limits on Soviet military power.

In the 1950s, the Eisenhower administration assumed that nuclear weapons
would be used in any war; it said that they should be treated just like any other
weapon. The carriers thus combined tactical and strategic roles. When the Kennedy
administration entered office, it reversed that policy, on the grounds that any use of
nuclear weapons might quickly escalate into an unrestrained nuclear holocaust. This
was much the view taken by later administrations during the Cold War. At about
the same time, the Navy deterrent role shifted from carriers to strategic submarines.
It seemed that Soviet strategy now favored supporting local wars of national liberation, which meant local insurgencies. Surely U.S. support of governments under
threat would entail the use of local airfields, which could support large land-based
air forces? It was no longer so obvious that a carrier, with a limited number of aircraft on board, was worthwhile.

The first (and only) U.S. war to stop local Communist insurgents was Vietnam.
The insurgent army in South Vietnam was in effect an arm of the North Vietnamese
army, and an important part of U.S. strategy was to convince the North Vietnamese
to pull back by threatening North Vietnam itself, by air strikes. North Vietnam
turned out to be a miniature version of the Soviet air defense situation. Land-based
aircraft flew predictable routes to their targets. Strikes from the sea turned out to
be quite useful, as they complicated the North Vietnamese air defense problem. It
also turned out that carriers in the Tonkin Gulf could deliver similar amounts of
ordnance to tactical aircraft in South Vietnam and Thailand. The carriers were well
worthwhile. Among other surprises, the Viet Cong in South Vietnam managed to
destroy many aircraft on the ground—carrier aircraft were immune to such strikes.
Aircraft in safer places like Thailand incurred their own costs.

After the United States withdrew from Vietnam, attention shifted back to the
Soviet threat to Western Europe. Again there was a question of whether strike carriers were worthwhile. It seemed to some that by the 1970s the Soviets had amassed
so much anti-carrier striking power that any attempt to operate carriers near the

Soviet Union would be suicidal (an author wrote about the ritual "dance of death" represented by carrier exercises in the Norwegian Sea). In the late 1970s the Carter administration planned a "sea control" fleet emphasizing submarines, frigates, and patrol aircraft specifically to deal with the large Soviet submarine fleet.

The new thinking, which denigrated carriers, distinguished between a power projection capability (carriers and amphibious forces) usable mainly in the Third World, and a sea control capability to defeat enemy submarines. This view, popularized by CNO Admiral Elmo Zumwalt Jr., responded in part to the Defense Department practice of categorizing forces for distinct missions. Critics within the Navy pointed out that the distinction between sea control and power projection might be a lot less clear-cut than the admiral, a surface force sailor, imagined. His strategy of concentrating on sea control in effect gave the Soviets the initiative. Many in the policy community thought that Admiral Zumwalt's ideas, which were the first explicit expressions of naval strategy they had ever seen, were actually mainstream Navy thinking.[4]

Many U.S. Navy strategists saw things differently. A new maritime strategy, actually a classic naval strategy, was framed beginning with the Navy's Seaplan 2000 response to the Carter administration's request for a study of the appropriate future of the fleet. One key point was that the Soviet fleet had changed dramatically. It had always had a large naval air arm, but by the 1960s it was deploying jet bombers with stand-off missiles. A fleet designed to defeat submarines could not provide sea control anywhere near Western Europe, because it could not beat the bombers. Only carrier-based fighters could (the bombers could get to sea-lanes without encountering land-based NATO fighters). By the 1970s the U.S. Navy was beginning to acquire the solution to the bombers, in the form of F-14 Tomcat fighters armed with the Phoenix missile, backed by the Aegis surface anti-aircraft missile system. The problem had always been that anti-ship missiles were so deadly a threat that fleet fighters would concentrate on them, allowing the bombers to launch, return to base, and launch again. Aegis was so effective a backstop that, once it was in service, the fighters could concentrate on the bombers, attacking "the archer rather than the arrow." Unless those archers were killed, they could easily destroy vital NATO shipping and also the surface ships intended to help fight Soviet submarines. Another factor in the change was the growing understanding that, while the Soviet view of land warfare was deeply offensive, the Soviets would start a war at sea on the defensive. An offensively oriented U.S. Fleet could keep them there.[5]

The strategists also emphasized the Soviets' flank problem. By 1969 the Soviet Union and China were bitter enemies. The Soviets began to move large forces to the Far East—to the detriment of those it could maintain facing Western Europe. In the late 1970s Pacific Fleet Commander Admiral Thomas B. Hayward pointed out that his fleet contributed to the defense of Europe by maintaining a threat in the Far East, in effect demonstrating to the Soviets that the United States would back China in a future global war. The alternative, which the Carter administration favored, was simply to swing the Pacific Fleet to the Atlantic to support the expected European war.

The new maritime strategy shaped the naval program of the Reagan administration. Secretary of the Navy Dr. John Lehman was a reserve carrier aviator who appreciated the efficacy of carrier air power, and who understood that the Navy could make a strategic contribution in any future war against the Soviet Union. His senior commanders already understood the way the Navy should fight (Lehman knew their views from his own participation in Seaplan 2000). Lehman had them combine their outline war plans into a single explicit maritime strategy that showed how a fleet built around carriers could seize and exploit naval supremacy. Dr. Lehman's own background probably made him particularly aware of the air threat not only to carriers but to NATO shipping, hence supportive of the use of U.S. carriers and their fighters to destroy that threat. The emerging maritime strategy built on classic sea power thinking: the U.S. Navy would neutralize the Soviet fleet (mainly land-based missile bombers and submarines) by confronting it with the choice between fighting a losing decisive battle in the Norwegian Sea or surviving as a fleet in being. Carriers and their aircraft were key both to forcing the Soviet fleet to fight (by mounting a threat the Soviet fleet would feel compelled to counter) and to destroying its strike bombers. As for the submarines, it seemed that the anti-submarine force built around the fleet would be far more capable than anything escorting NATO convoys. Although the new maritime strategy was a revival of classic thinking, many outside and even inside the Navy thought it was new and dangerous, contrasting it with the much less aggressive ideas publicized by Admiral Zumwalt. In Zumwalt's terms, the maritime strategy would achieve sea control by projecting naval power into the Soviet Union. U.S. naval exercises were conducted to dramatize the ability of the carrier-oriented fleet to survive and to project power in the crucial Norwegian Sea; Dr. Lehman himself considered the success of such exercises (Northern Wedding) a decisive Cold War victory.

When the Cold War ended, the U.S. Navy differed from most NATO navies in its emphasis on carrier-based power projection. That turned out to be an excellent idea, because the wars that followed required the United States to deal with local land power. Land-based aircraft were certainly vital, but the limitations of land bases became more and more obvious. Many governments were reluctant to allow basing, at least of combat aircraft. When NATO fought in the former Yugoslavia, the use of land bases was restricted not so much by politics as simply by weather, so that the large numbers of land-based aircraft could not conduct as many sorties as could much smaller numbers of sea-based aircraft. In Afghanistan, political limits on land basing led to the use of bases much farther from the battle area, and that in turn badly fatigued pilots, sometimes causing them to make fatal attack errors.

Perhaps Saudi Arabia in 1990 was the most interesting case of all. When the Iraqis invaded Kuwait that year, they threatened to continue on into Saudi Arabia. The natural Saudi reaction would have been to invite American forces into the country. Iraqi dictator Saddam Hussein warned that to invite unbelievers onto sacred Saudi soil would undermine the legitimacy of the Saudi government, and he had friends in country to back up that threat. Carriers made it possible for the United States to provide a degree of support for Saudi Arabia without moving troops into the country. Given that ability, it was no longer worthwhile for Saddam Hussein to risk having his bluff called. The Saudi government felt comfortable bringing in the coalition force, which ultimately ejected Saddam from Kuwait.

NEW CARRIERS—NEW AIRCRAFT

Even before the end of World War II the U.S. Navy convened a panel of experienced officers to ponder the future of the carrier, which it now saw as its primary weapon.[6] Panel members soon concluded that the main value of a future carrier would lie in its ability to deliver heavy bombs against land targets. A carrier could not accommodate many heavy bombers, but it seemed that relatively small numbers of heavy bombs delivered on a precision basis might be quite effective. Moreover, heavy bombs seemed to be the only effective antidote to the coming new generation of submarines. By spring 1945 the main characteristics of new German submarines (which it was assumed the Soviets would copy) were known, and they could clearly overcome most World War II convoy escorts. The submarines could, however, be destroyed in their pens. It seemed likely that the Soviets would adopt the wartime German practice of building heavily protected pens, hence the need for very heavy bombs to deal with them. It happened that a carrier-based heavy bomber could also drop atomic bombs, but that does not seem to have been the key consideration, at least initially.

The panel drew up a rough specification for a future carrier-based heavy bomber. A study by the Bureau of Aeronautics defined the largest bomber that could be launched by existing carriers, using their catapults. It fell far short of the ideal, but it was still worthwhile, and in December 1945 it was ordered as the North American AJ Savage.[7] President Truman agreed that the Navy should share the nuclear mission with the Army (hence with the Air Force established in 1947), thus the Savage design was modified in spring 1946 so that it could carry an atomic bomb. Meanwhile the Navy sought an interim nuclear attack capability. It had a new high-performance land-based patrol bomber, Lockheed's Neptune (P2V, later P-2). A Neptune could certainly deliver the 10,000-pound atomic bomb. Given sufficient boost, in the form of rockets, it could take off from the long flight deck of a *Midway*-class carrier. Neptunes and the carriers together amounted to an interim Navy nuclear attack system. The big airplanes were given tail hooks, but attempts to land them aboard a simulated carrier failed. In war, they would have been placed aboard their carriers by crane; they would have ditched on returning from their missions.

The limitations of the Savage and the Neptune were indications that existing carriers were too small for the key postwar mission. A rough specification was drawn up for the desired long-range bomber. The Bureau of Aeronautics (BuAer) produced an outline design as a guide to designing a carrier that could accommodate such aircraft. Meanwhile two much more ambitious specifications were released to aircraft companies.[8] One specification called for a long-range bomber fast enough to evade existing fighters. Maximum takeoff weight was 100,000 pounds, beyond what existing carriers could support; but some of the designs offered could operate from existing ships if they could be fitted with more powerful catapults. The second specification called for supersonic speed over the target, presumably to ensure immunity from interception. Nothing short of a much larger carrier could support such aircraft.

The main features of the special carrier were a very large flight deck without obstructions (a flush deck) and very powerful new catapults. The flush deck made it possible for the carrier to operate aircraft with long wingspans, which might otherwise collide with a ship's island.[9] Both involved technical problems. It would not be easy to vent the smoke produced by the ship's huge power plant, and a flush deck would greatly complicate placing the radars on which the ship would rely (for a time it seemed that radar and command facilities would be transplanted into an accompanying ship). Existing catapult technology was hydraulic, but the wires and sheaves such catapults used (to multiply the stroke of the hydraulic piston) could not take anything like the loads envisaged. The Bureau of Aeronautics became interested in a new technology, a cylinder whose piston would be moved by explosives.[10]

Perhaps the single greatest design problem was to provide a flight deck heavy enough and strong enough to accommodate aircraft weighing as much as ten times wartime types. The solution was to abandon the previous practice of building a light flight deck as a superstructure atop a hull. Instead, in the new carrier the flight deck was the upper strength element of the hull girder (especially creative solutions were needed to carry strength around the massive holes cut in the side of that girder). Given this approach, centerline elevators were abandoned. Initially it seemed that the new special-purpose carrier would have no hangar at all, her heavy bombers carried permanently on deck, but that idea was soon abandoned. Even placing the slots for catapults in the strength deck was a problem, but it could not be avoided. The ship was designed with four catapults, rather than the two of wartime carriers: two in the bow to launch heavy bombers, and two smaller ones in the waist to launch fighters or smaller bombers. The catapults were so spaced that airplanes could have been launched simultaneously from waist and bow catapults, to get an attack force into the air as quickly as possible (presumably in the event the ship was attacked).

By 1948 it seemed that the design of the new carrier was mature enough. It may also have seemed that this would be the Navy's last opportunity to decide for itself what it needed—before Service unification put much power in the hands of the Secretary of Defense and, more importantly, a Joint Chiefs of Staff dominated by the two ground Services, the Air Force and the Army. Surviving records suggest that neither of the key technical problems, the use of the flush deck and the catapult, had been solved. That was by no means obvious at the time.

The Navy did not expect to have many of the new carriers; the usual figure was four (or fewer). Navy plans called for modernization of existing carriers to form new task groups built around the heavy carriers. The existing carriers would operate jet fighters to protect the attack carriers when they conducted their strikes against Soviet targets. A task group would consist of one heavy carrier plus three smaller ones, for a total fleet of four new type carriers, three *Midway*s and ten modernized *Essex* class. Modernization for jet operation involved provision of much more fuel (jets were very thirsty), new heavier catapults (still hydraulic, hence within existing technology), and new arresting gear. In an *Essex*, the flight deck would be cleared to some extent by eliminating the gun mounts placed there and by shrinking the size of the island. The *Essex*-class carrier *Oriskany*, incomplete at the end of World War II, was suspended, redesigned, and rebuilt as the prototype of the modernized design, under SCB Project 27A. Modernization of the *Midway* class was deferred, probably because all three were badly needed to support the interim capability in the form of the Neptunes.

When he cancelled the new carrier on 23 April 1949, Secretary of Defense Johnson shifted the money to *Essex* modernization. He ordered the more visionary bomber designs cancelled, but he allowed a more conservative design, which could (in theory) operate from a modernized *Midway*, to proceed. It became the A3D (later A-3) Skywarrior. It was not obvious at the time that the BuAer catapult project was not very successful. In effect the cancellation of the supercarrier delayed that realization. However, to operate a Skywarrior from a *Midway*-class carrier required the new catapult. In 1950, as the big bomber approached its first flight, the catapult became the decisive item in the necessary *Midway*-class modernization, as without that modernization the Navy would never get its jet strategic bomber.

As defense funds shrank in 1949–1950, the Navy was ordered to lay up more and more of its attack carrier force. In spring 1950 it must have seemed that only anti-submarine forces would soon be left. Carriers certainly figured in such forces. Beginning in 1946 the U.S. Navy experimented with two captured high-speed U-boats, and soon it produced its own fast submarine in the form of the Guppy conversion of its fleet type. One possible counter to such submarines was to hunt them down. It was assumed, for the moment, that wartime HF/DF methods would provide the necessary wide-area surveillance (direction finding), and a pair of experimental task groups was created, built around a light carrier and a large escort carrier. This idea was so important that new specialized ASW aircraft (the AF Guardian) were developed on the basis of a late-war Grumman torpedo bomber (TB3F). There were two complementary roles: a hunter carrying sonobuoys and a big surface-search radar (to detect snorkels) and a killer, carrying one or more homing torpedoes. The wartime airframe was too small to combine the two roles, and it seemed that the available small carriers could not have supported anything much larger (even the Guardian was a difficult fit). However, in 1950 the Bureau of Aeronautics issued a requirement for a single-package (hunter and killer) carrier airplane, suitable to operate from the *Commencement Bay*–class escort carriers. Several companies offered single-engine aircraft, but Grumman won with a small twin-engine design, the S2F (later S-2) Tracker. A new CVE was included in the FY52 program, but it was not built. Several war-built escort carriers and light fleet carriers were modified for ASW.

The idea that future U.S. ASW would rely heavily on carrier aircraft cued by a wide-area surveillance system was established, and it shaped much of what carriers would do over the next decades. By the time the Tracker was ready, it was clear that not all *Essex*-class carriers would ever be modernized. Those not modernized were placed in a kind of second-class status as ASW carriers (CVS), operating in ASW task groups in the Atlantic and the Pacific. The carrier ASW mission survived because beginning in 1956 the United States had a new underwater ocean surveillance system (SOSUS) that could cue hunting aircraft both from carriers and from shore bases.

At this point there was little interest in providing the big strike carriers with their own ASW aircraft. It was assumed that their high cruising speed (over twenty knots) would give them effective immunity against even the fast submarines the Germans had deployed in 1945 (which the Soviets were expected to copy).

With the Korean War the project for a big carrier was revived, although at least in theory it was a flexible tool of limited war rather than a strategic weapon. The first of the post–World War II carriers, USS *Forrestal*, began as a slightly reduced version of the abortive supercarrier of 1949, USS *United States*, with the same flush deck and the same catapults.[11]

The close World War II relationship with the Royal Navy, the only other major carrier navy in the world, survived the end of the war. Royal Navy interest in heavy air attack was quashed by the Royal Air Force, which argued that the string of Commonwealth and Empire air bases made strike from the sea unnecessary. The Royal Navy found itself concentrating on sea control, largely in the seas close to Europe—hence close to Soviet naval bomber bases. The British military therefore considered air warfare key; it had to learn to operate jets from carriers much smaller than those of the U.S. Navy, and it had little chance of building supercarriers. These considerations forced the Royal Navy into innovation, from which the U.S. carrier force benefited enormously.

One idea was that aircraft could land on flexible (inflated) decks, without using landing gear. It appeared that an airplane might save substantial weight in this way, weight that could translate into higher performance. The British tested the flexible deck, and for a time it seemed the U.S. Navy might adopt it, but its problems (such as moving the airplane around the deck after it landed) were never really solved. The flexible deck did lead to a further, much more important idea. A British officer pointed out that the carrier landing area did not have to lie along the centerline of the flight deck; it could be angled to one side. That would simplify aircraft handling, since a crane could lift a landed airplane off the deck to clear the landing area. The prospective Commanding Officer of the new carrier *Ark Royal* suggested that this angled deck idea be applied to his ship.[12]

The angled deck would solve a major carrier problem. Landing aircraft sometimes bounced over the barrier to crash into the parked aircraft forward; the relatively small British carriers suffered particularly badly. Existing barriers, moreover, were ill-designed for jets. They were wires intended to stop a bolting airplane by winding around its propeller. A jet hitting the barrier would run the wire up over its nose to decapitate its pilot. Work was proceeding on a nylon net barrier to stop jets, but the angled deck solved the problem far more elegantly. If the airplane did not snag the arresting wires, it could simply power up and fly off the fore end of the angled deck. There was some question as to whether pilots could maneuver properly to land at an angle to the ship's centerline, but trials showed that was no problem. The U.S. Navy enthusiastically adopted the angled deck, more readily than did its inventor, the Royal Navy. The British were worried about operating relatively small high-performance aircraft, but the Americans had to operate very large aircraft—for them the greatest advantage of the angled deck was that it carried such aircraft well clear of the carrier's island. Thus the angled deck instantly solved the flush-deck design problem by eliminating the need for such a deck. The angled deck was tested in primitive form aboard USS *Midway* and then in more complete form aboard USS *Antietam*. Already under construction, *Forrestal* was quickly redesigned with a conventional island. Ironically, both she and the abortive *United States* had large sponsons angled out from their flight decks; they could easily have accommodated British-style angled layouts, but the arresting gear was never placed for such operation.

The small size of British carriers made catapults even more important than they were for the U.S. Navy. The U.S. problem was to launch super-heavy bombers. The British were more interested in high-performance fighters, with high stalling speeds. Jets needed catapults because they did not develop sufficient thrust for takeoff on a short deck (the power of a jet engine depends on how fast the airplane is moving, so jets need long runways to accelerate). A British catapult developer, Colin C. Mitchell, became interested in the steam catapult the Germans had developed to launch their wartime V-1 missiles. There was apparently no British interest in the explosive catapult the U.S. Navy was then developing; Mitchell's steam catapult was the alternative to the earlier (and too limited) hydraulic units and also to the wartime practice of sometimes using booster rockets (JATO) for takeoffs.

Initially the U.S. catapult developers showed little interest in the British steam catapult. By 1952 their situation was critical, because the heavy attack bomber that had survived the 1949 cuts was about to enter service. There was an urgent project to modernize the *Midway*-class carriers to accommodate it. The air branch of OpNav demanded quick action, and the U.S. naval attaché in London (an aviator) made sure that details of the steam catapult reached Washington. Ultimately he arranged for demonstrations by the British steam catapult test carrier. U.S. catapult developers maintained that the explosive catapult would ultimately succeed, but the steam catapult was a most satisfactory substitute. In effect the steam catapult and the angled deck made it possible for carriers to operate aircraft entirely equivalent to contemporary land-based types—they ensured the survival of carrier aviation. It appears that prior to the steam catapult episode, U.S. naval aviators showed little interest in British innovations, considering their own technology entirely superior. With the adoption of the steam catapult, this attitude reversed, probably accounting for the quick adoption of the angled deck.

A third British innovation can also be traced to the problem of small carriers. The British aircraft test establishment (Farnborough) analyzed in great detail the problem of landing high-performance jets. By the end of World War II the Royal Navy used the U.S. system, in which a Landing Signal Officer (LSO) watched the descending airplane. He signaled the pilot to correct errors and then to cut his engine while he was still in flight just prior to snagging the wire of the arresting gear. Thus the pilot and LSO were part of a feedback cycle. The faster the approaching airplane, the tighter that cycle should be—but it was limited by the reaction times of the pilot and the LSO. A British engineer realized that the pilot had to make his own corrections, based on something he could see, rather than on the LSO's observations. Using a paperclip and a makeup mirror, he proved to himself that a pilot could do what was needed on the basis of what he could see in a stabilized mirror mounted alongside the flight deck. This idea was quickly adopted (in modern form a Fresnel Lens replaces the mirror). The pilot watches banks of lights to indicate whether he is too high or too low or on the correct glide path. Again, the mirror landing sight was key to using high-performance jets on board carriers.

Angled decks and steam catapults were installed on board the three *Midways* and also on board modernized *Essex*-class carriers (as SCB 27C). The modernized carriers also received enclosed ("hurricane") bows; the idea may be traceable to the damage suffered by the carrier *Bennington* during a severe storm. U.S. carriers had suffered similar flight deck damage during the great 1944 typhoon, but that seems not to have affected early postwar designs such as SCB 27A and *United States*.

Forrestal was followed by three very similar ships (*Saratoga*, *Ranger*, and *Independence*). All represented the simplest possible redesign of the original flush-deck carrier, with elevators arranged so that one would feed each of the four cata-pults. When the angled deck was introduced, the forward elevator on that (port) side was relocated aft on the starboard side. It was soon clear that this arrangement was unfortunate, and in the fifth postwar carrier (*Kitty Hawk*) the positions of island and elevator were interchanged.

Convinced of the value of these powerful carriers, the Eisenhower administration adopted a policy of building one each year.

By this time another new technology, nuclear power, was nearing maturity. A carrier was a natural application; the first program for systematic reactor develop-ment (1955) included large surface ship plants for carriers and cruisers. Nuclear power offered effectively unlimited high-speed steaming, which in turn would make submarine attack nearly impossible (prior to the advent of Soviet nuclear subma-rines backed by ocean surveillance systems). The severe corrosion due to stack gases would be eliminated. Stack gases also affected aircraft approaching the carrier by reducing visibility. Because a nuclear carrier would not produce any smoke, her design became an opportunity to rethink the position of the island and hence carrier configuration. Possibilities included a pair of angled decks, one on each side of the island, crossing at the bow, and a two-deck configuration reminiscent of some pre-war British carriers. Ultimately all these possibilities were rejected, and the nuclear carrier used much the same flight deck configuration as *Kitty Hawk* (CVA-63). To attain the required power, the new ship needed eight reactors, all linked together into a single power plant. This massive structure in turn demanded a larger hull (not least for buoyancy), so the resulting *Enterprise* was considerably larger than the *Forrestals*. One unexpected feature of the design was a vast aircraft fuel capacity: fuel was part of the side protective system defending against torpedo hits, and the sheer size of the hull made for a larger system and hence for more tankage. The nuclear carrier was considered experimental, so the next carrier (USS *America*, CVA-66) was essentially a repeat version of *Kitty Hawk*.

Another new technology, long-range guided missiles, was also approaching maturity. In 1955 the U.S. Navy formed a Long-Range Objectives Group specifi-cally to work out the likely shape of the fleet fifteen years hence, and thus to pro-vide direction for naval research and development. The group's 1956–1957 reports were particularly significant, because they were of great interest to CNO Admiral Arleigh Burke. They give some idea of contemporary concerns; one was clearly

U.S. Navy, PH2 Geoffrey L. England

USS Abraham Lincoln, *typical of modern U.S. nuclear carriers, October 1994.*

the rising cost of attack carriers. Up to this point, carrier size had been set by the needs of heavy attack bombers. By 1956 it seemed that the fleet might shift to long-range cruise missiles (Regulus) as its heavy strike arm. It also seemed that within a decade there might be effective vertical takeoff fighters (the Navy was then helping fund the Ryan X-13 tail-sitting VTOL airplane, with delta wings). Both a tail-sitter and a cruise missile might operate from large surface ships, in which case big carriers might no longer be needed. Their remaining key mission would be tactical attack, which at the time involved tactical nuclear weapons. The 1956 Long-Range Objectives report envisaged a return to smaller (*Essex*-sized) carriers operating a new all-weather jet attack airplane—which the Marines would share. With its limited warload, it could be designed for short takeoff and vertical landing (STOVL) operation from fields ashore. This airplane emerged later as the Grumman A-6 Intruder. When it became obvious that limited wars would be fought with large numbers of non-nuclear weapons, it also became clear that the A-6 could never be a short take-off airplane, and the Navy felt fortunate that it was still operating large carriers. The tail-sitting VTOL fighter also never materialized, although the potential of VTOL was later raised again to justify an abortive shift to smaller carriers.

The long-range cruise missile was cancelled in favor of an even more futuristic weapon, the Polaris ballistic missile. Polaris did end the carriers' involvement in U.S. strategic war plans except for SIOP commitments that continued throughout the Cold War. To pay for the crash construction of the submarines and of the missile, the annual carrier program ended with USS *America*. Further carrier design continued, an important object being to find a less expensive way to build a nuclear carrier. Since the size of the *Enterprise* had been determined by her eight-reactor power plant, the next step was to use individually larger reactors and to reduce the total to four.

By the early 1960s the U.S. Navy was operating a large force of *Essex*-class ASW carriers (CVS) alongside its attack carriers. Their original mid-ocean ASW role was fading, because the new P-3 Orion could cover the whole Atlantic from coastal bases, the Azores, and Iceland. Moreover, it was fast enough to reach contacts before the original information (from SOSUS and other sources) became entirely stale. However, another CVS role opened. The Soviets began to deploy nuclear attack submarines. Carriers, particularly those using conventional power, were not fast enough to outrun such craft. Moreover, the Soviets built up their own ocean surveillance system, which could cue their attack submarines. They demonstrated it in spectacular fashion in February 1968, when such a submarine intercepted the carrier *Enterprise* despite her high speed, as she deployed to Vietnam. As they were withdrawn from the mid-ocean ASW role, the ASW carriers were assigned to work with attack carriers. The ideal formation was three attack carriers working with one ASW carrier. However, the *Essex*-class carriers were clearly ageing. How vital would it be to replace them, at a time when building any carriers at all seemed difficult? Proposals for a new CVS mentioned that it would both support troops ashore (S was sometimes taken to mean support) and conduct ASW. The idea died.

To a limited extent the U.S. Navy retained a kind of reserve carrier ASW capability. By 1956 the Marines were interested in helicopter assault from the sea (vertical envelopment), and a small carrier, based on the abortive CVE, was designed for them as the LPH. Its design specifically allowed for conversion to a helicopter ASW ship, as helicopters were now seen as effective ASW platforms. The contemporary Royal Navy mixed ASW aircraft with attack aircraft and fighters on its small carriers. It soon went so far as to consider building special ASW helicopter carriers (which it wanted to call escort cruisers) to clear its attack carriers of these aircraft. The U.S. LPH was too slow for that, but in the early 1960s un-modernized *Essex*-class carriers were converted into helicopter carriers for the Marines. Later much larger helicopter carriers were built as the *Tarawa* (LHA-1) class.

Carrier construction resumed fitfully, the Johnson administration deciding to build a further ship. Secretary of Defense Robert S. McNamara was skeptical of the carriers' value. Initially he did not want to build any carriers, but the Navy's effective operations in Vietnam convinced him that they were worthwhile. McNamara also questioned whether the nuclear power plant was worthwhile. Ultimately McNamara chose a conventional power plant for the next ship, USS *John F. Kennedy* (CVA-67). Although quite different in detail, the new ship was effectively a repeat version of *America*.

Work on more compact, less expensive reactor plants continued, so that by the time a further carrier was being considered for construction about 1966, there was a two-reactor plant nearly as powerful as the eight that powered USS *Enterprise*. It was possible to wrap them in a somewhat smaller hull, but still with roughly the same flight deck as had been adopted with USS *Kitty Hawk* more than a decade earlier. The resulting USS *Nimitz* (FY67 program) became the prototype for ten more nuclear carriers, built over two decades. The Nixon administration ordered two more ships (FY70 and FY74 programs).

The completion of USS *Nimitz* coincided roughly with the end of the Vietnam War. Money was very tight, and there was little prospect of building new carriers—and none replacing the worn-out ASW carriers. Since the carrier ASW mission was now mainly about self-protection, it occurred to CNO Admiral Zumwalt that this mission could be transferred onto the big carriers. Instead of their previous attack designation (CVA), they were re-designated CV. Admiral Zumwalt went further, arguing that a carrier should be able to "swing" her Air Group from mission to mission, adding and subtracting aircraft as needed. In effect he was using the fact that carriers are largely modular, their big hangars sized to accommodate a wide variety of aircraft. They were not quite as modular as might be imagined, because different aircraft needed different command and control facilities and different maintenance facilities. For example, part of the CV modification was installation of an ASW module, which equated to (but improved) the command and control and acoustic analysis facilities of a CVS. Installation was possible because the earlier manual facility could be automated. The computers involved were beginning to shrink dramatically. This degree of automation was linked to the appearance of a new carrier ASW aircraft, the Lockheed S-3 Viking, which was also highly automated, linked directly to the ASW module both while in flight and upon landing.

Before becoming Chief of Naval Operations, Admiral Zumwalt had been the last Chief of the Long Range Objectives Group. In that role he had had a good chance to think through what he considered the great challenges of the post-Vietnam world, as well as the technologies he thought would soon come to fruition. He particularly worried that Soviet silencing would render SOSUS, the key to American ASW, useless.[13] Without SOSUS, the U.S. Navy would find itself relying heavily on convoying, and on local mainly active sonar. In Zumwalt's view, that in turn would require a large force of small carriers, which he eventually called sea control ships. As CNO, Zumwalt considered the sea control ship a key program.[14] Zumwalt hoped that such ships could be built for a fraction of the price of a conventional carrier. They would have little or no strike capability. New VTOL technology would provide them with some fighter defense.[15] Instead of the usual airborne radar aircraft (E-2 Hawkeyes) they would rely on unmanned radar airships, which would lock onto them and follow them around the oceans.[16] Helicopters were already accepted as the key to local ASW defense.

In fact Zumwalt's sea control ship did not long survive his tenure as CNO, although the Spanish navy built a sea control ship to U.S. plans, and a Spanish shipyard built a scaled-down version for Thailand. Both navies operated British-designed Harrier attack fighters from their ships. In the United States, advocates of small but numerous carriers were defeated. The smaller the carrier, the more vulnerable to weapons (which were not of course scaled down). To mount the same air effort, the smaller carrier had to be replenished more frequently, and replenishment was both expensive and potentially dangerous. Moreover, the VSTOL aircraft that would make a small carrier practicable offered lower performance, including dramatically reduced payloads and shorter ranges (which would keep the carrier closer to hostile forces).

Admiral Zumwalt accepted that larger carriers retained a valid role, but he wanted to scale down from the big Nimitz. He proposed a conventionally powered 50,000- to 60,000-ton Tentative Conceptual Baseline (T-CBL) ship; in September 1972 Secretary of Defense Melvin Laird issued a program decision memorandum calling for the design of a $550 million carrier (the sea control ship was expected to cost $100 million, and the frigate $45 million). The third Nimitz (Carl Vinson, CVN-70) was bought instead for the FY74 program, but by this time T-CBL was regarded as a likely future carrier design, more affordable than the existing one, but not yet mature enough to buy.[17] Thus in July 1975 new Secretary of Defense James Schlesinger ordered the Navy to begin further studies of a non-nuclear carrier (the Navy appealed). Eventually Schlesinger approved work on a 50,000-ton CVNX, whose cost should not exceed that of USS Nimitz. The CVNX was to incorporate a variety of innovations in areas such as catapults, elevators, and command and control. However, in January 1976 a panel concluded that it would be more economical to buy a fourth Nimitz to retain the thirteen-carrier force beyond 1985. President Gerald Ford therefore included long-lead items for the ship in his draft FY77 budget. However, in response to criticism, he substituted plans for two oil-fueled carriers in FY79 and FY81. The cut in size (to something like T-CBL) was justified partly by hopes that a transition to a new generation of VSTOL aircraft would minimize demands for carrier size. The new carrier was tentatively designated CVV, the second V indicating VSTOL.

The Carter administration, which entered office in 1977, was far less interested in attack carriers, which it associated with power projection in the Third World (as it entered office, the administration view was that it was essential for the United States to make peace with Third World countries, as reflected in its decision to turn the Panama Canal over to Panama). Despite its reluctance to consider carrier construction at all, the Carter administration did support the reduced-price CVV. Designed within a severe price limit, it would be much smaller than the existing ships, and it would be non-nuclear. Instead of designing the ship to operate a tactically coherent Air Wing, it was designed with an Air Wing scaled to meet the price and size of the ship. It turned out that quite drastically shrinking a conventional carrier saved remarkably little money. Congress was unimpressed; it approved a fourth *Nimitz* in the FY79 program—which President Jimmy Carter then vetoed. The following year he felt compelled to reverse course, partly because operations in the Indian Ocean demonstrated the value both of nuclear power and of a large carrier Air Wing. Thus the fourth *Nimitz* was finally included in President Carter's final budget (FY80). By this time, too, hopes of a new VSTOL generation had generally been abandoned.

Then the situation changed dramatically. President Ronald Reagan's Secretary of the Navy, John F. Lehman, envisaged a fleet built around large carriers, consistent with the maritime strategy he supported. He knew that the war plans written by the Joint Chiefs of Staff required an unaffordable total of twenty-two; he settled for an affordable force of fifteen operational carriers. That meant more ships, because some carriers were always in long-term refit. Lehman was determined to build up the Navy at minimum cost; he was painfully aware that a build-up could easily cause gross inflation in defense products, so that it would buy almost nothing. Among his achievements was an agreement with the sole American yard capable of building nuclear carriers, Newport News, to invest in sufficient plant to build two ships simultaneously, so that each would cost considerably less than if ordered separately. Congress understood what he was doing, and it approved two pairs of carriers (CVN-72-3 and CVN-74-5).

Lehman also understood the potential of the large-deck amphibious ships. He replaced the ageing LPH fleet with much larger LHDs (*Essex* class), effectively improved versions of the LHA. By this time the Marines were operating STOVL fighters (versions of the British Harrier). Lehman required the LHD to be convertible into a sea control ship. The situation had changed dramatically since Zumwalt's time. Zumwalt had espoused the small sea control ship as an alternative to the expensive carrier, a way of killing off the big decks. Because he was so successful in building large carriers, Lehman saw the LHD as a potential supplement, to make up numbers in areas of less intense threat, and to extend U.S. naval presence.

Although Lehman's large decks looked much like their predecessors, the logic of their design had changed. USS *Forrestal* was designed to operate heavy attack bombers, which were then the largest U.S. carrier aircraft. Existing fighters were far smaller; they could operate even from an *Essex*. By 1980 the F-14 Tomcat was by far the most demanding carrier airplane, the one that set minimum carrier standards. The largest attack bomber, the Douglas A-3, could operate from a substantially smaller ship. However, it was the F-14 that could, it was hoped, fight the outer air battle, killing Soviet missile-bearing bombers and thus winning sea dominance.

As the Cold War ended, the logic of carrier operation began to change again. The role was again mainly attack. The emerging reality was that national air defense systems, like those of Iraq, could be knocked out in the initial stages of a war. Attack aircraft could operate at higher altitudes. They could more easily use the precision weapons, such as laser-guided bombs, which had emerged from the Vietnam War. Within a decade, the best such weapons were GPS-guided. Both kinds of weapons offered a new kind of attack. In the past, a carrier had launched mass raids against single targets. Mass was needed both to saturate enemy defenses and to ensure that hits were made, since the probability of hitting per bomb was limited. Precision weapons, delivered from outside enemy air defense range, could be used singly. One airplane could attack multiple targets on each sortie. A carrier with, say, forty-eight attack aircraft on board could hit at least forty-eight separate targets if her aircraft flew once per day.

The question became not how many airplanes the carrier could accommodate, but rather how many targets she could attack each day. That in turn depended on how rapidly her flight deck worked. *Nimitz*-class carriers reflected some much earlier ideas: that the bow catapults should be reserved for ready nuclear strikes, for example (to be launched at the outset before the ship could be vaporized), and that most strikes should be full-effort Alfa strikes, in which all available aircraft flew together to hit the same target. Flight deck turnaround time depended on how crowded the deck was, and on how weapons elevators were arranged in relation to aircraft elevators and catapults. Flight deck configuration really had not been rethought since the mid-1960s.

It gradually became clear that the new kind of operation could be conducted most efficiently if the deck were emptier, because airplanes could move around more easily. It also helped to move the island further aft, exchanging it with an elevator, so that airplanes could be fed to the catapults more efficiently. Weapons elevators should be rearranged. By the time the new configuration was being developed, it seemed likely that at some point the Navy would adopt unmanned armed aircraft (UCAVs). A new flight deck arrangement also seemed to offer the most efficient way of operating them. Big decks and big ships were still clearly best, but for very different reasons. On this basis the most recent carrier, USS *George H. W. Bush* (CVN-77), was designed.

Several studies showed not only that large carriers were far more efficient than smaller ones, but that even larger ones might be attractive. Just how large was never clear. By the late 1990s it could reasonably be argued that the *Nimitz* hull had more than run out of design margin, and that some redesign and enlargement was warranted. On the other hand, it was not clear how such growth could be controlled. Assistant Secretary of Defense Paul Wolfowitz personally decided to cap growth by requiring the next carrier (CVN-77) to fit within the same hull form as its predecessors. There were noticeable external changes: a large bow bulb, for better hydrodynamics, and a new island and mast.

The next carrier, CVN-78 (*Gerald R. Ford*), is a fresh design built around a new reactor (S9G instead of A1W) with a new flight deck arrangement (the island is further aft, and should be equipped with new fixed-array radars). As in other U.S. warships, systems are more electric—in this case the catapults and the arresting gear (which converts the energy absorbed as an airplane lands into electric power). The internal layout is more modular, for easier modification as systems and aircraft change. The new reactors are 25 percent more powerful than their predecessors, to provide three times the electric power of the earlier *Theodore Roosevelt* (a modified *Nimitz*). At least as importantly, the reactor requires many fewer operators and its core should last the lifetime of the ship (nuclear ships absorb much of their lifetime cost when they are re-cored). The redesigned flight deck should support 160 rather than 120 sorties per day.

The Marines, who operate from the large (carrier-like) amphibious ships, came to consider their shipboard attack aircraft integral with their helicopter-borne assault forces. When the time came to replace the big LHAs built in the 1970s, they initially chose a design about the size of a *Forrestal*, with two angled decks (converging at the bow): one for helicopters, one for VSTOL attack bombers. This "two tramline" design was initially accepted, but then dropped about 2004 as too expensive. Instead the LHD, which can accommodate VSTOL fighters, but which has only a single flight line, has been developed further. The great question is whether current plans for a follow-on to the Marines' Harrier (AV-8B) attack aircraft will materialize in the form of the F-35C. Without such an airplane, the Marines will no longer have the integral air attack capability they consider essential. However, the cost of the F-35C is escalating. Several foreign navies have also bet on the F-35C.

To operate conventional high-performance aircraft, a carrier must have a combination of catapults and arresting gear. Together they set a minimum size for an acceptable carrier—probably something like the French *Charles de Gaulle* (something less than half the size of a *Nimitz*); that is, at the least the ship must have sufficient length for arresting gear well clear of the after end of the flight deck, for pull-out once the wires are engaged, for a safety barrier, and for parking aircraft that have landed. The parking area must be clear of the catapults, whose length is set by the required end speed (a pilot can withstand only a certain acceleration).[18] More length can buy more catapults and more working space for faster turnaround. The smaller the carrier, the less numerous the Air Wing, with important tactical consequences. Sheer size also buys survivability and magazine space (so the carrier need not reload as often). STOVL aircraft like the Sea Harrier made it possible to produce a carrier of sorts within much smaller dimensions—the British *Invincible* is less than a quarter as large as a *Nimitz*. However, the smaller carrier cannot operate nearly as many aircraft (and often the ones she can operate are not particularly capable). Thus STOVL made it possible for several navies to operate affordable carriers—but they were not nearly so effective as large U.S. carriers.

Carriers have succeeded because they are, in effect, the first modular warships: they could operate successive generations of Navy aircraft without needing radical reconstruction for each change. As it happened, the outer limits on size, landing speed, and takeoff speed set by the postwar nuclear bombers sufficed for later aircraft such as the F-14 Tomcat fighter and the A-6 Intruder bomber. The current F/A-18 Hornet is smaller than either, and the coming F-35 is still within these limits. In a very broad sense a carrier is a broad flight deck and an open hangar deck ready for whatever aircraft she can launch. She still needs to carry specialized support equipment for each new airplane, but that entails far less effort than the sort of reconstruction surface that warships need to accommodate new weapons. The most important internal change to accommodate a new generation of aircraft was the installation of computer combat direction systems, which began in the 1960s. It radically changed carrier/Air Group capability, but again it was relatively easy to accommodate from a physical point of view. The same basically modular ship has supported multiple generations of air weapons, of self-defense weapons (beginning with 5-inch guns and now using short-range missiles), and of radars. Thus the same ship has offered dramatically different capability over the years.

NOTES

1. For more details of ships and of carrier designs see the author's *U.S. Aircraft Carriers: An Illustrated Design History* (Annapolis: Naval Institute Press, 1983). For British development see also this author's *British Carrier Aviation: The Evolution of the Ships and Their Aircraft* (Annapolis: Naval Institute Press, and London: Conway Maritime Press, 1988).

2. The April 1942 Doolittle raid on Tokyo by Army B-25s launched from the carrier *Hornet* seems to have inspired Navy interest in a carrier-borne medium (twin-engine) bomber, the abortive Grumman TB2F. Work on this airplane was cancelled in April 1944 on the explicit ground that, now that the Japanese had early warning radar, surprise air strikes were no longer possible. In 1945 OpNav suggested a program of carrier raids on Japan that, it claimed, would deliver about 60 percent of the bomb load the Army's B-29s could drop. The much smaller bomb loads of carrier bombers would be balanced off by their great numbers and by the much shorter turnaround (and greater readiness) of the carrier aircraft. Presumably the early 1945 carrier air raids on Tokyo were intended to demonstrate this capability. They were not particularly successful, but they did indicate intense interest in a new application of carrier air power. It should be kept in mind that the U.S. Navy had long required its torpedo bombers to fill an alternative heavy bombing role (with 2,000-pound bombs). Navy planning documents for the bombing campaign (Operation Hotpoint) are in the RG 38 collection, College Park division of the National Archives.

3. By way of contrast, the Royal Navy justified its postwar carrier fleet largely as a means of protecting shipping against just this threat. It had experienced large-scale land-based air attack both against convoys to Malta and against those to Russia. Too, the Royal Air Force was quick to slap down Royal Navy attempts to develop carrier-based land attack capabil-

ity. The new U.S. Air Force had similar hopes, but found them more difficult to realize, particularly since President Harry Truman explicitly gave both the Navy and the Army (later the Air Force) authority to develop the means to deliver nuclear weapons.

4. The later Maritime Strategy was much closer to earlier classic Navy thinking, which had never received much publicity outside the Navy. One consequence was that the Maritime Strategy was greeted by many in the wider defense world as a new and aggressive departure from a less "provocative" way of thinking. In his memoirs, Admiral Zumwalt explained that his approach had been much affected by his experience in the McNamara Defense Department, which originated the way of describing military forces in neatly defined compartments like "general purpose" and "strategic." When Admiral Zumwalt first enunciated his new strategy, an anonymous OpNav captain commented that reducing the Navy to a defensive sea control role fatally offered the initiative to the Soviets.

5. For years, readers of Soviet naval literature, such as Robert Herrick and Jamie McConnell, had made this point, but it was difficult to reconcile with the existence of a large Soviet submarine fleet. In recent years writers from the Office of Naval Intelligence have claimed a crucial role in the internal naval debate; sometime early in the 1980s, they say, they obtained direct evidence of Soviet thinking that backed up the U.S. analysts. Some unofficial accounts of U.S. naval activities in that period refer to interception of crucial Soviet undersea cables, which may have provided the evidence in question (alternatively, successful agent operations may have been involved). Exercises seemed to show clearly that, once the U.S. Navy showed its willingness to apply pressure to Soviet naval forces in waters nominally under their control, the Soviets would adopt a defensive stance. Yet another factor was the dawning realization that the one maritime resource the Soviets would feel compelled to defend was their fleet of ballistic missile submarines, which were designed to operate in just those waters.

6. On 27 April 1945 DCNO (Air) set up an informal advisory panel on carrier design. Its first task was to recommend characteristics for a follow-on to the wartime *Essex* class, which was then envisaged as a 35,000-ton carrier. Papers are in a SCB 6A file, naval air history collection, Naval History and Heritage Center. SCB 6A was the abortive supercarrier *United States*. While the new design was being developed, interim improvements to the *Essex* and *Midway* classes were authorized.

7. On 11 December 1945 BuAer Chief, Rear Admiral H. B. Sallada described alternatives to the Chief of Naval Operations: one class of bombers (A) that could operate from a *Midway*-class carrier; another class (B) that could operate from a *Midway* under more restrictive conditions (incapable of being struck below, but capable of landing-on in light condition and of taking off fully loaded); and a third class (C) that would require a new class of carrier. All of these aircraft would be powered by turboprops, and each would carry an 8,000-pound bomb. Class A would take off at 30,000 pounds (the heaviest existing carrier aircraft took off at less than 20,000), would achieve 362 knots at sea level, and would have a combat radius of 300 nautical miles. Class B would take off at 45,000 pounds, would achieve 500 knots at 35,000 feet, and would have a combat radius of 1,000 nautical miles. Class C would take off at 100,000 pounds (landing weight 45,000) and would achieve the same speed, but would have a combat radius of 2,000 nautical miles. Each could carry a single 12,000-pound bomb at a price in range. Alternative designs using piston engines or combining piston engines and jets would sacrifice speed and range. The letter recommended that a program be begun, beginning with an airplane in class B using piston engines and jets (so that it could be completed as quickly as possible). Based on an internal study, it should take off at 41,000 pounds, and should achieve 500 knots at 35,000 feet using jets to boost it; combat radius should be 300 nautical miles. This was the Savage. The follow-on A2J was conceived as the B airplane. A copy of this paper is in the SCB 6A file at the Naval History and Heritage Center, Naval Air Section. Admiral Sallada's letter in turn was prob-

ably based on a 12 October 1945 Aircraft Design Report prepared by the BuAer Aviation Design Research (ADR) Branch to determine the characteristics of a bomber limited by the existing carrier weight limit of 30,000 pounds and the arresting gear limit of ninety miles per hour, carrying a 7,000-pound bomb, responding to a verbal request. ADR practice was to sketch a design to test the effect of stated requirements; in this case it estimated a gross weight of 40,085 pounds and used a combination of two R2800 turbo-charged piston engines and three 24C jet engines (the type that powered the new FD-1 fighter). ADR estimated that such an airplane could reach 520 miles per hour (about 450 knots) at 35,000 feet, and that it would have a combat radius of 300 nautical miles, the minimum acceptable. The study is in the BuAer VV file for 1945 in RG 72 at the College Park National Archives center. Because the longer-range bomber was never designed, BuShips carrier designers used the product of another series of studies (ADR 62 and 64) to provide them with the footprint around which they designed the SCB 6A supercarrier. These studies were ordered on 13 February 1946, and performance objectives for the new airplane outlined in OpNav letters (from Op-05, DCNO for Air) laid out in letters dated 5 January 1948 and 10 March 1948. Of the two ADR studies, only ADR 64 was formally reported (11 June 1948). It became the basis for an informal design competition.

8. An outline specification (which apparently has not survived) dated 23 December 1947 was circulated within BuAer, comments being required by 5 January 1948. Comments from the Aircraft Specifications Branch suggest that maximum weight was 100,000 pounds and that the speed initially demanded seemed low; the branch wanted a minimum of 525 knots at 40,000 feet. Absolute minimum combat radius was set at 1,700 nautical miles. At this point the study was designated ADR 62. Meanwhile a second attack airplane (ADR 56) was also under consideration: the high performance seaplane that later materialized as the P6M Seamaster; however, it was also sometimes designated the attack aircraft with an unorthodox arrangement, a description that would apply to several of the abortive designs for aircraft to operate from the big new carrier. By September 1948, the weight limit was 100,000 pounds and the bomb load 10,000 pounds (i.e., an atomic bomb), with combat radius of 1,700 nautical miles (from a 24 September 1948 letter from the BuAer Chief to the Office of the Secretary of Defense, directed to Captain H. D. Riley, USN); this was Operational Specification OS-111. Lockheed regarded the 100,000-pound limit as impractical, and asked that it be extended to 125,000 pounds (BuAer refused). Several of the designs were clearly unsatisfactory, leaving four: three-engine designs by Convair and by Douglas Santa Monica and twin-engine designs by Curtiss and by Douglas El Segundo. The twin-engine designs offered marginal performance but the three-engine designs were already at the 100,000-pound maximum weight and would not meet the required radius of action. By this time it seemed that lighter nuclear weapons were in prospect, so BuAer suggested reducing the required bomb weight, thus making the twin-engine designs considerably more attractive (the reference to nuclear bomb weight is obvious in retrospect, but was not explicit in the document). The Douglas design was considered superior to the Curtiss. Moreover, the Douglas bomber could fit aboard a *Midway*, and it could operate from that ship if the deck were strengthened and a more powerful catapult installed. A 31 January 1949 memorandum therefore recommended beginning negotiations with Douglas, for what became the A3D (later A-3) Skywarrior. The Curtiss bid was somewhat lower, but Douglas was accepted as superior from an engineering point of view, and also because of Douglas' superior record of designing and building naval aircraft. Heavy attack was so important "to the future of naval aviation, and compromise in an engineering choice because of cost of the experimental airplane is certainly not to the best interests of the government." It seems clear that by this time the supersonic requirement had been abandoned, but it is not clear when that was done. No formal change was made in the required bomb load (because it would have required re-opening the competition),

but the prospect of a reduced bomb load certainly made the choice more attractive. There was some interest in buying both the Douglas and the Curtiss prototypes; as one senior BuAer staffer put it, "never before has the fate of the Navy been so dependent upon the success of a single ship and to tie the success of that ship down to a single [aircraft] design seems to be considerably less than prudent." Late in February 1949 Douglas was told to study the effect on range of reducing the bomb load to 6,000 pounds (while retaining sufficient structure to support a 10,000-pound bomb). The object was to reach the desired 1,700 nautical mile figure. In addition to the subsonic long-range bomber, BuAer became interested in a "special attack" airplane (OS-115): a single-shot or composite airplane capable of achieving higher speed over the target, only the crew element returning to the carrier (it was sometimes described as a piloted missile). This requirement was stated in February 1948. BuAer wanted a cruising speed of Mach 1.2 and a maximum speed above that. The competition was limited to seven companies: Martin, Grumman, Douglas El Segundo, Chance-Vought, Douglas Santa Monica, Fairchild, and Consolidated San Diego. Prior to the issue of the specification, three companies had submitted "superficial" studies. All offered composite aircraft that jettisoned most of their airframes before flying back to the carrier. Grumman's piloted module flew in tandem with the bomb carrier, which separated over the target. On this basis it could take off at 97,000 pounds and cruise at Mach 1.13 (which was also maximum speed). Martin, which specialized in flying boats, offered a droppable seaplane hull, taking off at 110,000 pounds, and achieving a cruising speed of Mach 0.85 and a maximum speed of Mach 0.93. Its crew module could operate conventionally from the carrier; otherwise it would drop the hull for the high-speed leg of the mission. Douglas El Segundo offered a piggyback arrangement (its crew module was essentially its X-3 research airplane), taking off at 65,000, cruising at Mach 1.4, and achieving Mach 2.0 over the target. The Douglas proposal showed that the attempt to reach Mach 2 (a remarkable figure for the time) was impracticable: radius was only 459 nautical miles with a 13-nautical mile run-in at maximum speed. Fairchild offered a 10-engine tailless airplane so heavy that it could operate only from the new supercarrier. Radius was given as 1,350 nautical miles with a 650-nautical mile run-in at Mach 1.1. Martin offered the same flying boat it had proposed for the heavy bomber competition, and it was rejected as subsonic. The proposal by Douglas El Segundo was attractive, with 1,700-nm radius (but supersonic run-in was reduced from the specified 1,000 nautical miles to 570 nautical miles). However, its engine ratings were considered unduly optimistic. The proposal was rejected because El Segundo was already heavily loaded with other Navy work. Convair's was the only proposal that met or exceeded the design requirements while showing an adequate understanding of the problem. Its droppable pod incorporated three J40 engines; the escape vehicle on top was much like the XF-92 delta. The bomb was dropped from the pod before the pod itself was jettisoned. Convair was therefore recommended for further development. The use of a pod to make a supersonic bomber practicable suggests the pod Convair incorporated in the B-58 Hustler, designed in the early 1950s. None of the designs incorporated the area rule, which later turned out to be a crucial feature of supersonic aircraft; and probably none could have achieved anything like the expected speed. The special attack project was cancelled on 2 May 1949, officially because of cuts to the FY51 budget, and more probably because the big new supercarrier *United States* had been cancelled. This material, including sketches of the design alternatives, is in the VA (attack aircraft) folder in the BuAer confidential correspondence series (RG 72, Box 158 in this series) in the National Archives College Park, MD, branch. The OS-111 and -115 designs are also illustrated, in greater detail, in Jared A. Zichek, *Secret Aerospace Projects of the U.S. Navy: The Incredible Attack Aircraft of the USS* United States, *1948–49* (Lancaster, PA: Schiffer Books, 2009).

9. Drawings showing the progression from the 35,000 ton carrier envisaged in 1945 to the much larger flush-deck carrier are in *Spring Styles,* vol. 4, a book of drawings held by the Cartographic Division of the National Archives, College Park branch. Studies C-1 and C-2 (15 February and 8 April 1946) show the more or less conventional carrier. The first real departure is CVB-X Study 1 (30 May 1946), followed by CVA-58 Study 1 (3 July 1947), and then by four more CVA-58 studies (26 August, 2 October, 10 October, and 12 December 1947). In retrospect, C-1 and C-2 had considerable impact on later designs, because they introduced the idea of a waist catapult. To clear the arresting gear aft, it had to be sponsoned off the centerline (to port, like the later angled deck—but for a very different purpose). C-1 was essentially a re-designed *Essex,* retaining the bow elevator of the earlier design, but with deck-edge elevators on the starboard side fore and aft of the island, and a port deck-edge elevator abaft the sponson. To reduce the effects of underwater hits, C-2 had her machinery separated into four units, the pairs of units being well separated; each pair of units had its own uptakes. Thus the island was split into two well-separated elements. War experience showed that elevators on the centerline tended to interfere with air operations, so in C-2 the forward elevator was replaced by a fourth deck-edge one, forward of the big sponson. In this design the flight-deck guns of an *Essex* were relocated to sponsons, and the after starboard deck-edge elevator was placed between the two island units and the port side elevators fore and aft of the big sponson. The ship was slightly larger than a wartime *Essex.* CVB-X was a special-purpose carrier to operate heavy attack aircraft: she had no hangar at all; the aircraft would spend their lives on the flight deck. She had an island much like that of the *Midway* class, but a single massive centerline catapult (using two parallel tracks) ran down much of the forward third of the flight deck. The ship would have been 1,190 feet long overall (1,124 feet between perpendiculars) with a beam of 130 feet (132 feet over the flight deck, 154 feet over the sponsons); standard displacement would have been 69,200 tons (about 82,000 tons fully loaded). Speed would have been 33 knots (240,000 SHP). In effect CVA-58 was a much-enlarged C-2 without any island (and with a second sponson for a fourth catapult), but with a hangar. CVA-58 Study 1 showed the flush-deck configuration adopted in all the studies: essentially an axial deck with two big sponsons abaft amidships, each carrying a long catapult, and another two catapults in the bow. The ship had two deck-edge elevators on the starboard side, one forward of the sponson, the other abaft it, plus a centerline elevator right aft; in addition, a ramp connected the hangar deck across from the forward deck-edge elevator with the flight deck, so that aircraft could be pushed up onto the flight deck. This ship would have been 1,000 feet long, 125 feet in beam (hull, not counting the flight deck), with a draft of 34.5 feet, displacing 60,000 tons standard (75,000 fully loaded); She would have made over 34 knots on 240,000 SHP. The air group was given as twelve heavy bombers (ADR 42) and fifty-four fighters (F2D-1s). The flight-deck arrangement was retained for the larger Study 5; intermediate studies showed no ramp. As in the later *Forrestal* class, there were gun sponsons on each bow and on each quarter, in this case each carrying two single 5in/54 guns and a twin 3in/70 (at that time the preferred anti-aircraft gun—only later did it turn out to be a dismal failure). The hull showed an open bow, with another twin 3in/70 on it, two more such guns on the stern, and another on a sponson abaft the forward starboard elevator. Study 4 showed a bow centerline elevator between the two bow catapults and a centerline elevator right aft, plus one deck-edge elevator on the starboard side abaft the starboard sponson. The drawing showed massive twin-engine bombers on the bow catapults, probably about the size of Neptunes, with a folded version on the elevator between the catapults. This sketch was marked with ship's data: 1,030 feet overall × 154 feet maximum beam × 34.5 feet designed draft; standard displacement would have been 67,200 tons (79,700 tons fully loaded). The ship would have made 33 knots on 260,000 SHP. This was much the configuration of Study No. 3, except that it was smaller, so the

flight deck extended further forward on its hull (No. 3 was 1,130 feet long, 69,000 tons standard). The album also includes a CVE dated 26 April 1952. Spring styles, so called to suggest women's fashions, were sketch designs from among which naval decision makers could choose which to buy.

10. BuAer first became interested in more powerful catapults in 1944, as it sought jet fighters. On 2 December 1944 BuAer circulated a requirement to its designers and to its catapult contractors: to replace the standard H4 on board carriers, it wanted a device that could accelerate a 5,000-pound airplane to about 250 mph in about 175 feet, and a 20,000-pound load to 125 mph in the same distance at a rate not to exceed 3.5 G. The only new catapult technology in sight was the slotted tube used by the Germans to launch V-1 missiles. BuAer considered various slotted-tube propellants and chose explosives; the same German technology inspired Mitchell in England to propose using steam (which BuAer rejected as impractical). Other alternatives were also explored, such as a Westinghouse "electropult." The 20,000 pounds clearly referred to a manned airplane; the 5,000 probably referred to a missile. The letter is in volume 4 of the confidential BuAer S83-2 file (College Park, National Archives). An 11 January 1946 letter from the director of the BuAer Military Requirements Division observed that existing catapults could not launch aircraft weighing more than 20,000 pounds with takeoff stall speeds of more than 100 mph, even with a 25-knot relative wind (the wartime H4B was rated at 18,000 pounds at 90 mph). The catapult division was to conduct a study to find the actual limits of existing catapults and to set out requirements for future ones. This applied both to jet fighters and to even the smallest of the projected heavy attack aircraft. About June 1946 the airplane requirement was changed to 45,000 pounds at 125 mph (BuAer S83-2 file, Vol. 8). As an interim step, BuAer developed the most powerful hydraulic catapult it could (H8) for installation in the upgraded *Essex*-class carrier *Oriskany*. It was rated at 15,000 pounds at 125 mph, hardly what BuAer had wanted in 1944. BuAer designed a more powerful H9, rated at 45,000 pounds at 120 mph (or 100,000 pounds at 90 mph), but it never entered service, and seems not to have been considered particularly practicable. H8 was more or less enough for the Savage. It took a slotted cylinder to provide much more power, but work on such catapults was slow (they may have been under-funded in the lean years of the late 1940s). On 10 November 1947 the Design Research Division provided relevant details of the new aircraft (ADR 42, ADR 45, XAJ-1, and XA2J-1): ADR 42 was expected to take off at 69,000 pounds and to stall at 78 knots; the 100,000-pound airplane would stall at 105 knots. Takeoff speeds would be about equal to stall speeds. That December BuAer completed the design of a catapult capable of accelerating a 100,000-pound airplane to 100 knots, which seemed to be what was required (S83-2 file, Vol. 9).

11. The North Koreans attacked on 25 June 1950. On 11 July the Joint Chiefs agreed to postpone any further consideration of carrier force level reduction, and the next day Secretary of Defense Louis Johnson, who had killed the *United States* slightly more than a year earlier, offered Chief of Naval Operations Admiral Forrest Sherman a new carrier (for the FY52 program). The Joint Chiefs adopted a twelve-carrier force level; a fourteen-carrier force was approved in February 1952 over Air Force objections. Representative Carl Vinson, the Navy's strongest advocate in Congress, informally suggested that Congress would approve a carrier significantly smaller than the *United States*, which meant a tonnage slightly below 60,000, compared to about 65,000 for the *United States*. As designed, *Forrestal* had the same four elevators (one right aft, two to starboard, and one to port) of the *United States*, but not the ramp up to the flight deck. She had an enclosed (hurricane) bow, and weight was saved by eliminating the twin 3in/70 guns of the earlier design. Detail changes included the use of individual smoke pipes rather than the two trunked smoke pipes of the earlier ship.

12. ADM1/31003 (The National Archive of the United Kingdom) gives details of various British angled-deck proposals. The key individual was Captain D. R. F. Campbell, prospective commanding officer of HMS *Ark Royal*.

13. This was a widespread fear. The great surprise was that the Soviets did *not* greatly quiet their submarines as they passed from first (HEN) to second (CVY) generation in the early 1970s. According to a Russian account published after the end of the Cold War, silencing of various sorts became an important Soviet R&D theme in the 1970s; the first really quiet Soviet submarine, Victor III, appeared in the late 1970s. The special Alfa class also showed substantial quieting, but it was never built in numbers comparable to those of the noisier conventional nuclear Victor I/II and Charlie (and many Soviet strategic submarines).

14. His other important new ship programs were an abortive austere Aegis ship (DG/Aegis), the *Perry*-class frigate, and the missile hydrofoil (PHM). Each convoy would be escorted by a sea control ship and frigates.

15. The most attractive prospect was blowing air through an airplane's wings to simulate the usual circulation of forward flight. Once in the air, such an airplane could cease blowing and devote all its power to forward propulsion; it seemed that it might avoid the usual VTOL performance penalties. Unfortunately the prototype built to demonstrate this technique, the XFV-12, never managed to fly (perhaps due to overweight).

16. The prospective Sea Control Ship Air Group varied. At one time it consisted of eleven ASW and three AEW helicopters and three Harrier fighter/attack aircraft; at others, it included the futuristic FV-12 VTOL fighter, and the AEW role was to have been filled by the remote-controlled airship. The fighters had multiple roles. In experiments, Harriers laid corridors of sonobuoys down that a simulated convoy would pass. A submarine trying to attack had to pass through the corridor, revealing itself and opening itself to attack.

17. T-CBL was sometimes compared with the 54,000-ton British CVA-01 design, cancelled in 1966; the existence of the British design seemed to show that a ship of that size would be a reasonable carrier. CVA-01 would have accommodated about half as many aircraft as a *Nimitz*.

18. Some of these factors were worked out explicitly during the CVNX studies (1976). An airplane passing over the ramp at the after end of the flight deck needs clearance for the tail hook (typically at least 11 feet). Given the standard glide path slope (3.5 degrees), the ramp had to be at least 180 feet from the second wire, which had to be at least 40 feet from the third wire; and the wire had to pull out 350 feet, with another 94 feet for barricade stretch, a total of 664 feet from the ramp to the fore end of the sponson carrying the angled deck. Ideally the airplane caught by the wires is then turned into a parking area abaft the bow catapults, which are 310 feet long. The landing area is at an angle to the rest of the hull, so that the fore end of the sponson is actually less than 660 feet from the stern, but total flight deck length is still over 900 feet, whatever the composition of the air wing.

CHAPTER 16

Conclusions

Douglas V. Smith

Nimitz-*class aircraft carrier USS* Ronald Reagan *(CVN 76) with guided-missile cruiser USS* Chancellorsville *(CG 62).*

Perhaps President George Herbert Walker Bush said it best in his much appreciated foreword to this book: "One of the first questions I always asked as Commander-in-Chief when American interests were threatened around the globe was '*Where are our aircraft carriers?*'"

It is interesting to note that there have been thirteen American presidents since World War II. Of these, six have worn the uniform of the United States Navy. Presidents Kennedy, Johnson, Nixon, Ford, Carter, and Bush (41) all came to their office aware of the options afforded by, and comfortable with the strategic and operational applications of, Navy—and particularly Carrier Air Wing—aviation as an instrument of national power. Of them, President H. W. Bush also had the advantage of being a Navy carrier pilot himself. It makes sense that these presidents would be predisposed to use of Navy aviation in times of national crisis, for precisely the reasons behind President George H. W. Bush's statement above.

A U.S. Navy carrier today represents the ability to bring considerable sustainable firepower near to an adversary or enemy's borders without the constraint of being subject to the political sovereignty of a nation providing a land base of operations. It can sortie considerable punch from a piloted aircraft, thus retaining the ability to cancel an attacking sortie before it strikes its targets. Moreover, if ordnance is expended, there remains sufficient capability to reload and attack again and again. Even if no strike is executed, a carrier can linger in proximity to an adversary for extended periods in a deterrent role. Thus a Navy aircraft carrier and her Air Wing gives the ability to execute immediately available options, unencumbered by the political objectives of even America's closest allies in time of national crisis.

In the preceding pages the evolving nature of the threat a carrier represents has been presented. In World War II for instance American carriers started the war in primarily a defensive posture, but moved to the offensive quickly on 4 June 1942 by sinking four of Japan's large carriers in the Battle of Midway and in the process adjusting the naval balance in the Pacific to near parity. This enabled contemplation of offensive American operations at sea and amphibiously on a limited basis. The carrier battles of the Eastern Solomons and Santa Cruz ensued on 24 August and 26 October 1942, which in large part made it possible for the Marine Corps' 1st Marine Division to land amphibiously on Guadalcanal, hold the island with support from the 164th U.S. Army Infantry Regiment of the Americal Division, and enabled Major General Roy Geiger's 1st Marine Air Wing to attrite a critical number of Japanese carrier pilots and their airplanes in the process. Moreover, it threw the Japanese back on their heels for long enough for forces generated by the Two-Ocean Navy Act of 1940 and associated appropriations to expand the U.S. Navy beyond Japanese ability to defend.

Holding Guadalcanal was critical to enactment of a two-pronged naval offensive through the Upper Solomons, Gilberts, Marshalls, Marianas, and Volcano Islands toward the Japanese home islands. So too was the expansion of the U.S. Navy and fielding of a second generation of wartime aircraft critical to the offensive. Splashing over four hundred Japanese aircraft and sinking three carriers (two by submarine attack, admittedly) in the Battle of the Philippine Sea/Marianas Turkey Shoot opened the back door at Saipan and Tinian to Japan itself.

Once the tide irrevocably turned against the Imperial Japanese Navy in the Pacific the American Navy transformed its carrier force to the role of attacking land targets. The versatility of carrier aviation, its destructive capacity, and assistance from land-based Navy aircraft in the reconnaissance and anti-submarine roles enabled the Navy gradually to move close enough to Japan to unleash the final destructive capacity of the Army Air Forces directly against the Japanese home islands.

So too was American Navy aviation critical in conflicts in Korea and Vietnam. It has remained so through countless conflicts and contingencies up to this very moment. The history of Navy aviation demonstrates its flexibility and ability to adapt in support of multiple and varied missions from a world war environment down to precise and limited missions in an evolving contingency. What remains constant through the range of military applications is that Navy aviation—land-based, helicopter, and carrier alike—gives the greatest flexibility to American presidents and political and military leaders of any form of military power available to them. From search and rescue, long-range surveillance, anti-submarine warfare, area defense to land attack, amphibious warfare, special operations, warfare at sea and nuclear strike, Navy carrier aircraft and their land-based counterparts excel at accomplishing their missions rapidly and precisely. But, as the chapters on aircraft and carrier developments over the last century point out, forethought and planning have to precede their use. Congressional and presidential support of programs that will continue the utility of Navy aviation in achieving a range of American goals and interests is essential to the continuation of the leading role the United States has played in world politics over the last century.

The question then becomes, What type of structure should U.S. Navy aviation take over the next century? Some might contend that aircraft carrier and anti-submarine operations will no longer be useful in crisis situations and are therefore costly additions to other options—such as unmanned drones—that are now available in the U.S. arsenal. The fact remains that of all existing options available to the national leadership only a carrier offers the combination of rapid response, considerable deliverable ordnance, sustainability, and above all the ability to gain air control rapidly over an objective area and maintain it. Then where and under what circumstances are carriers likely to be necessary?

The current strategic communication that structures the threat environment for the U.S. Navy for the next decade and beyond is "A Cooperative Strategy for the 21st Century." The "Cooperative Strategy" articulates the areas of the world where American—and by extension Allied—interests and goals lie, and the type of naval capabilities necessary to achieve and protect them. This document obviously focuses primarily on the Middle East and Western Pacific areas. Previous concentration on the Atlantic Ocean and Mediterranean Sea is conspicuously missing from the "Cooperative Strategy." However, possible emergent military requirements of a time-sensitive nature require American preparedness to respond. One can thus analyze the "Cooperative Strategy for the 21st Century" and see that aircraft Carrier Strike Groups must be able to respond to crises on short order in the northwestern Indian Ocean, in waters of the Sea of Japan and adjacent areas, and in the eastern Mediterranean Sea.

There has long been a paradigm of aircraft carrier availability based on the distance to sustain a Carrier Strike Group at sea in a particular crisis scenario; the proximity of the scenario to Underway Replenishment Group support; and the fact that, for every Carrier Strike Group on station, one will have just departed station for return to the continental United States and one will be in a U.S. port replenishing and resupplying. Given the two areas of vital U.S. concern delineated in the "Cooperative Strategy for the 21st Century," and the obvious need for rapid crisis response in distant areas or European waters, the above paradigm indicates that America will need at least nine carriers to retain a rapid-response posture in only its vital areas of interest for the foreseeable future. One additional carrier should be added to support training of pilots in the Advanced Pilot Training Program and the Replacement Air Groups located in the southeastern United States and another to maintain continuous crisis reaction capacity in that at least one carrier will of necessity be in the yards for overhaul and/or nuclear core removal and replacement or some other maintenance cycle in an almost continuous basis. Assuming that one of the proposed three aircraft carriers in the Atlantic/Mediterranean could be dual-purposed to meet this requirement, a minimum of ten American carriers should be maintained to secure American and Allied objectives around the world. If a dedicated training carrier is deemed necessary—and as a hedge against a multiple-area response requirement or the sinking of a carrier—an eleven-carrier American Navy is seen as the minimum requirement to sustain U.S. and Allied interests over the next several decades and beyond. Similarly, a modernized and substantial aviation surveillance and anti-submarine capability (particularly one capable of responding to the very real diesel submarine threat possessed by many potential aggressors) is needed.

The history of U.S. Navy air power has left a proud tradition that has rightfully shaped America's history of success in wars and in preserving American freedoms, moral imperatives, and interests. This volume is dedicated to all those who have flown against capable adversaries and often tremendous odds in securing them. In the Centennial Year of U.S. Navy air power it is hoped that all Americans pause to salute those patriots who have "carried America's flag into battle in pursuit of a just cause." They have shaped American history and will continue to do so in the second century of U.S. Navy air power.

CONTRIBUTORS

DR. STANLEY D. M. CARPENTER

Stanley D. M. Carpenter is a Professor of Strategy and Policy at the United States Naval War College in Newport, Rhode Island, and serves as the deputy Strategy and Policy Division Head for the College of Distance Education. He holds degrees from Florida State University (PhD in British Military History), the University of St. Andrews (Scotland) (MLitt in Scottish Military History), and the University of North Carolina at Chapel Hill (AB with honors in History). Dr. Carpenter is a retired U.S. Navy Captain, having served for thirty years on active duty and in the Navy Reserve as a Surface Warfare Officer. Professor Carpenter's publications include *Military Leadership in the British Civil Wars, 1642–1651: "The Genius of this Age"* (Cass 2005) and editorship of *The English Civil War* in *The International Library of Essays on Military History* (Ashgate 2007).

DR. DONALD CHISHOLM

Donald Chisholm has been Professor of Joint Military Operations at the Naval War College since 2000. Previously he taught at the University of Illinois, Chicago; University of California, Los Angeles; The Ohio State University; and University of California, San Diego. He earned his AB, MA, and PhD in political science at the University of California, Berkeley. His research has addressed planning and executing Joint military operations; cognitive and organizational limits on rationality; organizational failure and reliability; and privatization of public activities. He is the author of two books, *Coordination Without Hierarchy: Informal Structures in Multi-*

Organizational Systems (1989), and *Waiting for Dead Men's Shoes: Origins and Development of the U.S. Navy's Officer Personnel System, 1793–1941* (2001), which received the 2001 Rear Admiral Samuel Eliot Morison Award for Distinguished Contribution to Naval Literature. He has published in *Joint Force Quarterly*, *Parameters*, *Journal of Strategic Studies*, and the *Naval War College Review*.

CDR. KEVIN J. DELAMER, USN

Commander Delamer is a career helicopter aviator and a qualified test pilot. He has accumulated over three thousand hours over thirty type model series aircraft including various models of the H-3 and H-60. In addition to operational deployments, he has served in a variety of staff assignments including a tour with NASA, responsibility for political-military affairs for the U.S. Navy in the Middle East, and Executive Assistant to the Commander, Naval Forces, U.S. Central Command. He is currently serving as a military Professor in the Strategy Department at the U.S. Naval War College, where he also serves as a lecturer for the Fleet Seminar Program.

DR. NORMAN FRIEDMAN

Dr. Friedman has been concerned throughout his career with the way in which policy and technology intersect, in fields as disparate as national missile defense, nuclear strategy, and mobilization policy. An internationally known strategist and naval historian, he worked more than a decade at a major U.S. think tank, and another decade as consultant to the Secretary of the Navy. He has consulted for many major defense corporations. Dr. Friedman has written more than thirty-five books on naval strategy and technology, including an award-winning account of the U.S. Cold War strategy, histories of U.S. and British aircraft carriers (in the latter case including their aircraft), an account of carrier and naval aircraft technology, and a two-volume history of British (and Commonwealth) destroyers and frigates. He contributes a monthly column on world naval developments to the Naval Institute's *Proceedings* magazine and writes articles for journals worldwide. Dr. Friedman holds a PhD from Columbia University, New York. He lectures widely on defense issues in forums such as the National Defence University, the Naval War College, and the Royal United Services Institute. His current focus is on network-centric warfare, about which he has recently published *Network Centric Warfare: How Navies Learned to Fight Smarter in Three World Wars*. This year he is publishing a book on unmanned combat air vehicles and their possible effect on carrier aviation and also a history of British and Commonwealth cruisers.

HILL GOODSPEED

Hill Goodspeed is the author or editor of five books, one of which was named by Naval Institute *Proceedings* as one of the Notable Naval Books of 2001. Named a George C. Marshall Undergraduate Scholar while attending Washington and Lee University, he is the historian and Artifact Collections Manager at the National Naval Aviation Museum in Pensacola, Florida.

CAPT. JOHN EDWARD JACKSON, USN (RET.)

John Jackson has been a researcher and historian of lighter-than-air vehicles for over forty years. He has flown five different classes of modern commercial airships, as well as recreational hot-air balloons. He has authored numerous articles on the history and potential future of LTA platforms, and has contributed to a television documentary on the role of airships in the Battle of the North Atlantic. He served in logistics and education assignments over a twenty-seven-year career in the U.S. Navy, holds advanced degrees from Providence College and Salve Regina University, and is a graduate of the Management Development Program at Harvard University. He longs for the days when the phrase "Up Ship!" was exclaimed as Navy aviators took to the skies in buoyant flight.

TIMOTHY H. JACKSON

Timothy H. Jackson is a retired Navy officer, and formerly a special adviser to the President of the Naval War College, associate dean of Academic Affairs for Electives and Directed Research, and professor of Strategy and Policy at the United States Naval War College in Newport, Rhode Island. He is the former Director of Distance Education and Director of Academic Support, servicing more than 45,000 students from all branches of the military Services as well as students from other federal agencies. He is a published author of military studies and a guest lecturer at colleges and universities around the country. He was a guest speaker at the sixty-fifth anniversary of the attack on Pearl Harbor, when his "Two-Ocean Navy Act of 1940" was first presented.

EDWARD S. MILLER

Edward S. Miller, a Phi Beta Kappa graduate of Syracuse University, also attended the Harvard Business School Advanced Management Program. In his career at a Fortune 500 international mining corporation in New York he rose to Chief Financial Officer. He was later CFO of the U.S. government's Synthetic Fuels Corporation. From his interests in comparing corporate planning to war plans, and in the roots of the Pacific

War, he wrote *War Plan Orange: The U.S. Strategy to Defeat Japan, 1897–1945*, published by the Naval Institute Press. The book won five distinguished history prizes. He recently wrote *Bankrupting the Enemy: The U.S. Financial Siege of Japan before Pearl Harbor*. Mr. Miller lives in the now infamous Watergate in Washington, D.C.

DR. ALBERT A. NOFI

Albert A. Nofi, an educator, military historian, defense analyst, and game designer, has written or edited some forty books and wargames, most recently *"To Train the Fleet for War": The U.S. Navy Fleet Problems, 1923–1940*, released in 2010 by the Naval War College Press.

DR. GARY J. OHLS

Gary J. Ohls currently serves as Associate Professor of Joint Maritime Operations in the Naval War College Program at the Naval Postgraduate School. He received a PhD in History from Texas Christian University in Fort Worth, Texas, holds three master's degrees, and is a distinguished graduate of the U.S. Naval War College in Newport, Rhode Island. Prior to his current assignment, Professor Ohls served as a member of the Maritime History Department at the Naval War College in Newport, Rhode Island. Colonel Ohls served thirty-five years in the United States Marine Corps including duty as an enlisted man, a regular officer, a Reserve officer, and a Reserve officer on active duty. Additionally, he has worked in management positions with Northrop Grumman Corporation and the Aerospace Corporation. His professional publications include one book and five articles on various military issues.

DR. S. MIKE PAVELEC

Dr. Pavelec currently teaches at the School of Advanced Air and Space Studies at Maxwell AFB after teaching two years at the U.S. Naval War College and three years at Hawaii Pacific University. He received his PhD in History from The Ohio State University after BA and MA degrees from University of Calgary (Canada). His research focuses on military technology and innovation, and the interconnected nature of the military-industrial complex.

CAPT. ROBERT C. (BARNEY) RUBEL, USN (RET.)

Captain Rubel was a career light attack and strike fighter aviator and Landing Signal Officer. He commanded VFA-131 and accumulated over three thousand hours and nine hundred arrested landings in the A-7 and F-18. He is currently Dean of the Center for Naval Warfare Studies at the U.S. Naval War College; at this institution he directed the research and gaming effort that resulted in the current U.S. Maritime Strategy.

DR. DOUGLAS V. SMITH

Dr. Douglas V. Smith is Professor of Strategy and Policy and Head of the Strategy and Policy Division for the College of Distance Education at the Naval War College, Newport, Rhode Island. A career Navy officer and aviator, he earned his BS at the United States Naval Academy, his MAs at the Naval Postgraduate School and the Naval War College, and his PhD in Military History at Florida State University. He is the author of *Carrier Battles: Command Decision in Harm's Way* (Naval Institute Press, 2006), and a chapter titled "Gunboat Diplomacy: Presidential Use of Aircraft Carriers and Their Embarked Air Wings," part of the forthcoming *Statesmen and Air Power.*

DR. STEPHEN K. STEIN

A graduate of The Ohio State University, Dr. Stephen K. Stein teaches at the University of Memphis and also directs its online history program. His recent publications include *From Torpedoes to Aviation: Washington Irving Chambers and Technological Innovation in the New Navy, 1877–1913* (2007), and "The Greely Relief Expedition and the New Navy," *International Journal of Naval History* 5 (December 2006), which won the Rear Admiral Ernest M. Eller Prize in Naval History.

INDEX

A

A-1/AD Skyraider aircraft, 213, 270, 274, 275, 278, 280, 285, 286, 292, 314

A-3 Skywarrior aircraft, 247, 262, 331, 340, 345n8

A-4 Skyhawk aircraft, 247–48, 259, 265, 282, 285, 286–87, 290, 292

A-5 Vigilante bomber, 248, 266

A-6 Intruder bomber, 248, 256, 266, 267, 282, 285, 292, 336

A-7 Corsair II aircraft, 248, 249, 253, 255, 256, 259, 266, 267, 285

Abraham Lincoln, 336

aeronautics research, 12, 19, 20–22, 27–28

Air Force, U.S.: accident rate, 241, 265; bombing role of, 311–12; establishment of, 311; jet aircraft, transition to, 241; Korean conflict, 274–75, 277, 313; maintenance practices, 261; rescue operations, 226, 229; roles and missions of, 311–12, 318, 324; safety issues and initiatives, 262–63

air wings: number of aircraft in, 88, 159, 160, 167–68, 170–71, 193n12, 194n17, 194n19, 340; types of aircraft for, 87, 110, 147–48, 150n21, 173–74, 176, 188–89, 307–8

aircraft: advances in, 2, 3, 20–21, 35, 209–10, 264; bailing out, 259; control systems for, 20, 24; cost of, 148; crashes and accidents, 19–20, 25, 164, 165, 194n15, 241–42, 244–45, 265; design and development of, 8–10, 13–14, 210–15; early research and development, 6–8; funding for, 147, 303, 307; interwar development of, 199–200; loss of during Pacific campaign, 210; manufacturing of, 24–25, 151n40, 200, 209–10, 303, 307; orders for, 26, 139, 151n29; patent dispute over design of, 9, 14, 26; procurement of, 16, 17, 149n7, 167, 303; quality of, 24–25; range of, 31, 33–35, 37, 101; system of aircraft-type symbols, 156; technology transitions, dangers during, 49; for World War I, 154, 190n3, 200. *See also* air wings; jet aircraft; seaplanes and flying boats

aircraft carrier design: angled flight
decks, 258, 259, 265, 333, 335, 349n12;
armored flight decks, 172–73, 183–86;
characteristics proposed by Aviation
Division, 156, 190–91n4; construction
time and, 145–46; deck equipment
for landings, 84, 155–56; deck size
and specifications, 167–68, 194n18,
341, 342; elevators, 84, 165–66, 170,
330, 335; flexible decks, 333; guns on
flight deck, 160–61; larger carriers,
340–42; nuclear carriers, 335, 336–37;
preliminary characteristics, 157–58,
190n2, 192–93nn8–9, 329–31, 344–
48nn6–10; ship conversions, 24, 80,
97, 134, 153, 156, 157, 159, 186–88,
192n7, 193n10, 197–98nn29–32; size
and specifications, 89; smaller carrier
designs, 338–40, 349nn16–17; treaty
tonnage limits and, 146; for two-
ocean Navy, 177–82, 196–97nn27–28;
Washington Naval Treaty and, 167–75,
194n17, 194n19. *See also* catapults
aircraft carriers: annual building
program, 335, 336; carrier task force,
emergence of, 100–110; construction
and commissioning of, 138–39, 140,
141–45, 151n35, 156, 179–81, 189,
340; cost of, 141, 143, 191n5; crashes
aboard, 164, 165, 194n15, 257, 265;
deck park, 88; disarmament conference
and treaty and, 159–60; effectiveness
of, 53, 215, 343; first American, 6;
flexibility of, 325; flight deck hazards,
164, 261; flight-deck operations,
85; independent operations by, 101,
107–8, 115, 116, 122–23; launching
and landing procedures, 83–85, 134,
162–66, 193–94nn14–15, 254, 257–59,
330, 334, 342–43, 349n18; logistical
demands of operations with, 104; night

operations, 182–83; nuclear carriers,
337–38, 342; offensive missions with,
53, 81, 88–89, 97, 99–100, 104, 110,
189–90, 201; optical landing system,
258, 259, 265, 334; refueling of, 112;
role in fleet operations, 3, 133, 156–57,
191n5, 306, 322–29, 341, 343–44nn2–5,
351–54; sinking of and damage to, 101,
126n24; specialized air groups, 126–
27n33; system of ship-type symbols,
156, 185; tactics and operational
methods for, 80–83, 85–87, 89, 134,
182–83; technological advances, 343;
vulnerability of, 101, 108, 123, 177
airships: acquisition of, 44; blimps, 44,
49–50; capabilities and value of, 44,
106, 123; commercial airships, 43;
contributions of, 50; development
of, 6, 43; dirigibles, 24, 44, 304, 305;
interest in, 24, 302; military missions
with, 35, 43, 44, 46–50, 155, 194n16;
purchase of, 24; range of, 35; requests
for, 26; rigid airships, 44–49, 194n16,
208; scouting missions, 208–9; size
and specifications, 43, 47, 49, 50;
termination of operations with, 50,
305, 319n25; terminology, 44; value
of, 110
Akron, 35, 46–48, 106
Antietam, 258, 333
anti-submarine warfare: aircraft and
carrier operations for, 331–32, 337,
338–39; Battle of the Atlantic, 309;
helicopters and rotary-wing aircraft
for, 221, 223, 224, 227, 229–30, 231–32,
235, 236, 337, 339; Navy's role in,
313–14
Army/Army Air Force/Army Air Corps,
U.S.: Aeronautical Division, 8–9;
aircraft development and flight testing,
13–14; aviation program, development

of, 5, 6–8, 16–17, 302, 318n6; aviation
program, future of, 311; bombing
role of, 304, 309, 310; coastal defense
operations, 214, 306–7; fleet-based
versus land-based aircraft for Navy,
35, 208, 214, 305–7; funding for
aviation program, 16–17; helicopter
demonstration, 220, 221; Korean
conflict, 273–74, 276–79, 313; Navy
aviation, cooperation with, 14–15; roles
and missions of, 311–12, 324; Wright
brothers *Military Flyer*, 8–9
AV-8 Harrier, 251, 342
aviation: beginnings of military aviation,
6–8; Curtiss' contributions, 9–10;
first military aircraft, 8–9; German
development of military aviation, 12;
government funding for, 8; Wright
brothers flight research and testing,
8–9. *See also* naval aviation
aviation safety, 262–64

B
B-17 bombers, 310
B-24 Liberator aircraft, 214, 308, 309, 313,
316
B-25 bombers, 310
B-26 Invader, 271
B-29 Superfortress, 271, 282
B-36 Peacemaker, 243, 273, 312, 324–25
B-52 Stratofortress, 293
Badoeng Strait, 274, 276
balloons, 6, 10, 24, 303, 304
battleships: anti-aircraft capabilities,
89; capabilities of, 83, 319n29;
construction and commissioning of,
138, 143; design of, 153; expansion of
fleet, 10, 137, 140, 150n20, 151n31;
improvements to, 92n26; loss of, 143,
308; naval aviation and future of, 26–
28, 123, 124, 132; planes on, 15, 18, 22,

24, 26; treaty tonnage limits, 158–59,
193n11
Bennington (CV-20), 143
Birmingham, 5, 7, 12, 23, 153
bombing: aircraft for, 171, 195n23, 203–4,
210–15, 304, 309, 344–46nn7–8; dive-
bombing, 86–87, 106–7, 119, 123,
169, 212; effectiveness of, 203, 214–15;
horizontal bombing, 106–7, 119, 123
Bon Homme Richard (CV-31), 143, 289
Boxer, 272, 274
Bristol, Mark, 22–26, 27, 28, 190n2
Bunker Hill (CV-17), 141, 151n35, 179,
220, 221, 224–25
Bush, George H.W., 351

C
Carrier Strike Groups, 353
Carrier Task Force, 95, 123–24
Catalina aircraft. *See* PBY Catalina aircraft
catapults: advances in, 27–28, 330;
development of, 17–18, 153;
effectiveness of, 164; hydraulic, 186,
197n29, 258, 330, 334; importance of,
164–65, 178; installation of, 23–24, 161,
330–31; problems with, 25; purpose of,
161; steam, 258–59, 333–34
Chambers, Washington Irving:
aeronautics board chairmanship,
19; aircraft development and flight
testing, 13–14; aviation program,
control of, 18–19; aviation program,
promotion and development of,
5, 11–13, 15–16, 18, 27; catapult
development, 17–18, 23, 27–28; legacy
of, 27–28; pilot recruitment, 13; pilot
training, 13; replacement of, 22; role
in transformation of Navy, 11; safety
concerns of, 20; sea duty of, 18, 19;
seaplanes, interest in, 15
Civil War, 6

Coast Guard, U.S., 220–21, 222, 223, 224,
     227, 315
Cold War, 243, 273, 293–94, 311–16, 323,
     325–28
Constellation, 286–87
convoy escort operations. *See* escort
     operations
crew, 256, 260
Curtiss, Glenn: aircraft demonstration
     by, 12; aircraft demonstrations, 153;
     aircraft development and flight testing,
     9–10, 13, 21; aircraft manufacturing
     by, 24–25; flying boat development,
     17, 33–34; Navy's relationship with, 27;
     seaplane development, 12, 15, 16, 17,
     200; speed record, 9, 21

D
D-558-1 Skystreak, 247
D-558-2 Skyrocket, 247
Daniels, Josephus, 18, 19, 23, 24, 77n39,
     133
Desert Storm Operation, 236, 243
disarmament: peacetime reductions,
     54, 59–60, 64–65, 71, 72, 74–75n16,
     95–96, 272, 273, 304; post–World
     War II drawdown, 272, 273. *See also*
     Washington Naval Treaty
Drone Antisubmarine Helicopter
     (DASH) program, 232, 235
DT aircraft, 201–2

E
E-2 Hawkeyes, 338
EA-6B Prowler, 282
ejection seats, 259–60, 276
Ellyson, Theodore, 13, 15, 17, 18, 19, 27, 28
Ely, Eugene Burton, 3, 5, 7, 12–13, 19, 27,
     95, 153, 302
Enterprise (CV-6): Battle of Midway,
     89; construction and commissioning

of, 109, 135, 143, 152n54, 171; design
     of, 335; effectiveness of, 172; Fleet
     maneuvers, participation by, 117–19,
     130n68; nuclear carrier, 338; Vietnam
     War, 284
Enterprise-class carriers, 282
Erickson, Frank, 222, 223–24, 226–27,
     229–30
escort operations: air cover for shipping,
     309; Battle of the Atlantic, 308–9;
     blimps, 49–50; escort carriers (CVEs),
     146–47, 160, 187–88; sea control ships,
     338, 339, 349n14
Essex (CV-9), 137, 142, 145, 146, 177–79,
     196n27
Essex-class carriers, 89, 137, 146, 150n21,
     163, 172, 181, 284–85, 331, 344n6,
     347–48n9

F
F2H Banshee fighters, 244, 245, 246, 254,
     259, 282
F3D Skyknight fighters, 245, 246, 282
F3H Demon fighters, 246, 247
F-4 Phantom II fighter, 241, 248, 253, 255,
     266, 282, 285, 290, 291, 292
F4D Skyray fighters, 247, 251, 265
F4F Wildcat fighters, 87, 147, 148, 206,
     210
F4U Corsair fighter-bomber, 147, 148,
     210, 213–14, 260, 271, 272, 274, 275,
     280
F-5L flying boats, 33, 207
F6C Hawks, 203
F6F Hellcat fighter, 147, 148, 210
F6U Pirate fighters, 245
F7U Cutlass fighters, 244, 245, 246, 247,
     251, 266
F-8 Crusader fighter, 241, 242, 248, 251,
     265, 266, 282, 285, 286, 292
F8C aircraft, 204

F9F-2 Panther fighters, 244, 245, 246, 247, 251, 254, 266, 271, 274, 275, 276, 281

F9F-6 Cougar fighters, 246, 247, 254, 257–58, 266

F-11 Tiger fighters, 244, 247, 265

F-14 Tomcat fighters, 248, 249, 255, 315, 327, 340, 343

F-18 Hornet fighters, 248, 249, 252, 253, 264

F-35C aircraft, 342, 343

F-80 Shooting Star, 241, 271, 275

F-86 Sabre fighters, 247, 275, 282

F/A-18 Hornet fighters, 241, 243, 267, 315, 343

fan jet engines, 255

FF-1 fighter, 205–6

FH-1 Phantom fighters, 241, 245–46

fighter aircraft, 173–74, 204–6, 212–13, 244

Fiske, Bradley, 18–19, 22, 24, 27

FJ-1/FJ-3 Fury fighters, 245–46, 247

Fleet Plan WPPac-46, 41–42

Fleet Problems and joint exercises: air operations during, 97; areas used for, 98, 125n10; aviation's role in, 94–95; communications relay plane, 100, 125n22; contributions of, 123–24; deficiencies identified during, 39; diversion of fleet during, 96–97, 124–25n5; Exercise M, 109–10; FP I, 97; FP II, 97; FP III, 98; FP IV, 98; FP IX, 100–101, 206; FP V, 98–99; FP VI, 84; FP VII, 88, 99; FP VIII, 100; FP X, 101–3; FP XI, 103; FP XII, 103–4, 126nn28–29; FP XIII, 105–7, 123; FP XIV, 107–9; FP XIX, 116–17, 129nn64–65; FP XV, 109, 126n29; FP XVI, 110–12, 128nn50–51; FP XVII, 112–13; FP XVIII, 113–16, 129n58, 208; FP XX, 117–19, 126–27n22, 129–30nn67–68; FP XXI, 119–23; Grand Joint Exercises, 89, 94, 99, 100, 104–5, 126–27n33; naval force, creation of, 110–23; number held, 93n27; operational methods, doctrine, and tactics development during, 89, 94, 95, 134; phases of, 95

flight-deck cruisers, 175–76, 196n26

Flyer, 8

FM Wildcat aircraft, 210

Formosa, 269, 270

Forrestal, 243, 258, 289, 322, 332, 333, 335

Forrestal-class carriers, 282, 285, 347–48n9

France, 9, 17, 18, 21, 26, 139, 179, 303

Franklin (CV-13), 142, 151n35, 179

Franklin D. Roosevelt (CVB-42), 143

G

Germany: airships, 43, 45, 46, 154–55; aviation, funding for, 17; Battle of the Atlantic, 308–9; jet aircraft development, 242–43; naval aviation development, 12; number of planes, 26, 307, 320n40; Rainbow Five plan, 41

gold wings, 77n39

Grand Joint Exercises (GJEs), 89, 94, 99, 100, 104–5, 126–27n33

Great Britain, 41, 83, 303. *See also* Royal Air Force (RAF); Royal Navy

H

H-2 Sea Sprite helicopters, 231, 232, 235, 237

H-3 helicopters, 232

H-3 Sea King helicopters, 231–32, 234, 237

H-16 flying boats, 303

H-21 helicopters, 229

H-34 helicopters, 230

H-46 Sea Knight helicopters, 231, 234, 237, 292

H-53 helicopters, 236, 292

H-60 helicopters, 235, 237
Halsey, William F., 41–42, 73, 113, 158
Hancock (CV-19), 141, 144, 151n35, 287
Hawaii: exercises in waters around, 99, 100, 104–5, 107–8, 110–12, 116–17, 128nn50–51, 129n58, 129n65, 134; shore air facilities in, 137. *See also* Pearl Harbor
helicopters and rotary-wing aircraft: acceptance of and response to, 221, 222–24; anti-submarine warfare use, 221, 223, 224, 227, 229–30, 231–32, 235, 236, 337, 339; capabilities of, 227–28; changing role for, 236–37, 283; demonstrations of, 220–22, 223–25; design of, 230–34; development of program for, 220–27; flight tests, 225–26, 227; importance of, 237; Korean conflict use of, 230, 233, 276, 313; Light Airborne Multi-Purpose System (LAMPS) configuration, 232, 235, 236; LSTs as base for, 230; minesweeping operations, 234, 235, 236; procurement of, 223; rescue operations with, 222–23, 227, 228, 230, 232–34, 236, 237, 281, 313; training of pilots, 224, 227, 228–29; vertical replenishment missions, 234, 235, 281
HH-2C helicopters, 233
HH-3A helicopters, 233
HNS-1 helicopters, 226, 227
HO3S helicopters, 230, 276
HO4S helicopters, 229
Horne, Frederick J., 38, 76n35, 114, 115–16
Horne Board, 65, 70, 71–72, 76n35
Hornet (CV-8): construction and commissioning of, 137, 143, 176; loss of, 142; Pacific campaign, 310, 343n2; sinking of, 178
Hornet (CV-12), 89, 138, 142

Hornet-class carriers, 145–46
HOS-3 helicopters, 228
HRS helicopters, 229
HSS-1 helicopters, 229
HSS-1N Sea Bat helicopters, 230
HUP helicopters, 229

I
Independence-class light carriers, 143, 146, 180, 188
Intrepid, 138, 151–52n46

J
Japan: air wing, number of aircraft in, 163–64; aircrew, replacement of, 174–75; airship reconnaissance missions, 46; carrier-building program, 139, 156; China, dominance of by Japan, 31; conflict with, plans for, 134; disarmament conference and treaty, 158–59; Doolittle raid on Tokyo, 189–90, 342n2; number of planes, 307, 320n41; Pearl Harbor attack, 42, 176–77; Rainbow Five plan, 41–42; Russia, defeat of, 31; surrender of, 310–11; War Plan Orange strategy against, 31
jet aircraft: advances in, 3; carrier launching and landing procedures, 254, 257–59; cockpit design and system management, 255–56, 267; crashes and accidents, 241–42, 244–45, 252–53, 255, 260, 261–63, 264–65; design of, 241, 244; development of, 240; development of for carrier use, 242–45, 248–49; downing defective aircraft, 263–64; echelons of, 245–50, 252; ejection seats, 259–60, 276; engine design and performance, 240–41, 253–55; flight controls, 256–57; fuel management, 256; handling characteristics and performance of, 240–41, 245–46, 251–

53, 264–67; maintenance of, 260–61; man-made interferences, 255–57; naval aviation culture and transition to, 261–64; night/all-weather operations, 245, 252, 265, 267; nuclear weapons delivery operations, 245, 247; pilot training, 253, 263, 265; seaplanes and flying boats, 250; sorties with, increase in, 282; transition to, 241, 264–67; VTOL aircraft, 251. *See also* swept-wing jets

Johnson, Lyndon B., 286, 287, 294

Joint Strike Fighter, 249, 251

K

Kearsarge (CV-33), 143

Kimmel, Husband E., 41–42, 91

King, Ernest J.: aircraft demonstrations, 17; aircraft for War Plan Orange, 37, 208; airship reconnaisance missions, 46; attack role of aircraft, 38; aviation training, 158; contributions of, 73; Fleet manuevers, participation by, 103, 104, 105–6, 116–17, 126–27n22, 129n65; promotion criteria, 68–69, 78n44; ship construction, rate of, 141

kites and kite-balloons, 9, 10, 13

Kitty Hawk, 289, 335, 338

Korean conflict: American air superiority, 274–75; Battle of Carlson's Canyon, 280; carrier-based air support, 271–72, 274, 279–80; command arrangement for aviation units, 280; evacuation operations, 270–71, 281; ground forces, fighting by, 273–74; helicopter use during, 230, 233, 276, 281, 283, 313; jet aircraft and carrier operations, 243, 244, 246, 312–13, 320nn52–53, 325, 352; losses during, 313, 320n53; naval air power role in, 273–83, 294; start of, 269–70, 312

L

Landing Signal Officer (LSO), 193n14, 254, 257–58, 334

Langley (CV-1): air show demonstrations, 87–88; air wing, number of aircraft in, 88, 163; air wing, types of aircraft for, 87; capabilities and specifications of, 80; commissioning of, 80, 201, 305, 319n29; conversion to aircraft tender, 129n57; design of, 168; equipment modifications, 84; Fleet manuevers, participation by, 84, 88, 95, 97, 98–100, 101–2, 105, 109, 110–12; flight-deck operations, 85; launching and landing procedures, 83–85; in Pearl Harbor, 96; Reeves as commander, 80, 83; safety record on, 88; ship conversion, 80, 97, 134, 156; Washington Naval Treaty and, 170, 172

Langley, Samuel Pierpont, 6–8

Langley aeronautical laboratory, 21–22

Lexington (CV-2): air wing, number of aircraft in, 88, 169; capabilities of, 38, 80, 89; construction and commissioning of, 98–99, 143, 201, 319n29; Fleet manuevers, participation by, 95, 100, 101–3, 104–6, 107–9, 110–23, 129n64, 199; safety record on, 88; sinking of, 161, 178; specialized air groups, 126–27n22

Lexington (CV-16), 141, 144, 151n35

lighter-than-air craft. *See* airships

London Treaty, 175

Long Island (CVE-1), 146–47, 186

Los Angeles, 103–4, 106, 126n29

M

MacArthur, Douglas: fleet-based versus land-based aircraft for Navy, 35, 208, 214, 306; Japan, surrender of, 311;

Korean conflict, 270, 271, 276, 277, 279;
    Pacific campaign, 141
Macon, 35, 46, 47, 106, 109, 110, 126n29
Maddox, 286
Mahan, Alfred Thayer, 10, 27, 32, 137,
    150n19, 301
Marine Corps, U.S.: close air support,
    292–93; demise of and lack of support
    for, 272–73, 294; independence of, 311;
    Korean conflict, 276–80; officers in,
    73n4; promotion in, 68; roles and
    missions of, 311–12, 324; Vietnam War,
    290
Mars aircraft, 37
Midway: bases at, 40; Battle of Midway,
    89, 163–64, 179, 264; exercises in waters
    around, 110–12; Rainbow Five plan,
    41–42
Midway and *Midway*-class carriers,
    180–81, 292, 329–30, 331, 333, 344n6,
    347–48n9
Military Flyer, 8–9
missile development, 335–36
Mississippi, 22–23
Missouri (BB 63), 215, 311
Moffett, William A.: air attacks against
    ships, 107; airships, support for use of,
    35, 45, 48; bombing, effectiveness of,
    203; death of, 35, 48, 131; flight-deck
    cruisers, 175; as naval aviation observer,
    74n13; Naval Aviation Reserve Policy,
    61; naval aviation, support for, 131, 306

N
National Advisory Committee for
    Aeronautics (NACA), 22, 27
national aeronautical laboratory, 12,
    20–22
Naval Academy: appointments to, 59, 64;
    enrollment numbers, 60, 61, 62; length
    of coursework, 65

naval aviation: acceptance of and
    response to, 10, 54, 80, 131–32, 133–35;
    accident rate, 262; aircraft development
    and flight testing, 9, 13–14; airfield for,
    14–15; Army aviation, cooperation
    with, 14–15; birth of, 6, 16; under
    Bristol, 22–26; Centennial activities, 2;
    challenges of development of program,
    5, 8, 26–28; culture of, 261–64; demise
    of and lack of support for, 272–73,
    294; development of program for, 5,
    11–13, 15–16, 18, 19, 302–3, 318n6;
    effectiveness of, 53, 73, 215, 294,
    353–54; fleet-based versus land-based
    aircraft, 35, 208, 214, 305–7; funding
    for, 10, 12, 15, 16–17, 18, 24, 26, 28, 305;
    growth of, 148–49, 152nn53–54, 302–3,
    307–8, 319nn37–39; importance of,
    1–2, 243, 305; inattention to, 25–26;
    modernization of, 26; naval control of,
    166–67; responsibility and control of
    program, 11–12, 15–16, 18–19, 25–26;
    roles and missions of, 2–3, 52–53, 352;
    shore air facilities and bases and, 38–40,
    137, 148, 150n22, 303, 305; standards
    for, 134–35; technological advances, 3,
    315; wartime expansion and peacetime
    reduction, 54, 59–60, 64–65, 71, 72,
    74–75n16, 95–96, 304, 318n16
naval aviation cadets, 62–63, 64, 65, 76n31
Naval Aviation Maintenance Program
    (NAMP), 260, 265
naval aviation observers, 57, 67, 74n13, 83
naval aviation pilots, 57
Naval Aviation Reserve Act, 64
naval aviators: commanding officer
    qualifications, 135, 158; definition of,
    57; flight time, 123, 130n72; helicopter
    pilot qualifications, 228; hostility
    toward, 77n39; independence of and
    self-reliance characteristics, 261–62;

insignia for, 77n39; at Pensacola, 55;
uniform for, 77n39
Naval Reserve Officer Training Corps
(NROTC), 61, 65, 71, 75nn26–27
Naval Reserve, U.S.: creation of, 59,
74–75n16; disestablishment of, 61;
officers, number of, 59–60, 62–63,
64–65, 75nn19–20, 76n36; pilots
for, authorization of, 137, 150n17;
reorganization of, 64; training of
officers, 63–64, 75n19, 76n34; wartime
expansion and peacetime reduction,
59–60, 71, 74–75n16
Naval War College: instructors at, 11,
82–83; presidents of, 80, 90, 91n4, 133;
war games and concept generation at,
80, 81–83, 89, 133
Navy, U.S.: Aide System organization,
10, 15–16; aircrew, replacement of,
174–75; air-surface-undersea actions,
110, 128n46, 301; battleships of,
capabilities of, 83; Commander-in-
Chief of U.S. Fleet, 90, 96, 109; fleet
expansion, 10, 148–49; 152nn53–54,
157, 175, 304; fleet expansion, funding
for, 135–40, 150n27, 151n29, 151n31;
fleet expansion, public support for,
157; Fleet organization, 96; maneuvers
with aviation unit, 17; maritime
strategy, 327–28, 344n4, 352–53; roles
and missions of, 311–12, 318, 324; sea
duty requirement, 18, 19, 25, 57, 68–69,
78nn44–45; superiority of, 149, 274
Nimitz, Chester, 17, 81, 141, 149, 158, 311
Nimitz and Nimitz-class carriers, 282,
338, 339
North Carolina (ACR-12/CA-12), 23, 24,
25, 95, 153, 190n2
North Carolina (BB-55), 89, 90–91
nuclear weapons delivery operations, 245,
247, 326

O
officer personnel system: development
of, 54, 72–73; Marine officers,
73n4; naval aviation corps, 54–55,
56; number of officers, 58–66, 72,
75nn19–20, 318n16; promotion, 54, 61,
66–72, 73n6, 76–77n38, 77n40, 77n42,
78nn44–45; retirement, 61, 75–76n28;
specialization, 54–58; staff corps, 55;
structure and components of, 53;
transfer of officers, 60, 75n22, 76n36;
two-tier system, 66, 76n37
Oriskany (CV-43), 143, 181, 289, 290, 331

P
P-2 Neptune, 290, 313, 314, 329–30
P2Y aircraft, 34, 207, 208, 209
P-3 Orion, 290, 308, 315, 316–17,
321nn71–72, 337
P6M SeaMaster aircraft, 250, 315, 321n67
P-8 Poseidon, 317
PB-1 bombers, 310
PB2Y Coronado aircraft, 37, 209, 310
PB4Y-1 aircraft, 214, 308, 309, 310
PB4Y-2 Privateer aircraft, 214
PBJ Mitchell aircraft, 214
PBJ-1 aircraft, 310
PBM Mariner aircraft, 37, 209, 310
PBY Catalina aircraft, 34, 36–38, 40, 42,
113, 119, 176–77, 208, 215, 250, 309,
310
PBY-5A aircraft, 40, 214
Pearl Harbor: airship reconnaisance and,
49; attack on, 42, 105, 176–77; base
at, 41, 42; battleships lost at, 143, 308;
development of, 32; fleet transfer to,
41; investigation of, 91; Langley in, 96;
Navy expansion following attack on,
148–49
Pennsylvania, 3, 12–13, 15, 90, 92n26,
153, 302

Pensacola Naval Air Station: aviation unit
    relocation to, 22–23; bomb runs, 23;
    establishment of, 22, 137, 200; naval
    aviators at, 55; training at, 23–24, 228–
    29, 303; training of, 150n22
Philippine Islands, 31, 32, 33, 35, 41
Philippine Sea, 274, 277
pilots: aircraft crash injuries and deaths,
    19–20, 25, 164, 165, 194n15, 241–42,
    244–45; best two percent of humanity,
    2, 4n2; confidence of, 2, 4n2; courage
    of, 3–4; helicopter pilots, training of,
    224, 227, 228–29; increase in number
    of, 137, 147, 150n17; jet pilots, training
    of, 253, 263, 265; naval aviation pilots,
    57; number of for World War II, 308,
    320n42; training of, 13, 158, 263, 303,
    353
PM aircraft, 209
poem on aviation, 2
Pratt, William V.: Fleet manuevers,
    participation by, 100, 102; fleet-based
    versus land-based aircraft for Navy, 35,
    208, 214, 306; flight-deck cruisers, 175;
    Reeves, promotion of, 90
Princeton, 280–81
PV Ventura/Harpoon aircraft, 214

R
RA-5C Vigilante, 266
radar, 174, 182, 189, 215, 256
Rainbow Five plan, 41–42
Randolph (CV-15), 142, 144, 151n35
Ranger (CV-4): construction and
    commissioning of, 137, 149–50n10;
    design of, 168–72, 194n18,
    195–96nn20–24; Fleet manuevers,
    participation by, 110–19; launching
    of, 108–9; size and specifications, 89;
    speed of, 170, 195n22; Vietnam War,
    287, 289

Reeves, Joseph Mason "Bull": air show
    demonstrations, 87–88; air wing,
    types of aircraft for, 87; aircraft for
    War Plan Orange, 35, 37; carrier and
    air-strike tactics, development of, 80,
    82–83, 85–87, 89; carrier procedures,
    modification of, 83–85, 162–64; carrier
    scouting and offensive operations, 99–
    100; Commander positions, 80, 83, 90;
    Commander-in-Chief of U.S. Fleet, 90,
    109, 110; contributions of, 74n13, 79,
    88, 91; death of, 91; Fleet manuevers,
    participation by, 100, 104, 109, 110;
    General Board assignment, 90, 92n26;
    as naval aviation observer, 74n13, 164;
    naval aviation, support for, 135; Naval
    War College education and career, 81,
    82–83, 162; Pearl Harbor investigation,
    91; safety record of aircraft carriers,
    88; seaplane tenders, priority of, 39;
    wartime service, 91
Richardson, Holden C., 16, 17, 19, 23–24,
    27, 28
Roosevelt, Franklin: aeronautics board
    creation, 19; aircraft, funding for, 307;
    carriers, construction of, 180; Naval
    Aviation Reserve Act, 64; Navy, support
    for, 135, 136; Rainbow Five plan, 41;
    Reeves, promotion of, 90
rotary-wing aircraft. *See* helicopters and
    rotary-wing aircraft
Royal Air Force (RAF), 134, 166, 324, 332
Royal Navy: air wing, number of aircraft
    in, 162, 163–64; aircraft, quality of, 200;
    aircraft carrier design, 157–58, 160,
    183–86, 192–93nn8–9, 332–34; aircraft
    carriers, role of, 343–44n3; angled
    flight decks, 258; carrier operations,
    154–56, 164, 191–92n6; disarmament
    conference and treaty, 158–59; funding
    for, 15; helicopter purchases, 224;

naval aviation and the RAF, 166–67;
number of planes, 26; optical landing
system, 258; seaplane use by, 18, 155;
shipboard takeoffs by, 18, 190n2; steam
catapults, 258

S

S-2 Tracker aircraft, 262, 332
S-3 Viking aircraft, 237, 262, 315, 338
S-22 helicopters, 229
S-58 helicopters, 230
safety issues and initiatives, 20, 88,
262–64, 265
Saratoga (CV-3): air wing, number
of aircraft in, 88, 169; capabilities
of, 38, 80, 89; construction and
commissioning of, 98–99, 143,
152n54, 201, 319n29; Fleet manuevers,
participation by, 95, 100–103, 104–6,
107–9, 110–17, 120–23, 129n64,
199; Fleet Problem participation, 95;
landing on, 161; safety record on, 88;
specialized air groups, 126–27n22
SB2C Helldiver bomber, 147, 148, 210,
213
SBD Dauntless aircraft, 87, 147, 148, 204
seaplane tenders, 39–40, 172, 303, 305,
318n17
seaplanes and flying boats: acquisition
of, 16, 17; advances in, 27–28, 315;
attack role of, 37–38, 40–41, 209, 214;
bases for, 38–40; decline in use of,
313, 315; development of, 17, 33–34,
200, 208; effectiveness of, 207–8; Fleet
manuevers, participation by, 113,
206–7; flexibility of, 302; interest in,
12, 15; jet aircraft, 250; launching and
landing procedures, 17–18, 200–201,
206; manufacturing of, 303; Mexican
Civil War maneuvers, 23, 95; range of,
37, 208; scouting missions, 33–35, 38,

40–41, 99, 123, 124n4, 176–77, 207;
vulnerability of, 38
Selfridge, Thomas, 9
SH-2D/SH-2F helicopters, 235
SH-3A/HSS-2 helicopters, 231
SH-3H helicopters, 236
SH-60B Seahawk helicopters, 235
shipbuilding activities, 141–45, 151n40
ships: air attacks against, 106–7; anti-
aircraft capabilities, 89, 90–91; catapult
to launch aircraft from, 17–18, 23–24,
153; first take-off from, 5; system of
ship-type symbols, 156, 185; takeoffs
from, 3, 5, 7–8, 12–13, 18, 24, 153;
treaty tonnage limits, 158–60, 193n11
short takeoff and vertical landing
(STOVL) aircraft, 336, 340, 342–43
Sicily, 274, 276
Sims, William S., 46, 80, 81–82, 91n4, 133,
154, 215
sonar, dunking/dipping, 227, 229, 231–32,
309
swept-wing jets: carrier launching
and landing procedures, 257–59;
development of, 242–43; handling
characteristics, 246–47, 252–53;
transition to, 3

T

T3M/T4M torpedo planes, 202–3
TA-4J Skyhawk aircraft, 259
TBD Devastator aircraft, 87, 147, 148, 203
TBF/TBM Avenger bomber, 147, 148, 210
Tentative Conceptual baseline (T-CBL)
ships, 339, 349n17
Texas, 124n4, 174
Ticonderoga (CV-14), 142, 151n35, 286
torpedo bombers, 195n23, 201–3, 212,
332
Towers, John: aboard aircraft, 14; aircraft,
advances in, 20–21; aircraft, quality

of, 200; aircraft carriers, role of, 133;
aircraft demonstrations, 17; aircraft
for War Plan Orange, 37; aircraft
purchases, 25; career of, 28; carrier
deck operations, 85; Chambers Board,
19; as Chambers' replacement, 22;
contributions of, 73; contributions
to naval aviation, 27; dirigibles,
effectiveness of, 24; Fleet manuevers,
participation by, 104, 129n64; insignia
for naval aviators, 77n39; legislation,
role in drafting, 138; Mexican Civil War
intervention, 23; pilot training, 13; war
observation duties, 23
two-ocean Navy: carriers for, 177–82,
196–97nn27–28; Vinson-Walsh Act,
132, 136, 137–40, 149, 150n27, 151n29,
151n31, 152nn53–54

U
UH-1 Huey, 292
UH-1B helicopters, 234
UH-2A helicopters, 233, 234
UH-34 Seahorse, 292
UH-46A Sea Knight helicopters, 234
UH-60 Blackhawk helicopters, 235
United States, 243, 250, 273, 311, 312, 324,
325, 332, 348n11
Unmanned Combat Aerial Systems
(UCAS), 249–50, 341
Utah, 107, 117

V
Valley Forge, 271, 274, 275, 277–78
vertical takeoff and landing (VTOL)
aircraft, 251, 336, 338–39, 340, 342,
349n15
Vietnam War: anti-aircraft artillery
(AAA) fire, 287, 291; close air support,
292–93; end of U.S. involvement in,
293; Flaming Dart operations, 287–88;

Game Warden operation, 290–91;
Gulf of Tonkin incident, 286–87, 314;
helicopter use during, 232–34, 284;
jet aircraft and carrier operations,
243, 314–15, 326, 352; Linebacker
II operation, 293; Market Time
operation, 290–91, 314; naval air power
role in, 284–93; Rolling Thunder
campaign, 288–89, 292, 293; start of,
283–84; surface-to-air (SAM) missiles,
291–92; Vietnamization strategy, 293
Vinson, Carl, 131–32, 135–40, 149
Vinson-Trammel Acts, 35, 136–37, 141–
42, 151n40, 175–76, 196n25
Vinson-Walsh Act (Two-Ocean Navy
Act), 132, 136, 137–40, 149, 150n27,
151n29, 151n31, 152nn53–54
VP aircraft and VProns, 33–34, 35, 38–42

W
war: containment policy of U.S., 293–94;
fleet and force expansion, 54, 59–60,
64–65, 71, 72, 74–75n16, 95–96, 272,
273, 304, 318n16; naval warfare,
evolution of, 301, 318n3; naval warfare,
technology and, 301–2; strategy for,
283. *See also* anti-submarine warfare
War Plan Orange: aircraft range and, 31,
33–35, 37; bases for aircraft, 38–40;
cautionaries, 32–33; color plans for
war, 42n1; development of, 31; fleet to
carry out, 143–44, 149, 160; geographic
dilemma, 31; PBY Catalina aircraft,
34, 36–38, 40, 42, 208; phases of war,
31–33; strategic themes, 31; thrusters,
32, 33; VP aircraft and VProns, 33–34,
35, 38–42
Washington Naval Treaty, 158–61, 166,
167–75, 193nn10–11, 194n17, 194n19,
196n25

Wasp (CV-7), 109, 137, 143, 172, 178, 195n22
Wasp (CV-18), 141, 151n35
wings of gold, 77n39
World War I: aircraft built and used during, 154, 190n3, 200; Navy's role in, 304, 318n16; wartime expansion and peacetime reduction, 95–96, 304, 318n16
World War II: air-to-air combat, 210; Battle of the Atlantic, 308–9; carrier aviation, role of, 53; carrier operations, 182–83; Central Pacific campaign, 143–45, 149; Fleet Plan WPPac-46, 41–42; Lend-Lease Act, 91; multi-front war capabilities, 139; naval aviation buildup for, 308–9, 319nn37–39; Navy expansion during, 64–65; number of pilots for, 308, 320n42; Pacific campaign, 309–11, 351–52; Rainbow Five plan, 41–42; tactics for, development of, 81; V-J Day, 310–11
Wright, Orville, 8–9, 13–14, 16
Wright, Wilbur, 8–9, 13–14, 16

X
XF2Y-1 Sea Dart, 250, 315, 321n68
XFY-1 Pogo, 251
XR-4 helicopters, 220, 221, 224–25, 226

Y
Yorktown (CV-5): Battle of Midway, 89, 142, 179; construction and commissioning of, 109, 129n57, 135, 143, 171; design of, 171; Fleet manuevers, participation by, 117–19, 120–23, 130n68, 226; sinking of, 89, 142, 172, 174, 178
Yorktown (CV-10), 138, 142, 151–52n46
Yorktown-class carriers, 137, 145–46, 149–50n10, 163

The Naval Institute Press is the book-publishing arm of the U.S. Naval Institute, a private, nonprofit, membership society for sea service professionals and others who share an interest in naval and maritime affairs. Established in 1873 at the U.S. Naval Academy in Annapolis, Maryland, where its offices remain today, the Naval Institute has members worldwide.

Members of the Naval Institute support the education programs of the society and receive the influential monthly magazine *Proceedings* or the colorful bimonthly magazine *Naval History* and discounts on fine nautical prints and on ship and aircraft photos. They also have access to the transcripts of the Institute's Oral History Program and get discounted admission to any of the Institute-sponsored seminars offered around the country.

The Naval Institute's book-publishing program, begun in 1898 with basic guides to naval practices, has broadened its scope to include books of more general interest. Now the Naval Institute Press publishes about seventy titles each year, ranging from how-to books on boating and navigation to battle histories, biographies, ship and aircraft guides, and novels. Institute members receive significant discounts on the Press's more than eight hundred books in print.

Full-time students are eligible for special half-price membership rates. Life memberships are also available.

For a free catalog describing Naval Institute Press books currently available, and for further information about joining the U.S. Naval Institute, please write to:

Member Services
U.S. Naval Institute
291 Wood Road
Annapolis, MD 21402-5034
Telephone: (800) 233-8764
Fax: (410) 571-1703
Web address: www.usni.org